RELATING RELIGION

JONATHAN Z. SMITH

RELATING
RELIGION

ESSAYS IN THE STUDY OF RELIGION

THE UNIVERSITY OF CHICAGO PRESS
Chicago and London

The University of Chicago Press, Chicago 60637
The University of Chicago Press, Ltd., London
© 2004 by The University of Chicago
All rights reserved. Published 2004
Printed in the United States of America

13 12 11 10 09   3 4 5

ISBN: 0-226-76386-2 (cloth)
ISBN: 0-226-76387-0 (paper)

Library of Congress Cataloging-in-Publication Data
Smith, Jonathan Z.
    Relating religion : essays in the study of religion / Jonathan Z. Smith.
        p. cm.
    Includes bibliographical references and index.
    ISBN 0-226-76386-2 (alk. paper) — ISBN 0-226-76387-0 (pbk. : alk. paper)
      1. Religion—Study and teaching.   I. Title.

  BL41.S65 2004
  200'.71—dc22

                                                2004045967

For Jacob Neusner, Hans H. Penner, and Burton L. Mack — three quite different encounters of the closest kind — with affection, respect, and gratitude.

CONTENTS

Contents

PREFACE

ALTHOUGH I HAVE been delighted that an earlier collection of essays, *Imagining Religion* (1982), has made its way onto a number of course syllabi, it has been an unintended source of frustration. As I talk with individuals and come across references to my work in print, I seem to have been arrested somewhere in the 1970s when those essays were first composed. In 1990, recognizing this, Alan G. Thomas, who has served as the University of Chicago Press editor for my two more recent books, suggested that I assemble a new collection. At the time I resisted, being stubbornly committed to the completion of a bulky manuscript, *Close Encounters of Diverse Kinds: Studies in the Western Imagination of Difference*. As Columbus played a pivotal role in the work, I knew that I would have to complete it before the flood of new publications on the Columbian "enterprise" appeared in 1992 or face a delay of years while I worked to take these into account. I failed to make this self-imposed deadline, not in the least because I had accepted the general editorship of the *HarperCollins Dictionary of Religion* in 1988, a project of the American Academy of Religion, finally completed and published in 1995.

In 1997, I revisited the idea of a new collection. I began to assemble articles for possible inclusion and to draft an introductory piece with the working title "Thinking Religion." These efforts made clear that my work was in the process of taking several new turns and that I was not yet satisfied with their articulation in the essays then at hand.

In the past year, encouraged by friends and colleagues who asked for such a book, Alan Thomas and I returned to the notion of a collection. After several false starts, it seemed well to write a new piece, "When the Chips Are Down," to introduce the essays. This essay seeks, on the one hand, to answer the question I am most frequently asked by students, What led me to study religion, and to approach it in the way that I do? This portion of the essay describes early formative influences, breaking off at the point that I begin to publish articles that acknowledge intellectual engagements and debts more directly through their footnotes. On the other hand, the latter parts of the essay focus on persistent elements in my work over the years and suggest something of the close relationship between the studies in religion and thinking about education by discussing a good part of my previously printed articles and monographs. I have made some effort to relate the items printed in this volume to these earlier concerns, but I have refrained from summarizing, at any length, those texts, written between 1983 and 2002, that are now before you.

I define myself primarily as a writer of essays, which are often reworked versions of lectures. I understand the role of one who identifies himself as a generalist and comparativist to be that of interacting with the agenda and data of others. This has meant that much of my work is situational, designed for particular audiences, often discussing *their* assigned topics or questions. Of the hundreds of lectures, papers, seminar contributions, and responses delivered since 1961, only a relative handful have been general enough to justify publication; even fewer warrant republication. (See the appendix to this volume for a full listing of publications and reprintings.)

In this collection, I have organized the essays according to the topics in the "Persistent Preoccupations" section of the opening essay.

1. Chapters 2–6 consist of critical engagements with figures and scholarly traditions that serve to position these "preoccupations" within the larger setting of the discipline.

2. Chapters 7–10 take up a long-time interest in taxonomy and classification, carried over to the study of religion.

3. Chapters 11–13 consist of studies of the construction of difference and may be taken as sketches toward the work in progress, *Close Encounters of Diverse Kinds*, mentioned above. The movement from the language of 'incongruity' and 'gap' to that of 'difference' plots the trajectory of my work from 1970 to the present.

4. Chapters 14 and 15, taken together, illustrate the procedures of generalization and redescription that have become key to my understanding of the purpose of the comparative enterprise.

5. The final set, chapters 16–17, represents the deployment of elements that have become characteristic of my most recent work, especially the notion of translation.

Chapters 11–13, concerned with the construction of difference, especially in anthropological theories from the fifteenth through the eighteenth centuries, and chapter 16, which sketches some of the wider inquiries this has led to in Renaissance and Enlightenment anthropology and linguistics, especially as a foil against Romantic theories of cultural productions, suggest something of the directions of work in progress. Unrepresented in this collection is a second project, not unrelated to the critique of Romanticism, a set of structural studies of ritual. These have been delayed, in part, by the need to fully understand and take into account recent developments in cognitive theories of ritual, most especially the work of E. Thomas Lawson, Robert N. McCauley, and Harvey Whitehouse.[1]

I have been fortunate to have had as friends and as sometimes colleagues three extraordinary individuals: Jacob Neusner, since 1958; Hans H. Penner, since 1965; and Burton L. Mack, since 1974. Each has pioneered new ways of thinking in their chosen areas of specialization; each has engaged in the most provocative sort of general discourse about the study of religion. I have been given the opportunity of expressing to each of them, face-to-face, my sense of their significance to the field as scholars, as well as my abiding affection and indebtedness to them—Jack, on the occasion of his receiving an honorary degree from the University of Chicago; Hans, at the conference celebrating his years at Dartmouth College; Burt, at the presentation of a festschrift honoring his work. I can say of each of them the words that J.-P. Sartre perhaps misspoke in describing his relations to Pierre Victor (i.e., Benny Lévy), "There was real freedom between us—the freedom of endangering one's position."[2]

Chicago, September 2002

Notes

1. See, especially, E. T. Lawson and R. N. McCauley, *Rethinking Religion: Connecting Cognition and Culture* (Cambridge, 1990); MacCauley and Lawson,

Bringing Ritual to Mind: Psychological Foundations of Cultural Forms (Cambridge, 2002); H. Whitehouse, *Inside the Cult: Religious Innovation and Transmission in Papua New Guinea* (Oxford, 1995); Whitehouse, *Arguments and Icons: Divergent Modes of Religiosity* (Oxford, 2000). Important studies related to these projects are regularly published in the new serial *Journal of Cognition and Culture*.

2. J.-P. Sartre, in a 1977 radio dialogue with P. Victor, published in *Libération* and excerpted in S. de Beauvoir, *Adieux: A Farewell to Sartre* (1984; reprint, London, 1985), 36.

ACKNOWLEDGMENTS

THE BULK of the essays appearing in this volume have been reprinted, at times with some revision, from the following publications:

Chapter 2, "Acknowledgments: Morphology and History in Mircea Eliade's *Patterns in Comparative Religion* (1949–1999), Part 1: The Work and Its Contexts," along with chapter 3, was first presented as two History of Religions Lectures at the Divinity School of the University of Chicago in April and May 1999, commemorating the fiftieth anniversary of the French publication of Eliade's *Traité d'histoire des religions*. *History of Religions* 39 (2000): 315–31, © The University of Chicago; reprinted with permission.

Chapter 3, "Acknowledgments: Morphology and History in Mircea Eliade's *Patterns in Comparative Religion* (1949–1999), Part 2: The Texture of the Work," *History of Religions* 39 (2000): 332–51, © The University of Chicago; reprinted with permission.

Chapter 4, "The Topography of the Sacred," was first presented at a symposium, "Profane and Sacred," sponsored by the Department of Religious Studies at the University of California, Santa Barbara, in February 2001. It has not been previously published.

Chapter 5, "Manna, Mana Everywhere and /-/-/," was written for a conference sponsored by Dartmouth College, October 2000, in honor of Hans H. Penner on the occasion of his retirement. Nancy K. Frankenberry, editor, *Radical Interpretation in Religion* (Cambridge: Cambridge

Acknowledgments

University Press, 2002), 188–212, © The Syndicate of the Press of Cambridge University; reprinted with permission.

Chapter 6, "The Domestication of Sacrifice," was prepared for a "conversation" with Walter Burkert and René Girard on "Violent Origins" sponsored by the Institute for Antiquity and Christianity at the Claremont Graduate School and various institutions at Stanford University in the fall of 1983. Robert G. Hamerton-Kelly, editor, *Violent Origins: Walter Burkert, René Girard and Jonathan Z. Smith on Ritual Killing and Cultural Formation* (Stanford: Stanford University Press, 1987), 191–205, © The Board of Trustees of the Leland Stanford Junior University; reprinted with permission.

Chapter 7, "A Matter of Class: Taxonomies of Religion," was the 1996 William James Lecture for the Divinity School at Harvard University. *Harvard Theological Review* 89 (1996): 387–403, © The President and Fellows of Harvard College; reprinted with permission.

Chapter 8, "Religion, Religions, Religious," was written for the handbook by Mark C. Taylor, editor, *Critical Terms for Religious Studies* (Chicago: University of Chicago Press, 1998), 269–84, © The University of Chicago; reprinted with permission.

Chapter 9, "Bible and Religion," was a plenary address to the 1999 annual meeting of the Society of Biblical Literature. *Bulletin of the Council of Societies for the Study of Religion* 29 (2000): 87–93, © The Council of Societies for the Study of Religion, reprinted with permission.

Chapter 10, "Trading Places," was delivered as the opening address to an international conference on "Magic in the Ancient World," held at the University of Kansas in August 1992. Marvin Meyer and Paul Mirecki, editors, *Ancient Magic & Ritual Power*, Religions in the Graeco-Roman World, 129 (Leiden: E. J. Brill, 1995), 13–27, © E. J. Brill, reprinted with permission.

Chapter 11, "Differential Equations: On Constructing the 'Other,'" was the 1992 University Lecture in Religion at Arizona State University. *Differential Equations: On Constructing the 'Other,'* Annual University Lecture in Religion, March 5, 1992 (Tempe: Department of Religious Studies, Arizona State University, 1992).

Chapter 12, "What a Difference a Difference Makes," was the keynote address to the 1984 Brown University conference "To See Ourselves As Others See Us." Jacob Neusner and Ernest S. Frerichs, editors, *"To See Ourselves as Others See Us," Christians, Jews, 'Others,' in Late Antiquity*, Scholars Press Studies in the Humanities (Chico, CA: Scholars Press, 1985), 3–48.

Chapter 13, "Close Encounters of Diverse Kinds," was first written as the 1993 Lowe Lecture at MacAlister College. It was then delivered, each time in a somewhat different form, as the John Nuveen Memorial Lecture at the University of Chicago Divinity School (1994), the Boston University Lecture on Criticism (1997), and, in the form printed here, the Sir Isaiah Berlin Lecture at Wolfson College, Oxford (1999). Susan L. Mizruchi, editor, *Religion and Cultural Studies* (Princeton: Princeton University Press, 2001), 3–21, © Princeton University Press; reprinted with permission.

Chapter 14, "Here, There, and Anywhere," was the opening address at the 2000 conference "Prayer, Magic and the Stars in the Ancient and Late Antique World," sponsored by the Department of Near Eastern Languages and Civilizations at the University of Washington. Scott B. Noegel, Joel Walker, and Brannon M. Wheeler, editors, *Prayer, Magic, and the Stars in the Ancient and Late Antique World*, Magic in History, 8 (University Park: Pennsylvania State University Press, 2003), 21–36, © The Pennsylvania State University Press; reprinted with permission.

Chapter 15, "Re: Corinthians," was prepared as a contribution to the 2001 meeting of the Society of Biblical Literature Seminar on Ancient Myths and Modern Theories of Christian Origins. While it will appear in a forthcoming volume of seminar papers edited by Ron Cameron and Merrill Miller, it has not been previously published.

Chapter 16, "A Twice-told Tale: The History of the History of Religions' History," was a plenary address to the 2000 Quinquennial Congress of the International Association for the History of Religions. *Numen* 48 (2001): 131–46, © Koninklijke Brill NV; reprinted with permission.

Chapter 17, "God Save This Honourable Court: Religion and Civic Discourse," was first prepared as the Edward W. Snowden '33 Lecture at Wesleyan University (2001). In the form printed here, it was the second annual Ninian Smart Memorial Lecture, delivered in January 2003, sponsored by the University of California, Santa Barbara, and the University of Lancaster. It has not been previously published.

CHAPTER ONE

WHEN THE CHIPS
ARE DOWN

You and I ought not to die, before We have explained
ourselves to each other.
JOHN QUINCY ADAMS TO THOMAS JEFFERSON, July 15, 1813[1]

WHEN MIRCEA ELIADE occasionally recounted the tale of our early
meetings together, he always remarked that he had found it "very amus-
ing" that I so often used the phrase, "when the chips are down," when
commenting on one or another's work. He professed to have not previously encountered it. For my part, I had seen a version of the tag first as
the English translation (1948) of the title of J.-P. Sartre's play, *Les Jeux
sont faits* (1947). Both the French and the English phrases are gaming
terms that signal finality. With less urgency, I tended to employ it with the
connotation, "when all is said and done," as, for example, "despite so-
and-so's claims, when the chips are down, he's a functionalist."[2] In this essay, I want to turn the phrase on myself and account for my most persistent interests as a student of religion.

After several abortive attempts, I have settled on writing this account in the form of that awkwardly entitled genre, a bio-bibliographical
essay.[3] I am enough of a residual New Critic to largely discount the relevance of the *bios* part of that compound term, but chronology has its con-
veniences along with its conventional limitations.

I: Student

Growing up in Manhattan in the '40s and '50s provided both a foil
for my fascination with natural history, especially botany, and a nurtur-

ing setting for my initial interests in history and philosophy. Both sets of concerns have strongly influenced the sorts of problems and approaches I have taken when I turned to the study of religion.

My interest in natural history was at once both moral and intellectual. The former goes back to an early acceptance of the categorical imperative, "do no harm." Whether expressed in public gestures such as vegetarianism, conscientious objection, and passive resistance activities, or in my vocational plans to become an agrostologist, a grass breeder, with the hope of an atoning reclamation of those deserts that were the products of human failures to take care—it seemed clear to me, as a preteen, that those western religious traditions with which I had some superficial acquaintance provided no intellectual resources for such an ethic of "do no harm," insofar as they appeared to claim that the earth was ours to "subdue" and exploit. Writings from the late 40s and early 50s are filled with my excited reports of readings in Asian traditions, ranging from Buddhism and Jainism to Gandhi, as well as works on native religious traditions.[4]

At the same time, agrostology led, among other things, to a deep interest in taxonomy. My two bedside books during high school were the seventh edition of Asa Gray's *New Manual of Botany* and A. S. Hitchcock's *Manual of the Grasses of the United States*, soon replaced by the second edition, revised by Agnes Chase. This interest remains today; taxonomic journals are the only biological field I still regularly read in.

Putting these naturalist interests together with a concern for teaching, I started, and maintained for fifteen years, a small trailside museum in Westport, Connecticut. My first appearance in a scholarly publication is a 1954 report of a survey of the average number of milkweed plants (*Asclepias* sp.) per acre, undertaken in support of the Royal Ontario Museum's monarch butterfly migration project.[5]

In 1956, I abandoned my long held plans to study agrostology at Cornell Agricultural School. I instead went to Haverford College, where a remarkable philosopher and teacher, Martin Foss, inspired in me such a desire to emulate that I became a philosophy major. Haverford, at that time, still had a palpable connection with its origin as a Quaker school. The pacifism of the Society of Friends, as well as the austerity of their Meetings, was extraordinarily attractive and moved me to begin systematic readings in western religious traditions, working in Haverford's Rufus Jones collection of Christian mystical literature and studying with Douglas Steere.

These sorts of concerns coexisted with another set of philosophical and historical interests. By 1950, I had already discovered and taken full advantage of that distinctive West Side intellectual and political environment, bounded by Union Square and Brooklyn Heights, with Greenwich Village as its center. Within that universe of discourse, whether one's interlocutor be an old-time member of the International Jewish Labor Bund or a young Stalinist or Trotskyite, Marx was taken for granted, although what "school" of Marxism remained a matter for fierce debate. While accepting the model of both Marx and Lenin, that Hegel had always to be seriously and critically read, a central division of intellectual labor was the split between those who sought to reconcile Marx and Freud and those who worked on relations between Marx and Kant. In either case, there were strong fissures between the several Freudianisms or neo-Kantianisms. Although the project of reconciliation with Kant interested me more, I happily took part in both projects. I was especially intrigued by the so-called Austrian Marxists (especially Max Adler) who had made an industry of works with titles such as *Kant und Marx* (K. Vorländer) or *Kant und der Marxismus* (M. Adler). Their writings were studied in informal translations prepared by those who read German and distributed on purple hectograph or sepia-toned thermofax sheets.

By 1950–52, I had come to the view that language per se was a way of reconceptualizing the issues of Marxism and culture. For most of the anti-Stalinist groups, if the topic of language entered the discussion at all, it did so with reference to George Orwell's writings on the political manipulation of language—most famously in the twelve-page appendix to *1984* but more forcefully in some of his essays, especially, "Politics and the English Language."[6] (I do not recall anyone knowing of the journal *Politics and Letters*, coedited by Raymond Williams, until the 1958 publication of *Culture and Society, 1780–1950*, when he became a central figure). I found far more interesting one group that spent several months reading Joseph Stalin's *Marxism and Linguistics*, which had just become available in English translation. Stalin's insistence that "a Marxist cannot regard language as a superstructure on the base," and that language is not constituted by its vocabulary but rather by its grammar, which, like geometry, treats "relations" of entities "in general, without any concreteness,"[7] was a liberation from the mechanics of base/superstructure that dominated most of our discussions of cultural productions. Besides, this seemed to offer the possibility of a connection with Kant's formalism, which appeared hospitable to thinking about general linguistics.[8] In this connection I regularly quoted Hamann's remark on Kant, "the question is not 'What is Reason?' but 'What is Language?'. . . What we want is a Grammar of Reason"—a challenge paraphrased by Max Müller as a call for a "Critique of Language" to follow after Kant's first *Critique*.[9]

In the discussion of Marx and Kant, Marx and Freud, the under-

3

standing of Kant seemed enhanced by an appeal to language as grammar. On the other hand, Freud seemed more focused on a highly specific semantics. This had taught me to be shy of a quest for 'deeper' meaning (an abstention that largely remains intact), but the chapter "The Dream Work" in *The Interpretation of Dreams* was a brilliant syntactical proposal that informed my understanding of the project of relating Freud to Marx.

All of these inchoate musings became clearer when I accidentally came across a copy of a journal with E. Cassirer's 1945 article, "Structuralism in Modern Linguistics," in a 10¢ barrel in a Fourth Avenue used bookstore.[10] This introduced me to the names of Saussure, Trubetzkoy and Jakobson. In 1951–52, very little of their work was available in English, but I began to read in linguistic theory, especially L. Bloomfield, Z. Harris, and L. Hjelmslev.

Cassirer's article did more. He made a crucial analogy between morphology in biology and structuralism in linguistics—both of which would become lifelong preoccupations. (It was as a result of Cassirer that I read, for the first time, Goethe's *Metamorphosis of Plants*).[11]

I don't think I had ever been as impressed with a mind at work as I was with Cassirer's. As I came to read the bulk of his writings, he persuaded me of five foundational presuppositions.[12]

First, symbols are not expressive, they are a mode of thought.

Second, anthropological thought begins with thinking about language itself, for it is in the linguistic project that we see most clearly the creation of a distinctively human world, our "second environment." In crude terms, language "creates" the world; it does not merely "reflect" it. The various cultural forms that preoccupied Cassirer are differentiated modes of this linguistic project. To cite the peroration of Cassirer's *Essay on Man:*

> Language, art, religion, science are various phases of this process. In all of them man discovers and proves a new power—the power to build up a world of his own, an 'ideal world.' Philosophy cannot give up its search for a fundamental unity in this ideal world. But it does not confound this unity with simplicity. It does not overlook the tensions and deep conflicts between the various powers of man . . . They tend in different directions and obey different principles.[13]

The point at which I have learned to differ from this paragraph is with respect to its opening sentence, which repeats one of Cassirer's fundamental presuppositions: "human culture taken as a whole may be described as the process of man's progressive self-liberation." I would now reject the implications of the term "progressive" and would rather speak of a human cultural attempt at "liberation" from culturally created, culturally imposed, constraints through efforts at thought.

Third, Cassirer demonstrated that myth could be an object of inquiry that presumed its rationality, rather than denigrating it as irrational (as was common in so many triumphalist histories of philosophy and science) or celebrating it for its irrationality (as was common in so many Romantic works). I would now differ from Cassirer's grounds for postulating this rationality and seek to extend the logic to other modes of thought and action, especially to ritual, but for me the goal of Cassirer's project remains intact.

Fourth, Cassirer exhibited ways of thinking philosophically about ethnographies. They did not represent exotic or limit cases, extreme exaggerations of features we recognize in our own culture, but were to be taken as quite ordinary data for interrogation and constructive inquiry.

Finally, Cassirer illustrated by his practice that a prime way of doing philosophy was to think philosophically within the history of ideas, broadly construed, rather than against it (the latter, a mood rampant in the '50s, largely under British influence). What I learned from Cassirer was an ethic of careful reading, both contextually and critically, but without suspicion.

Beyond these fundamental elements, Cassirer sealed (as Durkheim would later confirm) my allegiance to neo-Kantianism and its relationship to aspects of the Enlightenment project, a conviction that persists to this day.

Cassirer was as well the source of what appears, with hindsight, to have been an enormous detour. When, in the preface to the first volume of the English translation of *The Philosophy of Symbolic Forms*, he described his project of studying cultural forms as a "morphology." I was certain I knew what he meant in light of both his 1945 article and my subsequent readings in the Germanic tradition of biological morphology. However, in the prefaces to the second and third volumes of the *Philosophy*, Cassirer went on to change his terminology from a Goethean one to a Hegelian, now describing his project as a "phenomenology."[14]

Beginning in 1955 and continuing through my four years at Haverford College, I read and reread Hegel, Husserl, Heidegger, and Sartre, each, always, in relation to Kant and the neo-Kantian tradition, in order to understand Cassirer's turn. By then, I had shifted from being a biology to a philosophy major and had the advantage of a series of reading courses with Martin Foss on these figures. (I shall never forget Foss sitting, week after week, in an old armchair in his living room, translating, line by line, Heidegger's *Sein und Zeit,* while I sat on a footstool furiously scribbling it down. This remains for me the archetypal image of a teacher at work.)

By the summer of 1958, both the readings in western religious and mystical traditions as well as those in phenomenology came together, and I began to outline a project on "the phenomenology of time and the structure of western mystical experience." I spent the summer writing a dense manuscript intended as a "methodological prolegomenon." While the attempt is, now, interesting largely for the bibliography, writing it convinced me that this was not a fruitful area for concentration.[15]

Paul Desjardins had joined the philosophy faculty at Haverford and introduced, among other things, a measure of focus on ancient Greek materials (along with careful readings of Kant's first and third *Critiques*). His passion was Plato; I found Aristotles's logical and taxonomic work far more intriguing. (Frank Parker, the fourth member of the department, was primarily interested in Aristotelian and Thomistic logic). Almost by way of a defense, I became fascinated with Francis M. Cornford's theory of the relationships between myth and philosophy, which, in turn, led to reading that collection of writers inappropriately collected together under the title the Myth-Ritual School. The Cornford thesis appeared to advance, in a historical way, Cassirer's philosophical interests in taking myth seriously. This led to a decision to focus on the possibility of treating Hesiod as a philosopher by setting his works within the larger framework of what I termed a "phenomenology of myth." At first, the older project was joined with this new one under the title "The Mythic Representation of Time: A Phenomenological Investigation" (1959), but was later generalized as "A Prolegomenon to a General Phenomenology of Myth," which was submitted as my senior thesis (1960).

Because I was convinced that myth could not be studied simply on the basis of antiquarian texts but required ethnographic materials as well, I attended during Columbia University's summer session (1958) a course in cultural anthropology with Morton Fried.[16] The course gave me some beginning measure of confidence in reading anthropology. The most striking feature of the much-revised 1960 "Prolegomenon" is the decline of citations of philosophical and theological writings and the increase in references to specific ethnographies and anthropological theories (including some early writings by Lévi-Strauss), along with an enlarged repertoire of Continental historians of religion. In the "Prolegomenon," the term "morphology" largely replaces "phenomenology." "Morphology" had been reencountered in Eliade but was equally resonant with past readings in Cassirer and in works cited by him.

I do not regret the "detour" into phenomenology. I read some wonderful books along the way. (I have read or reread Heidegger each summer for more than forty years). But by the end of 1959 I knew that the Romantic ontology and epistemology which characterized so much of the thought of both the phenomenologists and the historians of religions was profoundly nonanthropological and antihistorical and was, at its base, in curious ways, disturbingly nonrational. Neither Marx nor Kant could be satisfied.

In several papers written in 1959–60, I sharply criticized what was taken to be 'phenomenology of religion,'[17] coupled with a long paper in which I argued that Sartre's *Being and Nothingness* was a useful model for a properly anthropological phenomenology, even though I ended by confessing that I could not see how to apply it to problems of mythic thought. My work on Hesiod still retained too much phenomenological vocabulary; it was my excited reading of Lévi-Strauss's "Four Winnebago Myths" that purged that![18] I rewrote the Hesiod piece several times during 1960–61, striving to make it into a purely structuralist essay as I understood structuralism at that time.[19]

Having finished the B.A. at Haverford, I was not much interested in the analytic tradition that then dominated graduate programs in philosophy. Besides, my interests had clearly shifted to myth. After some uncertainty, I ended up going to Yale Divinity School with the initial intention of working in the New Testament where, thanks to Bultmann and his demythologizing project, I thought myth would be a topic of conversation. (I had seen Brevard S. Childs's 1955 dissertation, "A Study of Myth in Genesis I-XI," later reprinted as *Myth and Reality in the Old Testament*).[20]

As, at that time, the B.D. was the entry to M.A.-Ph.D. studies in religion, a two-year portion of the B.D.'s academic program was worked out for 1960–62. The required Divinity sequences were the first formal courses I took in religion.

In retrospect I have come to see that "the Protestant seminary curriculum, for all its inadequacies, constituted a general education in theological studies; religious studies, whether at the collegiate or graduate level, has been unable to construct a general education in religion." Rather, religious studies "made a decision to give up a (limited) coherence for a (limitless) incoherence."[21] In 1962, I moved to residency in the PhD. Program in the Department of Religion, newly severed from the Divinity School.

Yale was for me both a complex and an exhilarating experience. In many ways, interacting on a daily basis with tribal Protestants was analogous to an anthropologist's fieldwork.[22] I was, to a considerable degree, a participant-observer, making all the telling mistakes no native would, yet finding their indigenous quotidian practice and speech remarkable. (There was a set of friends who sometimes served as "native informants," willing to help me out on such awkward occasions as, for example, when I thought that the economic understanding of the Trinity might have something to do with Marx.) Furthermore, my fellow students' automatic assumption that, being Jewish, I would be as committed to that religious tradition as they were to theirs, prompted a considerable effort at reading in and thinking about Judaism.[23]

Both this undertaking and my studies in the New Testament and early Christianities—I had not read the New Testament, in its entirety, before coming to Yale—led to the question as to whether some of the concerns I had brought to the study of myth and ethnographic sources could be applied as well to Jewish and Christian materials. That is to say, in terminology I began to be comfortable with, was a history of religions approach to these western traditions possible?[24] Could such an approach overcome the exceptionalism with which they were commonly treated? At the same time, could such an approach be responsible to the thick history of scholarship on these traditions, a history whose extent I was beginning to learn?[25] I think it was generally understood that these issues would frame my future work. Largely unnoted by others was the fact that these questions had become more complicated due to a deeply felt tension between the strong focus of Yale's department on languages and history, which seemed to privilege particularities, and my growing acquaintance with complex statistical modes of comparison associated with Yale's Human Relations Area Files.[26] In retrospect, this discomfort was the beginning of what would become an interest in religion as a generic category, not limited to any particular tradition or canon.

This was clarified when I shifted from my initial plans to work at a degree in New Testament studies (I had drafted a dissertation that took as its starting point A. Guilding's work on the relation of the rabbinic lectionary cycle to the Gospel of John). I enrolled, instead, in a field listed in the catalog as a Ph.D. area but having neither faculty nor students at that time; History of Religions. By 1963–64, the problematics of comparison emerged as the place at which I could bring together responsibility to specific languages and histories with those philosophical issues concerning culture, religion, and language that I found most interesting. Having a first-class research library's stacks to rummage in,[27] I began a program of systematic reading in the history of comparison in the study of religion and in anthropology, abstracting both premodern and modern texts.[28]

At the same time, I began to think about a dissertation that would use

Frazer's *The Golden Bough* as a "laboratory for comparison."[29] The problem was the right one; but Frazer, as I already knew while drafting the dissertation, was the wrong choice. In my conclusion to the dissertation, written some six years later, I argued that the problem is neither with Frazer's data nor with his ever-changing and always weak theories, it is that "Frazer had no method, either explicit or implicit, for his innumerable comparisons." He offers no answer to the question, how shall we compare?[30]

II: Teacher

My first academic appointment was in the Department of Religion at Dartmouth College, for the year 1965–66, replacing faculty on leave. The teaching assignments were predetermined, courses that had already been scheduled.

That year at Dartmouth sealed my already existing friendship with Jacob Neusner. It was also where I met Hans Penner, who had come that year from the University of Vermont to begin teaching at Dartmouth. Hans was trained in History of Religions at Chicago; our association was the first opportunity I had to talk about the field with an individual rather than with a book. And talk we did . . . for hours each day. Whatever growing sense of security I felt as a neophyte in the history of religions I owed to these conversations.

In 1966, I joined the faculty of the Department of Religious Studies, University of California, Santa Barbara. This was a considered move. I had known its chair, Robert Michaelsen, through membership in the Society for Religion in Higher Education as well as through his writings. I shared his sense that teaching religion in state universities provided a new environment in which to think through our subject matter, and had hoped to have a career in public education.[31] The Department was small (Michaelsen, Walter Capps, Richard Comstock) and vigorous. I was expected to teach the large lecture class on world religions, to give an introductory course to the study of religion, and to offer introductions to the Old Testament, the New Testament, and Judaism.

While writing the bulk of the dissertation at Santa Barbara and reflecting on my growing sense of Frazer's inability to answer my questions on comparison, I had come to see that the problem needed to be framed differently. Implicit in the comparative project was a prior question, how can a morphological/structural approach be historically and anthropologically responsible? My initial experiments with this issue were the formats of the world religions course and the introduction to the study of religion. I had experienced, as well as taught in, survey courses, and I was convinced that their principles of coverage and of chronological ordering were uninteresting. One damn thing after another simply fails at problematizing the subject matter with respect to any intellectual capacity other than mnemonics. The two devices finally settled on, the exemplum and the test case, not only served as organizing principles for the courses but came to be stratagems I would deploy in most of my subsequent work.

The world religions course was structured around the notion that each of the major religious traditions should be taken as exemplifying particular structures of religious experience, behavior, and expression as identified by students of religion. (For example, Hinduism was paired with temple construction and sacrifice; Islam, with holy book and pilgrimage; Judaism, with holy land and the duality, pure/impure; Christianity, with myth and history and life-cycle rituals). The idea was to first understand the structure by acquiring what I termed a "vocabulary," a set of cross-cultural examples, quickly read, that gave some sense of a structure's range and attendant interpretative issues, then to study relevant materials within the particular religious tradition.[32]

The introduction to the study of religion was structured around the notion of test cases, significant texts that raised sets of questions as to both their meaning within the cultures that produced them, and their meaning within the history of scholarship on them.[33] This became a characteristic of much of my later work, a double archaeology of situating a text or artifact both in 'their' history and in 'ours.' The intellectual challenges of organizing the syllabi for both of these courses, the efforts at choice with respect to materials, gave rise to my careerlong preoccupation with the pedagogy of the introductory course.[34]

When I moved to the University of Chicago in 1968–69, the second course served, through the mid-1970s, at times as an offering in the College ("Basic Problems in the Study of Religion"), at times as the introductory course in the Divinity School to the History of Religions field ("Texts and Contexts in the History of Religions"). Each version had the same topics and primary readings, but had different supplementary bibliographies and final exercises. In 1974, I used some of these class materials as the armature for the Arthur O. Clarke Lectures at Pomona College. These were later rewritten as several of the essays subsequently reprinted in *Imagining Religion* (1982),[35] hence the reference in its introduction:

> The essays collected together in this volume are as well the efforts of a teacher. . . . Each had its origin in a specific classroom situation as I attempted to describe, through concrete example, the particular angle of vision of the historian of religion. As

such, each essay has a double pedagogic intent: to cast light upon a specific religious phenomenon and to do so in such a way that the characteristic preoccupations and strategies of the historian of religion be better revealed.[36]

The more than thirty years I have spent teaching at the University of Chicago has defined my work. With but two exceptions (1966, 1968), everything published has appeared during my tenure there. The University's commitment to letting a mind go where it will resulted in a diversity of appointments, until the ultimate freedom, granted in 1982, of being without departmental affiliation as the Robert O. Anderson Distinguished Service Professor of the Humanities.[37]

I have no intention, here, of reviewing these years in any chronological fashion. I shall only focus on a few items, postponing until the third part of this essay discussion of those persistent elements in my work which were formulated at Chicago. I have titled this third section "Persistent Preoccupations." As one who claims to be a generalist, I determined early on, at Chicago, that this entailed doing work in relation to the agenda of others. For this reason, the vast majority of papers, lectures, seminar contributions, and responses (largely unpublished) have been on topics that have been assigned. The question has always been what generalizing or comparative perspective could be brought to issues and to data stipulated as representing their interests. Thus my work represents less of a coherent system than it does a series of continuing foci, hence "Preoccupations."

It is not without significance that I was recruited by the New Collegiate Division of the College at the University of Chicago. Given my initial choice to work in a public university, I doubt I would have accepted appointment solely in the Divinity School. Charles Long was the voice behind the initiative, which was undertaken by James Redfield. The appointment was to a small, experimental program, the History and Philosophy of Religion, which had as its faculty Charles Long, Marshall Hodgson (who died, tragically, just before my arrival), and Henry Rago (the editor of *Poetry*). There were no set courses; teaching was in seminars or tutorials.

This said, it would be dissembling not to acknowledge that the Divinity School (to which I was offered a joint appointment in the History of Religions field) was a strong motivation in my decision to relocate. I had first met Mircea Eliade on February 14, 1968, in Santa Barbara, where he had arrived to begin a term as a Visiting Professor, the evening of my return from the interview at Chicago. We struck up an immediate

11

relationship with many hours of conversation, both about the history of religions and about literature. I had known Chuck Long through the Society for Religion in Higher Education since 1965; I had first met Joseph Kitagawa at a conference the year before. While I was not particularly eager to teach at the graduate level, I viewed an opportunity to work with these individuals as equivalent to a postdoctoral education in the history of religions, a field in which I was entirely an autodidact. Certainly the central role of Chicago in the profession, in those years, guaranteed a constant stream of visitors, an extraordinary group of graduate students, and entry into a variety of associations that would not have occurred had I been located elsewhere. By 1971–72, the program in the New Collegiate Division had been suspended, and I shifted my primary appointment, for a time, to the Divinity School, becoming chair of the History of Religions field.

I was restless. My interest was chiefly in college teaching, and I was increasingly being defined as a graduate instructor. In 1972, I received an offer from another university that specifically exempted me from having to participate in their graduate program. I was prepared to leave Chicago and had so informed the president and the dean of the Divinity School, when, fortuitously, a letter arrived at their offices from James Gustafson, who was about to assume an appointment at Chicago as University Professor, inquiring as to his College teaching responsibilities. (There were none.) In a hastily arranged meeting, President Levi and Dean Kitagawa asked me if I would stay at the University and form a College religion program.

I remained and worked on what would become the College's concentration in Religion and the Humanities—a program whose design both reflected my conception of religious studies[38] and my growing discontent with the traditional organization of the college major.[39]

The new concentration was approved in 1973, and I began offering seminars in it; I also designing two yearlong sequences, independent of the concentration, that would serve in the College's general education program.[40] In 1975, I was appointed to one of the first new chairs in the College, as the William Benton Associate Professor (later, Professor) of Religion and the Human Sciences. Apparently I had displayed sufficient political savvy in gaining approval for Religion and the Humanities to be asked to join the College administration, first as Master of the Humanities Collegiate Division, Associate Dean of the graduate Division of the Humanities, and Associate Dean of the College, 1973–77, then as Dean of the Faculty of the College, 1977–82. (I resigned from the Divinity School in 1977.) The decade spent in administration, in effect, provided me with a second career, as I began to speak at educational conferences and write on liberal learning nearly as much as I did on religion.[41]

III: Persistent Preoccupations

Moving to Chicago in the late 60s was to enter into Mircea Eliade's orbit at the height of his influence. Eliade had been, for me, a model of what it might be to be a historian of religion. He seemed to have read everything and to be able to place the most variegated data within coherent structures. While a graduate student, I had set out to read nearly every work cited by Eliade in his extraordinary bibliographies in *Patterns in Comparative Religion*, hiring tutors to teach me the requisite languages. These readings constituted my education in the field. I took Eliade to be my master, his power all the more palpable in that we had never met. Once, in 1965, while driving to a conference at Notre Dame, I had stopped off in Chicago and sat in a telephone booth for several hours trying, unsuccessfully, to gain enough courage to call Eliade and ask to meet with him. I doubt that I have ever been as apprehensive as on that first night's drive, two and a half years later, to meet Eliade at his villa outside of Santa Barbara. But Eliade proved to be a gentle giant, learned and funny, filled with curiosity, a master of exotica as well as a lively purveyor of gossip. He became the most generous of senior colleagues, both supporting my work and including our family within his wide circles of sociability. I count my association with him as one of the great gifts in my life and miss our conversations dearly.

Given this respect and affection, the issue became one of how to separate oneself from aspects of Eliade's thought without distancing oneself from the man. This dilemma came to speech in a paper delivered in 1971, with Eliade present, at a symposium on his work.

> In making these [few critical remarks], I feel acutely the stance of the pygmy standing on the giant's shoulders but without the attendant claim of having seen further (if one dares to so stretch this tortured phrase, fondly contracted as OTSOG, following Robert K. Merton's brilliant investigation of its history). The giant, in this case, has taught all of us how and what to see; and far more important, how to understand what we have learned to see. . . . It is for us, his students, only to bring forth the questions, blurrings, and shadows which result from our more peripheral vision.[42]

Much of my work in the early Chicago years was devoted to finding both constructive alternatives to the points of disagreement with Eliade and the appropriate rhetoric with which to express them.

1. Reversal and Rebellion; Locative and Utopian

In this latter regard, I place particular importance on a paper written for the 1968 annual meeting of the Society for Religion in Higher Education and delivered that August, quite literally while in transit from Santa Barbara to Chicago, "Birth Upside Down or Right Side Up?" (1970), treating the apocryphal traditions concerning Peter's upside down crucifixion.

From one perspective, the paper is a continuation of a series of explorations of gnostic themes and texts begun in 1962–63.[43] Here, the only novelty was a shift from a genetic interest in gnosticism to one more appropriately morphological: "My understanding of gnosticism is that it is a structural possibility within a number of religious traditions in the hellenistic-Mediterranean world, that it is not a new religion, or a Christian heresy, but rather a structure analogous to mysticism or asceticism."[44] The terms I chose to characterize this structure were "reversal" and "rebellion," especially with respect to archaic traditions, and the examples cited make clear that these elements were in no way limited to the "hellenistic-Mediterranean world."

From another perspective, the paper represents a series of breaks with previous work. (1) The first departure concerned the scope of the comparative materials, representing fidelity to the Eliadean tradition as I understood it. In "The Garments of Shame" (1966), I had ranged widely over traditions of nudity, and more narrowly, over exorcistic rituals on animal skins, but the examples were confined to either Mediterranean or Christian texts.[45] That is to say, there was a presumption of a genetic relationship guaranteed by spatio-temporal contiguities—a presumption I would later label as that of homology.[46] In "Birth," I was not so confined. The paper began with an Eliadean move to the "immediate apprehension" of the meaning of a symbol or archetype,[47] asking what the historian of religions could say about Peter's upside down crucifixion, "What does it mean to be upside down?" and answering, with an appeal to the phenomenological psychiatrist E. W. Straus, "Its most basic sense is to be nonhuman." It then goes on to give a variety of exempla from western and non-western traditions, from mythic, cultic, and literary texts.

(2) Unlike "Garments," which set the problem posed by the Gospel of Thomas within the context of a problem in a history of traditions approach to early Christianities, "Birth" placed the problem posed by the

Acts of Peter within a broad, largely anthropological, theoretical context, as represented preeminently by Claude Lévi-Strauss, Mary Douglas,
and Victor Turner, but also by E. Durkheim and M. Mauss, R. Hertz,
American ethnoscientists, and G. Dumézil.[48]

(3) The paper goes on to state a disagreement with Eliade, one that
came to dominate a number of essays written through 1974. After summarizing Eliade on the cosmogonic myth and arguing for its applicability
to aspects of ancient Mediterranean cultures (using Cornelius Loew's
summary of the conclusions of the Panbabylonian school),[49] I went on to
argue the alternative:

> One finds in many archaic cultures a profound faith in the cos-
> mos as ordered in the beginning and a joyous celebration of the
> primordial act of ordering as well as a deep sense of responsibil-
> ity for the maintenance of that order through repetition of the
> myth, through ritual, through norms of conduct, or through
> taxonomy. But it is equally apparent that in some cultures the
> structure of order, the gods that won or ordained it, creation it-
> self, are discovered to be evil and oppressive. In such circum-
> stances, one will rebel against the paradigms and seek to reverse
> their power . . .
>
> Rather than renewing the creation, reestablishing the pat-
> terns of destiny, the patterns are seen to be fundamentally per-
> verse. . . . Reality is discovered to lie not within the cosmos as
> ordered through creation but above the world, beyond it, and
> the aim of existence is seen to be to escape the constricted con-
> fines of one's place.[50]

I concluded that what was required was a "phenomenology of rebellion,"
adding that "It is my conviction that such a study is long overdue and, in
our present situation, might be of more than strictly academic relevance."[51]

All that was needed was to name this duality. After reviewing a number of options, I settled on 'locative' for the first, more Eliadean, pattern
in "The Influence of Symbols on Social Change" (1970), and 'utopian' for
the second, rebellious pattern in "The Wobbling Pivot" (1972),[52] yielding
the dichotomy, locative/utopian that I continue to use to the present day.

The culmination of this first effort at distancing was the 1971 conference on Eliade's work that resulted in "The Wobbling Pivot" (1972).[53] The
essay opens with an attempt to summarize, as fairly and accurately as possible, Eliade's categories of sacred space and sacred time—a necessary

prelude to criticism—before turning to the critique, diplomatically expressed in the form of a series of questions. Is chaos best understood as the equivalent of the profane? Has the category of the "Center" been too narrowly discussed in terms of geographical symbolism? Can one pay such attention to the "Center" without giving equal attention to the periphery? Are all mythic first times paradigmatic and to be ritually repeated? What about reversals and rebellions? What about those myths which express a fundamental tension in the cosmos? "Clearly these mythologies, many of which are extremely archaic, point to a different spiritual horizon than that described by Eliade as the fundamental 'archaic ontology.'" Are the materials Eliade describes best organized under the categories 'archaic' and 'modern?' Does the dichotomy between mythic-cyclical time and linear-historical time do justice to the rich patterns of temporal significance in various cultures? My attempt, here, was not so much to insist on a negative answer to each question as to propose a coherent alternative.

"Wobbling Pivot" is of interest in one other respect. After introducing for the first time the distinction, locative and utopian, it goes on to caution against imposing on this dichotomy "an explicit evolutionary scheme of development," as, for example, identifying the locative with primitive, archaic societies and utopian with modern. "Both have been and remain coeval existential possibilities. . . . While in this culture, at this time or in that place, one or the other view may appear to be the more dominant," this does not affect the "postulation of the basic availability of both at any time in any place."⁵⁴ This needs to be stressed as the Mediterranean examples I have frequently employed might lead to the perception that the locative, Classical traditions are always prior to the utopian Late Antique materials. (Unfortunately, my own language has, at times, given comfort to such an understanding.)⁵⁵

2. Situation, Incongruity, and Thought

In "Wobbling Pivot," I observed, almost by way of an aside, that "I have a sense that much will be learned from relating the cosmic views [i.e., locative and utopian] to the social worlds in which they are found."⁵⁶ I clearly had in mind the sort of situating of texts characteristic of my introductory classes. Beginning in 1972, I began to experiment with ways of carrying these efforts over into my writing.⁵⁷ In May 1974, when I was asked by the College of the University of Chicago to give an inaugural lecture to acknowledge receiving the William Benton Chair in Religion and the Human Sciences, I used the conventions of such an address both to summarize work already done and to forecast new directions. The lecture, "Map Is Not Territory" (1978), both bid farewell to my double project of appreciation and criticism of Eliade, and signalled a different tack. Rather than rebellion and reversal, the point of departure for understanding myth and ritual in a non-replicatory sense would be "incongruity" as experienced within quite particular "situations," with the premise that it is "the perception of incongruity that gives rise to thought."[58]

The lecture begins with a rehearsal of the locative cosmology, now termed a "map," but with a twist.[59] The argument is no longer one of accepting the pattern but juxtaposing it to another; rather, it has become one of suspicion with respect to the pattern in terms of its social situation, both within archaic cultures and within contemporary scholarship:

> I would term this cosmology a locative map of the world and the organizer of such a world, an imperial figure. It is a map of the world which guarantees meaning and value through structures of congruity and conformity.
>
> Students of religion have been most successful in describing and interpreting this locative, imperial map of the world— especially within archaic, urban cultures. . . . Yet, the very success of these topographies should be a signal for caution. For they are largely based on documents from urban, agricultural, hierarchical cultures. The most persuasive witnesses to a locative, imperial world-view are the production of well organized, self-conscious scribal elites who had a deep vested interest in restricting mobility and valuing place. The texts are, by and large, the production of temples and royal courts and provide their raison d'être . . . In most cases one cannot escape the suspicion that, in the locative map of the world, we are encountering a self-serving ideology which ought not to be generalized into the universal pattern of religious experience and expression.

The singular "universal pattern" was intended to refer to Eliade's "archaic ontology." But the critique was expanded: "I find the same conservative, ideological element strongly to the fore in a variety of approaches to religion which lay prime emphasis upon congruency and conformity, whether it be expressed through phenomenological descriptions of repetition [or] functionalist descriptions of feedback mechanisms. . . ."[60]

With this said, the lecture moved on to the chief implication of the criticism, not so much in terms of its ideological situation but, rather, in terms of its high valuation of congruency leading to a denial of the significance of efforts at thought and of intellectual criticism, especially as

projected upon so-called primitives. Using the perception of incongruency as the point of contention, the lecture went on to argue against the
consequences of such a view:

> On the conceptual level it robs them of their humanity, of those
> perceptions of discrepancy and discord which give rise to the
> symbolic project that we identify as the very essence of being
> human. It reduces the primitive to the level of fantasy where ex-
> perience plays no role in challenging belief . . . where discrep-
> ancy does not give rise to thought but rather is thought away.[61]

One implication of this emphasis on the relationship between discrepancy and thought was that, rather than according to Romantic theories of pristine myth,[62] myth was to be understood as a thoughtful "strategy
for dealing with a situation."[63] This was illustrated, in the course of the
lecture, by an Oceanic punning account of origins to account for a newly
introduced domesticated animal; African divination; the juxtaposition
between expectation and reality in Australian and African initiatory scenarios, and a lengthy discussion of the Ceramese myth of Hainuwele.[64] The
Late Antique materials previously used to establish the utopian themes
of rebellion and reversal were briefly mentioned but not discussed.[65]

The lecture had two sorts of conclusions. One reflected back on the
distinction of locative and utopian which had previously preoccupied
me, and suggested that these were but two "maps" among many. The lecture had sketched out one more of these maps: traditions which "are more
closely akin to the joke in that they neither deny nor flee from disjunction,
but allow the incongruous elements to stand"; traditions that seek "to play
between the incongruities, and to provide an occasion for thought."[66]
The other conclusion was offered with respect to the Hainuwele myth,
but intended to be generalized:

> The Ceramese myth of Hainuwele . . . does not solve the di-
> lemma, overcome the incongruity or resolve the tension. Rather
> it provides the native with an occasion for thought. It is a test-
> ing of the adequacy and applicability of native categories to new
> situations and data. As such, it is preeminently a rational and ra-
> tionalizing enterprise, an instance of an experimental method.
> The experiment was a failure. The white man was not brought
> into conformity with native categories, he still fails to recognize
> a moral claim of reciprocity. But this is not how we judge the suc-
> cess of a science. We judge harshly those who have abandoned

the novel and the incongruous to a realm outside of the confines of understanding and we value those who (even though failing) stubbornly make the attempt at achieving intelligibility, who have chosen the long, hard road of understanding.[67]

When I identify myself as having an intellectualist understanding of religion, it is the sense suggested by this quotation.

Several of the essays in *Imagining Religion* were devoted to the elaboration of these themes: in situations of intercultural conflict ("A Pearl of Great Price and a Cargo of Yams" [1976]; "The Unknown God" [1982]); in situations of intracultural discrepancies ("The Bare Facts of Ritual" [1980]);[68] as well as in scholarly discourse, when it classifies some phenomenon as unique and, therefore, unintelligible ("The Devil in Mr. Jones" [1982]).[69]

The most sustained investigation of situational incongruity was *To Take Place: Toward Theory in Ritual* (1987), based on the Merril L. Hassenfeld Memorial Lectures delivered at Brown University in 1985.[70] Here the issue was the displacement of two sets of systemic rituals, one Judaean, the other Christian, that had been carefully crafted for particular loci in Jerusalem, the Temple and the Church of the Holy Sepulchre. Each group, through the contingencies of history, lost access to the place. For each, the rituals had to be replaced by new intellectual constructions: the spatial systematics of pure/impure, as represented by texts such as *Mishnah*, and the systematics of temporality, as represented by the liturgical calendar.[71]

3. Taxonomy and Comparison

My early interest in botany and fascination with taxonomy, especially of the *Gramineae*, led directly to a concern with comparison. I spent hours puzzling through the implications of phrases such as "a natural classification of plants is one in which the different kinds of species are arranged in groups according to their resemblances, as shown by their structure"; "ideas of the relations of groups to each other are largely inferences based upon morphological resemblances"; "those individuals which are so much alike as to appear to be of one kind . . . are regarded as belonging to the same species"; "the question always arises whether there are several closely related but distinct species or a few distinct species each of which shows great variation," leading the author to distinguish between "well-marked varieties," "less well-marked varieties," and "additional forms."[72]

Chapter One

In the summer of 1952, one of the more ambitious exhibits I mounted in my small trailside museum was entitled *Same, Like, Different*, attempting to illustrate the issues attendant on taxonomy with examples of common wild plants. Put simply, taxonomy seemed a comparative enterprise which sought similarity across obvious individual variations and which asserted significant difference even in the face of apparent resemblances. Some thirty years later, this early perception was echoed in statements such as

> It is axiomatic that comparison is never a matter of identity. Comparison requires the acceptance of difference as the grounds of its being interesting, and a methodical manipulation of that difference to achieve some stated cognitive end. The questions of comparison are questions of judgment with respect to difference: What differences are to be maintained in the interests of comparative inquiry? What differences can be defensibly relaxed and relativized in light of the intellectual tasks at hand?[73]

By the time, as a graduate student at Yale, I began to take courses in anthropology, I was well prepared for their preoccupation with kinship. Kinship systems, after all, are one of humankind's more elaborate taxonomic constructions, and the comparative study of kinship systems by anthropologists have yielded some of their most impressive and successful efforts at classification. As with any young student of Marx and Engels, I was led, by them, to Lewis H. Morgan's pioneering studies, first, *Ancient Society,* and then, *Systems of Consanguinity and Affinity of the Human Family.* I had found my way, later, to Frazer, Durkheim, and Robertson Smith on totemism, and, by college, to Durkheim and Mauss on classification, as well as some of Lévi-Strauss's early writings on kinship. As I worked on a structural study of Hesiod's genealogies, I began systematic readings in the literature, published since the mid-1940's, on kinship in Native American, African, Australian and other Oceanic societies. At Yale, it was the controversies over the various formalizations of these systems that most interested me, an interest reawakened when the long-awaited second edition of Lévi-Strauss's *Elementary Structures of Kinship* appeared. Throughout this period, I continued, as well, to read in the theoretical literature on biological taxonomy and in journals devoted to botanical classification.

Given this history, I have always viewed comparison and classification as inseparable. In my published work, the one topic always entails the other. There are a set of writings more focused on taxonomic issues, often

20

relying on biological systematics: "Animals and Plants in Myth and Legend" (1974), "Fences and Neighbors" (1980), "What a Difference a Difference Makes" (1985), and "Classification" (2000). One subset concerns the problematic taxon, "world religions": "Map Is Not Territory" (1978), "A Matter of Class" (1996), "Religion, Religions, Religious" (1998), "Classification" (2000); and another concerns native taxonomic categories: "Earth and Gods" (1969), "Birth Upside Down or Rightside Up?" (1970), "Towards Interpreting Demonic Powers" (1978), *To Take Place*, esp. chapter 3 (1987), "Differential Equations" (1991), "Wisdom's Place" (1995), "Close Encounters of Diverse Kinds" (2001).[74] There are, as well, a group of programmatic essays more focused on comparison, which includes *"Adde Parvum"* (1971), "In Comparison a Magic Dwells" (1982), *Drudgery Divine* (1990), "Epilogue: The 'End' of Comparison" (2000), and "Acknowledgments: Morphology and History," parts 1–2 (2000).[75]

When first working on the problem of comparison, my chief concern was with the possibility of a rigorous method that would exclude what seemed all too typical of the practice of many scholars: *x* (which they happened to have noticed) reminds them of *y* (which they happen to have already known), therefore *x* must in some way be like *y*. The initial enthusiasm for the statistical procedures associated with George P. Murdock and the Human Relations Area Files was based on the hope that it offered such rigor. In fact, it was procedurally flawed, most tellingly with respect to its "sample." This said, the project's summary conclusion remains provocative, more than twenty thousand statistically significant correlations across a sample of sixty societies. By contrast, most students of religion, if they are interested in comparison at all, treat, at best, a few dozen.[76]

Then, too, so many comparisons in the study of religion were between single traits despite the fact that they were embedded in complex phenomena. Already in my historical studies ("The Garments of Shame" [1966]; "The Prayer of Joseph" [1968]) I had insisted on comparing a cluster of elements. But, even as I wrote these pieces Lévi-Strauss had convinced me of their inadequacy, that it is not the elements but the relations between the elements that are significant.[77] I worked through a good part of the '70s convinced that both the problems with comparison and, to a lesser degree, the remedies were correct: rigor through something like statistical procedures was desirable; multiple characteristics were crucial.

Renewed interest in these matters was prompted by an invitation to give one of the plenary addresses in honor of the centennial of the Society of Biblical Literature at the society's 1978 annual meeting. The hope was expressed that I might say something about the definitional problems associated with a field of increasing importance and activity but of un-satisfactory nomenclature—denoted by a variety of titles including in-tertestamental Judaism, postbiblical Judaism, early Judaism, late Judaism, hellenistic Judaism—such as would be suitable for the projected centen-nial volume, *Early Judaism and Its Modern Interpreters,* to be edited by Robert A. Kraft and G. W. E. Nickelsburg. I wrote several drafts of a lec-ture entitled "To Draw the Line" in response to this assignment, but it soon became clear that the problem was not confined to the anticipated one of the biases and interests reflected in the diversity of names. Of more gravity was a set of theoretical issues related to classification, com-parison, and by implication, definition. About the same time (1975–76), in preparation for the possibility of reoffering the Problems in the His-tory of Comparison course, I had been reading through a set of newer writings in phenetic (cladistic) and numerical classification which chal-lenged the evolutionary concerns of more traditional biological system-atics, insisting on taking all characteristics into account without regard for phylogenetic history. I was intrigued by echoes of Kant's early dis-tinction between complex contemporaneous similarities (*Naturbeschrei-bung*) and similarities that resulted from historical and genealogical rela-tions (*Naturgeschichte*), which I had taught in the "Problems" course, with special reference to the invention of the category of 'race.'[78]

In the centennial lecture, "Fences and Neighbors" (1980), I summa-rized only the new numerical taxonomic proposals as representing a "self-consciously *polythetic* mode of classification which surrendered the idea of perfect, unique, single differentia—a taxonomy which retained the notion of necessary but abandoned the notion of sufficient criteria for ad-mission to a class."[79] Comparison would be based on a multiplicity of traits, not all of which might be possessed by any individual member of the class. I then went on to describe two "experiments" toward a future polythetic description of the taxon, Judaism. The first mapped the "range" of one taxic indicator, circumcision; the second, the variety of indicators of Jewish identity gleaned from a corpus of funerary inscriptions. The conclusion was programmatic:

> What has animated these reflections and explorations is the conviction that students of religion need to abandon the notion of "essence," of a unique differentium for early Judaism. . . . The cartography appears far messier. We need to map the variety of Judaisms, each of which appears as a shifting cluster of charac-teristics which vary over time.
> As the anthropologist has begun to abandon a functional-

ist view of culture as a well-articulated, highly integrated mechanism . . . so we in religious studies must set about an analogous
dismantling of the old theological and imperialistic impulses toward totalization, unification, and integration. The labor at
achieving the goal of a polythetic classification of Judaisms,
rather than a monothetic definition of early Judaism, is but a
preliminary step toward this end.[80]

I returned to the problem of singularity in comparisons ten years
later, in the 1988 Louis H. Jordan Lectures, gaining an assist, this time,
from philosophical resemblance theory rather than from biology. Here
the suggestion was more formal, that rather than considering a comparative statement as being dyadic, '*x* resembles *y*,' it should be thought of as,
at least, triadic, as a "multiterm" expression such as '*x* resembles *y* more
than *z* with respect to . . . ,' or '*x* resembles *y* more than *w* resembles *z* with
respect to. . . .'[81]

In 1979, I brought together reflections growing out of these twin
concerns with rigor and singularity in response to an invitation from Jacob Neusner to deliver an opening paper to the newly reconstituted history of Judaism section of the American Academy of Religion. The paper, "In Comparison a Magic Dwells" (1982),[82] was less important in
itself than in the response it provoked by the distinguished anthropologist and specialist in Papua New Guinea, Fitz John Porter Poole. His paper, presented to a subsequent meeting of the same section of the Academy, remains, for me, the most suggestive treatment of comparison of the
past two decades. The sentence in it that interested me most reads,
"Comparison does not deal with phenomena *in toto* or in the round, but
only with an aspectual characteristic of them."[83] This was a far better way
of framing the issue than my usual language of suspicion concerning singularity and essence. It connected well with earlier criticisms of the holistic assumptions of conservative ideologies in the study of religion,[84]
and the term "aspectual" had, for me, a series of implications. I was able
to take up some of these in a paper for the 1988 annual meeting of the
American Society for the Study of Religion on the assigned, somewhat
oddly phrased, theme, "What Makes Some Categories Better for Comparison Than Others?" This paper served as a partial rough draft for the
second chapter of *Drudgery Divine* (1990), "On Comparison."

"On Comparison" sketches out the lineaments of what remains my
understanding of the comparative enterprise. Comparisons are not given;
they are the result of thought. Comparison in the service of disciplined
inquiry

brings differences together within the space of the scholar's
mind for the scholar's own intellectual reasons . . . [C]ompari-
son does not necessarily tell us how things 'are' . . . like models
and metaphors, comparison tell us how things might be conceived, how they might be 'redescribed' . . . [Comparison] lifts
out and strongly marks certain features within difference as being of possible intellectual significance, expressed in the rhetoric
of their being 'like' in some stipulated fashion. Comparison provides the means by which *we* 're-vision' phenomena as *our* data
in order to solve *our* theoretical problems. . . . Comparison, as
seen from such a view, is an active, at times even a playful, enterprise of deconstruction and reconstitution which, kaleidoscope-
like, gives the scholar a shifting set of characteristics with which
to negotiate the relations between his or her theoretical interests and data stipulated as exemplary.[85]

In a passage such as this, the notion of the "aspectual" has been extended.
It refers not only to the data but to the scholar's intellectual interests
as well.

In the course of this discussion in "On Comparison," there is a subordinate clause, "recalling . . . that a model is useful precisely when it is
different from that to which it is being applied."[86] At the time, I thought
chiefly of the map metaphor and of the notion of "defamiliarization," introduced by Soviet 'formalist' literary critics, which I thought to be one
of the important consequences of the juxtaposition inherent in comparison.[87] Later, in several of the essays reprinted in this volume, the notion
of an intellectual "object" being required to be different from the phenomenon in the interest of cognitive gain came to be a central element
in thinking about the study of religion.[88] (See section 5 below).

In *Drudgery Divine*, these latter implications were not taken up.
Rather, I revisited and expanded Richard Owen's influential eighteenth-
century distinction between homology and analogy to make a parallel
point.[89] For Owen, homology, resemblances explained by common descent, were "real." That is to say, they were the sorts of genealogical comparisons favored by historians in order to demonstrate filiation, contact,
diffusion. Analogies, by contrast, are "ideal." That is to say, they are mental constructions, they rest on postulated relations stipulated with respect
to particular points of interest. In *Drudgery*, I cited, with approval, J. S.
Mill's dictum, "if we have the slightest reason to suppose any real connection between . . . A and B; the argument is no longer one of analogy."[90] As already observed, while earlier essays such as "The Prayer of

Joseph" (1968) were homological in intent, I now insisted that analogy was the proper paradigm for comparison.[91]

Both *To Take Place* (1987) and *Drudgery Divine* (1990) represented ambitious attempts at comparison. *To Take Place* had as its major interest a comparison between the systemic constructions of rabbinic Judaism and post-Constantianian Christianities, between the sort of thoughtful endeavor represented by *Mishnah* and by the elaboration of the Christian liturgical calendar. In its initial discussion of the Tjilpa pole, it addressed comparison in relation to Eliade's taxonomic category of the "Center." *Drudgery Divine* is a thick critical description of the history of comparisons between earliest Christianities and the religions of Late Antiquity (especially the so-called "mysteries"), on a variety of topics. *Drudgery* goes on to sketch out a new comparison through redeploying the distinction of locative and utopian.

The issue of the manipulation of difference attendant on both comparison and classification led to a new focus on difference as the term under which I could bring together older vocabulary of 'reversal,' 'rebellion,' 'incongruity,' and 'gap' and older interests in the histories of comparison in anthropology and the study of religion with newer historical and theoretical concerns that have become characteristic of my work over the last decade. These are represented by a number of the essays reprinted in this collection: the relations of culture and difference; the 'discovery' of the Americas as the site where difference became an urgent intellectual problem, and its relations to the invention of the category of race; 'redescription' as the replacement term for older usages such as 'map,' 'model,' 'paradigm,' and the ways in which a set of intellectual operations, ranging from definition to explanation, may be understood as modes of redescription.

4. Culture, Difference, and Thought

In 1976, I was invited to give a presentation for a theological series sponsored by the United Methodist Foundation at the University of Chicago on the assigned topic, "The Persistence of the Sacred." As formulated, it seemed to me to be but a variant of the tired theme, humans have always been religious. After an initial interrogation of the title—a characteristic move in many lectures—I inverted the title to read "Sacred Persistence"[92] and chose the category of canon as its exemplification.[93] In the lecture, by way of preparation for the discussion of the latter, an illustration was introduced calling attention to three interrelated observations: the plenum of possible natural foodstuffs available to any culture; the all but arbitrary limitation of what any culture will, in fact, eat; and the fact that this limitation is, then, overcome by the variety of the foodstuffs' preparation. "If food is a phenomenon characterized by limitation, cuisine is a phenomenon characterized by variegation." While this was employed in "Sacred Persistence" primarily as an analogy to canon, it contains, as well, a more "general model of cultural activity" and, through the use of the term 'ingenuity,' a suggestion as to the relation of this cultural dynamic to thought.

> An almost limitless horizon of possibilities that are at hand (in nature) is arbitrarily reduced (by culture) to a set of basic elements. . . . This initial arbitrariness is, at times, overcome by secondary explanations which attempt to account for the reduction . . . Then a most intense ingenuity is exercised to overcome the reduction . . . to introduce interest and variety. This ingenuity is usually accompanied by a complex set of rules.[94]

That is to say, the dynamic of reduction and elaboration connects with earlier formulations on situation, incongruity, and thought (see section 2 above) but adds the notion that what was there called a "situation" could be internally generated as well as externally imposed and is a regular rather than an unanticipated occurrence. The response, a thoughtful process, was in earlier essays called "application," "experimentation," "rationalizing," "rationalization, accommodation and adjustment," or "casuistry." Here, it is called "ingenuity."[95] There is parity, as well, between the food/cuisine analogy and the earlier description of myth as a "limited collection of elements with a fixed range of cultural meanings which are applied, thought with, worked with, experimented with in particular situations."[96]

The most explicit deployment of this model is the Arizona State University lecture in religion, "Differential Equations: On Constructing the 'Other'" ([1992], reprinted in this volume), where I wrote that, beyond the "ubiquity of the construction of difference in human culture," it would seem that:

> culture itself is constituted by the double process of both making differences and relativizing those very same distinctions. One of our fundamental social projects appears to be our collective capacity to think of, and to think away, the differences we create.[97]

Earlier, in *"Adde Parvum"* (1978), I had generated a rudimentary classification of the sorts of constructed human differences, building on Robert

Redfield's discussion of the "primitive world view" as consisting of a pair of binary oppositions, often correlated, MAN/NOT-MAN and WE/THEY. I proposed "four specifications of the WE/THEY duality . . . (1) They are LIKE-US, (2) They are NOT-LIKE-US, (3) THEY ARE TOO-MUCH-LIKE-US (Robert Frost's "Good fences make good neighbors"), or (4) WE ARE NOT-LIKE-THEM (expressions and polemics concerning 'uniqueness')."[98] It is the third formulation that continued to fascinate me, for it is often the one that is most provocative of thought. In "What a Difference a Difference Makes" (1985) I termed this the problem of the "proximate other," arguing that 'otherness'

> is a matter of relative rather than absolute difference. Difference is not a matter of comparison between entities judged to be equivalent, rather difference most frequently entails a hierarchy of prestige and ranking. Such distinctions are found to be drawn most sharply between "near neighbors" . . . This is the case because "otherness" is a relativistic category inasmuch as it is, necessarily, a term of interaction. A "theory of otherness," is, from this perspective, essentially political.[99]
>
> [W]e know of thousands of societies and world views which are "different," but in most cases, their "remoteness" guarantees our indifference. By and large, Christians and Jews qua Christians and Jews have not thought about the "otherness" of the Kwakiutl or, for that matter, of the Taoist. The bulk of Christian theological thinking about "otherness" (starting with Paul) has been directed toward "other Christians" and, more occasionally, towards those groups thought of as "near-Christians," preeminently Jews and Muslims. Today, as in the past, the history of religious conflicts, of religious perceptions of "otherness" is largely intraspecific: Buddhists to Buddhists, Christians to Christians, Muslims to Muslims, Jews to Jews. The only major exceptions occur in those theoretically unrevealing but historically common moments when "proximity" becomes more a matter of territoriality than of thought.[100]

I have persistently returned to this theme of the "proximate other" in later works,[101] but it is in an unpublished manuscript (dated 1999) that an explicit connection was made with the 1976 food/cuisine analogy. I appealed to the discriminations of connoisseurship. There is no interest, for example, in distinguishing between red and white wine. They are sheerly different; nothing more needs be said. All the efforts at thought are directed toward distinguishing between two examples of the same varietal from different vineyards or between different years (vintages) of same vineyards's production. These differences among items that, to a lay palate, appear to be the same are the differences that count. As I argued in "Differential Equations" (1992), "the deepest intellectual issues are not based upon perceptions of alterity, but, rather, of similarity, at times, even, of identity."[102]

This is not to deny that there are occasions when a difference that is unrelated to the proximate other appears as a severe cognitive shock, when the question of placing the different becomes a pressing one because it calls into question prior anthropological and cosmological assumptions. I have long suggested that, in western discourse, such an occasion was the 'discovery' of the Americas and the unanticipated encounter with the Native Americans. It was this occasion that gave rise to the issues as to 'human nature' that conferred urgency on the human sciences. It led, as well, to the intellectual problematics associated with the invention of the category of 'race.' Although I have published several preliminary studies, reprinted in this volume, the full historical arguments for this case, as well as the implications for anthropological theory, remain a work still in progress (see below, note 95).

5. Redescription, Translation and Generalization

In 1995–96, two events occurred that pushed me to articulate a group of previously inchoate notions that had already begun to influence my way of speaking and writing in a number of unpublished lectures and seminar papers as well as in the college classroom. The first was the opening session of the Ancient Myths and Modern Theories of Christian Origins Consultation at the 1995 annual meeting of the Society of Biblical Literature.[103] The second was an invitation to give a keynote address to a 1996 conference of largely younger scholars, "Reconstructing a History of Religions: Problems and Possibilities," at Western Maryland College, in which my role appeared to be that of a ghost of Christmas past. The first event was as significant for Burton Mack's paper, which undertook in part to summarize aspects of my work with a clarity and conciseness I had not achieved, as it was for my own intervention. The second event, at which I was asked to speak on the question, "Why Imagine Religion?" I took as if it were a final testament.[104] Both events led to papers with a new interlocking set of elements and formulations that have continued to reappear in subsequent work, framing my discussions of a wide variety of topics.[105]

I first introduced the term 'redescription' in "Sacred Persistence" (1979), drawing on Max Black's and Mary Hesse's comparisons of metaphors and scientific models on the grounds that

> both invite us to construe one thing in terms of another (most usually that which is problematic in terms of that which is relatively better understood) so that we may see things in a new, and frequently unexpected, light. A model, in short, is a "redescription."[106]

As I used the term, it expressed a central goal, the redescription of classical categories in the study of religion to the end that these be 'rectified.'[107] Thus "Sacred Persistence" was subtitled "Toward a Redescription of Canon."[108] As that article made plain, the route to redescription and rectification is comparison, the latter predicated upon careful description. Burton Mack first formulated these "four operations" in my work in his contribution to the Consultation.[109] In a later restatement in 2000, I explained the relations between these operations as follows:

> The 'end' of comparison cannot be the act of comparison itself. I would distinguish four moments in the comparative enterprise: description, comparison, redescription and rectification. Description is a double process which comprises the historical or anthropological dimensions of the work: First, the requirement that we locate a given example within the rich texture of its social, historical, and cultural environments that invest it with its local significance. The second task of description is that of reception history, a careful account of how our second-order scholarly tradition has intersected with the exemplum. That is to say, we need to describe how the datum has become accepted as significant for the purpose of argument. Only when such a double contextualization is completed does one move on to the description of [at least] a second example undertaken in the same double fashion. With at least two exempla in view, we are prepared to undertake their comparison both in terms of aspects and relations held to be significant, and with respect to some category, question, theory, or model of interest to us. The aim of such a comparison is the redescription of the exempla (each in light of the other) and a rectification of the academic categories in relation to which they have been imagined.[110]

Because thought would be impossible without comparison, we could not stop comparing even if we wished to. The task, then, for those committed to the comparativist enterprise becomes one of clarifying our assumptions, rectifying our procedures, and justifying our goals.

In both my "Response" at the 1995 Consultation and in "Why Imagine Religion?" a new topic is advanced, partly with respect to the comparativist agendum, but extends beyond this role. I had long been fascinated with translation theories, accumulating a bulging file, offering a college seminar on the subject in the late 70s, and introducing translation as a pedagogical device for teaching Durkheim's project in *Elementary Forms* to college students in the early 80s. Now it was expanded to become a key notion in relation to that most challenging goal of the study of religion: explanation. The same sorts of arguments and, indeed, similar phraseology recur in both papers.

> Both explanations and interpretations are occasioned by surprise. . . . Surprise, in both the natural and the human sciences, is reduced by bringing the unknown into relations to the known—relations of similarity and difference, relations of metonymy and metaphor. The process by which this is accomplished, again in both the natural and the human sciences, is translation. That is to say, the proposal that the theoretical second-order language appropriate to one domain (the known/the familiar) may translate the theoretical second-order language appropriate to another domain (the unknown/the unfamiliar). Perhaps the strongest example of this procedure in the study of religion is Durkheim's translation in *Elementary Forms* of the language appropriate to "religion" (for him, in this work, the unknown) into the language appropriate to "society" (for him, in this work, the known). The point at which one might differ from Durkheim's project is with respect to his acceptance of a goal of explanatory simplicity. Better, here, Lévi-Strauss's formulation: "scientific explanation consists not in a movement from the complex to the simple but in the substitution of a more intelligible complexity for another which is less."

The argument goes on to offer one consequence of such an understanding:

> Too much work by too many scholars of religion takes the form of a description or paraphrase—particularly weak modes of translation, insufficiently different from their subject matter for

purposes of thought. To summarize: a theory, a model, a conceptual category cannot be simply the data writ large.[111]

I need only add that the preference for description and paraphrase is one more instance of the conservative interest in totality discussed above in connection with the notion of 'aspectual' (see part 3 above). Translation, by contrast, is necessarily incomplete. "Whether of a conceptual or a natural language, whether intercultural or intracultural, translation can never be fully adequate, it can never be total. There is always discrepancy. If there is not, then one is not translating but rather speaking the other language."[112] One cannot escape the suspicion that it is precisely this latter possibility (speaking the other language) that defines the goal of many students of religion. It is one means for avoiding the consequences of the necessary inadequacy of translation, submission to the "double requirement of comparison and criticism."[113]

This necessary incompleteness of translation means, as well, that it is corrigible. This interest in corrigibility leads to the last new term introduced into my work in the mid-1990s, that of 'generalization.'[114] The 'general' differs from the 'universal' in that it admits to exceptions; it differs from the 'particular' in that it is highly selective. Both characteristics guarantee that generalizations are always corrigible. As with comparison, generalization brings disparate phenomena together in the space of the scholar's intellect. As such, it often results in surprise, which calls forth efforts at explanation and rectification. One goal of the study of religion is the proposal of comparative generalizations based on a careful description of data that, nevertheless, remain firmly situated; generalizations that are advanced in the service of some stated intellectual task.

With the introduction of these newer notions of redescription, translation, and generalization, coupled with a more complex view of difference and its relation to thought, the sorts of problems I first associated with issues of taxonomy and then developed in my early essays on reversal, rebellion, and situational incongruity come together. The efforts at thinking about the status of theoretical constructs in the study of religion converge with interests in the data from religion and join with the long-standing critique of those scholars who would emphasize totality and congruency when describing religion. What these persistent preoccupations have in common is the insistence on the cognitive power of distortion, along with the concomitant choice of the map over the territory.[115]

I have attempted in this essay to provide a sense of both the career and the preoccupations of an individual who has been as much a student of the study of religion as a student of religion. I have sought to convey, through all the movements and experimentations, something of what has been constant, the argument that religion is not best understood as a disclosure that gives rise to a particular mode of experience. To the contrary, religion is the relentlessly human activity of thinking through a 'situation,' an understanding that requires assenting to Lévi-Strauss's dictum, "man has always been thinking equally well."[116]

Such a view carries, as well, as another consequence, the refusal to accept as an epitaph that phrase from one of Rudyard Kipling's *Plain Tales*, "Theory killed him dead." I am not so compulsive an academician as to claim that theory revivifies one or revives one's chosen field. Theory is not life, but I know with perfect surety that it is liveliness.

Notes

Complete references to publications by J. Z. Smith are located in the appendix.

1. L. J. Cappon, ed., *The Adams-Jefferson Letters* (reprint, New York, 1971), 358. The next sentence reads, "I shall come to the Subject of Religion, by and by." My interest in the Adams-Jefferson correspondence, which looms large in the first chapter of Smith, *Drudgery Divine* (1990), 1–9, 26–27, goes back to my 1959 encounter with Ezra Pound's 1937 essay, "The Jefferson-Adams Letters as a Shrine and a Monument" (now in E. Pound, *Selected Prose, 1909–1965*, ed. W. Cookson [London, 1973], 117–128), in connection with Pound's "Adams Cantos" (*Cantos: LXII–LXXIV*), which led to my reading the collected works of both presidents as well as to a systematic program of studying the Continental Encyclopedists to whom Pound persistently refers. The passage from Adams that serves as the epigraph, here, was quoted as the penultimate sentence of Pound's essay.

2. J.-P. Sartre, *Les jeux sont faits* (Paris, 1947); *The Chips Are Down*, trans. L. Varese (New York, 1948). For *les jeux sont faits*, see the "Vocabulaire" in J.-P. Sartre, *Les jeux sont faits*, ed. M. E. Storer (New York, 1952), 189; for its English equivalent, 'the game is up,' see, B. Kirkpatrick, ed., *Brewer's Concise Dictionary of Phrase and Fable* (London, 1993), 419. "The chips are down," omitting the temporal adverb *when*, represents Varese's attempt to provide a closer equivalent for the French. For the phrase "when the chips are down," see H. Wentworth and S. B. Flexner, *Dictionary of American Slang*, rev. ed. (New York, 1967), 101–2; E. Partridge, *A Dictionary of Catch Phrases* (New York, 1977), 33–34; *The Compact Edition of the Oxford English Dictionary*, 3, *Supplement* (Oxford, 1987), 126, s.v. "chip," 2.d; *Brewer's Concise Dictionary*, 206. The earliest citations for the phrase are from the 1940s.

3. In taking up this form, I want to acknowledge two stimuli. In 1995, Pro-

fessor Jon R. Stone (California State University, Bakersfield), then a Fellow of
the Center for the Study of Religion at the University of California, Santa Barbara, invited me to contribute an autobiographical essay for a project funded by
the Lilly Endowment. While I was unable to complete the assignment, the drafting of the introductory pages set off a train of reflections I have drawn on here.
Second, in 2001–2, in response to a request for theoretical clarification on behalf
of the Society of Biblical Literature Seminar, "Ancient Myths and Modern Theories of Christian Origins," a group that has been remarkably persistent in practicing both specialized knowledge and generalizing discourse, I wrote something
of an intellectual autobiography that was not intended for publication but was
addressed to three dear colleagues, Professors Burton Mack (Claremont School
of Theology, emeritus), Ron Cameron (Wesleyan University), and Merrill Miller
(Pembroke State University). I then wrote a public essay incorporating some aspects of these reflections as a seminar paper, "Conjectures on Conjunctures," for
the group's 2002 meeting in Toronto. I have cannibalized elements from both of
these writings here.

4. I still have a set of Hunter College Elementary School composition books
from 1948 in which I organized topics from these readings in alphabetical order—
largely taken from anthologies and popular series such as "The Wisdom of the
East." My major ethnographic source was the third edition of J. G. Frazer's *The
Golden Bough*. This latter interest led to the formation of an anthropology club
at my school in 1951. These same notebooks also record my excitement on first
reading Albert Schweitzer's reflections on "reverence for life" in his autobiography, *Out of My Life and Thought*, and in Ch. R. Joy's *Albert Schweitzer — An Anthology*; but there are several appended pages of more critical notes from 1953 on
Schweitzer's *The Philosophy of Civilization*.

5. F. A. Urquhart, *Report on the Studies of the Movements of the Monarch Butterfly in North America, July 1955* (Toronto, 1955), 33.

6. I returned to Orwell and language in a welcoming address to the University of Chicago's College class of 1984. Smith, "To the Entering Students, September 21, 1980," *The University of Chicago Record*, 14 (1980): 208–11.

7. J. Stalin, *Marxism and Linguistics* (New York, 1951), 14, 24, cf. 9–14, 22–26.

8. One of the remarkable features of the curriculum of the Horace Mann
School for Boys, which I attended from 1950 to 1956, was a first form class in general language, taught by Mr. Kovacs. This class and its readings constituted my
first introduction to linguistics. As Mr. Kovacs was an amateur botanist, an avid
collector of azaleas, we spent a number of hours outside of class talking about
both language and plants.

9. Both the Hamann quote and Max Müller's paraphrase are from the translator's preface to Müller's English translation of Kant's *Critique of Pure Reason*, 2d
ed. (New York, 1902), xlviii.

10. E. Cassirer, "Structuralism in Modern Linguistics," *Word: Journal of the Linguistic Circle of New York*, 1 (1945): 99–120.

11. I have discussed Goethe's *Metamorphosis of Plants* in *"Adde Parvum"* (1971), and "Acknowledgments . . . Part 1" (2000), 318–29.

12. In describing Cassirer, I have drawn on an unpublished 2001 talk on Cassirer's *Essay on Man*, prepared for the annual colloquium, "The Power of Books," sponsored by the University of Chicago College program, Fundamentals: Issues and Texts.

13. E. Cassirer, *An Essay on Man: An Introduction to a Philosophy of Human Culture* (New Haven, 1944), 228.

14. E. Cassirer, *The Philosophy of Symbolic Forms* (New Haven, 1953–57), 1–3. See, esp. vol. 1, *Language*, 69; vol. 2, *Mythical Thinking*, xv–xvi; and, most pointedly, vol. 3, *Phenomenology of Knowledge*, xiv: ". . . I am using the word 'phenomenology' not in its modern sense but with its fundamental signification as established and systematically grounded by Hegel." The problem for a young reader was to understand phenomenology's "modern sense," as well as its "fundamental signification . . . established by Hegel." It took some five years to gain confidence in my ability to understand Cassirer's differentiation and its entailments.

15. Works and authors quoted and discussed include (1) philosophers and theologians: S. Alexander, Aristotle, Aquinas, Augustine, K. Barth, H. Bergson, H. E. Brunner, E. Cassirer, J. Calvin, R. G. Collingwood, J. Dewey, W. Dilthey, A. S. Eddington; D. Emmet, M. Foss, G. Frege, M. Friedlander, I. Hocking, W. James, K. Jaspers, I. Kant, W. Kaufmann, G. Leibnitz, H. D. Lewis, Lucretius, J. Maritain, Meister Eckhart, M. Natorp, H. R. Niebuhr, B. Pascal, Plato, various pre-Socratics, J. H. Randall, E. Récéjac, H. Reichenbach, B. Russell, W. T. Stace, P. Tillich, E. Underhill, H. Vaihinger, and A. N. Whitehead; (2) phenomenologists (as I interpreted them): G. Bachelard, L. Binswanger, G. W. F. Hegel, M. Heidegger, J. Héring, E. Husserl, K. Kohler, E. Levinas, M. Merleau-Ponty (he receives the most extended discussion), E. Meyerson, J.-P. Sartre, M. Scheler, S. Strasser, J. van den Berg, and W. R. Worringer; (3) historians of religion: J. Darmstetter, M. Eliade, R. Otto, J. Prezywara, S. Reinach, and G. van der Leeuw; (4) anthropologists and sociologists: R. W. Codrington, E. Durkheim, J. G. Frazer, C. Kluckhohn, V. Lee, B. Malinowski, T. Parsons, H. Spencer, E. B. Tylor, and M. Weber; and (5) classicists et al.: F. M. Cornford, E. R. Dodds, A.-J. Festugière, H. Frankfort, J. E. Harrison, R. B. Onians, and H. Pépin, as well as C. Bell, S. T. Coleridge, S. Freud, N. Frye, Goethe, C. J. Jung, H. Pirenne, H. S. Sullivan, and A. J. Toynbee.

16. In fact, Fried had little interest in myth; a good sense of his concerns can be gained from his anthology, M. H. Fried, *Readings in Anthropology*, vol. 2, *Cultural Anthropology* (New York, 1959). Fried focused his course on the newer writings of the cultural materialists associated with Leslie White at the University of

Michigan. This opened up implications of Marx for anthropology in ways I would not have anticipated. The course was sufficiently exciting that I began regularly taking or auditing anthropology courses from 1958 to 1964.

17. Hans Penner's article, "Is Phenomenology a Method for the Study of Religion?" *Bucknell Review* 38 (1970): 29–54, remains for me the final word on the topic, both in its critique and in its specification of conditions that would have to be met by students of religions if phenomenology were to become a method within the field.

18. C. Lévi-Strauss, "Four Winnebago Myths: A Structural Sketch," in S. Diamond, ed., *Culture in History: Essays in Honor of Paul Radin* (New York, 1960), 351–62; reprinted in Lévi-Strauss, *Structural Anthropology* (New York, 1963–76), 2: 198–210.

19. One version of this paper, entitled "The Mystery of the Birth of Athene," was my first academic lecture, presented at Bryn Mawr College, February 1961. I returned to this topic in a paper presented to the inaugural faculty meeting of the Early Greek Seminar at the University of Chicago, November 29, 1976.

20. To be honest, it was a misunderstanding. I asked one of my Haverford teachers for advice as to where I could study myth. His answer, "Why don't you go to Yale and study the New Testament? It's the largest surviving collection of Greek myths," was, to his chagrin, taken seriously by me.

21. Smith, "Afterword: Religious Studies" (1995), 408.

22. The only other fieldwork analogue was my working on a dairy farm in the small town of Holland Patent, in upstate New York, for three months during a summer and one month during a winter as a prerequisite for admission to Cornell Agricultural School. See Smith, *Map* (1978), 291–92.

23. In part, my tutor in this respect was Jacob Neusner, whom I take to have refounded the study of classical Judaism in the United States. I first met Jack as we both walked out of a class at Columbia University summer session in 1958. We became reacquainted through the Kent Fellowship program and through our mutual friendship with Erwin Goodenough. Jack besieged me with bibliography and incorporated me in his various scholarly projects. Jack's unfailing generosity was responsible for everything from my first appointment (Dartmouth College, 1965–66) to a fair proportion of my publications through 1987.

Let me also note a profound indebtedness to the Kent Fellowship (and its parent, the Society for Religion in Higher Education). Kent understood (as did its sometimes partner, the Danforth Fellowship) how to nourish graduate students, intellectually as well as financially, and how to situate them comfortably in a transgenerational network of academics. À propos of the above, it was through the Kent Fellowship that I met, for the first time in my experience, a lively group of practicing Jewish intellectuals concerned with Judaica (along with Jack, most especially Yochanan Muffs, Baruch Levine, and Yosef Yerushalmi).

The position of "representing" Judaism at the Divinity School was clearly not always a comfortable one. For example, I resisted an assignment to write on "law and gospel in relation to the Christian life," turning it into a paper entitled "The Gospel of the Law." This, in turn, was rewritten as a lecture that was delivered first as a Divinity Wives Lecture at Yale (1963) and, subsequently, at five churches in the New Haven area.

24. While the term clearly depends on my earlier readings in Eliade and other European scholars, largely associated with the International Association for the History of Religions, I gained confidence in the use, in English, of "history of religions" with the publication of the first issue in 1961, of the journal *History of Religions*.

It is probably worth recalling that "history of religions" meant chiefly, at the Divinity School, the older German *Religionsgeschichtliche Schule* as it applied to the New Testament. Eliade was read in no class. A discussion of G. van der Leeuw's *Religion in Essence and Manifestation* in a course with John E. Smith, in the Philosophy Department, was, I think, the sole sign of interest in the tradition. This changed only when C. Colpe became a visiting professor in 1964, but largely in conversation rather than in class.

In my later work, I first employed the term 'historian of religions/history of religions,' then shifted to the singular, 'historian of religion/history of religion' (except when referring to others' work) before finally abandoning the terminology in favor of 'student of religion.'

25. My first experiments largely focused on traditions in the apocrypha and pseudepigrapha to the Hebrew Bible as well as apocryphal Christian texts. I note, especially, (1) a series of two lectures delivered at Bryn Mawr College (1963) entitled "The Manhood of Mary." The first lecture discussed the *Gospel of Thomas* 21, 22, and 37, part of which was later expanded in my first publication, "Garments of Shame" (1966); the second, *Gospel of Thomas* 114. This latter was revised as a lecture, "The Manhood of Mary: A Study in the Theology of Transvestism" presented in 1964 to a meeting of the Society for Religion in Higher Education and used as a sample lecture for job interviews in 1965. There is a book-length expansion of the latter drafted in 1964–65; reworked in 1965–67 to include "A Phenomenology of Christian Nudity." Neither version was submitted for publication because of a growing sense of unease with a focus on exotica (see below). (2) A "draft commentary" on the *Prayer of Joseph* (1963), which was the basis for both of my later articles on that text (1968, 1985). I should note that "Garments of Shame" and "Prayer of Joseph" both reveled in philological/historical details in Yale-ish fashion. In the preface to *Map* (1978, x), I retrospectively rehabilitated them by highlighting their implicit concerns with taxonomic questions. (3) A lecture, delivered as a collection address at Haverford College (1964), "The Twin Brother of Jesus," which focused on the Thomas traditions.

None of these avoided my sense that a truly successful history of religions approach to Judaisms and Christianities must deal with central formations and not exotica. (4) Far more successful, in that respect, was a 175-page manuscript (submitted, originally, as a course paper in 1963), "The Center: The Temple in Jerusalem." Parts of this paper were utilized in "Earth and Gods" (1969), delivered first as a lecture as part of the interview process that led to my appointment at the University of Chicago, "Jerusalem: The City as Place" (1986), and *To Take Place* (1987). It is not, I suspect, obvious, with respect to this latter topic (most especially "Earth and Gods"), that this subject was deliberately chosen as an exercise in empathy. As one who comprehended no intrinsic relation between Judaism and geography, except an archaic, now-irrelevant one—a reflection, no doubt, of the anti-Zionist Bundist circles that were an important part of my early political education—the thematics of exile and return, the tragic mythologization of exilic existence, were those elements in the tradition that were most profoundly alien to me.

While I have returned to the theme of a history of religions approach to Judaisms and Christianities at a number of points in my writings, its clearest early expression, widely distributed at the time in mimeographed form, was a 1967 manifesto entitled "Freedom Now: The Historian of Religions and Western Religious Traditions," first prepared for a Lilly Foundation conference and subsequently delivered on several campuses.

26. On the Human Relations Area Files, see Smith, "Fences and Neighbors" (1980) in *Imagining Religion*, 5; "In Comparison a Magic Dwells" (1982), in *Imagining Religion*, 25 and 139, n. 15; "Foreword" (2001).

27. It was during this period of 'playing in the stacks,' supported by a Yale Junior Sterling Fellowship, that, having read John Livingstone Lowes's description of Samuel Taylor Coleridge's reading habits (Lowes, *The Road to Xanadu: A Study in the Ways of the Imagination* [1927; reprint, New York, 1959], 30–36), I developed a set of reading rules I have followed ever since. These include: always read the entire chapter of a book in which a reference you are looking for occurs, then read at least the first and last chapters; always skim the entire volume of a journal in which you are seeking a particular article, then read the tables of contents for the entire run of the journal; after locating a particular volume on the shelves, always skim five volumes to the left and to the right of it; always trace citations in a footnote back to their original sources. (For one surprising result of the latter rule, see Smith, "Always Read the Fine Print," *Signs and Times of the Yale Divinity School* 3.6 [1963]: 5–8). Later, I added: do not teach or discuss a figure unless you have read the total corpus of their work as available to you.

28. Some of the early results of these readings formed the basis for two papers given at Fellows meetings of the Society for Religion in Higher Education, "When Is a Parallel a Parallel?" (1965) and "History of Religions in Herodotus

and the Herodotean Tradition" (1966). Portions of these papers were incorporated into Smith, *"Adde Parvum Parvo Magnus Acervus Erit"* (1971).

This project has continued to the present day, with particular attention to Late Antique, Renaissance, Reformation, and Enlightenment materials. I have drawn on these researches most heavily in "What a Difference a Difference Makes" (1985); *To Take Place* (1987); *Drudgery Divine* (1990); "Differential Equations" (1991); "Religion, Religions, Religious" (1998); "Close Encounters of Diverse Kinds" (2001); and "A Twice-told Tale" (2001), as well as in a number of unpublished lectures and in a yearlong graduate course, "Problems in the History of Comparison," taught several times at the University of Chicago. Special topics, such as the Alexander traditions and Columbus, have also resulted in both lectures and courses. I hope to publish some of these studies in a volume with the working title, *Close Encounters of Diverse Kinds: Studies in the Western Imaginations of Difference*.

29. I had clearly decided on examining Frazer's *The Golden Bough* as a "laboratory for comparison" by the summer of 1963. This decision was enhanced by Carsten Colpe's seminar on Frazer at Yale in 1964. As a souvenir of that course, I prepared a critical bibliography of Frazer's works (with corrections, it became an appendix to my dissertation [443–94]). The bulk of the dissertation, "The Glory, Jest and Riddle: James George Frazer and *The Golden Bough*" (1969) was written in 1966–68. Part of the delay was caused by an advisor's suggestion that Frazer be subjected to some sort of empirical test. This entailed a lengthy period of time learning the African materials concerning so-called "sacral regicide" which comprised part 2 (140–402). "When the Bough Breaks" (1973) is an abridged version of part 1 (8–138). I did not publish the companion essay, "The Golden Jest," announced in *Map* (1978), 239.

Frazer's *Golden Bough* was the subject of my first plenary presentation to an annual meeting of the American Academy of Religion, "Frazer and The Golden Bough: Milestone, Model or Idol?" in 1968. I returned to the subject in *Drudgery Divine* (1990), 89–93, and in a lecture, "James George Frazer and the Cambridge School" (1997) in the series "Anthropology, Theory and the Study of Ancient Religions," sponsored by the University of Chicago's Committee on the Study of the Ancient Mediterranean World.

30. Smith, "The Glory, Jest and Riddle" (1969), 427–28.

31. The issue as seen in the early 60s was "expressed as a choice between seminary studies and university studies, between the teaching of and the teaching about religion, between theological and religious studies. I have a good part of a bookcase in my office filled with publications devoted to such choices, all with respect to a single context: the teaching of religion in a state (public) university. It is a debate, a context, and a history that subsequent generations of

teachers in the field are the poorer for not engaging with." Smith, "Afterword: Religious Studies," (1995), 407.

32. For the "vocabulary," selections were read from M. Eliade's anthology, *From Primitives to Zen: A Thematic Sourcebook on the History of Religions* (London, 1967); for the particular traditions, the six-volume series on world religions published by George Braziller (New York, 1961) served as a base, supplemented with handouts. After one unsuccessful attempt to repeat this course at the College of the University of Chicago, I dropped it. The course could not survive a transition from a lecture to a seminar format.

33. The syllabus for this course was published in Smith, "Basic Problems" (1973) with an explanation of each unit. I reproduce it here.

Session 1
Introduction. What is a text?

Sessions 2–4
Reading: A. Heidel, *The Gilgamesh Epic*. Introduction to religion of an archaic, urban agricultural culture; the problems of editing a text when there is no complete text but only fragmentary versions. Question of whether there is an "original text," criteria for its reconstruction. Relations of epic materials to religious traditions. Possibility of pattern: hero, fertility deity, sacred kingship. Problem of assessing parallels: the Atrahasis epic, Genesis flood story.

Sessions 5–6
Reading: H. Hongi, trans., "A Maori Cosmogony." Highly developed "primitive" society. Problem of reconstructing history without written documents (diffusion, migration, etc.). Text is a cosmogonic myth: definition of myth; high god structure. Conditions under which text collected in field. Text is both myth and homily. Myth not naked text but encased in native exegetical tradition. Text is not, in fact, archaic, it is a late forgery containing Maori anti-Christian propaganda. Use of specific historical knowledge in interpreting the intentionality of a given text. Relation of evidence to theory: text is decisive for Eliade/Pettazzoni definition of myth and high god; does the fact that it is not archaic affect their theories?

Sessions 7–8
Reading: J. M. Kitagawa, "Ainu Bear Festival." Archaic hunting culture (relation to paleo-Siberian). Characteristics: hunt as religious activity,

shamanism, Master of the Animals, sacrifice. Ritual text rather than narrative. Observer's report rather than a primary document (do we interpret differently?). Problem of fieldwork, participant-observer. Do we believe what we are told?

Sessions 9–12

Readings: "Hainuwele Myth" and I. H. N. Evans, *The Religion of the Tempasuk Dusuns* (selections). Archaic agricultural materials, tuber and paleo-Asiatic rice cultures. *Kulturkreis* theory: relation of tuber, coconut, sago, grain. The structure of dema deity as present in Hainuwele, compared with other dema texts. Does pattern fit? Use of myth to reconstruct ritual. Multiple versions of same myth; how to assess? Introduction to folklore theories.

Sessions 13–15

Reading: K. Burridge, *Mambu* (selections): Etiology of cargo cult. Categories of cargo, problem of religious persistence and change, church/sect, prophet and charisma, initiation. A modern myth still evolving (4 collected versions). As text has best ethnography, detailed interpretation illustrating phenomenological, functional, psychological, and structural approaches.

Sessions 16–20

Reading: Purushasûkta (*Rig Veda* 10. 90). [Three texts in last sessions: Hainuwele, Mambu, and Purusha all narrate a primordial killing. Different cultures—is there a pattern? How would it be specified? Tension between morphology and history]. Problem of "canon," highly self-conscious literary-religious tradition. Oral/written. Use of a text both explicitly and implicitly in a self-conscious tradition. Notion of homology. What is a tradition? Exploration of parallel Sanskrit texts and commentaries. Relations of myth to theology. Use of text in Temple construction, Brahmanic sacrifice and Yoga.

As given in 1973, the syllabus proposed two requirements. "(1) Using the concepts and techniques gained in the course, each student will essay an interpretation (and an agendum of questions for further research) of the three versions of the origin myth of the Medicine rite of the Winnebago as published by Paul Radin. . . . (2) There will be a final examination: Write an essay on the following quotation from David Maybury-Lewis and indicate how you would go about solving his problem: 'If I read a myth, select certain elements from it, and arrange them in a pattern, that structure or pattern is bound to be in the material unless I have misread the text or demonstrably misrendered it. The fact of its being there does not, however, indicate that my arrangement is anything more than my personal whim. A myth is therefore bound to have a number of possible patterns or structures that are both in the material and in the eye of the beholder. The problem is to decide between them and to determine the significance of any of them.'"

34. See Smith, "Coup d'essai" (1969); "Basic Problems" (1973)—this was a part of an elaborate three-stage project on the undergraduate teaching of religion sponsored by the Lilly Foundation and undertaken by the Society for Religion in Higher Education in 1971–73, involving, at one stage, the presentation of sample syllabi at regional meetings of the American Academy of Religion, the Society of Biblical Literature, and the College Theology Society. I presented the syllabus at the San Francisco Bay Area College Theology Society meeting (Oakland, 1973) and at the New York-Philadelphia Area AAR meeting (New York City, 1973); "Puzzlement" (1987); "Narrative into Problems" (1988); *The Challenge of Connecting Learning* (1990); "The Introductory Course" (1991); "To Double Business Bound" (1993); "Double Play" (1995); "The Aims of Education" (1997)—a 1982 address; "Teaching the Bible" (1998); "Alternative Visions of General Education" (2000); "Private Sector Perspective" (2002).

35. An earlier draft of what were to become the Pomona Clarke Lectures was prepared for a two-lecture series at Hampshire College in April 1972, "Center and Periphery, Order and Rebellion in Archaic Religions." While these repeat many of the items that were characteristic of my engagements with Eliade, especially "The Wobbling Pivot" (1972), one lecture dwelt at length on Hainuwele. The Pomona lectures were entitled "No Need to Travel to the Indies: The Historian of Religions and the Worlds of Other Men." There were three lectures. The first, "The Congruous and the Incongruous: Towards a New Description of Archaic Religions," reworks a 1973 University of Maryland lecture and constitutes a draft of what would become "Map Is Not Territory" (1978), which I consider a crucial turning point in my work. The second, "The Disruptive Presence: Towards a New Description of Myth," takes up the Hainuwele text from the course (sessions 9–12) as well as the cargo materials (sessions 13–15) and constitutes a draft of "A Pearl of Great Price and a Cargo of Yams" (1976). The third, "The Challenge to Credulity: Towards a New Description of Magic and Ritual," takes up the Ainu materials (sessions 7–8) and constitutes a draft of "The Bare Facts of Ritual" (1980). In 1978, I recognized the importance of the Pomona lectures for my subsequent work when I returned to deliver a lecture in honor of the Colleges ninetieth anniversary, which I entitled "Imagining Religion." Besides, the Pomona lectures were the occasion of my first meeting with Burton Mack who has been my valued instructor, source of encouragement, and friend over the years.

While not included in the Pomona lectures, the Maori materials from the course (sessions 5–6) became what remains my favorite piece of work, "The Unknown God: Myth in History," first published in *Imagining Religion* (1982). A rather different version was delivered as a lecture at Yale University in 1981 and published as "Mythos und Geschichte" (1983).

36. Smith, *Imagining Religion* (1982), xiii.

37. At the University of Chicago, I have held the following appointments: (1) College Faculty (1968–); New Collegiate Division, History and Philosophy of Religion (1968–72); program coordinator, Religion and the Humanities (1973–), program coordinator, New Testament and Early Christian Literature (1974–); Social Sciences Core (1982–); Classical Civilization (1997–); New Collegiate Division, Fundamentals: Issues and Texts (1999–). (2) Faculty of the Graduate Division of the Humanities (1982–); New Testament and Early Christian Literature (1970–79); Committee on the Study of the Ancient Mediterranean World (1986–); Committee on the History of Culture (1990–95). (3) Faculty of the Divinity School (1968–77); Associate Faculty of the Divinity School (1990–). (4) Continuing Studies (1980–).

38. The initial prospectus for the Religion and the Humanities program, as approved by the College Council in 1973, reads in part:

> By locating the program within the Humanities Collegiate Division and by utilizing existing courses drawn from a variety of departments, we affirm our belief that the study of religion is a mode of humane inquiry, that the data of religion (its literature, history, etc.) are not the privileged possession of any single discipline. By proposing a core-curriculum of problem-oriented courses, we affirm our belief that there is an intellectual tradition of the study of religion which must be mastered. By this combination of breadth and sharp focus, by exploring religion within its widest cultural context and by reflecting on the act of understanding religion, the program presents a significant departure from the usual models for departments of Religious Studies.
>
> At the heart of this program is a core of four courses which serve as a focus of integration and coherence, and give the student a disciplined base which will allow him to make maximum use of other relevant [elective] courses. . . . The four courses, open to any student in the College, are described [with respect to their pedagogical goals] as follows:
>
> 1. Basic problems in the Study of Religion: The intent would be to isolate a key problem in the study of religion and critically examine a representative sample of the kinds of data which give rise to the problem and the sorts of answers that might be proposed. . . .

2. Approaches to the Interpretation of Religion: Recognizing that there is no single method adequate to the interpretation of religious phenomena, this course would ask the professor to stipulate an approach . . . and carry it through a given body of religious material with rigor and with self-criticism.

[This was later altered to, Basic Structures in the Interpretation of Religion: Recognizing that there are recurrent elements which serve as building blocks in any religion, the professor would be asked to choose one . . . and employing cross-cultural data, exhibit both questions of definition and significance as well as characteristic strategies for interpretation].

3. Basic Structures in the Self-interpretation of Religion: This course would recognize that each religious tradition has developed language and structures of thought for interpreting itself to its adherents and others. . . . Consequently this course would examine and analyze both internally and externally directed religious documents . . . focus[ing] either on the strategies and logic of one particular tradition . . . or venturing a cross-cultural comparison.

4. Religious Literature and Expression: This course . . . would examine forms of literature or other modes of expression which are characteristically . . . [employed by religions] either within a single tradition or comparatively . . . The course would aim at presenting those exegetical methods developed by modern scholarship (not necessarily within Religious Studies) as well as taking into account interpretations which are traditional within those religious traditions from which the texts have been taken.

Beyond these four courses, the program proposed that each student take one Western and one non-Western yearlong civilization sequence (that is to say, one sequence in addition to their general education requirement); and five electives anywhere in the University that enhanced, in the student's judgment, their understanding of religion. Three of these courses must, in the student's considered opinion, be related.

39. Reflections on the major include "Why the College Major?" (1983); *Integrity and the College Curriculum* (1985); "Reforming Undergraduate Education" (1986); *The Challenge of Connecting Learning* (1990); "To Double Business Bound" (1993).

40. These courses were taught in alternating years between 1980 and 1992. The first of these, Religion in Western Civilization, I–III, began with the ancient Near East and concluded with Islam. The second was far more interesting, The Bible in Western Civilization, I–III, which took the term, "Bible," to include the

Hebrew Bible, the Old and New Testaments, the Qur'an, and the Book of Mormon. The course devoted the first term to the history of literacy, the formation of the biblical texts, and handwritten Bibles; the second focused first on scripture in liturgies and lectionary systems as well as in iconographic program, then on printed Bibles and the development of textual and historical criticism; concluding, in the third term, with nineteenth- and twentieth-century critical approaches and with twentieth-century fundamentalist Christianity as a reaction to that scholarship. In this course, I attempted to fulfill Wilfred Cantwell Smith's fruitful notion of reading the Bible forward as well as backward; see J. Z. Smith, "Scriptures and Histories" (1992) and "Teaching the Bible in the Context of General Education" (1998). I should note that I have taught at least one course on biblical materials every year since 1963.

41. Articles on education include "Basic Problems in the Study of Religion" (1973); "What Is a Classic?" (1980); "Why the College Major?" (1983); "Here and Now" (1984); *Integrity and the College Curriculum* (1985); "Commentary on William J. Bennett's" (1985); "Symposium on the Academic Vocation" (1985); "Towards Imagining New Frontiers" (1986); "The New Liberal Arts" (1986); "Puzzlement" (1987); "Narrative into Problems" (1988); *The Challenge of Connecting Learning* (1990); "The Introductory Course" (1991); "To Double Business Bound" (1993); "Afterword: Religious Studies" (1995); "Double Play" (1995); "The Aims of Education" (1997); "Teaching the Bible" (1998); "Alternative Visions of General Education" (2000); "A Private Sector Perspective" (2002). Some of these were based on addresses on liberal learning and curricular issues delivered at more than eighty colleges, universities and professional associations, as well as at more than sixty national or regional educational conferences.

42. Smith, *Map* (1978), 90.

43. I had been led to the text in the Acts of Peter while working on the 1963 lectures on the Gospel of Thomas (see above, n. 25), especially logion 22, by Jean Doresse's reference (Doresse, *L'Évangile selon Thomas* [Paris, 1959], 212–213, *Les livres secrets des gnostiques d'Égypte*, [Paris, 1958], 2) to Antonio Orbe, "El misterio de la Cruz en los Acta Petri," in Orbe, *Los primeros herejes ante la persecución*, Estudios Valentinianos, 5, Analecta Gregoriana, 83 (Rome, 1956), 176–212.

44. Smith, *Map* (1978), 151, n. 12; cf. my review of U. Bianchi, ed., *Le origini dello gnosticismo: Colloquio di Messina* (Leiden, 1967), Supplements to Numen, 12, in *Kairos* 10 (1968): 298–302, esp. 299, for the same sentence. I continue to make this argument, even more sharply, when I have occasion to teach gnostic materials.

45. Smith, *Map* (1978), 2–18, with notes. In contrast to the more generic proposal for a "phenomenology of rebellion" in "Birth," I had proposed, in "Garments," a "forthcoming paper" with a more limited scope, a "phenomenology of Christian nudity" in the original publication of "The Garments of Shame," *His-*

tory of Religions 5 (1966): 223, n. 23. The reference was dropped when the article was reprinted in *Map,* 7–8, n. 23.

46. See, especially, Smith, *Drudgery* (1990), 47–48, n. 15. I first referred to the distinction, analogy/homology, in *"Adde Parvum"* (1971), n. 50.

47. See, for example, M. Eliade, *Patterns in Comparative Religion* (New York, 1958), 38–39, 154–57, 188, 216; cf. Smith, "Acknowledgments, Part 2" (2000), 339–40.

48. I would note that positive reference to anthropological theorizing, as opposed to the use of anthropologist's data, was not characteristic of history of religions in the '60s. See Smith, "On the Occasion of Frank Reynolds' Retirement" (2001), 11.

49. Aware of the ridicule associated with the Panbabylonian school, I diplomatically referred to Loew instead. I gave a lecture in 1970 (unpublished) comparing, in some detail, Eliade and the writings of the Panbabylonians (esp. A. Jeremias), some of which was briefly summarized in Smith, *Imagining Religion* (1982), 26–29, and "Mythos und Geschichte" (1983), 36–39. I first mentioned their work in print in "Wisdom and Apocalyptic" (1975).

50. *Map* (1978), 150–51, 170. I deliberately softened the disagreement by referring to Eliade's writings on transcendence (170, n. 64).

51. *Map* (1978), 170. The reference, here, to "more than strictly academic relevance" as well as the parallel reference, in "The Influence of Symbols" (1970) to "achieving cosmic freedom now" (140) clearly refers to political interests in California in the late '60s. In the choice of "rebellion" as the privileged term (rather than the later substitution, "utopian"), there are echoes of older debates between radical revolutionary socialism and ameliorating reform socialism which preoccupied the Socialist Labor Party in the 1950s; echoes buttressed by the quotation from Yeat's "Easter, 1916," as well as the citations of A. Camus, J.-P. Sartre, E. J. Hobsbawm, and E. da Cuna.

52. *Map* (1978), 134–38, 101–2.

53. "The Wobbling Pivot" was delivered at a symposium on Eliade's work held at Notre Dame, February 12, 1971 (just two days shy of the third anniversary of my first meeting with Eliade). The title is derived, most immediately, from Plutarch's anecdote concerning Alexander the Great and the Indian gymnosophist, Calanus (*Map* [1978], 102), but the ultimate source was a play on Ezra Pound's titling of the Confucian *Doctrine of the Mean* as "The Unwobbling Pivot," replacing the earlier "The Unwobbling Axis" ("L'Asse che non Vacilla"), after its first ideogram. (Pound's other renditions of the title, *Chung Yung,* which means, "Precisely Correct in Everyday Affairs," include "The Unwavering in the Middle," "The Standing Fast in the Middle," and most traditionally, "The Steadfast Mean.")

Three essays address the same point, often with the same language and examples: "Birth Upside Down or Rightside Up?" (1970), discussed above; "The Influence of Symbols upon Social Change: A Place on Which to Stand" (1970), and "The Wobbling Pivot" (1972). "The Influence of Symbols upon Social Change" was an assigned topic for a colloquium, Man and Symbol: The Anthropological and Sociological Sources of Ritual sponsored by *Worship*, the Institute for Ecumenical and Cultural Research at Saint John's Abbey (Collegeville, Minn.) and the Danforth Foundation. Victor Turner, whom I first met at a Dartmouth conference in 1967, had recommended my participation. In retrospect, it is most interesting in its concluding return to earlier interests, citing both Cassirer and "the tradition of Marx and Durkheim" (*Map* [1978], 144–45).

When I reprinted these three essays in *Map*, along with "Earth and Gods" (1969) to form a set, I deliberately disarranged the chronological order, placing "The Wobbling Pivot" first, as the more explicit critique of Eliade, in order to relativize my most Eliadean essay "Earth and Gods" (see above, note 25), which was, then, followed by "Influence" and "Birth."

54. *Map* (1978), 101.

55. See, for example, the preface to *Map* (1978), xiii. In "Here, There, and Anywhere" (2000), reprinted in this volume, I have employed, for the first time, a different set of categories to characterize Classical and Late Antique Mediterranean religious phenomena and placed them within a broad chronological relationship.

56. *Map* (1978), 101.

57. For the classes, see above, notes 33–34. As indicated in note 35, the Hampshire College lectures (1972) and the Pomona lectures (1974) served as drafts of portions of "Map Is Not Territory." In 1973, I gave two different lectures at several colleges, each entitled "Map Is Not Territory," which continued this drafting project. One of these, after repeating the critique of Eliade through the distinction between locative and utopian world-views, goes on to state, to the best of my knowledge for the first time, "More recently . . . I have become increasingly concerned with the category of incongruity, that which neither asserts a 'fit' between man and the world [i.e., locative] nor requires man not to fit [i.e., utopian], but rather one which plays with the slippage, the discrepancy inbetween."

58. *Map* (1978), 294. As the text acknowledged, I played, in this formulation, with Paul Ricoeur's well-known contention, "*le symbole donne à penser,*" Ricoeur, *Finitude et culpabilité*, vol. 2, *La Symbolique du mal*, Philosophie de la volonté, 2 (Paris, 1960), 324. I should note that I took courses with Ricoeur when he was a visiting professor at Haverford College.

From one point of view, my formulation, "perception of incongruity gives rise to thought," may be thought of as a neo-Kantian rewriting of the Marxist linkage between the perception of contradiction and (revolutionary) action—characteristically privileging thought over praxis.

59. The proximate cause for the use of 'map' as both the title for the lecture (and later, the volume in which it was printed) and as a substitution for terms such as 'cosmology' and 'world-view,' themselves replacements for Eliade's "ontology," was to emphasize the status of these patterns as 'constructs.' For this reason, I adapted a phrase from Alfred Korzybski, *Science and Sanity: An Introduction to Non-Aristotelian Systems and General Semantics*, 3d ed. (Lakeville, 1948): "A map is not the territory it represents, but if correct, it has a similar structure to the territory" (58). Also: "a language is like a map; it is not the territory represented" (498) and "a map is not the territory" (750); as well as the quote from E. T. Bell that Korzybski uses as an epigraph: "A map is not the thing mapped" (247). See also the stunning use of Korzybski by the science fiction writer, A. E. van Vogt, in his Null-A series, especially *The Players of Null-A* (1948; reprint, New York, 1974); where "the map is not the territory" is quoted (158). I had often used my abbreviated version of Korzybski's phrase in College papers, so much so that one of my English teachers, Gerhard Friedrich, incorporated it as the opening line of the first poem in Friedrich, *The Map within the Mind* (New York, 1957), "Map is not territory . . ." (7). See also, n. 115 below.

60. *Map* (1978), 292–93. I have returned to this critique of the nature of the sources on which the "archaic ontology" had been constructed, most especially in *To Take Place* (1987), 13–17.

When using the term 'conservative' to characterize scholarship that emphasizes congruity and conformity, I was thinking of Karl Mannheim's usage, as discussed in *"Adde Parvum"* (1971) and in "A Twice-told Tale" (2001), 140–41, now reprinted in this volume.

61. *Map* (1978), 297. One of my more extended treatments of this reduction to fantasy is in "Bare Facts of Ritual" (1960) = *Imagining Religion*, esp. pp. 61–62. "I am a Parrot (Red)" (1972) is the most direct confrontation with the issue of 'primitive thought.'

62. *Map* (1978), 299. Although not mentioned by name, the figure described was A. E. Jensen and his split between the primordial moment of "seizure" which led to a pristine myth, followed by its subsequent "semantic depletion" through "application." This is the beginning of a stratagem I would adopt in subsequent work, using Jensen as a stalking horse for Eliade. See, among other references, Smith, *Imagining Religion* (1982), 32, 42–47, 141 n. 13. Jensen's position was, for me, the enemy of enemies, leading, in its most extreme form, to an antihuman stance of silence before the sacred. (See the Eliade anecdote in what I believe to be the last time I returned to Jensen, in Smith, "A Slip in Time Saves Nine" [1991], 232, n. 15, cf. 72–74.) In an "in your face" move, I adopted Jensen's most negative term, "application," as one of my most highly valued terms. See, for example, Smith, "No Need to Travel to the Indies" (1983), 223–24, where, after summarizing Jensen, I insisted that "in culture, there is no text, it is all commen-

tary. . . . there is no primordium, it is all history. . . . all is application." Parts of this latter essay served as a rough draft for the introduction to *Imagining Religion*.

63. *Map* (1978), 299. I chose Kenneth Burke because he was one of the few figures I cited who would be well-known to the general College faculty attending the lecture. I knew I misread Burke's understanding of the term "situation," in his phrase, "a proverb is a strategy for dealing with a situation," which was for him, precisely not specific but, rather, "typical," "recurrent," even "timeless." K. Burke, *The Philosophy of Literary Form: Studies in Symbolic Action*, revised abridged ed. (New York, 1957), 256–60. Rather, I took "situation" in a more Sartrean sense, as a "condition" in which one finds oneself which calls forth a "project" or an "action." Since my emphasis was on thought (itself an action), I preferred the discussion of 'situation' in J.-P. Sartre, "Qu'est-ce que la littérature?" which makes up the bulk of Sartre, *Situations*, II (Paris, 1948), 55–330, to that of the powerful opening chapter of part 4 of *L'Être et le néant* (Paris, 1943), 507–642. "Situation" was, for me, primarily understood as a historical setting of "incongruity" between cultural norms and expectations and historical reality which calls forth thought as expressed in myth, in the instances adduced in the lecture. "Situation" was an attempt to critique notions of myth as archetypal, ahistorical, and cyclical. See, more explicitly, the use of Burke's phrase in the introduction to *Imagining Religion* (1982), xiii. For the emphasis on the specificity of "situation," and hence the historical placement of myth, see, Smith, "The Unknown God" (1982), researched and written during 1970–80, which remains my favorite piece of work.

64. *Map* (1978), 298–307. The example of the African diviner's basket became fundamental to the essay on canon, "Sacred Persistence" (1979). I used the initiatory juxtaposition of expectation and reality in a University of Chicago Convocation Address in June 1977 (Smith, "Birds, Beasts and Stubborn Little Stones," *University of Chicago Record* 11 [1977]: 135–37). Hainuwele was the centerpiece of "A Pearl of Great Price and a Cargo of Yams" (1976).

65. In the lecture, *Map* (1978), 302, I linked the Late Antique materials to Mary Douglas's discussion of the joke. Douglas, "The Social Control of Cognition: Some Factors in Joke Perception," *Man* 3 (1968): 361–76. This is because I had just completed the essay published as "Good News Is No News" (1975). In one of its several early drafts, it was delivered as a paper at the annual meeting of the American Academy of Religion (1974) under the title "Good News Is No News: The Gospel and the Joke."

The interest in 'situation' extended to Late Antiquity, see, among others, "The Social Description of Early Christianity" (1975); the "Preface" to *Map*: x–xv; "Too Much Kingdom/Too Little Community" (1978); and, most recently, "Re: Corinthians" (2001), reprinted in this volume.

66. *Map* (1978), 309.

67. *Map* (1978), 307–8. Compare the later version of the same paragraph in *Imagining Religion* (1982), 100–1.

68. It should be noted that "The Bare Facts of Ritual" (1980) is animated by a critique of congruency as expressed in the old categories of sympathetic, homeopathic, or mimetic magic, in the interests of emphasizing native thoughtfulness and ingenuity. See especially *Imagining Religion* (1982), 62–65. As in *To Take Place* (1987), I lay particular stress on the attempt to emphasize intellectual elements in ritual. There is a tradition of philosophizing about myth; but ritual, often characterized as habitual, thoughtless action (with close analogies to animal behavior), is the harder case. For a similar attempt, this time directed against more Romantic understandings, see Smith, "The Domestication of Sacrifice" (1986).

69. "The Devil in Mr. Jones," *Imagining Religion* (1982), 111–12; compare the discussion of the 'unique' in *Drudgery Divine* (1990), 37–46.

"The Devil in Mr. Jones" was first delivered as a lecture to College students at the University of Chicago, February 24, 1980. It was an address in my role as dean of the College that attempted to illustrate the value of our required Common Core curriculum for providing "an arsenal of classic instances which are held to be exemplary, to provide paradigmatic events and expressions as resources from which to reason, from which to extend the possibility of intelligibility" (*Imagining Religion,* 113). The examples for comparison to Jonestown, Euripides' *Bacchae,* and cargo cults were chosen because they were on the reading lists for the Humanities and Social Sciences Cores. Hence, the claim, "to have discussed Euripides' *Bacchae* is, to some degree, already to have discussed Jonestown" (ibid.).

The Woodward Court Lectures, the forum for the talk, was a remarkable community institution organized by Izaak and Pera Wirzup. There I also gave "The Bare Facts of Ritual" (1980) as a lecture in 1979, and "Now Wait for Last Year: The Future of Education's Past" in 1985, partially published as "A Commentary on William J. Bennett's *To Reclaim a Legacy*" (1985). There was also an unpublished 1982 lecture, "Up/Down/In/Out: Mapping an Ancient Culture," that anticipates some of the themes in the 2000 paper, "Here, There, and Anywhere," which is printed in this volume.

70. The stimulus for the approach taken in *To Take Place* (1987) was an invitation to participate in a 1982 symposium, *Civitas: Religious Interpretations of the City* sponsored by the Religion and Arts Program at Yale Divinity School. The convener, Peter S. Hawkins, invited me to speak on "The City as Place." I had not previously focused on the term, 'place,' being more accustomed to speaking of 'space,' but the new term provoked a set of reflections on social placement. The published lecture, "Jerusalem: The City as Place" (1986) contains, *in nuce,* much of the argument of chapters 2–4 of *To Take Place.* The Yale symposium was also significant in providing the occasion for meeting John F. Baldovin,

S. J., who was working on his dissertation, which has since been published as *The Urban Character of Christian Worship: The Origins, Development, and Meaning of Stational Liturgy*, Orientalia Christiana Analecta, 228 (Rome, 1987), and presented a preliminary report. The stational liturgy proved important for *To Take Place* (91–94), although I only had Baldovin's 1981 article (miscited in *To Take Place* [170, n. 83], as J. Baldwin). I should note that, through an error, the chart in *To Take Place* (93, figure 8) was truncated. In addition to what is printed, the chart, in manuscript, mapped twenty-one other feasts and locales for the liturgical period extending from Holy Week (beginning with Lazarus Sunday) through Pentecost; hence the reference (94) to the movement between eight locations on Pentecost.

71. As note 70 indicates, the additional materials in *To Take Place* largely occur in the first and fifth chapters. The first chapter is the reexamination of the Tjilpa and their pole, undertaken in the same style as the "Texts and Contexts" test cases (see above, note 33). I should note that this was the last critical piece on Eliade that I had the opportunity to show him in draft and discuss with him. Following his death in April 1986, I so keenly felt the loss of these conversations that I did not return to discussing Eliade's work in public at any length until the two-part "Acknowledgments" (2000).

The second element added to the work is the sustained interaction with the French anthropological tradition, from Durkheim to Dumont, as well as with Lévi-Strauss. This had several important consequences: an increased interest in social locations (taking place as "placement"), an extension of thoughtfulness to ritual (hence "theory *in* ritual"), and a distinction between myth and ritual:

> Ritual is a relationship of difference between "nows"—the now of everyday life and the now of ritual place; the simultaneity, but not the coexistence, of "here" and "there.". . .
>
> If ritual is concerned with the elaboration of relative difference that is never overcome, myth begins with absolute duality (. . . "then" and "now"); its mode is not that of simultaneity, but rather of transformation. In myth, through the devices of narrative and the manipulation of temporal relations, the one becomes the other—often after much conflict and a complex repertoire of relations. (*To Take Place* [1987], 110, 112)

I have set aside a lengthy manuscript, worked on over the past fifteen years, which focused on the thoughtfulness of ritual in relation to these sorts of distinctions between myth and ritual, and which continued the dialogue with various structuralisms. (See above, xi).

72. A. S. Hitchcock, *Manual of the Grasses of the United States*, 2d ed., revised

by A. Chase, Department of Agriculture, Miscellaneous Publication, 200 (Washington, D.C., 1950), 9–10.

73. *To Take Place* (1987), 13–14.

74. As best as I can determine, my earliest formal presentations on taxonomy were three papers given as a small series in 1970 to the History of Religions Club at Chicago, entitled "Taxonomy: From Aristotle to Linnaeus." After an introduction to philosophical and methodological problems, the lectures were concerned with the histories of biological and linguistic classifications. The presentations were prompted by the 1970 publication of the English translation of Michel Foucault's *Les Mots et les choses: Une archéologie des sciences humaines* under the title *The Order of Things: An Archaeology of the Human Sciences*. (My attention was first called to Foucault because of his work on Kant's anthropological writings for his *thèse complémentaire*. I had read his suggestive writings on space in *Critique*, 1963 and 1964. *Les Mots et les choses* was the first work of Foucault's that I studied and abstracted with care.)

75. As already suggested (see above, notes 28–29), my concern for the problems of comparison was long-standing. The 1963 original proposal for the dissertation was entitled "James George Frazer and The History of the Comparative Religions Method," which contemplated devoting one part to Frazer, one to a history of comparison from Herodotus to the Victorian period, and a concluding part on implications for present practice. Part 2 was obviously too ambitious for a dissertation, and the plan was abandoned. Nevertheless, the next two years were spent reading for part 2 (cf. note 28). In 1965, I outlined and drafted several chapters of a book to be called *Il y a fagots et fagots: Studies in the History of Comparison in History of Religions Research*, which intended to sample materials from Herodotus up to the Enlightenment. The surviving seven chapters are devoted to (1) Herodotus, (2) the Herodotean tradition, (3) the Alexander traditions, (4) the Classical and Christian Encyclopedists, (5) study and travel in the thirteenth century, (6) early understandings of Islam, and (7) parallelisms between "savage" and Christian rituals: antiquarians and ecclesiastical folklorists. These topics, in addition to the files accumulated on modern theories of comparison, led directly to the development of the fourfold typology of ethnographic, encyclopaedic, morphological, and evolutionary comparative modes in *"Adde Parvum"* (1971).

I have never stopped reading in these areas nor adding to the files on them set up in the early 60s. Indeed, over time, I extended the chronological range, both backward to the ancient Near East and forward to Enlightenment and post-Enlightenment texts. I have come to place particular emphasis on the Renaissance and Reformation, with the encounter with the Americas as the centerpiece. I have, as well, never ceased cannibalizing these files and early chapters. For example, the chapter on Herodotus was rewritten in 1966 as "Herodotus as an Historian of Religions," delivered at the annual meeting of the Society for Religion in Higher Education. This, in turn, was abbreviated as the section "Ethnographic" in *"Adde Parvum"* (1971). The materials on Conyers Middleton and pagano-papism from the draft of the seventh chapter were briefly summarized in the 1965 Society for Religion in Higher Education paper, "When Is a Parallel a Parallel?" which I took up at a pivotal point in *To Take Place* (1987), 96–98, finally, the broader topic of pagano-papism and Protestant-Catholic polemics became the argumentative spine of *Drudgery Divine* (1990).

These files and readings formed the basis of a two-quarter course sequence given four times, from 1974 to 1991, first in History of Religions, later in History of Culture, entitled "Problems in the History of Comparison." The topics treated, which I list here, both mimicked and expanded the earlier subjects: (1) "Introduction," (2) "The Ethnographic Mode: Herodotus and the Ionian Tradition," (3) "The Encyclopaedic Tradition, I: Graeco-Roman (especially Pliny)," (4) "The Encyclopaedic Tradition, II: Christian (especially Isidore of Seville and Vincent of Beauvais)," (5) "Skythika and Indika: The Alexander Traditions," (6) "The Mongol Mission," (7) "The 'Discovery' of America," (8) "The Native American and the Origin of Species" (9) "New Taxonomies, I: Renaissance— Enlightenment (with one session devoted to Linnaeus)," (10) "New Taxonomies, II: The Scottish Institutionalists," (11) "Morphological Comparison," (12) "Evolutionary Comparison," and (13) "Contemporary Issues in Comparison." These four occasions were crucial in spurring me to organize and summarize what had become an unruly mass of both primary and secondary materials.

76. See above, note 26.

77. See *To Take Place* (1987), 85.

78. "Acknowledgments . . . Part 1" (2000), 328.

79. *Imagining Religion* (1982), 4. My readings in numerical taxonomy were already reflected in my 1976 preface to *Map* (1978), ix, n. 2. "I intend a distinction between the enterprise of *classification* and that of *definition*. Definition is an essentially atemporal procedure that requires the specification of a unique principle of division thus resembling traditional, logical monothetic classification. Classification, in the sense I intend, is a polythetic grouping or clustering procedure which requires temporal specificity." I returned to numerical taxonomy and gave my most extended published discussion of phenetic/cladistic taxonomy in "Classification" (2000).

The strategy of turning to scholars in other fields who are "professionally concerned" with a topic I am discussing, in this case, taxonomists on classification (*Imagining Religion*, 8), has been a feature of a good bit of my teaching and published work over the years. It is one consequence of my rejection of the critique of "reductionism" which has characterized much scholarship in religion. Compare, for example, the initial move with respect to the category of "place" in *To Take Place* (1987, 28): "It is at this point that we ought to turn to our colleagues in geography who deserve to have their say. After all, in the economy of the academy's disciplinary labor, they are the ones charged with understanding place."

80. *Imagining Religion* (1982), 18. To the best of my recollection, this is the first time I employed in print the plural "Judaisms"—here in conscious opposition to the singular "Judaism." "Christianities," removed by the editor from the printed text of "The Social Description of Early Christianity" (1975), first appears in the subtitle to *Drudgery Divine: On the Comparison of Early Christianities and the Religions of Late Antiquity* (1990).

As an aside, let me note that the title was not derived from the quotation from Thomas Jefferson's *Notes on Virginia,* used as the book's epigraph, although the Jefferson quote was intended to echo and gloss my use of the phrase. Rather, "drudgerie divine" was taken from the fifth stanza of George Herbert's poem, "The Elixir," part of the collection *The Temple,* published posthumously in 1633. The poem had long intrigued me for its use of alchemical terminology in a Christian text—could "drudgerie divine" be a play on the alchemical use of the term *opus*? This interplay replicated some of the concerns in the lecture series. As the poem had been set to music as a British church hymn, I thought it might resonate with some members of my London audience.

81. Smith, *Drudgery Divine* (1990), 51. See the references to resemblance theory, p. 51, n. 21.

82. "In Comparison a Magic Dwells" was taken by some to be a rejection of the comparative enterprise itself. I had taken some pains to forestall such an understanding. When the essay was reprinted in *Imagining Religion,* I immediately followed "In Comparison a Magic Dwells" (chapter 3) with a set of comparative pieces (chapters 3–7), "Sacred Persistence: Toward a Redescription of Canon" (chapter 4) being, perhaps, the boldest comparative piece I had thus far published.

For some reflections on "In Comparison a Magic Dwells," see my "Epilogue: The 'End' of Comparison" (2000) when the article was again reprinted some twenty years after the paper's initial delivery.

83. F. J. P. Poole, "Metaphors and Maps: Towards Comparison in the Anthropology of Religion," *Journal of the American Academy of Religion* 54 (1986): 411–57; quotation from 53. Cf. *Drudgery Divine* (1990), 50–53.

84. See already *Map* (1978), 253–54. The connection between this criticism and Poole's statement is made explicit in *Drudgery Divine* (1990), 52–53.

85. *Drudgery Divine* (1990), 51–53. Influenced by Marx, Heidegger, and later by Bourdieu, the notion of activity was, for me, a crucial element in critiquing what has been termed above "conservative" approaches to the study of religion, whether these latter focus on human passivity in the face of the sacred or passivity before the "phenomenon." See already in *"Adde Parvum"* (1971; 253–54) "The Wobbling Pivot" (1972; *Map,* 91), and most recently, "A Twice-told Tale" (2001), 140–41; see further, note 62, above.

Catherine Bell quotes a sentence that often figured in my classes but never made it into print, "ritual is work" (C. Bell, *Ritual Theory, Ritual Practice* [Oxford, 1992], viii). The closest parallel is Smith, "The Domestication of Sacrifice" (1987), 198, where I say that ritual is "a quite ordinary mode of social labor." Compare the concluding paragraph of "The Unknown God" (1982; in *Imagining Religion*, 89), which speaks of the issue of "religious work" as repaying further study and of "*homo religiosus* as being, preeminently, *homo faber.*"

'Redescription' was first introduced in "Sacred Persistence" (1979, *Imagining Religion*, 36); see further, notes 92 and 106.

86. *Drudgery Divine* (1990), 51.

87. "Defamiliarization" first figures in the introduction to *Imagining Religion* (1982), xiii, citing V. Shklovsky, "Art as Technique." In my most recent unpublished work, I have returned to the procedure of defamiliarization, now coupling it with the notion of the necessity of distortion. A favorite example has become the well-known plate illustrating structural correspondences between a bird and a human skeleton in Pierre Belon, *L'Histoire de la nature des oyseaux* (Paris, 1555), sig. d, iii, in which the topological correspondences can be seen only because the bird's skeleton is distorted, pictured in the same "unnatural" vertical stance with dependent limbs as is more "natural" for the human. See now, Smith, "*Dayyeinu:* A Meta-reflection," and Smith, "Why Compare Religions?" forthcoming.

88. To the best of my recollection, I first introduced these reflections in a 1993 paper for a plenary symposium at the annual meeting of the American Schools for Oriental Research, "Religion Up and Down, Out and In" (2002), 4, with a formulation that makes explicit connection with the vocabulary of earlier concerns: "It is difference that generates thought, whether at the level of data or of theory. Thus, a model gains its cognitive power by not according in all respects to that which it models. 'Map is not territory' and is, therefore, of intellectual value . . . Hence, depending on one's philosophical orientation, the common employment of terminology for models such as 'simplicity' or 'approximation,' as well as the on-going debate on the relationship of models to both theories and analogies, witness to the intellectual necessity for incongruency. . . ."

This same paragraph, from the 1993 paper, also quotes the sentence from C. Lévi-Strauss's *The Savage Mind* (Chicago, 1966), 24, that "the intrinsic value of a small-scale model is that it compensates for the renunciation of sensible dimensions by the acquisition of intelligible dimensions," which is cited at almost every occasion I subsequently discuss the cognitive power of difference. It is clear from notes in my files (1988–92) that it was thinking about the implications of Lévi-Strauss's formulation, initially in the context of the discussion of miniaturization in *To Take Place* (1987), 87, that prompted this extension of the older notion of the relations of incongruency to thought. (Cf. my use of the passage from

Lévi-Strauss in two 1992 lectures concerned with miniaturization, "Constructing a Small Place" [1998], 21–22, 29, and "Trading Places" [1995], 27.)

The first extended public presentation of this set of notions was in a paper for the opening session of "Consultation on Ancient Myths and Modern Theories of Christian Origins" at the 1955 annual meeting of the Society of Biblical Literature, now printed as "Social Formations of Early Christianities" (1996), esp. pp. 272–74. This introduces the new language of "translation," developed first in the context of teaching Durkheim, which is discussed below.

Among the essays printed in this volume, see especially, in chronological order: "The Bible and Religion" (2000), plenary address to the annual meeting of the Society of Biblical Literature, 1999; "A Twice-told Tale" (2001), plenary address to the Congress of the International Association for the History of Religions in 2000; "The Topography of the Sacred," originally delivered at the third biennial Cultural Turn Conference on the topic "Profane and Sacred," University of California, Santa Barbara, 2001; "God Save This Honourable Court," originally delivered as an Edward W. Snowden, '33 Lecture, Wesleyan University, 2001.

89. The distinction between 'homology' and 'analogy' was first referenced in *"Adde Parvum"* (1971; Map, 258, n. 50). In *Drudgery Divine* (1990), 47–48, n. 15, I incorporated, without revision, three paragraphs on the distinction from the 1988 American Society for the Study of Religion paper on comparison. See also "Epilogue: The 'End' of Comparison" (2000), 240, n. 7.

90. *Drudgery Divine* (1990), 51, n. 20.

91. *Drudgery Divine* (1990), 51: "all comparisons are properly analogical." Building on a 1987 response to a panel on diffusion at the annual meeting of the American Academy of Religion, I have gone on to stipulate a set of "preconditions" that must be met for a successful homologous comparison, and to indicate some fields where these conditions are often fulfilled. "At present, none of these preconditions are fulfilled in the usual comparisons of religious phenomena, but there is nothing, in principle, to prevent their successful deployment." See Smith, "Social Formations of Early Christianities" (1996), 276; "Epilogue: The 'End' of Comparison" (2000), 238, 240–41, n. 8.

92. In its published form, "Sacred Persistence" (1979) followed the revised form of the paper as given at the 1977 Max Richter Conversations on Ancient Judaism at Brown University, sponsored by Jacob Neusner, with a few additions from subsequent versions. (These Richter Conversations, taken as a set, remain the most stimulating conferences I have attended. I owe Jack much for these opportunities of participating as a generalist with a brilliant and diverse group of specialists. This situation has served as a model ever since.) Acknowledging this setting, a new introductory paragraph was added relating the essay to Neusner's

work. When I gave the paper as a 1977 lecture at Scripps College, I followed this with a second new introductory paragraph, employing, for the first time, the category of "redescription." The original paper had begun with a critique of the assignment, "a few moments of reflection should drive one to the same conclusion I reached: it is really no topic at all" (*Imagining Religion* [1982], 37, now the third paragraph).

93. The topic of canon was much on my mind, having offered, in 1975, a course in the Divinity School with the committee-assigned title, "Scriptural Tradition," as a component of the school's newly instituted M.A. program. This gave rise to the question as to what a generalist and comparativist might bring to the question of scripture—one example of the power of a general education course in compelling new directions in one's thought.

At the 1978 annual meeting of the American Academy of Religion, I gave a paper, "Divining a Canon," which both revised and pressed further the analogies of canon to African divination procedures and made more explicit the relevance of the redescription to rabbinic and Islamic canon formation. Compare my later paper on canon, "Canons, Catalogues and Classics" (1998), which includes some reflections on "Sacred Persistence."

94. *Imagining Religion*, 40.

95. See these usages in *Map*, 307, 308; *Imagining Religion*, 62, 101, and the theme of "exegetical ingenuity" in "Sacred Persistence" (1979) = *Imagining Religion*, 39–44, 52. In the unpublished "Conjectures on Conjunctures", prepared for the 2002 Society of Biblical Literature seminar entitled Ancient Myths and Modern Theories of Christian Origins, I have brought these elements together under the term "experimental application."

As indicated in the preface, one of the two projects I have been working on steadily since 1990 is a work on difference in which these themes, and others discussed in this section, are embedded. The three articles grouped together in this collection—"What a Difference a Difference Makes" (1985), "Differential Equations: On Constructing the 'Other'" (1991), and "Close Encounters of Diverse Kinds" (2001)—may be taken as rough drafts of sections of this project. See note 28 above.

96. *Map* (1978), 308.

97. "Differential Equations" (1991), 11. As an example of this "project" I discuss an ethnographic report on the Hua people of Papua New Guinea (11–13).

98. *Map* (1978), 242–43.

99. "What a Difference a Difference Makes" (1985), 15.

100. "What a Difference a Difference Makes" (1985), 48.

101. See, among others, Smith, "Differential Equations" (1992), 13; "Scriptures and Histories" (1992), 104–5.

102. "Differential Equations" (1992), 13. Note that in this paper, I changed my classification: "while difference or 'otherness' may be perceived as being either LIKE-US or NOT-LIKE-US, it becomes most problematic when it is TOO-MUCH-LIKE-US or when it claims to BE-US" (ibid.).

103. The papers delivered at the Consultation were printed as a set in *Method & Theory in the Study of Religion* 8 (1966): 229–89. Therein see especially, B. Mack, "On Redescribing Christian Origins," 247–69, and Smith, "Social Formations of Early Christianities: A Response to Ron Cameron and Burton Mack," 271–78.

104. I subsequently delivered versions of "Why Imagine Religion?" on five other occasions between 1996 and 1998, but left it unpublished.

105. Formulations from both my response to Burton Mack, "Social Formations of Early Christianities" (1995) and "Why Imagine Religion?" recur in a number of articles printed in this collection. See note 88 above.

106. *Imagining Religion*, 36, cf. 141, n. 2 (especially the term "redescription" in M. Hesse). To the best of my recollection, it was Paul Ricoeur who pointed me to these discussions of redescription, either in conversations at the University of Chicago or through his book, *La Métaphore vive* (Paris, 1975); English translation, *The Rule of Metaphor* (Toronto, 1977), 239–46.

107. Redescription as a 'rectification' of scholarly categories was first used in *To Take Place* (1987), 103. This sense owes not a little to the Chinese philosophical project of the "rectification of the names," which I knew from both Hsün Tzu and from Maoist writings, as well as to Mack's description of my work in "On Redescribing Christian Origins," 256–59.

I had used the term 'rectification' regularly in earlier work, particularly in "A Pearl of Great Price" (1976), to denote the attempt to rectify a situation that was incongruous in light of past precedents through efforts at thought. See *Imagining Religion* (1982), 94–95, 99–101; cf. *Map* (1978), 308, n. 21; "The Domestication of Sacrifice" (1987), 194, n. 7, 211. Set in a different context, 'rectification' is the reinterpretation of tradition in the sense that has motivated most of my studies of Late Antique materials; see *Map*, xi; *Drudgery Divine* (1990), 106–107. In the newer sense, the precedents are no longer mythic but, rather, academic ones transmitted through the history of scholarship.

108. As noted above (n. 92), the paragraph on redescription was added to "Sacred Persistence" only when the paper was given at Scripps College in 1977; hence, the subtitle does not appear in the original manuscript but was inserted in the printed version.

109. Mack, "On Redescribing Christian Origins," 256–59.

110. Smith, "Epilogue: The 'End' of Comparison" (2000), 239; Mack's influence is acknowledged (241, n. 11). In a version of the same paragraph in "Bible

and Religion" (2000), 87, reprinted in this volume, I go so far as to claim that definition, classification, comparison, and explanation "have in common that they are all varying modes of redescription." To the prescriptive elements in this passage, compare the "three conditions" for choosing exempla in the introduction to *Imagining Religion* (1982), xi–xii.

111. "Why Imagine Religion?" To the criticism of paraphrase, compare the remark in "Connections" (1990), 10, delivered as an opening address at the 1989 annual meeting of the American Academy of Religion, "Too much of what we do . . . may be placed somewhere between show-and-tell and paraphrase." The quotation from C. Lévi-Strauss is from *La Pensée sauvage* (Paris, 1962), 328; compare the different rendering in Lévi-Strauss, *The Savage Mind* (Chicago, 1966), 248.

112. "Why Imagine Religion?"

113. "Social Formations" (1996), 273. For other consequences, see the articles cited in note 88 above.

114. I should note that my first inquiries into 'general' and 'generalization' were undertaken while I was Dean of the Faculty of the College in order to clarify some of the assumptions behind the use of the word in the term 'general education.' For a later use of the same sort of observations in this curricular context, see, "Teaching the Bible in the Context of General Education" (1998).

The most extended treatment of the subject is an unpublished 1997 paper delivered at the Annual Meeting of the North American Society for the Study of Religion on the assigned topic, "Origins, Universals, and Generalities."

115. In the unpublished 1996 lecture, "Why Imagine Religion?" I wrote:

> For all the clever turns of phrase I've endured when being introduced
> to audiences on the tag I adopted from Alfred Korzybski, "map is not
> territory," no one has ever turned the maxim into an interrogative, "why
> map territory?" A map is of such obvious utility that the question never
> seems to arise. And yet, since the 1970s, there has been an important
> cartographic literature of the epistemology of mapping by scholars
> such as Arthur H. Robinson, Barbara B. Petchenik, James Meyer and
> Roger M. Downs which calls into question the sorts of naive realism
> that underlies our confidence in a map's utility. After all, at the most
> basic level, a map is a graphic reduced re-representation of our mental
> representation of structures of spatial relations. Take, for example, two
> theses developed by the cartographer, J. S. Keates, concerning general
> topographic maps, a genre which, at first glance, appears to retain the
> most correspondence to their territory. "First, that for any feature, only
> a selection of the total information which it describes is shown by a
> map symbol; second, that the function of the symbol is mainly to clas-

sify or to categorize, that is, those features which have certain characteristics in common are grouped together, even though they all have individual differences and even though they all have different locations" (J. S. Keates, "Symbols and Meaning in Topographic Maps," *International Yearbook of Cartography* 12 [1972], 169). Maps are structures of transformation, not structures of reproduction.

What is at stake is an issue concerning which students of religion have been notably shy, the cognitive power of distortion, or difference, if you prefer a less strident term.

Recall, here, the example of the history of subway maps both in New York City and in London. In New York, one of the least successful experiments in civic map production was the 1979 Subway Map. As described in naïve realist terms in its promotional literature, it was based "on the principle that the relationship of the subway lines to the city above them is crucial. So the lines are laid over a real (though very slightly distorted) map [of the surface network of boroughs, avenues, streets, and blocks], making it possible to see where in the real city each subway stop is" (*New York Times*, August 2, 1979, C11). But this very attempt at reproductive realism made the map all but impossible to use. It has been replaced, today, by an abstract, generalized diagram of the subway system which has proved far more successful.

New York's experience recapitulated London's. In the 1920s, mapmakers superimposed a color-coded, accurately scaled map of the actual routes of the underground rail lines, with all their curved and intersecting paths, on a detailed London street map. It was unreadable, "geographically correct, yes, but useless." In 1931–32, a draughtsman, Henry C. Buck, revised the map with a format still in use today. Buck followed his immediate predecessor, F. H. Stingemore, in eliminating all representation of the streets above ground, but went further. He showed all routes as either straight lines or as bending at 90- or 45-degree angles, and represented all distances between stations as identical. In order to bring more clarity to the central London area, "he imagined that he was using a convex lens or mirror, enlarging the middle in relation to the whole." As A. de Forest writes of the Buck map, the "order that London's Underground map presents is an illusion, of course, a distortion of geographic fact. In actuality, the train lines don't follow a neat geometric pattern under the city, but twist and turn by necessity, just like the streets above. Distances on the map are not to scale; far-flung suburbs . . . seem much closer to the center than they are. In fact, the Underground map veers so far from geographic reality that . . .

those in the know call it simply '*The Diagram*'" (All quotations in this paragraph are from A. de Forest, "Mapping: Notes from the Underground," *Holiday Inn Express Navigator* [December 2001–January, 2002]: 2–7).

See also the use of J. L. Borges's parable, "Exactitude in Science," from Borges, *Collected Fictions* (New York, 1998), 325, in the conclusion of Smith, "Bible and Religion" (2000), 91, reprinted below.

116. C. Lévi-Strauss, "The Structural Study of Myth," in Lévi-Strauss, *Structural Anthropology* (New York, 1963–76), 1: 230.

ACKNOWLEDGMENTS

MORPHOLOGY AND HISTORY IN MIRCEA ELIADE'S *PATTERNS IN COMPARATIVE RELIGION* (1949–1999)

PART 1: THE WORK AND ITS CONTEXTS

The particular cannot be the model for the whole.

J. W. VON GOETHE, *Entwurf eine vergleichenden Anatomie* (1795)

I HAVE TAKEN particular care with the general title for this small series that commemorates the fiftieth anniversary of the first, French edition of Mircea Eliade's *Patterns in Comparative Religion*. Despite the word's awkward origins, merging two hitherto distinct Anglo-Saxon verbs, and adding both an imitative Latin prefix and a hybrid French suffix, 'acknowledgment' seems precisely right. Its semantic range includes a declaration of gratitude, a legal concession of validity, and the admission of that which cannot be denied by the senses. *Patterns* is a work that founded an influential approach to the study of religion. It is a work that can be thought with or against, but never thought around or away.

Confining myself to the public record, the history of *Patterns* is not entirely clear. Eliade's previous scholarly publications, largely in the form of journal articles, had three foci: alchemy, yoga, and Romanian folklore. While his omnivorous reading and curiosity are already apparent, these articles are not yet marked by the sort of global reach that informs his later work. The origin of *Patterns* appears to be a lecture course on religious symbolism delivered at the University of Bucharest in 1937. During 1940–41, Eliade began a manuscript, "Prolegomena to the History of Religions" or "Prolegomena to a Comparative History of Religions." He returned to the manuscript in 1945 in Paris. Two lecture series at the École des Hautes Études in 1946–48 formed the basis for, at least, the first two chapters of the work. In 1948, Eliade proposed the book to his publisher, Gallimard, with no response, and then to Payot. There is every indication of a feverish schedule of completing the manuscript and having the hybrid Romanian-French text translated into French by friends. Eliade continued to employ the working title, "Prolegomena to the History of Religions," and persistently referred to a second volume. The publisher found this title forbidding to readers and felt that the text was too long to be called a prolegomenon. Eliade's counterproposal was to entitle the work "The Morphology of the Sacred." But this too was rejected, although in hindsight it is apparent that much misunderstanding of Eliade's project might have been avoided if this title had been adopted. In 1948, the work was announced under the title "Manual of the History of Religions." On January 18, 1949, it appeared in print with the publisher's title, *Traité d'histoire des religions*.[1] This title was maintained in its Spanish, Italian, and Polish translations. Its German and English translations retitle the work, although not apparently at Eliade's initiative. In German it appears as *The Religious and the Holy: Elements of the History of Religions*, in English as *Patterns in Comparative Religion*.[2]

The publisher's choice, *traité*, is singularly ambiguous as to scope. It signals both introductory brevity and/or comprehensiveness. It promises, in either case, systematicity. As one dictionary defines 'treatise': "a formal or methodical discussion or exposition of the principles of the subject."[3] Eliade's work clearly intends to fulfill this latter characterization.

The first French edition of the work in 1949, with its authorizing "Preface" by Georges Dumézil, attracted sufficient attention for it to be reissued in 1953, followed by a series of new editions, consisting of slight bibliographical revisions, from 1964 (2d ed.) through 1975 (8th ed.). The 1958 English translation (several times reprinted) is of the first French edition with a handful of new bibliographical citations.

I wish I knew more about the circumstances of this 1958 English translation. By then, it was clearly no longer the sort of publisher's risk that Payot had taken in 1949 with but two postwar scholarly works by Eliade in print in France. By 1958, Eliade had become a figure of worldwide academic importance. The years 1946–48 had marked a shift to an expanded definition of 'archaic' from the ancient Eurasian agricultural civilizations to first articles, in French, on shamanism and "primitive" mythology.[4] The period from 1949 to 1957 was the most productive span in Eliade's academic career, seeing the French publication of *Patterns* (1949), *The Myth of the Eternal Return* (1949), *Shamanism* (1951), *Yoga* (1954), *The Forge and the Crucible* (1956), *The Sacred and the Profane* (1965)—as well as his most ambitious work of fiction, *The Forbidden Forest* (1955). By 1958, Eliade had already begun his association with the

University of Chicago, thereby attracting an English-language audience. With the exception of an unobtainable 1938, forty-seven-page pamphlet on alchemy and the 1955 translation of *The Myth of the Eternal Return*, 1958 marked a first and intense year for English translations of Eliade, with the successive printing, by separate publishers, of *Patterns*, *Birth and Rebirth*, and *Yoga*.

Rather than Eliade's usual skilled translator, Willard R. Trask, *Patterns* was translated by Rosemary Sheed (Mrs. Neil Middleton), the daughter of the publisher, Francis Joseph Sheed, and the sister of the founder of the American Catholic publishing house of Sheed & Ward, the original publisher of the English version of *Patterns*. There is no indication in the public record that Rosemary Sheed translated any other French text or that Eliade reviewed the translation.[5] It is not satisfactory. Sheed persistently mistranslates formulations or misconstrues the text. The English translation often conceals Eliade's technical vocabulary; it omits phrases; and, more troubling, it adds phrases, most frequently when Christian topics are discussed.[6]

With this much by way of a general introduction to both articles, let me turn and introduce the present topic.

Historians, by and large, have been notably uncomfortable with contemporary experiments in alternative history, a mode of narrative dependent on actualizing the question "What if?" It is a form that, itself, has a history, extending back, at least, to the taxonomy of Asclepiades of Myrlea in the first century B.C. with his category of "history that could have happened," and one that received its definitive form in Pascal's well-known *penseé* 162: "Cleopatra's nose: had it been shorter, the whole aspect of the world would have been altered." In this vein, a possible starting point for our meditation might be: What if, after 1948, Wittgenstein, instead of scribbling his second set of notes on Frazer's *The Golden Bough*, had read and jotted thoughts on Eliade's *Patterns*? At the very least, Wittgenstein's proposal of an alternative to Frazer's evolutionary/developmental hypothesis would have had a massive, concrete exemplar. Wittgenstein writes: "An historical explanation, an explanation as an hypothesis of the development, is only *one* kind of summary of the data—of their synopsis. We can equally well see the data in their relations to one another and make a summary of them in a general picture without putting it in the form of an hypothesis regarding the temporal development." Wittgenstein goes on to explain this alternative by quoting Goethe's 1798 poem, "The Metamorphosis of Plants": "'And all this points to some unknown law' is what we want to say about the material Frazer has collected. I *can* set out this law in a hypothesis of development [or, evolution] . . . but I can also do it just by arranging the factual material so that we can easily pass from one part to another and have a clear view of it—showing this in a *perspicuous* way." The translator, here, interrupts Wittgenstein to paraphrase his word, *übersichtlichen*, rendered by "perspicuous" as "a way of setting out the whole field together by making easy the passage from one part of it to another." Returning to Wittgenstein:

> For us the conception of a perspicuous presentation is fundamental. . . . This perspicuous presentation makes possible that understanding which consists just in the fact that we "see the connections." Hence the importance of finding *intermediate links*. But in our case an hypothetical link is not meant to do anything except draw attention to the similarity, the connection, between the *facts*. As one might illustrate the internal relation of a circle to an ellipse by gradually transforming an ellipse into a circle; *but not in order to assert that a given ellipse in fact, historically, came from a circle* (hypothesis of development) but only to sharpen our eye for a formal connection.[7]

This "perspicuous," synoptic viewing of formal relationships and connections that Wittgenstein juxtaposes to an evolutionary or developmental viewing of the *same* phenomena may also be denoted, as his explicit reference to Goethe makes plain, by the term 'morphological'—a term apparently invented by Goethe, who formally defined it in 1795.[8] What Wittgenstein has enunciated is the epistemological dualism, foundational in cultural studies, between a morphological and a historical approach. In the three-centuries-long intellectual history of this tension, first in the natural then in the human sciences, one may hear, again and again, the *cri de coeur* echoed by Carlo Ginzburg in 1986: "The relationship between typological (or formal) connections and historical connections . . . [has] to be confronted even in its theoretical implications. . . . In the case of my current work . . . the integration of morphology and history is only an aspiration which may be impossible to realize."[9]

It will be the burden of these articles to insert Eliade's *Patterns* into the history of the debate between these dual perspectives as well as that of the experiments in their integration. It is by placing the project of *Patterns* within this context that *Patterns* takes on its value. For Eliade, the emblem of this debate is Goethe.

The narrative of the intellectual influence, the reception history, of Goethe's morphological studies, most especially his 1790 monograph, *The Metamorphosis of Plants*, has yet to be written. Its trajectories through the history of nineteenth- and twentieth-century biological thought have been well documented: first of all, in the works of committed morphologists such as E. S. Russell's *Form and Function: A Contribution to the History of Animal Morphology* (1916), and in the writings of the incomparable Agnes Arber, especially her notes to her translation of Goethe's *Metamorphosis* (1946) and her general treatise, *The Natural Philosophy of Plant Form* (1950). These have been followed by more recent studies by historians of science such as William Coleman (1976), George A. Wells (1978), Timothy Lenoir (1982), Toby Appel (1987), Adrian Desmond (1989), Jane Maienschein (1991), Phillip Reid Sloan (1992), and Lynn K. Nyhart (1995). There have been, as well, more generalized studies by students of Germanic culture, culminating in the important collection edited by Frederick Amrine, Francis J. Zucker, and Harvey Wheeler, *Goethe and the Sciences: A Reappraisal* (1987), which contains Amrine's invaluable bibliography on the topic, as well as Amrine's more recent two-volume study, *Goethe in the History of Science* (1996–97).[10] But there are other, less obvious moments. To give but a few instances:

   a) The paragraphs on "The Plant" in the first edition of Hegel's *Encyclopaedia of Philosophical Sciences* (1817), which deploy Goethe's morphological notions to overcome the static and external classifications of Linnaeus by introducing the principle of dynamic unity. These few paragraphs were swollen to an eighty-page botanical treatise in Michelet's fourth edition of Hegel's work (1840–45) on the basis of students' notes. This expanded version is taken up and creatively played with in Derrida's *Glas* (1974), noting that "the Encyclopedia proposes a vast and meticulous deduction of the 'vegetable organism' . . . modelled, most often, on *The Metamorphosis of Plants* (Goethe)."[11]

   b) Rilke's careful study of Goethe's *Metamorphosis* influenced his *Sonette an Orpheus* (1923). This relationship is the culminating example in Elizabeth Sewell's *The Orphic Voice: Poetry and Natural History* (1960), a study which contains a long section, "Erasmus Darwin and Goethe: Linnaean and Ovidian Taxonomy," an essay that, along with Ernst Cassirer's "The Idea of Metamorphosis and Idealistic Morphology: Goethe," remains one of the two most provocative meditations on the topic.[12]

   c) Uncovering the relationship between "Humboldt's notion of 'organic form' in language and Goethe's much earlier theory of 'Urform' in biology" constitutes one of the crucial moments in the intellectual adventure of Noam Chomsky's *Cartesian Linguistics*. It suggests the central role Goethe's biological theories played in some formulations of the human sciences.[13]

   d) With more direct relevance to this latter project, there is Spengler's wholesale attempt to convert Goethe's botanical morphology into a "morphology of world history." Spengler begins *The Decline of the West* with an epigraph from Goethe and acknowledges that "the philosophy of this book I owe to the philosophy of Goethe." This indebtedness is exhibited with most clarity in the methodological section of the third chapter, entitled "Physiognomic and Systematic."[14]

The process of occluding Goethe's influence, especially for English readers, begins already with Spengler's work, whose subtitle, "Outline of a Morphology of World History," has been dropped from the title page of Charles Atkinson's "authorized translation." However, the most dramatic example remains the omission of four epigraphs from Goethe's morphological writings that head the foreword, as well as chapters 1, 2, and 9 of the Russian original of Vladimir Propp's *Morphology of the Wondertale* in both the first and second editions of its English translation. These omissions, according to Propp, led to Lévi-Strauss's misunderstanding of Propp's work as being structuralist rather than morphological, in Goethe's sense of the word—a correction that Eliade frequently repeated with considerable relish.[15]

It is not possible to determine with any security under what circumstances Eliade first encountered Goethe's morphological studies. Perhaps he found them in the course of his own wide reading and early interests in natural history. More probably, he was led to them by his studies, while still in his teens, of the books of Rudolf Steiner. Steiner, in addition to his anthroposophical writings, was the first, critical editor of Goethe's scientific works, for both the Kürschner edition (1883–97) and the great Weimar edition of 1887–1919. Steiner authored, as well, a set of influential studies that offered a holistic reading of Goethe's scientific achievements.[16] In any case, Eliade's devotion to Goethe, especially the 1790 monograph, *The Metamorphosis of Plants*, was intense. I can recall his delight in the unexpected discovery that this or that scholar knew Goethe's *Metamorphosis* well. (Toynbee is a case in point.) I remember as well his pleasure, when reading an early draft of my 1971 article, "*Adde Parvum,*" that I had isolated morphology as one of the four prime modes of comparison, suggesting along the way that it was morphology, rather than phenomenology, that most scholars of religion had in mind when they used the latter term. I had gone on to describe Goethe as foundational to the morphological enterprise and had situated Eliade's scholarly writings, especially *Patterns*, within that tradition, claiming that "the failure to recognize this [morphological and Goethean] ambience had been responsible for significant misinterpretation of the role of history and the status of patterns in Eliade's work."[17]

More telling than the above is Eliade's persistent testimony to the power of what he termed "this [morphological] method of delineating structures by reducing phenomena to archetypes." To give but two examples, the first from 1951 in Palermo: "When this history of the idea of *morphology* as Goethe understood it shall be written, it will be seen how fecund it has been, not only in the natural sciences, but also in the classification, analysis and interpretation of spiritual creations."[18] And, from Chicago in 1978:

> When Goethe was studying the morphology of plants, he came
> to the conclusion that it was possible to trace all vegetable forms
> back to what he called "the original plant," and he eventually
> identified that *Urpflanze* with the leaf. . . . For my own part, in
> my early days at least, I thought that in order to keep sight of the
> forest among so many trees—facts, figures, and rituals—the his-
> torian of religions would do well to search for the "original plant"
> in his own field, for the primal image. . . . In short, the kind of
> structuralism I consider fruitful consists in asking oneself . . .
> about the primordial order that is the basis of their meaning. . . .
> A historian of religions, whatever his opinions . . . thinks that
> his first duty, in practice, is to grasp the original *meaning* of a sa-
> cred phenomenon and then to interpret its history.[19]

Understanding Goethe's morphological project as appropriated by Eliade requires that we situate Goethe twice: once with respect to his immediate past context and then with respect to a more extended future. As is characteristic in any history of ideas, the morphological enterprise looks quite different from these two vantage points. The difference can be encapsulated by reference to the two philosophers' deployment of Goethe that have been cited above. For Hegel, placing Goethe within his immediate past context, and consonant with Goethe's own account,[20] morphology was dynamic, introducing 'development' as a privileged category of activity when compared with Linnaeus's static taxonomy. For Wittgenstein, writing out of the context of intellectual history posterior to Goethe, morphology is usefully synoptic and totalistic when compared with Frazer's evolutionary or developmental schema.

The one element common to both Hegel and Wittgenstein, as well as forming a part of Goethe's self-understanding, is that Goethe and his morphological project are perceived to be antithetical to the reigning scientific paradigm, whether this be the seventeenth- and eighteenth-century models associated with Linnaeus and Newton,[21] or the nineteenth- and twentieth-century systems for which Darwin and Frazer stand as emblems. Eliade clearly resonates with this contrarian stance.[22]

Allow me to summarize Goethe's proposal, drawing largely on the revised materials, including *The Metamorphosis of Plants*, collected in the 1817 printing of *On Morphology*, the first year the word 'morphology' appears in the title of a book.[23]

Writing in retrospect, Goethe dates his first "vision" of the vegetative system to a visit to the botanical garden in Padua on September 26, 1786. Three observations proved especially pregnant: (1) The extraordinary variability of plants; (2) the difference between variability that is the result of the internal dynamics of plant species and the external variations produced by environmental influences; (3) the serial nature of plant growth epitomized in the "sequence of modifications" in the leaves of a fan palm in which he saw "the simple, lance-shaped first leaves," then "the successive separation increased until finally the fan quality was discernible in complete development. From a spatulate sheaf, a branchlet with blossoms finally emerged."[24]

From these three observations, Goethe deduced a set of consequences. Starting with the observation of extraordinary variability—in the same parts of a single plant, between members of the same species, and between species—Goethe gained confidence in criticizing one of his intellectual heroes: Linnaeus. Goethe now argued that Linnaeus had focused only on particular parts (in the case of plants, on the reproductive organs) rather than on the "form of the whole" organism. Through this he had sought to "subjugate Nature" by arbitrarily privileging fixity over fluidity.

> To be sure, I recognized the necessity of this [Linnaean] procedure, which had as its goal the discussion of certain external plant phenomena, according to general agreement, and the elimination of all phenomena that are uncertain and difficult to represent. Nevertheless, when I attempted an accurate application of the [Linnaean] terminology, I found the variability of organs the chief difficulty. I lost courage to drive in a stake, or to draw a boundary line, when, on the self-same plant, I discovered first round, then notched, and finally almost pinnate stems, which later contracted, were simplified, turned into scales, and at last disappeared entirely.[25]

As the descriptive language of this last quoted sentence suggests variability, for Goethe, was not emblematic of riot and disorder. Beneath the multiplicity of forms were regular processes of formation: the simple expanding to the complex, then contracting, and finally vanishing. Beneath the apparent surface differences lay a deep similarity of process, the result of internal, logical, teleological principles of transformation that Goethe termed 'metamorphosis.'[26] The succession—in the particular example from Goethe just cited: round, notched, pinnate stems, contracted into scales, then disappearance—could be expressed in two "laws of transformation" (par. 3). On the one hand, "regular or progressive metamorphosis," which, in logical sequence, moves up the "ladder" from simplicity (i.e., relative undifferentiation) to complexity (i.e., relatively strong differentiation). On the other hand, "irregular or retrogressive metamorphosis," in which Nature steps "backward," resulting, again in logical sequence, in either halting differentiation prematurely: freezing differentiation into rigidity (e.g., leaf in the cactus is retrogressively transformed into a rigid spine); or, so compressing differentiation that the organ atrophies and disappears (pars. 6–7). Taken together, these two laws of progressive and retrogressive metamorphosis are but different expressions of the same organic process of growth: "a basic principle of alternation in expansion and contraction" (par. 73). Expansion is preeminently the serial, the "successive"—with respect to plants, their "vegetative" aspect. Contraction is preeminently the "simultaneous"—with respect to plants, their "reproductive" aspect (pars. 113–14). However, it must be stressed that these are alternative ways of viewing the *same* phenomena. "For we might equally well say that a stamen is a contracted petal, as that a petal is a stamen in a state of expansion" (par. 120).

While expressed in general language, this all turns back to Goethe's initial critique of Linnaeus. Linnaeus had, in Goethe's judgment, quite arbitrarily focused on the reproductive aspect of plants, which, in terms of Goethe's understanding of metamorphosis, limited Linnaeus's perspective to the aspects of regression, contraction, and simultaneity, to what I have termed 'freezing.' Hence, Linnaeus's rigidity. For Goethe, Linnaeus had ignored the progressive, vegetative aspects of plants and, by failing to place these two tendencies in relation to one another, had failed to perceive, as well, the dynamism of regressive metamorphosis.

Of considerable import to our overall inquiry into the relations between the morphological and the historical, Goethe names, and then sets aside, a third type of metamorphosis, "accidental metamorphosis . . . which we shall disregard . . . which is effected accidentally by external agents," and which may alter or thwart both internal sorts of metamorphoses—progressive or retrogressive—whether the "accident" be the effect of environment, disease, or insects (pars. 5, 8). With this move, Goethe explicitly excludes the historically contingent from his understanding of process.[27] His sequences remain formal and logically necessary.

For Goethe's chosen dynamic term, 'metamorphosis' (or, elsewhere, *Bildung*, 'form-change' or 'formation' as opposed to *Gestalt*, 'fixed form')[28] to have any meaning, the different must be a transformation of the same or the similar. Goethe's task was "to show, insofar as it was possible, that the various plant parts developed in sequence are intrinsically identical despite their manifold differences in outer form" (par. 67). This notion of the *innere Identität*, the internal same or similar, takes two directions in Goethe's morphological thought.

The first, the explicit thesis of *The Metamorphosis of Plants*, is summarized in Goethe's ejaculation, "Everything is leaf and through this simplicity the greatest diversity becomes possible."[29] A thesis that can be put more soberly, "we have sought to derive the apparently differing organs of the vegetating and reproducing plant from one organ—the leaf" (par. 119), or, more fancifully, as in Goethe's important letter to Herder (May 17, 1787): "It had occurred to me that in the organ of the plant, which we ordinarily designate as leaf, the true Proteus lay hidden, who can conceal and reveal himself in all forms. Forward and backward, the plant is always only leaf."[30]

The task in the *Metamorphosis* is to show the formal, logical processes of the successive exfoliations of leaf, progressively and regressively from the relatively undifferentiated cotyledon through simple leaves to various modes of leaf differentiation, achieving its highest degree in compound leaves composed of several leaflets. This expansion of leaf is followed by a compression of leaf around an axial point, forming a calyx. The corolla represents renewed expansion. Stamens and pistils are compressed leaves, resulting in the expansive fruit and concentrated again in seeds. While at times in the *Metamorphosis* Goethe takes his examples from a single species, the full series is illustrated from quite different plants, juxtaposed without regard for their taxonomic or geographic placement and without any implication that these logical successions had any chronological character.[31]

The second direction in Goethe's morphology that developed the notion of "inner identity" introduces a term that will recur as pivotal in Eliade, at least since 1937–38, that of the "archetype."[32] In botanical terms, the archetypal plant is the *Urpflanze*.[33] It is probably significant, although I remain uncertain as to how to evaluate it, that the notion and vocabulary of 'archetype' and 'Ur-plant' does not occur in any of Goethe's scientific writings.[34] It is rather to be found in poetic materials, in travel books, and in more informal genres such as letters, diaries, and reported conversations. While there are any number of such expressions, I choose this one from the letter to Herder of May 17, 1787, in the translation by Eliade's friend and fellow student of the *Metamorphosis*, Erich Heller: "I must confess to you that I am very close to discovering the secret of the creation and organization of plants. . . . The *Urpflanze* is to be the strangest creature in the world—Nature herself shall be jealous of it. With such a model . . . it will be possible to invent plants *ad infinitum*. They will be strictly logical plants—that is to say, even though they may not actually exist they could exist—they would not be mere picturesque or poetic shadows or dreams, but would possess an inner truth and necessity."[35] If Goethe, in the *Metamorphosis*, stressed succession or seriality, here the notion of the archetype emphasizes simultaneity. All transformations, both actual and possible, are present—at once.

In eighteenth- and nineteenth-century biological thought, the term 'archetype' proved fruitful as its understanding shifted from the logically generic, for those who stood in the Linnaean tradition, to the logically generative for those in the Goethean, and, then, to the historically genetic, as represented by Darwin, who redefined 'archetype' as a genealogically "ancestral" form.[36] Morphological thought, since Darwin, would adjust to this new understanding, restoring, as a consequence of the growing focus on adaptation, value to change as an effect of environment which Goethe had set aside, and transforming the interest of morphology from matters of form to questions of function.[37]

We may gain a glimpse, already, of these renewed historical concerns from an essay by Kant, published in 1777, recalling that Kant was a profound reader of Linnaeus, especially in part 2 of the *Critique of Judgement*.[38] Kant begins the 1777 essay, as Goethe had, with a critique of Linnaean taxonomy. However, unlike Goethe, he does so on the basis of Buffon's reproductive definition of species. "The [classificatory] divisions of the schools [i.e., Linnaeus] have to do with classes based on similarities; the divisions of nature, however, concern lineages which divide animals in terms of consanguinity in terms of their generation."[39] This shift, Kant argues, requires that artificial typologies be replaced with natural ones, built on natural laws. And this, in turn, presupposes the development of a new science of "natural history" which will substitute for the description of forms an account of how, over time, they came to be that way. This sort of natural history, Kant predicts, "would teach us about the changes in the form of the earth and at the same time about the [changes which] the creatures of the earth (plants and animals) underwent in the course of their natural wanderings, and the consequent variations from the original form of their ancestral line."[40] Because of the effect of what

Kant terms "natural wanderings," and we might term 'diffusion,' Kant suggests that natural history "would in all likelihood reinterpret a large number of apparently distinct types into varieties of the same species." Similarity is hidden, not in the Protean folds of leaf, but in history and genealogy.

What then of Eliade? We last left him sitting, in reverie, in the Sicilian botanical garden at Palermo, just twelve days short of the 164th anniversary, at that site, of one of Goethe's earliest written formulations of the *Urpflanze*. Eliade recollects: "In [this] public garden . . . Goethe 'contemplated' not only the lemon and orange trees but all those species of palm and cacti which allowed him to 'see' what he named the *Urplant*. (What I wouldn't give to be able to reread *here* that brilliant booklet. *The Metamorphosis of Plants*, from 1790!)"[41]

As best as I can determine, Eliade had no interest in the history of biological morphology apart from Goethe. But he did expect his readers to judge *Patterns* in light of the Goethean enterprise. He clearly knew and seriously thought about the sort of late nineteenth- and early twentieth-century cultural morphological proposals that took up, in a sense, the agendum of Kantian natural history in privileging diffusion as epitomized by the Panbabylonian, the Graebner and the Frobenius Schools, with which he held a lifelong dialogue, as well as something of its more enduring legacy in Scandinavian folkloristics. It will be a part of the burden of the close reading of *Patterns* in my second article to suggest that diffusion, an essentially spatial rather than temporal understanding of historicization, was persistently deployed by Eliade. This blunts, in part, the evaluation of his work as ahistorical.

But, there is more. In the essay by Carlo Ginzburg cited above, he notes that some scholars have utilized what might be termed a two-volume stratagem, with one volume a morphological treatment of its subject, and the other, a historical. Ginzburg's prime example is the two volumes by Propp, *The Morphology of the Folktale* (1928) and the *Historical Roots of the Wondertale* (1946).[42] While such a stratagem does not achieve an integration of the morphological and the historical—an integration Ginzburg rightly judges to be an urgent *desideratum*—it does, in the case of Propp, illustrate a virtue already referred to several times: the conception of the morphological and the historical as two ways of interpreting the *same* data analogous to synchrony and diachrony in Saussure's formulation (unlike Lévi-Strauss, who all but mythologizes them as opposing forces).

As a general methodological stance, this is to side with the south-west German Neo-Kantian School, as represented by Wilhelm Windel-band and Heinrich Rickert, and to assert that any object may be consid-ered *both* from a generalizing (in our term, morphological) point of view and from an idiographic, historical perspective.[43] Translated in terms of our issue, this is to say that the morphological and the historical comprise alternative views of the same object, rather than suggesting that they treat different objects, and to maintain that neither view is finally re-ducible to the other.

Some version of the two-volume stratagem appears to have been Eli-ade's intention while writing *Patterns*. At several points in the work, he refers to a second volume which will "enter upon the problem of the his-tory of religious phenomena. This study I have left for my companion volume."[44] It is generally held that this "companion volume" was never written. We should certainly resist the temptation to identify this miss-ing work with the awkward, multivolume, unfinished production of Eli-ade's last years, the *History of Beliefs and Religious Ideas*.[45] Rather, I would venture the suggestion that we *have* three chapters of what this compan-ion volume might have comprised: the two monographs, *Shamanism* and *Yoga*, and the briefer sketch, *The Forge and the Crucible*. The extraordi-nary length and complexity of the first two, largely confined to single cul-ture areas, and the cross-cultural breadth of the latter, for all its brevity, supplies reason enough why the full work could never appear.

This suggestion is strengthened when one recalls that the work on shamanism was being drafted during 1946–51, at the same time as the manuscript of *Patterns* was being completed, and that the "Foreword" to *Shamanism* remains Eliade's most comprehensive, though highly concen-trated, general statement concerning the historical enterprise. After dealing with alternative approaches to shamanism, Eliade begins his his-torical essay with a reference to the projected "complementary volume (in preparation) to *Patterns*" promising that it will address the urgent question "concerning the importance to be accorded to 'history'" in the work of the historian of religions, whose task is to present, for any reli-gious phenomenon, "a comprehensive view which shall be at once a mor-phology and a history."[46] It is difficult to escape the impression that this "Foreword" is, at the very least, a rough outline of what would have been the introduction to the companion volume. It is both constructive in terms of Eliade's own position and critical in counterdistinguishing his understanding of "history" in the history of religions from that of histor-ical ethnology, phenomenology, morphology, and historiography.[47]

In part 2 (see chapter 3), I shall turn from an exercise in intellectual history, from an exploration of context, to a close reading of text, utilizing this discussion of Goethe's morphological enterprise as one important assist in understanding the systematics, the logic of Eliade's *Patterns*.[48]

Notes

1. This account is drawn from three sources: M. Eliade, *Journal*, vol. 1, 1945–55 (Chicago, 1990), esp. 11, 13, 32, 44, 54, 57, 63, 67, 73, 76, 77, 79, 86, 87, *Autobiography*, vol. 2, 1937–1960, *Exile's Odyssey* (Chicago, 1988), esp. 93–94, 105, 107, 114–16, 119–20, 134, 138, 147, and "Avant-propos de l'auteur," in Eliade's *Traité d'histoire des religions*, 1st ed. (Paris, 1949), 14. The announcement of the title as *Manuel d'histoire des religions* appears in the frontispiece list of "Oeuvres de Mircea Eliade," in Eliade, *Techniques du Yoga* (Paris, 1948).

2. Eliade, *Tratado de historia de las religiones* (Madrid, 1954), *Trattato di storia delle religioni* (Turin, 1954), *Traktat o historii religii* (Warsaw, 1966), as compared with *Die Religionen und das Heilige: Elemente der Religionsgeschichte* (Salzburg and Munich, 1954) and *Patterns in Comparative Religion* (New York, 1958).

3. *The Oxford English Dictionary*, s.v. "treatise."

4. Eliade, "Le problème du chamanisme," *Revue de l'histoire des religions* 131 (1946): 5–52, "La mythologie primitive," *Critique* 27 (1948): 708–17. See, further, J. Z. Smith, "Mythos and Geschichte," in *Alcheringa oder die beginnende Zeit*, ed. H.-P. Duerr, 41–42. (Frankfurt-am-Main, 1983).

5. *Who's Who in America*, 37th ed. (Chicago, 1972), 2:2875, s.v. "Sheed, Francis Joseph."

6. I will revise the translation of quotations from *Patterns* as necessary below.

7. L. Wittgenstein, *Remarks on Frazer's Golden Bough*, ed. R. Rhees (Doncaster, 1979), 8e–9c, emphasis in the original. The citation is from Goethe's poem, "The Metamorphosis of Plants," line 6. Compare the allusion to this passage in Wittgenstein in the context of C. Ginzburg's brief discussion of morphology in C. Ginzburg, *Clues, Myths, and the Historical Method* (Baltimore, 1989) xii.

8. J. W. von Goethe, "Betrachtung über Morphologie überhaupt" (1795), English translation, D. Miller, *Goethe: Scientific Studies*, Princeton-Suhrkamp Collected Works of Goethe, 12. (Princeton, N.J., 1994), 57–60. Note, however, that this 1795 essay was first published in 1891. The earliest printed occurrence of 'morphology' is apparently its independent usage in a footnote in K. R. Burdach, *Propädeutik zum Studium der gesammten Heilkunst* (1800). Both Goethe and Burdach first employed "morphology" in titles of published works in 1817: Goethe, *Zur Morphologie* (Tübingen, 1817–20), vols. 1–2; Burdach, *Über die Aufgabe der Morphologie* (Leipzig, 1817). For the detailed history of the word, I am wholly dependent on G. Schmid. "Über die Herkunft der Ausdrücke Morphologie und Biologie: Geschichtliche Zusammenhänge," *Nova Acta Leopoldina*, n.s.,2

(1935): 599–620. As Schmid's title suggests, Burdach is credited as well with having introduced the term 'biology' in the *Propädeutik*.

9. Ginzburg, *Clues, Myths, and the Historical Method*, x, xii.

10. For the classic studies by morphologists, see E. S. Russell, *Form and Function: A Contribution to the History of Animal Morphology* (London, 1916), reprinted with an important introductory essay by G. V. Lauder (Chicago, 1982); A. Arber, *Goethe's Botany: "The Metamorphosis of Plants" (1790) and "Tobler's Ode to Nature" (1782)*, Chronica Botanica, vol. 10, no. 2 (Waltham, Mass., 1946) and *The Natural Philosophy of Plant Form* (Cambridge, 1950). For more recent studies by historians of science, see W. Coleman, "Morphology between Type Concept and Descent Theory," *Journal of the History of Medicine* 31 (1976): 149–75; G. A. Wells, *Goethe and the Development of Science, 1750–1900* (Alphen aan den Rijn, 1978); T. Lenoir, *The Strategy of Life: Teleology and Mechanics in Nineteenth Century German Biology* (Boston, 1982); T. Appel, *The Cuvier-Geoffroy Debate: French Science in the Decades before Darwin* (New York, 1987); A. Desmond, *The Politics of Evolution: Morphology, Medicine and Reform in Radical London* (Chicago, 1989); J. Maienschein, *Transforming Traditions in American Biology, 1890–1915* (Baltimore, 1991); P. R. Sloan, introduction to *The Hunterian Lectures in Comparative Anatomy, May and June, 1837*, by R. Owen (Chicago, 1992), 3–72; L. K. Nyhart, *Biology Takes Form: Animal Morphology and the German Universities, 1800–1900* (Chicago, 1995). For the Germanic studies, see F. Amrine, F. J. Zucker, and H. Wheeler, eds., *Goethe and the Sciences: A Reappraisal* (Dordrecht, 1987); and F. Amrine, *Goethe in the History of Science* (New York, 1996–97), vols. 1–2.

11. G. W. F. Hegel, *Enzyklopädie philosophischen Wissenschaften* (1817). See the translation of the first edition by S. A. Taubeneck, in G. W. F. Hegel, *"Encyclopedia of the Philosophical Sciences in Outline" and Critical Writings*, ed. F. Behler, German Library, 20 (New York, 1990), 183–85. The much-expanded fourth edition is translated by A. V. Miller, *Hegel's Philosophy of Nature* (Oxford, 1970), 303–51; note that pp. 311–21 constitute a small monograph on Goethe's *Metamorphosis of Plants*. J. Derrida, *Glas*, in the English translation by J. P. Leavey, Jr., and R. Rand (Lincoln, Nebr., 1986), 245.

12. For the relationship of Rilke to Goethe's *Metamorphosis*, see E. Sewell, *The Orphic Voice: Poetry and Natural History* (New Haven, Conn., 1960), esp. 380–81, building on E. Kretschmar, *Goethe und Rilke* (Dresden, 1937). For her essay, "Erasmus Darwin and Goethe: Linnaean and Ovidian Taxonomy," see *Orphic Voice*, 169–275. For Cassirer's essay, see E. Cassirer, *The Problem of Knowledge* (New Haven, Conn., 1950), 137–50.

13. N. Chomsky, *Cartesian Linguistics: A Chapter in the History of Rationalist Thought* (New York, 1966), 19–31; passage quoted, 23.

14. O. Spengler, *Der Untergang des Abendlandes* (Munich, 1922–23), vols. 1–2, esp. vol. 1, title page, epigraph, and 67, n. 1, 132–35.

15. The epigraphs from Goethe, which are unidentified in the Russian original edition, were tracked down first by R. Breymayer, "Vladimir Jakovlevič Propp (1895–1970), Leben, Wirken und Bedeutsamkeit," *Linguistica Biblica* 15 (1972): 60, and translated into English in A. Liberman's notes to A. Y. Martin and R. P. Martin, *Propp: Theory and History of Folklore* (Minneapolis, 1984), 205, n. 1. Propp's rejection of Lévi-Strauss's structuralist interpretation of his work and insistence that he was grounded in Goethe's morphology first appeared as an appended essay. "Struttura e storia nello studio della favola," in G. L. Bravo's translation of Propp, *Morfologia della fiaba* (Turin, 1966), esp. 205–9, which Eliade first called to my attention. (See J. Z. Smith, *Map Is Not Territory* [Leiden, 1978], 255, n. 41.) Eliade refers to this disagreement between Propp and Lévi-Strauss in M. Eliade, *Ordeal by Labyrinth: Conversations with Claude-Henri Rocquet* (Chicago, 1982), 142. Propp's essay now appears in English translation in Martin and Martin, *Propp*, 67–81.

16. For Eliade's early reading of Steiner, see Eliade, *Autobiography*, vol. 1, 1907–1937: *Journey East, Journey West* (San Francisco, 1981), 84. Beyond his editorial work, Steiner's most influential study of Goethe's science is the monograph, *Goethe's Weltanschauung* (Weimar, 1897), available in several English translations sponsored by the Anthroposophical Society, including H. Collinson (London, 1928) and W. Windeman (Spring Valley, N.Y., 1985). Some of the introductory materials in Steiner's 1883–97 five-volume edition of *Goethes Naturwissenschaftliche Schriften* have been translated as Steiner, *Goethe the Scientist* (New York, 1950), and *Goethean Science* (Spring Valley, N.Y., 1988).

17. J. Z. Smith, "*Adde Parvum Parvo Magnus Acervus Erit,*" *History of Religions* 11 (1971): 67–90, reprinted in Smith, *Map Is Not Territory*, pp. 240–64.

18. Eliade, *Journal*, 1: 126.

19. Eliade, *Ordeal by Labyrinth*, 142.

20. See, e.g., Goethe, "Entstehen des Aufsatzes über Metamorphose der Pflanzen" (1817) as translated in B. Mueller, *Goethe's Botanical Writings* (Honolulu, 1952), 165–66.

21. Goethe's polemical stance with respect to Newton does not affect his biological studies but comes to the fore in his *Zur Farbenlehre* (1810). It is of interest to note that the recently renewed interest in relating Goethe to phenomenology by some biologists and ecologists relies on the *Farbenlehre* rather than on the morphological writings. See, among others, the useful collection edited by D. Seamon and A. Zajonc, *Goethe's Way of Science: A Phenomenology of Nature* (Albany, N.Y., 1998).

22. While Eliade's general contrarian stance is expressed in his familiar critiques of "reductionism," it is worth noting that in 1931 he published a Romanian article, "Botanical Knowledge in Ancient India," contrasting, favorably, In-

dian descriptions and taxonomies of plants with the artificial taxonomies dominant in Western botany. Eliade, "Cunoştinţele botanica în vechea Indie," *Buletinul Societăţii de Ştiinţe din Cluj* 6 (1931): 221–37.

23. Goethe, *Zur Morphologie*, vols. 1–2, printed in the original with the wrapper title, *Zur Naturwissenschaft überhaupt besonders zur Morphologie*. Volume 1 adds prefatory and appended materials to the core reprinting (*Morphologie*, 1: 3–60) of the *Metamorphosis*. The whole work, with additional texts, forms the bulk of D. Kuhn, ed., *Goethe: Die Schriften zur Naturwissenschaft*, vol. 9, *Morphologische Hefte* (Weimar, 1954). For the first appearance of 'morphology' as a term in a book title, see n. 8 above.

24. Goethe, "Der Verfasser teilt die Geschichte seiner botanischen Studien mit" (1831 version); English translation, Mueller, *Goethe's Botanical Writings*, 161–62.

25. Mueller, *Goethe's Botanical Writings*, p. 160, compare Mueller, p. 165.

26. In citing Goethe's *Versuch über die Metamorphose der Pflanzen, zuerklären* (Gotha, 1790), commonly abbreviated to *The Metamorphosis of Plants*, I give the standard paragraph numbers in parentheses to facilitate reference to the various English translations.

27. Note that this interest in factoring out the externally contingent, especially 'accidental' environmental influences, was a prime motivation in the pioneering turn of late nineteenth-century morphologists to the study of embryology. The embryo, in effect, was understood to be sealed off from the external environment.

28. Goethe, *Zur Morphologie*, in Miller, *Goethe: Scientific Studies*, 63–64.

29. Goethe, "[Botanical Notes, Italian Journey]" (1786–87). This sentence, "*Hypothese: Alles ist blatt . . .*" appears as an interruption to a handwritten set of detailed botanical observations made by Goethe during his visit to Italy. It was first published in 1892 as an appendix, "Morphologische Studien in Italien," to the Weimar edition of the second volume of *Zur Morphologie*, in *Goethe's Werke*, Abteilung 2, *Goethe's Naturwissenschaftliche Schriften* (Weimar, 1892), 7: 273–88, passage quoted, 282.

30. Goethe's letter to Herder is printed in Goethe, *Italienische Reise* (1816–17), in Johann Wolfgang von Goethe *Italian Journey, 1786–1788*, trans. W. H. Auden and E. Meyer (New York, 1968), 305–6.

31. For the implications of this, see Smith, *Map Is Not Territory*, 256–62.

32. Without at all denying its Platonic origin and connotations, it is important to note that 'archetype' was a widespread technical term among biological morphologists through the late nineteenth century. See, among others, P. L. Farber, "The Type Concept in Zoology during the First Half of the Nineteenth Century," *Journal of the History of Biology* 9 (1976): 93–119. To the best of my knowl-

edge, 'archetype' first plays an important role in Eliade's work in *Metallurgy, Magic and Alchemy,* Cahiers de Zalmoxis, 1 (Paris, 1938).

33. As is well known, German can insert the prefix *Ur-* before almost any noun in a way that is not possible with the far less pregnant English *pre-*. As any number of literary critics have observed, Goethe availed himself of the possibilities of *Ur-* more than most German writers. In his writings, Eliade attempts to overcome this by deploying terms such as "archaic" or "original" as if they were prefixes.

34. Except in late, appended retrospective materials, such as Goethe's 1831 "Der Verfasser teilt die Geschichte seiner botanischen Studien mit," in Mueller, *Goethe's Botanical Writings,* 162.

35. E. Heller, *The Disinherited Mind: Essays in Modern German Literature and Thought* (New York, 1959), 10.

36. C. Darwin, *On the Origin of Species* (1859; facsimile ed., Cambridge, Mass., 1966), 435.

37. This is the explicit thesis of Russell, *Form and Function*.

38. The relationship of Kant to Linnaeus has been the subject of study by Cassirer, *Problem of Knowledge,* esp. 118–34, and has received important elaboration in J. H. Zammito, *The Genesis of Kant's Critique of Judgment* (Chicago, 1992), esp. 189–213. As is well known, the third *Kritik* caused Goethe to reevaluate his critical posture toward Kant. See the general discussion and texts cited in E. Cassirer, "Goethe and Kantian Philosophy," in his *Rousseau, Kant, Goethe* (Princeton, N.J., 1945), 61–98.

39. I. Kant, "Von den verschiedenen Racen der Menschen," in *Kants Gesammelte Schriften* (Berlin, 1902–83), 2: 429–43; quotation on 429; English translation in Zammito, 200.

40. *Kants Gesammelte Schriften,* 2: 434, and note; Zammito, *Genesis,* 200.

41. Eliade, *Journal,* 1: 125. Eliade refers to Goethe's account, dated April 17, 1787. See Goethe, *Italian Journey, 1786–1788,* 251–52.

42. Ginzburg, *Clues, Myths, and the Historical Method,* xii.

43. W. Windelband, "Geschichte und Naturwissenschaften" (1894), in Windelband, *Präluden: Aufsätze und Reden zur Einführung in die Philosophie,* 5th ed. (Tübingen, 1914), 2: 136–60; H. Rickert, *Kulturwissenschaften und Naturwissenschaft,* 5th ed. (Tübingen, 1921).

44. Eliade, *Patterns,* 463.

45. Eliade, *Histoire des croyances et des idées religieuses* (Paris, 1976–83), vols. 1–3; this uncharacteristic Eliadean title was abbreviated in the English translation, *A History of Religious Ideas* (Chicago, 1979–85). The bibliographical notes are, at times, revealing. For example, Albert Dieterich's, *Mutter Erde,* 3d ed. (Berlin, 1925), foundational for *Patterns,* 247–53, et passim, as well as other

works by Eliade (e.g., "Mother Earth and the Cosmic Hierogamies," in Eliade, *Myths, Dreams and Mysteries* [New York, 1960], esp. 163–68), is rudely dismissed in *History,* 1: 388 as "Dieterich's hasty generalizations."

46. Eliade, *Shamanism: Archaic Techniques of Ecstasy* (New York, 1964), xiii–xiv. I give a more detailed analysis of this "Foreword" in the second article of this series, see chapter 3 of this volume.

47. Even if these suggestions as to the "companion volume" prove unconvincing, I would note that it has long been my practice to set aside any study that claims to be a treatment of Eliade's project which is not centered on these four foundational works—*Patterns, Shamanism, Yoga, The Forge and the Crucible*—and relies, instead, on his essays, published lectures, and more occasional writings.

48. *Additional note:* In response to this essay, Professor Mac Linscott Ricketts, the foremost American authority on Eliade's works, published in the journal of the Association Roumaine d'Histoire des Religions a detailed account of the genesis of Eliade's *Traité* that supercedes the brief narrative provided above. He also offers evidence from Eliade's journals that Eliade considered, at least in retrospect, the *Histoire des croyances et des idées religieuses* to be the promised sequel to *Traité.* Ricketts, "The Tangled Tale of Eliade's Writing of *Traité d'histoire des religions,*" *Archaeus: Études d'histoire des religions* 4 (2000): 51–77.

ACKNOWLEDGMENTS

MORPHOLOGY AND HISTORY IN MIRCEA ELIADE'S *PATTERNS IN COMPARATIVE RELIGION* (1949–1999)

PART 2: THE TEXTURE OF THE WORK

To portray rather than explain

    J. W. VON GOETHE, *Betrachtung über Morphologie überhaupt* (1891)

IN A REMINISCENCE written forty years after the fact in the second volume of Mircea Eliade's *Autobiography*, Eliade recalls:

> In the middle of September in 1940 we moved . . . to Oxford . . . I read, took notes, and elaborated the plan of a vast synthesis of morphology and history of religions, a synthesis which I glimpsed instantaneously in an air raid shelter during an alarm. I shall return later to this book, *Prolegomena to a Comparative History of Religions* (which became *Traité d'histoire des religions* or *Patterns in Comparative Religion*).[1]

This report is notable in two respects. The first is a matter of genre: "The discovery of the archetype, as represented in the [morphological] literature, has a visionary quality; it appears to be the result of a sudden, intuitive leap to simplicity. Characteristic of morphological presentations will be a dated account of the vision—Goethe gazing at a palmetto in an Italian botanical garden on 17 April 1787: Lorenz Oken accidentally stumbling over a deer's skull while walking in the Harz Forest in the spring of 1806."[2] To these, and others that might be cited, can now be added Mircea Eliade in a London bomb shelter in the fall of 1940. The instantaneous glimpse seems to have been what will later become the two-volume stratagem described in "Part 1: The Work and Its Contents"(chapter 2). As Eliade characterizes it in the *Autobiography*, it was "a grand synthesis of morphology and history of religions," the same goal as that announced in the "Foreword" to *Shamanism* as "a comprehensive view which shall be at once a morphology and a history."[3]

The "Foreword" to *Shamanism*, which was described in part 1 as possibly being an outline of the opening chapter of the missing "companion volume" to *Patterns*, makes one contrast that may serve as a point of entry into *Patterns*. Eliade is in the midst of counterdistinguishing the historian of religions from the phenomenologist. The latter, despite some contemporary scholars of his work, is a term that Eliade usually stridently rejected as applicable to his approach. For example, in the 1949 review of the French translation of G. van der Leeuw's *Phänomenologie der Religion*, a review written in the same year as the original publication of *Patterns*, Eliade criticizes the ahistorical approach of phenomenology, deploying technical morphological vocabulary to charge that a phenomenological account ignores the "modifications" and "degradations" of the sacred brought about by cultural and historical "conditions."[4] In this review Eliade's Goethean terminology serves to distinguish what *he* understands to be the historical over against what *he* understands to be the phenomenological. In a different vein, in the contemporaneous "Foreword" to *Shamanism*, Eliade states the contrast with phenomenology as follows: "[The phenomenologist] in principle rejects any work of comparison, confronted with one religious phenomenon or another, he confines himself to 'approaching' it and divining its meaning. Whereas the historian of religions does not reach a comprehension of the phenomenon until after he has compared it with thousands of similar or dissimilar phenomena, until he has situated it among them; and these thousands of phenomena are separated not only in time but in space."[5]

This is surely one's first impression on encountering *Patterns*: the endless comparisons, juxtapositions, enumerations, classifications; the descriptions, but never, as this essay's epigraph suggests, explanations of "thousands . . . of phenomena." It is an impression akin to that riot of vegetative variation that first confronted Goethe when he launched his botanical studies. Indeed, sheer plentitude, sheer variegation, stands as one of the first principles of *Patterns*, enunciated in a passage that must be seen, in hindsight, as perhaps Eliade's most enduring contribution to the study of religion, the one element of his thought that can never be taken back: his all but limitless extension of the boundaries of potential data for the student of religion. Early on, in the first chapter of *Patterns*,[6] he argues in a mildly hilarious passage as Eliade attempts, quite futilely, to list everything:

We must get used to the idea of recognizing hierophanies absolutely everywhere, in every area of psychological, economic, spiritual and social life. Indeed, we cannot be sure that there is *anything*—object, movement, physiological function, being or game, etc.—that has not somewhere in the course of human history been transfigured into a hierophany. . . . It is quite certain that anything man has ever handled, felt, come in contact with or loved can become a hierophany. We know, for example, that, on the whole, the gestures, dances, children's games, toys, etc. have a religious origin. . . . The same is the case for musical instruments, architecture, means of transport (animals, wagons, boats, etc.). . . . It is unlikely that there is any animal or any important plant which has not participated in sacrality in the course of history. The same could be said for every trade, art, industry and technical skill which either had a religious origin or has been invested, over the course of history, with cultic value. This list could be carried on to include man's everyday movements (getting up, walking, running), his various employments (hunting, fishing, agriculture), all his physiological activities (nutrition, sexual life, etc.) . . . and so forth. (24/11–12)

What Eliade is coming close to proposing, in this passage, is that the science of religion is the study of everything and anything. What would then be required is the capacity to define what allows each of these objects and activities to be classified as 'religious.' For myself, Eliade's sacramental and incarnational view, signaled throughout this passage by the reiteration of the term 'hierophany,' and his use of eucharistic vocabulary, will not do. This negative judgment remains in place whether Eliade expresses this view ontologically ("we cannot be sure that there is *anything . . . that* has not in the course of human history been transfigured into a hierophany") or anthropologically ("somewhere, at a given historical moment, each human society transubstantiated a certain number of things, plants, gestures, etc. into hierophanies" [24/12]). But if we reject Eliade's conceptual frame, while accepting, as we must, his expansion of the data, then the issue still remains for contemporary students of religion to address at the levels of definition, classification, and theory.

Indeed, so wide was the horizon that Eliade here announced that he seems, at the outset, to shrink from its consequences and to preach a counsel of despair by appearing to argue that our theories should exhibit parity with the "blooming, buzzing confusion" (in William James's phrase) that we seek to study. He begins *Patterns* by quoting with approval a formulation by Roger Caillois, itself a critical paraphrase of Durkheim. Caillois had written: "The only helpful thing one can say of the sacred in general is . . . that it is the opposite of the profane. As soon as one attempts to give a clear statement of the modality of that opposition, one strikes difficulty. No formula, however elementary, will cover the labyrinthine complexity of the facts" (11–12/xii).[7] Eliade immediately adds to this quotation from Caillois what may be taken as a self-description of his life-long enterprise: "In my researches, what have primarily interested me are these facts, this labyrinthine complexity of elements which will yield to *no* formula or definition *whatever*. Taboo, ritual, symbol, myth, demon, god—these are some of the religious facts. But it would be an abusive simplification to present the list in this itemized fashion. In reality, we have to deal with a polymorphous heap, indeed, sometimes a chaotic mass of actions, beliefs and theories which constitute what one may call the religious phenomena" (12/xii). To follow such a counsel of despair, as Eliade surely did not, may yield utter difference's celebration, but it will not yield cerebration. It is this latter activity that calls forth the need for a conceptualizing confidence in the face of the limitless horizon, the sense of *de trop,* Eliade, here, described for himself, and, through his works, passed before our view. In Eliade's case, as he echoes with his scorn of the "itemized" list as an "abusive simplification," Goethe's critique of Linnaeus's artificial genera, this confidence rested, in *Patterns,* on adapting Goethe's morphological project, on reorienting it away from its focus on botanical objects to religious formations.

We may turn to a reading of *Patterns* with an eye toward the issue of morphology and history. We need to bear in mind that *Patterns,* as the morphological first volume in a projected two-volume set, the second to be devoted to history, necessarily and properly scants the historical.

The problem for the reader of *Patterns* is that the text works simultaneously on several interrelated levels of analysis, that each level has its characteristic vocabulary (rarely defined), and that Eliade fails to take pains, with any consistency, to make explicit these interrelations. Perhaps this is due to the haste in completing the work. Regardless, its problems remain.

There is both a surface and a deep architectonic to the work. The surface structure is enunciated early on in the "Foreword" to *Patterns* (12–13/xii–xiii), although its logic will not come clear until the conclusion. The deeper structure emerges only as the reader works and reworks her way through the book, and then only as a set of "approximations"—to borrow one of Eliade's terms (15/1).

What is most explicit in the opening chapter of *Patterns* is Eliade's polemic stance against what he views as reductionism, essentialism, and evolutionism, with Durkheim and, to a lesser degree, Frazer most often serving as the unnamed exempla of all three positions.

It is worth pausing to reflect on one implication of the fact that *Patterns* is now fifty years old. This means that the work is closer in time to Durkheim's *The Elementary Forms of Religious Life* and the massive third edition of *The Golden Bough* than it is to our own time. If one recalls that few European studies of religion were published during the war years, the separation between *Patterns* and the works of Durkheim and Frazer is foreshortened. It is from this ambience that Eliade seeks to counterdistinguish his work.

What Eliade criticizes is any proposal of explanatory, causal simplicity with respect to religious phenomena in favor of a descriptive, systemic complexity. He does this in part by adapting a central term from the school of Durkheim and Mauss, that of "religious facts" (e.g., 12, 15/xii, 1), which are as complex as their notion of "(total) social facts"—shorn, however, of all positivistic tendencies. Over against what appeared to be the implications of the introductory passage from *Patterns* just quoted, with its language of a "polymorphous heap" of phenomena yielding "to *no* formula or definition *whatever*," Eliade insists that these "religious facts" form coherent systems, deploying a vocabulary of "system," "coherence," "structure," "form," "modality," "element," and *"ensemble."*[8] While each of these terms are foundational in Eliade's morphological enterprise, none of them are defined at the outset or, indeed, in the rest of the work, leaving it to the reader to infer their meaning, gradually, from her or his growing sense of context.

Eliade states his intentions, with reference back to his meditation on Caillois, already quoted. "What I intend is to introduce my reader to the labyrinthine complexity of religious facts, to acquaint him with their basic structures, and with the diversity of culture-circles they bring into relief" (14/xiv–xv). This is a Goethean project: apparent diversity, deep structure, (cultural) environmental differentiation. Note that, in this endeavor, the "sacred" appears to function in a manner similar to leaf in Goethe's *Metamorphosis*, although in relationship to other agenda, this is not its only sense or function. Furthermore, as part of his introductory statement. Eliade promises that these "various modalities of the sacred" will be shown to "integrate themselves into a coherent system." For this reason, one must not "fragment . . . religious ensembles" inasmuch as "each class of hierophanies . . . forms, in its own way, a whole, from [both] the morphological and historical point of view" (14/xiv).

Eliade provides one clear map of his enterprise at the outset (fig. 1).

It is, in fact, a classification of the table of contexts of *Patterns* (12–13/xii–xiii). In addition, on the third page of the first chapter he provides a forecast of the central movement of the whole work in his abbreviated examples of the Indian Sacred Fig Tree (17/3). It is the argument of the book *in nuce*, but the reader will not know this until she or he has viewed the complex exfoliation of the rest of the work. I have supplied two more maps, which have already been characterized as part of a set of retrospective "approximations." The first of these (fig. 2) emerges by the time the reader has concluded chapter 4, "The Moon and the Lunar Mystique." The second approximation (fig. 3), which is in part a revision of the previous map, emerges in the reading of chapter 13, "The Structure of Symbols."

Figure 1 represents, in schematic form, Eliade's brief classification of the parts of *Patterns*, and constitutes, in its structure, a purely morphological construction (12–13/xii–xiii). After a first chapter entitled "Morphology of the Sacred," Eliade divides the remaining twelve substantive chapters into four groups.

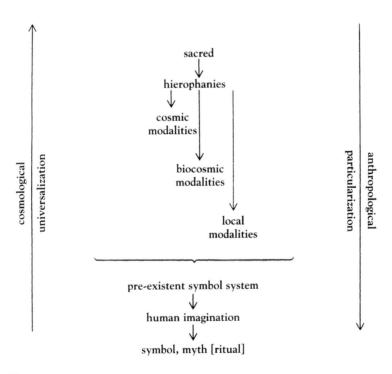

Figure 1

1. *Cosmic hierophanies* (chaps. 2–7): "Sky: Uranian Deities, Celestial Rites and Symbols"; "Sun and Solar Cults"; "The Moon and the Lunar Mystique"; "Waters and Aquatic Symbolism"; "Sacred Stones: Epiphanies, Signs and Forms"; "Earth, Woman and Fertility."

2. *Biological or bio-cosmic hierophanies* (chaps. 8–9): "Vegetation Symbols and Rites of Renewal" and "Agriculture and Fertility Cults."

3. *Local hierophanies* (chaps. 10–11): "Sacred Space: Temple, Palace, 'Center of the World'" and "Sacred Time and the Myth of the Eternal Beginning Again."

and finally, though of a seemingly different taxonomic order:

4. *Myths and Symbols* (chaps. 12–13): "Morphology and Function of Myths" and "The Structure of Symbols."

At the outset, it is important to observe that these four 'classes' exhibit a serial order, that of the 'downward path' which might be expressed as a movement from the cosmological to the anthropological or from the universalized to the particularized. Eliade expresses this downward movement in what I would term his first morphological law, one of some half dozen that recur through the work: "the progressive fall of the sacred into the concrete" (58/52), or with more drama, the "thirst for the concrete" (94/99). (One is entitled, I think, to read "fall" [*chute*] as both a directional term and as an allusion to Genesis 3.)

In Goethean terminology, while each element, in its "modalities," undergoes progressive and regressive metamorphosis, the entire series, as a downward movement, exhibits retrogressive metamorphosis.

Eliade's morphological law of the "fall into the concrete" can be given metaphysical force through his language of the "paradox of incorporation" (36/26), the "paradox of the sacred" (38/29–30), the "paradoxical *coincidentia* of the sacred and the profane, being and non-being, absolute and relative, the eternal and the becoming" (38/29), or the "dialectic of hierophanies" (394–95/461–63)—formulations that may be seen as ontologizations of Goethe's notion of environmental limitations, of specific variation, in relation to original form. But this needs, at the present stage of our inquiry, to be distinguished from Eliade's purely morphological system.

In Eliade's pure morphology, what is interposed between the hierophanies along with their modalities and the concrete human symbolic project is an "autonomous" symbol system "that manifest[s] more clearly, more fully, and with greater coherence, what the hierophanies manifest in an individual, local and successive fashion" (383/449). That is to say, the hierophanies, by their "manifestation," enter the historical; the "autonomous" symbol system remains suprahistorical. From a Goethean perspective, this autonomous symbol system has the same status as Goethe's archetypal plant—an *Urpflanze* that Nature herself will envy. "With such a model . . . it will be possible to invent plants *ad infinitum*. They will be strictly logical plants."[9]

It is worth noting that the three works by Eliade that I associated with his historical "companion volume" in part 1—*Shamanism, Yoga*, and *The Forge and the Crucible*—have in common that they reverse, by a variety of human activities, the downward path. Each technique has a directionality toward transcendence. Shamanism and Yoga annihilate the human condition, alchemy alters natural conditions. If this be correct, then the morphological volume portrays a movement of the transcendental toward the human; the possible partial contents of the historical volume would seem to illustrate a movement of the human toward the transcendental.

In *Patterns*, the general movement from the cosmological to the anthropological is expressed already through the simple enumeration of the titles of the chapters. If the explicit overall structure descends from the cosmic (group 1) to the anthropological world of myths and symbols (group 4), then the titles of the first two groups, the groups concerned with two different cosmic systems,[10] replicate this movement in nearly every case. They begin with the distinctive "modality" of the sacred "revealed" in each hierophany and end with a section of myth, ritual, or symbol: Sky/Celestial Rites and Symbols, Sun/Solar Cults, Waters/Aquatic Symbolism, Vegetation/Symbols and Rites of Renewal, Agriculture/Fertility Cults. This gives one reason to presume that the internal structure of each of these chapters will repeat the structure of the entire work.

Eliade is explicit about the replication of the downward movement in the internal structure of each chapter, which he describes as presenting first "a modality of the sacred," then "a series of relationships of man and the sacred," and finally, adding an element not found in the initial map, he will place "these relationships [in] a series of historical moments" (14/xiv).

Take, for example, chapter 2, "Sky: Uranian Deities, Celestial Rites and Symbols," which, as its triple title suggests, has a reduplicated replication of the overall structure of *Patterns*: sky is to sky deities as sky deities are to myths, rituals, and symbols. Both relationships exhibit the processes of increasing anthropologization. In the interests of space, I shall discuss only the first relationship, that of sky to sky deities.

Chapter 2 may be divided into two parts of unequal length: sky-itself, that is, sky in its most cosmic and universal form (47–63/38–58), and sky-gods (63–94/58–99), in which sky, through myths, rituals, and symbols, becomes increasingly particularized and personified, thereby becoming increasingly involved in human affairs. Each step of Eliade's presentation, buttressed by numerous examples, exhibits the same logic in a process of segmentary reduplication.

In the first instance, "the sky itself directly reveals its transcendence." "The transcendental quality of 'height' . . . reveals itself to man all at once" (47, 48/38, 39). In this transcendence of height, "in-itself, and prior to any mythological imagination or conceptual elaboration, sky presents itself as the divine realm par excellence" (60/54). Anthropologically, "the symbolism of its transcendence is deduced, so to speak" on the basis of a universal "simple recognition of its infinite height" (47/39).

Next, in logical order, sky-itself "became personified" through the operations of human mythological imagination. Rather than the height/transcendence characteristic of sky-itself, and immediately "given" to human perception and cognition, sky deities were imagined in forms of "supremacy" and "sovereignty" (49/40). This personification represents an anthropological particularization of the "simple recognition of . . . infinite height."

As a replication of previous relations, supreme deities are relatively immanent with respect to sky-itself but remain relatively transcendent with respect to human affairs. They are remote from human beings. There is a notable "cultic poverty" (53/46), matched by a diminished mythology. "Nowhere in primitive religion do we find Supreme Beings of the sky playing a leading role" (56/50). Therefore, they will be "replaced" by more anthropologized, more particularized forms. In Goethean terminology, they will either "degrade" into otiose deities, for most purposes disappearing (53–56/46–50) or, quite literally, petrify into idols.

At this point Eliade offers a carefully constructed morphological account of the "substitution" for supreme beings of the sky or of their "fusion" with divine figures more proximate to human affairs. He does so by presenting a variety of metamorphic processes: "replacement," "amalgamation," "assimilation," and "superimposition," with the resultant substitute/fused figures expressed in a variety of symbolisms and mythologies. This moves his analysis down to the fourth, most anthropological level of his initial four-fold schema represented in figure 1. These figures include solar or lunar deities, great goddesses, primordial pairs (husband/wife, brother/sister), demiurges, and mythological personifications of thunder or wind (56–60/50–54).

It needs to be stressed that while these transformations of sky-itself into supreme sky deities and supreme sky deities into substitute or fused deities are presented in serial order, the seriality is the result of internally logical metamorphic processes. It is a morphological series. The transformations are, here, not described as historical, in either a chronological or causal sense. For this reason, Eliade primarily confines his examples to what he terms "primitive peoples," presenting these 'primary' peoples in some sort of *Kultur-kreis* cartography, treating in order Australia, aboriginal India, Africa, Tierra del Fuego, and North America. For purposes of *this* morphological construction, Eliade takes the "primitive" to be without history.

The second section of the Uranic chapter, which both overlaps and replicates the first, focuses on sky deities among "polytheistic peoples" (63–94/58–99), by which he means 'secondary' Eurasian civilizations as well as 'tertiary' peoples (chiefly Central Asian) influenced by them. This difference in types of cultures is reflected in a difference of approach. For the first time the historical comes into play. The difference is relative, but, for Eliade, significant. "When we turn from the religion of 'primitive' peoples to religions called polytheist, the main difference we encounter comes from their own 'history.' Clearly 'history' has also modified primitive theophanies; none of the celestial deities of primitive peoples is 'pure,' none represent a dawning form. Their 'forms' have been modified, either under outside influences, or purely and simply because they have lived in a human tradition" (63/58). Here, history is the result of diffusion or contingency. Eliade remains in the ambience of Goethean morphology and its notion of accidental metamorphosis. With the "religions called polytheist," the historical is no longer external, it has become internalized. It is an expansive teleological force, going far beyond any Goethean principle of fulfillment of form. "But, in the religions termed polytheist, history has set to work with a completely different intensity. The religious conceptions, as well as the whole spiritual and mental life of these history-creating peoples, have undergone influences, symbioses, conversions, and eclipses" (63/58). The self-conscious historical activities of these peoples—Mesopotamian and Near Eastern Semites, Indo-Europeans, and culture areas dominated or influenced by them—their imperialisms, which constantly go beyond the borders of their 'environment,' have perturbed the internalized Goethean morphology of expansion and contraction, progression and regression. The result is a confusion of composite hybrids that resist morphological analysis. "Divine 'forms,' exactly as with all the other 'forms' produced by these civilizations, betray in their structure innumerable [different] components" (63/58).

The only countervailing force, which makes analysis still possible, is what I shall term Eliade's second morphological law: "the tendency towards the archetype" (58/63). In a more emphatic formulation, Eliade declares, "there does not exist a religious form that does not strive to draw as closely as possible to its own archetype, in other words, to purify itself of 'historical' accretions and deposits" (395/462).

The return to the archetype serves, in these formulations, as an internal feedback mechanism, achieving equilibrium by reverting to type. It allows Eliade to recognize the power of the historical, the processes of variation and combination, in the cultures of religious polytheism while, as a morphologist, holding that they may still be bracketed as the historical is capable of a kind of self-correction. Although factually these civilizations exhibit a historical complexity, when compared with the 'primitive,' the analytic, morphological strategies for their interpretation are able fundamentally to remain the same. "However multifarious, however diverse are the components that enter into any religious creation . . . their expression tends continually to return to the archetype. For this reason, in the course of our summary examination of several of the celestial divinities of polytheistic religions, we can dispense with knowing the 'history' of each in order to understand its structure and its fate; for each one, in spite of the 'history' that preceded it, tends to rediscover the original 'form,' to return to the archetype" (63–64/58–59).

For our purposes, we need not linger over the rich, forty-page display of examples and typologies that follows this argument. It is sufficient to note that the notion of "supremacy" found in the 'primitive' traditions is transmuted in the "polytheist religions" into a structure of "universal sovereignty." Then structure is specialized and further anthropologized in two lines of development expressed in two clusters of mythic motifs: (1) god of the sky/master of the world/absolute sovereign (or despot)/guardian of the law; (2) god of the sky/supremely male spouse of the great earth goddess/giver of rain. Each element of the clusters can not only be recombined but can be displaced and achieve independent development, as well as be subject to the metamorphic rules of replacement and fusion (63–94/58–99).

While Eliade continues chapter 2 by treating sky symbolism and celestial rituals (94–101/99–108), we may call a halt and move directly to Eliade's summary statements to this complex and highly structured chapter. These final statements are of two sorts. The first employs technical morphological terminology. The second introduces a theme that is central to Eliade's thought but one that is independent of, and I would argue, antithetic to, a morphological approach—namely, Eliade's ontological superstructure. He will not separate these two systems and vocabularies, and that must weigh heavily in evaluating Eliade's project. However, if we are interested in the constructive possibilities of a comparative, morphological approach to cultural phenomena (including religion), *we* must force them apart.

First, Eliade's morphological conclusion: "One could say that 'history' has succeeded in pushing towards the background the divine 'forms' of celestial structure . . . or has degraded [mongrelized] them . . . but that this 'history' which is, so to speak, humanity's always new experimentation and interpretation of the sacred, has not resulted in abolishing the direct and continual revelation of the *celestial sacred*" (103–4/111). Here, "history" means creativity and transformation, that is to say, metamorphosis, whether progressive or retrograde. Whereas in Eliade's ontological formulation, "history" means something quite different. The religious form can resist the historical because it is Other. As Eliade affirms: "The celestial symbolism has succeeded in maintaining itself in every religious ensemble simply because its modality of being is nontemporal" (104/111).

To understand this dual evaluation of history—the one from the point of view of morphology, the other from an ontological perspective—we must turn to the 'approximations' of the architectonic of *Patterns* as represented by figures 2–3. While for Eliade, this duality was indissoluble, with priority given to an affirmation of the reality and power of the ontological, for purposes of thought, as has already been suggested, *we* must separate them out.

The purely morphological schema, it has been argued, is represented by figure 1. Here, the sacred plays a role analogous to that of the leaf in Goethe. Even the hierophanies appear more as generic plants than as burning bushes. Eliade appears quite comfortable in describing the metamorphosis of sacrality through forms that must ultimately be understood as modes of human imagination in a series extending, downward, from the transcendental to the anthropological, from the universalized to the particularized. In the service of this enterprise, he deploys such Goethean (or Goethe-like) terms as "development," "transformation," "transfiguration" (which is, after all, but one Latinate translation of the Greek 'metamorphosis'), "change," and "modification." These processes are then further characterized in morphological terminology such as "substitution," "replacement," "fusion," "amalgamation," "assimilation," and "superimposition," or, to give their regressive forms, as "degradation," "devaluation," "displacement," and "infantilization." In this morphological trajectory, there is no special Eliadean vocabulary. Even when the term 'archetype' is employed, it carries strictly morphological connotations.

'History,' in this morphological tangent, is largely reducible to the notion of environment or habitat which acts, in Goethe's phrase, "from the outside" to alter and obscure the inner directionality of development. Even when historicity has been internalized, the morphological principle of "return to archetype" serves as an analytic corrective. This understanding of 'history' is what Eliade has in mind when he reiterates that every hierophany "takes place in some historical situation," that any attempt to understand religious phenomena must always be undertaken "in the framework [setting] of *history*" (16/2). As with Goethe, there are no existent archetypes. There is "no simple religion reduced to only elemental hierophanies" (12/xii). "We find ourselves everywhere in the presence of complex religious phenomena suggesting a long historical evolution" (15/1). This sense of the historical, what Goethe termed the accidental mode of metamorphosis which he "set aside," is expressed in Eliade through essentially spatial structures of historicization, through notions of habitat and diffusion. Such notions explain some sorts of modification, some types of change, but, for the morphologist, they cannot serve as explanation for aught but occlusions of a given phenomenon's inner logic of development.

Three quite different examples will have to suffice. The first is an illustration of the simple notion of habitat as an accidental cause of variegation. In his extraordinary fifth chapter on water, Eliade contrasts the rich elaboration of water symbolism among the insular Greeks (179–82/202–6) with the relatively unelaborated aquatic symbolism of Chinese myth, which is that of a "continental" [i.e., landlocked] people (184/208). While one might wonder what map of China he had consulted, the environmental correlation is clear.

The second example testifies to Eliade's long-standing preoccupation with questions of diffusion. His longest, and uncharacteristically critical, bibliographical note in *Patterns* concerns then current scholarly controversies over the Near Eastern diffusion of both agriculture and agricultural religious practices (309–13/362–65). What is at stake for Eliade in this discussion is the proper means of demonstrating coherence rather than giving way to despair in the face of their extraordinary "morphological variety" (232/265), "the almost unlimited abundance of vegetative hierophanies" (279/323). Eliade's morphological answer is, as it must be, a structural one: "the abundance and the morphological variation of these hierophanies are readily reducible to a coherent system" (279/323–24). At the historical level, this "reduction" must be based on deciding questions of monogenesis or polygenesis, of homology or analogy, and by understanding processes of diffusion and cultural variegation.

"It is natural that [representations of vegetative force] should vary from culture-type to culture-type, from one people to another, even if there were a single origin; such representations are, in turn, framed in different cultural and religious ensembles, and interpreted in different, even contradictory ways, even within the same population" (288/335).

The third example is perhaps the most telling. It comes from the "Foreword" to *Shamanism*, a work that differs from much contemporary usage in restricting the term 'shamanic' to the religions of circumpolar peoples and peoples who migrated from, or were affected by diffusion from, this arctic culture-circle. Analogous phenomena found elsewhere or of different pedigree were classified by Eliade as 'shamanistic.' The passage to be cited occurs in the service of his argument that "although the historical conditioning of a religious phenomenon is extremely important—for every human fact is in the last analysis a historical fact—it does not wholly exhaust it."[11] This argument concedes more to the historical than Goethe did in his morphology, a quite proper correction, on Eliade's part, for the translation of a botanical system into a cultural one. Eliade goes on to give an example:

> The Altaic shaman ritually climbs a birch tree . . . and it is extremely probable that the cosmological schema implied in this ritual is of Oriental origin. Religious ideas of the ancient Near East penetrated far into Central and North Asia and contributed considerably to giving Central Asian and Siberian shamanism their present features. This is a good example of what 'history' can teach us concerning the dissemination of religious ideologies and techniques. . . . Nothing warrants the supposition that influences from Oriental cosmology and religion *created* the ideology and ritual of the ascent to the sky among the Altaians; similar ideologies and rituals appear all over the world and in regions where ancient Oriental influences are excluded a priori. More probably, the Oriental ideas merely *modified* the ritual formula and cosmological ideas of the celestial ascent; the latter appears to be a primordial phenomenon.[12]

In technical terminology, derived from early nineteenth-century morphological disputes, the Central Asian traditions would be classified as 'homologous,' they share descent through diffusion, and to speak of the one modifying the other is proper. The "similar ideologies and rituals [that] appear all over the world and in regions where ancient Oriental influences are excluded a priori" would be classified as 'analogous.' Here, the language of modification would be inappropriate. In the nineteenth-century debates over diffusion, the alternative would be to appeal to "independent invention" or "the psychic unity of humankind." Eliade's appeal to a "primordial phenomenon" is of the same order. The distinction between homology and analogy is embedded, not only in biological thought, but in the normal science of the comparative historian. There is nothing exceptional in Eliade's argument.

What is exceptional is Eliade's persistent attempt to conjoin this morphological understanding of history with an ontology that rejects the historical. As I have already suggested and as I have written for more than thirty years, I find Eliade's move here profoundly troubling. It consists in encompassing morphology in a metaphysical hierarchy.

A useful illustration of the distinction between the morphological and the ontological system in Eliade is the notion of 'hierophany'—one of any number of words that Eliade employs constructed on the Greek *phaino:* hierophany, kratophany, theophany, epiphany, ontophany, and the like. As has already been observed, in Eliade's morphological system, hierophanies and their modes of appearance play a role analogous to plant organs in Goethe's system. In Goethe, these organs are metamorphised manifestations of leaf; in Eliade's system, the hierophanies are metamorphised manifestations of sacrality. Whereas in Eliade's onto-theological system, the hierophanies are a paradoxical self-display of Being in the realm of Becoming. To give but one, small, telling instance: For Goethe's morphology, environmental effects may be set aside because they are merely contingently historical, in his terms, because "they come from without."[13] For Eliade's ontology, the hierophany is to be supremely valued because it is suprahistorical, because it imposes "itself on man from without" (317/369). In Goethe's morphological view, externality is a mark of disposability; in Eliade's ontological view, it is a mark of indispensability. The difference is one between a focus on the mundane botanical world in Goethe's *Metamorphosis* and the supramundane, transcendental world in Eliade's *Patterns*.

In the second diagram (fig. 2), an approximation reached when the reader has progressed a little less than halfway through the work (to the conclusion of chap. 4), the anthropological implications of this ontological valuation are expressed under three categories of appearance: direct, mediated, and mimetic. The central column, focusing on structures of mediation, basically reproduces figure 1, the morphological map. But there are significant differences. The sacred is no longer analogous to Goethe's leaf. It is now an ontological power, and it is this reality that is being mediated through the morphological series. Furthermore, the

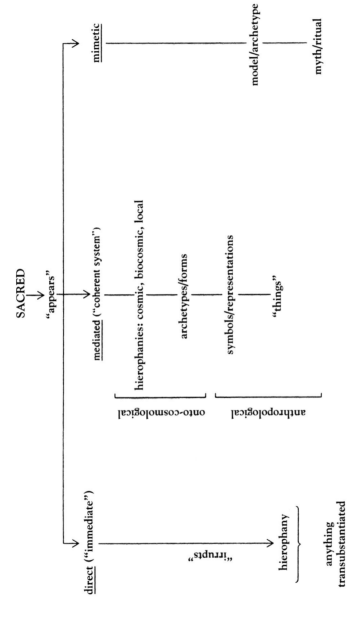

Figure 2

morphological (center column) is now bracketed by two theological systems. On the one hand, by modes of direct self-display—often conveyed in Eliade by extraordinarily active verbs such as "irruption," in which the sacred, now understood as the ultimately real, "transubstantiates" mundane reality into hierophanies. On the other hand, the morphological is bracketed by the mimetic, a theory of human participation in sacred realities by imitating divine archetypes, especially as revealed in the creative deeds of deities. This understanding of 'archetype' is utterly removed from its morphological meaning.

The third diagram (fig. 3), representing an approximation of the architectonic of *Patterns* reached toward the conclusion of the work, expands the morphological section of figure 2, that devoted to mediated modes of appearance, to include many more structural elements, explicitly relating these to a historical dimension. It now includes the mimetic as a form of mediation. However, the cost of this useful elaboration is high. As the gnostics imagined precosmic realms of powers, so now here, heading the system, is the construction of a vast ontological realm that has taken up, and made more complex, the immediate mode of appearance.

If there were to be a third article in this series, it would need to explore each of the terms in these latter two diagrams, focusing on their systemic relations, as well as describing the implications Eliade derives from the totalizing system. This would necessitate not only a line-by-line reading of the entire text of *Patterns*, but also the construction of a historical lexicon of Eliade's vocabulary. For unlike the morphological perspective which required no Eliadean linguistics, the onto-theological perspective is replete with special terminology.

Eschewing this option, let me head toward a conclusion. I want to insist that Eliade *has* addressed the issue of the relations of the morphological to the historical. He *has* creatively reworked morphological categories, and given the historical more prominence than it usually receives in morphological works by accepting into his analysis both historical modification and the effects of diffusion. He *has* achieved something of an integration of the historical and the morphological, but at an extraordinary cost—by encompassing both within an onto-theological hierarchy.

It is this latter stratagem of encompassment that both results in the usual critique of Eliade as ahistorical, as well as in Eliade's oft-cited violent language toward history, a language that plays almost no role in *Patterns*. As we do not have Eliade's second volume, we are not able to determine with certainty how these same relations might appear when viewed from a historical rather than a morphological perspective. As he

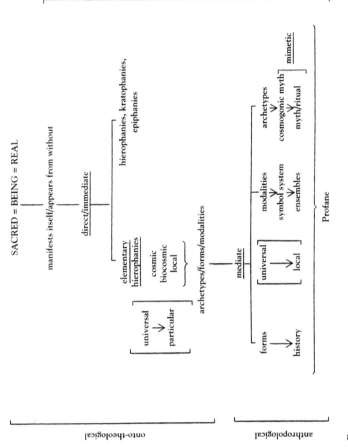

Figure 3

writes, five paragraphs from the end of *Patterns:* "In this volume we have avoided studying religious phenomena in their historical perspective; we limited ourselves to treating them as such, to know them, insofar as they are hierophanies" (394/461).[14]

If I am troubled by Eliade's encompassment, I am even more concerned that the apparent scanting of the historical in *Patterns* not be used as an excuse to jettison the morphological enterprise—an enterprise that I value. While he employs a more contemporary translation of the duality, I would join with the formulation of William H. Sewell, Jr.:

> I would argue that the study of history as transformation [as different from the study of history as temporal context] has typically been haunted by an excess of diachrony. . . . A proper appreciation of synchrony is the secret ingredient of diachronic history. I would argue that no account of historical transformation can be cogent unless it performs a dialectical oscillation between synchronic and diachronic thinking. We should, in my opinion, pay more literal attention to the word 'transform,' whose two roots—'trans' and 'form'—signal precisely the necessary joining of diachrony and synchrony. . . . No account of change will be judged deep, satisfying, rich or persuasive unless it is based on a prior analysis of synchronic relations.[15]

Different from Eliade, but responsive to the morphological impulse, is a project such as Max Weber's. Weber had an uncommonly rich documentary and multicausal sense of history. He worked with the notion of "ideal types" in order to pattern that history. He compared relations, not only at the level of historical data but also between types and between types and data. By borrowing from Goethe the notion of "elective affinity," he guaranteed that any relations between types will be based on their difference, indeed, their opposition.[16]

The status of the ideal type in Weber is closer to Goethe's notion of archetype, in one important respect, than it is to Eliade's. Both Weber and Goethe stress that it is a construct of the scholar's mind. Coming out of German Neo-Kantianism, Weber knew this from the beginning. Goethe had to be led, reluctantly, to that conclusion through furious debate with Schiller. As Goethe describes one such encounter: "I explained to him [Schiller] with great vivacity the Metamorphosis of Plants and, with a few characteristic strokes of the pen, conjured up before his eyes a symbolical plant. He listened, and looked at it with great interest and intelligence; but when I had ended, he shook his head saying: 'This has nothing to do with experience, it is an ideal.'"[17] Goethe ultimately accepted Schiller's correction, Eliade will not. For him, the cost would be too high.

I have often observed to students that a methodological or theoretical position is not some magic wand that makes problems disappear. Each position assumed entails costs and consequences. The question is not one of deciding on solutions but of choosing what set of costs one is willing to bear. In the case we have been studying in these two essays, Eliade accepted the price of his position while rejecting that implicit in Schiller's.

I am reminded of an incident at the University of Santa Barbara in the late 1960s when Eliade and I both taught there. We had held a public discussion on the study of religion. Afterward, one student rushed up to me with great excitement: "I get the issue between you! Smith says Eliade can't account for human beings; Eliade says Smith can't account for God!" I corrected neither the precision of his language nor the adequacy of his understanding, but responded, "OK . . . presuming you are right, I'd rather go to bed at night with my headache than with his."

The academy demands that we make great efforts at complex and varied modes of understanding before we venture critique. I hope this study of Eliade's *Patterns*, occasioned by the fiftieth anniversary of the first, French edition of this classic, has kept faith with that obligation. For all my deep appreciation of Eliade's effort, for his enterprise, for the complex intellectual history that lay behind his endeavor, and for the urgent nature of the central problems he sought to address, my response, finally, remains the same as I gave to that student some thirty years ago.

Notes

1. M. Eliade, *Autobiography*, vol. 2, 1937–1960, *Exile's Odyssey* (Chicago, 1988), 84.

2. J. Z. Smith, *Imagining Religion* (Chicago, 1982), 23–24.

3. Eliade, *Shamanism: Archaic Techniques of Ecstasy* (New York, 1964), xiii.

4. Eliade, "Phénoménologie de la religion et sociologie religieuse," *Critique* 39 (1949): 713–20. Cf. Eliade, *Autobiography*, 2: 138, where, in response to having his work characterized as a "phenomenology," Eliade responds, "for me, it was rather a morphology."

5. Eliade, *Shamanism*, xv.

6. In the following pages I will cite the pagination, in parentheses, first to the original French, Eliade, *Traité d'histoire des religions*, 1st ed. (Paris, 1949), and then to the English translation, *Patterns in Comparative Religion*, 1st ed. (New York, 1958). Subsequent reprints of the translation have kept the same pagina-

tion for the bulk of the work. However, in the most recent reprint (Lincoln, Nebr., 1996) Eliade's "Foreword" has been differently paginated. One needs to add 6 to the roman numerals in the first edition (e.g., p. xi in the 1st ed. becomes xvii in the 1996 reprint). Note that I have revised the English translation in nearly every quotation.

7. Eliade cites the opening lines of the "Foreword" to the first edition of R. Caillois, *L'homme et le sacré* (Paris, 1939); I cite the third edition (Paris, 1950), 11. Work needs to be done on the influence of Caillois on Eliade. Note Eliade's encomium to Caillois in Eliade, *Journal*, vol. 3, 1970–1978 (Chicago, 1989), 356–57.

8. Of all his structural terms, *ensemble* is the most often employed. Unfortunately it has been indifferently translated in the English *Patterns*.

9. Goethe to Herder, May 17, 1787, in the translation by E. Heller, *The Disinherited Mind: Essays in Modern German Literature and Thought* (New York, 1959), 10.

10. Note that the relation between these two systems replicates the same movement from the transcendental to the immanent.

11. Eliade, *Shamanism*, xiv. I have modified the English translation on the basis of the French, *Le chamanisme et les techniques archaïques de l'extase*, 1st ed. (Paris, 1951), 9.

12. Eliade, *Shamanism*, xiv.

13. Goethe, *The Metamorphosis of Plants*, par. 8. The German reads "von aussen."

14. While I have suggested, in my first essay, some clues as to the nature of the 'historical' volume, it would certainly not have been a "historiographical" work of the sort discussed and critiqued in the "Foreword" to *Shamanism*. Rather, it would have been something like a history of human religious imagination.

15. W. H. Sewell, Jr., "Geertz and History: From Synchrony to Transformation," *Representations* 59 (1977): 35–55, passage quoted, 41–42.

16. M. Weber, *Die protestantische Ethik und der "Geist" des Kapitalismus*, 2d ed. (1920), in the English translation by T. Parson, *The Protestant Ethic and the Spirit of Capitalism* (New York, 1930; reprint, 1958), 91, where the Goethean term, "elective affinities," is concealed under the bland translation "certain correlations." For a useful discussion of "elective affinities" in Weber's methodological project, see S. Kalberg, *Max Weber's Comparative-Historical Sociology* (Chicago, 1994), 102–17.

17. Heller, *The Disinherited Mind*, 7.

CHAPTER FOUR

THE TOPOGRAPHY OF
THE SACRED

I WAS IN MY near teens when I first encountered the rites of Roman boundary stones, the *termini*, in *The Evolution of Property from Savagery to Civilization* by Paul Lafargue,[1] Karl Marx's son-in-law. A footnote there led me to Fustel de Coulanges's classic, *The Ancient City*, a book that I continue to reread regularly with admiration and pleasure. In Fustel, I found not only a more satisfactory positive theory of religion and the rituals concerning the boundary stones but also an introduction to the Roman god Terminus, a name that in youthful enthusiasm I rendered as the god "Stop!"[2]

Lafargue, in passing, compared the Roman boundary stones with two passages in the Hebrew Bible, Deuteronomy 19:14, "You shall not remove your neighbor's landmark, which the men of old have set," and Job 24:2, which lists as the first class of evildoers, those who "remove landmarks."[3] A quick check in Strong's *Exhaustive Concordance*[4] added three parallels, Deuteronomy 27:17, Proverbs 22:28, and 23:10.[5]

In my English class, at the time, we were reading the King James Bible in that ubiquitous and pridefully titled anthology, *The Bible Designed to Be Read As Living Literature*,[6] and I was assigned a report on the episode of the 'Burning Bush' in Exodus 3. I used the god "Stop!" as well as the passages just enumerated, along with other passages, garnered from Strong's *Concordance*, which contained the idea of stopping (based, I confess, on English synonyms collected from dictionaries and thesauri),

101

to interpret the divine voice's command to Moses at the bush, "Do not come near; put off your shoes from your feet, for the place on which you are standing is holy ground" (Exodus 3:5)—most especially Isaiah 65:3–5 which spoke of people performing odd rituals in gardens and graves, consuming "swine's flesh and broth of abominable things," and saying, "Keep to yourself, do not come near me, because I am holy to you." That which was holy, it seemed to me, was a boundary, a place where one stopped. Removal of such a boundary, crossing such a boundary, was illicit or dangerous. The deity of the Burning Bush was the god "Stop!" Such a notion, I suggested, surely also lay behind such expressions as 'holy land.'

But there was more. At the same time, as well as for years afterward, my two bedside books, which I read in 'religiously' each night, were the seventh edition of Asa Gray's *New Manual of Botany*[7] and A. S. Hitchcock's *Manual of the Grasses of the United States*, soon replaced by the second edition, revised by Agnes Chase.[8] I was then intending to become an agrostologist and to study at Cornell Agricultural School. My interest in taxonomy (especially the varied genera of grasses) was intense. Therefore, I concluded my youthful paper on the Burning Bush by suggesting that holiness was a classificatory term designating a genus of places, people, and things before which one must stop. The classificatory nature of the distinction, sacred/profane, remains fundamental for my thinking about the topic.

When I went off to college, forsaking botany for philosophy and becoming interested in the Cornford thesis[9] on the relations of Greek mythology to Greek philosophy (an interest that subsequently landed me, quite by accident, in religious studies), I retained some of these earlier enthusiasms. My senior thesis was on systems of order and place especially in terms of Hesiod's *Theogony*. As a graduate student in religion at Yale, my longest manuscript short of the dissertation was on the symbolism of the 'center,' with special reference to Jerusalem. From my third published article, "Earth and Gods,"[10] to my later book, *To Take Place: Toward Theory in Ritual*,[11] I realize, in retrospect, that my careerlong preoccupation with sacred space began, years earlier, with *termini* and the god "Stop!" In the meanwhile, I had become at home in that French sociological and anthropological tradition of Coulanges, van Gennep, Hubert and Mauss, Durkheim, and Lévi-Strauss, each of whom began with an essentially spatial and classificatory understanding of the sacred and the profane.[12] Coulanges and van Gennep focused on the domestic threshold (the *limen*); Hubert, Mauss, and Durkheim on the duality of sacred/

profane with the prohibition of contact between them; Lévi-Strauss, on the notion of placement itself, "being in their place is what makes [sacred things] sacred, for if they were taken out of their place, even in thought, the entire order of the universe would be destroyed. Sacred objects therefore contribute to the maintenance of order in the universe by occupying the places allocated to them."[13] This approach stood in suggestive contradistinction to that Germanic tradition exemplified by scholars such as Otto, Söderblom, Feigel, Splett, and Baetke, which saw the sacred (or the holy) as a positive religious force and reality.[14] This deep conflict between two long-standing and influential traditions of scholarship gave rise to attempts at mediation, most famously by Eliade, to some degree influenced by Caillois.[15] The cost, however, which seemed (and seems) to me unacceptable, was a scanting of the anthropological in defense of the ontological. This is, in fact, a debate at least as old as Hume, now rephrased under the influence of various neo-Kantianisms, as to whether the sacred is best understood as an expression or an experience, as a representation or a presence. I side, with the French, in affirming the first member of these two oppositional pairs.

I would not have imposed upon you this remembrance of things past, which may seem an act of self-indulgence, were it not that the same kind of a history appears to underlie what remains for me the single most provocative treatment of our theme, that by Durkheim in *The Elementary Forms of Religious Life* (a title better translated as *The Elemental Forms of Religious Life*).[16] This history remained hidden until 1950 when a Turkish professor of law made available the complete text of Durkheim's lecture course, "The Physics of Morals and of Rights," delivered on a number of occasions between 1890 and 1912, based on a manuscript prepared by Durkheim between 1898 and 1900.[17] These *Lectures* constitute Durkheim's earliest persistent use of the distinction of sacred/profane, which is here presented as a set of spatial categories in the context of a sustained meditation on property rights. Until this publication, the only contemporary hint of such an important turn in Durkheim's thought was a cryptic note in favor of comparison in the preface to the first volume of *L'Année sociologique* (1898): "One cannot adequately describe a unique fact, or a fact of which one has only a single instance. . . . [For this reason, with reference to Coulanges,] the true character of the Roman *sacer* is very difficult to grasp and, above all to understand, if one does not see it in relation to the Polynesian *taboo*."[18]

The three lectures on "The Right of Property," forming part of "The Physics of Morals and of Rights" and framed as a critique of Kant, contain *in nuce* much of the argument of *Elementary Forms*. The most dominant influence is that of Durkheim's teacher at the École Normale Supérieure, Fustel de Coulanges, to whom Durkheim dedicated the 1892 publication of his Latin dissertation, and whose work, *The Ancient City*, is the chief cited secondary source in the *Lectures* on property.

Allow me to summarize the argument of these three *Lectures*, (133–70) which comprise numbers 12–14 in the series. Durkheim begins with Roman law, characteristically shifting attention from the usual focus on individual property rights to legal provisions concerning property that cannot be appropriated by any individual: sacred things (*res sacrae* or *religiosae*) and things held in common (*res communes*). In a move that anticipates one of the central argumentative strategies of *Elementary Forms*—the claim that if a given phenomenon is not natural, then it is social, with arbitrariness serving as the mark of that which is not natural—Durkheim concludes that it is not their "natural composition" that determines which items will be held as private and which held as sacred or communal. The same sort of 'thing' can be classified in either category (137–39). Nor is the distinction to be made on pragmatic grounds (139–42). This latter point is sharper in *Elementary Forms*, which views pragmatic understandings as characteristic of native interpretations which must always be set aside. In the *Lectures*, the characteristic of both individual and communal or sacred things is that their possession must be "exclusive" (142).

It is this characteristic of absolute separation that allows Durkheim to make a comparison with religion. For "the world over . . . the feature that distinguishes the sacred entities is that they are withdrawn from general circulation; they are separate and set apart." Durkheim illustrates this by describing Polynesian taboos.

> Taboo is the setting apart of an object as something consecrated. . . . By virtue of this setting apart, it is forbidden to appropriate the object of taboo under pain of sacrilege, or even to touch it. Those alone can have access to it who are taboo themselves or in the same degree as the objects. . . . There are only degrees of difference between the taboo of the Polynesians and the *sacer* of the Romans. We can see how close the connection is between this concept and that of ownership. Around the thing appropriated, as around the sacred thing, a vacuum formed. All individuals had to keep at a distance, as it were, except those who had the required qualifications to approach it and make use of it (143).[19]

Furthermore, in addition to property being exclusive, in the sense of being withdrawn from circulation, its second characteristic is that it may be transmitted. While the usual focus is on inheritance or transfer through sale, Durkheim shifts our attention to the provisions, again in Roman law, concerning rights of accession (*accessio*), namely, the right to all which one's property produces and the right to that which is united to it either naturally or artificially (148–49). While Durkheim does not entertain the intricacies of the law, a few examples from the six modes of accession distinguished in the Latin codes help clarify the point. "*First*, that which assigns to the owner . . . its products such as the fruit of trees, the young of animals. . . . *Fourth*, that which gives the owner . . . what is added to it by way of adorning or completing it."[20] On the latter, a contemporary American law dictionary provides the example, "if a tailor should use the cloth of B. in repairing A.'s coat, all would belong to A."[21] Durkheim compares this legal concept of the accession of property with the contagiousness of the sacred, which sacralizes anything it comes into contact with (147–49).

Having established the general parallelism between the concept of sacred and the concept of property, using materials from classical antiquity and Oceania, Durkheim now turns to Coulanges and the latter's further Greek and Roman examples, including my old friends, the *termini*. Coulanges describes a checkerboard-patterned landscape in which each field or holding was surrounded by a narrow belt of uncultivated land which was sacred, the property of the gods which could not be profaned, that is to say, which could not be privately acquired. This sacrality was regularly renewed and reinforced through sacrifices and rituals re-marking the *termini*, the boundaries that insulate the sacred ground (read, collective) from the family's individual plot (read, profane). Durkheim argues that there is no intrinsic difference between the two loci. They have been arbitrarily separated (150–58).

The fact that the structure of property and the structure of sacrality are parallel leads Durkheim to invoke a procedural 'scientific' rule often appealed to in *Elementary Forms*, "since the effects are identical, they can in all likelihood be attributed to similar causes" (144).

Let me pause here to take up this language of causation. Durkheim's positivism often leads to the suggestion that, for him as for common-sense usage, explanation is primarily the identification of causes. But his analytic procedures belie this claim. His favorite appeal is to concomitant variation, a parallelism that invites causal speculation but neither requires nor establishes it.[22] It would be better to take up a more linguistic view that insists that explanation is, at heart, an act of translation, of redescription. A procedure where the unknown is reduced to the known by holding that a second-order conceptual language appropriate to one domain (the known, the familiar) may, with relative adequacy, translate the language appropriate to another domain (the unknown, the unfamiliar). The cognitive advantage of such a proposal from language is that translation is, by its very nature, corrigible. Whether of a conceptual or natural language, whether intercultural or intracultural, translation can never be fully adequate, it can never be complete. There is always discrepancy. Central to any proposal of translation are questions of appropriateness and 'fit.' These are questions that must be addressed through the double methodological requirement of comparison and criticism. Furthermore, the cognitive power of any translation, model, generalization, or redescription (as, for example, in the imagination of 'sacred/profane') is, by this view, a result of its difference from the subject matter in question and not its congruence. (As an aside, this is the way in which I would rewrite Wayne Proudfoot's now-classic distinction between "descriptive" and "explanatory reduction.")[23] A second advantage to an understanding of explanation as an affair of language is that it is, thereby, in Durkheim's term, a "relentlessly social" activity, a matter of public meaning rather than individual significance. Focusing on translation at the level of second-order conceptual language requires that the public be the academic community and entails specifying the relations between, in our case, the study of "religion" and other disciplines' theoretical objects of study. This is a matter of locating oneself with respect to one's conversation partners, those with whom one will work out appropriate translation languages.

Perhaps the strongest example of this process in the study of religion is Durkheim's translation in *Elementary Forms* of the language appropriate to religion (for him, in this work, functioning as the unknown) into the language appropriate to society (for him, the known). The point at which one might differ from Durkheim's goal is with respect to his acceptance of explanatory simplicity. Better, here, is Lévi-Strauss's formulation: "scientific explanation consists not in a movement from the complex to the simple but in the substitution of a more intelligible complexity for another which is less."[24]

While the adequacy of any translation proposal may be debated, the only grounds for rejecting such a procedure *tout court* is to attack the possibility of translation itself, most often attempted through appeals to incommensurability.[25] Such appeals, if accepted, must entail the conclusion that the enterprise of the human sciences is, strictly speaking, impossible.

In the *Lectures*, as in *Elementary Forms*, Durkheim's explanation is relentlessly social. The gods whose property is marked off as sacred are to be translated as society projected in material form. (Durkheim, here, does not use the more adequate language of "collective representation.") Such projections are to the social order what perception is in the individual order. Both distort, but both can be interpreted and corrected by the scholar who knows how to "get through to the realities and to discover beneath the myths" the reality they "express" (158–59). The sacred is power that is in common; the profane is that which is individual (here expressed as private property). The eventual prioritizing of private property in western juridical discourse is the result, Durkheim suggests, of historical processes that eventuated in both social division and the supercession of landed property by personal or movable property (163–66). In a remarkable utterance that gives comfort to those of us who would see sacrality in terms of a socially spatial, topographical model, Durkheim insists that it is "only landed property that had the sacred character" (166).

There are only three aspects of the sacred in *Elementary Forms* that are not anticipated by the *Lectures*. The first is the lack of Durkheim's later linguistic analogy to sacrality, which I celebrate in *To Take Place*.[26] While I regret this absence, I do not mourn the lack of the second and third aspect of sacrality featured in *Elementary Forms*. This second aspect is Durkheim's positivistic assertion that the collective and, therefore, impersonal, social force that serves as his translation of the sacred is analogous to natural force as described by contemporary physics. This notion is encapsulated in his appeal to the Oceanic notion of *mana*—a notion I have discussed elsewhere that need not detain us here.[27] The third is his claim, toward the conclusion of *Elementary Forms*, that the sacred is ambiguous or ambivalent. This proposal has had a long and complex history and serves as the point of origin of both Mary Douglas's critique and positive proposals in her instant classic, *Purity and Danger*.[28] The ambiguity of the sacred has largely been argued in terms of two bodies of data, the Priestly tradition in the Hebrew Bible and the obscure Roman legal regulations surrounding "the sacred man" (*homo sacer*), recently the subject of an important monograph by Giorgio Agamben.[29]

I would argue that the alleged ambiguity in these cases is the result of the fusing, both in native and in academic discourse, of three systems (two cultic, one juridical) that need to be held distinct, at least in thought. First, the sacred and the profane (or, the holy and the common), which are binary, spatial, classificatory categories that must be kept apart. (You may picture them, if you like, as two separate circles.) Second, the distinction between the clean and the unclean, a set of hierarchical relative categories, which focus on the integrity of an individual container. (You may picture the clean as a balloon and the unclean as the result of a balloon bursting.) Third, the behavioral distinction between the permitted and the forbidden, including, in some systems, prohibitions against mixture, a set of interdictions often justified by reference to cosmogonic models. (You may picture this sort of instance of a category of the forbidden as that space resulting from two overlapping circles, Venn-diagram-like.) The three systems are homologous in important respects, but they are neither identical, nor are they interchangeable. In my own work, especially in *To Take Place*, I have tended to think of the sacred/profane distinction as essentially a royal one, the clean/unclean distinction as a cultic one, and the permitted/forbidden as a legal one. Given the reciprocal relations between king/priest, palace/temple, and law/cult it is not, then, surprising that the three systems coexist in texts that are the product of these relations.[30]

Allow me to illustrate aspects of Durkheim's mature understanding of the sacred with a contemporary American example. The Vietnam War Memorial in Washington, D.C., is one of three prime sites of present-day pilgrimage—along with Graceland and the Wisconsin farm that is home to a white bison. The memorial is preeminently sacred in Durkheim's sense of the term. That is to say, it may not be profaned. To see spray-painted graffiti, posters, or stickers on it would be felt a sacrilege.[31] Yet, it is only an expanse of black, polished stone. Like Durkheim's privileged example of the Australian *tjurunga*, which gives rise to his linguistic analogy, its "super-added" sacrality is signaled by arbitrary marks. (In the case of the memorial, by 58,132 proper names). Recalling Durkheim's prioritizing of nonrepresentational markings—a demonstration of their social rather than natural nature—there is, as well, a second memorial, erected as a result of political pressure, a realistic bronze statue of three "grunts." A few moments of observation at the site will be sufficient to convince you that, unlike the stone, the statue does not function as sacred.

The memorial was constructed at an arbitrary place, wherever there happened to be room in the park system. There is nothing natural about its location. There are no entombed bodies, such as at Arlington National Cemetery. It marks no site of historical significance, such as the memorial at Pearl Harbor, which eerily includes the remains of the actual actors (the ships and the sailors). There is, in my sort of language, no static, no noise. There is nothing to interfere with the Vietnam War Memorial's pure social representation. (Recall Durkheim's rejection of the theory by some natives and some anthropologists that the *tjurungas* are sacred because they embody either the souls or the bodies of the ancestors.)[32]

Visitors to the memorial form what Durkheim would term a "moral community," exhibiting high affectivity. Standing before the memorial, it is irrelevant whether one was once for or against the war. Divisiveness is overcome—at least for the moment. Hence, it is a community that requires periodic renewal.

At the memorial, Vietnam veterans are present in uniform. Like Durkheim's clan, this is a kinship socially created by insignia, not by natural processes of biological descent. One group of veterans stands in perpetual watch. Other veterans return to the memorial periodically to reestablish their solidarity with their brothers and sisters in arms, an extended community encompassing both the living and the dead in a web of reciprocal obligations. The latter characteristic defines, for Durkheim, a moral community.[33]

Behaviorally, there is a set of special relations between some of those who are at the wall and the memorial. In Durkheim's *Lectures,* these fit into the category of "qualified persons." In the more interesting characterization in *Elementary Forms*, they are participating in ritual which entails the notion of a "veritable sacrilege,"[34] that is to say, a rule-governed, socially sanctioned profanation. This subset of visitors (relatives, comrades, friends) touch the wall, especially the segments with which they feel associated. They often trace a name, which, while only an arbitrary mark, results in a deeply meaningful and highly emotional experience (one which Durkheim might label 'comm-union'). This subset, along with other visitors, often brings gifts (i.e., offerings), which are placed at the base of or against the wall. Some four thousand objects are left annually, each one of which is removed, nightly, by the Park Service and carefully preserved in climate controlled government warehouses in Lanham, Maryland. Having touched the wall, these gifts acquire sacrality by contagion. Furthermore, these gifts themselves are signs of that reciprocity that, for Durkheim, characterizes a moral community and are, therefore, "eminently social" representations. One set consists of letters, photographs, and household objects which assert the continuing community of the living and the dead. Another set consists of flags, military insignia and medals, parts of uniforms, cans of K-rations—each of which expresses, metonymically, the socially created kinship of military service; each of which is an emblem that maintains and renews solidarity.[35]

Sacred is not only a representation in the Durkheimian sense, it is also a word. We have been recently assisted in understanding its usage in the French anthropological tradition I have just reviewed by the semaisiological studies of Despland and Bourgeaud on the terminological opposition sacred/profane in French literature prior to Durkheim.[36] Then, too, there is the long scholarly tradition within both classical and Indo-

European studies of tracing the complex history of ancient usages, ranging from Benveniste to Palomé,[37] brilliantly summarized by Huguette Fugier in his monograph on the use of 'sacred' in Latin, the linguistic and religious system that most clearly distinguishes between the sacred and profane.[38]

English has been deeply influenced by Latin as a Christian ecclesiastical vocabulary and, by derivation, through Anglo-Norman French. It has been further enriched, at least since Middle English, by its Germanic heritage, which introduced a different, although parallel, terminology, for example, 'holy' for 'sacred' (*heilig;* cf. Middle English *holy* as well as *sacrid*); 'offering' for 'sacrifice' (*das Opfer;* cf. Middle English *offryng* as well as *sacrifise*). Staying only with the Latinate constructions, the essential elements of the Roman systematics are replicated in English.[39] 'Sacred' (Latin, *sacer*), functioning as an adjective, indicates what is set apart as wholly consecrated to the gods. Parenthetically, I know of no English dictionary that has recorded the substantive 'the Sacred,' so common in our field, a modern import from the French anthropological tradition and that was popularized by Eliade, although some dictionaries do note the archaic, usually plural, noun 'sacreds' denoting ritual objects. Continuing with the Latin system as exhibited in English, the 'sacerdote' (*sacerdos;* cf. Anglo-Saxon *sācerd*), literally 'the presenter of sacred gifts,' that is to say, a 'priest'—a word more common in English in its adjectival form, 'sacerdotal'—denotes the specialist in communication between the sacred and the profane through ritual, especially the 'sacrifice' (*sacrificium*) which, as Hubert and Mauss powerfully argued, effects this communication by transferring the offering from the profane to the divine realm through the agency of death which separates it from the mundane, thereby 'making it sacred' (the literal meaning of 'sacrifice,' in Latin, *sacer* + *facere*). 'Sanctified' (*sanctus*) focuses on the separative, inviolable, and prohibitive aspects of sacrality, at times expressed in legal formulations, a meaning carried over in the word 'sanction' and the pleonasm 'sacrosanct.' If portable, sanctified objects were protected in a special place, a 'sacrary' (*sacrarium*).

Of greater interest to me is a set of archaic, English, usually transitive, verbal forms (built on the Latin verb *sacrāre*, 'to make sacred'), such as in the Middle English *Merlin Romance* (III.502): "In the whiche he sacrefied first his blissid body and his flessh . . . that he sacred with his owene hande." The verbal forms are often paired with verbal nouns denoting the object resulting from the action. These usages are now listed as obsolete, the result of a process of semantic depletion, with its only survivor being the modern English 'consecrate' (*com-* or *con-* serves, here, as an intensifying prefix).⁴⁰ This archaic set includes the verb 'sacrate' with its noun, 'sacration'; the verb 'sacre,' with both its nominal and adjectival homophonic forms, 'sacre;' and the verb 'sacring.' These archaic forms reinforce the overall perspective of the Durkheimian tradition: 'sacred' is a product of human agency, this or that is made or designated 'sacred.' 'Sacred' is not the human response to a transcendental act of self-display.

In service of this conclusion, I offer, as a final and cautionary tale, an anecdote from the Africanist anthropologist, Colin M. Turnbull. The text addresses the sin of overseriousness, my version of the shrewdly perceptive Roman Catholic moral flaw of overscrupulousness, and exhibits both conscious and unconscious humor. Turnbull's work, *The Forest People: A Study of the Pygmies of the Congo*, focuses on the Mbiti. Turnbull describes their relations to their surrounding forest, which they view as a providing and protecting deity. He goes on to write of their most sacred object, an instrument called the *molimo*, which they understand to be "the voice of the forest." I pick up Turnbull's narrative as a group of males, accompanied by Turnbull, enter the forest in silence in order to "fetch" the molimo. One group of five breaks off and disappears from sight.

> Just as I was about to ask where the others had gone they returned, announcing their presence with low whistles. . . . They were in two pairs, each pair carrying between them, over their shoulders, a long, slender object. . . . They came on toward us. Madyadya was carrying the rear end of what proved to be a huge tube of some kind: fifteen feet long. He gestured proudly and said, 'See this is our molimo!' Then he turned and putting his mouth to the end of the trumpet, which it was, he blew a long, raucous raspberry. Everyone doubled up with laughter, the first sound they had made since leaving camp. I was slightly put out by this sacrilege and was about to blame it rather pompously on irreligious youth, when I saw something that upset me even more. I do not know exactly what I had expected, but I knew a little about molimo trumpets and that they were sometimes made out of bamboo. I suppose I had expected an object elaborately carved, decorated with patterns full of ritual significance and symbolism, something sacred, to be revered, the very sight or touch of which might be thought of as dangerous. . . . But now I saw that the instrument which produced such a surprisingly rude sound . . . was not made of bamboo or wood, and it certainly was not carved or decorated in any way. It was a length of metal drainpipe, neatly threaded at each end, though some-

what bent in the middle. The second trumpet was just the same, shining and sanitary, but only half the length. . . . I asked, keeping my voice low, how it was that for the molimo, which was so sacred to them, they should use water piping stolen from roadside construction gangs, instead of using traditional materials. Evidently now that they had the trumpets in their possession there was no longer any need for silence, for they answered calmly and loudly with a counter-question. 'What does it matter what the molimo is made of? This one makes a great sound, and, besides, it does not rot like wood. . . .' Ausu, to prove how well it sounded, took the end of the longer pipe . . . and all of a sudden the forest was filled with the sound of trumpeting elephants. The others clapped their hands with pleasure and said, 'You see? Doesn't it sound well?' My conservative feelings were still wounded however, and it gave me some pleasure to see the difficulty the Pygmies had on the way back, carrying a fifteen-foot length of drainpipe through the forest.[41]

In this essay, I have sided with the theoretical sophistication of the Mbiti with respect to the sacred—"What does it matter what the molimo is made of?"—over against Turnbull, who plays the role of the 'superstitious,' 'primitive' European who has apparently read too many books in the religious studies field and thinks of sacrality as something inherent, as something fraught with ambivalent danger. Besides, given his glee at the pygmies' discomfiture in threading the lengthy drainpipe through the thick density of trees, Turnbull exhibits a most unpleasant sense of retribution.

Notes

1. P. Lafargue, *La Propriété: Origine et évolution* (Paris, 1895). I cite the English translation, *The Evolution of Property from Savagery to Civilization* (Chicago, 1910), esp. 50–74. This material is not found in the better-known treatment by F. Engels, *Ursprung der Familie, des Privateigentums und des Staat* (Stuttgart, 1884); English translation, *The Origin of the Family, Private Property and the State* (London, 1986).

2. N. Fustel de Coulanges, *La Cité antique* (Paris, 1864). I cite the English translation, *The Ancient City: A Study of the Religion, Laws and Institutions of Greece and Rome* (Boston, 1896), esp. 76–92.

3. Lafargue, *Evolution of Property*, 58–59.

4. J. Strong, *The Exhaustive Concordance of the Bible* (New York and Nashville, 1890), s.v. "landmark."

5. "Landmark/landmarks" ($g^e b\hat{u}l/g^e b\hat{u}l\hat{a}$) in these passages refers to boundary stone(s), the moving of which constitutes land theft. It is not a matter of moving historical markers!

6. E. S. Bates, ed., *The Bible Designed to Be Read As Living Literature* (New York, 1936).

7. A. Gray, *New Manual of Botany: Handbook of the Flowering Plants of the Central and Northeastern United States and Adjacent Canada*, ed. B. J. Robinson and M. L. Fernald, 7th ed. (New York, 1908).

8. A. S. Hitchcock, *Manual of the Grasses of the United States* (Washington, D.C., 1935); 2nd ed., ed. A. Chase (Washington, D.C., 1951), in the series United States Department of Agriculture, Miscellaneous Publications, 200.

9. See, especially, F. Cornford, *From Religion to Philosophy* (London, 1912; reprint, New York, 1957); and Cornford, *The Unwritten Philosophy: The Origins of Greek Philosophical Thought* (Cambridge, 1952).

10. J. Z. Smith, "Earth and Gods," *Journal of Religion* 49 (1969): 103–27, reprinted in Smith, *Map Is Not Territory: Studies in the History of Religions*, Studies in Judaism in Late Antiquity, 23 (Leiden, 1978), 104–28.

11. J. Z. Smith, *To Take Place: Toward Theory in Ritual*, Chicago Studies in the History of Judaism (Chicago, 1987).

12. Fustel de Coulanges, *Ancient City*; A. van Gennep, *Les Rites de passage* (Paris, 1909), English translation, *The Rites of Passage* (London, 1960); H. Hubert and M. Mauss, "Essai sur la nature et la fonction du sacrifice," *L'Année sociologique* 2 (1899): 29–138, English translation, *Sacrifice: Its Nature and Function* (London, 1964); E. Durkheim, *Les Formes élémentaires de la vie religieuse: Le système totémique en Australie* (Paris, 1912), English translation, *The Elementary Forms of Religious Life* (New York, 1995); C. Lévi-Strauss, *La Pensée sauvage* (Paris, 1952), English translation, *The Savage Mind* (London and Chicago, 1966).

13. Lévi-Strauss, *Pensée sauvage*, 17, *Savage Mind*, 10. See, however, my correction to this passage in Smith, *To Take Place*, 121–22, n. 2.

14. R. Otto, *Das Heilige: Über das Irrationelle in der Idee des Göttlichen und sein Verhältnis zum Rationalen* (Breslau, 1917), English translation, *The Idea of the Holy: An Inquiry into the Non-Rational Factor in the Idea of the Divine and Its Relations to the Rational* (Oxford, 1924); N. Söderblom, "Holiness (General and Primitive)," in the *Encyclopedia of Religion and Ethics*, ed. J. Hastings (Edinburgh and New York, 1913), 6: 731–41; F. K. Feigel, *"Das Heilige:" Kritische Abhandlung über Rudolf Ottos gleichnamiges Buch*, 2d ed. (Tübingen, 1947), see the excerpt in C. Colpe, *Die Diskussion um das "Heilige,"* Wege der Forschung, 305 (Darmstadt, 1977): 380–405; J. Splett, *Die Rede vom Heiligen: Über ein religionsphilosophisches Grundwort* (Freiburg and Munich, 1971); W. Baetke, *Das Heilige im Germanischen* (Tübingen, 1942), excerpt in Colpe, *Diskussion*, 337–79.

15. M. Eliade, *Das Heilige und das Profane* (Hamburg, 1957), English trans-

lation, *The Sacred and the Profane* (New York, 1959); R. Caillois, *L'Homme et le sacré* (Paris, 1939), 3d ed. (Paris, 1963), English translation, *Man and the Sacred* (Glencoe, 1959). See further the useful summaries in H. Bouillard, "Le categorie du sacré dans la science des religions," in *Le Sacré: Études et recherches*, ed. E. Castelli, 33–56 (Paris, 1974); C. Colpe, "[The] Sacred and the Profane," *Encyclopedia of Religion*, ed. M. Eliade (New York, 1987), 12: 511–26; V. Anttonen, "Sacred," in *Guide to the Study of Religion*, ed. W. Braun and R. T. McCutcheon, 271–82 (London, 2000).

16. Durkheim, *Elementary Forms*, see above, n. 12.

17. E. Durkheim, *Leçons de sociologie: Physique des moeurs et du droit*, ed. H. N. Kuball, Publications de l'Université d'Istanbul, Faculté de Droit, III (Istanbul, 1950), with a simultaneous publication in France (Paris, 1950). I cite the English translation as *Lectures* from Durkheim, *Professional Ethics and Civic Morals* (London, 1957; reprint, London and New York, 1992), in parentheses in the text.

18. E. Durkheim, "Préface," *L'Année sociologique* 1 (1898): i–vii, English translation, K. H. Wolff, ed., *Emile Durkheim, 1858–1917* (1960; reprint, New York, 1964), 341–47.

19. Durkheim cites (144) as his source for Polynesian taboos, "Wurz, VI." This is a miscitation. The reference should be to T. Waitz, *Anthropologie der Naturvölker*, ed. G. Garland (Leipzig, 1859–72), vols. 1–6.

20. Cited in W. E. Baldwin, ed., *Bouvier's Law Dictionary*, 2d ed. (New York, 1928), s.v. "accessio."

21. *Ibid.*, s.v. "accession."

22. J. S. Mill, *A System of Logic*, 10th ed. (London, 1879), 1: 460–71.

23. W. Proudfoot, *Religious Experience* (New York, 1985), esp. 194–97.

24. Lévi-Strauss, *Pensée sauvage*, 328; compare the different translation of this sentence in *Savage Mind*, 248.

25. The issues of translation and incommensurability find their base in the fundamental work by W. Quine, *Word and Object* (Cambridge, Mass., 1960); see further, R. Feleppa, *Convention, Translation, and Understanding: Philosophical Problems in the Comparative Study of Culture*, State University of New York Series in Logic and Language (Albany, 1988). In thinking about this subject, I have been much helped by two quite different discussions, T. S. Kuhn, "Commensurability, Comparability, Communicability," in *Proceedings of the 1982 Biennial Meeting of the Philosophy of Science Association*, ed. P. D. Asquith and Th. Nickles, 2: 669–88 (East Lansing, 1983), reprinted in Kuhn, *The Road since Structure: Philosophical Essays, 1970–1993*, ed. J. Conant and J. Haugeland (Chicago, 2000), 33–57; and T. May, "From Linguistic Difference to Linguistic Holism: Jacques Derrida," in May, *Reconsidering Difference* (University Park, 1997), 77–128.

26. Smith, *To Take Place:* 105–8.

27. See J. Z. Smith, "Manna, Mana Everywhere and /-/-/," (2002), reprinted in this volume.

28. M. Douglas, *Purity and Danger: An Analysis of the Concepts of Pollution and Taboo* (New York, 1966).

29. G. Agamben, *Homo sacer: Il potere sovrano e la nuda vita* (Florence, 1995), English translation, *Homo Sacer: Sovereign Power and Bare Life* (Stanford, 1998), esp. 71–86.

30. Smith, *To Take Place*, 54–56 et passim.

31. I am indebted to Professor Ed Linenthal, University of Wisconsin, Oshkosh, for pointing out, in an oral communication, that such profanation has, in fact, occurred.

32. Durkheim, *Elementary Forms*, 122 and n. 125 et passim. Compare Lévi-Strauss, *Pensée sauvage*, 316–19; *Savage Mind*, 238–41 which rejects Durkheim at this point.

33. Durkheim's term for such a moral community, if religious, is *l'Église*, "Church" (*Elementary Forms*, 41–43). The English connotations of this word has caused some confusion. The French, *l'Église*, derived from the Greek *ekklesia*, carries the social sense of an assembly, as that which is 'called together.'

34. Durkheim, *Elementary Forms*, 342, cf. 38.

35. My general understanding of the memorial has been informed by William Lloyd Warner's classic work in the Durkheimian tradition, *The Living and the Dead: A Study of the Symbolic Life of Americans*, Yankee City, 5 (New Haven, 1959; reprint, Westport, Conn., 1975).

36. M. Despland, "The Sacred: The French Evidence," *Method & Theory in the Study of Religion* 3 (1991): 41–45; P. Borgeaud, "Le Couple sacré/profane: Gènese et fortune d'un concept 'opératoire' en l'histoire des religions," *Revue de l'histoire des religions* 114 (1994): 211–14. See also Boullard, "Le categorie du sacré," 33–38.

37. E. Benveniste, *Le Vocabulaire des institutions indo-européennes* (Paris, 1969), 2: 196–207, English translation, *Indo-European Language and Society* (Coral Gables, 1973), 445–69; [E. C. Palomé], "Indo-European Religion," in J. Z. Smith, ed., *The HarperCollins Dictionary of Religion* (San Francisco, 1995), esp. 488.

38. H. Fugier, *Recherches sur l'expression du sacré dans la langue latine*, Publications de la Faculté des Lettres de l'Université de Strasbourg, 146 (Paris, 1963). See also the summary in Agamben, *Homo Sacer*, 79–80.

39. In the following lexical summary, I have drawn on the following standard works: A. Blaise and H. Chirat, *Dictionnaire latin-français des auteurs chrétiens* (Strasburg, 1954); A. Ernout and A. Meillet, *Dictionnaire étymologique de la langue latine*, 4th ed. (Paris, 1959); J. R. Clark Hall, *A Concise Anglo-Saxon Dictionary*, 4th ed., Medieval Academy Reprints for Teaching, 14 (Cambridge, 1960; reprint,

Toronto, 1984); A. L. Mayhew and W. W. Skeat, *A Concise Dictionary of Middle English from* A.D. *1150 to 1580* (Oxford, 1887); J. A. H. Murray, ed., *The Oxford English Dictionary* (Oxford, 1882–1928), vols. 1–12; J. P. Pickett, ed., *The American Heritage Dictionary of the English Language*, 4th ed. (Boston, 2000); J. Pokorny, *Indogermanisches etymologisches Wörterbuch*, 3d ed. (Tübingen, 1994); M. Proffitt, ed., *Oxford English Dictionary Addition Series* (Oxford, 1997), vol. 3; A. Souter, *A Glossary of Later Latin to 600* A.D. (Oxford, 1949; reprint, 1996); A. Walde and J. B. Hofmann, eds., *Lateinisches etymologisches Wörterbuch*, 4th ed. (Heidelberg, 1965), vols. 1–3; W. D. Whitney, *The Century Dictionary and Cyclopedia* (New York, 1899–1910), vols. 1–10.

40. Alas, the modern verb and verbal noun pair 'sacralize' and 'sacralization,' which occurs from time to time in the writings of contemporary students of religion (including mine) carries, in dictionaries, only the medical sense of an operation that fuses the last lumbar vertebra with the sacrum.

41. C. Turnbull, *The Forest People: A Study of the Pygmies of the Congo* (New York, 1962), 74–79.

CHAPTER FIVE

MANNA, MANA
EVERYWHERE AND /ᴗ/ᴗ/

THE LABEL 'historian' is the one I am most comfortable with; that the focus of my interest is the history of religious representations and the history of the academic conceptualizations of religion does not alter this basic self-identification. Historians are a funny kind of folk. Whether of the species 'new' or of that sort thereby designated as 'old,' whether global in their reach or preoccupied with one limited segment of human activity, historians share an uncommon faith in the revelatory power of a telling detail, a small item that opens up a complex whole and that thereby entails a larger set of intellectual consequences. Given the anecdotal nature of their enterprise, historians are truly the descendents of Herodotus and thereby play the role of 'anthropologists' in Aristotle's sense of the term: people who delight in telling tales (*logoi*) about other folk (*anthrōpoi*), in a word, gossips (*Nichomachean Ethics* 1125a5).

Let me begin with one anecdote taken from the remote field of the textual criticism of Greek manuscripts, in which a major preoccupation is the determination of the filiation of late Byzantine copies, understood as a history of errors, based on distinctive or variant readings organized into genealogical stemmata. Günther Zuntz was working on the well-known problem of the relations between two important fourteenth-century codices of Euripides—designated L and P—from the same scriptorium. Which one was the exemplum? Which one was the dependent copy? Among a number of other details, both have a misplaced punctuation mark, an erroneous rhythmical period (a colon) in *Helen,* line 95. On June 3, 1960, Zuntz examined this reading in L at the Laurentian Library in Florence. The colon appeared to be of an odd color. After examining the paper manuscript under ultraviolet light, Zuntz asked the librarian, Anna Lenzumi, for her opinion. "She ran her finger over the place—and the 'colon' stuck to her finger. The heat of the lamp had loosened it. It was a tiny piece of straw . . . embedded in the coarse paper." It would appear that the scribe of P, which was a more expensive vellum manuscript, had mistakenly copied L's fragment of straw as a colon, thus proving that P was dependent on L. What interests me most in this narrative is the denouement. Zuntz writes, "the piece of straw is kept in a tiny box in the safe of the Laurentian Library as the decisive piece of evidence."[1] As the visual root (*videns/videre*) of the final word 'evidence,' indicates, the old Herodotean distinction between the probity of "seeing (for oneself)" over against "hearing (from an other)" is still in play, augmented by a characteristic positivism that holds such evidence to be self-evident. Hence, the scrupulous preservation of the little relic, the small piece of straw. As is so often the case in historical construction, the contingent accident has proven to be essential.

One cannot, of course, always count on the sheer presence of an object to guarantee its interpretative force. It is not the straw's quiddity, but the character of the argument it entails, that is probative.[2]

In this presentation, I should like to examine two instances of evidence that suggest different modes of significance and evaluation. The first concerns an episode in biblical narrative; the second is an Oceanic word/concept that has played a leading role in some anthropological theories of religion. All they have in common is a partial accidental homophony across two unrelated language systems. *Manna* and *mana* are what translators call "false friends."

In the biblical case, the evidence's 'being-there' is largely uninteresting; in the anthropological case, the evidence's not 'being-there' has, for some, not diminished in the least the theory's interest.

I: Manna

Manna, in the materia medica, the concentrated juice of some vegetable, naturally exsudating from it, soluble in water, and not inflammable.

> *Encyclopaedia Britannica,* 1st ed. (1771)

The Jews, however, with the majority of critics, for good reasons are of the opinion that it was a totally different substance from the

vegetable manna, and was specially provided by the Almighty for
His people. And this is confirmed by the language of our Lord,
John 6.

 J. N. BROWN, *Encyclopedia of Religious Knowledge* (1835)

Although immediate access to the German-born Israeli zoologist's
work was made impossible by World War II and was further occluded by
its initial announcements in relatively obscure publications, the conservative guild of Anglo-American biblical scholarship was electrified by
Frederick Simon Bodenheimer's 1947 English-language summary of his
earlier (1927) field researches in the Sinai Peninsula.[3] Manna (or, in Hebrew, *mān*) is neither the product of some form of Asiatic lichen (e.g.,
Lecanora esculenta) nor an exudation of the tamarisk tree (*Tamariscus gal-
lica* or *mannifer*), as had been previously argued.[4] It is the excretion, depending on geographic locale, of one of two species of scale insects—
Trabutina mannipara in the highlands, *Najacoccus serpentinus* in the
lowlands—found as parasites on the stems of tamarisks. As is, perhaps,
appropriate for an area of scholarly inquiry whose major publications are
classified "BS" in the Library of Congress system, manna turned out to
be a form of insect manure. (The latter word is, of course, another 'false
friend.') Notwithstanding its cloacal origins, manna was, with great relief, pronounced to be not a product of oriental imagination but rather a
fact. "On the basis of these findings, manna production is a biological
phenomenon of the dry deserts and steppes."[5] The little insects and the
product of their metabolism, like the "little piece of straw," can be preserved in "tiny" boxes in museums and figured in Bible dictionaries.[6]

There is, within the Hebrew Bible manna narratives, one brief notice of this sort of conservation: "Moses said, 'This is what YHWH has
commanded: "Let one omer [of the manna] be kept for future generations
in order that they may see the bread with which I fed you in the wilderness when I brought you out of the land of Egypt."' And Moses said to
Aaron, 'Take a jar and put an omer of manna in it and place it before
YHWH, to be kept for future generations.' Aaron did as YHWH had commanded Moses, and placed it before the Testimony [i.e., the Ark] for
safe keeping" (Exodus 16:32–34). Here, the Ark's confines serve as a 'cab-
inet of curiousities,' a sort of Ripley's Believe It or Not! Museum, where
strange objects are deposited like manna and, according to Numbers
17:10, Aaron's miraculously budded rod. While this way of telling the
tale emphasizes presentness—"here, you can see it" (compare the iron
bed of Og in Deuteronomy 3:11)—at the expense of the narrative motif
of the extreme perishability of the manna, it concludes with a learned

late scribal gloss giving voice to a sense of historical distance, "an omer is the tenth part of an ephah" (Exodus 16:36), an explanation of an obscure, possibly archaic, term of dry measure, a Hebrew word that occurs only in Exodus 16.[7]

By and large, however, it is not with matters of factuality that the biblical narratives of the manna incident are concerned. It is not what "biological phenomenon" manna denotes but rather what it connotes. In the varying accounts and mentions of manna, in some ten books of the Bible, we find the characteristic activity of the ancient mythographers, thinking with stories.[8] Understanding this activity requires that we make use of the identification of the variety of traditions within the Hebrew Bible as identified by more than two centuries of scholarship, but that we resist the tendency to conceive of these as 'sources' or to layer them chronologically. For purposes of this presentation, they may be seen as contemporaneous moments in an ongoing argument. In this case, the stimulus for the debate is a motif well-known to folklorists, that of a "marvel" expressed as an "extraordinary occurrence" in terms of "magic food." Thus, Stith Thompson classifies the two chief motifs concerning manna as D 1031.0.1 and F 962.6.2, respectively.[9] As translated into more specific terminology, we read different understandings of the significance of a narrated incident that, while in the wilderness, the Israelite ancestors received an unexpected source of food. (In some versions, they received both bread and meat, both manna and quails.)

One argument is expressed in the various framings of the incident. Is the story a positive or a negative one, a miracle tale or a cautionary fable?

We have already met one specification of the positive frame. YHWH, like a father, adopted Israel as his child when he led Israel out of Egypt. Like a father, he provided food for his children. In the passage already quoted, this takes on the character of a formula, "the bread with which I [YHWH] fed you in the wilderness when I brought you out of the land of Egypt" (Exodus 16:32). It is most common in long, poetic, *dayyênû*-like ["it would have been sufficient"] recitations of the gracious deeds of YHWH toward Israel, such as Psalm 105:37–45:

> Then he led forth Israel with silver and gold,
> and there were none among his tribes who
> stumbled. . . .
> He spread a cloud for covering,
> and fire to give light by night.
> They asked, and he brought forth quails,
> and gave them bread from the sky in abundance.

He opened the rock, and water gushed forth,
it flowed through the desert like a river.
For he remembered his holy promise,
and Abraham his servant.
So he led forth his people with joy,
his chosen ones with singing.
And he gave them the lands of the nations.

This is a celebratory hymn portraying a procession through the desert with YHWH showering his family with gifts and joy. It is also an occasion for further reflection on the nature of the deity: YHWH remembers his promise to Abraham. Here manna is but one instance in a long series of acts that form part of a divine strategy for realizing this seemingly unlikely promise.

This positive framing gains voice in one mode of telling the elaborated manna story. It also introduces a quite different set of reflections on YHWH's nature.

In Exodus 16:13–21, the picture is one of manna (and quails) covering the ground as far as one could see. As much as was gathered, there was more. Each day, yet more. That which was not collected turned rotten and bred worms. The controlling image of manna production in this way of telling the tale is one of a celestial cotton-candy machine gone amuck, spewing forth unending quantities of the sticky white stuff. It is *de trop*. When YHWH does something, he does it big! Manna here appears as a kratophany, a lavish, profligate display of power "that you should know that I am YHWH your God" (Exodus 16:12).

A quite different but equally positive picture is given in another mode of telling the elaborated manna story. In Exodus 16:22–30 the manna comes down in precisely measured quantities: just enough for one day and twice as much on the day before the Sabbath. Here YHWH is depicted as a law-abiding deity, one who keeps his own rules even in the midst of performing wonders. The implication is that of a "how much more so" argument. If YHWH keeps the Sabbath commandments, how much more so Israel. For this reason, the narrative includes a caution. "On the seventh day some of the people went out to gather and they found none. YHWH said to Moses, 'How long will you people refuse to keep my commands . . .'" (Exodus 16:27–28).

This last complaint introduces the other side of the central argument as to the significance of manna. If in the compositions just reviewed the major frame is that of the desert wandering as an almost paradisical time of intimacy with YHWH, the performer of mighty deeds, the

121

keeper of his law, the opposing frame—and the majority opinion within the Hebrew Bible—views the period of the wilderness wandering as a paradigmatic time of rebellion and disobedience, expressed in the narrative theme of Israel "murmuring" against YHWH.[10] This theme dominates the penultimate framing of the manna and quail stories in both Exodus 16 and Numbers 11.

In Exodus 16, the people are hungry, and they remember the good foods they ate back in Egypt (Exodus 16:3). In Numbers 11, the same complaint is better integrated into the narrative by being transposed from Israel's reproach before the appearance of manna, where manna is sent as a response to the complaint, to an effect of the provision of manna. In the Numbers version, Israel is bored with her constant manna diet: "O that we had meat to eat! We remember the fish we ate in Egypt . . . the cucumbers, the melons, the leeks, the onions, and the garlics. . . . Here there is nothing but this manna to eat" (Numbers 11:5). YHWH's response turns the blessing into a curse; the positive, kratophantic superfluity is reinterpreted as negative. The profligate provision of manna and quails is to be understood not as a demonstration of divine power but, rather, of divine anger. Indeed, as the people are stuffing themselves with quail, they are smitten with a great plague, and the resultant dead are buried in a cursed place called the "graves of craving" (Numbers 11:33–34; cf. Psalms 78:10–24; 106:13–16; and, for a later example, 2 Esdras 1). Here, the provision of food functions as part of a narrative reversal of the Exodus. Israel wishes to go back to Egypt; the divine feeding results in a plague.

The most complex form of this understanding of manna is given in Ezra's speech as composed in Nehemiah where it takes the form of two propositions: (1) even though YHWH provided "bread from the sky," the people rebelled; and (2) even though Israel rebelled, YHWH "did not withhold manna" (Nehemiah 9:15–17, 20). Moderating the more optimistic assimilation of the manna story to the promise to Abraham, this way of telling argues that YHWH remembers his promise even when Israel does not.

The ultimate framing of the manna incident relies on larger narrative structures in which the provision and cessation of manna serves to bracket the forty-year period of wilderness-wandering, marking it off as a 'time out of time,' which begins and ends with a water crossing. As with the Eden story, which in many ways parallels the wilderness period and which also revolves around eating, this is a segment, as we have seen, that can be assessed, positively or negatively, as a time of intimacy with YHWH and promise or as a time of rebellion against YHWH and curse. Taken as a whole, the manna narrative gives voice to both sides of this ambivalent understanding, with the positive assessment relativized by the more dominant negative evaluation. This is sequentially reenforced by redundancy: the provision of manna is itself bracketed by two incidents of water provision in which the negative interpretation prevails. Let me only outline the elements:

A) Beginning of the forty-year wilderness-wandering

1. Exodus 14:1–15:22. The Israelites cross the divided "sea of reeds" on "dry ground."
2. Exodus 15:22a. Israel immediately enters the "wilderness."
3. Exodus 15:22b–25. After three days, they have no water. The people "murmur." They come to a place of "bitter water." YHWH shows Moses a tree that, when thrown in the water, makes it "sweet" and potable.
4. Exodus 16. Manna (and quail).
5. Exodus 17:1–7 (cf. Numbers 20:2–13), Israel again lacks water. The people "murmur." YHWH tells Moses to strike a rock with his rod and that fresh water will flow. This element is a reversal of a previous incident where striking the Nile river with the rod made the Egyptians' waters "foul" and undrinkable (Exodus 7:14–24, alluded to in Exodus 17:5b).

B) End of the forty-year wilderness-wandering

1. Joshua 3:7–5.2. The Israelites cross the divided river Jordan on "dry ground." They enter Canaan thereby fulfilling the promise to both Abraham and Moses.
2. Joshua 5:12. Manna ceases. The Israelites return to eating ordinary, cultivated food, "the produce of the land," and "the people of Israel had manna no more."

If these opposing views make their points by integrating the manna incident into larger narrative structures, thereby framing it, other sorts of understandings can be found that do not require thinking with story but rather thinking about story. To cite only the best-known example, a homily attributed to Moses in Deuteronomy: "And he humbled you and let you hunger and fed you with manna, which you did not know, nor did your fathers know, *in order that* he might make you learn that humankind does not live by bread alone, but that humankind lives by everything that proceeds out of the mouth of YHWH" (Deuteronomy 8:3). Here manna is transposed from an ancient wonder to a present, recurrent phenomenon;

not a fact of nature, but rather a source of moral instruction. It is a symbol of every way in which YHWH every day nurtures his people—for the school of thought represented by this particular text, preeminently through the Law. Furthermore, the text, by referring to manna as that "which you did not know, nor did your fathers know," alludes to the learned scribal pun that claims that the etymology of manna is to be found in Israel's question, *mān hû,* "What is it?" (Exodus 16:15). This homily suggests that one should ask this question, quite literally, of everything and answer, "it is from YHWH."

Another constellation of manna speech focuses on this question, "What is it?" and seeks its answer in words taken to be synonymous with manna. Drawing on the full range of biblical and immediately postbiblical materials, manna is glossed as "bread from the sky" (Exodus 16:4; Psalms 78:24 and 105:40), "bread of angels" (Psalm 78:25; Wisdom 16:20; 2 Esdras 1:19), "heavenly food" (Sibylline Oracles 3:84), or "ambrosia" (Wisdom 19:21). These can be understood in an esoteric manner that gives rise to new questions. What might it mean for human beings to eat such food? Do they become, in some way, more than human?

I offer only one example, from the late first-century B.C. Greek Jewish work, the Wisdom of Solomon, which occurs in a now familiar frame, a catalog of the god's gracious deeds. "You did give your people the food of angels and, without their toil, you did supply them from heaven with bread ready to eat" (Wisdom 16:20). Here, manna is understood as a transfer of divine food to the human realm, perhaps to be contrasted with the attempt at an illegitimate transfer in the tree of life episode in Genesis 3:22. Likewise, the food is produced "without toil," perhaps in contrast to the curse found in Genesis 3:17–19. An event associated with the exodus here signals a new creation, a new beginning (an argument made explicit in Wisdom 19:6, 19:11).

For the purposes of this presentation, more interest attaches to the penultimate line of this text, which describes manna as a "crystalline quick-melting kind of ambrosial food" (Wisdom 19:21). This interpretation of manna as ambrosial divine food is more common than it appears. It has occurred every time I have written the word 'manna,' with its doubled consonant, rather than the Hebrew *mān. Mān* is carried over, in direct Greek transliteration, only in the Septuagint for Exodus 16; all other occurrences in the Hebrew Bible are rendered, in the Septuagint and in all other Greek versions, as *manna.* In a complex instance of interlinguistic relationship, *manna* is a Greek generic term (although possibly of Semitic derivation) referring to a powder or to granules of aromatic botanical substances, most commonly frankincense, used especially in ritual and medical procedures.[11] As such, it is part of the complex Greek system of vegetative scents elucidated by Marcel Detienne.[12] This is a transfer, introducing new denotations and connotations, which occurs entirely within the linguistic realm. It is a matter of philology, not entomology.

Manna, as a Greek word, can be associated with the immortalizing powers of ambrosia (Hesychius, s.v. "ambrosia") as well as with well-known classical traditions that the phoenix, symbol of immortality, feeds only on aromatic substances and dew.[13] The semantic field of the Greek term came to overlap the Hebraic, as may be seen in one late (first- to third century A.D.) pseudepigraphical Jewish text: "And what does it [the phoenix] eat? . . . The manna of heaven and the dew of earth" (3 Baruch 6:11, Greek version). The idiom of the answer is biblical, but the Greek mythic tradition is present in the question, as are the Greek associations of *manna* and dew in the answer.

What has interested me in thinking about the variety of manna texts is not so much a matter of historical confirmation or corroboration but rather one of narrative articulation and ratiocination.[14] It is not unlike the 'burning bush' of Exodus 3:2–4 (cf. Deuteronomy 33:16), which has been subjected to similar confirmative attempts to identify the particular species of an apparently thorny plant (s^{e}neh) by ransacking herbaria of Sinai flora for red-leaved shrubs or for bushes whose waxy leaves are capable of reflecting sunlight.[15] It has always seemed to me that the wonder of the plant is not so much that it was afire (bushes do burn) as that it was represented as coming to speech.

II: Mana

Mana, power, influence.
>   w. williams, *Dictionary of the New Zealand Language* (1845)

Ma-na, s. Supernatural power, such as was supposed and believed to be an attribute of the gods.
>   l. andrews, *A Dictionary of the Hawaiian Language* (1865)

It entered European consciousness as an italicized word, one of those glossed items of exotic native terminology that flavored nineteenth-century travel accounts by missionaries, administrators, and other colonial adventurers. *Mana,* "command, authority, power" (1843);[16] "mana, or power" (1855).[17] It first achieved general significance when F. Max Müller quoted a letter he had received from a British High Church missionary in Melanesia, Robert Henry Codrington, in Müller's 1878 Hibbert Lectures, *On the Origin and Growth of Religion*. Müller deployed the citation as part of his polemic against "fetichism" as a primitive stage in evolutionary theories of religion. Codrington had written, in a not altogether coherent report, that

> The religion of the Melanesians consists, as far as belief goes, in the persuasion that there is a supernatural power about belonging to the region of the unseen; and, as far as practice goes, in the use of means of getting this power turned to their own benefit. The notion of a Supreme Being is altogether foreign to them. . . . There is a belief in a force altogether distinct from physical power, which acts in all kinds of ways for good and evil, and which it is of the greatest advantage to possess or control. This is Mana. The word is common I believe to the whole Pacific. . . . It is a power or influence, not physical, and in a way supernatural; but it shews itself in physical force, or in any kind of power or excellence which a man possesses. This Mana is not fixed in anything, and can be conveyed in almost anything; but spirits, whether disembodied souls or supernatural beings, have it and can impart it; and it essentially belongs to personal beings to originate it, though it may act through the medium of water, or a stone, or a bone. All Melanesian religion consists, in fact, in getting this Mana for one's self, or getting it used for one's benefit—all religion that is, as far as religious practices go, prayers and sacrifices.[18]

The subsequent history of mana can be organized around six chronological points: 1891, 1902, 1904, 1912, 1915, and 1936 to the present.[19] The result has been a complex, century-long drama in which a word was transformed into an incarnate power only to be reduced to a word again.

1) In 1891, Codrington published what has been termed the "classic" account of mana in *The Melanesians: Studies in Their Anthropology and Folk-lore.*[20] In the same year, Edward Tregear's *Maori-Polynesian Comparative Dictionary*, dedicated to Max Müller, offered detailed illustrations of the meaning of 'mana' in ten Pacific island languages which gave confidence to the notion that it was a pan-Oceanic word/concept.[21]

2) In 1902, J. N. B. Hewitt's, "Orenda and a Definition of Religion,"[22] began the process of identifying a cluster of Native American terminologies subsequently held to be parallel to mana, which gave confidence to the emerging claim that mana was a universal religious concept.

3) 1904 saw publications by R. R. Marett[23] and H. Hubert and M. Mauss[24] which employed mana as a generic concept for theorizing about the origins of religion or magic.

4) In 1912, along with using mana as a central theoretical concept, mana was put forth as an explanatory principle for interpreting other non-Oceanic religious traditions in E. Durkheim's *Elementary Forms of Religious Life: The Totemic System in Australia*,[25] and Jane E. Harrison's *Themis: A Study of the Social Origins of Greek Religion.*[26]

5) In 1915, the first monograph, a dissertation devoted to a careful and critical comparative study of mana, was prepared by Friedrich Rudolf Lehmann.[27]

6) The period from 1936 to the present has been largely devoted to challenging the utility of mana as a generic concept through linguistic studies, either analyzing its specific meaning in particular cultures, supported by the detailed examination of mana's occurrences in a corpus of native sentences rather than constructing a composite portrait achieved by taking the term in isolation; or by arguing, on the basis of the same sort of data, that earlier accounts misunderstood its grammatical status, that mana is most commonly not a substantive noun naming an impersonal force, as had been common in the literature since Codrington,[28] but rather most frequently functions as a transitive stative verb. This critical process began with H. Ian Hogbin (1936), A. Capell (1938), and Raymond Firth (1940) and has culminated, for the present, in the work of Roger M. Keesing (1984).[29] Finally, using a quite different sort of linguistic analysis, Claude Lévi-Strauss, in a daring proposal, retheorized mana (1950), an undertaking recently critically examined, from quite different perspectives, by both Pascal Boyer (1990) and Maurice Godelier (1996).[30]

For the purpose of this presentation, we may focus on one segment of this history, the movement from Durkheim, who risked his argument on a mana that was not there, to Lévi-Strauss, who proposed mana as a category for objects that had no 'where.'

As is well known, Durkheim was able to present much of his theoretical understanding of religion in works prior to the 1912 *Elementary Forms*, most particularly in the 1898–1900 course of lectures at the University of Bordeaux, "The Physics (*physique*) of Morals and of Rights," in connection with an analysis of the origins and logic of private property.[31] Early on, in these pre-1912 writings, he links the sacred with the Oceanic word/concept *tabu*.[32] It is only with the *Elementary Forms* that he first invokes mana and couples it with the sacred, even though he had certainly read, by 1899, Codrington's 1877 letter on mana as published in Müller.[33] Doubtless, the theoretical use of mana by Hubert and Mauss, as well as by Marett provoked Durkheim's subsequent interest in the term.[34]

I take Durkheim, especially in the *Elementary Forms,* to be one of the great crafters of argument in the history of the study of religion. From the translation of "religion" by "society" in the very first sentence, his work has a rhetorical and intellectual momentum from which it is almost impossible to disengage. For this reason, it is striking when he violates the terms of his own agendum and introduces as a central concept the notion of mana, which cannot be found within his chosen ethnographic exemplum. There is no evidence for the presence of a term fully analogous to mana among the Australian aborigines.[35]

Durkheim deploys several compositional stratagems in facing this difficulty. For example, as is quite typical in *Elementary Forms,* there is the anticipatory mention. Codrington is first cited on the Melanesians early on, as part of Durkheim's discussion of a definition of magic, "in Australia as well as in Melanesia . . . the souls, bones, and hair of the dead figure among the tools most often used by the magician" (58–59/40). Codrington is next cited in the midst of a set of Australian exempla, as part of Durkheim's argument against animistic theories of religion (83/56, cf. 95/64). Four pages later, continuing the same discussion, Codrington on mana is directly quoted with the promise that Durkheim will "later make plain what the word expresses" (87–88/59). This "later" explanation will be deferred for eighty–nine pages (277/196), preceded immediately by another teaser in the course of an argument with Andrew Lang. "As we will see in the next chapter, the words *wakan* and *mana* imply the idea of *sacred* itself (the first word is taken from the language of the Sioux, the second from that of the Melanesian peoples)" (265/188).

This last citation, as well as the phrase already quoted, "in Australia as well as in Melanesia," gives voice to Durkheim's more ambitious stratagem: Australian data are comparable to Native American data; Native American data are comparable to Oceanic data; therefore, Oceanic data are comparable to Australian data. For Durkheim, it is the first proposition in this problematic syllogism that requires demonstration.

As you will recall, Durkheim begins *Elementary Forms* by setting forth as his overarching question the nature of the "simplest and most primitive religion" (1/1). Characteristically, he defers identifying that religion for four chapters, where it is finally argued that totemism is the simplest and most primitive genus of religion (124/85); Australian totemism, the simplest and most primitive species presently observable (132/90). In the course of this identification, Durkheim offers a brief history of scholarship. As the derivation of the word indicates, *totem* is a Native American term first brought to European awareness in the late eighteenth century. "For nearly half a century, totemism was known exclusively as an American institution. It was only in 1841 that Grey . . . drew attention to the existence of similar practices in Australia. From then on, scholars began to realize that they were in the presence of a system that has a certain generality. . . . McLennan was the first [1869–70] to try to connect totemism with general human history" (124–25/85). The history of ethnographic literature thereby justifies both the parallelism of Australian and Native American socioreligious terminology as well as the use of a native word as a generic, academic term of art.

Durkheim's second argument is more strictly sociological. He rejects the worldwide comparative use of 'totemism,' as, for example, employed by Frazer, inasmuch as this mixes "societies whose kind and degree of cultural development are quite disparate" (132/90–91). The relationship of the Native Americans to the Australians must be put with greater precision. With respect to social development, the Australians are 'simpler,' the Native Americans are more 'complex.' Thus he will focus on Australian data and will "supplement" it with American materials "only when it appears well suited to helping us understand the Australian data better" (132–38, esp. 138/91–93, esp. 93). In the bulk of *Elementary Forms*, Durkheim strictly follows the consequences of this placement: the Australian data are given first, then, if relevant, the Native American (e.g., 156, 159, 191–92, 205, 223, 254–55, 370, 373–74/109, 111, 135, 145, 158, 180–81, 261, 264). This procedural rule is broken only with the introduction of mana. Here, the presence of Native American mana-like terminology allows Durkheim to infer a mana-like concept among the Australian aborigines. I am tempted to suggest that Durkheim's entire proposal to "supplement" Australian data with Native American was made so that this one inference could be legitimized, thereby enabling Durkheim to "depart" from his precisely stipulated domain, the "circle of facts" (138, n.3/95, n.1) limited to Australia as his primary resource, with America as his secondary support, and to import the Oceanic word/ concept mana as the chief guarantor of his interpretation of his central second-order category, the sacred.

As might have been anticipated, Durkheim first makes this move in book 2, chapter six, which is subtitled "The Notion of the Totemic Principle, or Mana, and the Idea of Force" (268–92/190–206). Durkheim begins by deducing from his previous conclusions concerning totemism, the presence of "a common principle," a "kind of anonymous and impersonal force. . . . diffused in a numberless multitude of things," independent of, and yet imagined by, the native as taking particular forms, for example, as totems (269/191).

Durkheim's initial question is whether his deduction conforms to ethnographic fact; but his formulation already begins to shift attention from the putative focus on Australia. He asks "whether in societies akin to the Australian tribes or in those very tribes, we find—and in explicit form—conceptions that differ only in degree and nuance" from his deduction of the totemic principle? His first example is Oceanic, from Samoa. As Durkheim explains, it exhibits already a development beyond his deduction. Samoa has only "survivals" of totemism, hence the data exhibit "a totemic principle that the imagination has developed in somewhat personal forms" (273 and n. 1/193–94 and 193, n. 5).

His second set of examples from Native American traditions has been prepared for. Here they are placed, uncharacteristically but strategically, before the Australian materials. "In many American tribes, especially in those belonging to the great family of the Sioux. . . . [elements of totemic systems] are still identifiable in them. Among these peoples, there is a preeminent power above all the particular gods men worship, which they call *wakan*. . . . It is Power in the absolute" (274–75/194–45). Likewise the Iroquois, "whose social organization is still more markedly totemic. The word *orenda* . . . is exactly equivalent to the wakan of the Sioux" (276/195). "The same idea [with different names] is found among the Shoshone," the Algonquins, the Kwakiutl, the Tlingit, and the Haida (277/196). Parenthetically, it should be noted that this catalog is, in part, dependent on the list in Hubert and Mauss's essay on magic, as demonstrated by a mistake in bibliographic citation in the latter being repeated in Durkheim.[36]

Having established the presence of the "notion of impersonal religious force" in Native American traditions, Durkheim makes the comparison. "It is not peculiar to the Indians of America; it was first studied in Melanesia. On certain islands, it is true, the social organization is no longer based on totemism, but totemism is still visible on all of them . . . We find among these peoples, under the name 'mana,' a notion that is exactly equivalent to the wakan of the Sioux and the orenda of the Iroquois" (277/196). Rather than a detailed exposition, he quotes a long extract from Codrington's 1877 letter to Müller, which in Durkheim's French translation, as well as in his selectivity, highlights the element of impersonality (277–78/196–97).[37]

With this comparison in place, Durkheim rushes to his conclusion. Given the Native American and Melanesian materials, an analogous notion must be present in Australia. "We can legitimately infer the nature of each from that of the other" (283/200). "Is this [mana] not the same notion of a diffuse and anonymous force whose seed in Australian totemism we were uncovering a moment ago?" (278/201). It is a justifiable question to ask "whether a concept analogous to wakan or mana is altogether lacking in Australia" (283, n. 4/200, n. 41). It is "by no means reckless to impute" a similar force to the Australians (278/201). The absence of the same "degree of abstraction and generality" in the Australian instance, when compared with the Native American, is a difference in "social milieu" (280/198), a difference in their respective totemic organizations, which he had called attention to when he first suggested "supplementing" the Australian data with the Native American (132–38/91–93).[38]

To quote the old tag, "wishing does not make it so." Unlike Lévi-Strauss—recall the sloth in *The Jealous Potter* (1985, chs. 6–8)—Durkheim has no conceptual means of converting a logical and systemic requirement into an existent reality. There is nothing like the "little piece of straw," nor some vial of insect excretions to display. The Australian materials do not suggest the presence of a mana-like word or concept, setting aside the question as to whether mana and the presumed Native American cognates have been correctly understood, or what translation rule justifies the judgement that each term is "*l'équivalent exact*" (276–77/195–96) of the other.[39]

Durkheim's interest in establishing the facticity of the "totemic principle" in Australia was high. The notion of an "impersonal force" accomplished a set of important objectives. Impersonality insured a collective, social understanding of sacrality. It blocked, as well, any deistic definition of religion. Above all, social force, conceived as a parallel to force as conceptualized in the physical sciences, guaranteed facticity by providing an "objective correlative"—a goal persistently reiterated throughout Durkheim's career-long project of establishing the social sciences.[40] "When I speak of these [mana-like] principles as forces, I do not use the word in a metaphorical sense; they behave like real forces. In a sense they are even physical forces that bring about physical effects mechanically . . . The totemic principle is at once a physical force and a moral power" (270–71/192). "Religious forces are real, no matter how imperfect the symbols with whose help they were conceived" (292/206).

The last appearance of mana in the *Elementary Forms* is in relation to the "negative cult" and the connection of the sacred to "contagion." For the purpose of this presentation, this is not the element on which I wish to dwell, rather it is Durkheim's return to a previously enunciated argument that religious forces, being "transfigured collective forces," are in no way inherent in the "outward and physical forms in which they are imagined." Religious forces are "superadded," "they do not have a place of their own anywhere" (461–62/327; cf. 327–28/230, 603–4/424). As an illustration, Durkheim cites Codrington on mana, italicizing the quote, mana "is a force that is by no means fixed on a material object, but that can be carried on almost any sort of object" (461/327 [see above, n. 37]). However, Durkheim's most persuasive example of this understanding of sacrality does not require an appeal to mana, but occurs quite early on in his interpretation of the Australian data in the context of thinking about the *tjurunga* and its 'superadded' markings.

As I have argued elsewhere,[41] the linchpin of Durkheim's argument is the observation that "in themselves, the tjurunga are merely objects of wood and stone like so many others; they are distinguished from profane things of the same kind by only one particularity: the totemic mark is drawn or engraved upon them. That mark, and only that mark confers sacredness on them" (172/121). It is the nature of these "marks" that interests Durkheim and provides him with his key argument. The marks are nonrepresentational, they do not represent natural 'things.' Hence, they are to be derived from social rather than from sensory experience. While the argumentative move, not natural and therefore social, is a hallmark throughout Durkheim's work, here he develops a linguistic analogy. Although the Australians are fully capable of depicting natural phenomena with reasonable accuracy (e.g., in their rock or bark paintings), they do not do so when marking their tjurungas. Those marks "consist chiefly of geometric designs . . . having and only capable of having a conventional meaning. The relation between the sign and the things signified [*entre la figure et la chose figurée*] is so remote and indirect that the uninformed cannot see it. Only clan members can say what meaning they attach to this or that combination of lines. . . . The meanings of these drawings are indeed so arbitrary that the same drawing can have two different meanings for the people of two totems" (178–79/126).

Durkheim does not develop this linguistic analogy further. It remained for Claude Lévi-Strauss, in 1950, to propose a linguistic/taxonomic understanding of mana. Lévi-Strauss takes up the Durkheimian agendum in the context of writing on Hubert and Mauss's *General Theory of Magic*. "Conceptions of the mana type are so frequent and so widespread that we should ask ourselves if we are not in the presence of a universal and permanent form of thought which, far from being characteristic of only certain civilizations or alleged 'stages' of thought . . . will function in a certain situation of the mind in the face of things, one which must appear each time that this situation is given."[42] To elucidate this "situation," Lévi-Strauss calls attention to the "exceedingly profound remark" of Father Thavenet—quoted by Hubert and Mauss and, from them, by Durkheim—with respect to the Algonquin, that *manitou* "particularly refers to all beings which still have no common name, which are not familiar."[4³] After giving a set of ethnographic examples, Lévi-Strauss draws the striking conclusion: "Always and everywhere, notions of this [mana-]type intervene, somewhat as algebraic symbols, to represent a value of indeterminate signification, in itself empty of meaning and therefore susceptible to the reception of any meaning whatsoever. Thus [mana's] unique function is to make good a discrepancy between the signifier and the signified, or more precisely, to signal the fact that in this circumstance, on this occasion, or in this one of its manifestations, a relationship of inadequacy is established between the signified and the signifier to the detriment of the anterior relation of complimentarity."[44]

For Lévi-Strauss, the notion of mana does not pertain to the realm of an all but physical 'reality' but, rather, to that of thought. Mana is not a substantive category, it is a linguistic one. Mana has a "semantic function." Mana marks discontinuity rather than continuity by representing, with precision, floating or undecided signification. "It is the function of notions of the mana-type to oppose themselves to the absence of signification without allowing, by themselves, any particular signification."[45] He clarifies this function with three analogies: the phonological zero, as adumbrated by Jakobson; algebraic symbols; and the use of nominal 'place holders' (Boyer provides the English example of 'stuff') for objects not yet encompassed by native taxonomy or nomenclature. By such placement, thought can continue despite such occasions of discontinuity.[46] Rather than the popular, 'hot' analogy of electricity to mana, Lévi-Strauss has provided one of temporary cold storage. It is as if to the Israelites' question concerning manna, *mān hû*, "what is it?" the Maori and other Oceanic peoples would answer, "*mana*." It has been named as that whose name and taxon must be deferred.

This linguistic understanding drives Lévi-Strauss to the witty conclusion that "in one case at least the notion of mana does present those characteristics of a secret power, a mysterious force, which Durkheim and Mauss attribute to it—that [singular case] is the role which it plays in their own system. There, truly, mana is mana"![47]

As Hans Penner has persistently reminded his colleagues, "religion is constituted, or encompassed, by language. Language, in other words, is a necessary condition for the existence of religion: no language, no religion."[48] In this presentation, we have been concerned with two primary, serial, sense-making modes of linguistic activity: narrative and argument.

In the case of the biblical manna narratives, too much scholarly energy been expended on getting "behind" the word to some natural phenomenon as if that endeavor guaranteed its being of interest. If nothing else, the narrative interchangeability of the provision of manna, or quail, or water; the multiple examples of framing and reframing the provision tale in the service of larger reflective schemes; the consequences of substituting the Greek *manna*, carrying its own set of complex systemic relations, for the Hebrew *mān*—all argue against such a conclusion. In the case of the argumentative use of the Oceanic mana, too much scholarly energy has been expended on getting 'beneath' the word to either some supernatural 'reality,' as in the lineage from Marett to Eliade, or some powerful social 'reality,' analogous to a physical force, as in Durkheim, as if such an endeavor guaranteed its being of interest. In the service of this project, mana, and the words claimed to be its equivalent, were stripped of their linguistic status and removed from the sentences in which they were embedded. The result may be termed the "manic illusion."

I am far from certain, however, that we ought to rest content with reproducing native lexicography and, thereby, give in to the prevalent ethos of localism, branding every attempt at generalization a western imposition. It is one thing to argue for attention to the semantics and pragmatics of native speech; it is another to proclaim that "mana as an invisible medium of power was an invention of Europeans, drawing on their own folk metaphors of power and the theories of nineteenth century physics."[49] Merely substitute for 'invention' the term 'translation,' which always entails discrepancy and therefore always requires critical judgement, and the difference becomes clearer.[50] Besides, giving primacy to native terminology yields, at best, lexical definitions which, historically and statistically, tell how a word is used. But lexical definitions are almost always useless for scholarly work. To remain content with how 'they' understand 'mana' may yield a proper description, but little explanatory power. (I take Lévi-Strauss to have, in fact, proposed a proper explanation; one that can be challenged only on theoretical grounds.) How 'they' use a word cannot substitute for the systematic stipulative and precising procedures by which the academy contests and seeks to control second-order, specialized usage. This, too, Hans Penner has helped us to understand.[51]

Notes

1. G. Zuntz, *An Inquiry into the Transmission of the Plays of Euripides* (Cambridge, 1965), 14–15. Compare the use of Zuntz's account in H. Don Cameron, "The Upside-down Cladogram: Problems in Manuscript Affiliation," in *Biological*

Metaphor and Cladistic Classification: An Interdisciplinary Perspective, ed. H. M. Hoenigswald and L. F. Warner (Philadelphia, 1987), 232–33.

2. As a counter-example of the inappropriate use of a 'relic,' one might recall the jawbone, navel-string, and genitalia attributed to the Ugandan war-god, Kibuka [Kibuuka], "rescued when the Mohammedans burned down his temple in the civil wars of 1887–1890," and now preserved in the Ethnological Museum at Cambridge University. For James George Frazer, although only in the third edition of *The Golden Bough*, this could be deployed as evidence for his euhemerist theories, particularly for the origins of Osiris. If there were bodily organs, then Kibuka was once a historical king, subsequently elevated to the rank of a god. Perhaps the same could be said for Osiris on the basis of relics associated with the tomb of an early pharoah, excavated by Amélineau. While stated with all due caution, the fantastic connective tissues of the relevant paragraphs allow one to eavesdrop on Frazer's associative processes of thought. "We have seen that at Abydos . . . the tomb of Osiris was identified with the tomb of King Khent . . . and that in this tomb were found a woman's richly jewelled arm and a human skull lacking the lower jawbone, *which may be* the head of the king himself and the arm of his queen. . . . *It is possible*, although it would be very rash to affirm, that Osiris was no other than the historical King Khent . . . that the skull found in the tomb is the skull of Osiris himself, and that while it reposed in the grave this missing jawbone was preserved, *like* the jawbone of a dead king in Uganda, as a holy . . . relic in the neighboring temple. *If that were so*, we should be almost driven to conclude that the bejewelled woman's arm found in the tomb of Osiris is the arm of Isis." J. G. Frazer, *The Golden Bough*, 3d ed. (London, 1935), 6: 197–99, with notes (emphasis added). See further the discussion of Frazer's analogy of the Ugandan and Egyptian materials in B. C. Ray, *Myth, Ritual, and Kingship in Buganda* (New York and Oxford, 1991), 50–51, and Ray's discussion (184–88) of the similar treatment in E. A. W. Budge, *Osiris and the Egyptian Resurrection* (London, 1911), esp. 2: 92–96.

3. F. S. Bodenheimer, "The Manna of Sinai," *Biblical Archaeologist* 10 (1947): 1–6, reprinted in *The Biblical Archaeologist Reader*, ed. G. E. Wright and D. N. Freedman, 1: 76–80 (Garden City, 1961). The initial report appeared in F. S. Bodenheimer and O. Theodor, *Ergebnisse der Sinai-Expedition 1927* (Leipzig, 1929), 45–88. This was a survey undertaken when Bodenheimer, son of a distinguished Zionist leader, was staff entomologist at the Jewish Agency's agricultural experiment station in Tel Aviv, and published when he was research fellow in zoology at Hebrew University, Jerusalem. For an early notice of Bodenheimer's report, see the review by A. Kaiser, "Neue naturwissenschaftliche Forschungen auf der Sinaihalbinsel," *Zeitschrift des deutschen Palästina-Vereins* 53 (1930): 63–75. While Bodenheimer had wide-ranging interests in biology, ethology, and the history of zoology, he had special expertise in the *Coccidae* family of scale insects,

135

publishing a monograph, *The Coccidae of Palestine*, Zionist Organization Institute of Agriculture and Natural History, Agricultural Experiment Station Bulletin, 1 (Tel Aviv, 1924).

It should be noted that some earlier scholars had come halfway to Boden-heimer's thesis, providing an oral rather than a rectal cause, arguing that the manna that exuded from tamarisk trees did so as an effect of wounds in their stems resulting from having been pierced by scale insects. See, among others, T. Hard-wicke, *Asiatick Researches* 14 (1801): 182, as cited in A. MacAlister, "Manna," *Dictionary of the Bible*, ed. J. Hastings, 3: 236 (New York, 1900). The puncture thesis is still offered in the 1974 printing of the fifteenth edition of *Encyclopaedia Britannica*, IX: 792, or appears alongside the secretion thesis (VI: 571).

4. See the summary of these views by S. A. Cook, "Manna," *Encyclopaedia Biblica*, ed. T. K. Cheyne and J. S. Black, 3: 2929–30 (New York, 1902). Note that these two explanations still recur in an article by botanist R. W. Schery, "Manna" in the 1969 printing of the fourteenth edition of *Encyclopaedia Britan-nica*, 14: 797.

5. Bodenheimer, "The Manna of Sinai," 6. The same sentence appears, without attribution, in J. L. Mihelic, "Manna," *Interpreter's Dictionary of the Bible* (Nashville, 1962), 3: 260.

6. See, for example, Bodenheimer, "Fauna," *Interpreter's Dictionary of the Bible*, 2: 255, fig. 10.

7. Perhaps '*ōmer* is simply an archaic word that has become meaningless and is being translated in terms of a fraction of the well-known measure, an '*ēpâ*. Per-haps, because '*ōmer* might be confused with the common dry measure, a *hōmer*, equivalent to the load an ass might carry, it is here, by means of a note that it is equivalent to a tenth of an '*ēpâ*, being clarified as a much smaller amount, about two quarts.

8. I have been much influenced by the critical remark of C. Lévi-Strauss, *The Savage Mind* (Chicago, 1966), 95, that "[t]he mistake of Mannhardt and the Nat-uralist School was to think that natural phenomena are *what* myths seek to ex-plain, when they are rather the *medium through which* myths try to explain facts which are themselves not of a natural but a logical order."

9. S. Thompson, *Motif-Index of Folk-Literature*, rev. ed. (Copenhagen and Bloomington, Ind., 1955–58).

10. On this theme, see especially, G. W. Coats, *The Murmuring Motif in the Wilderness Traditions*, Catholic Biblical Quarterly Monograph Series (Washing-ton, D.C., 1968).

11. The citations in H. G. Liddell and R. Scott, *A Greek-English Lexicon*, rev. ed. (Oxford, 1968), s.v. "*manna*," are sufficient to give some idea of the semantic range.

In Greek Christian texts, *manna* refers to the food supplied during the exodus, but the ambrosial connotations are further developed through typological constructions that employ the contrast between the positive and negative framings of the manna narratives. Within the New Testament, see Paul, who already identifies manna as "spiritual food" yet interprets Israel's behavior as a cautionary fable (1 Corinthians 10:1–17). In John 6, this double evaluation is highly elaborated in the juxtaposition of the Mosaic manna with the Son as the "bread of life." In Revelation 2:7 and 17, the "Tree of Life" and the "hidden manna" are placed in parallel constructions as gifts given to "him who conquers." For later Christian usage, see the citations in G. W. H. Lampe, *A Patristic Greek Lexicon* (Oxford, 1961–68), s.v. *"manna."* The sole exception to the biblical referent is Hippolytus, *Refutatio omnium haeresium*, 4.31, where the word refers to a vegetable gum used in a recipe for poisoning oats.

Note that a standard reference work such as the *Encyclopaedia Britannica* could have an entry on "manna" (primarily in medicine), from the first through the eighth editions, without ever mentioning the biblical materials. The ninth through the eleventh editions add a single sentence to an appendix. It is only with the fourteenth that the biblical account of *mān* begins to overshadow the Greek understanding of *manna*.

12. M. Detienne, *The Gardens of Adonis* (Atlantic Highlands, NJ, 1977), 5–10 et passim.

13. While I have here focused on *manna* and spices as the phoenix's food, recall as well their role in the construction of the phoenix's nest and funereal pyre. See, in general, J. Hubaux and M. Leroy, *Le Mythe du Phénix dans les littératures grecque et latine* (Liège and Paris, 1939). R. van den Broek, *The Myth of the Phoenix according to Classical and Early Christian Traditions* (Leiden, 1972), especially 335–56, has a rich catalog of texts concerning the food of the phoenix. Detienne, *Gardens of Adonis*, 29–36, has a most important structuralist interpretation of the relation of the phoenix to spices.

14. I want to acknowledge three works on these traditions that offer important examples of approaches to biblical scholarship: B. J. Malina, *The Palestinian Manna Tradition* (Leiden, 1968); B. S. Childs, *The Book of Exodus: A Critical Theological Commentary* (Philadelphia, 1974), esp. 271–304; and W. H. Propp, *Water in the Wilderness* (Atlanta, 1987).

15. The identification of the bush as thorny depends on a claimed cognate to the term for the bush, *sᵉneh*, which occurs in the Hebrew Bible only in this incident in both the Exodus narrative and the briefer allusion in Deuteronomy. For a review of the various botanical identifications, see I. Löw, *Die Flora der Jüden* (Vienna and Leipzig, 1928–34), 3: 175–88.

16. E. Dieffenbach, *Travels in New Zealand* (London, 1843), 2: 371–72, as cited in the *Oxford English Dictionary, Supplement*, s.v. "mana." Dieffenbach, a German geologist, was a founding member of the London Ethnological Society.

17. R. Taylor, *Te Ika a Maui, or New Zealand and Its Inhabitants*, 1st ed. (London, 1855), 279, as cited in the *Oxford English Dictionary, Supplement*, s.v. "mana." Taylor, *Te Ika a Maui*, 2d ed. (London, 1870), 184, glosses the term "mana, virtue of the god." Note that J. White, *The Ancient History of the Maori: His Mythology and Traditions* (Wellington, 1887), 1: 35, 48; 3: 2 et passim, presents native sentences containing the word "mana" rather than simply deploying the isolated word.

18. R. H. Codrington, "Letter to Max Müller" (July 7, 1877), as quoted in Müller, *Lectures on the Origin and Growth of Religion, as Illustrated by the Religions of India*, 1st ed. (London, 1878), 53–54. Müller is concerned to challenge the notion of "fetichism" as the primitive stage of religion by appealing to the ubiquity of an "apprehension of the infinite." He uses Codrington's report as showing that the Maori had this notion in a "vague and hazy form." Perhaps confusing the uncertainties of Codrington with those he attributes to the natives, Müller describes mana as "one of the early, helpless expressions of what the apprehension of the infinite would be in its incipient stages" but goes on to note "the Melanesian Mana shows ample traces both of development and corruption" (loc. cit.).

Codrington reproduces his letter in *The Melanesians: Studies in Their Anthropology and Folk-lore*, 1st ed. (Oxford, 1891; reprint, New York, 1972), 118–19, n. 1. On Codrington, see G. W. Stocking, Jr., *After Tylor: British Social Anthropology, 1888–1951* (Madison, 1995), 34–46.

19. I note V. Valeri's comment, *Kingship and Sacrifice: Ritual and Society in Ancient Hawaii* (Chicago, 1985), 361, n. 15, "The history of the interpretation of mana remains to be written."

20. Codrington, *The Melanesians*, esp. 118–20, 191–92.

21. E. Tregear, *The Maori-Polynesian Comparative Dictionary* (Wellington, 1891; reprint, 1969), esp. 203.

22. J. N. B. Hewitt, "Orenda and a Definition of Religion," *American Anthropologist* n.s. 4 (1902): 33–46. While offering a wide ranging set of parallels, Hewitt does not mention mana.

23. R. R. Marett, "From Spell to Prayer," *Folk-Lore* 15 (1904): 132–65, reprinted in Marett, *The Threshold of Religion*, 1st ed. (London, 1909), 29–72. See further, Marett, "Pre-animistic Religion," *Folk-Lore* 11 (1900): 162–82 (*Threshold*, 1–28); "The Conception of Mana," *Transactions of the 3d International Congress of the History of Religions* (Oxford, 1908), 1: 46–57 (*Threshold*, 99–121); "The Tabu-Mana Formulation as a Minimum Definition of Religion," *Archiv für Religionswissenschaft* 12 (1909): 186–94 (reprinted in J. Waardenburg, *Classical Approaches to the Study of Religion* [The Hague, 1973], 1: 258–63); "Mana," *Encyclopaedia of Religion and Ethics*, ed. J. Hastings, 8: 375–80 (New York, 1916); "Mana," *Encyclopaedia Britannica*, 14th ed. (1929), 7: 770–71 (in later printings of this edition, Marett's article has been revised by R. M. Firth). See the recent treatment of Marett, with a useful bibliography, by M. Riesebrodt, "Robert Ran-

ulph Marett," in ed. A. Michaels, *Klassiker der Religionswissenschaft von Friederich Schleiermacher bis Mircea Eliade* (Munich, 1997), 171–84, 383–84.

24. H. Hubert and M. Mauss, "Esquisse d'un théorie générale de la magie," *Année sociologique* 7 (1904): 1–146; I cite the English translation, *A General Theory of Magic* (London, 1972), esp. 108–21. In a later autobiographical essay, Mauss stresses the importance of "Esquisse": "In particular, at the foundation of both magic and religion we discovered a vast common notion which we called *mana*, borrowing the term from the Melanesian-Polynesian language. The idea of mana is perhaps more general than that of the sacred." M. Mauss, "An Intellectual Self-Portrait," in P. Besnard, ed., *The Sociological Domain: The Durkheimians and the Founding of French Sociology* (Cambridge, 1983), 149. Cf. Hubert, "Étude sommaire de la représentation du temps dans la religion et la magie," *Annuaire de l'École Pratique des Hautes Études, section des sciences religieuses* (1905): esp. 30.

25. E. Durkheim, *Les Formes élémentaires de la vie religieuse: Le système totémique en Australie*, 2d ed. (Paris, 1922), esp. 268–92; compare the new English translation, *The Elementary Forms of Religious Life*, trans. K. E. Fields (New York, 1995), 190–206, which I cite below, in parentheses, with occasional modification, first giving the French and then the English pagination.

26. J. E. Harrison, *Themis: The Social Origins of Greek Religion*, 1st ed. (Cambridge, 1912); 2d ed. (Cambridge, 1927; reprint, 1962), 66–69, 84–85, 137–38 et passim.

27. F. R. Lehmann, *Mana: Eine begriffsgeschichtliche Untersuchung auf ethnologische Grundlage*, (Leipzig, 1915); 2nd ed., *Mana: Der Begriff des 'ausserordenlich Wirkungsvollen' bei Südseevölkern* (Leipzig, 1922); cf. Lehmann, "Versuche, die Bedeutung des Wortes Mana," in *Festschrift Walter Baetke*, ed. K. Rudolph, 215–40 (Weimar, 1966), 215–40.

28. Codrington, *The Melanesians*, 119, n. 1: "The word mana is both a noun substantive and . . . a transitive form of the verb."

29. While other work could have been mentioned, I have singled out H. I. Hogbin, "Mana," *Oceania* 6 (1936): 241–74; A. Capell, "The Word 'Mana': A Linguistic Study," *Oceania* 9 (1938): 89–96; R. Firth, "The Analysis of Mana: An Empirical Approach," *Journal of the Polynesian Society* 49 (1940): 483–510, reprinted in Firth, *Tikopia Ritual and Belief* (Boston, 1968), 174–94 and in *Cultures of the Pacific: Selected Readings*, ed. T. G. Harding- B. J. Wallace, 316–33 (New York, 1970); R. M. Keesing, "Rethinking Mana," *Journal of Anthropological Research* 46 (1984): 137–56. Keesing writes (138) that mana "is in Oceanic languages canonically a stative verb, not a noun. . . . Mana is used as a transitive verb as well. . . . Where mana is used as a noun, it is (usually) not as a substantive but as an abstract verbal noun denoting the state of quality of mana-ness (of a thing or act) or being-mana (of a person)." Note that this sort of understanding has en-

tered the wider public domain; see *Encyclopaedia Britannica*, 15th ed. Micropaedia, s.v. "mana."

For early examples of more general strictures on mana, see the harsh verdict of G. P. Murdock, *Our Primitive Contemporaries* (New York, 1934), xiii: "The author began with the intention of making full use of the concept [of mana]. In tribe after tribe, however, he found it inapplicable, the more so the more deeply he dug into the facts, and he ended without being able to use it at all. . . . In science, when a theory, however plausible, parts company with the facts, there is no choice; the theory must yield." Also, R. W. Williamson, *Essays in Polynesian Ethnology* (Cambridge, 1939), 264–65, who focuses on the issue of generalizability: "The beliefs, customs and usage connected with the Polynesian terms *mana* and *tapu* are so widely diverse that if we were to attempt to formulate definitions which would cover all of them, such formulations would be of such a general character that they might be attributed to any human culture."

30. C. Lévi-Strauss, "Introduction à l'oeuvre de Marcel Mauss," in Lévi-Strauss, *Sociologie et anthropologie par Marcel Mauss* (Paris, 1950), esp. xli–lii; compare the English translation, Lévi-Strauss, *Introduction to the Work of Marcel Mauss* (London, 1987), 50–66; P. Boyer, *Tradition as Truth and Communication: A Cognitive Description of Traditional Discourse* (Cambridge, 1990), esp. 27–30; M. Godelier, *L'Enigme du don* (Paris, 1996), I cite the English translation, Godelier, *The Enigma of the Gift* (Chicago, 1999), 18–29, et passim. The point of entry of Godelier's critique was to some extent anticipated in an essay first published in 1966 by J. Derrida; see Derrida, *Writing and Difference* (Chicago, 1978), 289–92. The proposal by Lévi-Strauss is prematurely dismissed by J. MacClancy, "Mana: An Anthropological Metaphor," *Oceania* 57 (1986): 148. I have discussed, with appreciation, the relationship of Lévi-Strauss to Durkheim at this point in J. Z. Smith, *To Take Place: Toward Theory in Ritual* (Chicago, 1987), 106–8. I draw on this discussion, below.

Because I have chosen to focus on the Durkheim/Lévi-Strauss trajectory, I omit discussion of the major monograph by Laura Makarius, *Le Sacré et la violation des interdits* (Paris, 1974), which constitutes a sustained and innovative reworking of the classical anthropological topoi associated with mana.

31. E. Durkheim, *Leçons de sociologie: Physique des moeurs et du droit*, ed. H. N. Kuball, Publications de l'Université d'Istanbul, Faculté de Droit, III (Istanbul, 1950), with a simultaneous publication in France (Paris, 1950), 133–75. For other important anticipations of central themes in *Elementary Forms*, see also Durkheim, *De la Division du travail social: Étude sur l'organisation des sociétés supérieures* (Paris, 1893); I cite the English translation, *The Division of Labor in Society* (New York, 1933), esp. 168–69; Durkheim, "De la Définition des phénomènes religieux," *Année sociologique* 2 (1899): 1–28; I cite the English translation, "Con-

cerning the Definition of Religious Phenomena," in W. S. F. Pickering, ed., *Durkheim on Religion* (Atlanta, 1994), 74–99.

32. The notion of tabu is central in Durkheim, "La Prohibition de l'inceste et ses origines," *Année sociologique* 1 (1898): 1–70; Durkheim, "Préface," *Année sociologique* 2 (1899): i–iv; as well as in the *Leçons de sociologie*.

33. Durkheim cites Müller's *Lectures on the Origin and Growth of Religion* (see above, n. 18) in "Definition," 76 and 98 n. 3.

34. See above, notes 23 and 24. See also Durkheim's discussion of both Marett and Hubert and Mauss in *Elementary Forms* (287–89/203–4).

35. Note that through either a mistranslation or a misprint, mana does appear in Australia in Fields's translation of Durkheim! In his chapter on positive rituals, Durkheim summarizes the account, in B. Spencer and F. J. Gillen, *The Native Tribes of Central Australia* (London, 1899; reprint, New York, 1968), 185–86, concerning the *intichiuma* ceremony of "the *Ilpirla* or manna totem." Spencer and Gillen had written that "*Ilpirla* is a form of 'manna' very similar to the well-known sugar-manna of gum trees but peculiar to the mulga tree (*Acacia aneura*)." Fields translates as follows: "In the clan of the Ilpirla (a sort of manna [*sorte de manne*]) . . . the group meets [in front of two groups of rocks]. . . . Both represent accumulations of manna [*des masses de manne*]. The Altjuna digs in the ground at the foot of these rocks and brings forth a churinga . . . that itself is like the quintessence of mana [*sic! comme de la quintessence de manne*] . . ." (470/333).

36. Hubert and Mauss, *General Theory of Magic*, 113–15. In connection with the Algonquin-Objibwa, *manitou*, Hubert and Mauss (114) cite the unpublished dictionary of Father Thavenet as quoted in "Tesa, *Studi del Thavenet*, Pisa, 1881, p. 17." In Durkheim (277, n.1/196, n. 21), the reference is given in even shorter form, "Tesa, *Studi del Thavenet*, p. 17," even though it had not been previously cited. The name of the author has been misspelled (Teza, not Tesa), and it is a serial rather than a monographic publication. The correct full reference should be E. Teza, *Intorno agli studi del Thavenet sulla lingua algonchina: Osservazioni di E. Teza*, Annali delle Università Toscane, 18 (Pisa, 1880), 17, as cited in A. M. di Nola, "Religione degli Algonchini centrali," *Enciclopedia delle religioni*, ed. A. M. di Nola, 1: 172–73 (Florence, 1970). The reference in Hubert and Mauss is largely corrected in a translator's note by F. Baker to her translation of C. Lévi-Strauss, *Introduction to the Work of Marcel Mauss* (London, 1987), 71, n. 13. Emilio Teza was a stunningly polylingual philologian whose work includes not only translations from many European languages but also an interest in Native American languages. See, among other publications, Teza, *Saggi inediti de lingua Americana: Appunti bibliografici* (Pisa, 1868).

37. Durkheim as translator is an insufficiently studied topic. I focus attention, here, only on Durkheim's translation of the pages in Codrington's *Melane-*

sians devoted to mana. Karen E. Fields, in her translation of *Elementary Forms*, 59, n. 26, 327, n. 102, has provided two brief notes on this topic. The first is mistaken. She claims that Durkheim's citation of Codrington, p. 125, is incorrect: "the quotation does not appear there." In my judgement, Durkheim's translation, "*des riens après comme avant la mort*" (88) is a reasonable translation of Codrington, "nobodies alike before and after death." The second observes correctly that Durkheim has provided two slightly different renderings of the same sentence in Codrington, p. 119, n. 1, continued, "This Mana is not fixed in anything, and can be conveyed in almost anything." Durkheim first translates, "*Le mana n'est point fixé sur un object déterminé; il peut être amené sur toute espèce de choses . . .*" (277), and later translates it, with added italics, as: mana is a force which "*n'est point fixée sur an object matériel, mais qui peut être amenée sur presque toute espèce d'objet*" (461). Both translations are reasonable; though Durkheim, for his own purpose, makes Codrington's vaguer "anything" into a more definite "*objet*." What is more disturbing about Durkheim's quotation of Codrington, in the first instance, is the ellipsis points indicating an omission; it is a full stop in the second instance. Durkheim is using this quotation, among other reasons, to support his view of impersonality. He, therefore, halts the quote at the point that Codrington continues, ". . . and can be conveyed in almost anything; but spirits, whether disembodied souls or supernatural beings, have it and can impart it; and it essentially belongs to personal beings to originate it, though it may act through the medium of water, or a stone, or a bone." I must agree with E. J. Sharpe that the notion that mana-like concepts have reference to impersonal forces "comes not from Marett but from Durkheim" (Sharpe, "Preanimism," in *Encyclopedia of Religion*, ed. M. Eliade, 11: 503 [New York, 1987]).

38. In their *General Theory of Magic*, 115, Hubert and Mauss follow their presentation of the Oceanic and Native American materials with a brief paragraph on "a concept of a similar kind" in Australia, noting that "here it is clearly restricted to magical activities, and more particularly to black magic." As would be anticipated, Durkheim reexamines this data at greater length (280–83/198–200). He offers two general arguments to explain this difference and, by implication, to give reasons for why he cannot find an unambiguous cognate for mana in Australia. His first argument is one of "social milieu," that clan autonomy, and the distinction of each totemic group from the other, mitigates against a notion "that these heterogeneous worlds were only different manifestations of one and the same fundamental force." For this reason, a true mana-like concept among the Australian aborigines would be unlikely. Second, in Australia, unlike clan-based totemism, magic is "not attached to any definite social division." Therefore, it is plausible that, there, a mana-like concept would be more likely to be associated with magic.

39. Because Irving Goldman is one of the few anthropologists to write im-

portant monographs on both Polynesian and Kwakiutl societies, I call attention to his brief comparison between the Oceanic term *mana* and the Kwakiutl term *nawalak*, held to be its synonym in Hubert and Mauss and in Durkheim. See Goldman, *The Mouth of Heaven: An Introduction to Kwakiutl Religious Thought* (New York, 1975), 2–3, 179–82; compare his discussion of Polynesian mana with Goldman, *Ancient Polynesian Society* (Chicago, 1970), 10–13, et passim. Note that throughout this latter work, Goldman takes great pain to characterize the specific understanding of "sanctity" (Goldman's general term for mana) in each society he discusses.

40. For an early statement, see Durkheim, *Le suicide: Étude de sociologie* (Paris, 1897); English translation (New York, 1951), 309–310: "Collective tendencies have an existence of their own; they are forces as real as cosmic forces, though of a different sort; they, likewise, affect the individual from without, though through other channels. The proof that the reality of collective tendencies is no less than that of cosmic forces is that this reality is demonstrated in the same way, by the uniformity of effects. . . . Whatever they are called, the important thing is to recognize their reality and conceive of them as a totality of forces which cause us to act from without, like the physico-chemical forces to which we react. So truly are they things *sui generis* and not mere verbal entities that they may be measured . . . as is done with the intensity of electric currents or luminous foci. Thus, the basic proposition that social facts are objective. . . . Of course it offends common sense. But science has encountered incredulity whenever it has revealed to men the existence of a force that has been overlooked."

41. J. Z. Smith, *To Take Place: Toward Theory in Ritual* (Chicago, 1987), esp. 106–8 and the notes on 174–75. I have drawn on these pages, above.

42. Lévi-Strauss, "Introduction à l'oeuvre de Marcel Mauss," xliii; cf. F. Baker's English translation, 53, which I have not quoted but have cited in parentheses below. Note Lévi-Strauss's quite different argument in *Totemism* (Boston, 1963), 31–32, where he argues on grounds of ethnographic accuracy against the Durkheimian confusion, resulting from the "totemic illusion," between totem, mana and tabu.

43. Lévi-Strauss, "Introduction à l'oeuvre de Marcel Mauss," xliii (54). On Thavenet, see above, note 36. The original Italian reads, "*Quando si tratta di un essere animato che non ha alcun nome di specie, o del quale non si conosce il nome, lo si distingue con il nome generico di manito.*" Note, however, that this citation is immediately preceded by a more conventional understanding of the term: "*Credo che questa parola Manito è il nome generico nel quale sono compresi tutti gli esseri animati, di qualsiasi specie . . .*" (Teza, *Thavenet sulla lingua algonchina*, 17). To Lévi-Strauss's understanding of this quotation and the ethnographic illustrations he adduces can be added others, such as W. K. Power, *Oglala Religion* (Lincoln, 1977), who offers a short list of compound names employing the element *wakan*,

"which were applied to items newly obtained from other Indians or the white man" (47).

44. Lévi-Strauss, "Introduction à l'oeuvre de Marcel Mauss," xliv (54).

45. Lévi-Strauss, "Introduction à l'oeuvre de Marcel Mauss," l, n. 1 (omitted in Baker's translation).

46. Lévi-Strauss, "Introduction à l'oeuvre de Marcel Mauss," xlvii–l (59–64); cf. Boyer, *Tradition as Truth and Communication*, 27. Lévi-Strauss cites, in a footnote (l, n. 1 [72, n. 18]), R. Jakobson and J. Lotz, "Notes on the French Phonemic Pattern," *Word*, 5 (1949), reprinted in Jakobson, *Selected Writings* (The Hague, 1962), 1: 426–34, for the notion of a "*phonème zéro.*"

47. Lévi-Strauss, "Introduction à l'oeuvre de Marcel Mauss," xlv (57).

48. H. Penner, "Holistic Analysis: Conjectures and Refutations," *Journal of the American Academy of Religion* 62 (1994): 989.

49. Keesing, "Rethinking Mana," 148.

50. See further, J. Z. Smith, "A Twice-told Tale: The History of the History of Religion's History," in *Numen*, reprinted below. Note that Keesing has given his views on translation in "Conventional Metaphors and Anthropological Metaphysics: The Problematic of Cultural Translation," *Journal of Anthropological Research* 41 (1985): 201–17. His most valuable caution is that he remains a "skeptic about attributing deeper salience to other people's conventional metaphors than we do to our own."

51. See, already, H. H. Penner and E. A. Yonan, "Is a Science of Religion Possible?" *Journal of Religion* 52 (1972): 107–33. See also S. I. Landau, *Dictionaries: The Art and Craft of Lexicography* (Cambridge, 1989), 20. With respect to mana, while intended critically, see the comments by R. Firth, "The Analysis of Mana," as reprinted in Harding and Wallace, 325 and 318: "To the Tikopia, *manu* I am sure has not the connotation of an isolatable principle, a force, a power, or any other metaphysical abstraction. . . . The interpretation in terms of such abstraction can only be the work of the anthropologist." "Treated in this manner, the word *mana* becomes something of a technical term describing a specialized abstraction of the theoretical anthropologist and, as such, may have little in common with the same term as used in native phraseology." Rather than being abjured, this difference needs to be accepted by students of religion. See further, J. Z. Smith, "Twice-told Tale."

THE DOMESTICATION OF SACRIFICE

In their eagerness to plumb ritual's dark symbolic or functional depths, to find in ritual more than meets the eye, anthropologists have, perhaps increasingly, tended to overlook ritual's surface, that which does meet the eye. Yet, it is on its surfaces, in its form, that we may discern whatever may be peculiar to ritual.

R. A. RAPPAPORT

I

ONE CONSENSUAL ELEMENT that appears to inform this "conversation on a theory of ritual" is a marked restlessness with the reduction of ritual to myth and a concomitant concern with "action" as a mode of human expression and experience that has a necessary integrity of its own.[1] In the elaboration of such a point of view, little will be gained by simply inverting past valences,[2] by adopting Goethe's stratagem of substituting "in the beginning was the deed" for "was the word." Although such an inversion could be questioned on logical grounds alone, there are other reasons more pressing to the concerns of this conversation. Chief among these is that, in the case of man, speech and action are given together. Neither is prior, in fact or in thought.[3] The connection is both so necessary and so intimate as to challenge all analogies where this duality is lacking (e.g., the animal on the one hand, the computer on the other). If action is not an "acting out" of speech, neither is speech a "secondary rationalization" of deed. In the history of this debate, much mischief has been done by the seemingly one-sided association of speech with thought and rationality, rather than perceiving action and speech, ritual and myth, as being coeval modes of human cognition.

Likewise, little will be gained by reinstating the old hierarchy by way of the back door. I have been struck by the desire of many who hold to the priority of action/ritual to find a story or a "primal scene" at the "origin" (itself, a narrative or mythological notion) of rite, be this expressed as tale or emotion, as articulate or inarticulate. In the one case, action has slid, all too easily, into "drama"; in the other, a consequence has been affirmed, all too readily, as a cause.

In thinking about a "theory of ritual," it would seem more fruitful to focus on the characteristics of those actions that, by one definition or another, *we* designate as 'rituals,' and to abstain from initial concern for content, which, among other problems, inevitably forces a premature return to myth. For me, in undertaking such an enterprise, the central theoretical works are two: Freud's brief essay "Zwangshandlungen und Religionsübungen" (1907) and the exasperating and controversial "Finale" to Lévi-Strauss's *L'Homme nu* (1971).

As is well known, Freud, in this first essay on religion, remarked on the resemblance between "what are called obsessive actions in sufferers from nervous afflictions and the observances by means of which believers give expression to their piety." The connection was to be found in the notion of "obsession," in the compulsion to do particular things and to abstain from others. The things done and the things not done are ordinary, "everyday" activities that are elaborated and made "rhythmic" by additions and repetitions. Obsessive acts in both individuals and rituals are described as the overwhelming concern for

> little preoccupations, performances, restrictions and arrangements in certain activities of everyday life which have to be carried out always in the same or in a methodically varied way . . . elaborated by petty modifications [and] little details [accompanied by the] tendency to displacement [which] turns apparently trivial matters into those of great and urgent import.

In this early essay, the defining characteristic of ritual is "conscientiousness [toward] details": "Thus in slight cases the ceremonial seems to be no more than an exaggeration of an orderly procedure that is customary and justifiable; but the special conscientiousness with which it is carried out . . . stamps the ceremonial as a sacred act."[4]

In Freud's essay, although a set of five summarized cases are offered as examples of individual obsessive behavior, no specific examples of religious ceremonial are provided. In the chapter in Lévi-Strauss, the religious examples are specified as those instances where "a ritual ceremony has been recorded and transcribed in its entirety," which may "fill a whole volume, sometimes a very large one" and take "days" to perform.[5] Lévi-Strauss's characterizations of ritual are drawn from "thick" ethnographic texts, from transcripts of an entire ritual rather than from a brief ethnographic "snapshot." As such, they are to be given particular value.

Lévi-Strauss begins with the two questions that confront any theorist of ritual: how are we to define ritual? how are the actions in ritual to be distinguished from their close counterparts in everyday life? He answers both of these questions (like Freud) by way of a characterization: "In all cases, ritual makes constant use of two procedures: parcelling out [*morcellement*] and repetition." Parcelling out is defined as that activity where, "within classes of objects and types of gesture, ritual makes infinite distinctions and ascribes discriminatory values to the slightest shades of difference."[6] Parcelling out is what he elsewhere describes as the processes of "micro-adjustment" (*micro-péréquation*), which he holds to be the characteristic activity of ritual.[7]

Alongside this "infinite attention to detail" is the second characteristic, that of a "riot of repetition." Lévi-Strauss proposes a further reduction of these two characteristics: "At first glance, the two devices of parcelling out and repetition are in opposition to each other. . . . But, in fact, the first procedure is equivalent to the second, which represents, so to speak, its extreme development."[8] One does not have to be persuaded of the cogency of this reduction to accept the accuracy of the two characteristics.[9]

I have not cited these two theorists in order to urge acceptance of their theories (which are, in fact, thoroughly incompatible) but rather to insist on the accuracy of their complementary characterizations of the surface appearance of ritual. They have presented us with a prima facie case for what is distinctive in ritual. Freely paraphrasing, both insist that ritual activities are an exaggeration of everyday activities, but an exaggeration that reduces rather than enlarges, that clarifies by miniaturizing in order to achieve sharp focus. Collecting their terms, ritual is the realm of the "little," the "petty," the "trivial." It is the realm of "infinite distinctions" and "micro-adjustments." Ritual is primarily a matter not of nouns and verbs, but of qualifiers—of adjectives and adverbs. Ritual precises ambiguities.

While I would derive a host of implications from these characterizations for a "general theory of ritual," one is of particular importance for this conversation. To put it crudely, ritual is "no big deal." The object of action that receives ritual attention is, more often than not, commonplace. The choice of this or that object for ritual attention often appears arbitrary. But what is of prime importance is its infinite and infinitesimal elaboration in the manner that Freud and Lévi-Strauss have suggested. One cannot single out a highly condensed or dramatic moment from the total ritual ensemble as if this, in some sense, was the "essence" of the ritual.

These considerations underscore the position that a theory of sacrifice (our specific topic for this conversation) cannot be found in a quest for origins but can only be found through the detailed examination of elaborations. The idioms of sacrifice are diverse; the everyday acts it elaborates are manifold (e.g., butchering, eating, exchanging, gift-giving, greeting, displaying); the contexts in which sacrifice gets applied and rationalized are highly variegated. Until there is an adequate typology accompanied by "thick descriptions" of exemplary ritual processes and ensembles, little progress will be made. To my knowledge, neither of these preconditions has been adequately fulfilled.

Let me make clear that this is not a request for more data, but a theoretical stance. I have tried to express this stance, in a quite different context, as a denial of

> the privilege given to spontaneity as over against the fixed, to originality as over against the dependent, to the direct as over against the mediated. . . . This is expressed in the learned literature in a variety of dichotomies: religion/magic, individual/collective, charisma/routinization, communion/formalism, the text as direct speech over against the commentary and the gloss, the original or primordial over against the secondary or historical. In elegant form this privilege is expressed in the writings of a scholar such as Adolf Jensen for whom all truth, meaning, and value is located in what he describes as a primal moment of ontic "seizure," a "revelation," a "direct cognition." The first verbal "formulation" of this experience, its first "concretization" is an "intuitive, spontaneous experiencing" which he terms, "expression." All subsequent "formalizations" and "concretizations" are reinterpretations of this primal experience which Jensen terms "applications" (for him, a pejorative). All "applications" fall under the iron "law of degeneration" resulting in the original "spontaneity" becoming a "fixed but no longer understood routine." [In contradistinction, I would propose an enterprise that would insist on] the value of the prosaic, the expository, the articulate. It is to explore the creativity of what I have termed in another context, "exegetical ingenuity," as a basic constituent of human culture. It is to gain an appreciation of the complex dynamics of tradition and its necessary dialectics of self-limitation

and freedom. To do these things . . . is to give expression to what I believe is the central contribution that religious studies might make, . . . the realization that, in culture, there is no text, it is all commentary; that there is no primordium, it is all history; that all is application. The realization that, regardless of whether we are dealing with "texts" from literate or non-literate cultures, we are dealing with historical processes of reinterpretation, with tradition. That, for a given group at a given time to choose this or that way of interpreting their tradition is to opt for a particular way of relating themselves to their historical past and their social present.[10]

Despite the above, although a quite different enterprise from my usual agendum, in accommodation to what appears to be one of the dominant concerns of the present conversation, I will venture a highly tentative suggestion on the possible activity that achieved prime elaboration in sacrifice.

II

From the immense variety of human ritual activities, a few have been lifted out by scholars as privileged examples on which to build theories of ritual—preeminently sacrifice, New Year's scenarios, and male initiatory rites. Each of these three seems to entail quite different consequences for scholarship. The choice of which one is to be taken as exemplary is one of great significance.[11] Having said this much, let me note that, among this small group, animal sacrifice has often appeared to be primus inter pares, primarily because it has seemed (at least to the scholarly imagination) quintessentially 'primitive.' Perhaps the first question that ought to be asked is, Is this the case?[12]

The putative 'evidence' for the primitivity of animal sacrifice is far from compelling. Though there are obvious questions of definition, of what counts, I know of no unambiguous instance of animal sacrifice that is not of a domesticated animal. The Paleolithic indications for sacrifice are dubious. I know of no unambiguous instance of animal sacrifice performed by hunters. *Animal sacrifice appears to be, universally, the ritual killing of a domesticated animal by agrarian or pastoralist societies.* Where it occurs in groups otherwise classified, it is still of a domesticated animal, usually in the context of a highly developed 'exchange (or display)' ideology. Furthermore, though I am unhappy with many of the interpretative implications developed from the familiar dual typology, where there are articulate native systems of animal sacrifice, they do appear to fall into the categories of gift-offering-display and/or pollution removal. Neither gives comfort to primitivity. The former seems to require a developed notion of property; the latter, the complex ideological and social hierarchies of pure/impure. As best as I can judge, sacrifice is not a primitive element in culture. Sacrifice is a component of secondary and tertiary cultures. It is, primarily, a product of 'civilization.'

Why, then, the preoccupation with the primitivity of sacrifice? Beyond its obvious resonances with elements of our past, with Greco-Roman and Judeo-Christian religious systems and practices, I suspect that sacrifice allows some scholars the notion that here, in this religious phenomenon at least (or at last), is a dramatic encounter with an 'other,' the slaying of a beast. As I have suggested elsewhere, such a notion rests on an agrarian mythologization of the hunt and is not characteristic of what we can learn of the attitudes of hunting-and-gathering peoples toward the activities of hunting.[13] This agrarian reinterpretation (interesting and important as it is in itself) has allowed the scholarly fantasy that ritual is an affair of the *tremendum* rather than a quite ordinary mode of human social labor. It has allowed the notion that ritual—and therefore religion—is somehow grounded in "brute fact" rather than in the work and imagination and intellection of culture.

It may well be for these reasons that one of the other privileged modes of ritual, initiation, has not been so vigorously put forth as the exemplum of primitivity. This is surprising in light of the fact that many of those early reports that asserted that this or that primitive group had "no religion" (reports that led, ultimately, to the overdrawn theses of *Urmonotheismus*, particularly in the form of the "otiose High God") specifically noted no sacrificial practices, but did report (often in lurid terms) the presence of initiatory practices and secret societies.[14] It is my sense, after surveying a wide sample of literature, that sacrifice and initiation stand in an inverse ratio to each other: where there are elaborate initiatory rituals, sacrifice seems relatively undeveloped; where there are complex sacrificial cycles and ideologies, initiation seems relatively undeveloped. Indeed, I am tempted to suggest that initiation is for the hunter and gatherer and primitive agriculturalist what sacrifice is for the agrarian and pastoralist. But initiation is relentlessly an affair of 'culture' rather than 'nature,' and one of making ordinary what appears to be an experience of the *tremendum*.[15] Furthermore, the temporal dimensions of initiation (at times an affair of twenty years, with highly ambiguous limits),[16] in contrast to the extreme binary compression and irreversibility of the sacrificial kill, make clear that initiation is an affair more of social labor than of drama.

Given these observations, I hazard the opinion that the starting point for a theory of sacrifice, that which looms largest in a redescription of sacrifice, ought no longer to be the verb 'to kill,' or the noun 'animal,' but the adjective 'domesticated.' Sacrifice is, in part, a meditation on domestication. A theory of sacrifice must begin with the domesticated animal and with the sociocultural process of domestication itself. In such an enterprise, we are aided by a recent rich literature on the historical processes of domestication, and on "domesticity" as a native, taxonomic category.[17]

Following current usage, domestication may be defined as the process of human interference in or alteration of the genetics of plants and animals (i.e., selective breeding). It is frequently, although not necessarily, associated with agriculture, which may be defined as the process of human interference in or alteration of the environment of plants and animals. Such processes of interference presuppose a variety of social developments and result in a variety of social consequences.

For an understanding of sacrifice (and other agrarian ritual activities), the most important consequence is an alteration of the sense of space and time. The most obvious spatial and temporal reorientation associated with domestication is signaled by the term "sedentary community." This marks a shift from the hunter-and-gatherer's social world of immediacy, skill, and chance to a social world of futurity and planning—of the capacity for continuity of time and place. This is apparent with respect to animals. Here the art of breeding is, as well, the art of selective killing. Some animals must be held separated out for several years until they reach sexual maturity. The bulk of the herd must be slaughtered while immature. In the domesticated situation (as the archaeological stratigraphy bears out), immature animals will be killed more frequently than mature ones, males more frequently than females, and so forth and so on. For the domesticator, killing is an act of precise discrimination with an eye to the future. It is dependent on the social acceptance of a "delayed payoff," as well as on the social acquisition of the intricate technology of sexuality and the concomitant pattern of settled dwelling.

If this everyday and continual activity of domestication is agrarian and pastoral man's prime mode of relating to the animal, then we can specify with precision the commonplace activity that is elaborated obsessively and intellectually in sacrifice, as well as its difference from the hunter's relationship to game: *sacrifice is an elaboration of the selective kill, in contradistinction to the fortuitous kill.*

Though I do not wish to strain the point, it does appear that the other elements characteristic of domestication have their concomitant elaborations in sacrifice. The notion of the "delayed payoff" is central to any but the most mechanical *do ut des* understanding of the gift structure of some sacrificial systems, but it is present in some pollution systems as well. (For example, in the Israelitic cult, washing with water works for immediate, advertent pollutions, whereas the *ḥaṭṭāt* is for inadvertent impurities that one may or may not be aware of, or for pollutions that last more than a week.) Furthermore, sacrifice is not fortuitous with respect to either time or place—it is highly determined and presumes a sedentary pattern.[18] Finally, in many sacrificial systems, the complex requirements for the physical and/or behavioral characteristics of a particular animal chosen (bred) for sacrifice, whether before or after the kill, represent to an extreme degree the same kinds of details that are sexually selected for by the breeder.[19]

All of these elements, governed in the majority of cases by elaborate, highly formalized rules, suggest that sacrifice is an exaggeration of domestication, a meditation on one cultural process by means of another. If domestication is a 'focusing' on selected characteristics in the animal, a process of sexual 'experimentation' that strives to achieve a 'perfection' or 'rectification' of the natural animal species (these terms are key elements in my vocabulary for ritual), then sacrifice becomes a focus on this focus, an experimentation with this experimentation, a perfecting of this perfection, a rectification of this rectification. It can do this precisely because it is a ritual. *Sacrifice, in its agrarian or pastoral context, is the artificial (i.e., ritualized) killing of an artificial (i.e., domesticated) animal.*[20] Because sacrifice is inextricably related to alimentation and, therefore, to what I have elsewhere described as a basic cultural process of reduction and ingenuity, of food and cuisine, it is, perhaps, especially suited for this sort of meditation.[21]

What has been proposed thus far could be further elaborated with respect to the taxonomies of domesticated animals in relation to humans, on the one hand, and to animals on the other.[22] Just as the role of the mask in initiation ceremonies, as interpreted by Victor Turner,[23] where the artificial, radical mixture or juxtaposition of anatomical features from humans and animals serves as an occasion for cultural meditation on difference and relationship; so too in the case of a domesticated animal, which is, in some sense, a hybrid, a fabrication. Furthermore, if the domesticated animal stands, in native taxonomies, between man and the wild animal, then, to invoke a more familiar scholarly idiom for sacrifice, the sacrificial animal stands in an analogous position between man and "the gods." The transactional character of both positions relativizes the apparent absolute difference. (Hence the frequently observed correspondence of kin taxonomies and rules for sexual relations to taxonomies for domesticated animals and rules for their eating or sacrifice.) Sacrifice accomplishes this not by sacramentalism, but by an etiquette of infinite degrees and baroque complexities.[24] But to develop such a thesis with any cogency and conviction demands particularities rather than generalities: the comparison of specific exemplary taxonomies of domesticates with specific exemplary sacrificial ensembles. The detail such a discussion would require goes well beyond the bounds of civil "conversation."

If Lévi-Strauss, through a discussion of wild animals in the "totemic" systems of hunters and gatherers, has taught us well that animals are "good to eat" and "good to think," then the domesticated animals in the sacrificial systems of agriculturalists and pastoralists may teach us, in analogous ways, that animals are "goods to eat" and "goods to think."

Appendix

As is well known, the observations that "ritual killing is completely absent in the oldest known strata of culture" and that animal sacrifices are "almost exclusively of domestic animals, for they all occur in agricultural cultures" stand at the foundation of A. E. Jensen's theory of sacrifice and ritual killing.[25] Jensen uses these observations to reason to a different set of conclusions than those proposed here.

It would require a lengthy monograph to review critically all the putative evidence that has been adduced for the primitivity of animal sacrifice and to cite the evidence for the stark assertions made above. Since the issue of primitivity is without interest for me, someone else will have to provide such a work. (I would propose J. van Baal, the distinguished scholar of *dema*, who has more than once offered a similar assessment, although I share none of his presuppositions.)[26] However, some brief indications may be provided:

1. The Paleolithic evidence remains opaque to interpretation. Since the work of F. E. Koby,[27] the evidence for Paleolithic bear sacrifice has been rendered exceedingly doubtful.[28] This is extremely important because the only contemporary putative evidence for a wild animal being used in sacrifice is the circum-polar bear festival.

In fact, the bear festival does not fit, although it was used as the hermeneutic key to interpret the Paleolithic remains. (a) The peoples who practice the bear festivals are pastoralists, not hunters. While the figure of the "Master of the Animals" appears to be shared by them and some hunters (especially the Amerindians), among the latter there is no recorded sacrifice of wild game. The conception of the "Master" among the reindeer pastoralists is in the idiom of pastoralism (penning the animals and the like). It is possible that this is a notion independent from that of the "Master" among hunters. If not, it is a radical reinterpretation that forbids any easy synthesis. (b) In the circum-polar bear ritual, the animal is domesticated for a period of years before being slain. (c) In the case of the Ainu (for whom there is the best ethnographic documentation), both the most distinguished native Ainu anthropologist, K. Kindaichi and the bear festival's most distinguished recent interpreter, J. M. Kitagawa, vigorously deny that the ritual should be classified as a sacrifice, seeing it instead as part of a complex structure of visit-and-return.[29] At the very least, the complex tissue of parallelism, invoked since the pioneering article by W. Koppers,[30] will have to be carefully reevaluated. Both terms of the proposed equation are in difficulty. The equation has been decisive in the literature on the primitivity of animal sacrifice.

2. On the issue of Paleolithic sacrifices, the evaluation of the evidence has been one of steady retreat from confidence to uncertainty. For example, J. Maringer, who confidently declared in 1952 that "the practice of sacrificing the head, skull and long bones of animals survived from earliest times right up to the Upper Paleolithic,"[31] retreated by 1968 to declaring that sacrifice is not evident in Lower and Middle Paleolithic deposits, and that it is possible to speak "with relatively great certainty" (*"mit mehr oder minder grosser Sicherheit"*) of animal sacrifices only in the Upper Paleolithic.[32] Yet even here, strong alternative hypotheses that account for the "evidence" as nonsacrificial have been proposed, as Maringer acknowledges.[33]

3. The fact that sacrifices are invariably of domesticated animals in contrast to wild ones (and hence from a different "sphere" than religious practices associated with hunters or Paleolithic man) was already quite properly insisted upon by L. Franz.[34] Several months of checking in a variety of ethnographic monographs have turned up no exceptions. Here, I distinguish between killing an animal in sacrifice and the postmortem offering of some portion of an animal routinely killed for food. The latter is certainly present among some hunters and gatherers.

There are occasions of the ritual killing and eating of wild animals in connection with initiatory rituals, most particularly initiations into secret societies. The Lele pangolin, made famous by M. Douglas,[35] would be an obvious example, although she gives no reliable description. I sharply distinguish this from sacrifice, and would classify the bulk of the instances known to me as modes of ordeal.

I would also note the interesting thesis—first developed by E. Hahn, C. O. Sauer, and others and recently revived by E. Isaac—that animals were first domesticated for the purpose of sacrifice.[36]

4. In the discussion of the primitivity of animal sacrifice, much depends on how one imagines hunters (Paleolithic or contemporary). I join in the consensus that there never was, and certainly is not now, a stage of pure hunting. Hunting is always in combination with gathering, with plant products making up the bulk of the diet (except in unusual cases, such as that of the Eskimos).

It is, of course, impossible to determine the diet of Paleolithic man. Only animal bones, mollusk shells, and the like can be preserved, not soft parts and vegetable substances. For contemporary hunters and gatherers, a figure that approximately 70 percent of their normal diet is vegetable occurs in a variety of cultural locales, from the Amazon to Australia.[37] Furthermore, if one examines a wide variety of ethnographic reports, it becomes clear that the meat portion of the diet, that which is the result of hunting, is composed largely of small mammals, birds, reptiles, eggs, insects, fish, and mollusks. *Mano a mano* combat with large carnivores is largely unreported. For example, among the Desana, although their mythology is largely concerned with jaguars, Reichel-Dolmatoff reports that "a man who goes to hunt for two or three days per week obtains approximately three catches, for example, a small rodent, an armadillo, and a few birds. In a month he can get three or four wild guinea pigs, two cavies and a monkey; a deer or a peccary every two months; and a tapir once a year."[38] If bored-through teeth (trophies?) are any indication of the results of a Paleolithic hunt, 56 percent of a wide sample of such teeth are those of fox and deer, and only 3 percent are of bear or wolf.[39]

Finally, as I insisted in "The Bare Facts of Ritual,"[40] we need to recognize the strong ideological component in hunting. Although men routinely gather, and women in some societies routinely hunt (e.g., Efe pygmies, Klamath Indians, Tasmanians, the Australian Tiwi), hunting is strongly marked as a prestigious male activity, even when the males rarely hunt. Though the native descriptions of killing strongly emphasize its *mano a mano* character, in some of those same societies, traps, stampedes, ambushes, and the like are widely employed.

5. I have not raised the issue, widely discussed in some German anthropological circles, that many of our present hunting-and-gathering societies may be derivative from earlier agricultural societies.[41] But this may need to be taken into account in evaluating a particular report, as

does the more recent influence of agrarians on pastoralists and hunters and gatherers (especially in Africa and northern Eurasia).[42]

Notes

1. Compare R. A. Rappaport, *Ecology, Meaning and Religion* (Richmond, Calif., 1979), 174: "It becomes apparent through a consideration of ritual's form that ritual is not simply an alternative way to express certain things, but that certain things can be expressed only in ritual." The quotation from Rappaport used as the epigraph, above, is from the same page.

2. I am speaking here at the level of theory. There is much to commend the detailed investigations of a variety of scholars, from C. Lévi-Strauss to S. Tambiah, which have demonstrated that, in a wide variety of cultural situations, myth and rite often stand in an inverse relationship to one another.

3. Here, as elsewhere, I mean "social man."

4. S. Freud, "Obsessive Acts and Ritual Practices," in J. Riviere, ed., *Sigmund Freud, M.D., L.L.D.: Collected Papers* (London, 1924), 2: 25–35, quotations on 26, 34. In presenting this aspect of Freud, I have deliberately abstained from his genetic account, which is here less important than his characterization, in that I am proposing, here, an analogy. A theory of ritual, in any case, could not be constructed on the basis of the 1907 essay, "Obsessive Acts and Ritual Practices," alone. A far more interesting genetic proposal—although one equally remote from the concerns of my essay—is Freud's late notion of a "compulsion to repeat" as sketched out in *Beyond the Pleasure Principle* (1920), ed. G. Zilboorg (New York, 1959), 40–46 et passim. See further, V. Gay, "Psychopathology and Ritual," *Psychoanalytic Review* 62 (1975): 493–507, and Gay, *Freud on Ritual: Reconstruction and Critique* (Missoula, 1979), esp. ch. 3.

5. C. Lévi-Strauss, *L'Homme nu* (Paris, 1971), 600–1, Mythologiques, 4; English translation, *The Naked Man* (New York, 1981), 672. His specific examples make clear that he is primarily thinking of the accounts of ritual in those thick, green Reports of the Bureau of American Ethnology, which he celebrates in "The Work of the Bureau of American Ethnology and Its Lessons," Lévi-Strauss, *Structural Anthropology* (New York, 1976), 2: 49–59.

6. Lévi-Strauss, *L'Homme nu*, 601, *The Naked Man*, 672.

7. C. Lévi-Strauss, *La Pensée sauvage* (Paris, 1962), 17; English translation, *The Savage Mind* (Chicago, 1966): 10.

8. Lévi-Strauss, *L'Homme nu*, 602, *The Naked Man*, 673.

9. As with Freud (note 4 above), so here I have abstained from accepting the implications that Lévi-Strauss draws from this characterization of ritual, that if myth and language are perceived as dichotomizing and contrastive, then ritual seeks to "counter" myth and "to move back from the discontinuous to the con-

tinuous" (*L'Homme nu*, 603, *The Naked Man*, 674). In my own work, I have taken, rather, the opposite view. See, for example, J. Z. Smith, *To Take Place: Toward Theory in Ritual* (Chicago, 1987), 110–12.

10. J. Z. Smith, "No Need to Travel to the Indies: Judaism and the Study of Religion," in J. Neusner, ed., *Take Judaism, For Example* (Chicago, 1983), 223–24.

11. In the discussion which followed the original delivery of this paper, I expanded on this point.

> Out of all the hundreds of types of ritual you could describe, those three [sacrifice, New Year's, and male initiations] have been plucked up, and each has a characteristic form of data associated with it, and each seems to involve one in a characteristic stance. . . . Those who favor New Year's have largely been people who really do want to emphasize the language of repetition, who want to try and get a cosmic dimension. It's not just Eliade . . . it's where the category of myth becomes terribly important. It's no accident that the myth-ritual school does its work best there. . . . If you are interested in stability, interested in repetition, interested in a kind of prioritizing of myth, then chances are you are going to build your theory on New Year's rituals. . . . If you are interested . . . in sacrifice or initiation, your stance will be commensurately different: there is a tendency for those who like otherness and drama to come down on sacrifice, and those who have the notion of a long-range social project to come down on the initiation material (*Violent Origins:* 208–9).

12. I have abstained from the question of human sacrifice and other modes of the ritual killing of humans, which are often too readily homologized to animal sacrifice in the scholarly literature. The evidence for these practices is frequently less certain than for animal sacrifice—often (but not always) being more illustrative of intercultural polemics than cultural facts. Nevertheless, a rapid review would indicate that well-documented human sacrifice is present only in agricultural or pastoral cultures. The other modes of ritual killing, while requiring their own interpretations, are not to be classed as "sacrifice."

13. J. Z. Smith, *Imagining Religion* (Chicago, 1982), 57–58.

14. Ibid., 66–89, 145–56.

15. On initiation as an affair of culture, consider, for example, the lack of correlation between biological puberty and the so-called puberty initiations, already clearly perceived, in 1909, by A. van Gennep, *Rites of Passage* (Chicago, 1960), 65–71. On making 'ordinary' what has been taken as an experience of the *tremendum*, consider, for example, the frequent phenomenon of the unmasking of the putative deities. See the survey in A. di Nola, "Demythicization in Certain

Primitive Cultures," *History of Religions* 12 (21972): 1–27, and the comments in Smith, *Map Is Not Territory*, 300–2.

16. For a detailed description of an elegant example, see D. F. Tuzin, *The Voice of the Tambaran* (Berkeley, 1980).

17. For the historical processes, see, among others, P. J. Ucko and G. W. Dimbleby, eds., *The Domestication and Exploitation of Plants and Animals* (Chicago, 1969); and E. Isaac, *Geography of Domestication* (Englewood Cliffs, 1970). For domestication as a taxonomic category, see, among others, E. Leach, "Anthropological Aspects of Language: Animal Categories and Verbal Abuse," in E. H. Lenneberg, ed., *New Directions in the Study of Language* (Cambridge, Mass., 1964), 23–63; S. J. Tambiah, "Animals Are Good to Think and Good to Prohibit," *Ethnology* 8 (1969): 423–59. See further, J. Z. Smith, "Animals and Plants in Myth and Legend," *Encyclopaedia Britannica*, 15th ed. (1974), "Macropaedia," 1: 911–18.

18. This characteristic was clearly perceived by A. E. Jensen, *Myth and Cult among Primitive Peoples* (Chicago, 1963), 162, who used it as a point of marked contrast to headhunting.

19. Each of these elements, presented here impressionistically, would have to be tested for frequency by means of detailed cross-cultural comparisons.

20. Perhaps this may account for the agrarian mythologization of the hunt, which exaggerates the 'otherness' (i.e., the nonfabricated nature) of the wild beast. See above, and Smith, *Imagining Religion*, 57–58.

21. Smith, *Imagining Religion*, 39–42.

22. See Leach and Tambiah as cited in note 17, above. Here is an excellent example of the relations of myth to ritual (see n. 9 above). The myths of domestication are relentlessly binary and contrastive. The etiquette and rituals concerning domesticated animals, in relation to both wild animals and humans, reduce this binary and contrastive character by providing instances of almost infinite degrees of difference. See Lévi-Strauss's description of the flattening of difference resulting in "continuity" in his ingenious and critical interpretation of sacrifice in contrast to totemism in *La Pensée sauvage*, 294–301; *The Savage Mind*, 222–26.

23. V. Turner, *The Forest of Symbols: Aspects of Ndembu Ritual* (Ithaca, NY, 1967), 105–8.

24. For a good example, see Tambiah, "Animals Are Good to Think," 142–43.

25. Jensen, *Myth and Cult*, 162–90, quotations from 162–63.

26. J. van Baal, "Offering, Sacrifice and Gift," *Numen* 23 (1976): 161–78, esp. 162; van Baal, *Man's Quest for Partnership: The Anthropological Foundations of Ethics and Religion* (Assen, 1981), 67–73, 219–25, et passim.

27. F. E. Koby, "L'Ours des cavernes et les paléolithiques," *L'Anthropologie* 55 (1951): 304–8.

28. See, among others, A. Leroi-Gourhan, *Les Religions de la préhistoire:*

Paléolithique, 2d ed. (Paris, 1971), 30–36; W. Burkert, *Structure and History in Greek Mythology and Ritual* (Berkeley, 1979), 167, n. 3.

29. K. Kindaichi, "The Concepts behind the Ainu Bear Festival," *Southwestern Journal of Anthropology* 5 (1949): 345–50; J. M. Kitagawa, "Ainu Bear Festival (Iyomante)," *History of Religions* 1 (1961): 95–151. See further, Smith, *Imagining Religion*, 59, and the literature cited on 144, n. 24.

30. W. Koppers, "Der Bärenkult in ethnologischer und prähistorischer Beleuchtung," *Palaeobiologica* 6 (1933): 47–64.

31. J. Maringer, *De Godsdienst der Praehistorie* (Romen, 1952), *non vidi*; I cite the English translation, *The Gods of Prehistoric Man* (New York, 1960), 90.

32. J. Maringer, "Die Opfer des paläolithischen Menschen," in *Anthropica: Gedenkschrift zum 100. Geburtstag von P. Wolhelm Schmidt* (Vienna, 1968), 249–71; quotation on 271.

33. H. Pohlhausen, "Zum Motive der Rentierversenkug," *Anthropos* 48 (1953): 987–90. Alternative interpretations are acknowledged by Maringer, "Die Opfer," 269–70.

34. L. Franz, *Religion und Kunst der Vorzeit* (Prague, 1937).

35. M. Douglas, "Animals in Lele Religious Symbolism," *Africa* 27 (1957): 46–58.

36. E. Isaac, "Myths, Cults and Livestock Breeding," *Diogenes* 41 (1963): 70–93, cf. Isaacs, *Geography of Domestication*, 105–10 et passim.

37. G. Reichel-Dolmatoff, *Amazonian Cosmos: The Sexual and Religious Symbolism of the Tukanao Indians* (Chicago, 1971), 11; M. J. Meggitt, "Notes on the Vegetable Foods of the Walbiri of Central Australia," *Oceania* 28 (1957): 143.

38. Reichel-Dolmatoff, *Amazonian Cosmos*, 13.

39. Leroi-Gourhan, *Les Religions de la préhistoire*, 28.

40. Smith, *Imagining Religion*, 53–65.

41. K. J. Narr, "Das höhere Jägertum: Jüngere Jagd- und Sammelstufe," in F. Valjavec, ed., *Historia Mundi* (Bern, 1952), 1: 502–22, esp. 504.

42. *Additional note:* Perhaps the most basic anthropological critique of the sacrificial theories of René Girard, one of the participants in the "conversations" for which this essay was prepared, was offered by the late V. Valeri, *Kingship and Sacrifice: Ritual and Society in Ancient Hawaii* (Chicago, 1985), 69. Valeri first notes that vegetable offerings are "of course . . . not in the least accounted for by Girard's theory." This shows one of the powers of redescription. The failure to account for vegetable offerings (as if animal sacrifices were primary) vitiates most understandings of sacrifice (including mine). Having redescribed sacrifice as vegetative, Valeri moves on to rectify Girard's interpretation: "decomposition, which marks the separation from the human and visible world, seems thus a more general and perhaps more important element than the violent act of killing, which is present only in animal and human sacrifices."

A MATTER OF CLASS

TAXONOMIES OF RELIGION

AS ROBIN WINKS has persistently and wittily demonstrated, there are striking and suggestive parallels between the methods of scholarship, especially in the human sciences, and detective fiction.[1] Perhaps the earliest self-conscious methodologist, therefore, is the redoubtable Sherlock Holmes. Some attention has been given to extracting his procedures and presuppositions from the prosaic, once-removed accounts of Dr. Watson, who plays a role in Doyle's fictions somewhere between one of Socrates' interlocutors, "I hadn't thought of that, please continue" and Jesus' disciples as represented by Mark, who, in one scholar's well-known formulation, progress from "nonunderstanding to misunderstanding."[2] In the literature on Holmes, however, I find surprisingly little attention paid to the manuscript writings and publications by the archetypical detective himself. There are fourteen in all, although four seem only sketches. While the two "memoirs" Holmes published in the *Anthropological Journal* are attractive, it is what appears to be his first publication, one of three translated into French, that catches my eye. Holmes describes this publication, which is primarily concerned with tobacco ashes, in *The Sign of the Four*:

> I have been guilty of several monographs. They are all on technical subjects. Here, for example, is one "Upon the Distinction Between the Ashes of the Various Tobaccos." In it I enumerate

a hundred and forty forms of cigar, cigarette, and pipe tobacco, with coloured plates illustrating the difference in the ash. It is a point which is continually turning up in criminal trials, and which is sometimes of supreme importance as a clue. If you can say definitely, for example, that some murder had been done by a man smoking an Indian *lunkah*, it obviously narrows your field of search. To the trained eye there is as much difference between the black ash of a Trichinopoly and the white fluff of bird's-eye as there is between a cabbage and a potato.[3]

Holmes's examples assume considerable skill on the part of the reader: the capacity to know the nomenclature of two sorts of Indian cheroots (*lunkah* and trichinopoly); to distinguish by name between pipe and cigar tobacco (bird's-eye and trichinopoly); and to know that bird's-eye will produce white fluff because the midribs have been removed from the leaves prior to shredding. This list of required knowledge is not uninteresting in itself as an indication of social location. What is of interest to me, however, is Holmes's enterprise. He uses taxonomy to "narrow your field," to arrive at a class of possible offenders, not the individual perpetrator. Although the technique was available to him, Holmes never uses fingerprints—the mark of a singular person. Such devices belong to the unimaginative and procedural Lestrade—but only for him, I think, in one instance ("The Adventure of the Norwood Builder"). At an early stage of investigation, Holmes seeks possibility, not probability. Such identification entails a number of physical and social indicators that further "narrow your field." To fail to make such discriminations, along with their attendant *typical* inferences, is to be in a world where cabbages may be potatoes or vice versa. This is a world without significant difference, though not difference at the level of the *infima species*, in human terms, the unique level of the proper name.

Varieties of Religion

I shall reflect here on the taxonomic enterprise as it applies to that form of scientific detection known as the academic study of religion. This agendum may appear odd in a lecture associated with the name of William James. James's work, *The Varieties of Religious Experience*, is the only book by an American-born author that has attained the status of a classic in the study of religion. There is hardly a single college major in religious studies who has not read the work. At one level James's work coincides with my own interests here. After all, the term "varieties" is itself a relentlessly taxonomic one. Indeed, James begins with a rudimentary classificatory endeavor, stipulating a definition of the taxon, religion, rejecting claims of its *sui generis* character, inquiring into "the *differentia* of religion" and describing, in a binary fashion, some of its genera.[4] While taxonomic language recurs rhetorically throughout the work, however, it is scarcely his interest. Despite some scholars' attempts to derive a Linnaean chart of families, types, and subtypes from *Varieties*,[5] James, with characteristic cheer, concludes that "in many instances it is quite arbitrary whether we class the individual as a once-born or twice-born subject."[6] This judgment of indifference guarantees that James will never be named by one of the strongest pejoratives he utters in his lectures, that of "systematizer."[7] What my college students derive from the book is their own take on religion read back to them: the priority of the individual, the centrality of experience and feeling, a vague but palpable sense of transcendence, a distrust of thought about religion (especially from "afar"), and the necessity of raising questions of ethical implications. None of these are helpful to a science of religion. If Harvard is to be our guide in the construction of such a science, I far prefer the lectures of James's colleague and critic, Josiah Royce. In his *The Problem of Christianity* Royce privileged both a theory of language and of community[8]—two essential elements in any theoretical proposal concerning religion. Both are notably lacking in James.

Nevertheless, James is not to be ignored, although it is James's *The Principles of Psychology*[9] rather than *Varieties* that proves to be provocative. Some thirty years ago, there was attention to the work on James's *Psychology* in an attempt to construct a kind of indigenous American "phenomenology,"[10] since the European import was never properly translated so as to work in religious studies.[11] While interesting, it is my impression that this phenomenological endeavor is largely a blind alley.

Within the tradition of anthropological thought that I am most comfortable with, James has had little impact. James does noticeably figure in one place, that is, in the most suggestive paragraph in Victor Turner's best-known article, "Betwixt and Between: The Liminal Period in *Rites de Passage*."[12] Turner's article is itself a reflection on the most relentlessly taxonomic work on social, religious phenomena, that of Arnold van Gennep's *The Rites of Passage*.[13] Turner is speaking about masks:

> If the exaggeration of single features is not irrational but thought-provoking, the same may also be said about the representation of monsters. . . . My own view is . . . that monsters are manufactured precisely to teach neophytes to distinguish clearly between different factors of reality, as it is conceived in their culture.

Here, I think, William James's so-called "law of dissociation" may help us clarify the problem of monsters. It may be stated as follows: when *a* and *b* occurred together as parts of the same total object, without being discriminated, the occurrence of one of these, *a* in a new combination *ax*, favors the discrimination of *a*, *b*, and *x* from one another. As James himself put it, "What is associated now with one thing and now with another, tends to become disassociated from either, and to grow into an object of abstract contemplation by the mind. One might call this the law of dissociation by varying concomitants.". . . [In masks] elements are withdrawn from their usual settings and combined with one another in a totally unique configuration, the monster or dragon. Monsters startle neophytes into thinking about objects, persons, relationships, and features of their environment they have hitherto taken for granted.[14]

This passage has three lessons for my enterprise. First, what is here described by Turner as the intellection characteristic of initiation is for me identical to the sort of thought prompted by comparison and classification basic to the human sciences. The theoretical enterprise, especially modes of explanation, is called forth by surprise, in this case, as in many taxonomic endeavors, by a process of "defamiliarization." Second, classification in relation to thought plays a central role in human cultures and, therefore, in religions. Cultures and religions themselves continuously engage in comparison and classification as well as becoming objects of our classifications and comparisons. Third, James was preoccupied with classification and with comparative issues of similarity and difference as fundamental to thought throughout *The Principles of Psychology*. Indeed certain chapters of *Psychology*[15] devoted to these topics prompted James's long dispute with the British philosopher, F. H. Bradley.[16]

Rather than belabor the exegesis of James, I shall instead take a Jamesean turn and "introspect" on my recent experience as general editor, on behalf of the American Academy of Religion, of the *HarperCollins Dictionary of Religion*.[17] This work is a fairly accurate snapshot of the current state of religious studies in America, of both its achievements and its problems.

The Genre and Taxonomy of a Dictionary

A dictionary differs from both an encyclopedia and a handbook by virtue of its necessary atomism; that is, a dictionary defines individual words in an arbitrary alphabetical order (a Roman alphabetical order which, in the *Dictionary of Religion,* violates the order of dozens of languages whose words appear in its pages). It focuses on the meaning of an individual word and includes other matter relevant to that verbal meaning such as pronunciation, etymology, and variation in usage. While often arranged alphabetically and sometimes including definitions, an encyclopedia is essentially topical in orientation, and attempts, at least in principle, to contain all information necessary to explore a topic as a whole. A handbook is an encyclopedia arranged by some stated principle of order that seeks to overcome the arbitrariness of the alphabet. In Manuila's useful taxonomy: an encyclopedia is "a comprehensive compilation of information on concepts pertaining to some or all fields of knowledge, arranged alphabetically under fairly broad subject headings."[18] Manuila terms a handbook a "classification" and defines it as

> a list of concepts, usually in a particular field of knowledge, arranged systematically in accordance with their characteristics and inter-relationships, either logical or ontological . . . [with] no necessary connection between the name of a concept and its position in a classification.[19]

According to Sidney Landau, a dictionary is "a collection . . . arranged alphabetically of the words of a particular language or a particular field of knowledge, giving some or all of the following information: orthography, pronunciation, etymology, definitions, use, history, synonyms."[20] Of course, these distinctions are more blurred in practice as all dictionaries include elements that are not, strictly speaking, lexical units. These elements range from nomenclature, that is, biographical and geographical entries, to conceptual elements. The latter are often quite prominent in a subject field dictionary, as they are in the *Dictionary of Religion.*

Thinking about dictionaries and their types is inseparable from thinking about definitions and their types. The general language dictionary works primarily at the level of lexical definition, a statistical and/or historical endeavor. Note well the slogan, made controversial at the time of the issuance of Webster's third edition: "dictionaries are descriptive, not prescriptive." A general language dictionary seeks to establish how a word is most commonly used. This task is frequently complicated by ranking usages in order of statistical frequency or by noting changes in usage over time. As such, lexical definitions are the only kinds of definitions that one can test by ordinary, common-sense criteria of accuracy. Lexical definitions comprise the vast majority of entries in the *Dictionary of Religion*, which seek to define, and often translate, native religious vocabulary.

Technical or subject-field dictionaries, such as a dictionary of religion, are a different matter. In principle, they are prescriptive; they oppose the statistical or historical reportage of lexical definitions with precising or theoretical definitions that often counter common usage and are persuasive rather than descriptive. As Landau expresses the distinction: in a general language dictionary

> general words are defined on the basis of citations illustrating actual usage: the meanings are *extracted* from a body of evidence. . . . The meaning of [technical] entries [in subject-matter dictionaries], on the other hand, are *imposed* on the basis of expert advice. The experts may have sources apart from their own knowledge and experience, but their sources are informative or encyclopedic rather than lexical, that is, they are likely to consist of authoritative definitions composed by other experts whose concern is maintaining the internal coherence of their discipline.[21]

Throughout the *Dictionary of Religion* one can see this attempt to reclaim from ordinary usage English terms that have a technical meaning, for example, "mysticism," "myth," and "cult."

If one understands the *Dictionary of Religion* as an essay in classification, its *summum genus*, or that which functions as the "unique beginner," is "religion." However, this is by no means explicit. There are a set of conjunctive articles, from "art and religion" to "society and religion," which suggest that the *summum genus* is human culture, with religion, along with other cultural forms, classed as subordinate taxa at the same level. The conjunctive articles rarely take up this question directly, save in those instances where disciplinary history has been preoccupied with a particular difference—for example, "magic, science and religion," "worldview" or "ideology" and religion, or "ethics and religion."

Either way, religion's *sine qua non*, the "that without which" it would not be an instance of religion but of something else, is held consistently, wherever the issue of definition is explicitly raised, to be "beliefs and practices that are related to superhuman beings." "No superhuman beings, no religion."[22] Thus, the definition serves to precise the common lexical definition that religion is belief in God and would suggest that "religion" is taken to be the "unique beginner" of the classification. Mel

Spiro, the most articulate defender of this definition, renders it thus: "an institution consisting of culturally patterned interaction with culturally postulated superhuman beings."[23] This theoretical definition, entailing acceptance of a broad theory of cultural creation signaled by the words "culturally patterned" and "culturally postulated," places human cultural activities or human institutions as the *summum genus* and religion as a subordinate taxon. Spiro's subsequent formulation makes this clear: "religion can be differentiated from other culturally constituted institutions by virtue only of its reference to superhuman beings."[24]

Notably lacking in such definitions are alternative taxonomic strategies, particularly those that do not take some modified form of essential definition as their model. There is no attempt at a polythetic classification which eschews the postulation of a unique differentium in favor of a large set of characteristics, any one of which would be necessary, but not sufficient, to classify a given entity as an instance of religion. Ernst Cassirer's notion of an overlapping chain of cultural forms is a weak example of such an enterprise.[25] Furthermore, there is little evidence of interest in reduction, that is, a proposal that the language that is appropriate to one domain (the known/the familiar) may translate the language characteristic of another domain (the unknown/the unfamiliar) such as in Durkheim's exemplary reduction of the language characteristic of religion to the language characteristic of society.[26] This is surprising as the only effective grounds for rejecting such a proposal, in either the natural or the human sciences, is to attack the possibility of translation itself, most often expressed through arguments of incommensurability. In a dictionary whose bulk consists of the translation of several thousand foreign-language terms, however, this is impossible. That is to say, the *Dictionary of Religion* lives by the premise of synonymy—a complex idea implicated in the very notion of the postulated inadequacy of translation. There is always discrepancy; translation is necessarily incomplete. To repeat the old tag: to translate is to traduce. Central to any proposal of translation and synonymy is the double requirement of comparison and criticism.

'World Religions'

Within the *Dictionary of Religion*, the category 'religion' is subdivided into 'religions' which function at some intermediate taxonomic level analogous to classes or orders. These are, in fact, of two sorts. First, a set of what appear to be common-sense divisions into the familiar seven 'world religions': Buddhism, Chinese Religion, Christianity, Hinduism,

Islam, Japanese Religion, and Judaism. A second set consists of three divisions of the sort structuralists would label "degree-zero"[27]: Religions of Antiquity, New Religions, and Religions of Traditional Peoples. At first glance, the first set seems to represent natural taxa; the second set is clearly artificial. In practice, all entries, except those devoted to the "Study of Religion," were parceled out among these ten categories, each the responsibility of an area editor. Despite the specious appearance of common-sense, this sort of division is fraught with difficulties of both theoretical and practical kinds.

Take first the taxon, 'world religions.' While seemingly a demographic category, including some 75.12 percent of the world's population in 1985, or 74.2 percent in 1993, this is not its basis. In fact, it is a sublimation of an earlier division—"universal" religions in contradistinction to "ethnic" or "national" religions. This division itself is ultimately a sublimation of the earliest and most fundamental dichotomous division: "ours" and "theirs," or "true" and "false."

While the distinction between "religions of the world" and "national" religions was first made by a member of the Tübingen School in 1827,[28] the earliest elaborated form of this taxonomy can be found in Cornelis Petrus Tiele's *Outline of the History of Religion to the Spread of Universal Religions*. This influential monograph appeared in Dutch in 1876, with two subsequent editions, and was rapidly translated into English (1877), French (1880), German (1880), Danish (1884), and Swedish (1887)—with the English and German versions going through as many as five or six later editions.[29] A convenient English summary may be found in Tiele's article, "Religions," in the ninth edition of the *Encyclopaedia Britannica*.[30]

Tiele begins by accepting the clearly apologetic distinction between "nature" religions and "ethical" religions, working out a complex taxonomy of nine types and subtypes of the former, but only two subdivisions of the latter: "national/nomistic" and "universalistic."[31] As the addition of the term "nomistic" makes clear, the contrast is essentially that between Judaism and Christianity, although the list of "national/nomistic" religions is expanded to include Taoism, Confucianism, Brahmanism, Jainism, "primitive Buddhism," Mazdaism (or Zarathustrianism), Mosaism (by which he means the religion of the Hebrew Bible), and Judaism (by which he means "rabbinism").[32] "Universalistic" religions is a class with only three members: Christianity, Buddhism, and Islam. The last is, in fact, generous. When Abraham Kuenen delivered his 1882 Hibbert Lectures, *National Religions and Universal Religions*, he demoted Islam to a national religion in conscious opposition to Tiele.[33] The "universalistic" religions are book religions, they are devoted not to the special interests of a nation or people but to humankind in general, and therefore, they are proselytizing traditions. In blunter language, after discussing the relative merits of the terms "universalistic," "universal," and "world religions," Tiele employed the term "world religions"

> to distinguish the three religions which have found their way to different races and peoples and all of which profess the intention to conquer the world, from such communities [that is, "national/nomistic" religions] as are generally limited to a single race or nation, and where they have extended farther, have done so only in the train of, and in connection with, a superior civilization. Strictly speaking, there can be no more than one universal or world religion, and if one of the existing religions is so potentially, it has not yet reached its goal. This is a matter of belief which lies beyond the limits of scientific classification. . . . Modern history of religions is chiefly the history of Buddhism, Christianity and Islam, and of their wrestling with the ancient faiths and primitive modes of worship, which slowly fade away before their encroachments, and which, where they still survive in some parts of the world and do not reform themselves after the model of the superior religion, draw nearer and nearer to extinction.[34]

Subsequent strict use of the term "world religions" has provided no improvements. The most recent full discussion of "world religions" as a taxonomic category is in Gustav Mensching's *Die Religionen: Erscheinungsformen, Strukturtypen und Lebensgesetze* (1959), translated into English as *Structures and Patterns of Religion*. Mensching continues the dichotomy "ethnic" and "world" religions, arguing that the distinction "does not concern geographical diffusion alone. Rather it is based upon a deeper structural differentiation of religion itself."[35] This difference points to "a fundamental change in human existence . . . the individual replaces the collectivity as the subject of religion" and is addressed with a soteriology that focuses on "a personal lack of salvation," relating to "the unredeemed condition of man."[36] Despite the substitution of a more Protestant version of Christianity as the paradigm, the same three "world religions" are singled out by Mensching: Christianity and Islam, which he terms "the prophetic world religions," along with Buddhism, "the mystic world religion."[37]

How did the mysterious symbolic number three permute into the equally mysterious and symbolic number seven? I find little explicit rationalization, but I cannot escape the sense that the change is due to a sort of pluralistic etiquette. If Christianity and Islam count as "world" religions, it would be rude to exclude Judaism (the original model for the opposite type, "ethnic" or "national" religion). Likewise, if Buddhism, then Hinduism. And again, if Buddhism, then Chinese religions and Japanese religions. The unprincipled nature of this list is made plain by the fact that some scholars list only five, omitting Judaism and Japanese religions,[48] while no typology includes Manichaeism, perhaps the first, self-conscious "world" religion.

I see little theoretical justification for the continued use of this taxon, which has, as I have written elsewhere, the following implications:

> A World Religion is a religion like ours; but it is, above all, a tradition which has achieved sufficient power and numbers to enter our history, either to form it, interact with it, or to thwart it. . . . We recognize both the unity within and the diversity between the 'great' World Religions because they correspond to important geo-political entities with which we must deal. All 'primitives' by way of contrast may be simply lumped together as may the so-called 'minor religions' because they do not confront our history in any direct fashion. They are invisible.[39]

Nowhere in the taxonomic literature on "world religions" is there a noticeable sense of the difficulties in defining particular religions. This has been a more recent concern, prompted as much by the area studies model for non-Western religions as from intellectual challenges such as the one mounted by Wilfred Cantwell Smith.[40] In the *Dictionary of Religion*, two strategies prevail. Judaism and Christianity are each defined in terms of an exemplum: for Judaism it is the "classical Judaism of the dual Torah" as expressed in the foundational rabbinic literature; for Christianity it is Roman Catholic tradition with confirmatory data from the Orthodox Church. The other "world religions" devote considerable space in their introductory essays to issues of definition and classification, one essay concluding that "there are at least as many conceptual difficulties in the definition of 'Buddhism' as there are in the definition of 'religion.'"[41] In contrast, and surprising to me was the persistence of an easy, unarticulated assumption of the universality of Christianity. As general editor I had to insert the adjective "Christian" into the defining sentence fragment of the majority of the Christian entries. Articles in no other area presented that editorial problem.

Negotiations over entry assignments revealed the pragmatic difficulties attendant on a division of labor into seven "world religions," at times resembling turf wars. Personifying the area editors by the religion for which they were responsible, neither Hinduism nor Islam wanted to commit much space to the Mughal period in India. Hinduism included the Sikhs with a full set of entries but scanted the Jains. The North Indian Sanskritic tradition predominated, somewhat at the expense of Dravidian materials and largely ignoring religion at the level of the village. Because Buddhism had to negotiate entries with both China and Japan, South Asian Buddhism was underrepresented. Buddhism ended up responsible for all entries on Tibetan religion. Korea, important for both the development of State Confucianism and for Buddhist transmission, was atomized without receiving a synoptic treatment comparable to China and Japan. Judaism correctly understood itself to be a new religion, as equidistant from the old religion of Israel as is Christianity, and hence refused to assign an article on Israelite religion. Religions of Antiquity responded quite properly that its category did not usually encompass ancient Israel. Islam drew the line at both Babism and Bahai. I can offer no reason for the total exclusion of Episcopalians from the dictionary save to plead editorial fatigue.

Despite these difficulties, the seven "world religions" function taxonomically at the level of a class or order. They are important conceptually if only for the exhibition of the processes of variation and adaptation—that is to say, of history and ecology—in the subordinate taxa, from the level of families through genera and species. This is acknowledged in the *Dictionary of Religion* by the provision of time-lines and "world distribution maps" for the seven "world religions" (though for no others). I should note that the original limited sense of "world religions" is illustrated by three graphs chronicling the "spread" of Buddhism, Christianity, and Islam. Whether graphically acknowledged or not, subordinate taxa in the case of "world religions" are essentially genealogical in nature. Whether at the level of general articles, specific entries, or cross-references, narratives are primarily concerned with pedigree, with locating topics, terminology, movements, and individuals in a vast diachronic web of descent and affiliation. Graphically, this is instantiated with respect to the privileged three, as the *Dictionary of Religion* provides "family-tree diagrams" for Buddhism, Islam, and Protestantism. The limitations of such an approach appear in the first two, where no direct line of descent can be figured for the Buddhist Tantric (Vajrayana) traditions or the Islamic Sufi traditions. In the case of Protestantism, two sorts of lines are drawn, a solid line indicating "filiation [or] direct descent" and a broken line indicating "affiliation [or being] influenced by."[42]

Given the triumphalist associations of the term "world religions," the maps and diagrams fail to display the ecological complexity of religions cohabiting contiguous space. Only one map, that illustrating "Religions in Southeast Asia,"[43] hints at this with its legend indicating distinctive shadings for Buddhist, Christian, Confucian, Hindu, indigenous, and Muslim traditions, but fails to convey the adaptive dimension made plain by the Philippine *Iglesia ni Cristo* or the Javanese *agama Djawa,* let alone Sri Lankan fire-walking, introduced by Tamils and now largely controlled and practiced by Buddhists. This is partially due to an ideological emphasis on purity of lineage. Hybridization, a positive adaptive mechanism in biological classifications, is denigrated in religious taxonomy, by terms such as 'syncretism' and 'accommodation.' That is to say, the notion of 'population' has yet to play the definitive role in cultural classifications that it has played in biological ones where it has all but replaced the notion of 'species.' This is an urgent future agendum.

What then of the other three categories not encompassed by the term "world religions": Religions of Antiquity, New Religions, and Religions of Traditional Peoples? In a sense these function as residual categories for those items not classifiable under the dominant system. In their introductory essays, each of their editors spent considerable space rationalizing the category; Traditional Religions added a spirited defense of its importance. At first glance, "antiquity" and "new" appear to be merely chronological indicators. This sense is especially apparent with "antiquity" since there has been a tendency in recent reference works to employ the category "world religions" as all but synonymous with the term "living religions."[44] But they are not synonymous. First, some of these "ancient" religions are still very much alive, such as the Samaritans and the Mandaeans. Second, as the editor indicated in her essay, it is not any religion of the past that is included, but only those with a particular pedigree:

> "Antiquity" in this article denotes those religions that either preceded Christianity in areas of its major expansion or were supplanted by it. It does not designate a simple chronological division. Neither Paleolithic religions nor the early religions of Asia (for example, Indus Valley culture) find a place within antiquity's domain. What is understood as "the ancient world" or "the classics" is hedged about with strictly patrolled borders and those who understand themselves as carriers and caretakers of the Western tradition look back to "antiquity" with a sense of ownership.[45]

"New Religions" is an even odder category, having only a vague chronological reference. This is the messy sphere in the sense of maximal adaptation. This point is driven home by the realization that while "New Religions" comprise the second-largest category in the *Dictionary of Religion* after "Christianity," more than a third of its entries are to groups arguably Christian that, nevertheless, received no place in Christianity's more centrist list of entries. Consonant with this centrism, various Gnostic entries were cheerfully abandoned to "Religions of Antiquity"; Protestantism did not appear on the proposed list of Christian entries. The editor defines "New Religions" as "independent groups that have arisen from the encounter of existing religious traditions, particularly through the latter part of the postcolonial period."[46] It is here, in a taxon in which few scholars have a stake, that some of the more interesting taxonomies have been developed, from Ralph Linton's formally satisfying classificatory paradigm for nativistic movements[47] to J. Gordon Melton's complex typology of American religions as consisting of seventeen families.[48] Ten are Christian in orientation, and continue, with greater breadth, the older conventions of American denominational studies. The others represent a new taxonomy with categories such as the Communal, the Metaphysical, the Psychic, and New Age, the Magick, the Eastern and Middle Eastern families, each with numerous subdivisions, largely generated by connections of filiation and affiliation. This taxonomy comes closest to the notion of 'population' discussed above.

The category "Religions of Traditional Peoples" is the best illustration of my previous remark that while we are capable of taking infinite pains at splitting "world religions" in an endless dialectic of unity and diversity we tend to lump together so-called 'primitive' religions. One of the most ambitious recent attempts to apply this dialectic to the religion of traditional peoples, in this case South America, is Lawrence Sullivan's *Icanchu's Drum*, but at the cost of considerable ontological overtranslation.[49]

In the *Dictionary of Religion* the "Religions of Traditional Peoples" are largely divided geographically, reinforcing the outdated notion that place rather than history and movement defines them. In most cases, the situation of being surrounded by water (whether an island or a continent) suggests a unity (thus, "African Traditional Religions," or "Australian and Pacific Traditional Religions"). This unity, however, is belied by linguistic and tribal diversities. As one entry reads:

> The ability to generalize effectively about Pacific religions is roughly proportional to the general cultural and linguistic diversity of the conventional groupings of societies. Diversity is least in Polynesia, greater in Australia and Micronesia, and

greatest by far in Melanesia, particularly in New Guinea with its seven hundred or more [largely unrelated] languages.[50]

The fact is that there is no satisfactory way of classifying these traditions. Neither geographical nor linguistic groupings have proved fruitful or gained wide assent. Until such is developed, we will continue to use prescientific categories, largely lumping these folk together by the putative absence among them of cultural indicators we associate with ourselves (from clothes to writing to historical complexity). To give one sadly comic example, the dictionary's photo editor submitted an image to illustrate "Traditional Peoples" of a group of five or six black male dancers, adorned with shells and feathers—perhaps being attracted to the image by the presence, along with drums and rattles, of a "boom-box" providing the music. Further investigation established that this was a photograph of Masira tribal members of the Anglican Church of Papua New Guinea celebrating the feast day of Saint Thomas à Becket, December 29, 1981.[51]

Classification and Thought

One hundred and twenty-six years ago, F. Max Müller, considered by some historians to be the progenitor of our field, in a lecture delivered at the Royal Institution in London and subsequently dedicated to Ralph Waldo Emerson, challenged religious studies with what is, in essence, a wager: "All real science rests on classification, and only in the case we cannot succeed in classifying the various dialects of faith, shall we have to confess that a science of religion is really an impossibility."[52] I would conclude that we have not yet met his challenge. For some, this will be an occasion for celebration rather than lamentation; in that, from the perspective of a late-twentieth-century reader, there are assumptions in Müller's statement that invite principled rejection. There is the positivism of his appeal to "science." There is the universalism of his notion of religion. Today, for many practitioners, there is an ethos of particularity that rubs up hard against Müller's presumption of generality, a presumption that some perceive as a sort of imperialism. Such an understanding would find support in Müller's sentences immediately preceding the one quoted:

> Let us take the old saying, *divide et impera*, and translate it somewhat freely by "Classify and conquer," and I believe that we shall then lay hold of the old thread of Ariadne which has led the stu-

dents of many a science through darker labyrinths even than the labyrinth of the religions of the world.[53]

I am aware of the new ethos that eschews classification, comparison, and explanation. In the satiric formulation of Kimberley Patton, "Thou Shalt Compare Neither Religious Traditions, Nor Elements of Religious Traditions, Lest Thou Totalize, Essentialize, or Commit Hegemonic Discourse"[54]—to which I might add, "Nor shalt thou consider thyself a member of the academy." This is counsel to be rejected, as it was by William James, in what has become, perhaps, the most oft-quoted paragraph in *Varieties*:

> The first thing the intellect does with an object is to class it along with something else. But any object that is infinitely important to us and awakens our devotion feels to us as if it must be *sui generis* and unique. Probably a crab would be filled with a sense of personal outrage if it could hear us class it without ado or apology as a crustacean, and thus dispose of it. "I am no such thing," it would say; "I am MYSELF, MYSELF alone."[55]

To fail to reject the crab's sentence is to condemn the study of religion to an inconclusive study of individuals and individual phenomena. I avoid the anti-intellectual term 'unique' in favor of the word 'individual,' which, at least, implies the notion of class. So classify we must—though we can learn from the past to eschew dual classifications such as that between "universal" and "ethnic" or the host of related dualisms, all of which finally reduce to "ours" and "theirs."

In the *HarperCollins Dictionary of Religion*, the article on "Typology, classification" makes the argument that scholars of religion have often substituted classification for explanation:

> Knowledge of any set of phenomena, whether natural or cultural, comes about not primarily from the application and development of taxonomies, but from explanatory theorizing. . . . This . . . does not deny the usefulness of taxonomies, it simply insists that any system of classification follow from whatever theories have been adduced to explain religion. Taxonomies are neither substitutes for, alternatives to, nor the generators of theories.[56]

I agree with the overall thrust, but not with the particular argument. As in Victor Turner's description of the relationship of classification to thought, so too here. Classification, by bringing disparate phenomena together in the space of a scholar's intellect, often produces surprise, the condition which calls forth efforts of explanation.

I shall offer one concrete example. 'Fundamentalism,' a term coined in the 1920s to describe a particular mode of Protestant Christianity and its relationship to biblical criticism, now extends as a generic category, largely applied to religions that have not yet experienced historical-critical readings of their sacred texts. It would be better to classify these other 'fundamentalisms' as instances of 'nativism' or 'revitalization' movements, thus emphasizing, among other matters, their setting in colonial and postcolonial histories, a setting that is not present in Christian fundamentalism. To read Islamic fundamentalism as a nativistic movement is to call for a different set of comparisons and other sorts of explanations than would occur when one foregrounds the Christian phenomenon.

In 1974, Charles J. Adams concluded his masterful survey of classifications of religion with an odd pluralistic counsel congruent with recent attempts to diminish concern for method with metaphors of toolboxes. He argues that

> the most fruitful approach for a student of religion appears to be that of employing a number of diverse classifications of religions, each one for the insight that it may yield. . . . The error that must be avoided is that of insisting on the validity of any single taxonomic effort. To confine oneself to a single, determined framework of thought about so rich and variegated a subject as religion is to risk the danger of missing much that is important.[57]

To be so generous is to run the risk of losing that very partiality, that casting of particular features into bold relief, those tensions of similarity and difference that give rise to thought. Scholarly labor is a disciplined exaggeration in the direction of knowledge; taxonomy is a valuable tool in achieving that necessary distortion.

Notes

1. Robin W. Winks, ed., *The Historian as Detective: Essays on Evidence* (New York, 1970).

2. Theodore J. Weeden, *Mark: Traditions in Conflict* (Philadelphia, 1971), 26–38.

3. Arthur Conan Doyle, *The Sign of the Four* (1893; reprint, Bedford, Mass., 1994), 9–10.

4. William James, *The Varieties of Religious Experience* (1902; reprint, New York, 1906).

5. J. E. Dittes, "Beyond William James," in Charles Y. Glock and Phillip E. Hammond, eds., *Beyond the Classics?* (New York, 1973), 291–354, esp. 298.

6. James, *Varieties*, 488 n. 1.

7. Ibid., 327.

8. Josiah Royce, *The Problem of Christianity* (New York, 1913), 2: 225–76 (lecture 13), 2: 279–325 (lecture 14).

9. William James, *The Principles of Psychology*, 2 vols. (1890; reprint, New York, 1950).

10. See James M. Edie, "William James and Phenomenology," *Review of Metaphysics* 23 (1970): 481–526; and Gerald E. Myers, *William James: His Life and Thought* (New Haven, Conn., 1986), 490 n. 35.

11. Hans H. Penner, "Is Phenomenology a Method for the Study of Religion?" *Bucknell Review* 38 (1970): 29–54.

12. Victor Turner, "Betwixt and Between: The Liminal Period in *Rites de Passage*," in *Symposium on New Approaches to the Study of Religion*, ed. June Helm (Seattle, 1964), 14.

13. Arnold van Gennep, *Rites of Passage* (London, 1960).

14. Victor Turner, *The Forest of Symbols: Aspects of Ndembu Ritual* (Ithaca, NY, 1967), 104–5; Turner cites James, *Psychology*, 1: 506.

15. James, *Psychology*, 1: 459–549 (chapter 12, "Conception"; and chapter 13, "Discrimination and Comparison"), and 2: 617–88 (chapter 28, "Necessary Truths and the Effects of Experience").

16. Francis H. Bradley, *Collected Essays*, 2 vols. (Oxford, 1969), 1: 287–302.

17. *HarperCollins Dictionary of Religion*, ed. Jonathan Z. Smith (San Francisco, 1995).

18. Alexander Manuila, ed., *Progress in Medical Terminology* (Basel, 1981), 58.

19. Ibid.

20. Sidney I. Landau, *Dictionaries: The Art and Craft of Lexicography* (1984; reprint, Cambridge, 1989), 23.

21. Ibid., 20.

22. *HarperCollins Dictionary of Religion*, s.v. "Religion, definition of."

23. Melford E. Spiro, "Religion: Problems of Definition and Explanation," in Michael Banton, ed., *Anthropological Approaches to the Study of Religion* (London, 1966), 85–126, quotation from 96.

24. Ibid., 98.

25. Ernst Cassirer, *An Essay on Man* (New Haven, 1944), 70–228.

26. Jonathan Z. Smith, *To Take Place: Toward Theory in Ritual* (Chicago, 1987), 35–40, 105–7.

27. Claude Lévi-Strauss, *Sociologie et anthropologie par Marcel Mauss* (Paris, 1950), xlii–l.

28. Pierre D. Chantepie de la Saussaye, *Manual of the Science of Religion* (London, 1891), 54.

29. Cornelius Petrus Tiele, *Outline of the History of Religion to the Spread of Universal Religions* (1876; reprint, London, 1877).

30. Idem, *Encyclopaedia Britannica*, 9th ed. (1875–89) s.v. "Religions," 20: 358–71.

31. Ibid., 369–70.

32. Ibid.

33. Abraham Kuenen, *National Religions and Universal Religions* (London, 1882).

34. Tiele, "Religions," 368, 371.

35. Gustav Mensching, *Structures and Patterns of Religion* (Delhi, 1976), 45.

36. Ibid., 51–55.

37. Ibid., 55.

38. For example, Joachim Wach, *Sociology of Religion* (Chicago, 1944), 268–69.

39. Jonathan Z. Smith, *Map Is Not Territory* (Leiden, 1978), 295.

40. Wilfred Cantwell Smith, *The Meaning and End of Religion* (New York, 1963).

41. M. David Eckel, *HarperCollins Dictionary of Religion*, s.v. "Buddhism," 149.

42. *HarperCollins Dictionary of Religion*, s.v. "Protestantism," 863.

43. *HarperCollins Dictionary of Religion*, s.v. "Religions in Southeast Asia," 1018.

44. See for example, Keith Crim, ed., *Abingdon Dictionary of Living Religions* (Nashville, 1981); recently reprinted as idem, *The Perennial Dictionary of World Religions* (San Francisco, 1989); and John R. Hinnells, *Who's Who of World Religions* (London, 1991).

45. Jorunn Jacobsen Buckley, *HarperCollins Dictionary of Religion*, s.v. "Religions of Antiquity," 56.

46. Carole A. Myscofski, *HarperCollins Dictionary of Religion*, s.v. "New Religions," 771.

47. Ralph Linton, "Nativistic Movements," *American Anthropologist* 45 (1943): 230–40.

48. J. Gordon Melton, *The Encyclopedia of American Religions*, 2 vols. (Wilmington, NC, 1978) 1: xv–xxxvi, 2: v–xxvi.

49. Lawrence Sullivan, *Icanchu's Drum* (New York, 1989).

50. *HarperCollins Dictionary of Religion*, s.v. "Australian and Pacific Traditional Religions," 94.

51. *HarperCollins Dictionary of Religion*, s.v. "Becket, Thomas a," 107.

52. F. Max Müller, *Introduction to the Science of Religion* (London, 1873), 123.

53. Ibid., 122–23.

54. Kimberly Patton, "The Comparative Study of Religion: Contemporary Challenges and Responses," American Academy of Religion Annual Meeting, Philadelphia, Penn., 21 November 1995, 1.

55. James, *Varieties*, 9.

56. *HarperCollins Dictionary of Religion*, s.v. "Typology, classification," 1102.

57. Charles J. Adams, "Religions, Classification of," *Encyclopaedia Britannica*, 15th ed. (1974), 15: 634.

CHAPTER EIGHT

RELIGION, RELIGIONS, RELIGIOUS

IN THE SECOND earliest account of the "New World" published in English, *A Treatyse of the Newe India* (1553), Richard Eden wrote of the natives of the Canary Islands that, "At Columbus first comming thether,
the inhabitantes went naked, without shame, religion or knowledge of
God."[1] In the same year, toward the beginning of the first part of his massive *Crónica del Perú* (1553), the conquistador-historian Pedro Cieza de
León described the north Andean indigenous peoples as "observing no
religion at all, as we understand it [*no . . . religion alguana, à lo question
entendemos*], nor is there any house of worship to be found."[2] While both
were factually incorrect, their formulations bear witness to the major expansion of the use and understanding of the term 'religion' that began
in the sixteenth century and anticipate some of the continuing issues
raised by that expansion: (1) 'Religion' is not a native category. It is not
a first-person term of self-characterization. It is a category imposed from
the outside on some aspect of native culture. It is the other, in these instances colonialists, who are solely responsible for the content of the
term. (2) Even in these early formulations, there is an implicit universality. 'Religion' is thought to be a ubiquitous human phenomenon; therefore, both Eden and Cieza find its alleged absence noteworthy. (3) In
constructing the second-order, generic category 'religion,' its characteristics are those that appear natural to the other. In these quotations
this familiarity is signaled by the phrases "knowledge of God" and "reli-

gion . . . as we understand it." (4) 'Religion' is an anthropological not a theological category. (Perhaps the only exception is the distinctively American nineteenth-century coinages, "to get religion" or "to experience religion.") It describes human thought and action, most frequently in terms of belief and norms of behavior. Eden understands the content of "religion" largely in the former sense ("without . . . religion or knowledge of God"), whereas Cieza articulates it in the latter ("no religion . . . nor . . . any house of worship").

The term 'religion' has had a long history, much of it, prior to the sixteenth century, irrelevant to contemporary usage. Its etymology is uncertain, although one of the three current possibilities, that it stems from the root *leig* meaning "to bind" rather than from roots meaning "to reread" or "to be careful," has been the subject of considerable Christian homiletic expansion from Lactantius's *Divine Institutes* (early fourth century) and Augustine's *On True Religion* (early fifth century) to William Camden's *Britannia* (1586). In both Roman and early Christian Latin usage, the noun forms *religio/religiones* and, most especially, the adjectival *religiosus* and the adverbial *religiose* were cultic terms referring primarily to the careful performance of ritual obligations. This sense survives in the English adverbial construction "religiously" designating a conscientious repetitive action such as "She reads the morning newspaper religiously." The only distinctively Christian usage was the fifth-century extension of this cultic sense to the totality of an individual's life in monasticism: "religion," a life bound by monastic vows; "religious," a monk; "to enter religion," to join a monastery.[3] It is this technical vocabulary that is first extended to non-Christian examples in the literature of exploration, particularly in descriptions of the complex civilizations of Mesoamerica. Thus Hernán Cortés, in his second *Carta de Relacíon* (1520), writes of Tenochtitlán:

> This great city contains many mosques [*mezquitas*, an eleventh-century Spanish loan word from the Arabic, *masjid*], or houses for idols. . . . The principal ones house persons of their religious orders [*personas religiosas de su secta*]. . . . All these monks [*religiosos*] dress in black . . . from the time they enter the order [*entran en la religión*].[4]

Cortés's relatively thoughtless language of assimilation is raised to the level of a systemic category two generations later in the encyclopedic work of the Jesuit scholar Joseph de Acosta, *The Natural and Moral History of the Indies* (1590; English translation, 1604). While the vast majority of the occurrences of the term "religious" refer to either Catholic or native members of "religious orders," sometimes expanded to the dual category, "priests and monks of Mexico" (*los sacerdotes y religiosos de México*), a number of passages strain toward a more generic conception. The work is divided into two parts, with the latter, "moral history," chiefly devoted to religion, governance, and political history. 'Religion' per se is never defined. Its meaning must be sought in words associated with it as well as its synonyms. For Acosta, "religion" is the belief system that results in ceremonial behavior. "Religion" is "that which is used (*que usan*) in their rites." "Custom" (*costumbre*), "superstition" (*superstición*), and "religion" (*religión*) form a belief series in conjunction with the action series of "deed" (*hecho*), "rite" (*rito*), "idolatry" (*idolatria*), "sacrifice" (*sacrificio*), "ceremony" (*ceremonia*), and "feasts" (*fiestas y solemnidades*).[5]

'Religion' in relation to ritual practice became an item in an inventory of cultural topics that could be presented either ethnographically in terms of a particular people, as in Eden or Cieza with reference to the "Indies," or in a cross-cultural encyclopedia under the heading of "ritual" or "religion." The encyclopedic version is illustrated by Joannes Boemus's popular *Omnium gentium mores, leges et ritus* (1520), in which *ritus* was translated as "customs" in the English translations by William Watreman, *The Fardle of Facions, Conteining the Aunciente Manners, Customes and Lawes of the People Inhabiting the Two Partes of the Earth* (1555) and by Edward Aston, *The Manners, Laws and Customs of all Nations* (1611); as well as by Sebastian Muenster's *Cosmographiae universalis . . . : Item omnium gentium mores, leges, religio* (1550). This focus on ritual had an unintended consequence. The myths and beliefs of other folk could simply be recorded as "antiquities," to use the term employed by Columbus. They raised no particular issues for thought. But ritual, especially when it seemed similar to Christian practice or when it illustrated categories of otherness such as "idolatry" or "cannibalism," gave rise to projects of comparative and critical inquiries. Similarity and difference, with respect to ritual, constituted a puzzle that required explanation by appeals to old patristic, apologetic charges of priestly deceit or to equally apologetic, patristic theories of accommodation, demonic plagiarism, diffusion, or degeneration. In the case of belief and myth, "their" words were primary; with ritual, "our" account superseded theirs.

Some two centuries later, this essentially Catholic understanding of 'religion' in close proximity to ritual has been decisively altered. Samuel Johnson, in his *Dictionary of the English Language* (1755), defines "religion" as "virtue, as founded upon reverence of God, and expectations of future rewards and punishments." The first edition of the *Encyclopaedia*   181

Britannica (1771) titled its entry "Religion, or Theology," defining the topic in the opening paragraph: "To know God, and to render him a reasonable service, are the two principal objects of religion. . . . Man appears to be formed to adore, but not to comprehend, the Supreme Being." Terms such as "reverence," "service," "adore," and "worship" in these sorts of definitions have been all but evacuated of ritual connotations, and seem more to denote a state of mind, a transition begun by Reformation figures such as Zwingli and Calvin who understood "religion" primarily as "piety." The latter term takes on a less awesome cast in subsequent Protestant discourse, for example, "Piety, a Moral vertue which causes us to have affection and esteem for God and Holy Things."[6]

This shift to belief as the defining characteristic of 'religion' (stressed in the German preference for the term *Glaube* over *Religion*, and in the increasing English usage of "faiths" as a synonym for "religions") raised a host of interrelated questions as to credibility and truth. These issues were exacerbated by the schismatic tendencies of the various Protestantisms, with their rival claims to authority, as well as by the growing awareness of the existence of a multitude of articulate, non-Christian traditions. The former is best illustrated by the first attempt to provide a distribution map for the various European Protestantisms: Ephraim Pagitt's *Christianographie; or, The Description of the Multitude and Sundry Sorts of Christians in the World Not Subject to the Pope* (1635). The latter is the explicit subject of the anthropological work by Edward Brerewood, *Enquiries Touching the Diversity of Languages and Religions through the Chiefe Parts of the World* (1614), which distinguished four "sorts" (i.e., "species") of the genus "religion"—"Christianity, Mohametanism, Judaism and Idolatry"—and provided statistical estimates for "the quantitie and proportion of the parts of the earth possessed by the several sorts."[7] It is the question of the plural *religions* (both Christian and non-Christian) that forced a new interest in the singular, generic *religion*. To cite what is perhaps the first widely read English book to employ the plural in its title, *Purchas His Pilgrimage; or, Relations of the World and the Religions Observed in All Ages and Places Discovered* (1613): "The true Religion can be but one, and that which God himselfe teacheth[,] . . . all other religions being but strayings from him, whereby men wander in the darke, and in labyrinthine errour."[8] What is implicit in Purchas becomes explicit in later seventeenth- and eighteenth-century debates concerning "natural religion," a term that became common only in the latter half of the seventeenth century, beginning with works such as the one by the prolific Puritan controversialist Richard Baxter, *The Reasons of the Christian Religion* (1667), in two parts: "Of Natural Religion, or Godliness," and "Of

Christianity, and Supernatural Religion." (Compare Baxter's earlier but congruent terminology, *Of Saving Faith, That It Is Not Only Gradually but Specifically Distinct from All Common Faith* [1658]).

As David Pailan has demonstrated, the notion of natural religion has been employed in the literature "to designate at least eleven significantly different notions, some of which have significant sub-divisions" ranging from "religious beliefs and practices that are based on rational understanding that all people allegedly can discover for themselves and can warrant by rational reflection" to "that which is held to be common to the different actual faiths that have been and are present in the world."[9] The former definition largely grew out of intra-Christian sectarian disputation and relied primarily on processes of introspection; the latter arose from study of the "religions" and involved processes of comparison. The essentially anthropological project of describing natural religion privileged similarity, often expressed by claims of universality or innateness; the explanation of difference was chiefly historical, whether it emphasized progressive or degenerative processes. This double enterprise had the effect of blurring the distinctions between questions of truth and questions of origins. For example, the title of Matthew Tindal's fairly pedestrian but widely read treatise, published anonymously as *Christianity As Old as the Creation; or, The Gospel, a Republication of the Religion of Nature* (1730), contains early English uses of the terms "religion of nature" and "Christianity." Tindal argues:

> If God, then, from the Beginning gave Men a Religion[,] . . . he must have giv'n them likewise sufficient Means of knowing it. . . . If God never intended Mankind shou'd at any Time be without Religion, or have false Religions; and there be but One True Religion, which ALL have been ever bound to believe, and profess[,] . . . All Men, at all Times, must have had sufficient Means to discover whatever God design'd they shou'd know and practice. . . . [He] has giv'n them no other Means for this, but the use of Reason. . . . There was from the Beginning but One True Religion, which all Men might know was their Duty to embrace. . . . By [this] *Natural Religion*, I understand the Belief of the Existence of a God, and the Sense and Practice of those Duties, which result from the Knowledge, we, by our Reason, have of Him and his Perfections; and of ourselves, and our own Imperfections; and of the Relations we stand in to him, and to our Fellow-Creatures; so that the *Religion of Nature* takes in every Thing that is founded on the Reason and the Nature of Things.[10]

183

While Tindal acknowledges some relativity—"I do not mean by This that All shou'd have equal Knowledge; but that All shou'd have what is sufficient for the Circumstances they are in"[11]—his usual explanation for variation is the historical institution and wiles of "priestcraft":

> Religion either does not concern the Majority, as being incapable of forming a Judgement about it; or must carry such internal Marks of its Truth, as Men of mean Capacity are able to discover; or else notwithstanding the infinite Variety of Religions, All who do not understand the Original Languages their traditional Religions are written in, which is all Mankind, a very few excepted, are alike bound in all Places to pin their Faith on their Priests, and believe in Men, who have an Interest to deceive them; and who have seldom fail'd to do so, when Occasion serves.[12]

In Tindal's self-description,

> He builds nothing on a Thing so uncertain as *Tradition*, which differs in most Countries; and of which, in all Countries, the Bulk of Mankind are incapable of judging; but thinks he has laid down such plain and evident Rules, as may enable Men of the meanest Capacity, to distinguish between *Religion*, and *Superstition*.[13]

When Tindal argued on logical grounds, the presumption of the unity of truth, that natural religion "differs not from *Reveal'd*, but in the manner of its being communicated: The One being the Internal, as the Other the External Revelation"[14] he signaled the beginning of the process of transposing "religion" from a supernatural to a natural history, from a theological to an anthropological category. This process was complete only when the distinctions between questions of truth and questions of origin were firmly established. While not without predecessors, the emblem of this transposition is David Hume's essay *The Natural History of Religion*, written between 1749 and 1751 and first published in his collection *Four Dissertations* (1757).

The question Hume sets out to answer in the *Natural History* is that of religion's "origin in human nature." He begins by disposing of the innateness thesis. If "religion" is defined as "the belief of invisible, intelligent power," then, although widely distributed, it is not universal, nor is there commonality: "no two nations, and scarce any two men, have ever agreed precisely in the same sentiments." "Religion" fails the minimal requirements for innateness, that it be "absolutely universal in all nations and ages

and has always a precise, determinate object, which it inflexibly pursues."
Therefore, "religion" is not "an original instinct or primary impression of
nature," and "the first religious principles must be secondary." In addition,
because they are "secondary," religious principles "may easily be perverted
by various accidents and causes." In this opening move, a major thesis is
forecast. There may well be a primary and valid human experience that
gives rise to the secondary religious interpretation, but the truth of the
experience is no guarantee of the validity of the interpretation.

The rich details of Hume's exposition need not concern us here but
only the argument with respect to this issue. "Polytheism or idolatry was . . .
the first and most antient religion of mankind." Its origin must be sought
in "the ordinary affections of human life." Filled with anxiety, human beings seek the "unknown causes" that "become the constant object of our
hope and fear." The primary human experience, "hope and fear," becomes
a secondary religious interpretation when these "unknown causes" are
personified through "imagination."

> There is a universal tendency amongst mankind to conceive
> all beings like themselves, and to transfer to every object those
> qualities, with which they are familiarly acquainted, and of
> which they are intimately conscious. . . . No wonder, then, that
> mankind, being placed in such an absolute ignorance of causes,
> and being at the same time so anxious concerning their future
> fortunes, should immediately acknowledge a dependence on in-
> visible powers, possest of sentiment and intelligence. The *un-
> known causes*, which continually employ their thought, appear-
> ing always in the same aspect, are all apprehended to be of the
> same kind or species [as themselves]. Nor is it long before we as-
> cribe to them thought, and reason, and passion, and sometimes
> even the limbs and figures of men, in order to bring them nearer
> to a resemblance with ourselves.[15]

What Hume here raises is the issue of the adjectival form 'religious.'
What sort of primary human experience or activity does it modify? What
constitutes its distinctive secondary interpretation? How may religious
interpretation be assessed in relation to other sorts of interpretation of
the same experience or activity? The 'religious' (the unknown that the
scholar is seeking to classify and explain) becomes an aspect of some
other human phenomenon (the known). As Walter Capps has argued, in
the eighteenth-century Enlightenment debates "the goal of the inquiry
was to make religion intelligible by discovering precisely where it is situ-

ated within the wide range of interactive human powers and faculties."[16] In which of the genera of common individual human capacities is the religious a species? Most frequently, the religious is identified with rationality, morality, or feeling.

A different set of taxonomic questions were raised by the 'religions' and became urgent by the nineteenth century: Are the diverse 'religions' species of a generic 'religion'? Is 'religion' the unique beginner, a *summum genus*, or is it best conceived as a subordinate cultural taxon? How might the several 'religions' be classified?

The question of the "religions" arose in response to an explosion of data. Increased mastery of non-European languages led by the latter part of the eighteenth century to a series of translations and editions of religious texts. Missionaries, colonial officials, and travelers contributed ethnographic descriptions. Encyclopedias of religions, lexica, and handbooks (the last of these frequently bearing the title "History of Religions") were produced to organize these materials. One of the earliest handbooks, *Historische-theologische Bericht vom Unterschied der Religionen die Heute zu Tage auf Erden sind,* by the Lutheran scholar Johann Heinrich Ursin (1563), focused heavily on the various Christian denominations, establishing a pattern that holds to the present day: that the history of the major 'religions' is best organized as sectarian history, thereby reproducing the apologetic patristic heresiological model. By the time of Brerewood's *Enquiries Touching the Diversity of Languages and Religions* (1614) this horizon had been extended to require inclusion of not only Christian data but also Jewish, Muslim, and "Idolatry." This fourfold schema was continued by other writers from the seventeenth century (for example, Guebhart Meier, *Historia religionum, Christianae, Judaeae, Gentilis, Mahumedanae* [1697]) until well into the nineteenth century (Hannah Adams, *A Dictionary of All Religions and Religious Denominations, Jewish, Heathen, Mahometan, and Christian, Ancient and Modern* [1817]; David Benedict, *History of All Religions, As Divided into Paganism, Mahometism, Judaism, and Christianity* [1824]; J. Newton Brown, *Encyclopedia of Religious Knowledge; or, Dictionary . . . Containing Definitions of All Religious Terms: An Impartial Account of the Principal Christian Denominations That Have Existed in the World from the Birth of Christ to the Present Day with Their Doctrines, Religious Rites and Ceremonies, as well as those of the Jews, Mohammedans, and Heathen Nations, together with the Manners and Customs of the East* [1835]; Vincent Milner, *Religious Denominations of the World: Comprising a General View of the Origin, History and Condition of the Various Sects of Christians, the Jews, and Mahometans, As Well as the Pagan Forms of Religion Existing in the Different Countries of the Earth* [1872]). The bulk of the subsequent expansion occurred in Brerewood's fourth category, "Idolatry," with data added on Asian religions and on those of traditional peoples. Beginning with Alexander Ross, *Pansebeia; or, A View of All Religions in the World from the Creation to These Times* (1614), there was a steady stream of reference works that undertook this task, including Bernard Picart and J. F. Bernard, *Cérémonies et coutumes de tous peoples du monde* (1723–43); Antoine Banier, *Historie général des cérémonies, moeurs, et coutumes religieuses de tous les peoples du monde* (1741); Thomas Broughton, *An Historical Dictionary of All Religions, from the Creation of the World to the Present Time* (1742); Christopher Meiners, *Grundriss der Geschichte aller Religionen* (1785) and *Allgemeine kritische Geschichte der Religionen* (1806–7); John Bellemy, *The History of All Religions* (1812); and Benjamin Constant, *De la religion considérée dans sa source, ses formes et ses développements* (1824–31). This undertaking invented the familiar nomenclature, "Boudhism" (1821), "Hindooism" (1829, which replaced the earlier seventeenth-century usages "Gentoo [from "gentile"] religion" and "Banian religion"), "Taouism" (1839), and "Confucianism" (1862). The urgent agendum was to bring order to this variety of species. Only an adequate taxonomy would convert a 'natural history' of religion into a 'science.'

The most common form of classifying religions, found both in native categories and in scholarly literature, is dualistic and can be reduced, regardless of what differentium is employed, to "theirs" and "ours." By the time of the fourth-century Christian Latin apologists, a strong dual vocabulary was well in place and could be deployed interchangeably regardless of the individual histories of the terms: "our religion"/"their religion," with the latter often expressed through generic terms such as "heathenism," "paganism," or "idolatry"; "true religion"/"false religion"; "spiritual (or "internal") religion"/"material (or "external") religion"; "monotheism" (although this term, itself, is a relatively late construction)/"polytheism"; "religion"/"superstition"; "religion"/"magic." This language was transposed to intrareligious disputation with respect to heresies and later revived in positive proposals of originary recovery in Christian Renaissance hermetism as well as, most massively and insistently, in Protestant polemics against Roman Catholicism. As such, it was at hand for the evaluation of the newly encountered religions beginning in the sixteenth century. Lifting up the fourfold enumeration of religions—Christianity, Judaism, Islam, and "Idolatry"—Christianity, in some imagination of its ideal form, became the norm in which Judaism and Islam problematically share. Adopting a term from Muslim discourse, these three "Abrahamic religions" form one set over and against an undifferentiated other:

It is indeed probable, that all the idolatrous systems of religion, which have ever existed in the world, have had a common origin, and have been modified by the different fancies and corruptions of different nations. The essence of idolatry is every where the same. It is every where "abominable" in its principles and its rites, and every where the cause of indescribable and manifold wretchedness.[17]

The initial problem for a classification of the religions is the disaggregation of this category.

One of the more persistent stratagems was the conversion of the epistemological duality natural/supernatural into a characterization of the object of belief (as in "nature worship") and the placement of these two terms in a chronological relationship.

The elements of nature were . . . the first divinities of man; he generally has commenced with adoring material beings. . . . Everything was personified. . . . Natural philosophers and poets [later distinguished] nature from herself—from her own peculiar energies—from her faculty of action. By degrees they made an incomprehensible being of this energy, which as before they personified: this abstract metaphysical being they called the mover of nature, or God.[18]

This simple schema of two religions could be greatly extended by the addition of intermediate stages in the temporal series.

Nineteenth-century anthropological approaches focused on increasing the number of "natural" religious categories, especially for "primitive" peoples, those held to be "nature peoples" (*Naturvolker*). Often mistermed "evolutionary," these theories conceded no historical dimensions to those being classified but rather froze each ethnic unit at a particular "stage of development" of the totality of human religious thought and activity. "Natural" religion was segmented into fetishism, totemism, shamanism, anthropomorphism, preanimism, animism, family gods, guardian spirits, ancestor worship, departmental gods, to name but a few. If the category "natural" were to be taken as including not only "primitives" but "antiquity," a set of peoples with whom the scholar more readily identified, then a meager note of historical dynamism would be introduced. For example, A. M. Fairbairn in his *Studies in the Philosophy of Religion and History* (1876), divided "Spontaneous or Natural Religions" into two classes, "Primitive

Naturalisms" (which included, among others, "primitives" and the "early" Greeks, Hindus, Teutons, and Slavs) and "Transformed Naturalisms" (e.g., "later" Greeks and Romans, Egyptians, and "ancient" Chinese).

The "high religions," which could be designated "spiritual," required a different technique for their division, one that recognized history. One proposal, establishing an alternative duality that remains current to this day, was set forth by the distinguished American Sanskritist, W. D. Whitney (1881): "There is no more marked distinction among religions than the one we are called upon to make between a race religion—which, like a language, is the collective product of the wisdom of a community, the unconscious growth of generations—and a religion proceeding from an individual founder." He cites as examples of the latter, Zoroastrianism, "Mohammedanism," Buddhism, and Christianity, noting that the last may be described as "growing out of one [Judaism] that was limited to a race."[19] Whitney here makes clear the dilemma posed by the study of the "religions" from the perspective of the spiritual. The older fourfold enumeration of the three "Abrahamic religions" plus "Idolatry" required revision. Judaism was to be demoted in that from a Christian apologetic perspective, it was the very type of a "fleshly religion"; Buddhism, formerly, the very type of "idolatry," was to be promoted because in the two-century history of the western imagination of Buddhism, it had become the very type of "spiritual religion."

Fairbairn adjusted his model such that the ultimate duality was between "spontaneous or natural religions" and "instituted religions," with the latter having two classes, each characterized by the same powerfully positive Protestant term: "Reformed Natural" (including the archaic religion of Israel ["Mosaism"], Zoroastrianism, Confucianism, Taoism), and "Reformed Spiritual," limited only to the new triad (Buddhism, "Mohammedanism," and Christianity). All other "religions" fell into one of three classes of "natural," the replacement term for the older category, "idolatry."

The most enduring device was the invention of the taxon "world" or "universal religions," a division that appeared to recognize both history and geography.[20] The term was introduced and placed in a classificatory scheme that synthesized previous taxonomic divisions in a work that stands as the first classic in the science of religion, Cornelius Petrus Tiele's work *Outline of the History of Religion to the Spread of Universal Religions* (1876), and was reworked in Tiele's article "Religions" in the ninth edition of the *Encyclopaedia Britannica* (1884). Tiele's "morphological" classification, which schematizes the "stage of development" each religion has "attained," has as its fundamental principle of division "natural religion" and "ethical religion," which he self-consciously correlates with Whitney's distinction between "race religion" and "founded religion." "Natural religion" has three families, one of which has two genera. The first family comprises "polydaemonistic magical religions under the control of animism." To this class "belong [all] the religions of the so-called savages or uncivilized peoples." Recognizing, perhaps, the effects of colonialism, he adds that their present forms are "only degraded remnants of what they once must have been."

The second family of "nature religions" is that of "purified or organized magical religions," which Tiele terms "therianthropic polytheism," according to which the "gods are sometimes represented in human form, more frequently in that of an animal." These are politically divided into two families, "unorganized" (tribal) and "organized" (imperial). The "unorganized" include the Japanese *kami* traditions, the Dravidians, the Finns, the "old Arabic religions, old Pelasgic religion, old Italiote religions, Etruscan religion before its admixture with Greek elements, [and] the old Slavonic religions." The "organized" include "the semi-civilized religions of America, . . . the ancient religion of the Chinese empire, ancient Babylonian (Chaldaean) religion, [and] the religion of Egypt."

The third family, "anthropomorphic polytheism," is characterized by the "worship of manlike but superhuman and semi-ethical beings" (the latter indicating that while the gods are often represented as being concerned with good and evil, they are also depicted as essentially amoral). Belonging to this class are "the ancient Vaidic religion (India), the pre-Zarathustrian Iranic religion, the younger Babylonian and Assyrian religion, the religions of the other civilized Semites, the Celtic, Germanic, Hellenic and Graeco-Roman religions."

Distinct from these "nature religions" are those belonging to the second major division, "ethical religions," which are subdivided into "national nomistic (nomothetic) religious communities" characterized by being "founded on a law or holy scripture," that is, "Taoism and Confucianism . . . Brahmanism, with its various ancient and modern sects, Jainism and primitive Buddhism, Mazdaism (Zarathustrianism) with its sects, Mosaism [and] Judaism," and "universalistic religious communities," a class with only three members: Islam, Buddhism, and Christianity. They are distinguished in not being devoted to the special interests of a nation or people but to humankind in general; they are proselytizing traditions.

After discussing at some length the relative merits of the labels "uni-

versalistic," "universal," and "world religions," Tiele employs blunt imperialistic language to defend his use of "world religions" to

> distinguish the three religions which have found their way to dif-
> ferent races and peoples and all of which profess the intention
> to conquer the world, from such communities [that is, "national,
> nomistic religions"] as are generally limited to a single race or
> nation, and, where they have extended farther, have done so
> only in the train of, and in connection with, a superior civiliza-
> tion. Strictly speaking, there can be no more than one universal
> or world religion, and if one of the existing religions is so poten-
> tially, it has not yet reached its goal. This is a matter of belief
> which lies beyond the limits of scientific classification. . . . Mod-
> ern history of religions is chiefly the history of Buddhism, Chris-
> tianity and Islam, and of their wrestling with the ancient faiths
> and primitive modes of worship, which slowly fade away before
> their encroachments, and which, where they still survive in some
> parts of the world and do not reform themselves after the model
> of the superior religion, draw nearer and nearer to extinction.

Furthermore, he apologetically insists, the three "world religions" are not
on an equal plane. Islam "is not original, not a ripe fruit, but rather a wild
offshoot of Judaism and Christianity," "in its external features [it] is little
better than an extended Judaism." Buddhism "neglects the divine" and
while "atheistic in its origin, it very soon becomes infected by the most
fantastic mythology and the most childish superstitions." Christianity
"alone preaches a worship in spirit and in truth . . . the natural result of
its purely spiritual character, Christianity ranks incommensurably high
above both its rivals." Despite the latter assertion, Tiele insists that "we
are giving here neither a confession of faith nor an apology. . . . we have
here to treat Christianity simply as a subject of comparative study, from
a scientific, not from a religious point of view."[21]

Later scholars expanded the number of world religions to seven by
collapsing Tiele's two classes of "ethical religions" in an odd venture of
pluralistic etiquette: if Christianity and Islam count as world religions,
then it would be rude to exclude Judaism (ironically, the original model
for the opposite type, "national nomistic religions"). Likewise, if Buddhism is included, then Hinduism cannot be ignored. And again, if Buddhism, then Chinese religions and Japanese religions.

It is impossible to escape the suspicion that a world religion is simply a religion like ours, and that it is, above all, a tradition that has achieved sufficient power and numbers to enter our history to form it, interact with it, or thwart it. We recognize both the unity within and the diversity among the world religions because they correspond to important geopolitical entities with which we must deal. All "primitives," by way of contrast, may be lumped together, as may the "minor religions," because they do not confront our history in any direct fashion. From the point of view of power, they are invisible.

Attempting to avoid such strictures and suspicions, other scholars have turned to alternative modes of classification. Following the implied correlation in Brerewood's *Enquiries Touching the Diversity of Languages and Religions*, F. Max Müller (1873) argued "that the only scientific and truly genetic classification of religions is the same as the classification of languages,"[22] while Brerewood's interest in statistics has led to geographical taxonomies, either demographic or in terms of spatial distribution.[23] Others combine these elements with ethnic classifications maintaining that any particular "religion derives its character from the people or race who develop it or adopt it" (Ward 1909).[24] All of these result in projects describing "the religion of" such and such a geographical region or folk, arguing that these eschew the imposed universalisms or barely disguised apologetics of their predecessors in the name of a new ethic of locality that often favors native categories. Thus, Clifford Geertz introduces his early work *The Religion of Java* (1960) by emphasizing the copresence of nativistic, Islamic, and "Hinduist" elements, arguing that "these three main subtraditions . . . are not constructed types, but terms and divisions the Javanese themselves apply. . . . Any simple unitary view is certain to be inadequate; and so I have tried to show . . . variation in ritual, contrast in belief, and conflict in values."[25] What remains uncertain is what he intends by the singular "religion" in his title.

As in the eighteenth century, so too in the late twentieth do the issues attending the religions force the definitional question of 'religion.' Two definitions command widespread scholarly assent, one essentially theological, the other anthropological. Paul Tillich (1959), reversing his previous formulation that religion is concern for the ultimate, argued that

> religion, in the largest and most basic sense of the word, is ultimate concern . . . manifest in the moral sphere as the unconditional seriousness of moral demand[,] . . . in the realm of knowledge as the passionate longing for ultimate reality[,] . . . in the aesthetic function of the human spirit as the infinite desire

to express ultimate meaning. [Religion is not a] special function of man's spiritual life, but the dimension of depth in all its
functions[26]

As Tillich's earlier concern with topics such as idolatry and the demonic
should suggest, this is not as generous and open-ended a definition as
might seem to be implied. There are insufficient, inadequate, and false
convictions of "ultimacy." Tillich has in fact provided a definition of the
"religious" as a dimension (in his case, the ultimate, unconditioned aspect) of human existence. This is explicit in William A. Christian's re-
formulation: "Someone is religious if in his universe there is something
to which (in principle) all other things are subordinated. Being religious
means having an interest of this kind" (1964).[27] If one removes Tillich's
and Christian's theological criteria, then it becomes difficult if not impossible to distinguish religion from any other ideological category. This
would be the direction that Ninian Smart (1983) points to in suggesting
that religion be understood as "worldview," with the latter understood as
a system "of belief which, through symbols and actions, mobilize[s] the
feelings and wills of human beings."[28]

The anthropological definition of religion that has gained widespread assent among scholars of religion, who both share and reject its
functionalist frame, is that formulated by Melford E. Spiro (1966), "an institution consisting of culturally patterned interaction with culturally
postulated superhuman beings." This definition requires acceptance of a
broad theory of cultural creation, signaled by the phrases "culturally patterned" and "culturally postulated," and places human cultural activities
or institutions as the *summum genus* and religion as a subordinate taxon.
This is made plain in Spiro's formulation that "religion can be differentiated from other culturally constituted institutions by virtue only of its
reference to superhuman beings."[29] Subsequent reformulations by scholars of religion have tended either to remove this subordination (for example, Penner [1989]) or to substitute "supernatural" for "superhuman"
(as in Stark and Bainbridge [1987]).[30]

It was once a tactic of students of religion to cite the appendix of
James H. Leuba's *Psychological Study of Religion* (1912), which lists more
than fifty definitions of religion, to demonstrate that "the effort clearly to
define religion in short compass is a hopeless task."[31] Not at all! The moral
of Leuba is not that religion cannot be defined, but that it can be defined,
with greater or lesser success, more than fifty ways. Besides, Leuba goes on
to classify and evaluate his list of definitions. 'Religion' is not a native

term; it is a term created by scholars for their intellectual purposes and therefore is theirs to define. It is a second-order, generic concept that plays the same role in establishing a disciplinary horizon that a concept such as 'language' plays in linguistics or 'culture' plays in anthropology. There can be no disciplined study of religion without such a horizon.[32]

Notes

1. R. Eden, *A Treatyse of the Newe India* (London, 1553), sig. M ii, in the facsimile published by the Readex Microprint Corporation as part of their Great Americana series (n.p., 1966); see also the printing of the *Treatyse* in E. Arber, ed., *The First Three English Books on America* (Birmingham, 1885; reprint, New York, 1971), 3–42. The *Treatyse* is a free English rendering of Sebastian Münster, *Cosmographiae universalis libri vi* (Basel, 1550), book 5.

The Columbus notice, from the *Journal* of the first voyage, is, in fact, more complex than has often been acknowledged. In the journal, the most common religious designation is "the Faith" or "the Holy Faith" (twenty-one times), referring always to Roman Catholicism. The term "religion" (used three times) is likewise reserved for Catholicism (O. Dunn and J. E. Kelly, Jr., eds., *The Diario of Christopher Columbus's First Voyage to America 1492–1493, abstracted by Fray Bartolomé de las Casas*, American Exploration and Travel, 70 [Norman, OK, 1989]: 140, 185, 395). Given this usage, Columbus never describes the natives as having no "religion"; rather Columbus insists, six times, that they have "no sect" (*Diario*, 68, 88, 126, 142, 184, 234). When "sect" is paired with "idolatry," it is unambiguously negative. Thus Columbus can speak of his contemporary Europe as a place where "so many peoples were lost, believing in idolatries and receiving among themselves sects of perdition," while the Spanish monarchs are praised for being sworn "enemies of the sect of Mahomet and of all idolatries and heresies" (*Diario*, 16, 18). At least twice, when Columbus reports that the natives have "no sect," he adds, "nor are they idolaters" thus easing their conversion to "our customs and faith" (*Diario*, 142, 184). See my comments in J. Z. Smith, "Classification," in W. Braun and R. T. McCutcheon, *Guide to the Study of Religion* (London and New York, 2000), 39–40.

2. P. Cieza de León, *Parte primera de la Chrónica del Perú* (1553), in the edition by E. de Vedia, *Historiadores primitivos de Indias*, Bibliotheca de Autores Españoles, 26 (Madrid, 1913–18), 2: 380.

3. See further, J. Z. Smith, "The Topography of the Sacred," printed in this volume.

4. H. Cortés, *Cartas de Relacíon* (1520), ed. M. Alcalá, Sepan Cuantos, 7 (Mexico City, 1971), 64.

5. J. de Acosta, *Historia natural y moral de las Indias* (1590), E. O'Gorman, 2d

ed., Biblioteca Americana, Serie de Cronistas de Indias (Mexico City, 1962), 215, 234, 267. The English translation is by Edward Grimston, *The Natural and Moral History of the Indies* (London, 1604), Hakluyt Society, 1st ser. (London, 1880; reprint, New York, 1973), vols. 1–2. Grimston's translations of the quoted passages may be found at 2: 295, 324, 372.

6. E. Phillips, *A New World of English Words; or, A General Dictionary Containing the Interpretation of Such Hard Words As Are Derived from Other Languages* (London, 1696), s.v. "piety."

7. E. Brerewood, *Enquiries Touching the Diversity of Languages and Religions through the Chiefe Parts of the World* (London, 1614), 118–19.

8. S. Purchas, *Purchas His Pilgrimage; or, Relations of the World and the Religions Observed in All Ages and Places Discovered . . . in Foure Parts* (London, 1613): sig. D 4r.

9. D. Pailan, "Natural Religion," an unpublished paper presented at the annual meeting of the American Academy of Religion, Chicago, 1994.

10. M. Tindal, *Christianity As Old as the Creation; or, The Gospel, a Republication of the Religion of Nature* (London, 1730), facsimile edition, ed. G. Gawlick (Stuttgart and Bad Cannstatt, 1967), 3, 7, 13.

11. Ibid., 5.

12. Ibid., 232.

13. Ibid., iii.

14. Ibid., 3.

15. D. Hume, *The Natural History of Religion*, in Hume, *Four Dissertations* (London, 1757). I cite the variorum edition, edited by A. W. Colver, in Colver and J. V. Price, eds., *David Hume on Religion* (Oxford, 1976), 25–34.

16. W. H. Capps, *Religious Studies: The Making of a Discipline* (Minneapolis, 1995), 9.

17. J. N. Brown, *Encyclopedia of Religious Knowledge; or, Dictionary . . . Containing Definitions of All Religious Terms: An Impartial Account of the Principal Christian Denominations That Have Existed in the World from the Birth of Christ to the Present Day with Their Doctrines, Religious Rites and Ceremonies, as well as those of the Jews, Mohammedans, and Heathen Nations, together with the Manners and Customs of the East* (Brattleboro, 1835), 279, s.v. "Budhism, or Boodhism."

18. M. Mirabaud [Paul Henry Thiery, Baron d'Holbach], *Système de la nature; ou, Des lois du monde physique et du monde moral* (London [Amsterdam], 1770), 2: 4.

19. W. D. Whitney, "On the So-Called Science of Religion," *Princeton Review* 57 (1881): 429–52, quotation from 451.

20. For further discussions of the taxon "world religions," see J. Z. Smith, *Map Is Not Territory* (Leiden, 1978; reprint, Chicago, 1993), 295–96 (cf. the comments on this article in J. M. Kitagawa, "Humanistic and Theological History of

Religions with Special Reference to the North American Scene," in P. Slater and D. Wiebe, eds., *Traditions in Contact and Change: Selected Proceedings of the XIVth Congress of the International Association for the History of Religions* [Waterloo, Ontario, 1983]: 559); Smith, "Classification" (cited, note 1, above), 41–42; Smith, "A Matter of Class," reprinted in this volume.

21. C. P. Tiele, "Religions," *Encyclopaedia Britannica*, 9th ed. (1884), 20: 358–71.

22. F. M. Müller, *Introduction to the Science of Religion* (London, 1873), 143.

23. K. G. Haupt, *Tabellarischer Abriss der vorzüglichsten Religionen und Religionsparteien der jetzigen Erdebewohner* (Leipzig, 1821) is an early example of a geographical taxonomy; P. Deffontaines, *Géographie et Religions* Géographie humaine, 21 (Paris, 1948) remains an important work on the geographical distribution of religions.

24. D. J. H. Ward, *The Classification of Religion* (Chicago, 1909), 64.

25. C. Geertz, *The Religion of Java* (Glencoe, 1960), 6–7.

26. P. Tillich, *Theology of Culture*, ed. R. C. Kimball (New York, 1959), 7–8.

27. W. A. Christian, *Meaning and Truth in Religion* (Princeton, 1964), 61.

28. N. Smart, *Worldviews: Cross-Cultural Explorations of Religious Beliefs* (New York, 1983), 2–3. See also R. D. Baird, *Category Formation and the History of Religions*, Religion and Reason, 1 (The Hague, 1971), for a persistent effort at removing Tillich's theological criteria.

29. Melford E. Spiro, "Religion: Problems of Definition and Explanation," in M. Banton, ed., *Anthropological Approaches to the Study of Religion*, Association of Social Anthropologists of the Commonwealth Monographs, 3 (London, 1966), 85–126, quotations from 96, 98. Spiro's definition, remains, for me, the most satisfying one.

30. For the removal of Spiro's subordination, see, for example, the important discussion by Hans H. Penner, *Impasse and Resolution: A Critique of the Study of Religion*, Toronto Studies in Religion, 8 (New York, 1989), 7–11. For the substitution of 'supernatural' for 'superhuman' (in my judgment, a retrograde step), see R. Stark and W. S. Bainbridge, *A Theory of Religion*, Toronto Studies in Religion, 2 (New York, 1987; reprint, New Brunswick, NJ, 1996): 39, et passim.

31. W. L. King, *Introduction to Religion* (New York, 1954), 63.

32. For an elaboration of this latter point, see J. Z. Smith, "A Twice-told Tale: The History of the History of Religions' History," reprinted in this volume.

BIBLE AND RELIGION

I HAD NOT known, until I received this year's annual meeting program book, that our conveners thought of this presentation in consort with my work in *Drudgery Divine*—an essay on methodological issues in comparison, using the rich documentation of the history of scholarship on the relations between early Christianities and Late Antique religions as the privileged example. As I wrote in the preface, quoting Vološinov, "what interests us here is not so much the connections between the phenomena as the connections between the problems."[1]

In the more than ten years since the writing of *Drudgery*, I have not so much altered the discussion of methods and models as I have sought to situate the comparative enterprise within the overall project of the study of religion, a project entailing definition, classification, comparison, and explanation. Each of these processes have in common that they are varying modes of redescription. From this perspective, the end of comparison cannot be the act of comparison itself. I would distinguish four moments in the comparative enterprise: description, comparison, redescription, and rectification. Description is a double process which comprises the historical or ethnographic dimensions of the work. A first requirement is that we locate a given example within the rich texture of its social, historical, and cultural environments that invest it with its local significance. The second task of description is that of reception-history, a careful account of how our second-order scholarly tradition has intersected with the exemplum, how the datum has come to be accepted as significant for the purpose of argument. Only when such a double contextualization is completed can one move on to the description of a second example undertaken in the same double fashion. With at least two exempla in view, one is prepared to undertake their comparison both in terms of aspects and relations held to be significant, expressed in the tropes of similarities and differences, and with respect to some category, question, theory, or model of interest to the study of religion. The aim of such a comparison is the redescription of the exempla (at the very least, each in terms of the other) and a rectification of the academic categories in relation to which they have been imagined.[2]

To keep faith with our conveners, my remarks can be taken as an epexegesis of the penultimate sentence of *Drudgery*, which speaks of the usefulness, for the student of religion, of comparisons between the religions of Late Antiquity and early Christianities and, by extension, to the value of the Bible as a datum: "a phenomenon will be privileged only with respect to its utility for answering a theoretical issue concerning the scholarly imagination of religion."[3] That is to say, I would like to reflect on the relationship of biblical scholarship to the enterprise of the study of religion (not the religions). That this is not a jejune question can be demonstrated by noting that, in the past decade, the North American Association for the Study of Religion has devoted four full sessions to theoretical questions raised by the New Testament research, as well as cosponsoring a panel on the same topic at a recent annual meeting of the Society for the Scientific Study of Religion.

This presentation acknowledges by its title the more than two thousand scholars who hold joint membership in the Society of Biblical Literature (SBL) and the American Academy of Religion (AAR). This is a massive syncretism, uncommon outside of North America, which holds out hope for the development of different practices and for experiments in reconceptualizations of both religious and biblical studies.

I intend as well to echo in my title some strains of an older element in this shared disciplinary genealogy. The immediate predecessor of the AAR was the National Association of Bible Instructors, bearing the portentous acronym, NABI, the Hebrew word for prophet.[4] Its previous name (1909–22) was more specific as to vocation: the Association of Biblical Instructors in American Colleges and Secondary Schools. This group self-consciously distinguished itself from the older Society of Biblical Literature and Exegesis. If the chief publication of the SBL was the *Journal of the Exegetical Society* (1881–89) and then the *Journal of Biblical Literature and Exegesis*, the house organ of NABI, replacing both its *Journal* (1933–

36) and its earlier proceedings published in *Christian Education* (1927–32), was, from 1937 to 1964, the *Journal of Bible and Religion*.

What was intended by this provocative and novel conjunction? We must, I think, resist the temptation to attribute a Barthian pedigree to it. Here the two nouns were not intended as antonyms, but rather as synonyms. If there was an antagonism, it was that "religion" was deployed as an oppositional term to both the more technical-sounding "exegesis" and to the more secular-sounding "literature" incorporated in the nomenclature of both the SBL and the *JBL*. NABI was concerned with values and education and thought of the SBL as concerned with texts and critical scholarship. This difference in vocation was expressed strongly in one NABI president's address:

> The professor who teaches Bible . . . is in for a discouraging time. He wants to emphasize religion, but critical and historical questions insistently bob up. No matter how hard he tries to keep them in a justly subordinate place . . . [he finds that] he has spent so much time clearing up [those] problems he had had little time for the truth.[5]

A similar sentiment informs an editorial in NABI's *Journal* devoted to the relations between the two societies:

> SBL has for its primary object technical and creative research. . . . NABI has a mission of its own, to it fall matters of pedagogy and education. It deals with methods and contents of courses of study, and the application of religion to character building.[6]

NABI's activist nature, in this latter regard, is signaled by the slogan on the front cover of each issue of the *Journal of Bible and Religion*, "To Foster Religion in Education."

"Religion," in such a context, was understood to be the beliefs, morals, and practices encoded in Scripture. NABI was, in fact, an implacable foe of the academic study of religion as we have come to understand it. As Chester Warren Quimby of Dickinson College lamented in his 1933 president's address:

> That all is not well with the teaching of the English Bible is a well-known and all too bitter axiom. The early hope that we [NABI] might become an influential national society has failed. The Southern section—the very core of the "Bible Belt"—was

stillborn. The Central and Western sections have become vague societies of religion. The Bible departments of our own [Eastern] section are fast changing to Departments of religion, so that now, although we only are left they are seeking our life to take it away.[7]

Four years later, in an editorial explaining the rationale for the change of name from the *Journal of the National Association of Bible Instructors* to the *Journal of Bible and Religion*, Ismer J. Peritz took some care to distinguish the *Journal*'s "unique function to center our interest in the Bible and in religion insofar as it relates to the religion of the Bible" from the "vast field of the discipline of religion."[8]

Despite these cautions, NABI morphed into the AAR in 1963. The AAR continued to publish the *Journal of Bible and Religion* as *its* journal from April 1964 to March 1967 when its name was changed to the *Journal of the American Academy of Religion* (JAAR).[9] It is due to this genealogy that, to this day, JAAR is not to be found on our libraries' shelves bearing the Library of Congress call letters "BL," along with other general serial publications in religious studies, but rather in quite another part of the library, under the official government classification "LC 351" which denotes "Education/Christian Education/Education Under Church Control." (In my university's library, JAAR is shelved between the volumes of the *Handbook of Christian Higher Education* published by the Council of Church Boards of Education, and a run of *Yearbooks* of the National Council of the Churches of Christ in the USA, Division of Christian Education.)

NABI's persistent unproblematized use of "religion" privileged a sharp focus on a locus of authority (the Bible) over against which a more generic notion of "religion" appeared, in the passages just quoted, to be both "vast" and "vague." If for NABI, "religion" had any meaning at all, it was in the sense of the title of a scarce, anonymous, seventy-two-page polemical pamphlet published in Dublin in 1840, *The Bible, The Religion of Protestants*. By contrast, for its successor, the AAR, "religion" is largely understood to be a highly contested academic construct. One that is contested with respect to definition, taxonomic status, strategies for explanation, and intellectual genealogy. These are matters that must be debated in terms of theory, rather than by appeal to some privileged set of data.

In this regard, two examples from NABI may stand for the whole.[10] "For the Bible is Religion. It is the Word of God. . . . Everywhere the Bible is religion—always Religion."[11] Or, "Let us look at the Bible as a religious document. Perhaps not many of us believe that one can make a

fast and easy distinction between biblical religion and biblical morality. . . . [Biblical religion is] the biblical ideas of God and man and sin
and salvation."[12] What interests me in these citations, as illustrative of a
far more widely shared position, is the matter of self-evidence. Neither
"Bible" nor "religion" are perceived as problematic terms, nor is there any
question as to their relationship. "Bible" and "religion" mutually entail
each other. There is no discrepancy between the datum (the Bible) and
its model ("religion"). The datum is coextensive with its model. While
presented here in naive form, this is a matter to which I shall want to return as it is characteristic of much biblical scholarship. For the members
of NABI, to judge from their association's publications, the King James
Bible functions, cognitively, as the prototype of "Bible." The present-day,
chiefly Christian, claimants to the category "biblical religion" function,
cognitively, as the prototype of "religion." This is a matter that requires
neither efforts at demonstration nor definition. Questions as basic as
"which Bible?" or "whose Bible?" or "the Bible when?" are not entertained. The self-evident referents of "Bible" and "religion"—thought of
as intact, definite objects—are taken to be a matter of common sense.

One source of this common-sense agreement, as the Latin implies
and as it was understood prior to Kant, is community. Unlike many of the
sorts of interpretative materials available to the student of religion, the
scholarly study of the Bible remains, to a remarkably large degree, an affair of native exegesis. That is to say, the sort of accounts that, for other
religious traditions, constitute data for the student of religion. One consequence of this is that, for all the hermeneutic subtlety at times displayed in wrestling with problems of historical and linguistic difference,
biblical scholarship, unlike most other fields in the western enterprise of
the study of religions, has not been formed by that cluster of urgent and
complex methodological and theoretical issues gathered together under
the label, "the insider/outsider problem." For the student of religion, that
problem is foundational.[13]

I want now to leave behind the particular set of scholars associated
with NABI and return to that conjunction with which I began, "Bible
and Religion," in order to begin the project of imagining what possibilities, problems, and costs might be latent in that construction.

While there are a few, European serial publications that conjoin Bible
and "religion" in their titles (e.g., *Religion och Bibel; Ricerche bibliche e religiose*), this is not common. The division of academic labor and the conventions of academic discourse have sundered the popular (and religious)
conviction that one is dealing with a singular book—indeed, the "Book
of Books"—so that scholars are both more at ease with the nomenclature

of Hebrew Bible and New Testament, as well as being specifically trained in graduate studies reflecting this distinction. While this presents some problems for the student of religion, of greater interest to me is the fact that this division is replicated by a sharp cleavage in scholarly practice with respect to the category "religion." There is no parity in the employment of the terminology of "religion" between scholars of the Hebrew Bible and scholars of the New Testament. The former appear comfortable with the term; the latter abjure it.

Recognizing the fragility of its probative character, and without subjecting you to the litany, based only on works I have had occasion to abstract, there are some forty important monographs, extending in time from 1835 to the present, which employ the terminology "religion of Israel," "Old Testament religion," or some closely parallel construction in their titles. This is the case whether these works are textually or archaeologically based.[14] Some of these works come close to entertaining, in their contents, the more appropriate plural, "Israelitic religions." Likewise, it is common to find important articles devoted to a survey of scholarship on "Israelite religion" in authoritative collective volumes on the state of current research on the Hebrew Bible sponsored by leading learned societies, including the SBL.[15] By contrast (and I should be grateful for correction at this point), except for a misrendering of Alfred Loisy's French title in English translation,[16] I can think of *no* important study of the New Testament or early Christianities that utilizes the term "religion" in its title. If the word does appear, it is with reference to other contemporary Late Antique religions or as a methodological label indicating that the author has adopted a "history of religions" approach. One simple example: Note the difference in titles between the first and second volumes of Helmut Koester's instant classic, *Introduction to the New Testament*. Volume 1 is entitled *History, Culture and Religion of the Hellenistic Age*; volume 2, *History and Literature of Early Christianity*. The anthropological situating of the Christian materials has dropped out. More commonly the nonemployment of the term is eloquent silence, resulting in the irony that, to judge again from titles, New Testament scholars are more comfortable with the term "magic" than they are with "religion." This disparity between the practice of Hebrew Bible scholars and New Testament scholars is a conundrum that invites thought.

While the collection of works on the "religion of Israel" are not distinguished, on the whole, for their prolonged meditation on definitional questions, there is enough to gain a sense of how they view the category, and why New Testament scholars might be recalcitrant towards its use. The nub of the problem appears to be that "religion," as understood with respect to the Hebrew Bible, is "eminently social" (to borrow Durkheim's phrase), institutional, and political. Scholars of the New Testament imagine their phenomena as anything but that.

Recall a foundational work, though by no means the earliest work, that establishes this agendum with respect to the Hebrew Bible: Abraham Kuenen's *The Religion of Israel to the Fall of the Jewish State*, first published in Dutch in 1869–70.[17] Kuenen was an important participant in the formulation of the historical-critical approach to the Hexateuch. He functioned, as well, as a general historian of religions, for example, entering into debate with his fellow Dutchman, C. P. Tiele—arguably the founder of the science of religion—over questions of taxonomy.[18] In this latter regard, he represents a characteristic of mid-nineteenth-century Hebrew Bible scholars. Lacking access to the languages of ancient Near Eastern and Mesopotamian texts, figures such as Kuenen, Wellhausen, and Robertson Smith were fluent Arabists (Arabic then providing the important assist to understanding Hebrew), who worked as comfortably in Islamic as they did in biblical topics. This inescapably drew them into broad contemporary discussions of what was then termed Comparative Religion.

Kuenen's book, *The Religion of Israel*, begins with a set of remarkable pronouncements:

> [This work] does not stand entirely alone, but is one of a number of monographs on "the principal religions." For us the Israelitish is one of those religions, nothing less, but also nothing more. In that general title, "the principal religions," it is by no means implied that there exists no difference in value between the forms of religion thus indicated. . . . On the other hand, however, this common appellation points to a certain mutual conformity. To be able to unite a number of phenomena into one group, we must regard them as homogenous. In a word, the idea of including the Israelitish and the Christian among the "principal religions" deserves approbation and applause, only if there exists no specific difference between these two and all the other forms of religion.[19]

Kuenen goes on to argue that those who would insist on "so great a gulf between these two and the rest of 'the principal religions'" exhibit a "want of thought" and have been misled by the "sacred records of the Israelites and Christians" who "attribute to each of these two religions a supernatural origin." This, he rightly insists, is an important element in their belief-system, and must be described by the scholar as such. But it can be no part of a critical study or explanation of these traditions, which must proceed despite the "testimony of their holy records."[20] As is characteristic of the nineteenth-century historical-critical school, Kuenen devotes the bulk of his work to a political and institutional religious history of Israel, correlated with a literary history of the Hebrew Bible, noting, with some consistency, where "popular religion" differed from "national religion."

Setting aside Kuenen's developmental schema, based on an inadequate theory of religion (summarized in the well-known formula, "from charisma to routinization"), let me abstract the presuppositions as to "religion" in his initial formulations. Religion is to be taken as neither a force nor an experience. It is, first of all, an artificial taxon applied by scholars. "To be able to unite a number of phenomena into one group, we must regard them as homogenous." This "uniting" does not, for Kuenen, entail the suppression of difference; indeed, difference is required. But he insists that there exists "no specific difference" (perhaps better translated, "no difference as to species") with respect to the criteria that qualify a particular set of data to be classified as a "principal religion" rather than as an instance of some other category. Within Kuenen's classification, there is a set of explicit or implied taxonomic levels: Religion is, at the very least, subdivided into principal religions and nonprincipal religions. Principal religions are subdivided, at the very least, into universal and national religions. Each of these, in turn, is subdivided, at the very least, into official and popular religions.[21] None of these conform either to natural kinds or to emic taxa. They are the results of an academician's comparative and logical division. This highlights the necessary gap that exists between the analytic categories of scholarship and native categories. (The latter are expressed, in the passages quoted from Kuenen, by reiterated reference to "their holy record," which must figure in any description but not in any scholarly redescription—a matter to which I shall shortly return.)

Finally, the indicia of "religion" are to be found, for Kuenen, in institutional structures. This implies a principle of classificatory subordination. "Religion" is not the unique beginner. Religion is a family within an encompassing order, that of human institutions. It is the act of subordination that, among other benefits, establishes, for the scholar, one's academic conversation partners.

Without taking time to offer the specifics, what was presented in declarative sentences in Kuenen was skillfully argued less than twenty years later in elaborate detail in William Robertson Smith's foundational *Re-*

ligion of the Semites. Smith's work, among its many other achievements, added to Kuenen's taxonomic and historical interests a rich, multifaceted social theory of religion.

Within New Testament scholarship the approach has, in the main, been quite different. "Religion" as a second-order artificial classificatory category has scarcely been entertained. Taxonomic subordination has been blocked, as *Drudgery,* among other matters, sought to demonstrate, by the deployment of the notion of the "unique." "Religion of the New Testament" or "religion of early Christianities" are not terms of art. The fact that neither of these recur as titles of scholarly works makes all the more striking the persistence of close exceptions: the tradition, extending from at least the mid-eighteenth century until today, of works entitled, *The Religion of Jesus* or *The Religion of Paul,* or more recent works that employ the adjective, "religious," usually modifying "experience," again often in relation to Jesus or Paul, less frequently in general titles such as *Religious Experience in Earliest Christianity.*[22] Each of these, in contrast to the assumption operative with respect to the Hebrew Bible, foreground "religion" as an individual affair rather than as a social formation.

While this shift is in fact a matter of complex theory—which requires argumentation rather than assertion or assumption—I am aware that a variety of prudential reasons have been adduced, at the level of the data, to account for this difference. It has been suggested that the time-span of the literature and collectivities of early Christianities is fore-shortened in comparison with the Israelitic. It has been noted that there are few, if any, archaeological remains from Christianities in the period in question, in contradistinction to the rich diversity of artifacts available to the student of Israelitic religion, and that, therefore, one is almost wholly dependent upon the literature of individual authors. It has been suggested that there are no institutions in the sense of hereditary priests or temples; that indeed, there appears to be a counter-institutional impulse. Such arguments from silence cannot be converted into positive principles, such as was common in earlier scholarship; for example, Shirley Jackson Case's proposition: "As yet the adherents of Christianity lacked an institutional equipment, such as the organized Jewish community possessed. . . . Hence they looked directly to God. . . ."[23] But, even if these claimed limitations at the level of data be accepted for purposes of argument, requiring us to set aside a variety of social structures, each having analogies in other Late Antique religious formations ranging from voluntary associations to trans-local communication networks, the student of religion knows full well that there are many parallel cases. For example, a similar situation pertains for early Islamic formations, which has not, in the least, prevented the development of sophisticated social analyses or the appropriate employment of the terminology of "religion." As I spoke, twenty-six years ago, at the founding meeting of the SBL Working Group on the Social Description of Early Christianity: "In a sense, I could wish for no higher success for our enterprise than that we someday achieve for early Christianity what W. Montgomery Watt has achieved for [early] Islam."[24] Works of subsequent scholarship in Islam, from Josef van Ess to Aziz al-Azmeh, only confirm me in this wish.

In fact, such prudential problems are not what are at issue. The marked preference for categories of individual experience, the equally strong reluctance to entertain the category "religion," signal a stance already spoken of with reference to NABI: that, with respect to early Christianities, there be no discrepancy between the datum and its model; that, for all its sometime sophistication in interpreting the literature, a model remains essentially at the level of a paraphrase.

While some scholars have complained that New Testament data have been excluded from contemporary discussions of general questions of theory in the study of religion,[25] it is rather the fact that New Testament data have characteristically been insufficiently redescribed to be of any general theoretical interest. It is furthermore the case that the current, preservationist tactic of many biblical scholars to reduce any theory and its necessary entailments to a method, to a procedure for reading texts, contributes to this lack of effort at redescription. This has notably been the case in many biblicists' procedural adaptations of literary and social theories which allow them to escape the "cost" of those theoretical positions. One needs to think, here, only of a number of putative applications of structuralism to biblical materials.

To speak first to the category of individual experience. At the very least, one must begin with the sort of candor expressed by Luke Johnson, "the category is, in all honesty, an extraordinarily difficult one with which to work."[26] At even the most modest level, these "difficulties" cannot be resolved by retelling narratives in a way that begs classic questions as to the relationship of experience and expression as well as to the relationship of the scholar to the expression. These questions have been made urgent again as the result of a succession of recent works by scholars from Wayne Proudfoot to Terry F. Godlove, Jr., that explore the complex relations between first-person authority and scholarly authority arguing that, at the level of description, the scholar must, at least, represent "the concepts, beliefs and judgments that enter into the subject's identification of his experience," but, at the level of explanation, in my sort of language, at the level of redescription, the scholar offers "an explanation of an experience in terms that are not those of the subject and might not meet with his approval. This is perfectly justifiable and is, in fact, normal procedure."[27] These are debates at the most general level of both method and theory and, therefore, can never be answered from data.

To join with such controversies is to enter into the most fundamental questions that have arisen from the century-old project of reconceptualizing the study of religion as one of the human sciences. The human sciences become conceptually possible largely through the acceptance of the argument that their objects of study are linguistic and language-like systems and that, therefore, they are the study of "eminently social" human projects.

One strong implication of this has been the rejection of the adequacy of the common-sense theory of "expressive realism," the notion that experience is anterior to language. While some continue to act as if the crucial question for the study of religion remains the relations of theological and religious studies, this is to miss the point. It is the debate about language and experience—whether experience can ever be immediate or is always mediated; the question as to whether we can experience a world independently of the conventional ways in which it is socially represented; the question as to whether the *re-* of re-presentation remains always at the level of re-presentation—that constitute the serious theoretical matters that sharply divide scholars in ways that thoroughly cut across the older, essentially political, division between theological and religious studies.

There are broader and more controverted matters at issue. My interest, here, has been the relationship of biblical materials and biblical scholarship to the student of religion. The imagination of "religion" as an intellectual category establishes a disciplinary horizon playing the same sort of role as "language" in linguistics or "culture" in anthropology. In each case, the generic category supplies the discipline with a theoretical object of study, different from, but complimentary to, their particular subject matters, the latter being appropriately investigated by historical and comparative methods. In our case, this is to speak of "religion" in relation to the "religions"—the theoretical *object* in relation to its empirical *subject* matter.

For this reason, it will not do to protest that, like "Bible," "religion" is a postbiblical term, appearing only in the Vulgate where, in several forms (*religio, religiositas, religiose, religiosus*) it translates, on twenty-one occasions, a small group of Hebrew and Greek words, or to argue that the mod-

ern sense of the word, as a generic term, bears no relation to its Latin connotations. It is the very distance and difference of "religion" as a second-
order category that gives it cognitive power.[28]

The particular subject matter provides the scholar with an occasion
for surprise. This becomes one point at which the outsider's view may be
privileged over the insider's view. The outsider's view has a greater likelihood of being surprised.

A recent book review in the *New York Times* concluded with a sentence of the sort I have often heard impatiently voiced at meetings of
both the SBL and the AAR: "no amount of theory can help an ornithologist to fly."[29] Precisely! An ornithologist is not a bird but one who studies birds. The ornithologist finds, as birds do not, flight surprising, and
therefore requires, again as birds do not, an explanatory theory in language surely different than that which birds might employ.

Surprise, whether in the natural or the human sciences, is always reduced by bringing the unknown into relations to the known, relations of
similarity and difference, relations of analogy and homology, relations
of metonymy and metaphor. The process by which this is accomplished
(again in both the natural and the human sciences) is translation; the
proposal that the second-order language appropriate to one domain (the
known/the familiar) may translate the second-order language appropriate
to another domain (the unknown/the unfamiliar). Perhaps the strongest
and best-known example of this procedure in the study of religion is
Durkheim's translation of the language appropriate to religion (the unknown) into the language appropriate to society (the known). The only
effective grounds for rejecting such an explanatory or interpretative
procedure is to attack the possibility of translation itself, most often attempted through arguments of incommensurability. But the latter land
one, again, in a complex set of theoretical arguments.

I would note two implications raised by surprise and translation.
First, translation, as an affair of language, is a relentlessly social activity,
a matter of public meaning rather than one of individual significance.
(In the study of religion, the public is the academic community.) Second—and this is crucial—whether intercultural or intracultural, translation is never fully adequate. There is always discrepancy. (To repeat the
old tag: "To translate is to traduce.") This holds equally for natural languages as for intellectual models.

Indeed, the cognitive power of any translation, model, map, or redescription—as, for example, in the imagination of "religion"—is, by
this understanding, a result of its difference from the phenomena in question and not its congruence. As already suggested, for this reason, a par-

aphrase, perhaps the commonest sort of weak translation in the human sciences, nowhere more so than in biblical studies, will usually be *insufficiently different* for purposes of thought. To summarize: a theory, a model, a conceptual category, *cannot be simply the data writ large*.

As this is a session of the SBL, whose members are practiced in biblical genres, let me conclude with a parable that imagines a map without distortion, a map with absolute congruency to its subject matter, and, hence, a map that is both absolutely useless for second-order intellection, as well as for finding one's way around: Borges's "Exactitude in Science" (1946), which I quote in its entirety.

> In that Empire, the Art of Cartography attained such Perfection that the map of a single Province occupied the entirety of a City, and the map of the Empire, the entirety of a Province. In time, these Unconscionable Maps no longer satisfied, and the Cartographer's Guild struck a Map of the Empire whose size was that of the Empire, and which coincided point by point with it. The following generations, who were not so fond of the Study of Cartography, as their Forebears had been, saw that that vast Map was useless, and not without some Pitilessness was it, that they delivered it up to the Inclemencies of Sun and Winters. In the Deserts of the West, still today, there are Tattered Ruins of that Map, inhabited by Animals and Beggars; in all of the Land there is no other Relic of the Discipline of Geography.[30]

For Borges, when map is the territory, it lacks both utility and any cognitive advantage with the result that the discipline which produced it, deprived of its warrants, disappears.

Notes

1. J. Z. Smith, *Drudgery Divine: On the Comparison of Early Christianities and the Religions of Late Antiquity* (Chicago, 1990), viii.

2. See, most recently, J. Z. Smith, "The 'End' of Comparison: Redescription and Rectification," in K. C. Patton and B. C. Ray, eds., *A Magic Still Dwells: Comparative Religion in the Postmodern Age* (Berkeley, 2000), 237–41.

3. Smith, *Drudgery*, 143.

4. As later described, "We do not know how this collection of letters [signifying our association] came about, whether it was due to purpose, coincidence or Providence, but it was nevertheless a striking fact. But we do know that the Prophet, reaching his climax in Jesus . . . is the unique contribution of the Bible

to universal religion" (quoted in E. W. K. Mould, "The National Association of Bible Instructors: An Historical Account," *Journal of Bible and Religion* [*JBR*] 18 [1950]: 13). While the source of the quote is not identified by name in Mould, it appears to be I. J. Peritz. Note that the *Journal of the National Association of Bible Instructors* (*JNABI*), the *JBR*, and the *JAAR* have consecutive volume numbers. *JNABI* ran from vols. 1 (1933) to 4 (1936); *JBR* from vols. 5 (1937) to 34 (1966); *JAAR* began with vol. 35 (1967).

5. C. W. Quimby, "The Word of God," *JNABI* 1 (1933): 4.

6. I. J. Peritz, "Editorial: The National Association of Bible Instructors and the Society of Biblical Literature and Exegesis," *JNABI* 1 (1933): 29.

7. Quimby, "The Word of God," 1.

8. I. J. Peritz, "Editorial: The Expansion of the Journal," *JBR* 5 (1937): 32.

9. Let me note a similar metamorphosis. William Rainey Harper's journal, *Hebrew Student*, became first, the *Old Testament Student*, and then, the *Biblical World*, before merging in 1921 with the *American Journal of Theology*, becoming retitled, at that time, the *Journal of Religion*, published by the Divinity School of the University of Chicago.

10. Within the first decade of publication of *JNABI* and *JBR* one can find less than a dozen instances where "religion" receives a passing definition or characterization, e.g., the Bible "is an adult book about adult religion" (H. Hartshorne, "The Future of the Bible in the American College," *JNABI* 1 [1933]: 10); religion is "the effort of man to relate himself in some intelligible way to the universe" (D. E. Adams, "The Study of Religion as an Integrative Discipline," *JBR* 5 [1937]: 28); "only as religion is made a matter of the mind as well as of the feelings . . ." (M. E. Lakenan, "Some Principles Governing the Formulation of a College Bible Curriculum," *JNABI* 1 [1933]: 16). Most frequently, when the educational goals are paramount, the Bible is religious because it contributes to "character formation," as, for example: the study of the Bible produces "trained religious attitudes . . . religious conduct and actions resulting ultimately in religious habits" (Lakenan, "Some Principles," 15); or, as expressed in another article, the study of "biblical religion" gives rise to an "ethical code," a "moral dynamic," a "personal religion or philosophy" (D. E. Adams, "The Teaching of Religion in the Liberal Arts College," *JNABI* [1934]: 57–58). At times, the unquestioning Christian character of these moral formations is explicit, as when A. E. Bailey characterizes the study of religion as the study of "God. . . . The Way of the Cross. . . . Worship . . . [and] Social Ethics" ("Religion and Education: At Home and Abroad," *JNABI* 3 [1935]: 27). Only once does the question of non-biblical religions also comprising "religion" explicitly enter *JNABI* or *JBR* during the period of NABI's sponsorship. In the first issue of the retitled *JBR*, Bernard Meiland argued for "comparative religion" as the appropriate introduction to the

study of religion in liberal arts colleges (Meiland, "The Study of Religion in a Liberal Arts College," *JBR* 5 [1937]: 62–68). L. H. Wild responded in the next issue; unsurprisingly, she insisted that the Bible serve as the foundation for the study of religion ("The Bible and the Foundation Course in Religion: A Reply to Professor Meiland," *JBR* 5 [1937]: 165–68).

What does emerge is an awareness of the growing field of religious studies and the political fact that departments of religion were beginning to replace departments of Bible (which often had required courses under their jurisdiction). There is a growing chorus of suspicion (see Quimby, "The Word of God") toward what one author terms, "non-biblical subjects . . . philosophy and psychology of religion, ethics, comparative religion, etc." (Hartshorne, "The Future of the Bible," 10). Professor Fowler writes in 1933: "the term Bible or biblical and the term religion or religious" is now occurring "with almost equal frequency in the names of the departments." He goes on to confess, "I find myself sometimes puzzled over the use of the term religion in these titles," concluding, not without some irritation, that it refers to an experience-far academic enterprise in which religion is a "subject of sociological or philosophical interest so far as it is really a subject for intellectual investigation" (H. T. Fowler, "The Place of the Bible in the Liberal Arts Curriculum," *JNABI* 1 [1933]: 26–27).

In contrast to the first decade's publications, in the years immediately following World War II, beginning with volumes 19 and 20 (1947–48), the *JBR*, without announcement, changes character. Articles and reviews treating world religions appear with some regularity; there are, proportionally less articles on biblical subjects. In 1954, there is the first explicit recognition of definitional problems associated with the *term* "religion," signaled by the placing of pips around the word. Its author observes, "Then there is the word 'religion.' Its omnifarious character is well known." Unfortunately, this important observation is followed by, perhaps, the most eccentric definition to appear on the journal's pages: "religion" is "any and every experience the meaning of which is derived from its relation to the Prime Mover, the source of axiogenesis and axiosoteria" (C. Milo Connick, "Achieving Religious Objectives," *JBR* 22 [1954]: 110).

11. Quimby, "The Word of God," 4. Several years later, Quimby repeats this assertion, "Everywhere the Bible is religion—always religion," and goes on to indicate that the "Bible as religion" means "God, ethical conduct and Jesus" (C. W. Quimby, "Teach the Bible as Religion," *JBR* 6 [1938]: 71–72). A respondent, who was not a member of NABI, writes, "I grant the contention of Mr. Quimby but I would be happier about it if I knew a little more specifically what he means by religion" (A. R. King, "Religion: A By-product in Education," *JBR* 6 [1938]: 74). Quimby responds that he was not speaking of the "wider subject of religion," and that it is the Bible "alone that I am here concerned . . . with the central religious

meaning of the biblical passages and their personal significance now." Besides, "I doubt any exact definition [of religion] is possible" ("Mr. Quimby Comments," *JBR* 6 [1938]: 76).

12. J. Haroutunian, "The Bible and Modern Education," *JNABI* 1 (1933): 11.

13. See now R. T. McCutcheon's outstanding anthology, *The Insider/Outsider Problem in the Study of Religion* (London, 1999).

14. See, among others: W. Vatke, *Die Religion des Alten Testamentes nach den kanonischen Büchern entwickelt* (1835), vol. 1 of *Die biblische Theologie wissenschaftliche dargestellt*, no further volumes published; A. Kuenen, *De Godsdienst van Israel tot den Ondergaang van der Joodschen Staat* (1869–70), English translation, *The Religion of Israel to the Fall of the Jewish State* (1873–75); W. von Baudissin, *Studien zur semitischen Religionsgeschichte* (1876–78); F. W. Baethgen, *Beiträge zur semitischen Religionsgeschichte* (1888); W. Robertson Smith, *The Religion of the Semites: First Series; The Fundamental Institutions* (1889), lectures delivered in 1888–89, the second and third series have been recently recovered and edited by J. Day, *Religion of the Semites, Second and Third Series* (1995); A. Duff, *Old Testament Theology; or, The History of Hebrew Religion from the Year 800* B.C. (1891), cf. Duff, *History of the Religion of Judaism, 500–200* B.C. (1927); C. G. Montefiore, *Lectures on the Origin and Growth of Religion as Illustrated by the Religion of the Ancient Hebrews* (1892); K. Marti, *Geschichte der israelitischen Religion* (1897, 2d ed., 1903), English trans., *The Religion of the Old Testament: Its Place among the Religions of the Nearer East* (1907)—Marti's work is a revision of T. Kaiser's *Theologie des Alten Testaments* (1st ed., 1813); K. Budde, *Religion of Israel to the Exile* (1899), German trans., *Die Religion des Volkes Israel bis zur Verbannung* (1900); Joh. Meinhold, *Studien zur israelitischen Religionsgeschichte* (1903), cf. Meinhold, *Einfuhrung in des Alte Testament: Geschichte, Literatur und Religion Israels* (1919; 2d ed., 1926); M.-J. Lagrange, *Études sur les religions sémitiques* (2d ed., 1905); S. A. Cook, *The Religion of Ancient Palestine in the Second Millennium* B.C. *in the Light of Archaeology and Inscriptions* (1908), cf. Cook, *The Religion of Ancient Palestine in the Light of Archaeology* (1930); A. Loisy, *La Religion d'Israël* (2d ed., 1908; 3d ed., 1933); F. Koenig, *Geschichte der alttestamentlichen Religion kritisch dargestellt* (1912; 2d ed., 1915); J. P. Peters, *The Religion of the Hebrews* (1914); R. Kittel, *Die Religion des Volkes Israel* (1921; 2d ed., 1929); G. Hölscher, *Geschichte der israelitischen und jüdischen Religion* (1922); M. Löhr, *Alttestamentliche Religionsgeschichte* (1930), English trans., *A History of Religion in the Old Testament* (1936); W. Oesterley and T. H. Robinson, *Hebrew Religion: Its Origin and Development* (1930; 2d ed., 1937); Y. Kaufmann, *Tôledôt Ha'emunáh Hayyiśēlît* (1937–56), abridged English trans., *The Religion of Israel* (1960); A. Lods, *La Religion d'Israël* (1939); W. F. Albright, *Archaeology and the Religion of Israel* (1st ed., 1942); B. D. Eerdmans, *De Godsdienst van Israël* (1947); A. Penna, *La religione di Israele* (1958); H. Ringgren, *Israelit-*

ische Religion (1963), English trans., *Israelite Religion* (1966; reprint, 1988); T. C. Vriezen, *De Godsdienst van Israel* (1963), English trans., *The Religion of Ancient Israel* (1967); G. Fohrer, *Geschichte der israelitischen Religion* (1969), English trans., *History of Israelite Religion* (1972); R. Albertz, *Religionsgeschichte Israels in alttestamentlicher Zeit* (1992), English trans., *A History of Israelite Religion in the Old Testament Period* (1994).

15. G. W. Anderson, "Hebrew Religion," in H. H. Rowley, ed., *The Old Testament and Modern Study* (Oxford, 1951), 283–310; W. Zimmerli, "The History of Israelite Religion," in G. W. Anderson, ed., *Tradition and Interpretation* (Oxford, 1979), 351–84; both of these published on behalf of the Society for Old Testament Study. P. D. Miller, "Israelite Religion," in D. A. Knight and G. M. Tucker, eds., *The Hebrew Bible and Its Modern Interpreters* (Chico, 1985), 201–37, in celebration of the centennial of SBL.

16. A. Loisy, *Naissance du Christianisme* (Paris, 1933), English trans., *The Birth of the Christian Religion* (London, 1948). Since delivering this lecture, Professor Christopher R. Matthews, Weston Jesuit School of Theology, has called my attention to the recent publication of Gerd Theissen's *The Religion of the Earliest Christians: Creating a Symbolic World* (Minneapolis, 1999), an English translation of the announced German original, *Die Religion der ersten Christen: Eine Theorie des Urchristentums* (Gütersloh, 2000).

17. A. Kuenen, *De Godsdienst van Israel tot den Ondergang van den joodschen Staat* (Haarlem, 1869–70), vols. 1–2; English trans., *The Religion of Israel to the Fall of the Jewish State* (London, 1873–75), vols. 1–3.

18. See Kuenen, *Volksgodsdienst en Wereldgodsdienst* (Leiden, 1882); English trans., *National Religions and Universal Religions* (London, 1882). For the more dominant taxonomy of Tiele, see J. Z. Smith, "Religion, Religions, Religious," in M. Taylor, ed., *Critical Terms for Religious Studies* (Chicago, 1998), esp. 278–79, reprinted in this volume.

19. Kuenen, *Religion of Israel*, 1: 5.

20. Kuenen, *Religion of Israel*, 1: 5–11.

21. I combine here Kuenen's *Religion of Israel* and his *National Religions and Universal Religions*.

22. The earliest title I have seen for the first is John Reynolds, *The Religion of Jesus* (1726); for the second, E. Synge, *St. Paul's Description of His Own Religion*, which I have read only in the third edition (1744). Perhaps the most interesting distinction is in G. A. Deissmann's English-language Selly Oak Lectures for 1923, published as *The Religion of Jesus and the Faith of Paul* (1923; I am unaware of a German edition of this work). For religious experience with reference to Jesus/Paul, see, among others, P. Gardner, *The Religious Experience of Saint Paul* (1911); for the title generalized, see among others, L. T. Johnson, *Religious Expe-*

rience in *Earliest Christianity* (1998). J. D. G. Dunn combines both in *Jesus and the Spirit: A Study of the Religious and Charismatic Experience of Jesus and the First Christians as Reflected in the New Testament* (2d ed., 1997).

23. S. J. Case, *Experience with the Supernatural in Early Christian Times* (New York, 1925), 25.

24. J. Z. Smith, "The Social Description of Early Christianity," *Religious Studies Review* 1 (1975): 21.

25. See, for example, H. D. Betz, "Christianity as Religion: Paul's Attempt at Definition in Romans," *Journal of Religion* 71 (1991): esp. 315–16.

26. Johnson, *Religious Experience*, 46.

27. W. Proudfoot, *Religious Experience* (Berkeley, 1985), passages quoted, 194–97. See also T. Godlove, Jr., "Religious Discourse and First Person Authority," *Method & Theory in the Study of Religion* 6 (1994): 147–61. Both authors supply excellent preliminary bibliographies.

28. See, for example, one of the rare instances where Bible dictionaries have an entry for "religion," F. D. Gealy, "Religion," *Interpreter's Dictionary of the Bible* (Nashville, 1962): 4: 32: "The words translated 'religion' are used almost exclusively in the later, more Hellenistic NT writings. . . . The infrequent use of 'religion' in the Bible is due to the fact that the concept of 'religion' is itself alien to the core of biblical thought [which employs 'faith']. . . . Primary for faith is man's relation to God, not his relation to faith structure or cult practice. The introduction of the general concept of 'religion' into the late NT writings meant the weakening, if not the abandonment, of the revelation character of Christianity. 'Religion,' now meaning the Christian religion, becomes a system of doctrine, an organization, an approved pattern of behavior and form of worship. Thus the primary importance of the term 'religion' in the NT is in its pointing to the shift which was taking place in the Hellenistic churches, from the Hebrew understanding of faith as concrete obedience of the whole man to God, to faith as an ecclesiastically approved system of doctrine, worship, and behavior." This sort of argument, generalized, is at the heart of W. C. Smith's *The Meaning and End of Religion* (New York, 1963). Cf. the discussion of Smith and by Smith in M. Despland and G. Vallee, eds., *Religion in History: The Word, the Idea, the Reality* (Waterloo, 1992). For a discussion of the history of the term in sixteenth- to twentieth-century academic discourse, with a preliminary bibliography, see Smith, "Religion, Religions, Religious," 269–84, reprinted in this volume.

29. D. Cohen, "Review: Clement Greenberg: *Homemade Esthetics*," *New York Times Book Review*, September 12, 1999, 34.

30. J. L. Borges, *Collected Fictions* (New York, 1998), 325.

CHAPTER TEN
TRADING PLACES

AS THE NOVELIST Tom Robbins has observed, all human beings may be divided into just two classes: those who think that everything can be divided into just two classes, and those who don't. The putative category "magic" is a prime example of such duality. Indeed, in the history of its imagination, it has been doubly dual, being counter-distinguished from *both* elements in another persistent and strong duality—from both "science" *and* "religion." On logical grounds alone, this reduplicated dualism should give rise to some suspicion of duplicity, for, if something is the opposite of one member of another opposition, it ought to have, at the very least, a close affinity to the second member of the pair. But, in the "prelogical" modes of thought that so often characterize anthropological and religious studies discourse within the human sciences (and so rarely characterize the thought of those peoples they claim to study), the law of the excluded middle has long since been repealed, most commonly by means of a shift from a logical to a chronological rhetoric. Employing an evolutionary hierarchy, the one ("magic") is encompassed by either one of its opposites ("religion" or "science"), with "magic" invariably labeled "older" and "religion" or "science" labeled "newer." (Note that this same hierarchy is often applied to the relations between "religion" and "science.") In this strategic model, as Rick Shweder describes it,

The image is one of subsumption, progress and hierarchical inclusion. Some forms of understanding are described as though
they were incipient forms of other understandings, and those
other forms of understanding are described as though they can
do everything the incipient forms can do plus more.[1]

Hence, many accounts of "magic" adopt a *privative* definition of
their subject matter. "Magic" resembles "religion" (e.g., Rodney Stark
and William Bainbridge[2]) or "science" (e.g., Robin Horton[3]) lacking only
some of the latter's traits. In such formulations, a promised difference in
kind turns out to be a postulated difference of degree—or, more pointedly, of development—and one is entitled to ask what sort of difference
that sort of difference makes?

This is, perhaps, the largest single family of theoretical, substantive
definitions of "magic": "magic" is "religion" or "science," or an incipient
form of "religion" or "science," but for the lack of this or that—or, less commonly, but for an excess of this or that. (More popular in early apologetic
accounts but still present in scholars such as H. D. Betz,[4] is the reverse
ploy, which sees "magic" as a degraded form of "religion" or "science.")

This dominant understanding is an odd sort of definition. Not only
does it break the conventional definitory rules (especially those against the
use of a negative definiens), but also because it is typically inconsistent
in its application of differentia. For example, many phenomena that we
unhesitatingly label "religious" or understand to be "religions" (notwithstanding the long and tortured debates over how those terms are to be defined) differ among themselves, on some scale of absent or excessive characteristics, at least as much, if not more, than "magic" does from "religion"
in many theories. What privileges the characteristics chosen for the
"magic/religion" duality? Or, to ask this question another way, if the purpose of a model in academic discourse—if the heart of its explanatory
power—is that it does *not* accord exactly with any cluster of phenomena
("map is not territory"), by what measurement is the incongruency associated with those phenomena labeled "magical" by scholars (rather than,
say, "religious") judged to be so great as to require the design and employment of another model?

This becomes clearer if we turn to the second major family of theoretical, substantive definitions of "magic." While exhibiting many of the
strategic features of the first, this second group adopts an atemporal
rather than an explicit (or implicit) developmental perspective. This approach holds that "magic" is essentially *synonymous* with this or that aspect of the total ensemble of "religion." (Note that this understanding

mimics the first family in viewing "magic" as encompassed by "religion" and as exhibiting either a lack or an excess. The old notion of magic as "compulsion," for example, judges "magic" to be either an inadequacy or an exaggeration, depending on the overall theoretical [and apologetic] stance of the scholar.) Thus, Stanley J. Tambiah, in his recently published Morgan Lectures, *Magic, Science, Religion and the Scope of Rationality,* reviews and criticizes the usual roundup of suspects—from Tylor and Frazer to Malinowski and Evans-Pritchard—in order to make his main point, that magic is essentially "performative utterance."[5] True, but even leaving aside the ongoing arguments with and reformulations of Austin's original proposals in differing ways by both philosophers and linguistics, so are a whole host of human utterances in a wide variety of concrete, pragmatic contexts, including a large number of expressions, as Tambiah would acknowledge, usually classified as "religious" rituals.

The second family of theoretical, substantive definitions depends, as has been already suggested, upon a notion of some aspect of "magic" being synonymous with some aspect of "religion" (albeit often with a different valence). Synonymy is theoretically useful precisely in that two (or more) terms are thought to be so close that their microdistinctions take on enormous clarificatory power. While of no use whatever for scholarly purposes, I refer, for a sense of what I mean, to the entry "magic" in *Webster's New Dictionary of Synonyms* (1968 edition):

> Magic, sorcery, witchcraft, witchery, wizardry, alchemy, thaumaturgy are comparable rather than synonymous in their basic senses. In extended use they are sometimes employed indifferently without regard to the implications of their primary senses and with little distinction from the most inclusive term, magic, but all are capable of being used discriminatingly and with quite distinctive implications.

But if one cannot specify the distinctions with precision, as is usually the case in definitions of this second type, the difference makes no difference at all.

From E. B. Tylor's notion of "magic" as misapplied logic (a strong example of the first family) to Claude Lévi-Strauss's understanding of magic as an exaggeration of human analogies (an equally strong example of the second family), substantive definitions of "magic" have proven empty in concrete instances and worthless when generalized to characterize entire peoples, whole systems of thought, or world-views. Such substantive definitions have failed for the logical and procedural reasons already suggested (among others). In their turn, these flaws have been brought about by the fact that in academic discourse "magic" has almost always been treated as a *contrast* term, a shadow reality known only by looking at the reflection of its opposite ("religion," "science") in a distorting fun-house mirror. Or, to put this another way, within the academy, "magic" has been made to play the role of an evaluative rather than an interpretative term and, as such, usually bears a negative valence.

While such negative valuations can, at times, be traced to specific ideologies, causality is rarely that clear. The notion of "magic" as "other" is far more deeply engrained. It is already present, to be used rather than created by these ideologies. As is the case with the majority of our most disturbing and mischievous hegemonic formulations, the negative valence attributed to "magic" has been, and continues to be, an element in our commonsense—and, therefore, apparently unmotivated—way of viewing cultural affairs.

Consider the shifting taxonomies and genealogies we employ (without ever troubling to account for the shift). For example, in most late nineteenth- and early twentieth-century works, shamanism is the very type of "magic." In more recent treatments, shamanism has been transferred to the "religious." (For Mircea Eliade it is the most transcendent form of "archaic religion"; for Tom Overholt it is the very type of "prophetic religion.") What has changed is *not* the data—by and large, the old, circumpolar ethnographies continue to be the prime sources. What has changed is the attitude of the scholar.

For these (and for other) reasons, I see little merit in continuing the use of the substantive term "magic" in second-order, theoretical, academic discourse. We have better and more precise scholarly taxa for each of the phenomena commonly denoted by "magic" which, among other benefits, create more useful categories for comparison. For any culture I am familiar with, we can trade places between the corpus of materials conventionally labeled "magical" and corpora designated by other generic terms (e.g., healing, divining, execrative) with no cognitive loss. Indeed, there would be a gain in that this sort of endeavor promises to yield a set of middle-range typologies—always the most useful kind—more adequate than the highly general, usually dichotomous, taxa commonly employed ("sympathetic/contagious," "witchcraft/sorcery," "benevolent/malevolent"—or even Christina Larner's more sophisticated typology of three types with two subtypes[6]). Similarly, such midrange taxa would be more adequate than the highly specific categories employed for particular cultures, usually constructed either anthropologically by function or philologically by native vocabulary, formulae, or text-type.

John Middleton was right in his meditation on Lévi-Strauss, although he shrunk from its consequences:

> If magic is a subjective notion . . . then it can have little or no meaning in cross-cultural analysis or understanding. The concept of magic is in itself empty of meaning and thus susceptible to the recognition of any meaning we care to give it; following this, Lévi-Strauss has implied that the category of magic must be "dissolved."[7]

The matter, however, will not be so simply disposed of. As with a large class of religious studies vocabulary (e.g., "myth"), the name will not be easily rectified. Abstention, "just say 'no'," will not settle "magic." For, unlike a word such as "religion," "magic" is not only a second-order term, located in academic discourse. It is as well, cross-culturally, a native, first-order category, occurring in ordinary usage which has deeply influenced the evaluative language of the scholar. Every sort of society appears to have a term (or, terms) designating some modes of ritual activities, some beliefs, and some ritual practitioners as dangerous, and/or illegal, and/or deviant. (Even some texts, conventionally labeled "magical" by scholars, themselves contain charms and spells against what the text labels "magic."[8])

These ethnoclassifications differ widely and can be quite complex. Moreover, it is far from clear that, in many cases, these native distinctions as to dangerous, illicit, and/or deviant practitioners and practices can be properly rendered, in all their nuances, by the common English terms "magic," "witchcraft," "sorcery." Nevertheless, the observation of these native categories has generated a number of important interpretative strategies, although it is now becoming clear, despite earlier enthusiasms, that these have often complicated rather than simplified the problem.

First, as pioneered by Africanists, the focus on native categories has shifted attention away from the act and actor to the accuser and the accusation. "Magic," in this sense, is almost always a third-person attribution rather than a first-person self-designation, and it becomes essential for the interpreter to explain the charge. Note that this presents a set of extraordinary documentary problems that have been overcome in only a relatively few areas of research. Pay attention to one Africanist's research protocol, which catalogs the kinds of data required:

> The significant point about a given instance of accusation is not that it is made . . . but that it is made in a given field situation. (An account of) this situation would include not only the struc-

> ture of the groups and subgroups to which the accuser and ac-
> cused belong but also their extant division into transient alli-
> ances and factions on the basis of immediate interests, ambi-
> tions, moral aspirations, and the like. It would also include as
> much of the history of these groups, subgroups, alliances and
> factions as would be considered relevant to the understanding of
> the accusation. . . . It would further include . . . demographic
> data about subgroup and factional fluctuations over the relevant
> time period together with information about the biological and
> sociological factors bearing on these such as epidemics, rise and
> fall in the birth and death rates, labor migrations, wars and
> feuds. . . .[9]

Due, in large part, to the absence of the sorts of data required, I know of
no convincing application of this interpretative strategy, for example, to
ancient accusations of magic. In this latter area of research, generalities
abound concerning power relations—many of which I find intuitively satisfying—but they lack the sociological specificity, the documentary gravity that confers plausibility to some of the work of colleagues in African,
European, and American studies, to name the most obvious examples.

Second, focus on the accusation and the accuser implies that one
can usually speak only of the "magician" rather than of "magic." Almost
any act, or in some cases, no act at all (this latter possibility alluding to
the long-standing discussion engendered by Evans-Pritchard's Zande materials[10]) can give rise to the accusation. It is the accused individual or
group, along with their network of social relations and loci in relation to
the accusing individual or group, that is held to be the prime motivation
for the charge. The "evidence" adduced by the native accuser is held by
the scholar to be secondary, and usually utterly conventional.

This has led to a noticeable bias in the literature toward the powerless. But this is an unwarranted simplification. While the accusation of
"magic" may well be a power ploy that marginalizes the accused, the accusation may equally well be between members of elite groups (as the
practice of "magic" may well be directed by the marginal against elites).

One cannot have it both ways. The shift to a social understanding
of the relations between the accuser and the accused *forbids* any attempt
at a substantive, theoretical definition of "magic." As Victor Turner has
observed,

> Almost every society recognizes such a wide variety of mysti-
> cally harmful techniques that it may be positively misleading to

impose on them a dichotomous classification. Their name is legion, their form is protean for the very reason that individual *spite* is capricious.[11]

I wish I could share the confidence of some scholars that, although a substantive definition of "magic" is rendered impossible by a sociological approach, the sorts of social fissures and conflicts revealed by the accusations are generalizable. A review of the ethnographic, historical, and analytic literature makes clear that they are not. Any form of *ressentiment,* for real or imagined reasons (see Aberle on "relative deprivation"[12]), *may* trigger a language of alienating displacement of which the accusation of magic is *just one possibility* in any given culture's rich vocabulary of alterity.

Third, by focusing scholarly attention on the accusation, and given most scholars' work-a-day common-sense positivism, it is all too easy to reduce the charge of "magic" to one of mere social placement. One can read entire monographs, especially on European materials, without gaining the sense that anyone might have "actually" practiced "magic" or "witchcraft." As an example, I would call attention to the lively debate that has exercised social historians of Salem for the past decade and a half. While their social analyses agree to a significant degree, they sharply disagree over the question as to whether the accused (or others) "actually" practiced "magic."[13]

Fourth, and closely related to the above, the social approach, ironically, cannot seem to handle those cultural instances where "magicians" function as a craft, as a profession, either as a hereditary office or as a guild with procedures for both training and incorporation. The accusatory model's bias toward the powerless often ignores the positive association of native conceptions of "magic" with power. (The latter was one of the strengths of the evolutionary understanding that stressed, although often in naïve or polemical forms, the power relations between what it termed "magic" and priestcraft or kingship.) The same issue recurs in those cultural instances where "magic" is a "high-class" phenomenon or where its practice confers social prestige.

A fifth and final caution is more strictly methodological in nature. Giving primacy to native terminology yields, at best, *lexical* definitions that historically and statistically, tell how a word is used. But lexical definitions are almost always useless for scholarly work. To remain content with how "they" understand "magic" may yield a proper description but little explanatory power. How "they" use a word cannot substitute for the *stipulative* procedures by which the academy contests and controls second-order, specialized usage. However, this returns us to the beginning of this essay and the problematics of a proper, theoretical definition of "magic."

I should now like to turn to the Preisendanz corpus of Graeco-Egyptian texts, as modified and translated in Betz's edition, and offer some reflections by a generalist for whom the label "Greek Magical Papyri" constitutes something of a distraction.[14] After all, compared with the fragments, contextless quotations, literary descriptions and artistic representations, the corpus, even as it now stands, represents something quite precious: *one of the largest collections of functioning ritual texts, largely in Greek, produced by ritual specialists that has survived from Late Antiquity.* The fact that the size of the collection could have been more than doubled by the inclusion of parallel materials from other Greek and Greek-based corpora only serves to reinforce its importance.[15]

My own interest in Late Antique "magical" texts has stemmed, primarily, from my long-standing preoccupation with themes related to place, especially the shift in the locus of religious experience and expression from a permanent sacred center, the archaic temple, to a place of temporary sacrality sanctified by a mobile religious specialist (in this case, the so-called "magician").[16] I propose to continue that meditation by calling attention to some features of the Preisendanz-Betz corpus that have little to do with issues of "magic" as conventionally perceived.

As part of a larger pattern of religious persistence and change in late antiquity, and for a diversity of reasons ranging from the economic to the aesthetic, from the political and demographic to the ethical and theological, in a number of traditions, temple sacrifice, especially that requiring animal victims, declined. As sacrifice was the raison d'etre of the archaic temple, the chief currency of both its divine and human economies, this meant that temples must either be revalorized or abandoned. A temple, an altar, without sacrifice is a mere monument. (See, already, the admittedly polemic account in Joshua 22:10–34.) This meant, as well, that sacrifice would have either to be dis-placed or re-placed.

The rationales and strategies for these latter processes were varied. Sometimes, as in the case of Orphic, Neoplatonic, and Neo-Pythagorean traditions, a moral cast—no bloodshed—was given to older cultic rules prohibiting pollution by dead animal products, corpses, and blood with a consequent recovery and refocus on archaic practices of cereal and incense offerings. (See, for example, the fumigation recipes that form part of the titula of seventy-eight of the eighty-seven late third-century "Orphic" Hymns.)

In the case of the emergent Judaisms and Christianities, spurred only in part by the destruction of the Temple in Jerusalem, the locus of sacrifice was shifted from Temple to domicile, and the act of sacrifice was wholly replaced by narrative and discourse. Early rabbinic traditions talked endlessly about sacrifices no longer performed, in many cases, never experienced and, in its ritual praxis, substituted speech for deed. The best-known example is the dictum attributed to Rabbi Gamliel: "Whoever does not say these three things on Passover has not fulfilled his obligations," with the first of the three being the sacrifice of the Paschal lamb (M. *Pesahim* 10.5). This is a sentence *about* ritual speech that, by virtue of its inclusion in the later *Passover Haggadah*, has itself *become* ritual speech.

Some early Christians developed the utterly rhetorical metaphor of sacrifice as an important component of their narrative understanding of Jesus' death. Over time, the Christian use of the sacrificial analogy was extended to characterize a whole host of human phenomena by traditions that never "actually" sacrificed, including the sacrament of marriage post–Vatican II.

Christian liturgy maintained the language of "altar," "smoke," and of the sacrificial elements—now wholly metaphorized; the eucharistic flesh and blood was subsumed to a narrative of paradigmatic institution which was set in a domestic, nonsacrificial context.

Of all the documents from late antiquity, I know of *none* more filled with the general and technical terminology and the praxis of sacrifice than those texts collected by modern scholars under the title Greek Magical Papyri. They are all the more important because they display, as well, a thoroughly domesticated understanding of sacrifice.

Within the papyri,[17] while a small number of the ritual *topoi* are outside—in an open place (IV.900), a deserted place (III.616), a tomb (III.25,286) or by a river (III.286; IV.27)[18]—the vast majority of rituals that give a locale are set in domestic space, in the practitioner's house (e.g., I.83, 84; II.148; III.193; IV.2188) or more rarely, in the client's place of business or home (VIII.59; XII.104; cf. IV.2373–2440 where it is implied). As a substantial number of rituals are for procuring some sort of dream oracle, "your bedroom" predominates (e.g., II.1–182; IV.62; VII.490, 593–619, 628–42, 664–85). There are, as well, a number of references to rituals performed on "your housetop" (I.70; IV.2711; LXI.6), "lofty roof" (I.56; IV.2469, 2711), or upper room (IV.171), chiefly as a place for receiving a celestial power who is then conducted to "the room in which you reside" (e.g., I.80–84).

Within this domestic space, there is a high concern for purity in both the rituals of preparation and reception. The practitioner is to abstain from sex, from animal food (including fish), and from "all uncleanness" (I.40–1, 54, 290–92, et passim). The ritual site is to be a "clean room" (IV.2189), a "pure room" (VII.875[?])—"let your place be cleaned of all pollution" (II.148).

Within the "clean," domestic place, the chief ritual is that of sacrifice, most commonly of generic incense (e.g., IV.215; V.395; VIII.58), with frankincense the most frequently specified (e.g., I.63; IV.908, 1269, 1909). Some dozen other aromatic plant substances, from gums (e.g., III.23) to spices (e.g., III.308; IV.919), were also employed. Other vegetable offerings include roses (IV.2235), sumac (IV.2235), mulberries (III.611), beets (III.614), moss (LXXII.3), cakes (XII.22), and fruits (XII.22), along with libations of wine and/or milk (e.g., III.694).

By contrast to these common vegetable offerings, sacrifices *wholly* made up of animal victims or products are rare. The largest group requires the sacrifice of a white cock (IV.26–51, 2189–92, 2359–72; XIII.364–82 [+ pigeon]). The only instance of the whole offering of a mammal remains an editorial conjecture (IV.2394–99).

More common than purely animal sacrifices, though less common than purely vegetable offerings, are sacrifices of mixed animal and plant substances. Their usual form is a series of plants plus one animal part, usually its dung or an organ (e.g., I.285; IV.1309–15, 3092). If it is a vegetable series plus a whole animal, the latter is invariably a bird (e.g., IV.2892). Some of the animal *materia* (e.g., dung, eggs, a snake's shed skin) do not require the killing of the animal, while other *materia*— "wolf's eye" (I.285), "frog's tongue" (V.203)—may well be code names for plants (see XII.401–44), as is certainly the case for the ingredient, "pig's snout" (III.468; V.198, 371). Other texts appear to place differing valences on animal and plant offerings, for example IV.2873–79:

> For doing good, offer storax, myrrh, sage, frankincense, a fruit pit.
> But for doing harm, offer magical material of a dog and dappled goat [(gloss:) or, in a similar way, of a virgin untimely dead].[19]

The impression that animal offerings were not the central focus is strengthened by the fact that a sharp knife, the one, indispensible requirement in animal sacrifice, is mentioned as an implement just three times in the corpus (XIII.91–96, 373–75, 646–51).

The other ritual implements mentioned introduce another important and highly characteristic element. They are not only highly portable, but appear to be *miniaturized*. The table, the throne, the tripod, and the censer seem, themselves, to be small and to hold relatively small objects. The sacrificial altar—most often constructed of two or more (unbaked) bricks, but never more than seven—seems especially so. What must be the scale of an altar on which is sacrificed "on grapevine charcoal, one sesame seed and [one] black cumin seed" (IV.919)?

In addition to these common, though miniaturized, implements is a set of small wooden shrines. Eight appear to be mentioned in the corpus: a juniper wood shrine that holds a mummified falcon (I.21–26); a small, wooden shrine, set up on a table covered with pure linen, enclosing a tripod, censer, and small figurine (III.290–320); a lime wood shrine in which lies a small figurine of Hermes made of dough (V.370–99); a shrine of olive wood containing a statuette of Selene (VII.866–79); a small temple, standing on a table, into which a small dish is placed in which the first morsels of food from a meal are offered (X.1–9); two small (?) temples connected by a single sheet of papyrus (V.159–60, admittedly obscure); and, most suggestive of all, IV.3125–71, which contains a ritual for fashioning a phylactery that will cause any "place or temple" to flourish, to become a "marvel," and to be "talked about throughout the whole world." (It would appear that this "place or temple," for which favor is being asked, is the shop of the ritual's patron [IV.3170, editorial conjecture].) The ritual involves the construction of a small, three-headed wax statue, "three handbreadths high," which is deified by animal (?) sacrifice and placed within a "little juniper wood temple" wreathed with olive. The practitioner is enjoined, "Now feast [with the god], singing to him all night long."

As this last text makes plain, the "little" temples and shrines, in this latter case one housing a figure 0.3 meters high, are treated as if they were major edifices housing a divine image and a cult table. Sacrifice is held before them; a cultic meal follows with a liturgy sung. In other cases, incubation is practiced before the miniature (e.g., V.390–423) rather than sleeping within the large temple precincts. In still other rituals, the divine being is conducted to a small throne, in an ordinary but purified room, from which it gives oracles or provides a powerful guiding presence (e.g., I.293–347; cf. I.74–90), just as in the throne room of a major temple complex. These quite typical procedures within the Greek Magical Papyri suggest that the practitioner's "clean room" and the rituals performed therein are to be understood, to no small degree, as *replacements* of (and for) temple space and rituals.

Alternatively, while the small shrines resemble the portable *naiskoi* commonly carried in religious processions, the little shrines, ritual implements, small statues, and ritual practices have their closest parallels, as Fritz Graf has convincingly argued, in small-scale, private, domestic rituals conducted by ordinary householders for their household deities and/or ancestors[20] (a comparison that deserves further detailed study). From this point of view, the domestication of ritual has *already* occurred. What is different about the Greek Magical Papyri is that these practices have been divorced from a familial setting, becoming both highly mobile and professionalized.

In either case, the sacrality of the place is established, *temporarily*, through ritual activities, and by virtue of the direct experience of a mobile, professional ritualist (the "magician") with an equally mobile deity.

One further matter. If one reads through the entire corpus with an eye toward ritual activities, it is not purification, nor incubation, nor even sacrifice that predominates. Rather, the chief ritual activity within the Greek Magical Papyri appears to be *the act of writing itself*. The vocabulary of inscription constitutes one of the larger groups. Alongside the evident concern for the accurate transmission of a professional literature marked, among other features, by scribal glosses and annotations, is an overwhelming belief in the efficacy of writing, especially in the recipes that focus on the fashioning of amulets and phylacteries—themselves, miniaturized, portable, powerful written texts of papyrus, metal, stone, and bone.

The most common writing material is a sheet of papyrus, often described as "clean," "pure," "choice," or "hieratic." While blood and other *magica materia* occasionally function as writing fluids (most dramatically, VIII.70–72), most of the inks, some of which are quite complex, are variants of the common, everyday combination of a burnt substance for pigment (e.g., charcoal, soot, lampblack) and a gum as a fixative. The most frequent combination is "myrrh ink" (*smurnomelan*, or *zmurnomelan*).

The technology of ink mimics the technology of the vegetable sacrifice, with burning and aromatic gums serving as their common denominators:

> The (preparation of the) ink is as follows: In a purified container, burn myrrh, cinquefoil, and wormwood; grind them to a paste and use them (II.36; cf. I.244–46).

Within the corpus, the instructions for the preparation of ink are often given a liturgical rubric, *skeuē melanos* (e.g., I.243; IV.3199; VII.998), at times in immediate juxtaposition to the rubric for the sacrificial offering.

The ritual of writing is more than a replacement of the archaic temple as a major site of scribal activities and library of ritual books—although, at times, use is made of the familiar motif of allegedly finding a book or spell in a prestigious temple, as in one of the older, surviving papyri, CXXII.1–4. It is, rather, a displacement of ritual practice into writing, analogous, in important respects, to the displacement of sacrifice into speech in the emergent Judaisms and Christianities (discussed above), as well as a continuation of the impulse towards miniaturization.

In a difficult analogy in *La Pensée sauvage*, Lévi-Strauss has written of "the intrinsic value of a small scale model" as a process of compensating "for the renunciation of sensible dimensions by the acquisition of intelligible dimensions."[21] In a somewhat similar vein, the literary critic and folklorist, Susan Stewart, who has written the most extended meditation on miniaturization,[22] insists that small does not equal insignificant (in both senses of the term), that

> a reduction in the physical dimension of an object depicted can, in fact, increase the dimension of significance. . . . The miniature always tends towards exaggeration—it is a selection of detail that magnifies detail in the same movement by which it reduces detail.[23]

If ritual, with its characteristic strategies for achieving focus, with its typical concern for "microadjustment," often is, itself, a miniaturization that is, at one and the same time, an exaggeration of everyday actions, as major theorists of ritual from Freud to Lévi-Strauss have rightly maintained,[24] then miniaturization, when applied *to* ritual, as is the case in the Greek Magical Papyri, becomes a sort of *ritual of ritual*, existing, among other loci, in a space best described as discursive or intellecual.[25]

Notes

1. R. A. Shweder, *Thinking Through Cultures* (Cambridge, Mass., 1991), 118.

2. R. Stark and W. S. Bainbridge, *A Theory of Religion* (New York, 1987), 40 et passim.

3. R. Horton, "African Traditional Thought and Western Science," *Africa* 37 (1967): 50–71, 159–87.

4. See, for example, H. D. Betz, "Magic and Mystery in the Greek Magical Papyri," in C. A. Faraone and D. Obbink, eds., *Magika Hiera: Ancient Greek Magic and Religion* (Oxford, 1991), 244–59, esp. 253–54.

5. S. J. Tambiah, *Magic, Science, Religion and the Scope of Rationality* (New York, 1990), 58, 82–83, et passim. Cf. Tambiah, "The Magical Power of Words,"

Man, n. s. 3 (1968): 175–208; and Tambiah, "A Performative Approach to Ritual," *Proceedings of the British Academy* 65 (1979): 113–69. These latter two articles are a more sophisticated presentation of his thesis than that in *Magic, Science, Religion*.

6. C. Larner, *Witchcraft and Religion: The Politics of Popular Belief* (Oxford, 1985), 80–82.

7. J. Middleton, "Theories of Magic," in M. Eliade, ed., *Encyclopedia of Religion* (New York, 1987), 9: 88.

8. See, for example, the well-known "Moses Phylactery" from Acre, most recently edited by R. D. Kotansky, "Texts and Studies in the Greco-Egyptian Magic Lamellae" (Ph.D. diss., University of Chicago, 1988), text no. 36 (esp. 220–22) and his general treatment of "counter-magic" in the introduction (8–10).

9. V. Turner, "Witchcraft and Sorcery: Taxonomy versus Dynamics" (1964), reprinted in Turner, *The Forest of Symbols* (Ithaca, 1967), 11:5.

10. E. E. Evans-Pritchard, *Witchcraft, Oracles and Magic among the Azande* (Oxford, 1937), 21: "A witch performs no rite, utters no spell and possesses no medicines. An act of witchcraft is a psychic act." If this distinction be accepted as generalizable beyond the Zande (by no means an uncontroversial proposal), then so much for Christian apologetic New Testament scholars who would acquit Jesus of magic on the grounds that he employed no spells or magic *materia*. In Zande terms, Jesus may be no sorcerer, but might well be a witch!

11. Turner, "Witchcraft and Sorcery," 124–25, emphasis added.

12. D. Aberle, "A Note on Relative Deprivation Theory as Applied to Millenarian and Other Cult Movements," in S. Thrupp, ed., *Millennial Dreams in Action* (The Hague, 1962), 209–14.

13. This debate was largely engendered by the publication of Chadwick Hansen's *Witchcraft at Salem* (New York, 1969).

14. K. Preisendanz, *Papyri Graecae Magicae* (Leipzig and Berlin, 1928–41), hereafter referred to as *PGM*; K. Preisendanz and A. Henrichs, *Papyri Graecae Magicae*, 2d ed. (Stuttgart, 1973–74); H. D. Betz, ed., *The Greek Magical Papyri in Translation* (Chicago, 1986–). All citations will be to the Betz translation with occasional small emendations.

15. Additional "handbook" materials could have been included from the Byzantine documents published by A. Delatte, *Anecdota Atheniensia* (Paris and Liège, 1927), and the Coptic materials published by A. M. Kropp, *Ausgewählte koptische Zaubertexte* (Brussels, 1930–33), cf. P. A. Mirecki, "The Coptic Hoard of Spells from the University of Michigan," in M. Meyer and R. Smith, eds., *Ancient Christian Magic: Coptic Texts of Ritual Power* (San Francisco, 1994), 293–310, and the greatly expanded version in Mirecki, "The Coptic Wizard's Hoard," *Harvard Theological Review* 87 (1994): 435–460. Likewise the amuletic materials collected by R. D. Kotansky, "Texts and Studies in the Greco-Egyptian Magic Lamellae" (Ph.D. diss., University of Chicago, 1988). But such expansions ac-

cept whatever common-sense criteria for inclusion Preisendanz-Betz had in mind. There are, as well, individual pieces in *PGM* that could trade places with individual items in other Greek collections and vice versa, especially, M. Bertholet, *Collection des anciens alchemistes grecs* (Paris, 1887–88) and the *Catalogus codicum astrologorum graecorum* (Brussels, 1898–), not to speak of the relations of individual items in *PGM* to even wider circles of texts from herbaria and oracles to Gnostica and Hermetica.

16. See, among others, J. Z. Smith, *Map Is Not Territory* (Leiden, 1978), 172–207; Smith, "Towards Interpreting Demonic Powers in Hellenistic and Roman Antiquity," in *Aufstieg und Niedergang der römischen Welt*, 2.16.1: 425–39.

17. Please note that my citations from the Betz edition are exemplary and not exhaustive.

18. Other outside loci include a bathhouse (II.49); a stadium (II.43); the eastern section of a village (IV.58–59); a bean field (IV.769); "a place where grass grows" (IV.3091); and a crossroad (LXX.16).

19. For a most complex example of differing evaluation, in several recensions, see the slander spells involving "hostile" offerings, IV.2571–2707.

20. F. Graf, "Prayer in Magic and Religious Ritual," in Faraone and Obbink, *Magika Hiera*, 195f.

21. C. Lévi-Strauss, *La Pensée sauvage* (Paris, 1962), 34–36; English translation, *The Savage Mind* (Chicago, 1966), 23–24, esp. 24.

22. S. Stewart, *On Longing: Narratives of the Miniature, the Gigantic, the Souvenir, the Collection* (Baltimore, 1984), chapter 2.

23. S. Stewart, *Nonsense: Aspects of Intertextuality in Folklore and Literature* (Baltimore, 1980), 100–1.

24. Cf. J. Z. Smith, *To Take Place: Toward Theory in Ritual* (Chicago, 1987), 103–12 et passim.

25. The second part of this essay has been adopted from my paper, "Constructing a Small Place," delivered at the Joshua Prawer Memorial Conference, "Sacred Space: Shrine, City, Land," sponsored by the Israel Academy of Sciences and Humanities, Jerusalem, June 1992, now published in Smith, "Constructing a Small Space" (1998).

DIFFERENTIAL EQUATIONS
ON CONSTRUCTING THE OTHER

To be confused about what is different and what is not, is to be confused about everything.

DAVID BOHM

DURING THE PAST few years, a quick trip through any reasonably stocked bookstore would reveal a significant shift in intellectual concern. The shelves devoted to literary criticism and anthropology—the two fields in which the most interesting philosophical work is presently being done—as well as philosophy—itself, show a decline in the number of linguistic and language-related titles and an absolute increase in titles concerned with the 'other' and with 'difference' (the latter spelled in different ways with different understandings). The Columbus anniversary will surely give rise to even more such works. While the social historian may find particular reasons to account for why such matters preoccupy so many minds at this time, there is nothing inherently strange in the topic—it is a subject for thought at least as old as humankind.

I

Setting aside ethological notions of animal territoriality, perhaps the most basic sense of the 'other' is generated by the opposition IN/OUT. That is to say, a preoccupation with boundary, with limit (in the primary sense of threshold) seems fundamental to our construction of ourselves and our relations to others. Expressed with respect to the self, the stressed notion is that of containment, especially with respect to cultural understandings of the body, which, as Mary Douglas reminds us,

230

is a model which can stand for any bounded system. Its boundaries can represent any boundaries which are threatened or precarious. . . . Any structure . . . is vulnerable at its margins. We should expect the orifices of the body to symbolize its especially vulnerable points. Matter issuing from them is marginal stuff of the most obvious kind. Spittle, blood, milk, urine, faeces or tears . . . bodily parings, skin, nails, hair clippings and sweat.[1]

Hence their role as agents of pollution. That is to say, what pollutes is what leaks out, what cannot be contained, thereby transgressing the boundary between the self and world.[2] Indeed, pollutants are primarily bodily fluids that disperse in an indeterminate fashion, adhering to other beings and things, thereby further dissipating the self and its identity.

If the notion of self-containment focuses on the idea of keeping-in, then the dualities of external relations center on the idea of keeping-out, particularly with respect to access to cultural goods. It is the notion of the threshold which separates those who belong, those who are welcome, from those who are not; those who are received by a host (in the sense of one who provides food) from those who are repelled by a host (in the sense of armed force). Expressed in its most neutral form, as a part of Robert Redfield's influential argument that the universal worldview is governed by two binary oppositions, WE/THEY and HUMAN/NOT-HUMAN:

It is probably safe to say that among the groupings of people in every society are always some that distinguish people who are my people, or are more my people, from people who are not so much my people.[3]

Such global generalizations are a useful starting point for stimulating thought—they give a sense of the elemental structure of our topic; but I wish to look at a more specific (though scarcely narrow) tradition: the history of the western imagination of the 'other.'

Abstracting from a large collection of historical data, I would propose, as an initial move, that three basic models of the 'other' have been employed. (1) The 'other' represented metonymically in terms of the presence or absence of one or more cultural traits. (2) The 'other' represented topographically in terms of center and periphery. (3) The 'other' represented linguistically and/or intellectually in terms of intelligibility. This third model, which I will go on to suggest is the most problematic and mischievous, is the only one of the three to be raised to the status of a modern theory.

(1) The metonymical model most frequently occurs in connection with naming. One group distinguishes itself from another by lifting up some cultural feature, expressed as the lack of some familiar cultural trait, the use of some unfamiliar cultural object (e.g., "fish-eaters," "garlic-eaters"), the presence of some marked physical feature (e.g., "whites," "blacks"),[4] or the characterization of difference by naming the other as a nonhuman species.[5]

The metonymical model is found in the oldest surviving texts from the western tradition. For example, the Sumerians (Ur/III period) distinguish themselves from the Amorites because the latter "do not know barley," they have "never known city life," they eat "uncooked meat," and after death, "will not be buried."[6]

Following the lead of William Scott Green, we may see in these metonymies more than the rhetorical act of taking one marked feature for the whole. Rather, we must understand them as suggesting a complex structure of reciprocal determination. Taking the example of a group that calls itself "human beings" and a neighboring group, "crocodiles," Green observes that from one point of view this is an essay in caricature. "The neighboring peoples, after all, are not really crocodiles . . . but some trait of their collective life makes the label fitting and plausible to those who invent it." From another point of view, it is reflexive.

> To evoke the significant disparity . . . the symbol must correspond powerfully to the naming society's sense of its own distinctiveness . . . it must reach inside the culture of the people who employ it, correlate to some piece of themselves that they believe prominently displays who they are and induce response, perhaps fear or disgust, but also perhaps envy and respect.

Seen this way there is, in fact, a "double metonymy."

> In creating its others, a society confuses some part of its neighbor with its neighbor and a piece of itself with itself, and construes each in terms of the other. Although designed to mark and certify divergence and discontinuity, such correspondences can forge enduring reciprocal patterns. . . . They can reshape the naming society's picture of itself, expose its points of vulnerability, and spark in it awareness of, or reflection about, the possibility or the reality of otherness within. The boastful proposition 'we are men and they are crocodiles' implies that 'we were, or could have been, or might yet be crocodiles too.'

Such metonymies are, then, not solely exercises in domination by the power of naming. They also "are means by which societies explore their internal ambiguities and interstices, experiment with alternative values . . . and question their own structures and mechanisms."[7]

In the Sumerian example, the primary metonymic determination of the Amorites as "people-who-know-not-grain" likewise determines the Sumerians as "people-who-know-grain." They have projected this distinction back into their primordial history, acknowledging that there was a time when they "knew-not-grain," as in *The Dispute between Cattle and Grain* which depicts a time when their gods, as well as their ancestors, "knew-not-grain."

> Like humankind when first created
> They [the gods] knew not the eating of bread,
> Knew not the weaving of garments,
> They went around with skins on their bodies,
> Ate plants with their mouths like sheep,
> Drank water from the ditch.[8]

Likewise, the same distinction can describe the Sumerians' threatened future. In the *Lament over the Destruction of Nippur,* when the city is destroyed, the "people ate all (kinds of) grasses like sheep."[9] Finally, in the Old Babylonian versions of *Gilgamesh,* Enkidu, the wild man within, is described in a manner that suggests a Sumerian prototype:

> He [a]te spring grass,
> The milk of wild creatures
> He was want to suck.
>
> . . . .
>
> Enkidu does not know how to eat bread,
> (How to) drink beer.[10]

This is to say, the metonymy know-grain/know-not-grain is not an uncomplicated statement of Sumerian superiority. It is a highly ambivalent construct. Domesticated grain is a fragile achievement, little distant from the wild grasses from which it was bred. It can be taken away, as the fragile cities can, whether by drought, or warfare, or sin, leaving the Sumerian indistinguishable from the Amorite. As with Enkidu, the Sumerians are but a generation away from wildness; ferality is, therefore, an ever present possibility. Finally, as the *Dispute* text maintains, the condition of both the gods and the Sumerian ancestors receiving the arts of cultivation is that humankind serve as slaves of the gods; indistinguishable, in this respect, from any subject people.

(2) The model of center and periphery, is often found in the form of a contrast between the inhabitants of cities and the hinterlands. As such, it characteristically takes the form of an imperial model with replication. The king especially guards the center and the borders—for example, Nebuchadnezzar's throne name, *Nabukudurri-usur* meant "O Nabu, preserve the boundary stone"—beyond the king's realm lies danger, lies another world. In royal epic traditions, the cosmopolitics of center/periphery take two forms: in some texts, such as *Gilgamesh*, high value is placed on the centripetal act of ordering and maintaining the center; in other texts, such as the complex *Alexander Romance*, emphasis is placed on the centrifugal value of establishing the periphery. It is the latter pattern that displays spatial 'otherness' most frequently.

In the third-century Greek *Alexander Romance*,[11] the bestseller of the Late Antique world, the travels of Alexander, beginning with his journey, at the age of fifteen, to the athletic contests at Pisa (1.15) and ending with his death, at the age of thirty-three, in Babylon, after subduing "twenty-two barbarian nations and ten Greek" (3.33), are framed by the contrasting accounts of stay-at-home rulers. At the very beginning of the *Romance* stands Nectanebo, the last native king of Egypt and, in the *Romance*, Alexander's actual father, who "by magic and reason" defends his kingdom, not by going forth into battle but by retiring to his palace and manipulating figurines of his enemies while chanting incantations (1.1). Toward the conclusion of the narrative, the Amazons, the last ethnic group to be trafficked within the *Romance*, fight fiercely to defend their borders, but they and their queen never cross the boundaries of their land (3.25). Philip, Alexander's adoptive father according to the *Romance*, represents the conventional king. He goes forth to battle in foreign lands but returns home (e.g., 1.9). In contrast to Nectanebo and the queen of the Amazons, on the one hand, and to Philip, on the other, Alexander is represented as a thoroughly utopian or cosmopolitan figure. While he founds thirteen cities (3.33), he dwells in none of them. Indeed, the foundation ritual (a modified *mundus*) of his most important city, Alexandria, was accompanied by a suggestive omen:

> He ordered that the circumference of the city be plotted. They took meal and outlined the area; and birds of various species picked up the meal and flew off in all directions. And Alexander, anxious about the meaning of this, hastened to summon soothsayers and told them what had happened. And they said,

'This city which has been built shall feed the entire world; and
the men born in it shall be everywhere; like birds, *they shall travel
through the entire world*.' (1.85 in Armenian; cf. 1.32 in Greek.
Emphasis added).

Within the *Romance*, it is the Indian campaign, occupying fully one-
third of the narrative, which establishes the farthest boundary of the inhabited world. Beyond India "there is nothing but beast infested wilderness" (3.17, Armenian). The map of the *Romance* is accordingly skewed
eastward, with the Amazons occupying the northeastern boundary and
India marking the southeastern extremity. Alexander's travels reverse the
solar route (3.26), taking him "near to the land of sunrise" (3.4). In the
older, third-century B.C. Onescritan Alexander tradition, so influential
on the later *Romance*, this oriental limit becomes joined with a topos that
in India, because the sun stands always directly overhead, there are no
shadows and, therefore, India is a never-never land where time cannot be
reckoned (Pliny, *Natural History* 2.185) and where its gigantic inhabitants live long and die without signs of old age (7.28).

Materials describing the monstrous and alien peoples of India (the
Indika traditions) represent the largest set of interpolations into the *Romance*,[12] often circulating independently as well as achieving a separate
and elaborately illustrated existence in the complex *Marvels of the East*
literature, beginning in the sixth century and culminating in the fourteenth,[13] as well as being systematized in works such as Thomas of Cantimpré's *Book of the Monstrous Men of the Orient* (c. 1230) which carefully
classifies forty-one kinds.[14] In these texts one encounters the full range of
imagined monstrous peoples, some of which, such as the beings with one
large foot or peoples with ears so large as to cover their back and arms, retain the solar motif as these appendages are employed as parasols to shield
them from the unrelenting sun. Others represent reversals characteristic
of never-never lands: people with no anuses, people with no nostrils,
people with no mouths who live on odors, people whose heels are in front
and whose toes point backward, people with head and feet reversed,
people born with gray hair that turns black as they age. Still others have
a composite character, reduplicated organs or other features expressive of
the lack of order, the excess, of a world beyond the pale: people with dog's
heads or tails, people with dog's ears and a single eye on their foreheads,
headless people with a face between their shoulders, people with eight
fingers and toes or six heads, people who live a thousand years, pygmies
whose testicles drag along the ground. Etc., etc., etc.

Shorn of its epic dimensions, an analogous cartography appears in the *Inquiries* (i.e., *Histories*) of Herodotus with complex segmentations, a plurality of centers and multivalent systems of cultural evaluations. Taken as a cultural geography rather than a physical one (the latter Herodotus organizes on different principles), and giving only the broadest outline, there is a north-south axis, with the north carrying a relatively negative valence and the south a relatively positive one. At the outermost limits, north and south, is the monstrous realm. Moving inward, next is the realm of autonomous cultures who borrow from no one: Scythia, to the north, is largely negatively evaluated; Egypt, to the south, is largely positive. The center is the realm of mixture, with Persia, to the north, negatively evaluated; Greece, to the south, positively evaluated (borrowing most heavily from prestigious Egypt); and Ionia, in the center, caught between Greece and Persia.[15]

If the center/periphery model in traditions such as the *Alexander Romance* depicts cultural values as a sort of Doppler effect, a thickness of cultural similarity in the center, relative to the observer, a thinness, an alienation, at the margins; the Herodotean map adopts the figure of the Venn diagram with overlapping spheres of influence.

The simplest form of the center/periphery model is binary. Its most frequent expression is the contrast between the settled city and the roving nomad, between *nomos* and anomie. Thus, the sole criterion by which the Sumerians judged a group to be a "people" was their sedentary character,[16] as opposed to folk such as the Amorites, "who have never known city life," "a tent dweller buffeted by the wind." For the Greeks, the Scythians are the nomads par excellence. For the Romans and successor Christians, the contrast was between them and a series of Turko-Mongolic steppe peoples from the Huns through the Mongols. The bombastic rhetoric of Tertullian (207 A.D.) concerning the Scythians makes the point with precision:

> The fiercest nations dwell there, if indeed one can be said to dwell in a wagon. They have no fixed abode, their life is rude, their lust promiscuous. . . . They devour the bodies of their parents. . . . Their climate, too, exhibits the same rude nature. . . . The whole year is winter. . . . Nothing there is hot except ferocity.[17]

The simple dichotomy of city and outlands was generalized into universal types that have proven to be the longest lived designations for 'others' in native, western vocabulary: 'Pagan,' the rustic village or country dweller (built on the same root as 'peasant') in contrast to town or city folk. 'Heathen,' the heath dweller, one who lives on wild, uncultivated land. 'Civilized,' those who possess the virtues and qualities associated with city living. 'Savage,' literally, forest dweller, a term originally applied in adjectival form to wild animals and plants or to uncultivated land then to feral individuals ('wild boys,' *homo sylvestris*) represented as prowling the margins of settlements, naked or dressed in leaves, and finally applied to other peoples, first as an adjective, then in the mid-sixteenth century, as a substantive. Note that each of these terms has been applied both to 'others' without and to those perceived as 'others' within.

As has been argued with respect to the metonymical model, so here too there is a deep ambivalence to the mapping of 'others' by center/periphery. While the peripheral can be evaluated as bestial or monstrous, the limit case of humanity, its distance from the center can also be viewed positively. Separation from the city suggests virtues uncontaminated by the city and its effete and sinful ways. Nomadism, from this viewpoint, suggests freedom and transcendence from material values. Therefore, it is only in this model that the duality, Wild Man/Noble Savage, appears in which the very remoteness of the marginal allows the projection of a host of positive features unaffected by the daily compromises that make up the familiar world. Whether represented as ferocious or philosophical, the peripheral is preeminently the realm of the strong. In the positive picture of the periphery, as Hayden White has shrewdly observed, rather than a return to the archaic, so characteristic of nostalgic writers from Hesiod to Eliade, "reform is envisaged . . . as the throwing off of a burden [civilization and its corruption] that has become too ponderous. . . . Like archaism, then, primitivism holds up a vision of a lost world; but unlike archaism, [primitivism] insists that this lost world is still present in modern, corrupt and civilized man—and is there for the taking."[18]

The first two models, while seemingly harsh in their initial dualisms between 'us' and 'them,' have each turned out to imply complex reciprocal relationships. The third model, where the 'other' is represented linguistically and/or intellectually in terms of intelligibility, admits no such ambivalence. Here, the 'other' remains obdurately 'other' in a most basic sense: the 'other' is unintelligible and will remain so. The third model differs from the previous two in another regard, it is the only one to be raised to the level of a modern theory.

To my knowledge, the view that the 'other' is essentially unintelligible is not widely held in the earliest western sources. Indeed, quite the opposite.[19] Although there are Babylonian terms such as *nû'u*, which mean both 'stupid' and 'foreigner,'[20] and Sumerian texts that express a Babel-like sense of linguistic diversity—in the time of Enlil, all humans spoke one language; this was altered during the reign of Enki[21]—the Sumero-Akkadian culture was built, to no small degree, around translation. A substantial part of the intellectual effort and the preserved production of their scribes was devoted to foreign language vocabularies and grammars, to the production of bilingual texts correlating the archaic non-Semitic Sumerian with the later Semitic Akkadian. Loeb Library–like, the Sumerian materials were "classics" for the Akkadians. Similarly, within the Hebrew Bible, where linguistic diversity along with genealogy and territory are the central criteria for ethnic classification (Genesis 10:32, cf. 10:5, 10:20, 10:31), and where domination by "foreign speech and a hard language which you will not understand," by people who "stammer in a language which you cannot understand" (Ezekial 3:5–6; Isaiah 33:19; Psalm 114:1) is a powerful threat, multilingualism (aided by the Aramaic lingua franca) and glosses with respect to foreign speech (e.g., Deuteronomy 3:8–9; Esther 3:7 and 9:24) are not unknown.[22]

How different the Greeks! While Arnaldo Momigliano's contention that no Greek learned a foreign tongue,[23] in contradistinction to the Jews, Romans, Egyptians, Phoenicians, Babylonians, Indians, and others who not only learned Greek but translated their native writings and undertook original compositions in Greek, might be judged "an exaggeration in the direction of the truth"—the point remains. Their most fundamental anthropological dualism was linguistic: the *Hellene* who spoke rational speech in opposition to the onomatopoeic *barbarian* (buh! buh! buh!) who spoke unintelligible, stammering, animal- or child-like speech. (A distinction found elsewhere, ranging from Mesoamerica, where *Nahuatl* means "people who explain themselves and speak clearly," to the white South African designation of a group of natives as *Hottentots,* combining *hateren,* "to stammer," and *tateren,* "to stutter"). In the Greek geographer Strabo's formulation:

> A person will be called a barbarian in comparison with another because he is strange in his ways of speaking and because he pronounces the other's language badly. (*Geography* 14.2.28)

On the one hand, this renders the 'other,' the one designated 'barbarian,' opaque and nonhuman, for without speech there can be no understanding, without reason and language, no humanity. On the other hand, the same designation, 'barbarian,' reduces the 'other' to being utterly transparent. Difference becomes insignificant, in the strict sense of the term and, therefore, requires no decipherment, no exegetical labor, no hermeneutic projects. It is for the vocal opposite, for 'us,' to speak for 'them.' Difference has become in-difference.[24] In native ethnographies ranging from that of the Slavs to the Mayas and Aztecs, the 'other' is represented as mute and unable to speak or, at best, can only, like a parrot, mindlessly mimic their vocal opposite.[25]

While a history of opacity has yet to be written, within the modern western tradition a starting point is surely the early humanist historiography as epitomized in Petrarch, who coined the term, "Dark Ages," to stand for that never-to-be-overcome distance that stretched between what he saw as the golden era of classical antiquity and the European present.

> The culture, customs and institutions of ancient Greece and Rome . . . had flourished, declined and finally disappeared and any hope of returning to them or resurrecting them was utterly in vain.[26]

'Our' past was no longer to be thought of as being immediately accessible. At best, "we see through a glass but darkly." Beginning in the fourteenth century, there was a keen sense of historical distance which could be but partially relaxed through philological endeavors and hermeneutic projects. The past could be mimetically present only in acts of imagination and empathy. It could no longer speak directly to us. In this view, the historical 'other' stood within one's own heritage, occult, yet indissolubly linked to one's self-understanding. An understanding now tempered by the full realization of the force of L. P. Hartley's well-known phrase that opens *The Go-Between:* "The past is a foreign country; they do things differently there."

This sense of ancestral opacity became even more acute in western discourse with the nineteenth-century discovery of the antiquity of the human species. This magnified the notion of temporal distance and alienation, symbolized by the word 'prehistory,' a term first introduced into English by Daniel Wilson in 1851, a word that we have become so accustomed to that we fail to flinch at its shock. For artifacts and bones do not speak. History cannot be undertaken without story, and so the early literature on prehistory is filled with confessions of unintelligibility. To quote William Palgrave: "We must give it up, the speechless past. . . . Lost is lost, gone is gone forever."[27]

To overcome this silence, nineteenth- and early-twentieth-century scholars employed a strategy pioneered in the seventeenth and eighteenth centuries to understand Greco-Roman antiquity by the present

practices of 'savages.' An homology between their material cultures led
to a postulation of an analogy between their intellectual cultures. As La
Créquinière wrote in 1704:

> The study of the customs of the Indians is in no way useful in it-
> self. I make use of it only to understand the ancients and to ex-
> plain it. The understanding of antiquity is my only aim.[28]

As redeployed in the later writings of those scholars we group together as
practitioners of "The Comparative Method," the comparison was between "living Stone Age peoples" and the prehistoric Stone Age on the
grounds that they both shared the same "primitive mentality." Thus
Spencer and Gillen introduce their classic monograph on the Australian
Arunta (1927) by claiming that

> Australia is the present home and refuge of creatures, often
> crude and quaint, that have elsewhere passed away and given
> place to higher forms. This applies especially to the Aboriginal
> as to the platypus and the kangaroo. Just as the platypus laying
> its eggs and feebly sucking its young reveals a mammal in the
> making, so does the Aboriginal show us . . . what early man must
> have been like before he learned to read and write, domesticate
> animals, cultivate crops and use a metal tool. It has been pos-
> sible to study in Australia human beings that still remain at the
> cultural level of men of the Stone Age. . . . [The Aborigines are]
> a people that afford as much insight as we are now ever likely to
> gain into the manner of life of men and women who have long
> since disappeared in other parts of the world and are now known
> to us only through their stone implements, which, together with
> rock drawings and more or less crude carvings, were the only
> imperishable records of their culture that they could leave be-
> hind them.[29]

Yet paradoxically embodied in this hope for comparison was a process
of impeaching the witness which forbade projects of meaning: "primitive mentality" was held to be fundamentally irrational, exhibiting *Ur-
dummheit*. Both the peoples of the old Stone Age and "contemporary
Stone Age peoples" were lumped together as essentially prehistoric; the
former being before history, the latter having no history. Either way, neither are finally intelligible, therefore we must speak for them. (I remind

you that the original Greek meaning of "anthropologist," as found in Aristotle, was a "gossip," one who likes to talk about other human beings).[30] For the nineteenth- and early-twentieth-century comparativists, there was no point in directly interrogating the 'savage,' just as there was no point in speaking to a Paleolithic worked stone. As a leading contemporary scholar complains, in his presidential address to a royal learned society, on the matter of using Australian rock engravings and cave paintings to interpret Paleolithic cave art: "few Aborigines have made comments worth recording about the engravings."[31]

As with the linguistic version of the model, so with the intellectual one, both exhibit the curious paradox of an initial sense of opacity which is, subsequently, held to be transparent. The focus on the 'other' as unintelligible has led, necessarily, to 'their' silence and 'our' speech.

II

To this point, we have been reflecting on models of the 'other'—always a dualistic term ('other' means, literally, 'other of two')—which, nevertheless, in two of the models implied reciprocal relations even as the designation insisted on utter separation, alienation, and estrangement. This is not surprising. Even in theological discourse and imagination, where the notion of the "totally Other" is most strongly maintained, the distinction can never be held to be absolute. As H. W. Turner remarks in his commentary on Rudolf Otto:

> When Otto describes this experience of the Numen as 'Wholly Other,' he cannot mean *wholly* 'Wholly Other.' We could never have this knowledge of a Being quite cut off from us. It must therefore be present in our experience without losing its 'otherness.' [But] to be present in our experience, the Numen must have some affinity with men.[32]

Despite such cautions, it must be insisted that the language of the 'other' always invites misunderstanding, suggesting, as it does, an ontological cleavage rather than an anthropological distinction. Much better is the language of 'difference,' which is as relational and relative a terminology as the 'other' is absolute. 'Otherness' blocks language and conceptualization; 'difference' invites negotiation and intellection. For 'difference' is an active term—ultimately a verbal form, *differre*, 'to carry apart'—suggesting the separating out of what, from another vantage point, might be

seen as the 'same.' By contrast, 'other' has no verbal form, except, perhaps, 'alienate,' which, tellingly, most often appears in the passive voice.
Viewed in this light, difference is the more interesting phenomenon,
which has not received the attention it merits. Among other gains, the
making of difference allows for an understanding of the construction of
internal distinctions as well as external ones.

I am told by one of the many nature shows, which allow public television to appear educational while avoiding controversy, that there are
flocks of birds in Africa that elude carnivores by erupting suddenly, in the
tens of thousands, from the ground into flight with the result that the at-
tacker is unable to focus its attention on anyone. Their collective strategy is to make themselves *de trop*.

There are many days when the cultural comparativist feels like the
frustrated hunter of the African plains must feel when confronting the
myriad of historical and ethnographic details that cross her or his desk.
There is so much that it seems impossible to find significance in any one.
There is so much that the comparativist spends most of the working day
deciding what *not* to study, what facts to refuse to take up as potential data.

I want to share with you one such report that almost did not make it
into my files. It was like so many others I have read that it scarcely seemed
worth a second glance. Yet, I want to suggest, it is its very commonplace
character that commands attention by highlighting, in a concrete fashion, not only the ubiquity of the construction of difference in human culture, but also by suggesting that culture-itself is constituted by the double
process of both making differences and relativizing those very same distinctions. One of our fundamental social projects appears to be our collective capacity to think of, and to think away, the differences we create.

The report concerns the Hua people, a relatively small group of
3,100 individuals (in the 1970s), distributed in eleven traditional villages, ranging in size from 80 to 300 persons, practicing slash and burn
agriculture on the slopes of Mount Michael in the Eastern Highlands
province of Papua New Guinea.

In native ideology, all eleven villages, collectively, constitute "the
people," but four of the villages, plus four more that are thought of as
their "offshoots," are held to be the direct descendants of the four ancestral brothers celebrated in their myths.

> Welded together by an idiom of common patrilineal descent,
> marriage within this eight-village unit was traditionally prohib-
> ited. The three remaining villages of Hua people are bound to
> the first eight through ties of marriage.

In native idiom, these three villages live "inside" the eight and intermarriage is between the larger "outer" circle of eight and the smaller "inner" circle of three. Here, difference is encompassed within the larger unit.

The eight "outer" villages are divided into "two hostile camps" of four villages each (or, two pairs, each made up of one of the "original" four villages and its "brother/offshoot") termed the "upper inhabitants" and the "lower inhabitants." There is no native consensus as to how the three "inner" villages relate to this split. All options were expressed: they are allied with the "upper," they are allied with the "lower," they are neutral.

Thus far, at the level of the "people," a relatively small group, which to the outsider's eye, is homogenous, exhibiting only the usual individual variations characteristic of any set, has been divided and distinguished, by native intellectual labor, into spheres of relative difference through the creation of traditions of descent (four "original" villages + four "offshoot" + three) and by mental maps ("inner"/"outer" and "upper"/"lower") while, at the same time, the postulations of difference have been at least partially overcome through structures of alliance, both marital and martial.

That these distinctions are best understood as theoretical postulations of difference can be illustrated at the level of kinship, recalling Durkheim's essential insight that kinship is never 'natural,' but always a social taxonomy. If, at the level of "the people," marriage is between the "outer" eight and the "inner" three villages, marriage, at the level of lineage, is theoretically between allied villages (the pairs of "original" + "brother/offshoot") in the "upper" and "lower" topography. However, the ethnographer reports, "the fact that the upper and lower inhabitants, although still in some sense enemies, are cautiously beginning to marry suggests some complications." Rather than interpreting this as some breakdown, is it not the case that the different theories of difference are in tension; that while difference is maintained at the systemic level, the potentiality of difference for relativization is employed in practice?

The same sort of tension can be illustrated at the third, intermediary level of organization, that of the village. (Not to speak of the tensions, available to native thought, by the juxtaposition of these three levels, each with their characteristic multiple postulations of both difference and affinity). The village system of difference is expressed and mapped through the "idiom of men's houses," the exclusive residences of initiated males and postmenopausal females. (This detail calls attention to at least two other systems of difference which will not be discussed, gender and age-grade, each, like kinship, not "natural" but rather social constructions). Each village has from one to three such houses, prominent buildings, centrally located, on an east-west axis (yet another topography).

> Each men's house ideally housed two lineages, each identified
> with the door over which it had exclusive right of use. . . . Each
> village is paired with a second . . . with which it supposedly
> shared a men's house. [Again, the "upper" and "lower" pairs of
> "original" and "brother/offshoot"]. . . . Further, the villages that
> comprise each people are divided into two groups representing
> the original descendants of the opposite doors of the original
> [mythic] men's house.

Here an architectural system of differences divides the unit of the village
at the same time as it reaffirms cross-cutting dual alliances with other villages. Overlaying the marriage system on this village map, rules and prohibitions can be expressed in terms of "doors":

> In matrilineal marriage ego cannot take a woman from ego's
> mother's door and in patrilineal marriage ego cannot marry a
> daughter of ego's own door. . . . Hua males say they like to marry
> from the opposite door of one of their own men's houses.

But again, the three "inner" villages provide the opportunity for relativization. They are thought of as having no "doors" and, therefore, marriage
with these "outer" villages "is not only frequent but indiscriminate."[33]

In fact, despite the above, most Hua marriages are not internal to the
Hua people.

> The Hua are typical Eastern Highlanders in that they reside pa-
> trilocally: that is, on marriage women go to live in the village of
> the husband. For generations, perhaps for centuries, the Hua
> have contracted most of their marriage alliances with the Gimi,
> Siane, and Chimbu peoples, whose languages differ from Hua,
> impressionistically, as much as French, German and Russian dif-
> fer from English. Children born of such marriages grow up bilin-
> gual. When they in turn marry, they learn the first language of
> their spouse, which may be different from that of either their
> mother or their father. Prolonged intermarriage has made the
> community phenomenally multilingual. In a survey of 359 adult
> speakers in 1974, it was found that 305 were fluent in Gimi, 287
> in Siane, and 103 in Chimbu. A smaller number of people spoke
> at least a half a dozen other languages. Only two respondents
> claimed to be totally monolingual, and only eleven knew only
> one other language besides Hua. All the others spoke at least

two, and many were fluent and at ease in four or five. Within the last twenty-five years, another language, Neo-Melanesian, also known as Pidgin English, has gained currency in the Highlands, replacing all others as the most widely spoken second language among the young.[34]

What this last item reveals is of utmost importance to our inquiry. "Real" difference, here represented by language, is negotiated with ease. Specific, different languages are learned when it is socially valuable to do so; Pidgin, a language equally different from all native languages, is employed when pantribal communication is required. Differences that are "there" are simply overcome when it is necessary to do so; differences that are constructed are thought about and thought away.

The issue of difference as a mode of both culturally encoding and decoding, of maintaining and relativizing internal as well as external distinctions, raises the last point, the observation that, rather than the remote 'other' being perceived as problematic and/or dangerous, it is the proximate 'other,' the near neighbor, who is most troublesome. That is to say, while difference or 'otherness' may be perceived as being either LIKE-US or NOT-LIKE-US, it becomes most problematic when it is TOO-MUCH-LIKE-US or when it claims to BE-US. It is here that the real urgency of theories of the 'other' emerges, called forth not so much by a requirement to place difference, but rather by an effort to situate ourselves. This, then, is not a matter of the 'far' but preeminently of the 'near.' The deepest intellectual issues are not based upon perceptions of alterity, but, rather, of similarity, at times, even, of identity.

There is a further matter. While all the previous constructions of 'otherness' and of difference we have considered have been essentially affairs of the history of culture and, therefore, also relevant to the history of religion, the issue of problematic similarity or identity seems to be particularly prevalent in religious discourse and imagination. Thus the ancient Israelites created a myth of the conquest, fabricating themselves as outsiders and therefore as different from their encompassing and synonymous group, the Canaanites, from whom they cannot otherwise be distinguished. Paul never writes against Jews or members of Greco-Roman religions but always against fellow Christians from whom he insists on counterdistinguishing himself and his teachings. John of Pian del Carpini and William of Ruysbroeck, thirteenth-century missionaries to the Mongols, have no difficulty in recording scores of positive comparisons between the feared Tartars and their own Christian European culture, even though they are at war; rather, their deepest perceptions of problematic difference are focused on the Nestorian Christians who remain largely unintelligible to them. From heresy to deviation to degeneration to syncretism, the notion of the different which claims to be the same, or, projected internally, the disguised difference within, has produced a rich vocabulary of denial and estrangement. For in each case, a theory of difference, when applied to the proximate 'other,' is but another way of phrasing a theory of 'self.'

There are thousands of societies and world-views. In most cases, their actual remoteness guarantees mutual indifference. For example, by and large Christians and Jews have not thought much about the 'otherness' of the Hua or the Kwakiutl, or, for that matter, the Taoist. The bulk of Christian and Jewish thought about difference has been directed against other Christians and Jews, against each other, and against those groups thought of as being near neighbors or descendants: in this case, most especially, Muslims.

Today, as in the past, the history of religious conflicts and of strong language of alienation is largely intraspecific. The major exceptions occur in those theoretically unrevealing but historically common moments when proximity becomes more a matter of territoriality than of thought.[35]

As Lévi-Strauss, among others, has convincingly demonstrated, when we confront difference we do not encounter irrationality or bad faith but rather the very essence of thought. Meaning is made possible by difference. Yet thought seeks to bring together what thought necessarily takes apart by means of a dynamic process of disassemblage and reassemblage, which results in an object no longer natural but rather social, no longer factual but rather intellectual. Relations are discovered and reconstituted through projects of differentiation.

In the bulk of the models and strategies we have considered, thought is provoked by postulations of reciprocity, by the mutual determinations of difference. A distance, initially formulated, is relativized—or, in the case of the last instance, a proximity initially perceived as too close is distanced. The only model that fails in these respects, the only model, I repeat, that has been raised to the level of a second-order theory, is one that is formed in terms of thought itself; but an inadequate notion of thought as either transparency or opacity. The model of unintelligibility denies both the work of culture and the study of culture. It sets aside the reason that most of the human sciences are, first and foremost, linguistic enterprises. For it is the issue of translation, that 'this' is never quite 'that,' and, therefore, that acts of interpretation are required that marks the human sciences. It is thought about translation, an affair of the in between that is always relative and never fully adequate; it is thought about translation across languages, places, and times, between text and reader, speaker and hearer, that energizes the human sciences as disciplines and suggests the intellectual contributions they make. *Vive la différence!*

Notes

1. M. Douglas, *Purity and Danger: An Analysis of Concepts of Pollution and Taboo* (New York, 1966), 115, 121.

2. Douglas, *Purity and Danger*, has done an important theoretical service by relating the body to containment as a central model of pollution. This model ought not to be confused with the model of mixture that, at least within the Levitical system on which she bases an important segment of her work, is part of the system of permitted/forbidden rather than the clean/unclean. The dietary laws in Leviticus 12, central to her understanding, experiment (unsuccessfully) in combining these two systems (as elsewhere in Leviticus 1–16)—but systematically, the animals are permitted and forbidden, not clean/unclean. The awkward combination of these two systems in the summary passage (Leviticus 12:47) indicates consciousness, at the level of redaction, of this experimentation: "to make a distinction between the clean and the unclean and between the living creature that may be eaten and the living creature that may not be eaten."

3. R. Redfield, *The Primitive World and Its Transformations* (Ithaca, 1953), 92.

4. Such a metonymical construction lies behind the earliest extant example of Greek comparative religions, Xenophanes (c. 570–475 B.C.): "The Ethiopians say their gods are snubnosed and black; the Thracians say that their gods have light blue eyes and red hair." H. Diels-W. Kranz, *Die Fragmente der Vorsokratiker*, 5th ed. (Berlin, 1934), frag. 16(B). See the discussion of this text in R. Pettazzoni, "Alle origini della scienza delle religioni," *Numen* 1 (1954): 136–67.

5. C. Lévi-Strauss, *The Savage Mind* (Chicago, 1966), 115–16 quite rightly insists that the logic of totemism is "homology between *two systems of differences*, one of which occurs in nature and the other in culture" yielding the notion, for example, that "clan 1 differs from clan 2 as . . . the eagle differs from the bear," and that "this structure would be fundamentally impaired" if it were held that "clan 1 is like the eagle and clan 2 like the bear." Nevertheless, he goes on to offer instances of the latter, arguing that, in this case, "the idea of diversity is likely to prevail over that of unity."

6. The fundamental collection of these materials is in G. Buccellati, *The Amorites of the Ur III Period* (Naples, 1966), 92–95, 330–32. See further, J. H. Tigay, *The Evolution of the Gilgamesh Epic* (Philadelphia, 1982), 198–205, on which I draw heavily for this section.

7. W. S. Green, "Otherness Within: Towards a Theory of Difference in Rabbinic Judaism," in J. Neusner and E. S. Frerichs, eds., *"To See Ourselves As Others*

See Us": Christians, Jews, "Others" in Late Antiquity (Chico, 1985): 49–69, quotations from 50–51.

8. Cited in Tigay, *Evolution*, 203.

9. Tigay, *Evolution*, 204.

10. Tigay, *Evolution*, 199.

11. In citing the *Alexander Romance*, I follow the Greek alpha-recension as edited by W. Kroll, *Historia Alexandri Magni (Pseudo-Callisthenes)*, vol. 1, *Recensio Vetusta* (Berlin, 1926). There are two excellent English translations: E. H. Haight, *The Life of Alexander of Macedon by Pseudo-Callisthenes* (New York, 1955) and K. Dowden, "Pseudo-Callisthenes: The Alexander Romance," in B. P. Reardon, ed., *Collected Ancient Greek Novels* (Berkeley, 1989), 650–735. I have compared, and occasionally cite, the Armenian version of the alpha-recension translated by A. N. Wolohojian, *The Romance of Alexander the Great by Pseudo-Callisthenes* (New York, 1969) from the edition by R. T'reanc (Venice, 1842).

12. These interpolations occur in two major forms. The first is the teratological narrative of the "wonders of India" in the *Letter of Alexander to Aristotle*, which in some manuscripts (3.7–17) replaces the briefer epistle (3.17). See, in general, W. W. Boer, *Epistula Alexandri ad Aristotelem* (Masenheim am Glan, 1973). The second is the more positive philosophical traditions represented by the pseudo-Palladian, *Treatise on the Brahmans* (3.7–16); the pseudepigraphical correspondence between Dindamus and Alexander in the Latin traditions; and the brief (Cynic) treatise attributed to Dindimus. For all three texts, see P. Pfister, *Kleine Texte zum Alexanderroman* (Heidelberg, 1910), 1–20 and the rich study by J. D. M. Derrett, "The History of Palladius on the Races of the Indians and Brahmans," *Classica et Medievalia* 21 (1960): 351–80.

13. P. A. Gibb, "Wonders of the East: A Critical Edition and Commentary," (Ph.D. diss., Duke University, 1977).

14. Thomas of Cantimpré, *De natura rerum*, book 3, *Liber de monstrosus hominibus orientis*, which, to my knowledge, remains unpublished. The only relatively accessible version of this text is an edition of an Old French translation. A. Hilka, "Eine altfranzösische moralisierende Bearbeitung des Liber de monstruosis hominibus orientis aus Thomas von Cantimpré, De naturis rerum, nach der einzigen Handschrift Paris Bibl. Nat. fr. 15106," *Abhandlungen der Gesellschaft der Wissenschaften zu Göttingen*, Philologisch-historische Klasse, 3d ser., 3.7 (Berlin, 1933). Hilka apparently treated the Latin text of the *Liber* in a contribution to the *Festschrift zur Jahrhundertfeier der Universität Breslau am 2 August 1911* (Breslau, 1911), 151–65, which I have been unable to obtain.

15. For the mapping of Herodotus, see J. Redfield, "Herodotus the Tourist," *Classical Philology* 80 (1985): 97–118, esp. 106–13.

16. H. Limet, "'Peuple' et 'humanité' chez les Sumériens," in G. van Driel et al., *Festschrift F. R. Kraus* (Leiden, 1982), 258–67, esp. 260.

17. Tertullian, *Adversus Marcionem* I.1 in A. Lovejoy and G. Boas, *Primitivism and Related Ideas in Antiquity* (reprint, New York, 1973), 342–43.

18. H. White, "Forms of Wilderness: Archaeology of an Idea," in E. Dudley and M. E. Novak, eds., *The Wild Man Within: An Image in Western Thought from the Renaissance to Romanticism* (Pittsburgh, 1972): 3–38, quotation from 26.

19. Although I would not go so far as A. L. Oppenheim, "The Position of the Intellectual in Mesopotamian Society," *Daedalus* (spring 1975): 38, in declaring that Mesopotamian texts exhibit a "consistent absence of any expression of that civilization's uniqueness in the face of an alien background. Thus no need is felt to contrast native ways of thinking or doing things with those of the outside world. Nor are its merits and achievements ever set forth in contradistinction to foreign views and values." Compare the comments on Oppenheim's view by P. Machinist, "On Self-consciousness in Mesopotamia," in S. N. Eisenstadt, ed., *The Origins and Diversity of Axial Age Civilizations* (Albany, 1986), 183–202, esp. 184, 188–90.

20. *Assyrian Dictionary* (Chicago, 1956–), 11:2: 356–57, s.v. "*nû'u.*" See also M. Liverani, "The Ideology of the Assyrian Empire" in M. T. Larsen, ed., *Power and Propaganda: A Symposium on Ancient Empires* (Copenhagen, 1979): 297–317, esp. 310: "As regards knowledge, the Assyrians are physically and linguistically normal, comprehensible, fully human; whereas the foreigners are strange (*nak(i)ru* 'different, strange' → 'stranger' → 'enemy') . . . belonging rather to the animal world, and as a matter of fact frequently compared to animals."

21. *Epic of Enmerkar*, 136–55: "The people in unison spoke to Enlil in one tongue . . . Enki, lord of wisdom . . . changed the speech in their mouths (bringing) contention into it. Into the speech that (until then) had been one." See S. N. Kramer, "Man's Golden Age: A Sumerian Parallel to Genesis 11:1," *Journal of the American Oriental Society* 63 (1943): 191–93 and Kramer, "The 'Babel of Tongues': A Sumerian Version," *Journal of the American Oriental Society* 88 (1968): 108–11.

22. M. Fishbane, *Biblical Interpretation in Ancient Israel* (Oxford, 1985), 45–46 and note 5.

23. A. Momigliano, *Alien Wisdom: The Limits of Hellenization* (Cambridge, 1975), 7–8, 91–93 et passim.

24. I have taken this play on words from H. Lefebvre, *Le manifeste différentialiste* (Paris, 1970), 53–101, esp. 94, where he writes of the "reduction of difference to the indifferent (or repetitive) . . . of the plural to the monotonous . . ."

25. For a brief list of examples, see T. Todorov, *The Conquest of America* (New York, 1984), 76. For parroting, see L. Hanke, "Pope Paul III and the American Indians," *Harvard Theological Review*, 30 (1937): 84.

26. E. Cochrane, *Historians and Historiography in the Renaissance* (Chicago, 1981), 15. For Petrarch, see T. E. Mommsen, "Petrarch's Concept of the Dark

Ages," in Mommsen (E. F. Rice, Jr., ed.), *Medieval and Renaissance Studies* (Ithaca, 1959), 106–29.

27. W. Palgrave as quoted in the opening paragraph of J. Lubbock (Lord Avebury), *Prehistoric Times as Illustrated by Ancient Remains and the Manners and Customs of Ancient Savages* (London, 1865), 1.

28. M. de La Créquinière, *The Agreement of the Customs of the East Indians with Those of the Jews and Other Ancient Peoples* (London, 1705), vii, from the French original (Brussels, 1704).

29. B. Spencer and F. J. Gillen, *The Arunta: A Study of a Stone Age People* (London, 1927), 1: vii.

30. Aristotle *Nichomachean Ethics* 1125a5.

31. F. D. McCarthy, "Presidential Address," *Journal and Proceedings of the Royal Society of New South Wales* 91 (1957): 10.

32. H. W. Turner, *Rudolf Otto, the Idea of the Holy: Commentary on a Shortened Version* (Aberdeen, 1974), 19.

33. A. S. Meigs, *Foods, Sex and Pollution: A New Guinea Religion* (Rutgers, 1984), 4, 6–8, 11–12.

34. J. Haiman, "Hua, a Papuan Language of New Guinea," in T. Shopen, ed., *Languages and Their Status* (Cambridge, Mass., 1979): 36–37; cf. Haiman, *Hua: A Papuan Language of the Eastern Highlands of New Guinea* (Amsterdam, 1980), 515–16.

35. I have drawn some sentences from my article, "What a Difference a Difference Makes," in Neusner-Frerichs, *"To See Ourselves As Others See Us,"* 3–48, esp. pp. 46–48, reprinted in this volume.

CHAPTER TWELVE

WHAT A DIFFERENCE A DIFFERENCE MAKES

The discourse of difference is a difficult one.   𝒹. 𝒹. 𝒹

T. TODOROV, *La conquête de l'Amérique: La question de l'autre*

"TO SEE OURSELVES as Others See Us: The Theory of the Other in the Formative Age of Christianity and Judaism." What a formidable topic to set before an international gathering of scholars as the focus for a summer's weeklong period of papers and reflections! Only the title's points of chronological reference to the first centuries strike me as bearing a measure of self-evidence. Quite rightly, they have supplied the skeletal outline for the proceedings of our conference. Abstaining from the question of the referent for "Christianity" or "Judaism," what is by no means clear is what was intended by the framers of our topic when they employed the portentous phrase "the theory of the other." I take it to be the obligation of one charged to give a "keynote" address to inquire into this most general aspect of our subject.

For this reason, in what follows I shall not dwell at all on the stated chronological period, nor venture to anticipate the welter of historical particularities and exempla concerning Christians and Jews which the full program promises. Rather, I shall direct my inquiries toward that phrase "the theory of the other" and attempt to discern several senses in which the "other" can be framed as a theoretical issue. That is to say, I shall want to ask, from the perspective of intellectual history, what difference does difference make? My point of entry into this difficult matter has been supplied by the poetic apostrophe in our conference's title.

Chapter Twelve

I

There is no settling the point of precedency between a louse and a flea.

DR. JOHNSON

I would like to believe it was far from accidental that our conveners chose to introduce our topic with a line from the concluding stanza of a poem by Robert Burns. First published in the historic Kilmarnock edition of 1786, it has, detached from its context, since become a piece of proverbial lore.

> O wid some Power the giftie gie us
> To see oursels as ithers see us!
> It wad frae mony a blunder free us,
>   An' foolish notion:
> What airs in dress an' gait wad lea'e us
>   An' ev'n devotion![1]

In quoting Burns's lines, we have already gained an initial purchase on our topic. What language was the poem written in? The language seems not-quite-English, yet, is it different enough to be classified as "other"? To quote one distinguished scholar of Scottish literature on Burns:

> Though all of this is still unmistakably Scots, only a small change of spelling is required to make these couplets visually indistinguishable from English ... [but] they have to be pronounced with a Scottish accent. Thus they fall within the compass of Scottish speech and the language employed in them cannot strictly be called 'English'; perhaps it should rather be termed 'near-English.'[2]

It may be fairly asked, how "near" is near? How "far" is far? How different does difference have to be to constitute "otherness"? Under what circumstances, and to whom, are such distinctions of interest?

The question of interest reminds us of yet another facet to our theme, one that is contained within the original sense of "interest" as continued in legal and economic usage. Difference is rarely something simply to be noted; it is, most often, something in which one has a stake. Above all, it is a political matter. As the proximate historical setting of Burns suggests, following the Union of the Crowns in 1603 and the Parliamentary Union of 1707, and contemporary with the establishment in Edinburgh of a "Select Society for the Promoting of the Reading and Speaking of the English Language," what appears from a linguistic point of view to be "near" appears from a political vantage to be exceedingly "far."[3] How far might be measured by comparing Burns's self-consciously vernacular poems with the equally self-conscious classic English prose of his Scottish contemporary, Adam Smith. Difference is seldom a comparison between entities judged to be equivalent. Difference most frequently entails a hierarchy of prestige and the concomitant political ranking of superordinate and subordinate.

[margin note: Language v. politics]

Yet, as the Scottish example illustrates, such distinctions are usually drawn most sharply between "near neighbors." For a Scotsman to opt for either Scottish or English (both being Anglo-Saxon dialects) is a more politically striking decision than to have chosen to speak either French or Chinese.[4] The radically "other" is merely "other"; the proximate "other" is problematic, and hence, of supreme interest.

[margin note: White v. Black]

But there is more. The choice of our conveners proved to be of even greater prescience. For the poem that contains the line "to see ourselves as others see us" is entitled "To a Louse: On Seeing One on a Lady's Bonnet at Church." Perhaps this will seem an unsuitable topic; it has appeared so to many of Burns's deepest admirers. But the louse has provided the subject for a wide variety of poets and painters,[5] although it has been eclipsed in this regard by the equally parasitic flea[6] in the works of poets ranging from John Donne to Roland Young, in operatic works by Mussorgsky and Ghedini, and not forgetting its place in the anonymous Victorian pornographic novel, *Autobiography of a Flea, told in a Hop, Skip and Jump, and recounting all experiences of the Human and Superhuman Kind, both Male and Female; with his Curious Connections, Backbitings and Tickling Touches.*[7] Burns's poem will not repay further study—it's lousy; but its pediculine subject will.

There is, perhaps, no scientific area of scholarship in which more sustained attention has been devoted to the taxonomy and definition of "otherness" than parasitology. Rare for biology, here is a subdiscipline devoted not to a natural class of living things but, rather, to a relationship between two quite different species of plants or animals. It is the character of the difference and the mode of relationship that supplies both the key characteristics for classification and the central topics for disciplinary thought. This is especially apparent in the literature of the last half of the nineteenth century, while parasitology was achieving status as an independent field of inquiry.[8] Observations about some of the larger parasites on animals and man may be found throughout antiquity.[9] However, awareness of parasitism's ubiquity had to await the late seventeenth-century development of the microscope.[10] This resulted in a decisive shift of intellectual interest to the scientific, philosophical, and literary topos of the intricately small.[11] Even after this point, despite the enormous increase in data,[12] theoretical issues with respect both to taxonomy[13] and "spontaneous generation" had to be settled before the discipline of parasitology could emerge.[14]

While the majority of biology's historians have focused their attention on the aetiological issues associated with the theory of "spontaneous generation" (*generatio aequivoca* or "abiogenesis"), it was, in fact, the taxonomic implications that were more serious for our theme. Until the stunning monograph by J. J. S. Steenstrup (1842),[15] it was by no means clear that many parasites go through both free-living and parasitic stages of development (at times, with sex changes) that bear no resemblance to each other and often with an invariant sequence of hosts. It is the generation of parasitologists that immediately followed upon this discovery that developed the classificatory systems of most interest to us.[16] It was first thought that one biological class could contain all zoological parasitic forms, and so the older nomenclature of external form which presented the parasite as "wormlike" (whether expressed through the Greek, *helminth*, or the Latin, *vermis*) yielded to a neologism of relative position, the *Entozoa* (animals who live within).[17] This was a major shift in taxonomic strategy, creating a class of animals joined together by their "mode of existence" even though, judged by other criteria, they belonged to different zoological classes.

Regardless of what biological class the individual parasitic species belonged to, they might be classified qua parasites by the mode of their relationship to their hosts. From this point of view, parasitology is not the study of parasites, it is the study of the host-parasite relationship. Parasites are classified by their relationship to the "other," by the modes and degrees of "otherness."

The initial move in this complex taxonomic endeavor was to attempt a general definition of "parasitism" within the animal kingdom. (Plant parasitism posed a different set of issues). A "parasite" was defined as an organism of one species that obtained benefits (most usually food) from an organism of another species with whom it was in direct contact and that served as "host." It was understood that this definition was both relative and nonreciprocal. The definition was relative in that the parasite must be smaller than its host (e.g., the leech, which, when it preys on smaller animals, is properly termed a "carnivore," is rightly called a "parasite" when it attaches itself to larger animals). It was nonreciprocal in

[handwritten margin note:] Americans; regardless of color or creed.

that the host must derive no benefit from the parasitic association. Indeed, most usually the association is detrimental to the host. This latter, nonreciprocal criterion is understood to imply that the negative effect must be the direct result of the benefit derived by the parasite (e.g., the destruction of the host's cells by feeding) and not indirect, such as in the case of diseases transmitted to the host by the parasite.[18]

Concealed within such late nineteenth-century attempts at a generic definition of "parasitism" were a set of thorny taxonomic distinctions. If attention was focused on the criterion of "benefit," then the attempt was made to distinguish the nonreciprocal benefit to the parasite from closely related phenomena such as "symbiosis" (a term invented in 1879 by A. de Bary) in which both species derived necessary mutual benefits from their association, "mutualism" (a term introduced by Beneden in 1876) in which one species derived benefit without affect on the other, and "commensalism" (likewise created by Beneden) in which one species lives on or in another without apparent benefit or harm to either.[19]

Note that such taxonomic distinctions, by virtue of their concern for matters of association, are explicitly political. The definitions are based on hierarchical distinctions of subordination and superordination, on mapping structures of benefits and reciprocity. Such political interests are continued in those taxonomic distinctions made with respect to the nature and character of the direct relationship between host and parasite which constitute a virtual typology of "otherness."

Perhaps the most influential of these was that developed by R. Leuckart in *Die menschlichen Parasiten* (1863–76). His first distinction was between what he termed "ectoparasites" (or "epizoa") and "endoparasites" (or "entozoa"). Ectoparasites "live on" their hosts; endoparasites "live in" their hosts. Both may be further subdivided into two classes on the basis of whether the relationship of parasite to host is "temporary" or "permanent."

In general, ectoparasites are temporary. They seek their hosts in order to obtain food or shelter and leave them when they have been satisfied. They tend to inhabit the surface of their host's body or its immediately accessible orifices. Their bodily form is little modified by their parasitic habit when compared with closely related nonparasitic forms.

In general, endoparasites are more complex. They tend to have both parasitic and nonparasitic life stages, the former being highly modified when compared with the latter. In their parasitic stages, the relation to their host is stationary. They more usually inhabit the internal organs of their host.

With primary reference to endoparasites, Leuckart introduced a further set of classificatory differentia based on "the nature and duration of their strictly parasitic [stage] of life." (1) Some have "free-living and self-supporting" embryos which become sexually mature only after they have reached their hosts. (2) Others have embryos which are parasitic but "migratory," moving (a) to a "free life," (b) to another part of their host, or (c) to a different host, before becoming sexually mature. (3) Others are parasitic during every stage of their lives, having no migratory embryonic stage and passing their entire lives on a single host.[20]

In the above, it should be noted that Leuckart's entire classificatory project is based on the differing forms of relationship between parasite and host. It is a relativistic, economic or political system that does not follow the traditional anatomical/morphological criteria for taxonomy.

Before continuing, it may be well to pause and to make explicit what considering this brief history of late nineteenth-century parasitology has contributed to the question of a "theory of the other."

Perhaps the most important point is that reiterated by Leuckart: "no broad line of demarcation can be drawn between parasites and free-living animals."[21] That is to say, "otherness" is an ambiguous category. This is so because it is necessarily a term of interrelation. "Otherness" is not so much a matter of separation as it is a description of interaction. As the taxonomy of parasitism makes clear, the relation to the "other" is a matter of shifting temporality and relative modes of relationship. There are degrees of difference, even within a single species.

While at one level the taxonomy of parasites (and, hence, of "otherness") appears to be reducible to the ancient legal question, *Cui bono?* at another level the distinctions between "parasitism," "symbiosis," "mutualism," "commensalism," "epiphytism," and the like are distinctions between types of exchange. A "theory of the other" must take the form of a relational theory of reciprocity. "Otherness," whether of Scots or of lice, is a preeminently political category.

It might have been thought that I would go on and attempt to make a further contact with this symposium's theme by cataloging the varied roles parasites have played in western religions[22]—not forgetting the Roman deity, Verminus.[23] Indeed, parasites, and most particularly, the louse, have supplied a variety of Christian theological conundrums ranging from the justification for their existence in terms of natural law (a matter still raised by Immanuel Kant)[24] to ticklish questions as to whether Adam and Eve had lice in Paradise prior to the Fall (I remind you that what is alleged to be the shortest poem in the English language reads, in full, "Adam Had 'em"),[25] whether Eve contained in her body not only the seed of all future human beings but also of all future human parasites,[26] and whether lice and other parasites found a place on Noah's Ark.[27] Nor should we ignore Charles Bonnet's triumphant demonstration of the Virgin Birth's scientific credibility when he observed parthenogenesis in plant lice.[28] But I have another sort of connection in mind.

It would appear that the term "parasite" came into technical discourse as a generic category only in the last decades of the nineteenth century. A search of lexica, encyclopaedia, and earlier scientific works reveals that it was in common use in botany at the beginning of the century,[29] and was taken over only at a later stage by zoologists, replacing, as we have seen, "entozoa," and "helminths."[30] This is not the first time the word "parasite" has replaced a previous set of terms. Such a substitution had occurred once before, in ancient Athens during the first half of the fourth century B.C. This earlier shift established "parasite" as bearing a cultural connotation. And this sense persisted through the middle of the nineteenth century as the prime meaning of "parasite," while laying the ground for the later European scientific usage.[31]

As is well known, the figure of the fawning Parasite was a stock character in ancient Greek comedy. The type is archaic, going back at least to the first half of the fifth century and the play *Hope or Riches* by the Sicilian, Epicharmus. But while the character is old, its name, "Parasite," is at least a century younger. It first appeared in Alexis's play by that name (c. 360–50 B.C.) and replaced the older names for this stock figure, the "Flatterer" (*kolax*) and the "Sycophant."

Much ink has been expended on this name change by modern scholarship,[32] but the issue was posed centuries earlier in a lengthy (now lost) lexicographical work preserved in excerpted form by the third-century A.D. rhetorician, Athenaeus.[33]

The relevant passage, in a manner typical of Athenaeus, is in the form of a quotation within a quotation.

> Plutarch said, The name, parasite, was in earlier times a dignified and sacred name. Take, for example, what Polemon[34] writes about parasites. . . . Parasite is nowadays a disreputable term, but among the ancients we find it used of something sacred, equivalent to companion [*synthoinos*, "messmate"] at a sacred feast. (6.234d)

Six examples are given to illustrate this archaic, cultic use of the term "parasite" before a series of quotations are marshalled to illustrate its transformation into a comedic term of opprobrium.[35] It is the first cultic example that is of greatest interest to us—that of the annual celebration of Herakles at Kynosarges, outside Athens.

The gymnasium at Kynosarges[36] was open to membership by Athenian residents lacking the status of full citizens, most particularly, since the law of Pericles in 451–50,[37] the children of mixed marriages (*nothoi*) between Athenian males and foreign women.[38] According to Polemon, the Herakleion at Kynosarges possessed a stele with a law from Alcibaides:

> The priest shall sacrifice the monthly offerings in company with the parasites. These parasites shall be drawn from men of mixed descent [*ek tōn nothōn*] and their children according to ancestral custom.[39] And whoever shall decline to serve as parasite, the priest shall charge him before the tribunal. (6. 234e)

In addition to their monthly sacrificial duties, the chief annual cultic activity of the parasites was to eat a meal, during the month, Metageitnion, together with Herakles—hence the derivation of "parasite" from *para + sitos*, (to eat) grain beside (another).[40]

With this last piece of information on the most archaic use of the term "parasite," we may briefly come to rest. The earliest use of the term referred to a rule-governed, legally required relationship of commensality between representatives of a community of not-quite-Athenians (the *nothoi*) and a cult figure (Herakles) who was neither quite hero nor quite god.[41] To think about parasites, whether in the most ancient or most modern sense of the term, is to think about reciprocal relations of relative "otherness."[42]

Before attempting a fresh start on the question of a "theory of the other," it might be well to collect and restate the conclusions that might be drawn from this first set of reflections on the topic which began with an eighteenth-century poem by Robert Burns and ended with an archaic cult law, after rapidly passing through the history of late nineteenth-century parasitology.

In this first stage of our inquiry, even though three quite different sorts of data were explored, the conclusions drawn were symmetrical. "Otherness," it is suggested, is a matter of relative rather than absolute difference. Difference is not a matter of comparison between entities judged to be equivalent, rather difference most frequently entails a hierarchy of prestige and ranking. Such distinctions are found to be drawn most sharply between "near neighbors," with respect to what has been termed the "proximate other." This is the case because "otherness" is a relativistic category inasmuch as it is, necessarily, a term of interaction. A "theory of otherness" is, from this perspective, essentially political and economic. That is to say, it centers on a relational theory of reciprocity, often one that is rule-governed.

While I shall return to this set of contentions in my conclusion, it seemed useful to inquire as to whether there was a stronger "theory of the other" than the political; that is to say, were there situations that led to a more radical theory of "otherness"? It is to this essentially anthropological question that I turn by way of making a second start on our theme. Such a theory, we shall see, is essentially a project of language.

II

The Sioux have a saying, 'With all beings and all things we shall be as relatives.' Our Hillel said, 'Separate thyself not from the community.' Mazel Tov to Rabbi Glaser and his excellent programs linking Judaism to brothers and sisters of Indian cultures and for reminding us that we are all members of one tribe.

LETTER TO THE EDITOR, *Reform Judaism* 12.4 (1984): 32.

The social and cultural awareness of the "other" must surely be as old as humankind itself. "Cultures are more than just empirically comparable; they are intrinsically comparative."[43] As Robert Redfield has argued, the world-view of any people consists essentially of two pairs of binary oppositions: MAN/NOT-MAN and WE/THEY.[44] These two oppositions are often correlated, i.e., WE = MAN; THEY = NOT-MAN. Indeed, the distinction between "us" and "them" is present in our earliest written records.[45] It is an omnipresent feature of folk taxonomies.[46] The distinction is most ubiquitous in the complex rule-governed matter of kinship in institutions such as endogamy, exogamy, and the incest taboo.[47] Likewise, it is universal in the detailed etiquette and laws concerning "the stranger,"[48] as well as in those devoted to its less-studied opposite, "the friend."[49] Social and cultural awareness of the "other" is also the centerpiece of the most persistent ethnographic traditions.[50] As times, cultural differences appear merely to have been noted (for example, as "curiosities" in travel reports). More frequently, "difference" supplied a justificatory element for a variety of ideological postures, ranging from xenophobia to exoticism, from travel, trade, and exploration to military conquest, slavery, and colonialism. The "other" has appeared as an object of desire as well as an object of repulsion; the "other" has rarely been an object of indifference.

On rare occasions, meditation on cultural difference, on "others," itself became one of a culture's dominant features. Such was the case in fifth-century B.C. Ionia[51] and in the Chinese periods of the T'ang and Southern Sung,[52] and such may be inferred from the preconquest court of Moctezuma with its remarkable zoological collections of all types of birds and animals and human forms.[53] This living museum appears to be quite similar to that all-but-contemporary "human zoo" maintained by Cardinal Ippolito de Medici, which consisted of "a troop of barbarians who talked no fewer than twenty different languages and were all of them perfect specimens of their races."[54]

As this last example hints, the cultural meditation on difference received its most massive institutionalization in the vast modern western enterprise of anthropology: a xenological endeavor which began with the savants of the Renaissance and Enlightenment was fueled by the discoveries of the "Age of Reconnaissance" and continued into the present. Indeed, the most distinctive feature of modern anthropology is its relatively recent requirement that the anthropologist have living experience of the "other." It is fieldwork that makes anthropology a distinctive enterprise among the human sciences.[55] Because of this, anthropology may be described as the science of the "other." As Claude Lévi-Strauss bluntly states:

> Anthropology is the science of culture as seen from the outside. . . . Anthropology, whenever it is practiced by members of the culture it endeavors to study, loses its specific nature [as anthropology] and becomes rather akin to archaeology, history and philology.[56]

That is to say, anthropology holds that there is cognitive power in "otherness," a power that is removed by studying the "same." The issue, as Lévi-Strauss has phrased it in the passage quoted above, is not the sheer distance of the object of study,[57] but rather the mode of relationship of the scholar to the object. In anthropology, the distance is not to be overcome, but becomes, in itself, the prime focus and instrument of disciplinary meditation.[58]

To be sure, even within contemporary anthropology, "otherness" remains a relative category in at least two important senses. First, unlike parasitism, the "other" is of the same species. Despite wide variation, it is man studying man; it is *Homo sapiens* and not some Martian that is the object of attention. (It may be noted that, since 1970, the American Anthropological Association has sponsored a section at its annual meeting on the issues raised by the possibility of the future study of extraterrestrial beings. However, to date, such matters have been better explored by science fiction writers, for example, the profound work of Michael Bishop).[59]

Matters with respect to this first qualification are, in fact, more complex. Anthropologists have at times explored other cultures (or particular institutions within them) in such a way as to suggest that they might be conceived of as "limiting cases,"[60] that they represent so extreme a development of something known and familiar that they appear to be radically "other."[61] More usually, they have insisted on just the opposite: in some often unspecified way, the "other" is to be seen as "typical." While the field encounter is most frequently described as an extremely traumatic, disorienting kind of experience, the result, as reported in the monograph, reads as an encounter with "Everyman." Edmund Leach has characterized this quixotic element with precision:

> When we read Malinowski we get the impression that he is stating something which is of general importance. Yet how can this be? He is simply writing about Trobriand Islanders. Somehow . . . he is able to make the Trobriands a microcosm of the whole primitive world. And the same is true of his successors; for Firth, Primitive Man is a Tikopian, for Fortes, he is a citizen of Ghana.[62]

Second, anthropological investigation is, by nature, relational. What an anthropologist reports is almost always solely based on his or her interaction with a particular people. For this reason, anthropology has tended to develop and embrace theories that factor out time and the historical, that eliminate all past before the fieldworker's presence.[63] Hence, the evolutionism of the late nineteenth-century "armchair" anthropologists was jettisoned by workers in the field in favor of a functionalism that depended on the observation of a given society at time "t," or, later, in favor of the atemporalism of a variety of structuralist approaches. For this reason, as well, the anthropological report, no matter how great a period of time had elapsed between the field experience and publication, is almost always written in the "ethnographic present," in what Jan Vansina has called the "zero-time fiction."[64]

The effect of these two qualifications (and there are more) has been to relativize "otherness" in anthropological discourse—if not in experience. Anthropology has become largely an enterprise of "decipherment," attempting to "decode" an encrypted message from "another" with the firm prior conviction that, because it is human, it will be intelligible once it is "broken."[65] That is to say, anthropology is essentially a project of language with respect to an "other," which concedes both the presence of meaning and the possibility of translation at the outset. Indeed, without these two assumptions, "all the activities of anthropologists become meaningless."[66] As such, contemporary anthropology is to be seen as part of the Anglo-American philosophical tradition, which has tended to view "otherness" as a problem of communication in contradistinction to the Continental philosophical tradition, which has tended to conceive of the "other" in terms of transcendence and threat.[67]

This contemporary anthropological viewpoint stands in sharp contrast to the classical ethnographic tradition where, from Herodotus on, there is rarely the perception of an opacity to be overcome. Difference is, itself, utterly transparent. The "other" is merely different and calls for no exegetical labor. Within the classical ethnographic sources, differences may be noted; at times, differences may be compared, but they are most frequently set aside. Difference is insignificant—that is to say, difference signifies nothing of importance and therefore requires no decipherment, no hermeneutical projects. In classical ethnography, the "other" does not speak. This topos can be illustrated from traditions as far apart as the notion that the "other" is a "barbarian," that is, one who speaks unintelligibly[68] (or, in stronger form, one who is mute),[69] and the conventions of "silent trade."[70] For the classical ethnographer, the labor of learning an "other's" language would be sheer folly.[71] Classical ethnography manipulated a few basic explanatory models to account for "others." Briefly put, similarity was, above all, to be explained as the result of a temporal process: common descent and genealogy in remote times; contact, borrowing, and diffusion in more recent times. Difference was, above all, to be explained as the consequence of a spatial condition, preeminently climate. This would later become known as "environmental determinism."

To be sure, there were perturbations, encounters with "others" that appeared to present cognitive shocks—the Greek experience of Egypt; the thirteenth-century "Mongol Mission"—but these were rapidly assimilated to the prevailing models. However, there was one perturbation that was not so readily assimilable, that of the so-called "discovery" of America. It is here that the anthropological issue of the "other" as preeminently a project of language most clearly begins.[72]

If there was one cosmographical element that could be taken for granted in the west prior to the "voyages of discovery," it was that the inhabitable world, the *oikoumenē,* was divided into three unequal parts.[73] It was this tripartition, Ovid's *triplex mundus,* that allowed the classical traditions to be so readily merged with the biblical. For most of western history, Pliny and Genesis 10 contained all that was necessary for both anthropological and geographical theorizing.[74] If there was one cosmographical element that became increasingly apparent to the west after the impact of the "voyages of discovery," it was that there were additional inhabitable landmasses, and that neither the classical nor the biblical traditions could be easily harmonized with this new world-view. To Europe, Asia and Libya/Africa must now be added the neologism "America"[75]— the *quarta orbis pars*.[76] This "fourth part," eventually recognized as what the ancients had theoretically termed an *orbis alterius*,[77] for the first time in western intellectual history raised the theoretical issue of the "other" as a project of language and interpretation. For this reason, we must pause and examine this cosmographical shift more carefully.

The classical cosmography may be summarized in terms of four elements.

(1) The earth, most usually thought of as spherical, was pictured as a great terraqueous globe, divided into Northern and Southern hemispheres. The earth's most distinctive feature was a large island in the Northern Hemisphere—the *orbis terrarum*.[78]

(2) Of greater significance than the division into hemispheres was the marking off of the terrestrial globe into "zones" (most usually five) in which only the intermediate (temperate) zones were presumed inhabitable.[79] That is to say, the extreme northern and southern (polar) zones and the middle (equatorial) zone were judged too severe to support human life in any recognizable form.[80] Habitation was possible only in the northern and southern temperate zones.

(3) The distinction as to habitability became central and was expressed by the term *oikoumenē*.[81] Geographically, the *oikoumenē*, the "inhabitable world," was that portion of the northern earth-island south of the Arctic Circle, north of the Tropic of Cancer, bounded on the east and west by Ocean, that was known to be inhabited. Theoretically, the possibility was entertained that there might be a corresponding "inhabitable land" in the Southern Hemisphere—a possibility most usually advanced for reasons of geometric symmetry.[82] If so, it would be "another world . . . an other *oikoumenē* . . . not inhabited by ones such as us" but by other species of men.[83]

(4) The northern *oikoumenē* was divided into three lobes:[84] Europe, Asia, and Libya/Africa.[85] These were most frequently distinguished from one another by river boundaries.[86]

In time, these four essential classical cosmographic elements received distinctively Christian interpretations. Combining the speculations of the Greco-Roman geographers and Genesis 10, the three lobes of the world-island became identified with the three sons of Noah who repopulated the *oikoumenē* after the Flood.[87] In turn, the tripartition became identified allegorically with a range of specifically Christian elements ranging from the Trinity[88] and the "Three Wise Men"[89] to the triple papal tiara (the *triregnum*).[90]

Such a view, with its striking monogenetic implications, made all but impossible Christian belief in the existence of other inhabited worlds apart from the northern, tripartite *oikoumenē*. As Augustine declared of the monstrous races as described by encyclopaedists such as Pliny, so, too, of "other worlds":

> Either the written accounts of certain races are completely unfounded; or, if such races do exist, they are not human; or, if they are human, they are descended from Adam.[91]

That is to say, either "other worlds" do not exist or, if they exist, they are uninhabited or, if they are inhabited, then they must (somehow) be descended from Adam and have been populated by the sons of Noah. All Christian discussion of "antipodes" and "austral" landmasses took place within the framework of this logic.[92]

With this brief sketch, the stage for the emergence of our theme has been set: how to make room for an "other world," for an inhabited fourth part of the globe, a "world," an *oikoumenē*, unanticipated by either the Greco-Roman or the biblical traditions?

It is simple, in retrospect, to appreciate the impact of the "discovery" of America, and to sense its challenge to both biblical and classical worldviews.[93] But this is anachronistic. What was apparent by the middle of the sixteenth century was by no means clear half a century earlier.[94] It is a distinctly modern voice that we hear in the remark of the sixteenth-century Florentine historian, Francesco Guicciardini, suppressed until the Freiburg edition (1774–76):

> Not only has this navigation confounded many affirmations of former writers about terrestrial things, but it has given some anxiety to the interpreters of the Holy Scriptures.[95]

A voice echoed by his contemporary, the Parisian lawyer, Étienne Pasquier:

> It is a very striking fact that our classical authors had no knowledge of all this America which we call 'new lands.'[96]

A voice so modern that it has called forth recent reinterpretations of the very words "discovery"[97] and "conquest"[98] as they appear in the fifteenth-

and sixteenth-century literature. But the earlier voices are less clear. The anthropological perception of the "other" had yet to occur and to find its voice.

For the cognitive issue of the "otherness" of America to emerge, America first had to be perceived as truly "other." Despite an emerging vocabulary of "otherness" (from Columbus's *otro mundo* to Vespucci's *un altro mondo*, or *mondo nuovo* and Peter Martyr's *nova tellus*, *alter* or *alius orbis*, *novus orbis*, and *de orbe novo*),[99] the moment at which this perception first emerged in intellectual discourse is far from clear.

It is tempting to place the emergent perception no later than the point at which Balboa first saw the Pacific (September 25, 1513),[100] or the point at which the reports of the survivors of the Magellan trans-Pacific circumnavigation of 1517–21 became available.[101] But this is by no means certain. It can be no earlier than the report of the first voyage of Columbus (April, 1493).[102] But this is premature. There can be no doubt that Columbus interpreted all of his sightings and land-falls in terms of the classical, tripartite *oikoumenē*, perhaps expanding, in theory, only the classical limits of inhabitability to all five "zones" of the world-island.[103] From the first to the last, he was convinced that he had reached the Asian coast, the easternmost boundary of the *orbis terrarum*.

His persistence was remarkable and unrelenting. The day after his first landfall at San Salvador (October 14, 1492), he wrote that "in order not to lose time" he will set off immediately to "see if I can find the island of Cipango [Japan]."[104] In a letter dated July 7, 1503, at the conclusion of his fourth and final voyage, he wrote that he was only nineteen days' journey westward from "the river Ganges."[105]

Throughout his writings, what was in fact new and previously unknown was translated endlessly and effortlessly by Columbus into what was old and well-known. For example, on November 26 and again on December 11, 1492, having "understood"[106] the Arawaks to speak of a nearby man-eating tribe which they feared, "the *Carība*," Columbus misunderstood them to have pronounced the name as *Caniba*—a misunderstanding we perpetuate every time we utter the word "*cannibal*." This misperception was further compounded by being placed within Columbus's preexistent interpretative scheme. *Caniba* sounded to him like the familiar *cane*, "dog." Therefore, Columbus concludes, the *Caniba* must be the cynocephalic monsters of European travel lore, associated especially with India.[107] Alternatively, *Caniba* reminded him of the word *Can* (i.e., Khan), therefore, he declared, "Caniba is nothing else but the great Can who ought now to be very near."[108]

At only one juncture does Columbus's confidence appear shaken and the easy verbal translations and associations seem to falter. During his third journey, on August 5, 1498, Columbus became the first European to set foot on the South American mainland, on the Paria Peninsula on the coast of what is now called Venezuela. Although he first believed the peninsula to be another island, by August 15th, he correctly interpreted the physical evidence as requiring the landmass to be "a great mainland, of which nothing has been known until now."[109] Remarkably, Columbus was able to fit even this "discovery" into the tripartite schema in its Christian interpretation. For concealed within the Christian topography was a "wild card"—an option hitherto of merely theoretical status, that, in addition to the tripartite world-island, there was a terrestrial Paradise.[110] It is this mythic landmass that Columbus understands himself to have discovered, in the process altering the commonly accepted view of the globe as spherical into something rather more eccentrically bulbous. The letter to the Spanish court of October 14, 1498, is devoted almost entirely to this remarkable proposition.[111]

Columbus begins his Letter with a sort of preamble, summarizing his accomplishments in all three voyages and making plain his conservative intention to place his "enterprise . . . which was foretold in the writings of so many trustworthy and wise historians" (including Isaiah!) within the context of the "sayings and opinions of those [ancients] who have written on the geography of the world."[112] Nevertheless, the land of which he will now write is "another world [*otro mundo*] from that which the Romans, and Alexander, and the Greeks made mighty efforts . . . to gain possession of."[113] What does this portentous phrase, "another world," mean?

In the body of the letter, two interpretative options are proposed. The landmass is either "an immense tract of land situated in the south" (i.e., a new austral world-island) or it is "terrestrial paradise." Columbus opts for the latter interpretation. Citing the opinions of patristic authorities, he states, "the more I reason on the subject, the more I become satisfied that the terrestrial paradise is situated on the spot I described."[114]

From our perspective, it would appear that rather than opting for the "correct" choice—that he had indeed discovered a previously unimagined landmass—Columbus persuades himself of the opposite.[115] He does so by arguing for an essential difference between the two hemispheres. The southern is not spherical like the northern,[116] for "Ptolemy and the others who have written on the globe had no information respecting this part of the world which was then unexplored, they only established their arguments with respect to their own hemisphere."[117] In a bizarre image, Columbus declares:

I have come to another conclusion concerning the world, namely that it is not round as they describe, but is in the form of a pear, which is very round except where the stalk grows, at which point it is most prominent; or like a round ball, upon one part of which is a prominence, like a woman's nipple.[118]

At the height of this nipple-like protrusion is

the spot of the earthly paradise whither none can go without God's permission, but this land which your Highnesses have now sent me to explore is very extensive, and I think there are many others [countries] in the south [*otras muchas en el austro*] of which the world has never had any knowledge.[119]

In this manner, Columbus had it both ways. All of the lands previously sighted and explored in his voyages were part of the "Indies"—part of the Asian lobe of the tripartite *orbis terrarum*. This newly discovered *otro mundo* was not contained within the bounds of the tripartite division, but it was not an *orbis alterius*. Rather, it was the only possible exception within Christian topography—terrestrial paradise.[120] It was an "old" land in terms of biblical tradition; a "new" land in terms of Spanish possession.[121] Peter Martyr's nearly contemporary verdict (1501) will suffice: "*fabulosa mihi videantur.*"[122]

To understand the Columbian "fantasy," it is insufficient to characterize him as possessing a "medieval mind," as many recent commentators have done,[123] or to depict him as being deluded through an extreme case of wish fulfillment—an interpretation as old as his early chronicler, Las Casas, who, writing of Columbus's fixation on establishing his proximity to the courts of the Khan, comments: "How marvellous a thing it is how whatever a man strongly desires and has firmly set in his imagination, all that he hears and sees at each step he fancies to be in its favor."[124] What we must see in Columbus is primarily a failure of language, the inability to recognize the inadequacy of his inherited vocabulary and the consequent inability to project a new. At best, there is a muddle. Things are either "like" or "unlike" Spain, but nothing is "other." In a manner similar to the classical ethnographers', Columbus recognizes nothing that requires "decipherment"; all is sheerly transparent.

We must leave, then, the explorer and turn to the scholar for our purposes, the towering figure of Peter Martyr, whose *De Orbe Novo* represents the first, systematic, historiographical reflection on the Columbian "discoveries" by a nonparticipant.[125]

The most striking element in Peter Martyr's earliest writings on Columbus's "enterprise" between 1493 and 1495 is an absence: he scrupulously avoids the term "Indies" and, hence, the Columbian identification.[126] This is apparent, already, in his earliest reaction. In May 1493, less than two months after Columbus's return from his first voyage—if the epistolary record is to be credited[127]—he refers to Columbus as having travelled to the "western antipodes."[128] In September 1493, he augments this description by locating the "western antipodes" in the "new hemisphere of the earth." Here, novelty clearly refers to their previously unknown status; the islands have been "hidden since Creation."[129]

By November, 1493, Martyr reports (in the first book of the first *Decade*) the existence of "recently discovered islands in the western ocean,"[130] but he remains ambivalent as to their identification. He knows that Columbus understands this "unknown land" to consist of "islands which touch the Indies,"[131] but he is not convinced. He suggests that they are a previously unknown group of westerly Atlantic islands, thoroughly analogous to the long-familiar Canaries.[132] Furthermore, when reporting on "Hispaniola," he notes that Columbus believes it to be the rediscovered ancient Solomonic site of Ophir (an identification, like terrestrial paradise, which shows forth Columbus's attempt to locate his "enterprise" within the framework of biblical cosmography). Martyr rejects the identification, suggesting instead the legendary western Atlantic islands, the Antilles.[133] All three of Martyr's interpretations (the "western antipodes," the analogy with the Canaries, and the Antilles) show Martyr as rejecting Columbus's oriental fantasy. All three place his discoveries in the western Atlantic in terms that recall Greco-Roman geography.

There is, however, a hint in this 1493 account of something more. Columbus claims to have found "indications of a hitherto unknown *alterius terrarum orbis*."[134] Martyr will later report, in 1501, that Columbus believes it to be "the continent of India"—an identification that Martyr firmly rejects.[135] But for now, Martyr supplies no identification.

In November 1493, Peter Martyr employs a different terminology, one for which he will become famous. In a letter to Cardinal Sforza, he writes of a *novus orbis* that Columbus has discovered.[136] Again, we must inquire as to the meaning of this portentous phrase.

Martyr's earliest usage of the term *novus orbis* is closely akin to his even earlier phrase, "the new hemisphere of the earth" (*novo terrarum hemispherio*). It means newly discovered parts of the familiar globe. When Martyr writes of the *novus orbis*, he is not identifying a new geographic entity in the sense we are familiar with when we capitalize the "New World" as the Americas in contradistinction to the "Old World." Martyr's *novus orbis* is neither Columbus's *otro mundo* (which he understands, as we have seen, to be terrestrial paradise), nor Vespucci's *mundus novus* (which he understands to be a previously unknown extension of Asia),[137] but like these terms, it does not challenge the old world-view. This will not occur in explicit fashion until the *Cosmographiae Introductio* of 1508 with its declaration that Vespucci had discovered a previously unsuspected "fourth part of the world."[138]

At any rate, Martyr does not employ the phrase "new world" in his *Decades* until those portions of the work composed after 1514.[139] Here, it may well carry the connotation of an *orbis alterius*, but only after the period of the initial responses, when the notion of the inadequacy of the tripartite *oikoumenē* had become commonplace in intellectual discourse.

What has been learned thus far from the first explorer and the earliest interpreter of that exploration is the difficulty in conceptualizing "otherness." Something "different" has been sensed but has as yet gained no distinctive voice. Rather, the old language has been stretched to accommodate it. Perhaps this "stretching" is what was meant by the curious phrase the sixteenth-century historian Hernan Pérez de Oliva used to describe the Columbian "enterprise." He speaks of an enterprise in which Columbus "sought to unite the world and give to those strange lands the form of our own."[140] The "other" emerges only as a theoretical issue when it is perceived as challenging a complex and intact world-view. It is only then that the "different" becomes the problematic "alien." The incapacity of imagination exhibited by Columbus and Peter Martyr stands as eloquent testimony to that intactness. Yet, once the question is admitted, once alienation is even fleetingly glimpsed, it cannot be silenced or ignored. It will give rise to thought as expressed in speech. What was inconceivable in the last decade of the fifteenth century became commonplace, for some, by the first decade of the sixteenth. The "Americas" were, as the 1508 *Introductio* named and described them—in an act of language, not of exploration—a "fourth part" of the world. Like us, in that it was inhabited; unlike us, in its geographical form. For the familiar three parts were contiguous landmasses (i.e., continents); the newly discovered "fourth part" was discontinuous, it was understood to be an island surrounded by a vast expanse of water.[141] It was the insular nature of the unexpected "discovery" of a "fourth part" of the "world" that gave rise to the more intense debate over "otherness"—that respecting the land's inhabitants: its humans, animals, and plants.

For Columbus, knowing that he was in the "Indies," the presence of human inhabitants, of animals and plants which seemed both familiar and strange, presented no major intellectual problems. True, the naked men and women did not resemble the high civilization of the "great Khan" that Marco Polo and Toscanelli had led him to expect. But, no matter. As he endlessly repeats, he has heard that the capital of the Khan is just a short journey away. Because he is in what he believes to be both a contiguous and an unfamiliar land, he can recognize differences and impose similarities without giving these matters a second's thought. Because he cannot speak directly to the natives, except through ambiguous "signs," he can impose his language on whatever or whomever he encounters without impediment.[142] He "gives to these strange lands the form of our own" precisely because he did not know what Olivia knew decades later, that in some profound fashion, the lands were truly "strange." The most obvious example of this is also the most enduring: six days after landing, Columbus was able to easily and unquestioningly call the indigenous population "*Indios.*"[143]

Less often noted but, in fact, far more massive a feature of Columbus's writings is his constant Europeanization of the indigenous flora and fauna.[144] Take, for example, the matter of the nightingales (the common name for a group of small Eurasian thrushes of which no species is to be found in the Americas). Even before making land-fall, Columbus found one night on board ship so agreeable that, according to Las Casas, "the Admiral said that nothing was wanting but to hear the nightingale."[145] Columbus was not to be disappointed. On at least three occasions after landing in the "Indies" he heard "the singing of the nightingales and other birds of Castile."[146]

For all the unconscious humor that might be found in these and other examples,[147] the point as to "Indians," "nightingales," and the like is far more serious. As Terrence Hawkes reminds us, "a colonist acts essentially as a dramatist. He imposes the 'shape' of his own culture embodied in his speech on the new world, and makes that world recognizable" and, hence, "habitable" for him.[148] So long as Columbus and the other early explorers were successful in giving "to those strange lands the form of our own," the lands could not emerge as truly "strange"; they could not be perceived as objects of thought; there could be no language and, hence, no theory of the "other."

The early records must therefore be searched for moments of heightened self-consciousness, for crises of confidence in the sheer translatability of "here" to "there," of "old" to "new," of "familiar" to "strange." Such moments are difficult to find and to pinpoint with chronological precision. Nevertheless, a set of such essentially linguistic "turns" can be discerned—although a determination of their contemporary influence must remain problematic.[149]

The "issue of the Indians," that is to say, the question of how the "New World" came to be populated[150] was, as best as can be determined, first raised in interrogatory form[151] in a play printed circa 1519 and attributed to John Rastell, brother-in-law of Sir Thomas More. Rastell, a minor Tudor poet and major early English printer, had himself attempted a journey to the "New Founde Lands" in 1517.[152]

In the play *A New Interlude and a Mery, of the Nature of the iiij Elementis, declarynge many proper poyntys of philosophy naturall and of dyvers straunge landys*,[153] the author, in the guise of describing a globe, knows that there is a single mass of "new landes . . . westwarde . . . that we never harde tell of before thus/by wrytnge nor other meanys."[154] It stretches from the "north parte" where "all the clothes/That they were is but bestis skins" to the "south parte of *that contrey*" where "the people there go nakyd alway/the lande is of so great hete."[155] The poet immediately goes on to pose the query:

> But howe the people furst began
> In that contrey or whens they cam,
> For clerkes it is a questyon.[156]

The first explicit attempt to answer this question,[157] to go beyond narrative and description to the level of explanation, was Gonzalo Fernández de Oviedo y Valdés's encyclopaedic work,[158] *Historia general y natural de las Indias islas y Tierra Firme del Mar Oceano*, specifically, in those parts published in 1535.[159] Oviedo offers two hypotheses: (1) the land had been populated by the ancient Carthaginians,[160] (2) his more persistent argument, that the lands were ancient Spanish possessions (identified with the Hesperides) associated with the mythical Spanish king Héspero, who was alleged to have reigned circa 1680 B.C.[161] Thus for Oviedo, there was no "new discovery" or problematic population; "through the agency of Columbus, God had returned the Indies to their [original and] rightful owner—the Spanish Crown."[162]

While attempts persisted to deny "otherness" by arguing, in one form or another, that the "new" land was in some sense rediscovered "old" land that was a part of the tripartite *oikoumenē* and a part, as well, of classical geographical lore, these would remain minority positions.[163] More usually, given the monogenetic interpretations of Genesis 1–10, three kinds of theoretical options were proposed. (1) The new land was not wholly insular. It was connected (most usually by a land bridge) to the tripartite *oikoumenē* and thus, though an "other world" geographically, it was populated by an overland migration of familiar peoples. It should be noted that this remains, today, the leading explanation. (2) There was a "second Ark"—one not recorded in Scripture, with all that implied. (3) There was some form of miraculous intervention—the *locus classicus* being Augustine, *De Civitate Dei*, 16.7, which posed the hypothesis that angels transported animals to remote islands after the Flood.

These interpretative options were taken up and systematically reviewed for the first time by Joseph de Acosta in his remarkable, *Historia natural y moral de las Indias*, a work begun circa 1580.[164] Acosta rejected the hypotheses of the "second Ark" and of angelic intervention,[165] while supporting in a sophisticated manner the hypothesis of a land bridge or a narrow strait separating the "Indies" from the "old world."[166] He rejected all attempts to deny difference: the "Indies" were not Ophir or Atlantis; the "Indians" were not Hebrews.[167] His understanding of the process of population was complex and suggestive. The inhabitants of the "new world" came over from the "old" at different times in the past. They gradually lost their previous cultures and developed their own indigenous ones, becoming first hunters, then agriculturalists.[168] Therefore, there will be cultural similarities between the "new" and the "old," but these similarities are the result of similar development, and may not be used, in themselves, as clues to origin.[169] Finally, note must be taken of the publication in 1607 of the first book wholly devoted to the question of the Indians' origins, Gregorio García's *Origen de los indios de el Nuevo Mundo, e Indias occidentales*. It is a massive, 535-page review of all possible interpretative options.[170]

The concomitant issue, the origin of the flora and fauna and their similarities and differences to those of the "old world," was largely addressed by the same sort of theorizing as attended the human. But there was one difference. Given the monogenetic interpretations of Genesis 1–10, the "Indians," if identified as human (and there is little evidence that they were not),[171] could never be absolutely "different." Animals and plants could be so perceived. Thus, it is in their naturalistic observations and writings that we find the clearest early statements of "otherness" framed in terms of the linguistic implications of "difference."[172] I shall content myself with citing three telling examples from the rich, sixteenth-century Spanish naturalistic literature. First, perhaps the earliest and most extreme statement of "otherness," from a work by Oviedo published in 1526, which describes what appears to be a jaguar.

> In my opinion, these animals are not tigers, nor are they panthers, or any other of the numerous known animals that have

spotted skins, nor some new animal [of the "old world"] that has a spotted skin and has not [yet] been described. The many animals that exist in the Indies that I describe here, or at least most of them, could not have been learned about from the ancients, since they exist in a land which had not been discovered until our own time. There is no mention made of these lands in Ptolemy's *Geography,* nor in any other work, nor were they known until Christopher Columbus showed them to us. . . . But, returning to the subject already begun . . . this animal is called by the Indians, *ochi.*[173]

This last sentence is of crucial importance. Given the stated inadequacy of "old world" taxa, Oviedo self-consciously shifts to native terminology. Our second example is Acosta's protest against the imperialism of names (as in Columbus and the nightingales).

> The first Spaniards gave many things found in the Indies Spanish names taken from things which they somewhat resembled . . . when, in fact, they were quite different. Indeed, the difference between them and what are called by these names in Castile are greater than the similarities.[174]

Finally, Acosta makes a complex, theoretical statement concerning "difference."

> What I say of the *guanacos* and *pacos* I will say of a thousand varieties of birds and fowls and mountain animals that have never been known [previously] by either name or appearance, nor is there any memory of them in the Latins or Greeks, nor in any nations of our [European] world over here. . . . It is well to ask whether these animals differ in kind and essence from all others, or if this difference be accidental. . . . But, to speak bluntly, any one who in this way would focus only on the accidental differences, seeking thereby to explain [away] the propogation of the animals of the Indies and to reduce them [to variants] of the European, will be undertaking a task that he will not be able to fulfill. For, if we are to judge the species of animals [in the Indies] by their [essential] properties, they are so different that to seek to reduce them to species known in Europe will mean having to call an egg a chestnut.[175]

Can't reduce to essential as it would then the represent other.

The "new world" is not merely "new," not merely "different"—it is "other" *per essentiam*. As such, it calls forth an "other" language.

As this review has suggested, although slow to start, the theoretical issues posed by the "otherness" of "America" were raised in sharp form as a project of language by the end of the sixteenth century. But they could not be solved—not for want of data, but because theory was inadequate. This deficiency at the level of theory persisted for centuries. The nineteenth century finally established the principle of polygenesis—above all, through that major contribution to anthropological theory now discredited, the notion of "race." The nineteenth century also contributed an early understanding of genetic variation's processes and the procedures for polythetic classification. It is only in the last decades, following upon the long and arid debates over independent variation versus diffusion, that we are beginning to develop adequate theories and well-formulated criteria for diffusion.[176]

III

"Few questions have exerted so powerful a grip on the thought of this century than that of the "Other". . . . It is difficult to think of another topic that so radically separates the thought of the present . . . from its historical roots."

M. THEUNISSEN, *Der Andere*

In the first part of this essay, in relation to the notion of "parasite," attention was focused on what might be termed the political aspects of a "theory of the other." That is to say, we were largely concerned with the figure of the "proximate other," with questions of the relativity of "otherness," of its modes and degrees,[177] often perceived hierarchically. We were led to postulate that "otherness," by its very nature, required a relational theory of reciprocity (in other words, politics), and that a "theory of otherness," in this sense, must be construed as a rule-governed set of reciprocal relations with one socially labeled an "other."

In the second part of this essay, that concerned with the "discovery" of "America," we shifted to what might be termed the linguistic aspects of a "theory of the other."[178] In the same way that, according to one historian of science, "Ptolemy's model of the earth was the weapon by which the real earth was conquered intellectually,"[179] so, too, here. The "conquest of America," for all of its frightful human costs, was primarily a linguistic event.[180] Once recognized (in the face of an intact, linguistically embedded world-view), "otherness" was, on the one hand, a challenge to "decipherment"; on the other hand, it was an occasion for the "stretching" of language—both for the creation of new linguistic entities ("new world" and the like) and the attempt, through discourse, to "give to these strange worlds the shape of our own."[181] "Otherness" is not a descriptive category, an artifact of the perception of difference or commonality. Nor is it the result of the determination of biological descent or affinity.[182] It is a political and linguistic project, a matter of rhetoric and judgment.

It is for this reason that in thinking about the "other," real progress has been made only when the "other" ceases to be an ontological category. That is to say, "otherness" is not some absolute state of being. Something is "other" only with respect to something "else." Whether understood politically or linguistically, "otherness" is a situational category. Despite its apparent taxonomic exclusivity, "otherness" is a transactional matter, an affair of the "in between."[183]

In our historical review, this situational and transactional character loomed large through the notion of the "proximate other." That is to say, absolute "difference" is not a category for thought, but one that denies the possibility of thought. What one historian has stated about the concept, "unique," may be applied as well to the notion of the "wholly other" (with the possible exception of odd statements in even odder Continental theologies):

> This word 'unique' is a negative term signifying what is mentally inapprehensible. The absolutely unique is, by definition, indescribable.[184]

The "otherness" of the common housefly can be taken for granted, but it is also impenetrable. For this reason, its "otherness" is of no theoretical interest.[185] While the "other" may be perceived as being either LIKE-US or NOT-LIKE-US, he is, in fact, most problematic when he is TOO-MUCH-LIKE-US, or when he claims to BE-US. It is here that the real urgency of a "theory of the other" emerges. This urgency is called forth not by the requirement to place the "other," but rather to situate ourselves. It is here, to invoke the language of a theory of ritual, that we are not so much concerned with the drama of "expulsion," but with the more mundane and persistent processes of "micro-adjustment."[186] This is not a matter of the "far" but, preeminently, of the "near." The problem is not alterity, but similarity—at times, even identity. A "theory of the other" is but another way of phrasing a "theory of the self."

In the examples discussed above, the parasite was the object of intense theoretical interest not merely because it was "there," but because it invaded intimate human space. The parasite was apart from and yet a part of our personal bodily environment.[187] So too, with the "Indian"—although matters here are necessarily more complex. The aboriginal Amerindian became a figure of high theoretical interest only when he was gradually thought of as being "in between"—neither the well-known though exotic citizen of the fabled "Indies," nor a separate species of man (as in Linnaeus's remarkable proposal to establish the types *Homo americanus*, *Homo monstrosus patagonici*, and *Homo monstrosus plagiocephali* to describe three forms of Amerindians).[188] Rather, especially in the latter half of the eighteenth century, he became a figure of intense and long-lasting speculation precisely to the degree that Amerindian culture was seen as revelatory of the European's own past.[189] "In the beginning," to cite John Locke, "all the world was America."[190]

By way of conclusion, this may be pressed in a direction closer to the explicit theme of this conference. Due to the emergent disciplines of anthropology, history of religions and the like, we know of thousands of societies and world views which are "different," but in most cases, their "remoteness" guarantees our indifference. By and large, Christians and Jews qua Christians and Jews have not thought about the "otherness" of the Kwakiutl or, for that matter, of the Taoist. The bulk of Christian theoretical thinking about "otherness" (starting with Paul) has been directed toward "other Christians" and, more occasionally, towards those groups thought of as being "near-Christians," preeminently Jews and Muslims. Today, as in the past, the history of religious conflicts, of religious perceptions of "otherness" is largely intraspecific: Buddhists to Buddhists, Christians to Christians, Muslims to Muslims, Jews to Jews. The only major exceptions occur in those theoretically unrevealing but historically common moments when "proximity" becomes more a matter of territoriality than of thought.

A "theory of the other" rarely depends on the capacity "to see ourselves as others see us." By and large, "we" remain indifferent to such refractions. Rather, it would appear to imply the reverse. A "theory of the other" requires those complex political and linguistic projects (necessary) to enable us to think, to situate, and to speak of "others" in relation to the way in which we think, situate, and speak about ourselves.

Notes

1. Robert Burns, *Poems Chiefly in the Scottish Dialect* (Kilmarnock, 1786), 192–94, esp. 194.

2. K. Wittig, *The Scottish Tradition in Literature* (Edinburgh, 1958), 201.

3. The social and political settings of Scottish vernacular have been well studied by D. Craig, *Scottish Literature and the Scottish People* (London, 1961). I have taken the detail of the "Select Society" from D. Murison, "The Language of Burns," in D. A. Low, ed., *Critical Essays on Robert Burns* (London, 1975), 56.

4. For the ideological issues and their relation to continental theories concerning language, see F. W. Freeman, "The Intellectual Background of the Vernacular Revolt before Burns," *Studies in Scottish Literature* 16 (1981): 160–87.

5. See the study by H. Meige, *Les pouilleux dans l'art* (Paris: 1897). For a catalog of old, scientific illustrations, see G. H. F. Nuttall, "The Systematic Position, Synonymy and Iconography of *Pediculus humanus* and *Phthirus pubis*," *Parasitology* 1, no. 1 (1919): 329–46, esp. 337–39.

6. For a study of the flea in literature, see B. Lehane, *The Compleat Flea* (New York, 1969).

7. Title page, *Autobiography of a Flea* in the edition published by the Erotica Biblion Society (New York, 1901). The first edition, published for the Phlebotomical Society, London, bears the date 1789. This is false. The *Autobiography* is clearly a work of Victorian England. For a bibliography devoted to the special topic of the flea in erotic literature, see H. Hayn and A. N. Gotendorf, *Floh-Literatur (de pulicibus des In- und Auslandes vom XVI Jahrhundert bis zur Neuzeit* (Dresden [?], 1913).

8. I know of no good history of parasitology. For the present, W. D. Foster, *A History of Parasitology* (Edinburgh and London, 1965) remains the most serviceable.

9. R. Hoeppli, *Parasites and Parasitic Infections in Early Medicine and Science* (Singapore, 1959) is a rich repertoire of ancient sources (especially valuable for its inclusion of Chinese materials). There are a series of comprehensive notes on the Greco-Roman parasitological literature in F. Adams, *The Seven Books of Paulus Aeginela*, 3 vols. (London, 1844–47), esp. 2: 139–53.

10. See, in general, A. N. Disney et al., *The Origin and Development of the Microscope* (London, 1928); R. S. Clay and T. H. Court, *The History of the Microscope* (London, 1932). The introductory material to the English translation of Leeuwenhoek's writings by C. Dobell, *Antony van Leeuwenhoek and His "Little Animals"* (London, 1932) is invaluable. It will be recalled that an early term for microscope was "louse-lens."

11. Much work remains to be done on the topos, "small is more interesting than large." While such a notion is as old as Pliny (*Historia naturalis* 11.1), it became a dominant motif only after the fashioning of lenses, both for the telescope and, most especially, for the microscope. For the former, one thinks of Galileo's encomium to the "little moons" of Jupiter, which concludes with a defense of and hymn of praise to tiny things (Galileo, letter dated May 21, 1611, in P. Dini, *Epistolario Galilei* [Leghorn, 1872], 1: 121–22). The latter is summarized, at a late stage of its development, in the well-known dictum in Emerson's essay "On Compen-

sation": "The microscope cannot find the animalcule which is less perfect for be-ing little," (R. L. Cook, ed., *Ralph Waldo Emerson: Selected Prose and Poetry [New York, 1950], 109*). The fundamental study of this topos is M. Nicolson, *The Microscope and English Imagination* (Northhampton, Mass., 1935), in the series Smith College Studies in Modern Languages, 16.4, which should be read in conjunction with her analogous studies of the telescope, "The Telescope and the Imagination," *Modern Philology* 32 (1935): 233–60; "The New Astronomy and the English Literary Imagination," *Studies in Philology* 32 (1935): 428–62, cf. Nicolson, *The Breaking of the Circle: Studies in the Effect of the "New Science" upon Seventeenth-Century Poetry*, 2d ed. (New York, 1960). For other studies of this topos, see A. Lovejoy, *The Great Chain of Being* (Cambridge, Mass., 1936), 236–40; A. Gerbi, *The Dispute of the New World: The History of a Polemic, 1750–1900* (Pittsburgh, 1973), 16–20.

12. It is the special merit of E. Mayr, *The Growth of Biological Thought* (Cambridge, Mass., 1982), 1: 134–40, to place the increase in knowledge about the number of parasitic species within the context of the general eighteenth-century increase in the knowledge of the number and diversity of animal and plant species. The article by P. Geddes, "Parasitism, Animal," *Encyclopaedia Britannica*, 9th ed. (1875–89) is an eloquent witness to the perception of parasitism's ubiquity: "we observe not only the enormously wide prevalence of parasitism—the number of parasitic individuals, if not indeed that of species, *probably exceeding that of non-parasitic forms*—but its very considerable variety in degree and detail" (18: 260, emphasis added).

13. For some of the taxonomic implications, see F. B. Churchill, "Sex and the Single Organism: Biological Theories of Sexuality in the Mid-19th Century," *Studies in the History of Biology* 3 (1979): 139–77.

14. For an overview, see J. Farley, *The Spontaneous Generation Controversy from Descartes to Oparin* (Baltimore, 1977), 18–19, 34–38, 58–66 focus on parasites. I have been much helped by the treatment in E. Guyénot, *Les sciences de la vie au XVIIᵉ et XVIIIᵉ siècles* (Paris, 1941), 211–19. With particular reference to parasites, see R. Hoeppli and I. H. Ch'iang, "The Doctrine of Spontaneous Generation of Parasites in Old-Style Chinese and Western Medicine," *Peking Natural History Bulletin* 19 (1950–51): 375–415, reprinted with revisions in Hoeppli, *Parasites and Parasitic Diseases*, 113–56.

15. J. J. S. Steenstrup, *Über den Generationswechsel; oder, Die Fortpflanzung und Entwicklung durch abwechselnde Generationen, eine eigenthümliche Form der Brutpflege in den niederen Thierklassen* (Copenhagen, 1842). This German translation (by C. H. Lorenzen) is the first publication of Steenstrup's manuscript, *Om Fortplantning og Udvikling gjennem vexlende Generationsraekker*. An English translation was rapidly published by the John Ray Society, *On the Alternation of Generations; or, The Propogation and Development of Animals through Alternate Genera-*

tions (London: 1845). On Steenstrup and his contributions, see E. Lagrange, "Le centenaire d'une découverte: Le cycle evolutif des Cestodes," *Annales de Parasitologie* 27 (1952): 557–70.

16. A. W. Meyer, *The Rise of Embryology* (Stanford: 1939), 43, supports the notion that the decisive generation in parasitology was the period 1840–70. In what follows, I have surveyed the following widely used texts: J. Leidy, *A Flora and Fauna within Living Animals* (Washington, D.C., 1853); F. Küchenmeister, *Die in und an dem Körper des lebenden Menschen vorkammenden Parasiten* 1st ed. (Leipzig, 1855), 1–2; C-J. Davaine, *Traité des entozoaires et des maladies vermineuses de l'homme et des animaux domestiques* (Paris, 1860); T. S. Cobbold, *Entozoa, An Introduction to the Study of Helminthology* (London, 1869); P.-J. van Beneden, *Les commensaux et les parasites dans la règne animal,* 2d ed. (Paris, 1878); R. Leuckart, *Die menschlichen Parasiten und die von ihnen herrührenden Krankheiten* 1st ed. (Leipzig and Heidelberg, 1863–76), 1–2, Leuckart, *Die Parasiten des Menschen und die von ihnen herrührenden Krankheiten,* ed. G. Brandes, 2d. ed. (Leipzig and Heidelberg, 1879–1901), 1–2 (all citations are to the second edition). For contrast to the "newer" parasitology, C. Rudolphi, *Entozoorum sive vermium intestinalium historia naturalis* (Amsterdam, 1808–10), 1–2 was employed.

17. This process of changing nomenclature may be illustrated by the compound titles in the works by Davine, Cobbold, and Rudolphi in note 16 above.

18. This last distinction creates a new series of definitional issues still unresolved in the literature. From one point of view, every disease produced by a microorganism might be considered a parasitic disease. In practice, parasitic diseases are more narrowly defined, but the criteria remain unclear.

19. To these distinctions were added others chiefly derived from botany, such as "epiphytism," in which one species derives physical support but not nourishment from another species. (For example, mistletoe is a parasite; English ivy is not).

20. I stress that the above is a summary of an influential late-nineteenth-century taxonomy. For the current state of the question: (1) the most significant work on the *theory* of parasitism has been done by Russian scientists. Their work has been made available in the English translation of V. A. Dogiel, *General Parasitology* (New York, 1966) with rich bibliography. (2) For a review of the complex contemporary state of the question with regard to *taxonomy,* see the distinguished collection edited by G. D. Schmidt, *Problems in the Systematics of Parasites* (Baltimore, 1969).

21. Leuckart, *Die Parasiten des Menschen,* 1: 3.

22. For a wide-ranging survey, see the chapter, "Parasites and Parasitic Infections in Religion," in Hoeppli, *Parasites and Parasitic Infections,* 396–409.

23. Verminus is known from only one Latin inscription, *Corpus Inscriptionum Latinarum,* 7.1: no. 3732= H. Dessau, *Inscriptiones Latinae Selectae* (Berlin, 1892–1916), 2.1: no. 4019. See E. Buchner, "Verminus," *Real-Encyklopädie der*

classischen Altertumswissenschaft, 2.8: 1552–53; Hoeppli, Parasites and Parasitic Infections, 397–98.

24. I. Kant, Allgemeine Naturgeschichte und Theorie des Himmels (1755) in P. Mesiger, ed., Kant: Populäre Schriften (Berlin, 1911), 127.

25. Leuckart, Die Parasiten des Menschen, 1: 35; Meyer, Rise of Embryology, 67; H. Zinsser, Rats, Lice and History (Boston, 1935), 182; Hoeppli, Parasites and Parasitic Infections, 401; Guyenot, Les sciences de la vie, 218–19. For the poem, Lehane, Compleat Flea, 96–97.

26. Meyer, Rise of Embryology, 66.

27. D. C. Allen, The Legend of Noah (Urbana, 1963), 72, 185; Hoeppli, Parasites and Parasitic Infections, 401.

28. B. Glass et al., Forerunners of Darwin, 1745–1849 (Baltimore, 1959), 51.

29. "Parasite" is standard in English as a botanical term in the early eighteenth century. See, for example, Chamber's Encyclopaedia (Edinburgh, 1727–41), s.v. "parasite." For its massive use in an influential, early botanical work, see A. P. de Candolle, Physiologie végétale (Paris, 1832), vol. 3, Des parasites phanerogames.

30. I have been unable to locate the first self-conscious use of the term "parasite" as a zoological term. It gained early currency among the first generation of parasitologists as the result of the comprehensive article by the distinguished biologist, Carl von Siebold, "Parasiten," in R. Wagner, ed., Handwörterbuch der Physiologie (Brunschweig, 1844), 2: 641–92, but there is no explicit reflection on the name. (Siebold's article was a major influence in the acceptance of Steenstrup's work, op. cit. 646–47). From a review of the citations in the early works cited above (note 16) and a survey of the titles in J. Ch. Huber, Bibliographie der klinischen Helminthologie (Munich, 1895), it would appear that Küchenmeister, Die in und an dem Körper des lebenden Menschen vorkommenden Parasiten, was the first comprehensive work to use "parasite" in its title. Again, I can find no explicit meditation on the use of the term. This was strengthened in the title of the English translation of the second edition, On Animal and Vegetable Parasites of the Human Body (London, 1857), 1–2. As best as I can determine, the Zeitschrift für Parasitenkunde (Jena, 1869–75) was the earliest journal to employ "parasite" in its title.

31. In this regard, the articles on "Parasiten" in J. Ersch and T. Gruber, eds., Allgemeine Encyklopädie der Wissenschaften und Künste (Leipzig, 1838), 3.2: 417–23 are revealing. There is a brief, one-paragraph article consisting of two sentences which provides a botanical definition of "parasite" by A. Sprengel (423a). This is preceded by a long article of seven pages (thirteen columns) on the social meaning of parasite by M. H. E. Meier—a brief treatment of its cultic use (417a–418a) and a long essay on the figure of the Parasite in ancient comedy (418b–423a). This proportion has been reversed by the turn of the century. For example, in the eleventh edition of the Encyclopaedia Britannica (1910–11), there is an anonymous one-paragraph article on the cultic and literary sense of "parasite"

(20: 770a–b), followed by a twenty-two-page article on "parasitic diseases" (20: 770b–793b) and a five-page article on botanical and zoological "parasitism" (20: 793b–797b).

32. The fundamental study remains O. Ribbeck, *Kolax: Eine ethologische Studie* (Leipzig, 1883) in the series *Abhandlungen der Königl. Sächischen Gesellschaft der Wissenschaften*, Phil.-hist. Klasse, 9.1: 1–113. See further, M. H. E. Meier, "Parasiten," in Ersch-Gruber, *Allgemeine Encyklopädie*, 3.2: 418–23; J. E. B. Mayor, *The Thirteen Satires of Juvenal* (London, 1901), 1: 271–72; A. Giese, *De parasiti persona capita selecta* (Kiel, 1908); F. M. Cornford, *The Origin of Attic Comedy* (London, 1914—I cite the new edition edited by T. H. Gaster [Garden City, 1961]), 143–45; J. O. Loftberg, "The Sycophant-Parasite," *Classical Philology* 15 (1920): 61–72; cf. Lofberg, "Sycophancy at Athens" (Ph.d. diss., University of Chicago, 1917); M. E. Dilley, "The Parasite: A Study in Comic Development" (Ph.d. diss., University of Chicago, 1924); J. M. G. M. Brinkhoff, "De Parasiet op het romeinsche Toneel," *Neophilologus* 32 (1948): 127–41; L. Ziehen, E. Wüst and A. Hug, "Parasitoi," *Real-Encyklopädie der classischen Altertumswissenschaft*, 18: 1377–1405; T. B. L. Webster, *Studies in Late Greek Comedy* (Manchester, 1953), 63–5; W. G. Arnott, "Studies in Comedy (1): Alexis and the Parasite's Name," *Greek, Roman, and Byzantine Studies* 9 (1968): 161–68.

33. Athenaeus, *Deipnosophistae*, 6. 234d–248c, in the edition and translation by C. B. Gulick in the Loeb Classical Library series (Cambridge, Mass., 1929), 3: 54–119. That Athenaeus was dependent on a lost lexicographical work was argued by V. Rose, *Aristoteles Pseudepigraphus* (Leipzig, 1863); 457–59.

34. On Polemon, fragment 78 (Preller)= Jacoby, *Fragmente der griechischen Historiker*, 3: 137–38, see L. Preller, *Polemonis periegetae fragmenta* (Leipzig, 1838), 115–23.

35. On the cultic term, *parasitos, parasitoi,* in addition to the works cited above in note 32, each of which devote some pages to the subject, see A. von Kampen, *De parasitis apud Graecos sacrorum ministris* (Göttingen, 1867), A. Tresp, *Die Fragmente der griechischen Kultschriftsteller* (Giessen, 1914), 209–11; R. Schlaifer, "The Cult of Athena Pallensis," *Harvard Studies in Classical Philology* 54 (1943): 141–74, esp. 152; L. Ziehen, "Parasitoi (1)," *Real-Encyklopädie der classischen Altertumswissenschaft*, 18.3: 1377–81; H. W. Parke, *Festivals of the Athenians* (Ithaca, N.Y., 1977), 51.

36. On Kynosarges, see J. E. Harrison, *Mythology and Monuments of Ancient Athens* (London, 1890), 216–19; W. Judeich, *Topographie von Athen*, 2d ed. (Munich, 1931), 422–24.

37. For the Periclean law, see Aristotle, *Constitution of Athens*, 26.3. See further, the excellent discussion of this law in relation to the *nothoi* in A. Diller, *Race Mixture among the Greeks before Alexander* (Urbana, 1937), 91–100, in the series Illinois University Studies in Language and Literature, 20.1–2.

38. For the *nothoi* in Athens—which means a person of mixed descent instead of its more usual meaning, "bastard"—in connection with Kynosarges, see Demosthenes, *Orations*, 23.216. See further, U. E. Paoli, *Studi di diratto attico* (Florence, 1930), 272–76; K. Latte, "Nothoi," *Real-Encyklopädie der classischen Altertumswissenschaft*, 33: 1066–74, esp. 1069–71.

39. The requirement that the *parasitoi* be chosen *ek tōn nothōn* appears to be burlesqued in the fragment from Diodorus of Sinope, *The Heiress*, quoted in Athenaeus, 6.239d–e (= T. Kock, *Comicorum Atticorum Fragmenta* [Leipzig, 1880–88], 2: 420).

40. The *parasitoi* of Herakles are mentioned in Athenaeus's citations of fragments from Kleidemus (6.235a) and Philocorus (6.235d). Other mentions include Aristophanes, *Daitales* (Kock, *Comicorum Atticorum Fragmenta*, 1: 438) and Alciphron, *Parasites*, 3.42. For a collection of testimonia concerning the cult of Herakles at Kynosarges, see S. Solders, *Die ausserstädtischen Kulte und die Einigung Attikas* (Lund, 1931), 78–80.

41. There is, thus, an irony in Beneden's attempt to distinguish between *les commensaux* and *les parasites* in his work by that title (see above, note 16). The former is synonymous with the latter.

42. While this would take us far from our theme, see the important monograph by D. Whitehead, *The Ideology of the Athenian Metic* (Cambridge, 1977) for another aspect of "relative otherness" in Athens.

43. J. A. Boon, *Other Tribes, Other Scribes: Symbolic Anthropology in the Comparative Study of Cultures, Histories, Religions, and Texts* (Cambridge, 1982): 230.

44. R. Redfield, "Primitive World View," *Proceedings of the American Philosophical Association* 96 (1952): 30–36, reprinted in Redfield, *The Primitive World and Its Transformations* (Ithaca, 1953), 84–110, quotation on 92.

45. See the Sumerian materials in S. N. Kramer, *The Sumerians* (Chicago, 1963), 275–88. Cf. R. Labat, *Manuel d'epigraphie akkadienne* (Paris, 1948), nos. 60 and 74, for the terminology. A particularly instructive example is provided by G. Buccellati, *The Amorites of the Ur III Period* (Naples, 1966), 92–5. Cf. M. Liverani, "Per una considerazione storica del problema amorreo," *Oriens Antiquus* 9 (1970): 22–26.

46. While the literature on this subject has become vast in the past several years (see H. C. Conklin, *Folk Classification: A Topically Arranged Bibliography* [New Haven, 1972]), the most useful essay, from our perspective, is B. E. Ward, "Varieties of the Conscious Model: The Fishermen of South China," in M. Banton, ed., *The Relevance of Models for Social Anthropology* (London, 1965), 113–37.

47. See the important remarks on "true endogamy" in C. Lévi-Strauss, *The Elementary Structures of Kinship* (Boston, 1969), 46–47. The close relationship of social sanctions with respect to sexuality and "otherness" is made starkly plain in the title of the published proceedings of the Twelfth Conference of French Jew-

ish Intellectuals (1971), edited by J. Halpérin and G. Lévitte, *L'autre dans la conscience juive: Le sacré et le couple* (Paris, 1973). "Otherness" and "sacrality" are reduced to questions of intermarriage!

48. See the famous "Exkurs über den Fremden" in G. Simmel, *Soziologie*, 3d ed. (Leipzig, 1923), 509–12. This is developed in M. M. Wood, *The Stranger: A Study in Social Relations* (London, 1934). For an excellent collection of thirty-three essays that focus on the legal relations to the "stranger," see the collective volume, *L'Étranger* (Brussels, 1958), 1–2, which appeared as volume 9 in the series Recueils de la Société Jean Bodin. The definitional article by J. Gilissen (1: 5–57) is of particular merit. There are vast collections of data regarding "strangers" from an anthropological perspective—e.g., J. G. Frazer, *The Golden Bough*, 3d ed. (London, 1935), 3: 101–16; P. J. Hamilton-Grierson, "Strangers," in J. Hastings, ed., *Encyclopaedia of Religion and Ethics* (Edinburgh, 1921), 11: 883–96. A. van Gennep, spatializing the "stranger," gained the generative model for *Rites de Passage* (Paris, 1909). There are a set of important theoretical notes in Lévi-Strauss, *Elementary Structures of Kinship*, 60, 402–3. P. Gauthier, *Symbola: Les étrangers et la justice dans les cités grecques* (Nancy, 1972) provides a model monograph for the study of the topic in an ancient society.

49. From an anthropological perspective, this theme has been a consistent object of attention by Africanists. See, among others, M. Wilson, *Good Company* (London, 1951); and D. Jacobson, *Itinerant Tribesmen: Friendship and Social Order in Urban Uganda* (Menlo Park, 1973).

50. M. Duala-M'bedy, *Xenologie: Die Wissenschaft vom Fremden und die Verdrängung der Humanität in der Anthropologie* (Munich, 1977) collects much interesting data in the service of an unsatisfying and confused thesis.

51. The standard monographs remain K. Trüdinger, *Studien zur Geschichte der griechisch-römischen Ethnographie* (Basel, 1918); and L. Pearson, *Early Ionian Historians* (Oxford, 1939).

52. See the various studies by E. H. Schafer, including *The Golden Peaches of Samarkand: A Study of T'ang Exotics* (Berkeley, 1963), *The Vermilion Bird: T'ang Images of the South* (Berkeley, 1967), *Shore of Pearls: Hainan Island in Early Times* (Berkeley, 1970).

53. Cortés, "2nd Dispatch," in D. Enrique de Vedia, *Historiadores Primitivos de Indias* (Madrid, 1918), 1: 34b–35a in the series Biblioteca de Autores Españoles, 22. Translation in I. R. Blacker and H. M. Rosen, *Conquest: Dispatches of Cortes from the New World* (New York, 1962), 60–61.

54. J. Burckhardt, *The Civilization of the Renaissance in Italy* (New York, 1929), 291–92.

55. For the history of fieldwork, see A. I. Richards, "The Development of Field Work Methods in Social Anthropology," in F. C. Bartlett, ed., *The Study of Society* (London, 1939), 272–316; P. Kaberry, "Malinowski's Contribution to

Fieldwork Methods and the Writing of Ethnography," in R. Firth, ed., *Man and Culture*, 2d ed. (London, 1960), 71–91, esp. 72–76; G. W. Stocking, Jr., ed., *Observers Observed: Essays on Ethnographic Fieldwork* (Madison, 1983), in the series History of Anthropology, 1. See further, P. C. W. Gutkind and G. Sankoff, "Annotated Bibliography on Anthropological Field Work Methods," in D. G. Jongmans and P. C. W. Gutkind, eds., *Anthropologists in the Field* (New York, 1967), 214–71.

56. C. Lévi-Strauss, *Structural Anthropology* (New York, 1976), 2: 55.

57. History, to take up Lévi-Strauss's example, treats the temporally remote at least to the same degree as anthropology treats the spatially remote.

58. Such is most explicitly the case in C. Lévi-Strauss, *Tristes Tropiques* (Paris, 1955) and J.-P. Dumont, *The Headman and I: Ambiguity and Ambivalence in the Fieldworking Experience* (Austin, 1978).

59. For a collection of papers from the 1974 meeting on "Cultural Futuristics," see M. Maruyama and A. Harkins, eds., *Cultures beyond the Earth: The Role of Anthropology in Outer Space* (New York, 1975). For science fiction novels that make extraterrestrial anthropology their central theme, see, among others, the sophisticated works of Michael Bishop, *Transfigurations* (Berkeley, 1979), and Chad Oliver, *Unearthly Neighbors* (New York, 1960). See further, Smith, "Close Encounters of Diverse Kinds," reprinted in this volume.

60. For the notion of "limiting case," see L. Dumont, *Homo Hierarchicus*, 2d ed. (Chicago, 1979), 24–27.

61. Colin Turnbull's novelistic study of the Ik would be an extreme example, *The Mountain People* (New York, 1972).

62. E. R. Leach, *Rethinking Anthropology* (London, 1961), 1.

63. For a profound meditation on this theme, see J. Fabian, *Time and the Other: How Anthropology Makes Its Object* (New York, 1983).

64. J. Vansina, "Cultures through Time," in R. Naroll and R. Cohen, eds., *A Handbook of Method in Cultural Anthropology* (Garden City, N.Y., 1970), 165. See further, Fabian, *Time and the Other*, 80–97, and the shrewd characterization of the "functionalist monograph" in J. Boon, *Other Tribes, Other Scribes*, 13–14.

65. For a profound meditation on "decipherment," see M. V. David, *Le débat sur les écritures et l'hiéroglyph aux XVIIᵉ et XVIIIᵉ siècles, et l'application de la notion de déchiffrement aux écritures mortes* (Paris, 1965).

66. E. R. Leach, *Political Systems of Highland Burma*, 2d ed. (Boston, 1965), 15.

67. This distinction between the Anglo-American tradition of the "other" and the Continental deserves further study. For the present, D. Locke, *Myself and Others: A Study in Our Knowledge of Minds* (Oxford, 1968) may be taken as an exemplary review of the Anglo-American tradition; M. Theunissen, *Der Andere: Studien zur Sozialontologie der Gegenwart*, 2d ed. (Berlin, 1977) may be taken as an exemplary review of the Continental.

68. One need do no more than appeal to the onomatopoeic derivation of *bar-*

baros from "ba! ba! ba!," that is, unintelligible, stammering, animal- or child-like speech (already in the *Iliad* 2.867). See, among others, the semaisiological study by A. Eichhorn, *Barbaros quid significaverit* (Leipzig, 1904). The same notion is found in the sparse Israelitic ethnographic tradition (e.g., Ezekiel 3: 5–6; Isaiah 33: 4–19; Psalm 114:1), and underlies narratives such as Judges 12:5–6. Compare the Mesoamerican analogue. "The Indians of this New Spain derive, according to what is generally reported in *their* histories, from two diverse peoples; they give to the first the name, Nahuatlaca, which means '*People who explain themselves and speak clearly*,' to be differentiated from the second people, at the time very wild and uncivilized, concerned only with hunting, to whom they give the name, Chichimecs, which means, 'People who go hunting'." Juan de Tovar, *Historia de los indios mexicanos*, in the edition and French translation by J. La Faye, *Manuscrit Tovar: Origines et croyances des Indiens du Mexique* (Graz, 1972), 9, emphasis added.

69. See the collection of examples in T. Todorov, *The Conquest of America* (New York, 1984), 76. A variant of this is to treat the "other" as a "parrot" with no native language, but imitating European speech. See, for example, the report by Bernardino de Minaya cited in L. Hanke, "Pope Paul III and the American Indians," *Harvard Theological Review* 30 (1937): 84.

70. L. Olschki, *Marco Polo's Precursors* (Baltimore, 1943), 4–5 and note 9 citing the earlier literature. See further, H. Hart, *The Sea Road to the Indies* (New York, 1951), 21n.; and P. Wheatley, *The Golden Khersonese: Studies in the Historical Geography of the Malay Peninsula before* A.D. *1500* (Kuala Lumpur, 1961), 130–31.

71. The observations of A. Momigliano, *Alien Wisdom: The Limits of Hellenization* (Cambridge, 1975), 7–8, 91–93, et passim may be generalized. Note further the observation that, even with an interpreter, the barbarian may prove unintelligible, as in Hanno, *Periplus*, 11, in the English translation by R. Harris (Cambridge, 1928), 26.

72. Of the many formulations, that by W. Franklin, *Discoverers, Explorers, Settlers: The Diligent Writers of Early American* (Chicago, 1979), 7, is most useful for our theme. "More than anything else, the West became an epistemological problem for Europe. . . . It was simply the fact of 'another' world which most thoroughly deranged the received order of European life. The issue was not merely an informational one. It involved so many far-reaching consequences that the very structure of Old World knowledge—assumptions about the nature of learning and the role of traditional wisdom in it—was cast into disarray. . . . Faced with a flood of puzzling facts and often startling details, the East was almost literally at a loss for words. Having discovered America, it now needed to make a place for the New World within its intellectual and verbal universe."

73. For a brief overview of the classical conception of the *triplex mundus*, see F. Gisinger, "Geographie," *Real-Encyclopädie der classischen Altertumswissenschaft*, suppl. vol. 4: 521–685, esp. 552–56. See further, the standard histories: E. H. Bun-

bury, *A History of Ancient Geography* (London, 1879), 1: 145–6; E. H. Berger, *Geschichte der wissenschaftlichen Erdkunde der Griechen*, 2d ed. (Leipzig, 1903), 82–90; H. F. Tozer, *A History of Ancient Geography*, 2d ed. (Cambridge, 1935), 67–70.

74. For Pliny's centrality, see E. W. Gudger, "Pliny's 'Historia naturalis': The Most Popular Natural History Ever Published," *Isis* 6 (1924): 269–81, which provides a census of printed editions from 1469 to 1799. Of direct relevance to our topic, see Columbus's copy of Pliny with his annotations in C. de Lollis, *Scritti di Cristoforo Colombo* (Rome, 1894), 2: 471–72 in the series Raccolta di Documenti e Studi Pubblicati dalla R. Commissione Columbiana, 1.2. In the early "New World" scientific and historical literature, Pliny serves as the standard of classical knowledge, e.g., E. Alvarez López, "Plinio y Fernández de Oviedo," *Annales de Ciencias naturales del Instituto J. de Acosta* (Madrid, 1940), 1: 46–61 and 2: 13–35.

On Genesis 10, see the commentary and full bibliography in the magisterial work of C. Westermann, *Genesis* (Göttingen, 1966–), 662–706. From our perspective, the most useful work is G. Hölscher, *Drei Erdkarten: Ein Beitrag zur Erdkenntnis des hebraischen Altertums* (Heidelberg, 1949), esp. 45–56.

75. The origin and derivation of the name "America" remains a matter of some controversy. J. A. Aboal Amaro, *Amérigho Vespucci: Ensayo de bibliografía crítica* (Madrid, 1962) provides a representative summary of the various proposals. See pp. 15, 18, 20, 31, 53, 55, 56, 60, 61, 64, 65, 66, 67, 68, 71, 79, 89, 90–94, 123, 124–25, 127–28, 129, 131, 134–35, 136, 144–45, 147–48, 148, 149. See further the important study by C. Sanz, *El Nombre América: Libros y mapas quo lo impusieron* (Madrid, 1959) and the review of scholarship by J. Vidago, "América: Origem e evolucão deste nome," *Revista Ocidente* 67 (1964): 93–110.

The figure of "America" as a "fourth" entity was developed through a process of experimentation. This is seen most clearly in the development of "America's" iconography. See, among others, J. H. Hyde, "L'iconographie des quatres parties du monde dans les tapisseries," *Gazette des Beaux-Arts* 66 (1924): 253–72; C. Le Corbeiller, "Miss America and Her Sisters: Personifications of the Four Parts of the World," *Metropolitan Museum Bulletin*, n.s. 19–20 (1960): 209–23. On the general theme, see E. Köllmann, et al., "Erdteile," *Reallexikon zur deutschen Kunstgeschichte* (Munich, 1967), 5: 1107–1202.

76. The first occurrence of this phrase is in M. Waldseemüller[?], *Cosmographiae Introductio* (St. Dié, 1507), a iii. See the facsimile edition by J. Fischer and F. von Wieser (reprint, New York, 1969), xxv.

77. The theme of the *orbis alterius* was first developed at length in Pomponius Mela, *De situ orbis*, 1.4, 3.7 (in the edition of G. Parthey [Berlin, 1867]). See, in general, A. Rainaud, *Le continent austral: Hypothèses et découvertes* (Paris, 1893).

78. As is well known, there was a conceptual debate as to whether water or land was primary—the former (and most widely held view) gave rise to the picture of land as insular; the latter reduced the oceans to landlocked lakes. See A.

Norlind, *Das Problem des gegenseitigen Verhältnisses von Land und Wasser und seine Behandlung im Mittelalter* (Lund and Leipzig, 1918) in the series Lunds Universitets Årsskrift, n.s. 1.14.2.

79. The "zonal" division is attributed either to Parmenides (Strabo, 2.2.2) or Pythagoras (Aetius, *De placitis philosophorum*, 3.14.1). Both attributions have been the subject of debate. See, among others, W. A. Heidel, *The Frame of the Ancient Greek Maps* (New York, 1937), 76, 80, 91, in the series American Geographical Society Research Series, 20; W. Burkert, *Lore and Science in Ancient Pythagoreanism* (Cambridge, Mass., 1972); 305–6. The division by *zonai* must not be confused with the division into *klimata* (which were later correlated with the Ptolemaic parallels). See E. Honigmann, *Die sieben Klimata und die Poleis Episemoi* (Heidelberg, 1929), 4–9, 25–30.

80. Posidonius, fragment 28 (Jacoby) in Strabo, 2.2.3.

81. See, in general, F. Gisinger, "Oikoumenē," *Real-Encyclopädie der classischen Altertumswissenschaft*, 17.2: 2123–74. From our perspective, the most useful study is J. Partsch, *Die Grenzen der Menscheit* (1): *Die antike Oikoumene* (Leipzig, 1916) in the series Berichte über die Verhandlungen der König. Sächsischen Gesellschaft der Wissenschaften zu Leipzig, Phil-hist. Kl. 68 (1916), 1–62.

82. For an influential form of this argument, see Macrobius, *Commentarius in Ciceronis Somnium Scipionis*, 2.5.9–36 in the translation by W. H. Stahl, *Macrobius: Commentary on the Dream of Scipio* (New York, 1952); 200–6. Note that the view that the southern temperate zone "is also inhabited *is inferred* solely from reason" (2.5.17, emphasis added). This symmetrical argument goes back to the speculation of Krates that the northern *oikoumenē* is but one of four inhabited landmasses. See H. J. Mette, *Sphairopoiia: Untersuchungen zur Kosmologie des Krates von Pergamon* (Munich, 1936), 76–77.

83. Strabo, 2.5.13. Cf. 2.5.34, 2.5.43. Strabo here denies that such "other worlds" are part of the study of geography, confining geography to "our *oikoumenē*." For an important discussion of this limitation, see C. van Paassen, *The Classical Tradition of Geography* (Groningen, 1957), 4–31. This limitation persisted on the part of some geographers even after the "discovery" of America, e.g., the preface by Johannes Cochlaeus to the 1512 edition of Pomponius Mela, *De situ orbis:* "In our lifetime, Amerigo Vespucci is said to have discovered that new world . . . [that] is quite distinct from [Africa] and bigger than our Europe. Whether this is true or a lie, it has nothing . . . to do with Cosmography or History. *For the peoples and places of that continent are unknown and unnamed to us.* . . . *Therefore, it is of no interest to geographers at all*" (emphasis added). The passage has been quoted in E. P. Goldschmidt, "Not in Harrisse," in *Festschrift Lawrence C. Wroth* (Portland, 1951), 133–34 and J. H. Elliott, "Renaissance Europe and America: A Blunted Impact," in F. Chiappelli, ed., *First Images of America* (Berkeley, 1976), 1: 14. Both Goldschmidt and Elliott have drawn negative conclusions

from the passage rather than setting it within the context of the Strabonian limitations on "geography."

84. It is important to avoid the anachronism of imposing our insular notion of "continent" on this tripartition. I have not been able to locate a history of the term, but it would appear that it referred to a contiguous (*continens*) landmass, e.g., W. Cunningham, *The Cosmographical Glasse* (London, 1559), 113, "Continens [margin: continent] is a portion of the earth which is not parted by the seas asounder." Thus Waldseemüller, in 1508, distinguished between the traditional three contiguous landmasses, which made up the northern earth-island, and the newly discovered "island" of "America": *et sunt tres prime partes continentes, quarta est insula* (Fischer and Wieser facsimile edition, xxx). The application of the term "continent" to all of the major landmasses occurs only in the late sixteenth century. F. Gagnon, "Le thème médiéval de l'homme sauvage dans les premières représentations des Indiens d'Amérique," in G. H. Allard, ed., *Aspects de la marginalité au Moyen Age* (Quebec, 1975), 96, attempts to discern an evaluative opposition in the early iconography of the "Indies"—"la terre ferme européenne est opposée à l'île primitive."

85. While the division of the world-island into three landmasses is already presumed by Herodotus (e.g., 2.16), it was, perhaps, implied by the arrangement of Hecateus's *Periodos* into two books (Europe and Asia) with Libya as an appendix. See F. Gisinger, *Die Erdbeschreibung des Eudoxos von Knidos*, 2d ed. (Amsterdam, 1967), 14–18, 35–36.

86. See R. von Scheliha, *Die Wassergrenze im Altertum* (Breslau, 1931), esp. 34–42, in the series Historische Untersuchungen, 8.

87. This is graphically depicted in the Noachie "T-O" maps. The study by M. Destombes, *Mappemondes*, A.D. 1200–1500 (Amsterdam: 1964) in the series Monumenta Cartographica Vetustioris Aevi, 1, supercedes all previous publications.

88. E.g., Hrbanus Maurus, *De Universo*, 2.1 (Migne, *Patrologia cursus completus, series Latina*, 111: 54), 12.2 (111: 353–54). See also the expanded edition of the *Glossa ordinaria* ad Mt 2.11 (Venice, 1603), 5:62. This identification is not found in the *Glossa* as printed in Migne, *PL* 114:75.

89. The identification depends on first identifying the unnumbered magi of Mt 2 as "three kings" (Leo, *Sermon* 33 [Migne, *PL* 54: 235] is an early example) and then identifying the three kings with the three continents. See [pseudo] Jerome, *Expositio Quatuor Evangeliorum* ad Mt. 2.1 (Migne, *PL* 30: 537); Hrbanus Maurus, *Commentariorum in Matthaeum* ad Mt. 2.1 (Migne, *PL* 107: 760); [pseudo] Bede, *In Matthaei Evangelium exposito* ad Mt. 2.1 (Migne, *PL* 92: 113); Michael Scot, *Liber introductorius* (MS. Bodleian 266), f. 3 (as cited in L. Thorndike, *A History of Magic and Experimental Science* [New York, 1923], 2: 318). J. Duchesne-Guillemin, "Jesus' Trimorphism and the Differentiation of the Magi," in E. J. Sharpe and J. R. Hinnells, eds., *Man and His Salvation* (Manches-

ter, 1973), 97, asserts, in passing, that the identification is as old as Augustine, but I have not located a reference. On the identification, see in general, H. Kehrer, *Die "Heiligen Drei Könige" in der Legende und in der deutschen bildenden Kunst* (Strasbourg, 1904), 23; and H. Baudet, *Paradise on Earth: Some Thoughts on European Images of Non-European Man* (New Haven, 1965), 17–8.

90. The triple tiara appears to be a fourteenth-century innovation, most usually explained as symbolizing the pope's authority over heaven, earth, and hell (see J. Braun, *Encyclopaedia Britannica*, s.v. "Tiara," 11th ed., 26: 911–12). However, Pedro Simón, *Primera parte de las noticias historiales de las conquistas de Tierra-Firme en las Indias Occidentales* (Cuenca, 1627), 1: 9, suggests that a fourth crown be added to symbolize the pope's authority over "America"—the other three crowns being associated with the traditional tripartition. As this latter suggests, the numerical symbolism can be dazzling, e.g., Gregory Horn, *Arca Noe* (Leiden and Rotterdam, 1666), 35, 183, passim, who attempts to correlate the three sons of Noah, the four "world empires," and the five "continents."

91. Augustine, *Civitate Dei*, 16.8 (in the Loeb Library edition and translation). Being "human" means, above all, having reason—as in Augustine, *De Trinitate*, 7.4.7. (*Corpus Christianorum*, 50: 255).

92. In addition to Rainaud, *Le continent austral*, see W. Wright, *The Geographical Lore of the Time of the Crusades* (New York, 1925), 157–65 and P. Delhaye, "Le théorie des antipodes et ses incidences théologiques," which appeared as note "S" in his edition, *Godfrey de Saint-Victor: Microcosmus* (Lille and Gembloux, 1951), 282–86. The arguments against the inhabitability of the austral island or the antipodes are elegantly summarized in Pierre d'Ailly, *Imago Mundi*, 7 (in the edition of E. Buron [Paris, 1930] and the English translation by E. F. Keever [Wilmington, N.C., 1948]).

From our perspective, the most interesting argument (in terms of the Augustinian options) is that while the *orbis alterius* is real, its inhabitants are not. This is already implied by the influential encyclopaedia of Isidore of Seville, *Etymologiae*, 14.5.7 (Migne, *PL* 82: 512); cf. 9.2.133 (82: 341). For Isidore's view, see G. Boffito, "La leggenda degli antipodi," *Festschrift A. Graf* (Bergamo, 1903), esp. 592 and n. 4. Isidore's view of the antipodes found graphic representation in the "Beatus" maps—see K. Miller, *Mappae Mundi* (Stuttgart, 1895–98), 1: 58; T. Simar, *Le géographie de l'Afrique centrale dans l'antiquité au moyen age* (Brussels, 1912), 150–58; and J. Marquis Casanovas et al., *Sancti Beati a Liebana in Apocalypsin Codex Gerundensis* (Olten and Lausanne, 1962), ff. 54v–55r. Note, however, that in the later figures, which are attached to Isidore's discussion of the "zones" in *De natura rerum* 1.10 (Migne, *PL* 83: 978–79 with figs.), two inhabitable "zones" are shown. (See the discussion of this in E. Brehaut, *An Encyclopedist of the Dark Ages: Isidore of Seville* [New York, 1912], 50–54). Furthermore, the outline of Isidore's geographical section in the *Etymologiae*, appending a section on islands after sections on the tripartite *oikoumenē*, suggests yet a third pattern (see Wright, *Geographical Lore*, 259, 460, n. 12).

93. The issue of the geographic impact has been often studied since the pioneering work of K. Kretschmer, *Die Entdeckung Amerika's in ihrer Bedeutung für die Geschichte des Weltbildes* (Leipzig, 1892).

94. This issue has been the special burden of the important and controversial works by Edmundo O'Gorman, which have been fundamental to my construction of this section. See especially, *La idea del descubrimiento de América: Historia de esa interpretación y crítica de sus fundamentos* (Mexico City, 1951) and the similarly titled, though quite different work, *The Invention of America: An Inquiry into the Historical Nature of the New World and the Meaning of Its History* (Bloomington, 1961).

95. F. Guicciardini, *Storia d'Italia* (1561) in the edition of C. Panigara (Bari, 1929), 2: 130–31 as cited in H. Honour, *The New Golden Land: European Images of America from the Discoveries to the Present Time* (New York, 1975), 84.

96. É. Pasquier, *Les oeuvres* (Amsterdam: 1723), 2: 55, as cited in J. H. Elliott, *The Old World and the New, 1492–1650* (Cambridge, 1970), 8.

97. W. E. Washburn, "The Meaning of 'Discovery' in the Fifteenth and Sixteenth Centuries," *American Historical Review* 68 (1962–3): 1–21. Note that this article is conceived as a fundamental attack on O'Gorman's work (note 94 above).

98. C. Gibson, "Conquest and the So-Called Conquest in Spain and Spanish America," *Terrae Incognitae* 12 (1980): 1–18.

99. See the useful collection of such terms in Kretschmer, *Die Entdeckung Amerika's*, 360–69.

100. There are no primary sources. See J. Toriboio Medina, *El descubrimiento del Oceano Pácifico* (Santiago, 1914) for a thorough review of the early historians who mention Balboa's discovery, none of whom appear to emphasize its cosmographic implications.

101. The best reviews of the complex Magellan literature are M. Torodash, "Magellan Historiography," *Hispanic American Historical Review* 51 (1971): 313–35, esp. 313–26, and F. Leite de Faria, "As primeiras relações impressas sobre a viagem de Fernão de Magalhães," in A. Teixeira de Moto, ed., *A Viagem de Fernão de Magalhães e a questo de Molucas* (Lisbon, 1975), 473–518, in the series Estudos de cartografia antiga, 16. Surprisingly, while the older sources relate the drama and novelty of the circumnavigation, none of them draw cosmographical implications. (1) Fugger Newsletter: *Eine schöne Newe zeytung so Kayserlich Mayestet ausz getz nemlich zukommen sind* (Augsburg, 1522), 8 (in C. Sanz, *Últimas Adiciones* to H. Harrisse, *Bibliotheca Americana Vetustissima* [Madrid, 1960], 2: 909–12). (2) Maximilian of Transylvania, *De Moluccis Insulis* (Cologne, 1523), on which see Faria, "As primeiras relacões", 479–500. See esp., in the English translation by J. Baynes printed in Ch. E. Nowell, *Magellan's Voyage around the World: Three Con-*

temporary Accounts (Evanston, 1962), 274, 275–76, 277, 279–80, 291–92, 309. (3) Antonio Pigafetta, *Primo viaggio intorno al mundo,* written c. 1523. On the complex history of this text, see Faria, "As primeiras relacões," 506–16. The earliest printed version, in French (Paris, 1525), is now available in a facsimile edition and translation by P. S. Paige, *The Voyage of Magellan* (Ann Arbor, 1969), esp. 20. See also the Ambrosian manuscript in Nowell, *Magellan's Voyage,* 64. (4) *Roteiro* of the anonymous "Genoese Pilot," in H. E. J. Stanley, *The First Voyage Round the World by Magellan* (London, 1874), 9.

The earliest work that I can find that appreciates the cosmographic implications of the circumnavigation is Richard Eden's paraphrastic translation of Peter Martyr's *Decadas* — *The Decades of the Newe Worlde or West India* (London, 1555), facsimile edition (New York, 1966), 214r–215r, who sets the reports of Maximilian, Pigafetta, and Peter Martyr in the context of the classical tripartition ("the hole globe or compase of the earth was dyvyded by the auncient wryters into three partes") and concludes with a clear statement of novelty ("the antiquitie had never such knowledge of the worlde . . . as we have at this presente by th'industrye of men of this oure age").

102. Columbus's first report, *Epistola de Insulis Nuper Inventis* (dated February 15, 1493) was first printed prior to Columbus's arrival at Barcelona (between April 15–20, 1493). There were eleven printed editions by 1497. See C. Sanz, *La Carta de Colón* (Madrid, 1958) for facsimiles of the first seventeen printed editions. Cf. Sanz, *Bibliografía general de la Carta de Colón* (Madrid, 1958). See further, the useful tabulation in R. Hirsch, "Printed Reports on the Early Discoveries and Their Reception," in F. Chiappelli, ed., *First Images of America,* 2: 537–52 and appendices 1–3 (unpaginated).

103. It is reported by his son that Columbus wrote a *Memoria anotacion para probar que las cinco zonas son habitables,* c. 1490. If so, it is now lost. Ferdinand Columbus, *Vida del Almirante Don Cristóbal Colón,* chap. 4, in the English translation by B. Keen (New Brunswick, N.J., 1959), 11.

104. The *Journal* written by Columbus during his first voyage has had a complex history. The document itself has been lost. It was massively excerpted in Bartolomé de las Casas, *Historia de las Indias,* book 1, chaps. 35–75, a work composed between 1527 and 1560 but not published in full until the Madrid edition of 1875–76. (There are excerpts as well in Ferdinand Columbus, *Vida,* which permit some cross-checking). The *Columbus Journal* was first printed separately by M. Fernández de Navarrette, *Colección de los viajes y descubrimientos que hicieron por mar los españoles desde fines del siglo XV* (Madrid, 1825–37), 1: 1–166. C. Sanz, *Diario de Colón* (Madrid, 1962), 1–2, has published a facsimile edition of the Las Casas manuscript (Madrid MS.V.6, n. 7). For the distinction between Columbus and Las Casas, see A. Vásquez, "Las Casas' Opinions in Columbus' Diary," *Topic* 11 (1971): 45–56. I cite the convenient edition by G. Marañon, *Diario de Colón*

(Madrid, 1968), and the English translation by C. R. Markham, *The Journal of Christopher Columbus* (London, 1893). Quotations are from Marañon, *Diario,* 29 and Markham, *Journal,* 40.

105. The so-called *Lettera rarissima,* addressed by Columbus to the king and queen, July 7, 1503. Text and translation in R. H. Major, *Christopher Columbus: Four Voyages to the New World. Letters and Selected Documents* (London, 1847; reprint, New York: 1961), 169–203. I have combined two separate figures: Ciguane is "nine days' journey westward" (Major, 175), the "river Ganges" is "ten days" from Ciguane (Major, 176).

106. It must be recalled that Columbus could not "speak" with the natives, despite his frequent (and, sometimes lengthy), translations of what they said. He communicated with them in "signs."

107. Marañon, *Diario,* 81; Markham, *Journal,* 87. For the appearance of man-eating cynocephali in the Orient in a book owned by Columbus, see H. Yule and H. Cordier, *The Book of Ser Marco Polo,* 3d ed. (London, 1921), 2: 309. The argument by D. B. Quinn, "New Geographical Horizons: Literature," in F. Chiappelli, *First Images of America,* 2: 637, that Columbus elicited the information concerning the cynocephali by showing "pictures to his Arawak informants" from illustrated editions of Marco Polo and Mandeville is without evidence.

108. Marañon, *Diario,* 103; Markham, *Journal,* 106.

109. Excerpt by B. Las Casas from the Columbus *Journal* of the third voyage in *Raccolta di documenti e studi publicata dalla R. Comisione Columbiana* (Rome, 1892–96), 1.2: 22.

110. While most frequently placed in the East, there was a speculative tradition that Paradise lay beyond the earth-island, inaccessible to man. See J. K. Wright, *Geographical Lore of the Time of the Crusades,* esp. 262.

111. *Raccolta,* 1.2: 26–40; text and translation in R. H. Major, *Christopher Columbus,* 104–46.

112. Major, *Christopher Columbus,* 105–6.

113. Major, *Christopher Columbus,* 109, cf. 143.

114. Major, *Christopher Columbus,* 142.

115. The most remarkable instance of this "persuasion" is the oft-cited *Información y testimonio acerca de la exploración de Cuba* printed in Navarrete, *Colección,* 2: no. 76.

116. Major, *Christopher Columbus,* 129–30, 133.

117. Major, *Christopher Columbus,* 131.

118. Major, *Christopher Columbus,* 130. The image is repeated twice, Major, 131 and 137.

119. Major, *Christopher Columbus,* 137 (in revised translation); cf. 135, 136, 142, 145.

120. This distinction between two types of land—the "Indies" and the "Paradisical"—is maintained in two other documents associated with the third voyage: the *Letter* to Dona Juana de la Torres (1500) in Navarrete, *Colección*, 1, esp. 267–68; and the so-called *Papal Letter* (February, 1502) in *Raccolta*, 1.2: 64–66.

121. See Major, *Christopher Columbus*, 143. The Spanish Crown appears to have taken up Columbus's rejected option. As they had doubted his earlier identification of the newly discovered islands with the "Indies" (see the texts cited in O'Gorman, *Invention*, 81–82, 157, n. 18), settling on the ambiguous phrase, "islands and firm land . . . in the western part of the Ocean sea, toward the Indies [*versus India*]," (papal bull, *Inter caetera* [May 3, 1493] in Navarrete, *Colección*, 2: no. 17), so, now, they inferred the existence of a large southern landmass and dispatched no less than six expeditions during the period 1499–1502 to make territorial claims (O'Gorman, *Invention*, 104).

122. Peter Martyr, *De Orbe Novo*, 1.6. *Opera*, 64; MacNutt, 1: 139 (see note 125, below for bibliographical references).

123. E.g., C. O. Sauer, "Terra firma: Orbis novus," in A. Leidlmair, ed., *Festschrift Hermann von Wissmann* (Tübingen, 1962), 258, 260, 263; T. Todorov, *The Conquest of America*, 12–3, et passim.

124. Bartolomé de las Casas, *Historia de las Indias*, 1.44. I cite the edition published in Madrid, 1927(?), 1: 224.

125. The major work of Peter Martyr, *De Orbe Novo*, has had a complex history that affects its interpretation. The first *Decade* devoted to Columbus and Martin Alonso Pinzón was completed (with the exception of book 10) between 1493 and 1501. An Italian version, which survives in only two copies, was published (most probably without Martyr's consent) by P. Trevesan under the title *Libretto de tutta la navigatione de Re des Spagna de le isole et terreni nouvamente trovati* (Venice, 1504)—now available in a facsimile edited by L. C. Wroth (Providence, 1930). It is uncertain whether this text is an abridgement of Martyr's first *Decade* as eventually published or an accurate copy of Martyr's first version which he later expanded. The *Libretto* received wide circulation when it was incorporated as book 4 of Francanzano Montalboddo's collection, *Paesi Novamente Retrouati* (Venice, 1507), which rapidly went through fifteen editions. (See D. B. Quinn, "Exploration and Expansion of Europe," in the *Rapports* of the twelfth International Congress of Historical Sciences [Vienna, 1965], 1: 45–59.)

The first *Decade*, in Martyr's final version, was first published in a collection of his works, *P. Martyris Angli Mediolanensis Opera: Legatio babylonica, Oceani Decas, Poemata, Epigrammata* (Seville, 1511), d–f. The first three *Decades* were published under the title *De Orbe Novo Decades* (Alcala: 1516). The fourth *Decade* was published under the title *De Insulis nuper repertis simultaque incolarum moribus* (Basel: 1521). All eight *Decades* were published posthumously, *De Orbe Novo Petri*

Chapter Twelve

Martyris (Alcala, 1530)—now available in a facsimile edition by the Akademische Druck- und Verlangsanstalt, *Petrus Martyr de Angleria: Opera* (Graz, 1966), 35–32, 73. Until this facsimile (which I cite), the full text of *De Orbe Novo* was most readily available in the edition by Richard Hakluyt (Paris, 1587).

An English translation of the first four *Decades* was made by Richard Eden, *The Decades of the Newe Worlde or West Indies* (London, 1555)—facsimile edition (New York, 1966), 25–161. An English translation of the entire work was first made by M. Lok, *De Orbe Novo; or, The Historie of the West Indies* (London, 1612). The standard English translation (which I cite with minor revisions) is that by F. A. MacNutt, *De Orbe Novo* (New York, 1912; reprint, New York, 1970), 1–2.

A more difficult question is the correlative use of the extensive correspondence, first published as *Opus Epistolarum Petri Martyris* (Alcala, 1530)—facsimile edition, *Opera* (Ganz, 1966), 275–707, which are available in the important Spanish translation by J. López de Toro, *Epistolario de Pedro Mártir de Angleria* (Madrid, 1953–57), 1–4, in the series Documentos inéditos para la historia de España, 9–12. A selection of the *Letters* which relate to the "new world" were published in French translation by P. Gafferal and l'Abbé Louvot, *Lettres de Pierre Martyr Anghiera relatives aux découvertes maritimes des espagnols et des portugais* (Paris, 1885).

The evidence of the *Letters* must be used with extreme caution. While their authenticity has been challenged, this seems unlikely. It is certain that their chronology is unreliable; many appear to have been backdated. See, among others, J. Bernays, *Petrus Martyr Anglerius und sein Opus Epistolarum* (Strasbourg, 1891).

For the relative chronology of the individual books of the various *Decades*—a matter crucial for their interpretation—I have followed that given by E. O'-Gorman, *Cuatro historiadores de Indias* (Mexico City, 1972), 43–44.

126. This is, quite rightly, insisted upon by C. O. Sauer, "Terra Firma: Orbis Novus," 260–61; 262, n. 7.

127. On the problems attendant on using the *Epistles*, see above, note 125.

128. *Epistle*, 130. *Opera*, 360; *Epistolario*, 1: 236. The term *antipodes* recurs in *Epistles* 134 (September, 1493); 140 (January, 1494); 144 (October, 1494).

129. *Epistle*, 134. *Opera*, 361; *Epistolario*, 1: 244.

130. *De Orbe Novo*, 1.1. *Opera*, 39; MacNutt, *De Orbe Novo*, 1: 57.

131. *De Orbe Novo*, 1.1. *Opera*, 41 and 39; MacNutt, *De Orbe Novo*, 1: 65 and 57.

132. *De Orbe Novo*, 1.1. *Opera*, 39; MacNutt, *De Orbe Novo*, 1: 58.

133. *De Orbe Novo*, 1.1. *Opera*, 40; MacNutt, *De Orbe Novo*, 1: 61, cf. 1: 87, 114 et passim. For this claim, see Columbus's *Papal Letter* (February, 1502) in *Raccolta*, 1.2: 472, and Columbus, *Libro de las Profecías* (1501–52), in *Raccolta* 1.2: esp. 150–56. The identification persists through the early literature. See the important study by G. Gliozzi, *Adamo e il nuovo mondo* (Florence, 1976), 147–74.

134. *De Orbe Novo*, 1.1. *Opera:* 41. MacNutt's translation (1: 65) is inadequate at this point.

135. *De Orbe Novo*, 1.4. *Opera:* 54; MacNutt, *De Orbe Novo*, 1: 105, cf. 1: 92, 139–40, 178, 330 et passim. Compare further, *Epistles*, 135 and 142.

136. *Epistle*, 138. *Opera:* 360; *Epistolario*, 1: 250. The phrase recurs in *Epistles* 142 (October 20, 1494) and 154 (February 2, 1494).

137. For the Asian extension, see Vespucci, *First Letter* (July 18, 1500) in R. Levillier, ed., *El Nuevo Mondo: Cartas relativas a sus viajes y descubrimientos* (Buenos Aires, 1951), 277, cf. 299.

The term "new world" occurs only five times in Vespucci's writings, only in the letter now entitled, *Mundus Novus* (n.p., n.d. [c. 1502–4]). See the summary bibliography in J. A. Aboal Amaro, *Amérigho Vespucci*, 99–111. Its most important occurrence is in the first paragraph: "On a former occasion I wrote to you at some length concerning my return from those *new regions* which we found and explored with the fleet. . . . And these we may rightly call a *new world*. Because our ancestors had no knowledge of them, and it will be a matter *wholly new* to all those who hear of them." (English translation by G. T. Northup, *Mundus Novus* [Princeton, 1916], 1, [emphasis added], in the series Vespucci Reprints, Texts and Studies, 5). The phrase "*quasque novum mundum appellare licet*" may be taken as indicating the author's self-consciousness at coining a term, but what does it mean? The context makes plain that *novus* refers to the fact that the lands were unknown and unexpected, i.e., (a) that they could not be harmonized readily with any of the lands described by the ancient authorities, and (b) that they occurred in the Southern Hemisphere which, according to the ancients, was entirely ocean. *Mundus* refers to the fact that the lands were inhabited, i.e., that they constituted a "world" in the sense of *oikoumenē*. The question of whether they were a previously unknown extension of the familiar tripartite *oikoumenē* or constitute a "new" geographical entity was not raised in the *Mundus Novus*.

However, extreme caution must be used in evaluating this text. "Vespucci's writings have had a strange and complicated history. They have suffered at the hands of translators, copyists, printers. . . . The texts on which we base our judgements are *vastly different* from those which left the author's hand." (G. T. Northup, *Amerigo Vespucci: Letter to Pietro Soderini* [Princeton, 1916], 1, in the series Vespucci Reprints, Texts and Studies, 4 [emphasis added]). While it may be too extreme to label the *Mundus Novus* and the *Soderini Letter* "forgeries" as has been done by F. J. Pohl, *Amerigo Vespucci: Pilot Major* (New York, 1944), esp. 144–67, C. O. Sauer, "Terra Firma: Orbis Novus," 268, n. 19 and 269; R. Iglesia, *Columbus, Cortés, and Other Essays* (Berkeley, 1969), 253, among others, they are most certainly not, in their printed form, by Vespucci. They represent Latin versions by anonymous translators that probably ill accord with Vespucci's original. See A. Magnaghi, *Americo Vespucci: Studio critico* (Rome, 1924),1–2; the careful textual and philological study of the *Soderini Letter* by Northup (op. cit.), and the review of the current state of the question in R. Levillier, *Américo Vespucci* (Madrid, 1966), 339–62.

Regardless of authorship (or the original meaning), the phrase took on independent power and was widely disseminated, shifting, in time, from a preeminently geographical to a social-political context. See, on this, C. Ginzburg, *The Cheese and the Worms: The Cosmos of a Sixteenth Century Miller* (Baltimore, 1980), 81–86.

In letters subsequent to *Mundus Novus* attributed to Vespucci, the term does not recur. The phrase is dropped in favor of the less suggestive "new lands" in the conventional sense of lands of which there was previously no knowledge. See Levillier, *El nuevo mundo*, 201, 203, 204–5, 233, 251, 259, et passim.

138. Martin Waldseemüller, *Cosmographiae Introductio* (St. Dié, 1507), a iii—facsimile edition by J. Fischer and F. von Weiser (reprint, New York, 1969), xxv. I am aware in giving the traditional attribution, that many authorities consider the *Introductio* to be the work of Matthias Ringmann. See the excellent review of the state of the question by F. Laubenberger, "Ringmann oder Waldseemüller?" *Erdkunde* 13 (1959): 163–79.

139. The first use of the term is in *De Orbe Novo*, 3.1. *Opera*: 105; MacNutt, *De Orbe Novo*, 1: 281, written in 1514. Here, as elsewhere, the term occurs in the dedication. The term appears as the title for the first three books in the Alcala edition of 1516.

140. H. Pérez de Oliva, *Historia de la Invención de las Yndias*, in the edition of J. Juan Arrom (Bogota: 1965), 53–54 as quoted in J. H. Elliott, *The Old World and the New*, 15.

141. *Cosmographiae Introductio*, facsimile edition: xxx, "*et sunt tres prime partes continentes, quarta est insula.*" See above, note 84.

142. In his marginal notations to Columbus's *Journal* of his first voyage, Las Casas frequently comments on Columbus's linguistic limitations. See Vásquez, "Las Casas' Opinions," esp. 53–54.

143. Marañon, *Diario*, 37; Markham, *Journal*, 48.

144. Rarely, Columbus recorded native names for useful or edible species, e.g., *aje, aji, cazave*, although some of these may be interpolations by Las Casas (Vásquez, "Las Casas' Opinions," 51–52). At times, Columbus does recognize difference, but in a somewhat casual manner. For example: "The trees are as unlike ours as night from day, as are the fruits, the stones, and everything. It is true that some of the trees bore some resemblance to those in Castile, but most of them are very different, and some were so unlike that no once could compare them to anything in Castile." Marañon, *Diario*, 38; Markham, *Journal*, 49. See in general L. Hughes, *L'opera scientifica di Cristoforo Colombo* (Turin, 1892).

145. Marañon, *Diario*, 16; Markham, *Journal*, 30.

146. Marañon, *Diario*, 100, cf. 62, 106; Markham, *Journal*, 103, cf. 71, 109. On the significance of this see Menéndez Pidal, "La lengua de Cristóbal Colón," *Bulletin hispanique* 42 (1940): 27 and n.1, criticizing the important essay by L. Olschki, "Il lusignuolo di Colombo," in Olschki, *Storia letteraria delle scoperte geografiche* (Florence, 1937), 11–21. See further, Gerbi, *The Dispute of the New World*, 161, n. 12 and index, s.v. "nightingales."

147. Compare the incident of the nutmegs and cinnamon, Marañon, *Diario*, 58–59; Markham, *Journal*, 67.

148. T. Hawkes, *Shakespeare's Talking Animals* (London, 1973), 211. Barry Holstun Lopez, in his short story, "Restoration," makes effective use of this motif. Lopez, *Winter Count* (New York, 1982), 1–14, esp. 8–12.

149. See the wise comments on the difficulty of establishing criteria for "impact" and "influence" in J. H. Elliott, "Renaissance Europe and America: A Blunted Impact?" in Chiappelli, ed., *First Images of America*, 1: 11–24.

150. This question was made infinitely more complex by the encounter with the "high" civilizations of Mesoamerica. See, for an overview, the important monograph by B. Keen, *The Aztec Image in Western Thought* (New Brunswick, N.J., 1971).

151. See L. E. Huddleston, *Origins of the American Indians: European Concepts, 1492–1729* (Austin, 1967), 8, 110, in the series University of Texas, Latin American Monographs, 11. Huddleston's survey of the topic is the finest to date.

152. For biographical information on Rastell, see A. W. Reed, *Early Tudor Drama* (London, 1926), 1–28, 187–233. For the attempted 1517 voyage, see the summary account in D. B. Quinn, *England and the Discovery of America* (London, 1974), 162–69.

153. The text survives in only a single, imperfect printed copy in the British Museum. It lacks a title page and other introductory material, hence neither its author, date, or place of publication are beyond dispute. The play was first attributed to Rastell in 1557. The attribution has been accepted by all scholars. The date is more controversial. Estimates range from 1517 to 1530, with the majority of scholars suggesting 1519–20.

I have not seen the facsimile edition in the series Tudor Facsimile Texts (London, 1908). I have used the recent edition by R. Axton, *Three Rastell Plays* (Totowa, N.J., 1979), 29–68, esp. 48–52. The more familiar edition is that by J. O. Halliwell, *"The Interlude of the Four Elements": An Early Moral Play* (London, 1848), esp. 27–33, in the series Percy Society: Early English Poetry, Ballads and Popular Literature in the Middle Ages, 22. It is accessible, as well, in E. Arber, ed., *The First Three English Books on America* (Westminster, 1895), xx–xxi. (In 1971, a modernized and abridged form of the play was performed at Cambridge University. See R. E. Coleman, ed., *"The Four Elements" as Performed at the University Printing House* [Cambridge, 1971]; B. Critchley, ed., *Siberch Celebrations, 1521–1971* [Cambridge, 1971], 83–131, esp. 106–11.)

There has been considerable scholarship devoted to the cosmographical elements in the play. See G. P. Park, "The Geography of *The Interlude of the Four Elements*," *Philological Quarterly* 17 (1938): 251–62; M. Borish, "Source and Intention of *The Four Elements*," *Studies in Philology* 35 (1938): 149–63; E. M. Nugent, "The Sources of John Rastell's *The Nature of the Four Elements*," *Publications of the Modern Language Association* 57 (1942): 78–88; G. P. Park, "Rastell and the Waldseemüller Map," *Publications of the Modern Language Association* 58 (1943): 572–74; J. Parr, "More Sources of Rastell's Interlude of the Four Elements," ibid. 60 (1945): 48–58; H. C. Porter, *The Inconstant Savage: England and the North American Indian, 1500–1660* (London, 1979), 34–37.

154. Axton, *Rastell*, 49 (lines 737–38).

155. Axton, *Rastell*, 51 (lines 811–15). Emphasis added.

156. Axton, *Rastell*, 51 (lines 817–19).

157. Huddleston, *Origins*, 15–16.

158. On the encyclopaedic nature of this work, see Enrique Alvarez López, "Plinio y Fernández de Oviedo," *Annales de Ciencias naturales del Instituto J. de Acosta* (Madrid, 1940), 1: 46–61; 2: 13–35; D. Turner, "Oviedo's *Historia*. . . . The First American Encyclopedia," *Journal of Inter-American Studies* 5 (1960): 267–74.

159. Oviedo, *Historia general y natural de las Indias islas y Tierra-Firme del Mar Oceano*, 1st ed. (Seville, 1535) containing the prologue, books 1–19 and book 50.1–10. The bulk of the *Historia* remained in manuscript until the edition of José Amador de los Ríos (Madrid, 1851–55), 1–4. See the careful account of the publication history in D. Turner, *Gonzalo Fernández de Oviedo y Valdés: An Annotated Bibliography* (Chapel Hill, 1966), 7–13. I cite the edition by J. Pérez de Tudela, *Historia general y natural de las Indias* (Madrid, 1959), 1–5, in the series Biblioteca de Autores Españoles, 117–21, which reproduces the 1851–55 text.

160. *Historia*, 2.3; Pérez de Tudela, 1: 17. See Gliozzi, *Adamo e il nuovo mondo*, 247–58. The Carthaginian tradition is based on an altered version of Aristotle, *Mirabiles auscultationes*, 84 (see A. Giannini, *Paradoxographorum Graecorum* [Milan, 1965], 258–9).

161. *Historia*, 2.3; Pérez de Tudela, 1: 17–20. See Gliozzi, *Adamo e il nuovo mondo*, 28–30. This identification is based on the pseudo-Berossus forgeries of Annius of Viterbo, *Commentaria super opera diversorum auctorum de antiquitatibus* (Rome, 1498), on which see D. C. Allen, *The Legend of Noah*, 114–15. Ferdinand Columbus, *Historie*, 10 (Keen: 28–34) responds with heat to both of Oviedo's contentions.

162. Huddleston: 16. Cf. O'Gorman, *La idea del descubrimiento*, 80–3.

163. The most popular version of this thesis identified the new lands with Atlantis. See I. Rodríguez Prampolini, *La Atlántida de Platón en los cronistas del siglo XVI* (Mexico City, 1947); Gliozzi, *Adamo e il nuovo mondo*, 177–246.

164. The first two books of Acosta's *Historia*, those most relevant to our interests, were begun c. 1580 and published in Latin as *De natura novi orbis libri duo* (Salamanca, 1589). Acosta translated these two books into Spanish, added five others, making up the whole, *Historia natural y moral de las Indias*, 1st ed. (Seville, 1590), 2d ed. (Barcelona, 1591), 3d ed. (Madrid: 1608). The *Historia* was translated into Italian, French, Dutch, German, and Latin by 1602. An English version was prepared by E. G. [= Edward Grimston], *The Naturall and Morall Historie of the East and West Indies* (London, 1604). I cite the critical edition by E. O'-Gorman, *Historia natural y moral de las Indias* (Mexico City, 1940); and C. R. Markham's reedition of Grimston's translation, *The Natural and Moral History of the Indies* (London, 1880), 1–2.

165. *Historia*, 1.16; O'Gorman, *Historia*, 61; Markham, *History*, 1:45.

166. *Historia*, 1.20–21; O'Gorman, *Historia*, 75–81; Markham, *History*, 1: 57–64.

167. *Historia*, 1.22–23; O'Gorman, *Historia*, 83–88; Markham, *History*, 1: 64–69

168. *Historia*, 1.24; O'Gorman, *Historia*, 89–90; Markham, *History*, 1: 69–70.

169. In addition to the valuable preface in O'Gorman's edition (reprinted in O'Gorman, *Cuatro historiadores*, 165–248), see Th. Hornberger, "Acosta's *Historia* . . . A Guide to the Source and Growth of the American Scientific Tradition," *University of Texas Studies in English* 19 (1939): 139–62; Gliozzi, *Adamo e il nuovo mondo*, esp. 371–81; Huddleston, *Origins*, 48–59.

170. García, *Origen de los indios de el Neuvo Mundo, e Indias occidentales* (Valencia, 1607). This first edition is exceedingly scarce. The second edition (Madrid, 1729) is most commonly cited. It contains extensive notes by its editor, Andres González de Barcia Carballido y Zúñiga. Unfortunately, these have not always been distinguished from García's words in subsequent scholarship. A facsimile of the second edition has been edited by F. Pease (Mexico City, 1981), in the series Biblioteca Americana. Pease's introduction is of great value. Huddleston, *Origins*, 60–76, gives an overview.

Huddleston's overall conclusion deserves notice. "Two clearly distinguished traditions [as to the origin of the Indians in the period 1492–1729] have emerged from my investigations: the Acostan and the Garcian. The first, marked by a skepticism with regard to cultural comparisons, considerable restraint in constructing theories, and a great reliance on geographical and faunal considerations, is named for Joseph de Acosta, who gave it its earliest clear expression. . . . The Garcian tradition, named for the author of the *Origin de los Indios* . . . is characterized by a strong adherence to ethnological comparisons, a tendency to accept trans-Atlantic migrations, and an acceptance of possible origins as probable ones." Huddleston, *Origins*, 13.

171. The various writings by Lewis U. Hanke have been crucial in gaining perspective on this matter. See, among others, "Pope Paul II and the American Indians," *Harvard Theological Review* 30 (1937), 65–102; *Aristotle and the American Indians* (Chicago, 1959); *The Spanish Struggle for Justice in the Conquest of America* (Boston, 1965).

172. To insist on the importance of the naturalistic materials has been the special contribution of A. Gerbi, *The Dispute of the New World* (Pittsburgh, 1973); and *La natura delle Indie nove: Da Cristoforo Colombo a Gonzalo Fernandez de Oviedo* (Milan, 1975). I have also profited from observations in C. E. Chardon, *Los naturalistas en la américa latina: Los siglos XVI–XVIII* (Cuidad Trujillo, 1949), 1.

173. Oviedo, *De la natural hystoria de las Indias*, 1st ed. (Toledo: 1526), 11—facsimile edition (Chapel Hill, 1969), 37–39; English translation by S. A. Stoudemere, *Natural History of the West Indies* (Chapel Hill, 1959), 47–48. This work, frequently called the *Sumario*, must not be confused with Oviedo's larger and later, *Historia general de las Indias* (see above, note 159). A parallel passage does occur in the *Historia*, 1.12.10, Pérez de Tudela, 2: 39–42, esp. 40.

174. Acosta, *Historia*, 4.19; O'Gorman, *Historia*, 275. The Grimston translation is not useful at this point.

175. Acosta, Historia, 4.36; O'Gorman, *Historia*, 325–26. The Grimston translation is not useful at this point.

176. For an important overview of the present state of the question, see the monograph by A. Laming-Emperaire, *Le problème des origines américaines* (Lille, 1980), in the series Cahiers d'archéologie et d'ethnologie d'Amérique du Sud.

177. For an interesting attempt to describe "relative otherness" with more precision, see E. S. Bogardus, "A Social Distance Scale," *Sociology and Social Research* 17 (1933): 265–71. J. C. Mitchell, *The Kalela Dance* (Manchester, 1956), 22–28, in the series Papers of the Rhodes-Livingstone Institute, 27, has adapted the scale for a tribal context with interesting results for our theme.

178. By emphasizing in separate sections the political and linguistic aspects of a "theory of the other," I do not mean to imply their separation. As is well known, especially in matters of colonialism, the two go hand in hand. This is well illustrated in an incident that has become emblematic for historians of the period. "In 1492, in the introduction to his *Gramática [de la lengua castellana]*, the first grammar of a modern European language, Antonio de Nebrija writes that language has always been the partner [*compañera*] of empire. And in the ceremonial presentation of the volume to Queen Isabella, the bishop of Avila, speaking on the scholar's behalf, claimed a still more central role for language. When the Queen asked flatly, 'What is it [good] for?' the Bishop replied, 'Your Majesty, lan-

guage is the perfect instrument of empire.'" (S. J. Greenblatt, "Learning to Curse: Aspects of Linguistic Colonialism in the Sixteenth Century," in Chiappelli, *First Images of America*, 2: 562). The story is told in a variety of historical works including: J. B. Trend, *The Civilization of Spain* (London: 1944), 88; Hanke, *Aristotle and the American Indian*, 8 and 127, n. 31; Lach, *Asia in the Making of Europe* (Chicago, 1977), 2.3: 504; Todorov, *The Conquest of America*, 123.

179. J. Leighly, "Error in Geography," in J. Jastrow, ed., *The Story of Human Error* (New York, 1938), 92–93.

180. It is in this sense that O'Gorman is quite right to insist on *la invención de América* (see above, note 94). Cf. H. B. Johnson, "New Geographical Horizons: Concepts," in Chiappelli, ed., *First Images of America*, 2: 623, "[in early German reports] the fourth part of the world was always *erfunden* not *endeckt.*"

181. For an important attempt to describe the "grammar" of such discourse, see B. Bucher, *Icon and Conquest: A Structural Analysis of the Illustrations of de Bry's Great Voyages* (Chicago, 1981), 24–45.

182. See, from a quite different perspective, the arguments by F. Barth, introduction, in Barth, ed., *Ethnic Groups and Boundaries: The Social Organization of Cultural Difference* (Boston, 1969), esp. 9–15. Barth's theoretical work is of crucial importance for our topic.

183. While I place no confidence in the probative force of etymological arguments, it is, perhaps, of interest to note that **an*, the hypothetical root of the Germanic-English, "other," contains the notion of duality: the second or other member of a pair, e.g., Anglo-Saxon, *ōder* (J. Pokorny, *Indogermanisches etymologisches Wörterbuch* [Bern-Munich, 1959–69], 1: 37–38). **Al*, the hypothetical root of the Greco-Roman *alien* and the Germanic-English, "else," contains the notion in extended form, the other of more than two (1: 24–26).

184. A. J. Toynbee, *A Study of History* (Oxford, 1961), 12: 11. Cf. the delicious comment in H. W. Turner's *Commentary on Otto's Idea of the Holy* (Aberdeen, 1974), 19, "when Otto describes this experience of the Numen as 'Wholly Other,' he cannot mean *wholly* 'Wholly Other.'"

185. See, however, the stunning exception in the work of the biologist Johannes von Uexküll. In his work (published with the collaboration of the artist G. Krizat), *Streifzüge durch die Umwelten von Tieren und Menschen: Ein Bilderbuch* (Berlin, 1934), he begins with a "tick's eye view of the world" (pp. 1–2, 8–9) and procedes to present several pictures as they would appear *für die Menschen* and *für die Fliege* (fig. 11c [p. 24], fig. 15 [p. 29], fig. 31 [p. 58], fig. 32 [p. 62]).

186. I owe the phrase "micro-adjustment," to C. Lévi-Strauss's formulation of ritual as processes of *micro-péréquation* in *La pensée sauvage* (Paris, 1962), 17.

187. This intimacy is well symbolized by two closely related folk beliefs, that of the "heartworm" carried in each individual's heart from birth; and the worm which serves as "life index," when it dies, its human host dies as well. See, H. Pa-

genstecher, *Vermes* (Leipzig, 1878–93), 1: 38; R. Hoeppli, *Parasites and Parasitic Infections*, 64, 160.

188. C. Linnaeus, *Systema natura*, 10th ed. (Holmiae: 1758) as cited in T. Bendyshe, "On the Anthropology of Linnaeus," *Memoirs of the Anthropological Society of London* 1 (1863–64): 424–25.

189. This has been the special burden of the important monograph by R. L. Meek, *Social Science and the Ignoble Savage* (Cambridge, 1976).

190. This quotation, from the second of John Locke's *Two Treatises of Government*, ed. P. Laslett (New York, 1965), 343, appears as a major theme in Meek, *Social Science*.

CHAPTER THIRTEEN
CLOSE ENCOUNTERS OF
DIVERSE KINDS

Noah sail'd round the Mediterranean in Ten Years, and divided the World
into Asia, Afric and Europe, Portions for his three Sons. America then, it
seems, was left to be his that could catch it.

JOHN LOCKE, *Two Treatises of Government* (1698)

I

To signal at the outset, as Steven Spielberg has done, the indebtedness of
my title, I remind you of the labors of the late Chicago-area professor, J.
Allen Hynek, to put the study of unidentified flying objects (UFOs) on a
scientific basis.[1] In Hynek's typology, "close encounters of the first kind"
are where alien ships are sighted; in the "second kind," the UFOs leave
some physical mark of their presence; "close encounters of the third
kind" are where contacts with the occupants of a UFO are made.[2] It will
be with a variant of the third "kind" with which we shall initially be concerned, considered, recently, by some to be a distinctive new type, "close
encounters of the fourth kind."[3]

Since the fall of 1957, when a Brazilian farmer, Antonio Villas Boas,
reported that a spaceship had landed on his farm, the occupants taking
him aboard and performing a variety of physical acts on him,[4] a specific
mode of American UFO tale has emerged, and found a secure, iconic
place in popular culture: the Abduction Report.[5]

The first North American version was that of Betty and Barney Hill
in the White Mountains of New Hampshire on the evening of September 19, 1961; it was widely disseminated through the television movie,
The UFO Incident, and more recently reconfigured in a characteristically
ingenious fashion in the late, lamented TV series, *Dark Skies.*[6] The Travis

Walton narrative (Arizona, November 1975), recounting his five-day capture, the subject of the Paramount film, *Fire in the Sky*, is, perhaps, best known, having received nationwide media attention.[7] The most developed, all but canonical report, is the Betty Andreasson narrative.[8] The most popular account remains Whitley Strieber's bestseller, *Communion* (1987), presented as an autobiographical recounting of a series of experiences undergone by this well-known writer of horror stories.[9]

In all, by 1987, some 1,200 North American abductions were filed under the name of the abductee; 600 to 700 narratives had been collected; 300 of these were carefully studied by the folklorist, Thomas E. Bullard, with 103 considered by Bullard to be "high information cases."[10] Bullard's comparative studies suggest that there is a persistent structure to Abduction Reports, with the same episodes recurring in invariant order in 80 percent of the "high information" narratives.[11] "A single deviation accounts for failure of sequence in almost all of the remainder."[12] Bullard distinguishes eight episodes.[13] By his own statistics, I would reduce the number to seven.

1. *Capture*. The aliens take the individual aboard a UFO.[14]

2. *Examination*. The aliens subject the individual to both physical and mental tests.[15] The first two episodes, capture and examination, are the most developed segments of the abduction reports. With the obvious addition of the penultimate episode, the return, they recur most frequently and contain the highest degree of repetitive elements.

To elaborate on the examination episode: once aboard, the human is taken to the examination room, a central, circular location, with a dome, dominated by an examination table, and usually lacking all other furniture. The placement of the room suggests that the ship was constructed with examination as its primary purpose. The abductee is stripped, cleaned, and placed on the table where she or he is subjected to a searching physical examination. The first stage is manual; the second, scanning with a mechanical device. Next, various needle-like instruments probe beneath the skin, with specimens of various sorts, especially bodily fluids, being taken. Either the ovaries or the testicles are probed in what seems to be the preoccupation of the examination with the reproductive system. (In one report, a male's examination was terminated and he was abruptly released because he had had a vasectomy). Finally, neurological tests are administered, at times climaxed by the insertion of some sort of miniaturized electronic device in the brain.

Significantly, it is most often in the context of the examination episode that we are given the fullest physical description of the aliens. While more than one hundred types of alien beings have been described in UFO reports and classified in taxonomic studies by Jadar U. Pereira, Eric Zurcher, David Chance, Patrick Huyghe, and Kevin Randle and Russ Estes,[16] most commonly, in North American abduction narratives, they are represented as humanoids, three to five feet tall, with soft gray skin. Popularly referred to as "the Grays," they have large hairless heads with tapering chins. Their eyes are large, extending around the sides of their heads like wraparound sunglasses. Their ears are tiny or absent; the nose and mouth are small holes. Their limbs are thin, with arms that reach to their knees. Their fingers are elongated, with less than five visible digits. Their legs are often short and oddly jointed, producing an awkward gait. They are most often represented as clothed in a neutral-colored, close-fitting garment which appears to be a uniform, at times belted or with a hood. There are usually no discernable sexual characteristics. One alien, in some reports taller than the others, in other reports indistinguishable from the rest, serves as leader and liaison, both directing the examination and communicating with the human, frequently in a reassuring manner.[17]

3. *Conference*. The effects of the examination on the abductee are often described in terms ranging from discomfort and embarrassment to pain and terror consistent with its nature as a rape-like violation of a helpless subject. However, following the examination, the next reported episode is a conference between the aliens and the human, usually by means of telepathic communication, which, without supplying the reasons, claims a shift in attitude by the abductee towards the aliens from fear and hostility to friendly, positive feelings.[18]

Beginning in the mid-1980s, a different sort of narrative has emerged which describes the examination as sexual abuse, often related to an alien project of producing human-alien hybrids. This focus brings about a concomitant decline in the number of reports of a positive conference, the conference often being replaced by a horrified viewing of the hybrid embryos or children.[19]

4. *Tour*. The conference is usually followed by an escorted tour of the ship.[20]

5. *Journey*. The ship then leaves its landing site and conveys the human to a "strange place," usually not identified as the aliens' home base. In a very few cases, a "divine" figure is encountered.[21]

6. *Return*. A necessary part of the narrative structure of the Abduction Report, the return tale is usually quite brief, often reversing the capture sequence. The human is escorted out of the ship, frequently to the place of initial contact, and watches the UFO's departure.[22]

7. *Aftermath*. A distinctive feature of Abduction Reports is that they do not conclude with the reintegration of the abductee into society or the resumption of ordinary life. She or he remains strongly marked by the experience, exhibiting a variety of often puzzling symptoms.[23] Acute thirst and the need to bathe are the most immediate. Later, there will be nightmares, flashbacks, anxiety attacks, and noticeable personality changes, often relieved by remembering the experience under hypnosis. Others report further paranormal experiences, incidents of extrasensory perception, or visions of "men in black," a subtype studied by Peter M. Rojcewicz, which seems to be one of a number of subordinate elements that interpret the abduction experience as demonic. (Note that the recent Columbia-Amblin film, *Men in Black,* has quite inverted the significance of these figures).[24] In a few cases, further abductions, or recollections of previous abductions, are reported.

It will serve little purpose, here, to pause over the question of the truth of these reports or to rehearse the various theories, from the psychoanalytic to the folkloristic, that have been brought to their interpretation.[25] For our reflections, their nature as narratives allow them to be linked with Mark Rose's "paradigm" for science fiction: texts that "are composed within the semantic space created by the opposition of human . . . and non-human,"[26] and our attention is directed to their most elaborated episode and theme, the examination.

It may seem a simple conclusion to assert, with Bullard, that in these narratives, "the examination appears to be the real purpose of the encounter,"[27] and yet, this is quite remarkable. When one reads in the wider UFO literature, and, most particularly, in the alien contact or encounter literature produced by the stunning variety of UFO religions,[28] a variety of other motivations prevail: they are from a superior culture and bring us wisdom; they are from a threatened culture and bring us warning; they are from a dying planet or species that needs something from us; they come to lead; they come to share; they come to give; they come to exploit; they come to punish; they come to replace; they come to destroy. Whatever the scenario, there are interests at stake, be they ours, theirs, or mutual. By contrast, in the Abduction Reports, there are rarely explicit motivations.[29] Rather than interests, there seems only to be interest, or, better, disinterested observation, a curiosity often felt to be prurient by the abductee.

At one level, the Abduction Reports seem to be a modernist version of the literary subgenre, reverse anthropology, well known through texts such as *Gulliver's Travels*. Americans are captured as specimens. They are helpless. They are manipulated (literally) without regard to their feelings as if they were not of the same order as their examiners. The humans are stripped, cleaned, and probed for incomprehensible reasons. Their only acknowledged function is that of providing data. And yet, faithful to the all but pornographic male fantasy of the ethnographic enterprise, the abductees' own emotions at being violated begin with fear and hostility and end with good will. It is only the concluding episode, the aftermath which challenges this dominant scientific romance as the narratives go on to record the aftershocks, the posttraumatic effects of the encounter. Once examined, nothing is (or will be) ever the same again.

While it is tempting to develop these themes into a contemporary fable, one that would invoke a host of images from discipline and panopticons to the ambivalences of postcolonial discourses, something does not fit. Above all, it is the silence—not a lack of communication, but a lack of interrogation.[30] The aliens betray no interest in human culture; and impart nothing of their own. There is no trace of the interspecific, interlocutory agendum of cultural encounter which informs ethnographically sophisticated science fiction novels such as Chad Oliver's *Unearthly Neighbors* (New York, 1960); which underlies the recent essay by Jonathan vos Post, "How to Talk to an Extraterrestrial"[31]; or which was raised at the 1970 Annual Meeting of the American Anthropological Association in their symposium, "The Role of Anthropology in Outer Space."[32] Indeed, as has been noted, while not the explicit subject of the reports, there is a silent, mutual examination of bodies, ours and theirs. It is from a comparison of these bodies that I shall derive my fable for our reflection.

What the aliens seem to be interested in, above all, what they appear to most want to understand, is difference. As their bodies are represented to us in the Abduction Reports, it does not matter whether they are clothed or unclothed; either way they are uniform, neutral gray, with no distinguishing features, whether of physiognomy or status. This uniformity was strikingly replicated in the 1997 collective suicide of the Heaven's Gate group with their erasure of difference by means of identical dress, haircuts, and traveling cases as well as the neutered males, as they awaited transportation to an alien ship hidden behind the Hale-Bopp comet.[33] In the Abduction Reports, the aliens are neither naturally nor culturally marked in any way visible to their human subjects. Their observed activities—search, seize, probe, release—could just as readily and interchangeably be performed by NASA-style robots. In archaic language, they are "protoplasts," "homunculi," existing permanently in this prefor-mative state without any apparent imprinting mechanism to give them characteristics. They lack even the mysterious contagious processes of mimicry, of simulation, by which the protoplasts in the pods in the now thrice-made film, *Invasion of the Body Snatchers*, assume the personal ap-pearance, habits, character, and memory of those human individuals to which they are placed in close proximity. In the Abduction Reports, there is no transfer, only collection; and while there is concentrated interest in the human reproductive system, there are no processes of reproduction.

The aliens' attention to the body, to that which is, at one and the same time, most typical and most individual in any complex species, is an examination of that site at which difference, whether evaluated as natu-ral or cultural, is most immediately apparent. The aliens' preoccupation with probing beneath the surface of the skin, both the human reproduc-tive system and the brain, while ignoring other, equally significant phys-iological systems,[34] is to focus on precisely those systems in which the problematics of difference are most complex and rich in information.

The comparison of bodies, theirs and ours, which underlies the cen-tral episode of the Abduction Reports might be expressed in the technical terminology of classical taxonomy as follows: the aliens' bodies, in their performative uniformity, appear as essential; the humans' bodies, in their variegation, appear as accidental. The fable I want to construct out of the Abduction Reports for our further reflection is one of singularity and di-versity. While the genre of fable requires relative brevity, this very char-acteristic often compels its exegesis and application to take the "long way round." In this case, the detour is necessarily historical, an element in the histories of the western imaginations of difference, which will lead us to isolate the intellectual moment that made the invention of "race" neces-sary—the first, new, influential anthropological theory since the classical period, and one that made urgent the emergence of the human sciences.

II

It is a commonplace to speak of western intellectual history as an in-terrelationship between Athens and Jerusalem. Within the sphere of an-thropological thought, at least through the sixteenth century, it is un-doubtedly true. The biblical account of human origins and subsequent relations, especially the genealogical and territorial map of Genesis 10, was overlaid upon the rich Greek and Roman ethnographic tradition, es-pecially as categorized and transmitted by classical and Christian ency-clopaedists. The resultant system exhibited remarkable flexibility, ever accommodating to new elements. For example, as late as the fifteenth and sixteenth centuries, aided by the pseudo-Berossian forgeries of Annius of Viterbo,[35] new segments were added to both the Noachic genealogies and migrations to account for the origins of the population of all of known Europe, as well as Africa and Asia, as may be seen, for example, in the well-known ninth chapter of Jean Bodin's *Method for the Easy Comprehension of History* (1565).[36]

It was a system that, by its very elasticity, prevented surprise whenever similarities or differences were encountered in the peoples mapped upon it. For the genealogies that underlay the system, as well as the biblical narration of anthropogony, guaranteed the essential unity of humankind. All were children of Adam and Eve, even though their lineages must be traced through Noah's three sons: Shem, Japhet, and Ham. Differences were, therefore, accidental. Drawing upon Greek and Roman theories, these were explained by the effects of climate, especially for somatic characteristics, and as the results of migration or diffusion for cultural divergencies. Similarities and differences were perceived as having documentary characteristics, allowing the mapping of spatial and temporal associations. Adopting the archaic Christian apologetic language for the relations of Christianity to classical culture, a notion of anthropologically significant survivals was developed in which the Christian scholar sought "seeds," "sparks," "traces," "footprints," "remains," or "shadows" of the original, essential unity of humankind amidst its palpable, contemporary diversity, and through which one could discern placement and reconstruct historical relations.[37]

Take, for example, the encounter with the Mongols (or, Tartars) in the thirteenth and fourteenth centuries, the occasion for the first new ethnography in the west since Roman times. Older Christian pseudo-Sibylline oracles were updated to place the Mongols within the framework of an apocalyptic scenario that associated them with the Scythians, one of the borderlines of humanity on the old Herodotean ethnographic map, and, through them, with the release of the feared, biblical tribes of Gog and Magog, walled in by Alexander the Great in Jewish and Christian versions of the *Alexander Romance*.[38] In support of this, a new version of the pseudepigraphical *Letter of Alexander to Aristotle Concerning the Wonders of India* was produced, proclaiming the presence of apocalyptic trials and associating them with the advent of the Mongols.[39] Other initial reports of the Mongol incursions displayed more positive biblical placements: the first notice (1221) identified Genghis Khan with King David,[40] while the Hungarian Dominican, Brother Julian (1238), as well as the *Alexander to Aristotle* letter, declared them to be "sons of Ishmael."[41] An interpolation into a set of fourteenth-century French manuscripts of *Mandeville's Travels*, confusing Khan and (C)ham, connected the Mongols with the Noachic Hamitic lineage.[42] The Mongols were hitherto unknown to the west, but their presence constituted no surprise; they could be classified as another "remnant" of biblical ethnography. The literature on the Mongols, taken as a whole, demonstrates the power of the amalgamation of the Greco-Roman ethnographic tradition and the biblical. Even in times of extreme distress and military conflict, the flexibility of the system proved able to assimilate new elements while holding the map intact. Differences remained in the realm of accident; similarities in that of essence.

I know of no serious challenge to this interpretative system until the post-Columbian debates over the nature of the Americas. It is here, for the first time, that a strong language of alterity emerges. America is an "other world," a "new world."[43] I shall not take time, here, to review the slow and difficult history of this perception,[44] but pause only to note that, as such, the American continent was a world wholly unknown to either the Greco-Roman or the biblical authors. In that regard, both sets of writings were irrevocably impeached. True, the Noachic model was reexamined, including the suggestion that there were two Arks, one that re-populated the familiar three-lobed world island of Africa, Europe, and Asia, a second that sailed, with its cargo of quite different species, to the new world[45]—an hypothesis most likely based on an observation of the effects of interweaving the so-called "J" and "P" Flood narratives, which, among other doublets, results in Noah, his family, and the animals entering the Ark twice (Genesis 7:7–9[J]/Genesis 7:13–15[P]).

Other authorities expanded the migratory model in the face of the dilemma created by Noah having three rather than four sons. For example, in Gregorio García's enormous encyclopaedic work *Origin of the Indians of the New World and the West Indies* (1st ed., 1607), theories that the Americas were populated by Jews, Carthaginians, Greeks, Romans, Phoenicians, Egyptians, Africans, Ethiopians, French, Cambrians, Finns, Frisians, or Scythians are reviewed.[46] As an appendix to this naval, Noachic, transatlantic catalog, another possibility is raised, returning to the original Columbian misidentification of the native Americans as "Indians," but, in fact, now a correct understanding, that the Americas were populated by an overland migration of Chinese or, more likely, Mongols.[47] Once this theory was isolated and disseminated, most famously by Edward Brerewood's *Enquiries Touching the Diversity of Languages, and Religions through the Chiefe Parts of the World* (1614)[48] and by John Ogilby's *America, Being the Latest, and most Accurate Description of the New World* (1671),[49] the old genealogical enterprise was resumed as to the Noachic genealogy of the Mongols, with descent from Japhet now being the most frequently argued connection.[50] But the haunting and shattering conclusion could not be long avoided; the elasticity of the old system finally proved insufficiently flexible. The Americas were a novelty that resisted absorption. There were no "traces." The native Americans were untraceable. The "new world" was not merely newly discovered, it was not merely different, it was "other" in its very essence—a radical conclusion first and more readily made with respect to its flora and fauna. Thus Acosta (1590), in a passage much discussed in seventeenth-century works on the implications of America for biblicist anthropology:

> What I say of the *guanacos* and *pacos* I will say of a thousand varieties of birds and fowls [in the Americas] that have never been known [previously] by either name or appearance, nor is there any memory of them in the Latins or Greeks, nor in any nations of our [European] world over here. . . . It is well to ask whether these animals differ in kind and essence from all others, or if this difference be accidental. . . . But, to speak bluntly, anyone who in this way would focus only on the accidental differences, seeking thereby to explain [away] the propagation of the animals of the Indies and to reduce them [to variants] of the European, will be undertaking a task he will not be able to fulfill. For, if we are to judge the species of animals [in the Americas] by their [essential] properties, they are so different that to seek to reduce them to species known to Europe will mean having to call an egg a chestnut.[51]

This radical zoological conclusion could even be deployed analogically in seventeenth-century arguments for extraterrestrial life, as in Otto von Guericke (1672): "Anyone who would deny the presence of living creatures on the planets because he is not capable of imagining any creatures other than those he sees here on earth should know that in America there is no wild animal of exactly the same kind as in Europe, Asia or Africa."[52]

The zoological and botanical discoveries of essential difference with respect to the Americas foreshadowed the same sort of revision within anthropology. The novelty and the alterity of the Americas introduced surprise.

III

It is in the context of this disarray with respect to the centuries-old amalgam that a previously refused resource within theories associated with Greco-Roman ethnography was recovered and resituated at the center of the European anthropological enterprise. The biblical narrative, and, therefore, western ethnologic theory was, up to this point, relentlessly monogenetic. There was a single ancestral pair from whom all humankind descended; there was a single locus, traditionally understood as somewhere in the Armenian mountains, from which all the intrafamilial diversities of humankind ultimately diffused. However, such an account could not be sustained if, as the novelty and the alterity of the Americas suggested, difference was an affair of essence rather than of accident.

Deep within the Greco-Roman theories of migration and diffusion, mixture and borrowing, climate and ecology as the explanations for cultural similarities and differences, a second, oppositional structure coexisted that emphasized immobility and originality: that of autochthony.[53] While best known as an Athenian political topos (autochthony equals autonomy), the notion, more widely applied as in emergence myths, suggested not only that some people were sprung from the very soil they inhabit, but implied, as well, plurality of places of origination. Rejected by the monogenetic presuppositions of the biblically oriented Christian anthropology, autochthony was a theory of polygenesis.

Even at the present time, when we have returned to a Darwinian rather than a biblical notion of monogenesis, the concept of polygenesis persists in some of our most common ethnic designations: "aborigine" (classically understood as the Latin equivalent of autochthony), a people who has been in this or that place from their beginning; "indigenous," "creole," and "native," a people first born (or, created) in the place they inhabit. Ironically, these terms in colonialist discourse shifted from expressing their firstness to ours, becoming a designation of the inhabitants found in a place when we first "discovered" it.

Some scholars find anticipations of polygenetic theory in the Renaissance hermeticists, especially Paracelsus and Bruno.[54] The scattered references are far from clear and seem to reflect speculations about spontaneous generation. By the seventeenth century, these hints would be fully developed. One of the earlier, unambiguous polygenetic accounts of the Americas is by an anonymous author, L. P., Master of Arts, in a work entitled *Two Essays, Sent in a Letter from Oxford, to a Nobleman in London* (1695):

> The West Indies and the vast regions lately discovered towards the South abound with such a variety of inhabitants and new animals not known or even seen in Asia, Africa or Europe that the origin of them doth not appear so clear . . . especially seeing

that there are no records or monuments of their migrations out of Asia or any other known parts of the world, either before or after the Flood; and their differences from all the rest of the Globe, in manners, languages, habits, religions, diets, arts and customs as well as in their quadrupeds, birds, serpents and insects, render their derivation very obscure and their origin uncertain, especially in the common [biblicist] way and according to the vulgar opinion of planting all the earth from one little spot. [In their] great zeal to maintain a Jewish tradition . . . every corner of the earth is searched to find out a word, a rite, or a custom in order to derive from thence many millions of different peoples. . . . [But] all nations agree in some words and in some customs, therefore a resemblance in a few of them is no proof. . . . I can see no way at present to solve this new face of nature by old arguments fetched from Eastern rubbish or rabbinical weeds. . . . Let them all [i.e., the new world humans, flora, and fauna] be *aborigines*.[55]

Although L. P.'s essay was not widely circulated, it contains, *in nuce*, the paradigmatic logic of the polygenetic argument: (1) given the utter novelty of the Americas, (2) the biblical account must be rejected (here the rejection contains an anti-Semitic element), (3) as must be the quest for "traces"; (4) the solution is that the life forms of the Americas are autochthonous: "let them all be *aborigines*."

The polythetic logic had already been fully elaborated in its theological rather than its anthropological implications in one of the most controversial and widely known works of the seventeenth century, Isaac de La Peyrère's books collectively entitled *Prae-Adamitae* ("The Preadamites," 1655; English translation, *Men before Adam*, 1656).[56]

Peyrère represents that longstanding fear of Catholicism, the lay Bible reader. He tells us that he has spent twenty years pondering Romans 5:12–14, the classic Augustinian and Reformation proof text for original sin, itself a monogenetic notion.[57] On the basis of the phrases "sin was not imputed when the Law was not" and "even over those whose sin was not like the transgression of Adam," he concluded that "sin was in the world before Adam" although "it was not imputed until Adam." Therefore, there were many sorts of humans before Adam; Adam was not the ancestor of humankind.

With this established, he turns to an exegesis of the opening chapters of Genesis. Genesis 1.26–27 shows that God created, by the power

of the Word, vast numbers of humans (i.e., Gentiles) just as the deity created all of the different sorts of animals and plants. Genesis 2 records the
special creation of Adam, the first Jew, out of clay. Turning his attention
to a set of well-known conundrums, Peyrère notes that the Cain and
Abel story indicates the presence of numerous other peoples: If the
brothers were farmers and shepherds, who made the knife that killed
Abel? Where did Cain's wife come from? Who are the others who would
kill Cain? Who inhabited the cities that "covered" the world at that time?

More generally, he asserts, the Jewish biblical chronology is strictly
limited. It comprises no more than some 5,000 years. But Peyrère knows
of older histories: the Chaldaeans record 470,000 years of history, the
Mexicans and Peruvians write of thousands of suns, and Chinese history
extends back 880,000 years.

Drawing upon the biblical criticism of his friend Richard Simon,
Peyrère then argues that Moses wrote an epitome of earlier records at a
comparatively late date. In Genesis 1–11, Moses compressed a series of
long works into several brief chapters, being more interested in his own
time than in prehistory. Thus, Moses was being no more than hyperbolic
when he declared Adam to be the first human rather than the first Jew;
the Flood was a limited phenomenon, confined to parts of Palestine
which were easily repopulated by Noah's three sons. Hence all parallels
between the biblical account and other cultures are merely superficial.

The polygenetic accounts of L. P. and Peyrère in principle freed anthropology from its biblical framework. The Bible was reduced to a
parochial document, the history of the Jews of a relatively early period.
It was no longer to be understood as the universal history of humankind.
Human diversity now became an urgent intellectual problem. While
these radical conclusions would be debated throughout the seventeenth
and eighteenth centuries, they contributed to the formation of the first,
new western theory for explaining human similarities and differences,
the theory of race, the possibility that the genus *homo* might be divided
by essential rather than accidental characteristics into separate species of
differing lineages—a possibility first put forth by François Bernier in an
article in the *Journal des Savants*, April 24, 1684.[58]

It was neither Orientals nor Blacks, who had long been mapped on
the old Greco-Roman and biblical taxonomy, that gave rise to the intellectual problematics of race. Rather it was the unanticipated presence of
native Americans, a surprise of profound implication, rendered even
more certain once it was clear beyond doubt, post-Magellan, that America was not a part of Asia.

IV

To expand fully on the history of race theories and polygenesis would require a lengthy study, recalling the judgment of George Stocking, Jr.: "It seems fair to say that polygenism—or more broadly the problem of race—was the central concern of pre-Darwinian anthropology."[59] I can, here, give only a few conclusions, shorn of their necessary historical narratives which would, among other matters, have to trace the development of two complex terms and ideas, the new sixteenth-century coinage, "race," and an old term, now reconfigured, "species."

Simply put, monogenesis celebrated similarity; polygenesis, diversity—the latter leading, for the first time, to the development of a complex vocabulary for describing and explaining difference, limited by the unfortunate eighteenth-century decision to correlate biological and cultural characteristics. From the point of view of difference, with respect to biology, the intellectual choice was whether to understand the human "races" as "varieties" (i.e., accidents) or "species" (i.e., essences). If difference was understood to be accidental, a monogenetic account could be fashioned where difference was accounted for by environmental and historical causes. If difference was understood to be essential, then a polygenetic account which held the races to be irreducible was required. From the point of view of similarity, with respect to culture, a monogenetic account would need to refurbish the old language of diffusion and derivation. A polygenetic theory would have to emphasize parallel, independent development. In the biological language introduced by Richard Owen in the nineteenth century, for monogenetic approaches, cultural resemblances would be "homologies"; for polygenetic approaches, they would be "analogies."[60] From these choices, combined with questions of hierarchy, a necessary component in any classical taxonomic enterprise, one can generate the central debates that dominated eighteenth- and nineteenth-century anthropological discourse and, still, to a large degree, rule popular perceptions, processes, and notions of cross-cultural comparison.

Having undertaken a historical detour, we can return to the Alien Abduction Reports. The central episode, the examination, appears to be a displacement onto "them" of our popular notion for understanding human difference as chiefly an affair of bodies, as being only "skin deep." The uniformity of their bodies, in contradistinction to the differentiation of ours, is a striking exaggeration of our common-sense belief, derived from the Greco-Roman and biblical amalgam, that there is an essential core of human sameness and, therefore, that difference is accidental, transferred, in the narratives, to the imagination of an unambiguously polygenetic situation: alien and human. But in the examination episode it is the silence that remains, be it expressed in the lack of either the interrogative or the indicative with respect either to the aliens' culture or to ours, or in the lack of recognition of the problematics of communication, within and between cultures, let alone across phyla, expressed in the reports as the aliens' too ready use of English or extralinguistic mental telepathy.

To this one must respond, whether with respect to popular belief or professional procedure, that the issue of human differentiation will not be settled by more observation at the somatic level, but rather by theories of an intellectual sort. It will not be settled by taxonomies of differential exclusion but by comparative structures of reciprocal difference. It will be settled, at the level of culture, only by thoughtful projects of mediated discourse, by enterprises of translation, recalling that, whether intracultural or intercultural, translation is never fully adequate, there is always discrepancy. *Traduttori traditori*. And that, therefore, central to any proposal of translation are questions as to appropriateness or "fit," expressed through the double methodological requirement of comparison and criticism. As Isaiah Berlin framed it, in the course of one of his meditations on Vico: "In a sense, the mere existence of an extraordinary variety of very dissimilar languages . . . is itself an index or, one might say, a model of the irreducible variety of human self-expression, such that even in the case of cognate languages, complete translation of one into any other is in principle impossible; and the gap—indicative of difference in ways of perceiving and acting—is at times very large indeed."[61] To which I need only add that in culture as in language, it is difference that generates meaning.

The novelty of the Americas gave the west its first compelling language of difference, shattering, thereby, the older synthetic theory of essence and accident. We have yet to set forth a set of equally compelling cultural and comparative theories adequate to this new language. This remains, today, the unfulfilled challenge to the human sciences.

Notes

1. J. A. Hynek, Epilogue in S. Spielberg, *Close Encounters of the Third Kind* (New York, 1977), 253–56.

2. J. A. Hynek, *The UFO Experience: A Scientific Inquiry* (New York, 1974), 31–34, et passim; Hynek, Epilogue, 253–54.

3. The terminology gained some currency by its inclusion in the glossary of A. Pritchard, D. E. Pritchard, J. E. Mack, P. Kasey, and C. Yapp, eds., *Alien Discussions: Proceedings of the Abduction Study Conference held at MIT, Cambridge,*

MA (Cambridge, Mass., 1994), 680: "CE-IV is not part of Hynek's original classification but is used to mean abduction by entities." C. D. B. Bryan entitled his
account of the conference *Close Encounters of the Fourth Kind: Alien Abduction,
UFOs, and the Conference at M.I.T.* (New York, 1995). In fact, the new terminology was little used in the published proceedings. My understanding of the abduction narrative is echoed by David Webb at the conference, "We have a huge
catalogue of CE-III cases of which the abduction cases are a subset" (Pritchard et
al., *Alien Discussion*, 99).

4. G. Creighton, "The Amazing Case of Antonio Villas Boas," in *The Humanoids*, ed. C. Bowen, 200–38 (Chicago, 1969); C. and J. Lorenzen, *Encounters
with UFO Occupants* (New York, 1976), 61–87; K. Randle and R. Estes, *Faces of
the Visitors: An Illustrated Reference to Alien Contact* (New York, 1997), 133–41.
As Boas's reported experience included compelled sexual intercourse, it more
closely resembles a later stage in the development of abduction narratives (see below, n. 19).

5. See T. E. Bullard's classic work, *UFO Abductions: The Measure of a
Mystery*, vol. 1, *Comparative Study of Abduction Reports*, vol. 2, *Catalogue of Cases*
(Mount Rainier, MD, 1987). He gives a general definition of the Abduction Report as a narrative where a "witness is captured and held in unwilling temporary
detention by extraordinary and apparently alien beings usually aboard a flying
craft of unconventional design and usually for purposes something like a medical
examination" (1: vii). See below, for Bullard's description of typical plot elements.

6. J. G. Fuller, *The Interrupted Journey* (New York, 1968) is the richest account, widely known through its abridged serialization, "Aboard a Flying Saucer,"
Look, October 4, 1966, 44–48, 53–56; October 18, 1966, 111–21. The television
film, *The UFO Incident*, first aired on NBC, October 20, 1975. See further the important synoptic treatment of the Hill narratives in Bullard, *UFO Abductions*, 2:
79–93.

7. T. Walton, *The Walton Experience* (New York, 1979).

8. R. E. Fowler, *The Andreasson Affair* (Englewood Cliffs, NJ, 1979); Fowler,
The Andreasson Affair, Phase Two (Englewood Cliffs, NJ, 1982).

9. W. Strieber, *Communion: A True Story* (New York, 1987). Strieber's narratives have continued in a series, from *Transformation: The Breakthrough* (New
York, 1988) to *Confirmation: The Hard Evidence of Aliens among Us* (New York,
1998). Strieber's relations with the wider UFO community have become increasingly tense. See the account by S. Casteel, "Q&A: Strieber Sounds Off," *UFO* 8:
5 (1993): 20–23.

10. Bullard's works, since his dissertation, "Mysteries in the Eye of the Beholder: UFO's and Their Correlates as a Folkloric Theme Past and Present"
(Ph.D. diss., [Indiana University, 1982]), have been central. In addition to his
foundational study, *UFO Abductions*, also summarized in Bullard, *On Stolen Time:*

A Summary of a Comparative Study of the UFO Mystery (Mount Rainier, Md., 1987), see, among others, "UFO Abduction Reports: The Supernatural Kidnap Narrative Returns in Technological Disguise," *Journal of American Folklore* 102 (1989): 147–70; "Hypnosis and UFO Abductions: A Troubled Relationship," *Journal of UFO Studies*, n.s. 1 (1989): 3–40; "Folkloric Dimensions of the UFO Phenomenon," *Journal of UFO Studies*, n.s. 3 (1991): 1–57; as well as his several contributions in Pritchard et al., *Alien Discussions*, "A Comparative Study of Abduction Reports: Update," (45–48), "The Rarer Abduction Episodes," (72–74), "The Well-Ordered Abduction: Pattern or Mirage" (81–82), "The Variety of Abduction Beings" (90–91), "The Relation of Abduction Reports to Folklore Narratives" (389–92), and "Addendum: The Influence of Investigators on UFO Abduction Reports: Results of a Survey" (571–619; on the latter, cf. Bullard, *The Sympathetic Ear: Investigators as Variables in UFO Abduction Reports* [Mount Rainier, Md., 1995]).

11. Bullard, "Folkloric Dimensions," 23; Bullard, *UFO Abductions*, 1: 52–57.

12. Bullard, *UFO Abductions*, 1: 47–57, et passim; Bullard, "UFO Abduction Reports," 153–54.

13. Bullard, *UFO Abductions*, 1: 58–63.

14. Bullard, *UFO Abductions*, 1: 58–63. Bullard distinguishes four subelements in this segment of the narrative. (a) Alien intrusion by the UFO. (b) Entry into a "zone of strangeness" where ordinary physical laws seem suspended. (c) A time lapse in which the individual becomes, in some way, mentally impaired. Most frequently expressed as amnesia, it remains a curious (and troubling) feature of the abduction experience that the majority of them have been recovered under hypnosis. (See Bullard, "Hypnosis and UFO Abductions"). (d) The actual procurement of the individual is often described as a series of events: a beam of light strikes the individual, pulling him or her toward the ship; aliens approach and a brief conversation, by speech or telepathy, follows that pacifies the subject who is then escorted (frequently "floated") to the ship. If there has not been a previous impairment of the faculties, the abductee often experiences "doorway amnesia" upon entering the craft, which is usually described as the familiar "flying saucer." Inside, there is uniform antiseptic lighting with no visible source. Temperatures are cold; the atmosphere is misty and it is difficult to breathe. Doors open and close without apparent seams. See, now, B. Hopkins "The Abduction Experience: Acquisition," in Pritchard et al., *Alien Discussions*, 49–52, which reflects the shift, in the later phase of Abduction Reports, from outdoors to the subject's bedroom. See the perceptive remarks on this shift in J. Dean, *Aliens in America: Conspiracy Cultures from Outerspace to Cyberspace* (Ithaca, NY, 1998): 100–1.

15. Bullard, *UFO Abductions*, 1: 81–103. Compare the section, "Medical Examination and Subsequent Procedures," in Pritchard et al., *Alien Discussions*, 53–64.

16. J. U. Pereira, "Les Extra-Terrestres," *Phénomènes spatiaux*, special issue 2 (1974); E. Zurcher, *Les apparitions d'humanoides* (Nice, 1979); P. Huyghe, *The Field Guide to Extraterrestrials* (New York, 1996); D. Chance, *A Visual Guide to Alien Beings* (n.p., 1996); K. Randle and R. Estes, *Faces of the Visitors*. Cf. Bullard, *UFO Abductions*, 1: 239; D. M. Jacobs et al., "Descriptions of Aliens," in Pritchard et al., *Alien Discussions*, 86–99.

17. Bullard, *UFO Abductions*, 1: 238–99.

18. Bullard, *UFO Abductions*, 1: 104–11.

19. The sexual-abuse narrative provides the focus of works such as B. Hopkins, *Intruders: The Incredible Visitations at Copley Woods* (New York, 1987); D. M. Jacobs, *Secret Life: Firsthand Accounts of UFO Abductions* (New York, 1992); Jacobs, *The Threat: The Secret Alien Agenda* (New York, 1997); and J. E. Mack, *Abduction: Human Encounters with Aliens* (New York, 1994); and it was a major component in the reports and discussions at the 1992 M.I.T. Abduction Conference, see Pritchard et al., *Alien Discussions*, esp. D. M. Jacobs, "Subsequent Procedures," (64–68); C. D. B. Bryan, *Close Encounters of the Fourth Kind*, 17–20 et passim. As articulated in the pithy comment of J. Dean, *Aliens in America*: 101: "Rather than an outside event, happening mostly to men on the road . . . in the early sixties and . . . in the seventies, abduction in the late eighties happens inside, in bedrooms." See the few instances of this element in earlier reports in Bullard, *UFO Abductions*, 1: 91–92, 350–60; 2: 66–75.

20. Bullard, *UFO Abductions*, 1: 111–12.

21. Bullard, *UFO Abductions*, 1: 112–17. Bullard classifies the encounter with a divine being as a sixth separate episode (1: 117–18). On the basis of his statistics, it is uncommon enough to be subsumed as a component in the journey episode.

22. Bullard, *UFO Abductions*, 1: 63–66.

23. Bullard, *UFO Abductions*, 1: 143–73.

24. P. M. Rojcewicz, "The 'Men in Black' Experience and Tradition: Analogues with the Traditional Devil Hypothesis," *Journal of American Folklore* 100 (1987): 148–60. Compare the novel by S. Perry, based on the screenplay by E. Solomon, *Men in Black* (New York, 1997), which represents the Men in Black as a government agency dedicated to tracking down, regulating, and/or destroying alien life forms disguised as humans.

25. See the review of the literature in Bullard, "Folkloric Dimensions."

26. M. Rose, *Alien Encounters: Anatomy of Science Fiction* (Cambridge, Mass., 1981), 31–32.

27. Bullard, "UFO Abduction Reports," 157. This has been a persistent theme in Bullard's work; see *UFO Abductions*, 1: 90: "the examination is the major goal of the abduction, perhaps its only goal"; 1: 358: "examinations are the heart of abductions"; see further, 1: 122–23, 354 et passim.

28. For a valuable overview, see the collection, J. R. Lewis, ed., *The Gods Have Landed: New Religions from Other Worlds* (Albany, 1995).

29. A few narratives do give reasons comparable to those listed above (Bullard, *UFO Abductions*, 1: 108–9, 123, 125–26, 136–38), but they are a distinct minority. The narratives of sexual abuse (see above, note 19) often provide hybridization as a rationale.

30. Bullard, *UFO Abductions*, 1: 110–11, 119–20.

31. J. vos Post, "How To Talk to an Extraterrestrial," in B. Fawcett, ed., *Making Contact: A Serious Handbook for Locating and Communicating with Extraterrestrials* (New York, 1998), 54–98.

32. M. Maruyama and A. Harkin, eds., *Cultures beyond the Earth: The Role of Anthropology in Outer Space* (New York, 1975).

33. I rely on contemporary news reports. It should be noted that the Heaven's Gate group, under a variety of names, had been active with respect to UFO mythology since 1973, and had been well studied by sociologists since 1975. See R. W. Balch, "Waiting for the Ships: Disillusionment and the Revitalization of Faith in Bo and Peep's UFO Cult," in Lewis, *The Gods Have Landed*, 137–86, and the bibliography by J. G. Melton and G. M. Eberhart, 275–76.

34. Bullard, *UFO Abductions*, 1: 90–91.

35. Johannes Annius of Viterbo, *Commentaria super opera diversorum auctorum de antiquitatibus* (Rome, 1498). See the discussion of this work in D. C. Allen, *The Legend of Noah* (Urbana, 1963), 114–16, and, at greater length, in W. Stephens, *Giants in Those Days: Folklore, Ancient History, and Nationalism*, Regents Studies in Medieval Culture (Lincoln, Neb., 1989).

36. Jean Bodin, *Methodus ad facilem historiarum cognitionem* (1565), in the English translation by B. Reynolds, *Method for the Easy Comprehension of History by Jean Bodin* (New York, 1969), 334–64.

37. See further, M. T. Hodgen, *The Doctrine of Survivals: A Chapter in the History of Scientific Method in the Study of Man* (London, 1936).

38. R. E. Lerner, *The Powers of Prophecy: The Cedar of Lebanon Vision from the Mongol Onslaught to the Dawn of the Enlightenment* (Berkeley, 1983), 9–24 et passim. For the Gog-Magog traditions, see A. R. Anderson, *Alexander's Gate, Gog and Magog, and the Enclosed Nations* (Cambridge, Mass., 1932; vol. 12 in the series Publications Medieval Academy of America), esp. 58–86.

39. Lerner, *Powers of Prophecy*, 12, n. 5, referring to an unpublished text, MS UB Innsbruck 187 (fol. 8r–v).

40. F. Zarnacke, *Der Priester Johannes* (Leipzig, 1879–83), 4–59. Note that King David, while understood as a "recirculation" of the biblical figure, is here identified as the son of Prestor John.

41. G. A. Bezzola, *Die Mongolien in abendlandischer Sicht, 1220–1270* (Bern, 1974), 41–43.

42. For example, Fitzwilliam Additional MS 23, fols. 144–45, in J. B. Fried-man, *The Monstrous Races in European Art and Thought* (Cambridge, Mass., 1981), 102–3 and 237, n. 68. See also, M. Letts, ed., *Mandeville's Travels: Texts and Translations* (London, 1953), 1: 154–55.

43. See the useful collection of the terminology of novelty in K. Kretschmer, *Die Entdeckung Amerika's in ihrer Bedeutung für die Geschichte des Weltbildes* (Leipzig, 1892), 360–69.

44. See my discussion of this, with the essential bibliography, in J. Z. Smith, "What a Difference a Difference Makes," (1985), reprinted in this volume.

45. See the critique of this view of an *"otra Arca de Noé,"* in José de Acosta, *Historia natural y moral de las Indias* (Seville, 1590), book 1, chapter 16, in the edition of E. O'Gorman (Mexico City, 1962), 45.

46. G. García, *Origen de los Indios de el Nuevo Mundo e Indias occidentales*, 1st ed. (Valencia, 1607); 2d ed., ed. A. Gonzalez de Barcia (Madrid, 1729). I cite the reprint of the second edition, edited by F. Pease (Mexico City, 1981), 41–308.

47. García, *Origen*, 239–48, 315.

48. E. Brerewood, *Enquiries Touching the Diversity of Languages, and Religions through the Chiefe Parts of the World* (London, 1614), 96–102.

49. J. Ogilby, *America, Being the Latest, and most Accurate Description of the New World* (London, 1671), 35–42.

50. See, among others, A. Tornielli, *Annales sacri, ab orbe condito ad ipsum Christi Passione repartum, praecipus ethicorum temporibus apte ordinateque dispositi* (Milan, 1610), 2: 239; A. de la Calancha, *Cronica moralizada de la Orden de San Augustin en el Perù* (Barcelona, 1639), 1: 41–46.

51. Acosta, *Historia natural y moral*, IV.36 in O'Gorman, 202–3. For its use in debates, see, among others, Matthew Hale, *The Primitive Organization of Mankind, considered and examined according to the Light of Nature* (London, 1677), 198–201.

52. Otto von Guericke, *Experimenta nova (ut vocantur) Magdeburgica de Vacuo spatio* (1672; reprint, Aalen, 1962), 216, as cited in K. S. Guthke, *The Last Frontier: Imagining Other Worlds from the Copernican Revolution to Modern Science Fiction* (Ithaca, NY, 1990), 178.

53. The classic study remains that of N. Loraux, "L'Autochthonie: Une topique athénienne," *Annales, Economies, Sociétés, Civilisations* 34 (1979): 3–26, English translation, N. Loraux, *The Children of Athena* (Princeton, 1993), 37–71. See further, E. Montanari, *Il mito dell'autoctonia* (Rome, 1981); V. J. Rosivach, "Autochthony and the Athenians," *Classical Quarterly* 81 (1987): 294–306.

54. For example, Paracelsus, *Astronomia magna* (1537–38), in K. Sudoff and W. Mattiessen, eds., *Paracelsus: Sämtliche Werke* (Munich, 1922–33), 12: 35, 114, 469. Giordano Bruno, *De immenso, innumerabilibus et infigurabilibus* (1590) in F. Fiorentino et al., eds., *Jordani Bruno Nolani. Opera latine conscripta* (Naples, 1879–86), 1.2: 282.

55. L. P., Master of Arts, *Two Essays, Sent in a Letter from Oxford, to a Noble-man in London. The First, concerning some Errors about the Creation, General Flood, and the Peopling of the World. In Two Parts. The Second, concerning the Rise, Progress, and Destruction of Fables and Romances. With the State of Learning* (London, 1695), reprinted in J. Somers, *A Third Collection of scarce . . . Tracts* (London, 1751), 3: 291–308 (reprint, London, 1814). I follow the convenient reprint of extracts from the latter in J. S. Slotkin, *Readings in Early Anthropology* (New York, Viking Fund Publications, 40, 1965): 82–83. Another reprint of the relevant passages may be found in T. Bendyshe, *The History of Anthropology* (London, 1865): 365–71 (same as *Memoirs of the Anthropological Society of London* 1 [1863–64]: 335–458). See the polemic rejoinder by J. Harris, *Remarks on some late Papers (by L.P.) relating to the Universal Deluge* (London, 1697). The only extended treatment of this important essay is G. Gliozzi, *Adamo e il nuovo mondo* (Florence, 1976), 585–93.

56. Isaac de La Peyrère, *Prae-Adamitae, sive Exercitatio super Verbibus duodecimo, decimotertio et decimoquartyo, capitia quinti Epistolae D. Pauli ad Romanos. Quibus inducuntur Primi Homines ante Adamum conditi* (n.p. [Amsterdam], 1655); anonymous English translation, *Men before Adam. Or a Discourse upon the twelfth, thirteenth, and fourteenth Verses of the fifth Chapter of the Epistle of the Apostle Paul to the Romans. By which are Prov'd that the first Men were created before Adam* (London, 1656). See further, D. Pastine, "La origini del poligenismo e Isaac La Peyrère," *Miscellanea Seicento*, Instituto di Filosofia della Facolta di Lettere e Filosofia dell' Universita di Genova, 1 (1971): 7–234; R. H. Popkin, *Isaac la Peyrère, 1596–1676* (Leiden, 1987), with rich bibliography.

57. Hence Pius XII's attack on polygenesis, along with other modern scientific theories, in the encyclical, *Humani Generis*, August 12, 1950.

58. F. Bernier, "Une nouvelle division de la Terre d'après les différentes espèces des races d'hommes qui l'habitent," *Journal des Savants* (April 24, 1684).

59. G. W. Stocking, Jr., *Race, Culture and Evolution: Essays in the History of Anthropology* (New York, 1968), 40.

60. R. Owen, *Lectures on the Comparative Anatomy and Physiology of the Invertebrate Animals* (London, 1843). See further, E. R. Lankester, "On the Use of the Term Homology in Modern Zoology, and the Distinction between Homogenetic and Homoplastic Agreements," *Annals and Magazine of Natural History* 6 (1870): 34–43.

61. I. Berlin, *The Crooked Timber of Humanity: Chapters in the History of Ideas*, ed. H. Hardy (1990; reprint, Princeton, 1997), 61.

CHAPTER FOURTEEN
HERE, THERE, AND ANYWHERE

THE ORGANIZERS of this conference have presented me with a double rhetorical task. According to their initial formulation, I was to write for both an interested public and for an international group of experts. The general topic contemplates a geographical range of more than two and a half million square miles of land, "from Iran and Mesopotamia in the East to Canaan, Egypt and the Aegean in the West."[1] Concealed in these boundaries is the intense interactivity of these various cultures across the entire southern Eurasian continent: for example, Sumer and the Indus Valley in trade relations in the third millennium (B.C.);[2] F. J. Teggert's calculation that, of the forty occasions of war in the western Roman empire between 58 B.C., and 107 A.D., twenty-seven were directly traceable to changes in the commercial policy of the Han Chinese government.[3]

The invitation projects a literate time-span of some 3,800 years as it considers religious phenomena within this broad region in their "Ancient, Classical and Late Antique forms." It defines "religion" comprehensively as the "manifold techniques, both communal and individual, by which men and women . . . sought to gain access to divine power." I would revise only the last clause, substituting "sought to gain access to, or avoidance of, culturally imagined divine power by culturally patterned means."[4]

As the recent turn of the millennium has resulted in much celebratory rhetoric concerning the duration of one new Late Antique religion—one of six new Late Antique religions to continue into modern times[5]—

it is worth recalling that the assigned region and time-span encompasses a set of religious traditions most of which have had two or three millennia-old histories. To understand these phenomena is to think through the dynamics of religious persistence, reinterpretation, and change; to think through the ways in which a given group at a given time chose this or that mode of interpreting their traditions as they related themselves to their historical past and to their social and political present.

In fulfilling my assigned task, there are only two stratagems available to me, either to focus in thick detail on a particular instance as exemplary of the whole or to generalize, recognizing that generalization falls between particularity and universality and, therefore, is always both partial and corrigible. In this essay, I will take the latter tack, and I will do so in the form of a topography.

I have signaled this intent with my title, which I owe to Dr. Seuss's character, Sam, and his canonical rejection of green eggs and ham by means of a formula that recurs some half-dozen times in the work with only a change of verb. To cite just one occurrence:

> I will not eat them here or there,
> I will not eat them anywhere.[6]

My confidence in this tripartite division of every place was strengthened when Dr. Seuss's doggerel brought to mind Robert Orsi's important 1991 article, "The Center Out There, In Here, and Everywhere Else: The Nature of Pilgrimage to the Shrine of St. Jude, 1929–1965." In this study, Orsi seeks to answer a quite particular question:

> A peculiar anomaly has characterized the National Shrine of Saint Jude Thaddeus, patron saint of hopeless causes and lost causes, since its founding by . . . a Spanish order of missionaries in Chicago in 1929. On the one hand, Jude's shrine was seen by both the saint's devout and the clerical caretakers of the site as a specific and special place of power, desire and hope, which is how such locations have always been imagined in the Catholic tradition; on the other hand, the devout were never encouraged nor did they feel compelled to go to that place in order to secure the benefits they sought from the saint.[7]

Orsi proposes that the solution to this "spatial decentering" was the formation of a voluntary association, the League of Saint Jude, which communicated with the shrine by writing. Through this association a "center out there" was established and maintained by means of "writing as going." This transformed a local shrine into a national one. Equally important, this transformation shifted attention from a notion of space "as the primary focus of devotional life to time"—a Late Antique strategy I have explored at some length in *To Take Place*.[8]

In this essay I should like to propose a topography in terms of three spatial categories: (1) the "here" of domestic religion, located primarily in the home and in burial sites; (2) the "there" of public civic and state religions, largely based in temple constructions; and (3) the "anywhere" of a rich diversity of religious formations that occupy an interstitial space between these other two loci, including a variety of religious entrepreneurs and ranging from groups we term "associations" to activities we label "magic."

While modes of access to and means of protection from imaginations of divine power differ in all three of these loci, I would locate one significant difference between the ancient/classical and Late Antique forms of the Mediterranean religions under review as being the expansion and relative prominence of the third locus (the religions of "anywhere") in Late Antiquity over against, and sometimes at the expense of, the persistence and transformations of the first two loci (the religions of "here" and "there").[9]

1. "Here": The Sphere of Domestic Religion

Considered globally, domestic religion is the most widespread form of religious activity; perhaps due to its very ubiquity, it is also the least studied. This is especially true of domestic religion of the past. Being largely nondramatic in nature and largely oral in transmission, domestic religion does not present itself to us as marked off as "religious" in any forceful manner. Its artifacts, if any, are small-scale and often of common materials, resulting in what one scholar has termed an archaeology of clay rather than of gold. Such artifacts tend to fill up museum basements rather than display cases. While their interpretation remains insecure, to make the point I need only refer to the decades-old debate between scholars of ancient Mediterranean religions as to whether the common small clay nude female figurines associated with household sites are dolls for children or goddesses for ritual.[10] The domestic realm, "here," precisely because it is not "there," because it is not situated in separated sacred space, invites ambiguity as to significance. This ambiguity is only increased when such artifacts are assigned to the dubious place-holding category of "popular religion." For these reasons, one can only applaud important recent works, such as the study by Karel van der Toorn, *Family Religion in Babylonia, Syria, and Israel* (1996), which begin to redress the imbalance.[11]

Domestic religion, focused on an extended family, is supremely local. It is concerned with the endurance of the family as a social and biological entity, as a community, as well as with the relations of that community to its wider social and natural environs. While no doubt pressing the matter to an extreme, one thinks of Fustel's insistence that each family, in classical Greek and Roman tradition, constituted a separate "religion."[12]

While the parallel is remote from Mediterranean cultures and therefore serves as an analogy, I have been most helped in imagining the category of domestic religion by Marcel Granet's portrait of a rural Chinese peasant household.[13] Several feet below the ground is buried a receptacle containing the bones or relics of ancestors. Directly above this is a subterranean storage vessel containing next year's seed rice. Placed above this, on the surface of the ground, is the bed of the primary householder couple. These three loci interact through symmetrical relations of exchange. The power of the ancestors enlivens the seed rice and the conjugal bed. The rice feeds both the ancestors and the householders. The sexual activity of the husband and wife quickens the seed rice and the ancestors. There is no apparent distance to be overcome. Relations are intimate; their continuity is expressed in terms of circulation and exchange.

Although the idiom differs within and between the religions of the regions we have under review, an analogous set of symmetrical relations pertains. It is a continuity that remains as long as the familial community is itself maintained. Extinction is its most obvious threat—whether by war, disaster, disease, or demonic attack. While the religious avoidance of these general traumas remains primarily an affair of civic or national modes of religion, the presence in many domestic sites of small divine figurines with apotropaic inscriptions suggests similar concerns with avoidance within the sphere of household religion.[14]

For domestic religion, dislocation is another sort of threat bearing a similar religious value. While scholars have tended to focus their attention on the civic and national implications of exiles and diasporas, forced distance from hearth, home, and especially, the familial burial site is a profound rupture of the presumed endless accessibility of the ancestors, which stands at the heart of domestic religion. One needs only to recall the solemn oath Joseph made the Israelites in Egypt swear, "When God comes to you, you shall carry up my bones from here" (Genesis 50:25) and the narration of the fulfillment of that promise by Moses at the time of the Exodus from Egypt (Exodus 13:19), the bones finally being reburied at a familial site: "The bones of Joseph, which Israel had brought up from

Egypt, were buried at Shechem, in the portion of ground that Jacob bought ... it became an inheritance of the descendants of Joseph" (Joshua 24:32). If, from the temple-centered perspective of the religions of "there," the dead constitute a pollution, interfering with sacred trans-actions, in the religions of "here," the dead are an indispensable medium for such transactions.[15]

Finally to any list of threats to domestic continuity must be added the danger of forgetfulness; hence, the importance of formal and infor-mal genealogies as well as family sagas. This threat raises, as well, a dif-ferent set of potential interruptions to the community and continuity of the family. As both Durkheim and van Gennep already perceived,[16] these are the issues addressed by those life-crisis rituals surrounding birth, pu-berty, marriage, and death with their attendant dilemma of increasing or decreasing the community. Such entrances and exits, such incorpora-tions and dissolutions, require social/ritual markings and memorializa-tions. While van Gennep's over-reliance on the metaphor of "threshold" may require revision, for domestic religion the *limen* is central inasmuch as it highlights issues of external rather than familial relations. The thresh-old separates those who belong or who are welcome through complex codes of hospitality from those who are not. It separates those who are re-ceived by a host (in the sense of one who provides food) from those who are repelled by a host (in the sense of armed force). The central locus of this difference, expressed as inclusion or exclusion, and, therefore, the most elaborated form of the domestic religion of "here," is the familial meal with its attendant ethos of commensality.

The meal might be routinely marked as "religious" by verbal formu-lae or through ritual business with food—although almost always these employ ordinary domestic utensils or common fire and consist of small elaborations of quotidian acts of eating, drinking, cooking, serving, pour-ing—but its prime mode of domestic sacrality consists in acknowledging who is there, both the familial living and the familial dead. The latter present something of a paradox. On the one hand, it is crucial that the dead remain in the sphere of the dead. Ghosts, the undead, the resur-rected, constitute, from this perspective, a threat to be protected against while protecting them against others. On the other hand, it is equally cru-cial that there be controlled contact with the dead, that there be a conti-nuity of relationship and appropriate modes of the dead's presence. Hence practices that range from memorializing the dead at meals, to sharing food with the dead, or eating with the dead, often at burial sites.[17] (Regarding burial sites, there is archaeological evidence at selected sites for *refrigeria*, often by holes drilled in tombs or tombstones through which foodstuffs and drink could be introduced).[18] The appropriate form of the presence of the dead is expressed also in general categories such as "blessing," as well as in their oracular or intercessionary roles within familial settings.[19]

2. "There": The Sphere of Civic and National Religion

It is possible to be briefer in describing the religion of "there," as this is what most of us think of first when we imagine ancient religion: the dominant deities and their attendant mythologies and liturgies, the impressive constructions associated with temple, court, and public square. Wherever one's domicile, these latter locales are someplace else, are "over there" in relation to one's homeplace. To some degree, access to such constructions is difficult, as expressed in the architectural language of walls and gates, of zones and nested interiors.[20]

The religion of "there" appears, cross-culturally, as the result of the co-occurrence of at least six elements, although causal priority cannot be ascribed to any one member of the nexus: urbanism, sacred kingship, temple, hereditary priesthood (as well as other religious specialists often organized as craft guilds), sacrifice, and writing.[21] As this list suggests, the religion of "there" has to do primarily with relations of power. These relations are expressed, religiously, through modes of replication and rectification, characteristically employing the dual idioms of sacred/profane, pure/impure, permitted/forbidden.[22] Skill in the strategic deployment of these relations requires complex specialized knowledge (rather than largely oral, familial knowledge), as well as the mastery of intricate modes of interpretation ranging from the technologies of divination to the devices of casuitry.[23]

Central to these "imperial" religious formations is a principle first enunciated by the so-called Panbabylonian school who understood their early reading of cuneiform texts to reveal a world-view dominated by the equivalence, "as above, so below."[24] Rather than the immediate and symmetrical reciprocities of the religion of "here," the religion of "there" postulates a distance between the realm of the gods and the human realm. This distance is a relative one. Unlike today's all-but-infinite cosmos, the ancient calculation of distance was a matter of hundreds of feet (the distance at which the smoke of sacrifice disappears from view). Nevertheless, this distance was mediated by structures such as kingship and temple, in which the "above" served ideologically as a template for the "below," in which a variety of human activities served to bring the "below" ever closer to the "above" through ritual works of repetition and, when breaches occurred, through ritual works of rectification.

This essentially imperial cosmology is concerned with defending both the center and the periphery. These are frequently first established as the result of a cosmogony through combat in which a new king of the gods overthrows the previous king, thereby gaining the right to reorganize the world according to his like. (Note that, despite many scholars' formulations, this is not a movement from chaos to order, but rather from a previous system of order to a new system of order). Aspects of the predecessor's cosmos are typically recycled and re-placed in the new order, thus introducing a potentially destabilizing element if the new order is not scrupulously maintained. (Another mode of destabilization is the possibility, inherent in royal combat, of a new challenger). Following the new king of the god's victory and coronation, through an essentially bureaucratic taxonomy, the various parts of the cosmos, both celestial and terrestrial, are assigned their stations, have their roles and honors established, their names pronounced, their powers placed, and their destinies fixed.[25] For human activity to be successful in achieving replication and rectification, the intricacies of this order must be known—a knowledge that implies both an initial difficulty of discovery, and an evidence, once discovered, that is celebrated in genres ranging from wisdom texts to omens, from law codes to mythic and historical narratives. In each of these kinds of texts, individually acquired insight is rendered into public discourse through the mediation of precedent.

Rather than commensality among an extended family with ordinary foodstuff, the central ritual of the religion of "there" is the sacrifice, a meal among unequals, often coded in complex hierarchies (as, for example, in the division of the corpse and the distribution of the meat), with at least one, usually sacerdotal, figure serving not as the presence but rather as the representative of the god(s), with concern for transporting the meat (itself not a usual item of diet) to the divine realm, which is "over there."[26] Sacrifice is primarily food for the god(s), but it also becomes linked with complex systems of sacred/profane, purity/impurity, permitted/forbidden. As such, sacrificial praxis invites learned exegesis and complex systematics unthinkable apart from writing. While I do not share the implications they draw, I commend the observation of some scholars that sacrifice is "as much a textual enterprise as one of actual practice; the sacrifice system begins to develop a level of significance independent, though not inseparable, from cultic practice."[27]

3. The Religion of "Anywhere"

At times more closely related to the familial model characteristic of the religions of "here," at other times closer to the imperial model characteristic of the religions of "there," there is a third pattern of religion, which takes many forms, but has in common the element that it is tied to no particular place. It is, in the strict sense, "neither here nor there." It can be anywhere. In archaic or classical formations, religions of "anywhere" include religious clubs and other forms of associations, entrepreneurial religious figures (often depicted as wandering), and religious practitioners not officially recognized by centers of power.[28] In many cases, to use an old sociological distinction, they are associations or figures of status but not of rank. What they offer are means of access to or avoidance of modes of culturally imagined divine power not encompassed by the religions of "here" and "there." At times they may imitate, at other times they may reverse, aspects of these two other dominant forms of religion.

What has interested me for much of my scholarly career is the fact that throughout the Mediterranean world in the period of Late Antiquity these religions of "anywhere" rise to relative prominence, although the religions of "here" and "there" continue, often in revised forms.[29] Much energy by several generations of scholars has been devoted to accounting for this change.[30] While the explanations have been highly variegated, reflecting, no doubt, that we are treating with a multicausal phenomenon, I would lift out three elements as especially relevant to our theme: a new geography, new cosmography, and a new polity.

1. First, the New Geography

While there were experiments in imperialisms from Sumer on, and dislocations due to invasions or colonizations, there is a difference in disruptive scale resulting from the newer imperialisms ranging from the Persian and Macedonian to the Roman. An anthology of texts could be gathered that expresses both the positive and negative evaluations of displacement, of being a citizen of no-place. But if, as for many, the extended family, the homeplace, as well as the burial place of the honored dead, are no longer coextensive *topoi*, then the religion of "here" has been detached from its roots.

In such a situation, the religion of "here" must be transmuted in such a way as to overcome this dislocation. One solution will be sociological, the association as a socially constructed replacement for the family.[31] The other solution will be mythological. In these traditions dislocation is cosmologized by a new, vertical myth, which overlays the horizontal reality (much as in Philo, where the terrestrial migrations of the Israelitic ancestors have been revalued as celestial ascents). In some forms, humans are depicted as dispersed, as exiled from their heavenly home, as having been mis-placed into bodies. Through death or by undergoing rituals that are deathlike, individuals may ascend back to their true home, "on high," thus overcoming distance. Locale, having been dis-placed, is now re-placed.[32] These transformations give comparative advantage to religions of "anywhere."

2. Second, the New Cosmography

While not without elaboration, the archaic two-story cosmos (above/below) or three-story (above/earth/underworld) cosmos allowed for points of mediation between strata imagined as being relatively adjacent. Communication was largely unimpeded.[33] Each realm could have the other always in its sight (hence, archaic structures such as covenant). Each displayed its appropriate order to the other, an order that was to be affirmed and replicated, an order that could be rectified if breached. The cosmos, as the Greek implies (Gk. *kosmos*, lit. "ornament" "order"), was essentially good and beautiful because its elements were in their appropriate place. These were the essential presuppositions for the religions of "there."[34]

The new Late Antique cosmography, articulated from Eudoxus (390–340 B.C.) to Ptolemy, (fl. 127–148) proposed a far different picture. The earth was now conceived as a sphere, surrounded by the circular orbits of other planetary spheres which either comprised or were transcended by divine realms.[35] In a common literary topos, the view back from the vast expanse of celestial space rendered the earth small, the human activities on its surface were seen as miniscule, as insignificant.[36] As the planets revolved around the earth, they spent much of their time period out of sight. We can't see them; they can't see us. What are they up to? Do they know what we're up to? How is the elevation of the food of sacrifice possible with such a remote and movable target? (The dilemma is not unlike that of the Houston Space Center, which can fire a rocket only when there is a "window of opportunity.") Transcendence of earth, both as an experience and as a source of knowledge, becomes a goal—giving comparative advantage to a religion of "anywhere." (It is important, in the understanding of these traditions and their transcendental horizon, not to substitute the notion of "everywhere" for that of "anywhere.")

I will give but one example. It is one thing to observe the movements of the heavenly bodies and discern from them both knowledge of the regularities of the cosmos and of the destinies of terrestrial affairs, the collection of which remains, especially in the vast Mesopotamian omen-series, one of the chief intellectual achievements associated with the religions of "there." It is quite another matter to claim experience of having ascended to the stars or through the planetary spheres and to assert one's kinship with them in order either to obtain celestial knowledge directly or to press past them to reach even higher realms and even more hidden divine knowledge.

3. Third, the New Polity

The creation of new political ideologies, post-Alexander (356–323 B.C.), are the result of the total cessation of native kingship.[37] The unique, mediating role of the king was one of the foundations of the religion of "there." His removal from the scene was decentering. In some Late Antique traditions, the old forms of kingship became idealized objects of nostalgia, as in messianism. At the same time, archaic combat myths were revisioned as resistance myths to foreign kings resulting in new religious formations such as apocalypticism and millenarianism.[38] Other traditions appear to have pressed the logic of archaic sacred kingship even further. If the king was the image of the deity, and if the wrong king, that is to say, the foreign or illegitimate king, now sat on the throne, then there must be a wrong, or counterfeit, king of the gods on high, a concomitant variation explored in gnosticizing reinterpretations of archaic traditions.[39]

The new mode of kingship, post-Alexander, was not only foreign, it was remote. Positively, as Eric Petersen has suggested, the model of the distant emperor, mediated by satraps, governors, or vassal kings, played a significant role in the elaboration of the new formations of monotheism, along with the king-god's ubiquitous attendant subordinate and secondary divinities, principalities, and powers.[40] All of these actors were capable of being readily assimilated to the new, expanded cosmography. Similarly, there could be claimed experiences of celestial journeys to or the receipt of messages from the true king of the gods who was above, or antagonistic to, the king-god of this world.[41]

In illustrating the effects of these three new elements, I have largely confined myself to examples from the mythological response to the new geography, cosmography, and polity. Let me turn, now, to the social with respect to two formations: associations and magic. In so doing, I will highlight reconfigurations and reinterpretations of elements characteristic of the religions of "here" and "there."

Associations, as religions of "anywhere," may be understood primarily as re-placements of the religion of "here" in modes appropriate to the new world order. They do so, at least in part, by adapting elements more characteristic of the religions of "there." Responding to the experience of dislocation, they provide a new, predominantly urban, social location. Some were formed first as immigrant societies, initially retaining strong bonds to the homeplace. Others associate around divine figures, gods and goddesses, usually, but not exclusively, of the sort more characteristic of the civic and state religions of "there." The archaic domestic preoccupation with familial relations of inclusion/exclusion is here translated into a concern for boundaries that enclose a restricted and tested membership. While entire households may join such a club, the primary relations are between individuals as members of a fictive kin group, addressing one another as "brother" and "sister." This apparent egalitarianism stands in notable contrast to the hierarchical ordering of members, bearing an often bewildering diversity of titles, some of which echo those in the highly organized bureaucracy of the religions of "there."[42] Kinship is forged by rituals of acceptance, of initiation and expulsion, as well as legalistically by the formal acceptance of rules, the taking of oaths, the paying of dues. In this sense, group identity is not genealogical but, rather, contractual. Indeed, some groups are chartered by the state; all are subject, at least in principle, to government regulation.[43]

The meal shared by these "brothers" and "sisters" continues to be the prime repetitive ritual for expressing their relations, now undertaken in the setting of a privately owned cult place or burial site, at times with hieratic practices that reflect priestly concerns characteristic of the religions of "there" (as, for example, in the Pharisaic *havurah*).[44]

In some associations, rather than forgetfulness representing a threat to the maintenance of the community, disclosure now menaces the group. Secrecy, with respect to those outside, has become an important value.

Finally, I should note that these associations have the potential of working at cross purposes to the older conceptualizations of family in the religions of "here," as when differing memberships divide genealogical siblings while at the same time establishing new, intimate relations and loyalties among their socially created fellow "brothers" and "sisters."

I have written elsewhere on the problematic of magic and shall, therefore, not rehearse that here.[45] For the purposes of this essay, it is sufficient only to note that Late Antique magic, often conceptualized as a religion of "anywhere," represents, among other things, a fascinating and creative combination and re-formation of elements characteristic of both the religion of "here" and of "there." Like the religion of "here," its prime space is domestic, its rituals are small-scale. It may seek relations with the dead or with exceedingly local divinities. But just as frequently it treats with the sorts of deities more commonly associated with the religions of "there." In either case, it does so in the insistent idiom of oracle and sacrifice. Finally, as is characteristic of the religions of "there," magic is a learned profession, presupposing both written texts and complex techniques for their interpretation.⁴⁶

From another perspective, however, Late Antique magic is primarily a religion of "anywhere." As is the case with associations, it deploys ritual distinctions, especially initiations, with a highly developed sense of inclusion/exclusion. As with associations, its greatest threat is the divulging of its secrets.⁴⁷ As is characteristic of religions of "anywhere," it places great value on direct experience of transcendent beings, both as a demonstration of power and as a means of gaining esoteric knowledge.

In the vast panorama of religions this topography encompasses, it is possible to propose a final taxonomic generalization, one that depends on contrastive world-views and their attendant soteriologies. We may distinguish between religions of "sanctification," which celebrate the present ordered world, having as their goal its maintenance and repair, and religions of "salvation," which seek to escape the structures and strictures of this world through activities having as their goal a constant working toward transcendence. While perhaps having an apparent affinity with one or the other, the religions of "here," "there," and "anywhere" have been adapted to either world-view. The contestations, permutations, and combinations generated by these two *ethoi*, whether within or between any particular tradition, constitute what we take to be the history of religions.

Notes

1. I cite here the formulations of the original conference document. The general assumptions parallel an important contemporary redescription of the ancient Mediterranean world as an interactive site of transformative contact as well as divisive conflict. See, for example, the Melammu initiative of the Neo-Assyrian Text Corpus Project devoted to "the intellectual heritage of Babylonia and Assyria in East and West," in S. Aro and R. M. Whiting, eds., *The Heirs of Assyria: Proceedings of the Opening Symposium of the Assyrian and Babylonian Intellectual Heritage Project Held in Tvärminne, Finland, October 8–11, 1998*, Melammu Symposia, 1 (Helsinki, 2000).

2. See, for example, David Potts, *The Arabian Gulf in Antiquity*, vol. 1 (Oxford, 1990); E. C. L. During-Caspers, "Harappan Trade in the Arabian Gulf in the Third Millennium B.C.," *Mesopotamia* 7 (1972): 167–91; S. Ratnagar, *Encounters: The Westerly Trade of the Harappa Civilization* (Delhi and New York, 1981).

3. F. J. Teggart, *Rome and China: A Study of Correlations in Historical Events* (Berkeley, 1939), vii–viii, et passim.

4. As is readily recognizable, I adapt here Melford Spiro's definition of reli-

gion as "an institution consisting of culturally patterned interaction with culturally postulated superhuman beings," specifying the interactions in terms of access and avoidance in keeping with the conference's announced theme. See M. Spiro, "Religion: Problems of Definition and Explanation," in *Anthropological Approaches to the Study of Religion*, ed. M. Banton, Association of Social Anthropologists of the Commonwealth Monographs, 3 (London, 1966), 96.

5. I include as the new Late Antique religions surviving to modern times Judaism, Samaritanism, Christianity, Mandaeanism, Islam, and depending on how one dates the Iranian formations, the Parsis (as well as the Gabars).

6. Dr. Seuss, *Green Eggs and Ham* (New York, 1960), no pagination. It is important to my topography that "anywhere" not be read as "everywhere."

7. R. Orsi, "The Center Out There, In Here, and Everywhere Else: The Nature of Pilgrimage to the Shrine of St. Jude, 1929–1965," *Journal of Social History* 25 (1991): 213–32.

8. J. Z. Smith, *To Take Place: Toward Theory in Ritual*, Chicago Studies in the History of Judaism (Chicago, 1987), 86–95, et passim.

9. While the topographical strategy remains constant, I would not wish this scheme to be identified with the distinction "locative/utopian" developed, among other applications, to explore continuities, revaluations, and differences in archaic and Late Antique Mediterranean religions in J. Z. Smith, *Map Is Not Territory: Studies in the History of Religions*, Studies in Judaism in Late Antiquity, 23 (Leiden, 1978), xi–xv, 100–3, 130–42, 147–51, 160–66, 169–71, 185–89, 291–94, 308–9, as well as in subsequent publications.

10. For a summary of these debates, see P. J. Ucko, *Anthropomorphic Figurines of Predynastic Egypt and Neolithic Crete with Comparative Material from the Prehistoric Near East and Mainland Greece*, Royal Anthropological Institute, Occasional Paper, 24 (London, 1968).

11. K. van der Toorn, *Family Religion in Babylonia, Syria, and Israel: Continuity and Change in the Forms of Religious Life*, Studies in the History and Culture of the Ancient Near East, 7 (Leiden, 1996).

12. N. D. Fustel de Coulanges, *The Ancient City: A Study of the Religion, Laws and Institutions of Greece and Rome* (Boston, 1896), 41, 46–48, et passim. This usage is especially dominant in Fustel's description of the marriage rituals (53–60).

13. M. Granet, *La Civilisation chinoise: La vie publique et la vie privée*, L'Évolution de l'humanité: Synthèse historique, 25 (Paris, 1929), 205; Granet, *La Religion des Chinois*, 2d ed. (Paris, 1951), 21–25.

14. See, for example, the inscriptions cited in D. Rittig, *Assyrisch-babylonische Kleinplastik magischer Bedeutung vom 13.–6. Jh.v. Chr.* (Munich, 1977), 185–208.

15. For a suggestive attempt to account for the historical reasons for this shift in archaic and classical Greek religion, see I. Morris, "Attitudes toward Death in Archaic Greece," *Classical Antiquity* 8 (1987): 296–320.

16. E. Durkheim, *The Elementary Forms of Religious Life* (New York, 1995), esp. 405; A. van Gennep, *The Rites of Passage* (London, 1960), 41–165.

17. See my treatment of these themes in J. Z. Smith, *Drudgery Divine: On the Comparison of Early Christianities and the Religions of Late Antiquity,* Jordan Lectures in Comparative Religion, School of Oriental and African Studies, University of London, 14; and Chicago Studies in the History of Judaism (London, 1990; and Chicago, 1990), 122–32. There have been a number of important specialized studies of some of these themes, ranging from A. Scurlock, "Magical Means of Dealing with Ghosts in Ancient Mesopotamia" (Ph.D. diss., University of Chicago, 1988) to T. J. Lewis, *Cults of the Dead in Ancient Israel and Ugarit,* Harvard Semitic Monographs, 39 (Atlanta, 1989). J. Bottéro, *Mesopotamia: Writing, Reasoning and the Gods* (Chicago, 1992), 279–84, offers a set of subtle generalizations concerning the familial dead.

18. The starting point for any analysis remains A. Parrot, *Le "Refrigerium" dans l'au delà* (Paris, 1937). See further, *The Assyrian Dictionary of the Oriental Institute of the University of Chicago* (Chicago, 1956–), A/2, 324, s.v. "*arûtu.*" For a rare Greek example, see Martin P. Nilsson, *Geschichte der griechischen Religion. 1, Die Religion griechenlands bis auf die griechische Weltherrschaft,* Handbuch der Altertumswissenschaft, 5,2(1) (Munich, 1976), 1: 177, and n. 1. For these traditions in Late Antiquity, see, among others, G. F. Snyder, *Ante Pacem: Archaeological Evidence of Church Life before Constantine* (Macon, GA, 1985), 172, s.v. "meal for the dead"; and compare the use of Snyder in Smith, *Drudgery Divine,* 129–32. For later, North African Christian *refrigeria,* largely associated with martyria, see J. Quasten, "*Vetus Superstitio et Nova Religio:* The Problem of Refrigerium in the Ancient Church of North Africa," *Harvard Theological Review* 33 (1940): 253–66.

19. The oracular materials are often subsumed under the broader category of necromancy (a term of enormous fluidity, as, for example, in J. Tropper, *Nekromantie: Totenbefragung im Alten Orient und Alten Testament,* Alter Orient und Altes Testament, 223 [Neukirchen-Vluyn, 1989]). See, among others, the significant recent studies of I. L. Finkel, "Necromancy in Ancient Mesopotamia," *Archiv für Orientforschung* 29–30 (1983–84): 1–17; K. van der Toorn, "The Nature of the Biblical Teraphim in the Light of the Cuneiform Evidence," *Catholic Biblical Quarterly* 52 (1990): 203–22; B. B. Schmidt, *Israel's Beneficent Dead: Ancestor Cult and Necromancy in Ancient Israelite Religion and Tradition,* Forschungen zum Alten Testament, 11 (Tübingen, 1994). See also the shrewd comments on oracular dreams of the dead in a Melanesian context in K. Burridge, *Mambu: A Study of Melanesian Cargo Movements and Their Social and Ideological Background* (London, 1960), 252–53; and Burridge, *Tangu Traditions: A Study of the Way of Life, Mythology, and Developing Experience of a New Guinea People* (Oxford, 1969), 164–66.

20. Smith, *To Take Place*, 48–73. Compare the recent remarkable work by S. M. Olyan, *Rites and Rank: Hierarchy in Biblical Representations of Cult* (Princeton, 2000).

21. This complex has been best adumbrated by P. Wheatley's work on "urban genesis," especially Wheatley, *The Pivot of the Four Quarters: A Preliminary Enquiry into the Origins and Character of the Ancient Chinese City* (Chicago, 1971). See further the bibliography of Wheatley in Smith, *To Take Place*, 149, n. 16, as well as my comments on Wheatley (50–54).

22. These three systems, while often parallel, ought not be confused as they are in the classic work by M. Douglas, *Purity and Danger: An Analysis of Concepts of Pollution and Taboo* (New York, 1966).

23. See Smith, *Map Is Not Territory*, 70–72; Smith, *Imagining Religion: From Babylon to Jonestown*, Chicago Studies in the History of Judaism (Chicago, 1982), 48–49.

24. On the Panbabylonian School, see Smith, *Imagining Religion*, 23–29; Smith, "Mythos und Geschichte," in H. P. Duerr, ed., *Alcheringa oder die beginnende Zeit: Studien zu Mythologie, Schamanismus und Religion* (Frankfurt am Main, 1983), 36–41.

25. This summarizes both the Divine Combat Myth and the Kingship in Heaven Myth, which are widely distributed throughout the Mediterranean. See, among others, C. Scott Littleton, "The 'Kingship in Heaven' Theme," in J. Puhvel, ed., *Myth and Law among the Indo-Europeans* (Berkeley, 1970), 83–121; J. Day, *God's Conflict with the Dragon and the Sea* (Cambridge, 1985); N. Forsyth, *The Old Enemy: Satan and the Combat Myth* (Princeton, 1987); B. F. Batto, *Slaying the Dragon: Mythmaking in the Biblical Tradition* (Louisville, 1992); H. R. Page, *The Myth of Cosmic Rebellion: A Study of Its Reflexes in Ugaritic and Biblical Literature*, Supplements to Vetus Testamentum, 65 (Leiden, 1996).

26. I draw here on C. Lévi-Strauss, *The Savage Mind* (Chicago, 1966), 32; and his valuable contrast between games and rituals. "Games thus appear to have a *disjunctive* effect . . . Ritual, on the other hand, is the exact inverse; it *conjoins*, for it brings about a union (one might even say communion in this context) or in any case an organic relation between two initially separate groups . . . [In ritual] there is an asymmetry which is postulated in advance between profane and sacred, faithful and officiating, dead and living, initiated and uninitiated, etc." Compare the view of sacrifice as communication in H. Hubert and M. Mauss, *Sacrifice: Its Nature and Function* (Chicago, 1964), 97–98. I have presented an account of sacrifice in J. Z. Smith, "The Domestication of Sacrifice," in R. G. Hamerton-Kelly, ed., *Violent Origins: Ritual Killing and Cultural Formation. Conversations Between W. Burkert, R. Girard, and J. Z. Smith* (Stanford, Calif.: 1987), 278–304, reprinted in this volume. On the division of meat, see both M. Detienne, "Culinary Practices and the Spirit of Sacrifice," in M. Detienne and

J.-P. Vernant, eds., *The Cuisine of Sacrifice among the Greeks* (Chicago, 1989), 13; and J.-L. Durand, "Greek Animals: Toward a Topology of Edible Bodies," in *The Cuisine of Sacrifice among the Greeks*, 87–118.

27. G. A. Anderson, "Sacrifice and Sacrificial Offerings," in D. N. Freedman, ed., *The Anchor Bible Dictionary* (New York, 1992), 5:873. For a similar perception of what Anderson calls "sacrifice as a textual phenomenon" (loc. cit.), see Hubert and Mauss, *Sacrifice*, 16.

28. See, for example, W. Burkert, "Craft Versus Sect: The Problem of Orphics and Pythagoreans," in B. F. Meyer and E. P. Sanders, eds., *Self-Definition in the Graeco-Roman World*, Jewish and Christian Self-Definition, 3 (Philadelphia, 1982).

29. See note 9 above.

30. Smith, *Map Is Not Territory*, 143.

31. See the important collection of studies in J. S. Kloppenborg and S. G. Wilson, eds., *Voluntary Associations in the Graeco-Roman World* (London, 1996); and the brilliant overview of the state of the question by R. S. Ascough, *What Are They Saying about the Formation of Pauline Churches?* (New York, 1998).

32. Smith, *Map Is Not Territory*, xii–xv, et passim.

33. The issue of the communication between the realms as well as the dilemma of the blockage of communication between the upper and lower worlds has led to an important revisionary understanding of the *Homeric Hymn to Demeter* by J. Rudhardt, "À propos de l'hymne homérique à Déméter," *Museum Helveticum* 35 (1978): 1–17, now available in a slightly abridged English translation in H. P. Foley, ed., *The Homeric Hymn to Demeter: Translation, Commentary, and Interpretive Essays* (Princeton, 1994), 198–211. See also J. S. Clay, *The Politics of Olympus: Form and Meaning in the Major Homeric Hymns* (Princeton, 1989), 202–66, esp. 208–13, 219, 220–21, 256–57, 260–66.

34. Compare the essay by J. Bottéro, "The Religious System," in Bottéro, *Mesopotamia*, 201–31, esp. 218–31.

35. See, among others, M. P. Nilsson, "The New Conception of the Universe in Late Greek Paganism," *Eranos* 44 (1946): 20–27; cf. Nilsson, *Geschichte der griechischen Religion*, 2, *Die hellenistische und römische Zeit*, 4th ed., Handbuch der Altertumswissenschaft 5,2(2) (Munich, 1988), 702–11; Nilsson, *Greek Piety* (New York, 1969), 96–103.

36. See the treatment of this topos in E. R. Dodds, *Pagan and Christian in an Age of Anxiety*, Wiles Lectures, 1963 (Cambridge, 1968), 7–8.

37. See, in general, S. K. Eddy, *The King Is Dead: Studies in the Near Eastern Resistance to Hellenism*, 334–31 B.C. (Lincoln, 1961), a pioneering work on the consequences of the cessation of native kingship.

38. On these themes, see Smith, *Map Is Not Territory*, 67–87. For the Egyptian materials there cited, see now the superb treatment by D. Frankfurter, *Elijah*

in Upper Egypt: The Apocalypse of Elijah and Early Egyptian Christianity, Studies in Antiquity and Christianity (Minneapolis, 1993), 159–238.

39. I have persistently maintained that rather than thinking of "gnosticism" as a separate religious entity, it should be viewed as a structural possibility within religious traditions, analogous to categories such as mysticism or asceticism, and needs to be seen in relation to exegetical, reinterpretative practices. The wrong king/wrong god element discussed above should be compared to M. A. Williams's category of "biblical demiurgical" in his important work, *Rethinking "Gnosticism": An Argument for Dismantling a Dubious Category* (Princeton, 1996), 51–53, et passim.

40. E. Petersen, *Der Monotheismus als politisches Problem: Ein Beitrag zur Geschichte der politischen Theologie im Imperium Romanum* (Leipzig, 1935).

41. Cf. Forsyth, *The Old Enemy.*

42. See T. Schmeller, *Hierarchie und Egalität: Eine sozial-geschichtliche Untersuchung paulinischer Gemeinden und griechisch-römischer Vereine,* Stuttgarter Bibelstudien, 162 (Stuttgart, 1995).

43. See the literature cited in note 31 above.

44. J. Neusner, *From Politics to Piety: The Emergence of Pharisaic Judaism* (Englewood Cliffs, 1973), 83–90.

45. Smith, *Map Is Not Territory,* 172–89; Smith, "Towards Interpreting Demonic Powers in Hellenistic and Roman Antiquity," *Aufstieg und Niedergang der römischen Welt* (Berlin, 1978), 16.1:425–39; Smith, "Trading Places," in M. Meyer and P. Mirecki, eds., *Ancient Magic and Ritual Power,* Religions in the Graeco-Roman World, 129 (Leiden, 1995), 13–27. The last essay is reprinted in this volume.

46. H. D. Betz, "The Formation of Authoritative Tradition in the Greek Magical Papyri," in Meyer and Sanders, *Self-Definition in the Graeco-Roman World,* 161–70.

47. See, among others, H. D. Betz, "Secrecy in the Greek Magical Papyri," in H. G. Kippenberg and G. G. Stroumsa, eds., *Secrecy and Concealment: Studies in the History of Mediterranean and Near Eastern Religions,* Numen Book Series, 65 (Leiden, 1995), 153–75.

RE: CORINTHIANS

But capitalization does not convert a muscular twitch into a god.

    P. BUCK (TE RANGI HIROA), *The Coming of the Maori*

"There is something strange about the Corinthians, to be sure. They fanta-
sized about themselves and their achievements, as Paul himself did. We must
wonder, however, if some of their strangeness is not due to the way in which
Paul presents them."

    R. M. GRANT, *Paul in the Roman World: The Conflict at Corinth*

I

IF BURTON MACK is correct in his understanding of the cunning of
Mark, then surely Mark's gospel is one of the most contaminating texts
for the understanding of early Christianities. How much more so 1 Corinthians! This text, especially, although not limited to, those aspects that
have been traditionally viewed as resonating with Luke's Pentecost narrative, has contaminated the general field of the study of religion well beyond any limitation to Christian data. It has affected not only scholarly
constructions such as charismatic movements, "ecstatic religions," and
models of both archaic and contemporary cult associations but also native religious self-representations. Indeed, in the latter case, at times in a
sort of feedback loop, 1 Corinthians has influenced anthropological data
and theories that then have been used by New Testament scholars to interpret early Christian data.[1]

    1 Corinthians has also been used more than any other New Testa-
ment text (with the possible exception of Luke's composition of the Are-
opagus speech) for direct Christian (missionary) interpretation of the religions of other folk—most especially their rituals. The so-called Chinese
Rites Controversy is, perhaps, the classic example,[2] but a more commonplace instance would be the twenty years of Dutch Calvinist missionary
debate (1914–34), as summarized by Webb Keane,[3] over native sacrificial

practice in West Sumba (Indonesia), an island separated on the east by the Savu Sea from its better-known neighbor, Timor. The question was the native practice of commensalism with respect to meat resulting from sacrifice, a central index of Sumbanese sociality. "To demand of converts that they withdraw from this commensuality is to threaten their participation in society altogether."[4] The issue was joined with the publication of a latitudinarian article by D. K. Wielenga in 1914, whose title, "On the Eating of Flesh Offered to Idols,"[5] displays its Corinthian genealogy, and was officially resolved by its prohibition proclaimed by a Special Assembly of Missionaries in 1934:

> A Christian, through the accepting and eating of meat brought to the house [that comes] from animals slain according to pagan *adat* [custom], of which he knows the source, has objective communion with the worship of the devil. Moreover, the accepting and eating of [such] meat . . . is (a) unworthy of the Christian, (b) dangerous for the Christian and the young Christian congregation, (c) contrary to the commandment of brotherly love. Also on the ground of all these considerations, the accepting and eating of such flesh is in conflict with God's Word, for which reason . . . our Christians must hate and eschew such a thing from the heart.[6]

What official documents fail to indicate is the sort of commonplace, common-sense resolutions in practice of such a social dilemma that can, at times, be captured by an observer's ethnographic report. For example, as the number of individuals following the traditional Sumbanese practice declined over the years, due, largely, to successful missionizations, the sacrificial rituals became increasingly dependent on native Christian support. Hence, since the 1980s, "one pig" would be "often omitted from the offering prayers" so it could "be fed to the Christian visitors."[7] That is to say, a 'legal fiction' was created that one pig was slaughtered in an ordinary act, in contradistinction to its fellows, which were ritually slain. Alternatively, from the Christian side, a notion of "functional equivalence"[8] could be invoked. Rather than meat being brought home as gifts for the traditional spirits, it could be "transposed" as being brought home to be distributed as "support for the poor";[9] rather than a piece of meat, cut from the shoulder of the victim being presented to the head man, a different cut of meat could be offered "on the grounds that the shoulder cut was pagan, but the substitute gift still bore the secular display of deference."[10]

While a reception history of 1 Corinthians in both theories of reli-

gion and Christian praxis with respect to other religions deserves attention, I turn now to the task at hand and attempt a redescription of the
Corinthian situation in relation to a set of data from Papua New Guinea.

II

Papua New Guinea was, in the 1960s and 70s, an important site for
theorizing about religion in terms of data from indigenous 'cargo cults'—
an interest that has largely disappeared among students of religion.[11]
Later, in the 1980s and '90s, it became a site for important anthropological theorizing about sexuality—materials that have not, by and large,
been taken up by students of religion.[12] Most recently, Papua New Guinea,
along with Melanesia, has been the site of important discussions of a widespread 'new' religious pattern: a concomitant increase, within the same
locale, in both native Christianities, especially Pentecostalisms (whether
independent of or affiliated with North American churches), and nativistic movements (that is to say, the invention of new traditionalisms).
One important point of intersection between these two 'new' religious
forms has been healing, often spirit-healing. These matters are just beginning to find place in the agenda of scholars of religion.[13]

The particular group under discussion is the Atbalmin (or, Nalumin),[14] comprised of some 3000 individuals, clustered in settlements of
some 30–40 folk. They inhabit the Telefolmin area in the Star (or, Ster-
ren) mountain range, part of the continuous mountain-range running
northwest-southeast that divides the world's second-largest island. On a
contemporary map, their settlements are sited at the border between the
nominally Christian and independent Papua New Guinea and the Muslim state Indonesian territory of Irian Jaya (or Irian Burat, or West New
Guinea, or West Papua). It is a region that as late as 1969 could be described in the *Encyclopaedia Britannica* as "still little known." While there
was some European exploration after 1910, there was no direct contact
until government officials of the Australian Trust Territory made periodic visits after 1950. In the same period, a station of the Australian
Baptist Missionary Society was established. Following independence in
1975, a small airport was constructed, along with copper mines, a health
clinic and a primary school. The Christian mission made little progress
until this period (1976–79), when, using native "pastors" from the neighboring, and linguistically related, Urapmin and Tifalmin tribes, the majority of Atbalmin converted, seeing "themselves as part of a much larger
Christian community that encompassed Europeans as well as Melane-

sians." Unlike the successive colonial administrations, Christian conversion required abandoning their indigenous religion. Clearly, indigenous religion was so intercalated into the fabric of everyday Atbalmin social and material relations that such abandonment was, practically speaking, impossible. From kinship with its structure of ancestral myths and requirements of exchange relations to place names to ritual roles for household implements and utensils, indigenous religion defined quotidian life. Beyond this 'background,' cult sites, particularly those associated with the ancestors, such as men's houses and temples, which focused on ritual performances and the transmission of traditional wisdom, were 'foregrounded' concentrations of the old traditions which continued postconversion.[15] While the ethnographer I am here following unfortunately gives little detailed account of these traditions, and Frederick Barth's important study of the region makes plain the significant variations among these geographically proximate and linguistically related groups that prevent secure inference from the practices of neighboring tribes, the overall Atbalmin pattern is similar enough to allow reporting Jack Goody's generalization concerning one aspect of Barth's work:

> Since knowledge is held largely in the minds of men . . . the older are inevitably at once the most experienced, and the most privileged communicators, as well as the most likely to die, taking their knowledge with them to the world of the ancestors. The dead must therefore know more than the living; the forefathers are also the forebearers, the carriers of 'tradition.' And it is in the cult of the ancestors that the dead reveal some of their superior, more comprehensive knowledge.[16]

For the Atbalmin, it was the Christian language of "sin" that gave voice to this tension between indigenous and Christian.[17] "The Atbalmin found in Christianity a source of both desires and fears; a new way of living but also a disturbing ongoing critique of their lives individually and collectively."[18]

This tense new identity negotiating relations between indigenous/Christian was complicated, within a very few years, by the appearance of two 'new' religious movements that occurred almost simultaneously.[19]

The first was a Christian 'revival' (in English-based Tok Pisin pidgin, *rebaibel*) movement that had as its apparent catalyst a powerful wind that struck an Atbalmin settlement on March 21, 1985, building as well on a general Christian enthusiasm during the previous months (September

1984–February 1985) brought about by the return to the community and the renewed baptizing activities of James, one of the native 'pastors' responsible for their first conversions.[20]

> This wind . . . [was] widely understood to be the work of the Holy Spirit. [A] number of women became possessed. Over the next two days, women in other settlements became possessed by what they and others believed to be the Holy Spirit. In their possessed state, the women emphasized that Christ was about to return and that the people had to prepare themselves. . . . 'Finally,' a number of people told me, 'we will have our own Revival!' In saying this, they were drawing on their knowledge of another Christian religious movement known as the Rebaibel . . . that had taken place in 1977–78 among a people who lived east of the Atbalmin. It involved widespread possession by the Holy Spirit, most often by women, and destruction of many temples of the indigenous religion. Many Atbalmin had been disappointed when the movement had failed to enter their area. Now people felt they had another chance. On March 25, I awoke to find people ridding the settlement of things they linked with indigenous ways. . . . A young man told me, 'If we give up all the non-Christian ways and only go to church, they say God will send his spirit—the Holy Spirit, a new life—into all of us and heat us up.' The next day, on March 26, [at an] intense Sunday service at the church at Okbil . . . there was a great emphasis on disclosing and ending forever the kinds of routine concealment of non-Christian practices and beliefs that had been occurring. . . . [A woman] suddenly became possessed and began beating the floor and yelling for people to rid their house of evil. A few days later, the same possessed woman began to urge people to destroy the crucial temple at Bomtem. She said she was willing to enter it first herself to exorcize Satan.[21]

The temple was, in fact, never destroyed. It stands—a structure of wood and vine—at the highest point of the settlement.[22]

The second religious movement was a nativistic one spurred, in the early 1980s, by the arrival of West Papuan refugees from conflicts in Irian Jaya with the Indonesian government who settled in villages close by the Atbalmin. Related to the larger "Free Papua Movement" (Organisasi Papua Merdeka):

The leaders of these refugees sought to unite all Melanesians against outside forces, a category that included not only Indonesians but also Christians and the existing Papua–New Guinea government (which was seen to serve outside interests). They emphasized the need to reject new influences and to return to ancestral Melanesian social and religious practices. . . . They also said that they had special ties to the dead ancestors themselves, who would insure their victory.[23]

This general agendum took a more specifically cargo cult–like form just a few days after the Christian revivalist episodes. On April 5, 1985, an Atbalmin returned from a visit to one of these refugee settlements. He announced that

ancestors were on their way back bringing the wealth and power that had been promised. "They [the refugees] say we will clap our hands," he reported, "and the Europeans will cry out once and will trade positions with us. They will carry things for us, they will work for us for money. We will look after them and pay them." The Atbalmin who remained Christian after the return of the ancestors would not get any benefits and might perhaps be killed.[24]

These two, apparently oppositional, movements did not cancel each other out. "For a period of several months, from April to June, both were active in the same area at the same time."[25] By December, 1985, both 'new' religious movements had declined,[26] though not without affecting the post-1976 situation: "What was indigenous in Atbalmin Christianity in the early to middle 1980s was . . . not so much how they were Christian but how they were both Christian and non-Christian at the same time."[27]

In this abstract, I have largely prescinded from Bercovitch's analytical framework, which emphasizes the creativity of multiplicity. In the service of this viewpoint, he maps the Atbalmin world in terms of "landscapes," which may serve us as a summary of his ethnographic report.

Despite their conversion to Christianity, people commonly seemed to situate themselves in an indigenous landscape of settlements, territories, and descent groups constituted from a long history of indigenous social and religious relations. Sacred narratives of the indigenous religion explained many features of this visible world, such as physical or social differences between people and the existence of prominent natural landscapes. At other times, people showed their knowledge of a landscape defined by the government and business. It was marked by a profound difference in wealth and power between New Guineans and Europeans, and by a hierarchy of places beginning with the nearest government outpost and leading up through the provincial government capital at Vanimo, larger cities, the national capital at Moresby, and finally the place of the Europeans. . . . The West Papuans had contributed another landscape. It had its center far away in the lowlands of Irian Jaya, where the place of the dead was located. . . . The last landscape was provided by Christianity. It encompassed an even vaster world, including Christians as well as all pagans, Satan (and a host of devils) as well as God and Jesus, and Hell and Heaven as well as the visible world.[28]

One last comment. Based on Bercovitch's ethnography, it is the Christian myth of the Holy Spirit and not the Christ myth that seems of greatest interest to the Atbalmin. It is the Spirit that appears associated with particular acts ('sins'), which are named in public confession.[29] The Pauline sense of 'Sin' as a cosmic power that defines a view of human nature and, therefore, entails some sort of Christ myth with both cosmic and anthropological implications does not seem present. There appears to be some native Christian Christ mythology in the formulations concerning "the sending of the Spirit," at times associated with the "return of Christ," that would eliminate "sin" as the tension between native and Christian practices by an erasure of indigenous practices.[30] It is impossible to judge the degree to which the "sending" and/or the "return" is homologized to the quite different indigenous concept of a return of the ancestors, a concept reinterpreted in the cargo cults.[31] (For ways in which the Christ myth is interpreted in coastal Papua New Guinea, see the materials quoted in note 41 below).

As I have understood the term, 'redescription,' at the level of data, is neither a procedure of substitution nor of synonymy; it is the result of comparison across difference, taking cognitive advantage of the resultant mutual distortion. (For this reason, among others, I have preferred analogical comparisons, such as the Atbalmin to the Corinthians, over homological ones). Redescriptions, at the level of data, are in the service of a second, more generic revisionary enterprise: redescribing the categories employed in the study of religion.[32]

In the cases at hand, I should like to focus on two different fields. The first encompasses the social situation; the second, various mythic formations. One might, in a quite commonsense fashion, suppose the first to be relevant to the attraction of the second.

Two major elements stand out in which the New Guinea materials make more plausible the imagination of some early Christian social formations. The first is the ability of a small relatively homogenous community[33] to absorb a stunning series of situational changes within a brief span of time through strategies of incorporation and resistence. In the case of the Atbalmin, we might list, in rough chronological order, first contact with Europeans; European presence; Christian missionization (both Australian and, more successfully, by neighboring native Christians); the adoption of nonnative language (Tok Pisin) to denote central elements of this new religion; European alteration of the landscape (esp. the copper mines); intrusion of ethnically distinct natives (the West Papuans); a disastrous storm; and the destruction or interruption of some traditional sacra.[34] The West Papuans, with whom the Atbalmin interacted, having experienced the intrusion of foreign governments and Europeans at home, now, within the same time frame, underwent displacement from their land and their honored dead. The second element is the capacity of a small relatively homogenous community to experiment, simultaneously, with multiple modes of religion. (Bercovitch described four). The Atbalmin have exhibited, within their social and religious history, the dialectical relations of processes of reproduction and transformation that constitute, with particular clarity, what Sahlins has termed "structures of conjuncture."[35]

As a generalization, all of this makes more plausible the presumption of the coexistence of multiple experiments by early 'Christian' communities as well as their localism. It alerts us to the presence of sorts of changes not necessarily captured by the historical record. The small, relatively homogenous communities of the Atbalmin resemble more closely our imagination of the Galilean villages associated with Q and the Jesus traditions. However, in a locale such as Corinth, the clear presence of face-to-face communication networks, and the relative prominence of "households" suggest the existence of analogous communities within the larger urban landscape that served as the primary sites of earliest Christian experimentations. This suggests the possibility of thinking of Paul (and others) as intrusive on the native religious formations of the Corinthians addressed in 1 Corinthians, analogous, to some degree, to intrusions on the Atbalmin.

We would expect (and therefore may find less surprising or interesting) more diversity and historical complexity in pluralistic urban settings, especially those coastal cities engaged in translocal commerce. This has been a historical truism for circum-Mediterranean settlements; it holds as well for the Papua New Guinea coast, as any number of ethnographies that focus on so-called 'syncretism' would indicate. (See the coastal Ngaing example, note 41, below). Corinth has been taken as a 'usual' exemplar of such pluralisms. Yet, there is more. The Corinthians are the result of a relatively recent displacement and re-placement: the resettlement of Corinth (44 B.C.), involving the movement of non-Roman populations of freed slaves from Greece, Syria, Judaea, and Egypt.[36] In this respect they bear some situational analogy to the West Papuan refugees.

Informed by this analogy, I would propose, as an initial move, deploying the West Papuans interest in ancestors and the land of the dead in order to interrupt the usual lexical chain that moves from "Spirit" (*pneuma*) and "Holy Spirit" in the New Testament to *rûaḥ* in the Hebrew Bible with, more recently, a crucial detour to Qumran, before rushing on to invoke the dominant paradigm within New Testament scholarship of Easter/Pentecost. If careful, the usual semaisiological litany pauses briefly to note some aberrations (F. W. Horn terms them "unique uses of *pneuma*" [*Anchor Bible Dictionary*, 3: 266]) such as *pneuma* meaning 'ghost' in Luke 24:37, 39, or *pneumata* as referring to the (righteous) 'dead' in Hebrews 12:23. (Depending on how the scholar decides the undecidable "spirits in prison," 1 Peter 3:19 may be cited as a parallel to the plural usage in Hebrews). I would like to suggest, on the basis of our ethnographic comparative example, that, for some Corinthians with whom Paul interacts, such usages, linking spirit(s) with the dead, are by no means aberrant but rather constitute the norm.

If this be maintained, a different genealogy for 'spirit' in Corinth suggests itself: one that begins in the Hebrew Bible with the scattered, polemic references to ʾôb or the word pair ʾôb and yiddᵉʿônî (more frequently, the plural ʾōbôt wᵉyiddᵉʿōnîm), with newer translations, such as the *Revised Standard Version*, and the *New Revised Standard Version*, rendering ʾôb as "medium."[37] While the *Oxford Annotated Bible* (*Revised Standard Version*) glosses ʾôb as "necromancy" ([1965] *ad* Leviticus 19:31), Jacob Milgrom, in the *HarperCollins Study Bible* to the *New Revised Standard Version* ([1993] *ad* Leviticus 19:31 and 20:5–6), glosses the term as "mediums or [consulting] 'ancestral spirits.'" Our Papua New Guinea materials would strongly support the latter reading, requiring us to delete the sanitary pips.

What has brought about this revisionary understanding of the biblical term, that *'ōbōt* means 'ancestral spirits' or 'spirits of the dead,' is a set of studies of comparative Near Eastern materials effectively summarized by Joseph Tropper (1995).[38]

Analogous notions of oracular relations to the ancestors and the more proximate dead, within the context of a set of cultic relations and responsibilities to the dead, are thus found in Papua New Guinea, Israel, and the ancient Near East and are likewise present in each of the culture areas from which the resettled population of Corinth was derived. While such relations are often seen as problematic from the perspective of temple-based religion, they are an essential component of domestic religion. Drawing on my previous work on this theme[39] and influenced by the Papua New Guinea materials, we might imagine two different sorts of essentially familial practices obtaining for some groups in Corinth (I separate here what may, in fact, be joined in practice). One would focus on cultic relations with the spirit(s) of the now dislocated ancestors left behind, in the homeland. Such relations would include attempts to obtain oracular esoteric wisdom. Another would focus on cultic relations with the more immediate dead, now buried in Corinth, and would include a range of activities from memorial meals with the dead to oracles guiding present behavior, including moral guidance. I see nothing that would have prevented both sorts of honored dead being referred to as *pneumata* (analogous to the honored dead being termed *'ĕlōhîm* in 1 Samuel 28:13, cf. less unambiguously, Isaiah 8:19; Micah 3:7; also 2 Samuel 14:16)[40] or collectively, as *pneuma*.

It would be my suggestion that Paul has misconstrued these relations, understanding the variety of cultic activities with respect to the spirit(s) of the dead as being related to his already formed notion of the (holy) spirit (1 Thessalonians 1:6, etc.) as well as his already formed notion of tripartite anthropology (1 Thessalonians 5:23). This is the same sort of mistranslation the Atbalmin Christians and Revivalists employed with their specifically Christian Tok Pisin term 'Holy Spirit,' and their recasting of spirit-possession relations to the ancestors in the specifically Christian vocabulary of 'possessed by the Holy Spirit.'

Thus, I think, Paul would have understood one thing, some groups of Corinthians another, when *pneuma* is associated with *gnōsis;* when Paul claims to have authority for guiding present behavior because he "has the spirit of God" (1 Corinthians 7:40) or when he himself can be present "in spirit" (1 Corinthians 5:3–4) at the occasion of a communal moral dilemma; when they meet together for a meal for/with the dead (the celebratory meal of 1 Corinthians 11:20–21, which seems both traditional and non-Christian) to which a Lord's Supper has apparently been added; or, when they are concerned about baptism for the dead (1 Corinthians 15:29).

The imagination of such an understanding among some Corinthians requires another sort of redescription, at the level of the data, with respect to our scholarly imagination of the "divisions" at Corinth (the strong/weak, the spiritists, let alone claims for the presence of proto-gnostics). What I have been terming, with deliberate vagueness, "some Corinthians," does not map a group (or groups) that accords with the to-pography of 'parties' provided by those fragments conventionally identi-fied as 'slogans' quoted by Paul from his opponents. However, I am not prepared, in this essay, to offer a counter-proposal.

One consequence of this hesitation is that I have made no mention of "speaking in tongues." I suspect that Paul himself is straining to un-derstand the phenomenon that he encounters in Corinth as suggested by his (surprising?) appeal to the Delphic model of ecstatic speech inter-preted by a prophet. Paul may well have misunderstood the practice. I am tempted to suggest that if the communication is with the spirits of the ancestral dead, and if the Corinthians are, at most, second-generation immigrants to Corinth, then perhaps the ancestral spirits are being ad-dressed in their native, homeland language. Such language is frequently maintained for ceremonial and religious purposes by second-generation immigrants. If this be the case, Paul has taken xenoglossia (the *lalein het-erais glossias* of Acts 2:4) to be glossolalia.

I raise these matters as having relevance to my assigned topic: Paul's Christ myth at Corinth. If what I have redescribed is at all plausible, then Paul is implausible. Perhaps this is why, except for formulae (e.g., the re-peated "Christ crucified"), the myth is rarely elaborated in 1 Corinthians. It appears to play a role chiefly in those instances where Paul is palpably in difficulty: his shift on "idols" from being meaningless to meaningful (1 Corinthians 10:14ff); the polemic against Corinthian meal practice (1 Corinthians 11:23ff) where his strongest argument, finally, is not myth-making but rather the threat of supernatural sanction (1 Corinthians 11:31–32); and the discourse on resurrection (1 Corinthians 15).

It is this last issue that makes clear why a Christ myth would be, strictly speaking, meaningless to some Corinthian groups.[41] If Christ, having died, is no longer dead, then this violates the fundamental pre-supposition that the ancestors and the dead remain dead, even though they are thoroughly interactive with their living descendents in an ex-tended family comprising the living and the dead. For the ancestral dead, it is the fact of their death, not its mode and significance (for example, topoi of martyrdom, sacrifice, enthronement) that establishes and sustains their power.[42]

The problematic, for both the West Papuans and for the Corinthians here imagined, is not death but rather distance. To take the West Papuan refugee immigrants at their word, there is a problem because their "center" is "far away in the lowlands of Irian Jaya, where the place of the dead is located."

Some Corinthians may have understood Paul as providing them, in the figure of Christ, with a more proximate and mobile ancestor for their new, nonethnic 'Christian' *ethnos*.[43] Certainly, celestial figures often have a mobile advantage over chthonic ones who are more readily bound to a place. Perhaps some Corinthians found support for a new sort of ancestor in Paul's first/last Adam language in 1 Corinthians 15 (esp. 15:45), but this is vitiated by its context as part of a defense of resurrection, unless it was previously heard in another context. Perhaps some Corinthians found support for a new sort of ancestor in the complex set of registers played by Paul on *sōma*, with the body of Christ understood in a corporate sense (1 Corinthians 12:23) as a new collective ancestor. (Compare the term that used to be popular with respect to Israel, "corporate personality"). This new ancestor continues to be experienced in a traditional way, in a meal (1 Corinthians 10:17).

However, none of this will do without a major effort in non-Pauline myth-making by some Corinthians. For the continuing present liveliness of the ancestors and the dead is predicated on their continuing status as dead. This effort at myth-making would need to be coupled with their apparent ritual experimentation on new modes of relations to the dead, such as that suggested by 1 Corinthians 15:29.

One might go on to redescribe other themes in 1 Corinthians as a result of the Papua New Guinea comparison. For example, 'sin' as a term for expressing the tension between traditional indigenous and native Christian behavior, especially in matters of sexual conduct, kinship, eating and 'idolatry'—to list topics the Atbalmin have in common with the Corinthians.[44] Or, one might explore the attraction of the promise of participation in an enlarged Christian landscape for a relatively small group, as described for the Atbalmin, and as suggested in 1 Corinthians with its multiple references to an extended Christian 'family' present in other locales, but bound together by a communications network of letters, travels, and gifts.

I shall let matters rest at this point. This experiment in redescription suggests that a Christ myth, as represented by Paul in the course of his intrusion on the Corinthians, would have been uninteresting to some

Corinthians; that a spirit myth, as they appear to have understood it, might have been interesting to some Corinthians in that it was "good to think." The Corinthian situation may well be defined as the efforts at translations between these understandings and misunderstandings.[45]

Notes

1. This is by no means a singular contamination. For example, one needs to use extreme caution in evaluating the Christian influence on 'native apocalyptic' traditions, which are then redeployed, on the basis of ethnographic reports and anthropological theories, to interpret both Jewish and Christian apocalypticisms. See, for example, J. Z. Smith, "Too Much Kingdom/Too Little Community: A Review of J. Gager's *Kingdom and Community,*" *Zygon* 13 (1978): 123–30.

Early examples of such feedback often gave rise to secondary mythologies, such as the presence of Native American versions of biblical stories, which had been received from missionaries but which were taken to be indigenous 'originals' (see, already, S. Thompson, *European Tales among the North American Indians,* Colorado College Publications, 2 [Colorado Springs, 1919]). The alleged parallels were then deployed as proof that the Native Americans were the "lost tribes" of Israel.

E. B. Tylor's 1891 article remains, to the best of my knowledge, the first responsible discussion of the question of Christian contamination of 'native tradition.' E. B. Tylor, "The Limits of Savage Religion," *Journal of the Royal Anthropological Institute* 21 (1891): 283–301. See further, J. Z. Smith, "The Unknown God," in Smith, *Imagining Religion* (Chicago, 1982), 66–89 and 145–56.

2. The Chinese Rites Controversy was a seventeenth- and eighteenth-century Catholic argument over the degree of 'accommodation' with Chinese ritual practice by recent Roman Catholic converts, part of a wider, chiefly Jesuit, missionary strategy that was first experimented with in Japan in the mid-sixteenth century and later applied to India and China. Not at all irrelevant to issues raised later in this paper, the controversy concerned participation by Chinese Christians in domestic rituals honoring the ancestral dead, as well as in public and state rituals honoring Confucius. The controversy was sparked by Matteo Ricci's position that these were civil and social rituals and, therefore, not idolatrous. (See Y. Bettray, *Die Akkomadations-methode des Matteo Ricci,* Analecta Gregoriana, 76 [Rome, 1955]). Ricci's position was reenforced by a decree of the emperor, K'ang Hsi. (See the widely read proaccommodation treatise by C. Le Gobien, the procurator in Paris of the Chinese Mission, *Histoire de l'édit de l'Empereur de la Chine en faveur de la religion chrétienne, avec un éclaircissement sur les honneurs que les Chinois rendent à Confucius et aux morts* [Paris, 1698]). The question was debated until prohibited by Benedict XIV in the bull *Ex quo singulari* (1742).

Just short of two centuries later, Ricci's position on China was reaffirmed by Pius XII. The 1939 reversal began with pressure by Japanese Christians concerning their participation in State Shinto rituals for the emperor, defined by the state as a civil, and not a religious, act. At the request of then Commander (later Admiral) Yamamoto, Louis Bréhier and Pierre Batiffol prepared a brief, seventy-three-page monograph, *Les Survivances du culte impérial romain: À propos des rites shintoistes* (Paris, 1920), defending the participation by indicating the accommodation with imperial cult practices and themes in Roman Christianity. While this work was surely not a direct cause of the reversal, it played a role in a subsequent series of diplomatic exchanges and conferences that led to the relaxation of the prohibition against participation, first for Manchuria (1935), then Japan (1936), then China (1939, reconfirmed in 1941)—and, later, citing these precedents, Catholic Vietnamese being permitted to 'honor' ancestors (1964). See J. Guennou, "Les Missions catholiques," in H.-C. Puech, ed., *Histoire des religions*, Encyclopédie de la Pleiade (Paris, 1972), 2: 1167–71.

For the seventeenth-eighteenth–century controversy, F. Bontinck, *La Lutte autour de la liturgie chinoise aux XVIIe et XVIIIe siècles* (Louvain and Paris, 1962), remains the most important account. From a wider perspective, see the fascinating study by D. E. Mungello, *Curious Land: Jesuit Accommodation and the Origins of Sinology* (Stuttgart, 1985). See also the judicious summaries in one of the great historiographical achievements of our time, D. F. Lach (with E. J. Van Kley), *Asia in the Making of Europe* (Chicago, 1965–93), 3.1: 260–69, 385–86, 423–24, 429–30, 3.4; 1674–80, et passim. Many of the relevant documents are translated in A. S. Rosso, *Apostolic Legations to China of the Eighteenth Century* (South Pasadena, 1948). The richest guide to the voluminous controversy literature remains R. Streit, et al., *Bibliotheca missionum* (Münster and Aachen, 1916–75), 5: 803–961, 7: 1–44. See also H. Cordier, *Bibliotheca Sinica*, 2d ed. (Paris, 1904–24), 2: 869–926, 1279–94.

We still await a definitive study of the effect of the Rites Controversy on seventeenth- and eighteenth-century European theories of religion as part of a wider preoccupation with Chinese philosophy and religious practice. (See the effective summary in P. Hazard, *The European Mind, 1680–1715* [Cleveland, 1963]; 20–25). A major source for these theories was the proaccommodation work by Louis Le Comte (sometimes, Le Compte), *Nouveaux mémoires sur l'état présent de la Chine* (Paris, 1696–98; reprint, 1701), vols. 1–3; rapidly translated into English (1697, reprinted at least four times by 1738), Dutch (1697), and German (1699). Le Comte's work was condemned by the faculty of the Sorbonne (1700)—partly under pressure from a powerful French Catholic secret society, the Compagnie du Saint Sacrement. For the influences of the Rites Controversy on some strands of European religious and philosophical thought, see V. Pinot, *La Chine et la formation de l'esprit philosophique en France, 1640–1740* (Paris, 1932; reprint, Geneva,

1971), and D. P. Walker, *The Ancient Theology: Studies in Christian Platonism from the 15th to the 18th Century* (Ithaca, NY, 1972), 194–230.

3. For the Sumbanese materials, see W. Keane, "Materialism, Missionaries, and Modern Subjects in Colonial Indonesia," in P. van der Veer, ed., *Conversion to Modernities: The Globalization of Christianity* (New York and London, 1996), 137–70. In presenting the historical narrative, Keane is largely dependent on T. van den End, ed., *Gereformeerde Zending op Sumba, 1859–1972: Een Bronnenpublicatie* (Alphen aan den Rijn, 1987), *non vidi*.

4. Keane, "Materialism," 149.

5. Wielenga's article is briefly summarized in Keane, "Materialism," 147–48.

6. Keane, "Materialism," 152.

7. Keane, "Materialism," 153.

8. Keane, "Materialism," 160.

9. Keane, "Materialism," 156.

10. Keane, "Materialism," 160.

11. One of the earliest attempts to relate 'cargo cults' to the wider phenomenon of nativistic movements is the classic work by the Italian Marxist scholar, Vittorio Lanternari, *Movimenti religiosi di libertà e di salvezza dei popoli oppressi* (Milan, 1960), English translation, *The Religions of the Oppressed: A Study of Modern Messianic Cults* (New York, 1963). See, in general, the bibliographies by I. Leeson, *A Bibliography of Cargo-cults and Other Nativistic Movements in the South Pacific*, South Pacific Commission Technical Papers, 30 (London, 1952); and W. La Barre, "Materials for a History of Studies of Crisis Cults," *Current Anthropology* 12 (1971): 3–44. For an important, detailed ethnography of a New Guinea Highlands movement that resulted in the formation of an independent church, see P. Gesch, *Initiative and Initiation: A Cargo Cult–type Movement in Sepik Against Its Background in Traditional Village Religion*, Studia Instituti Anthropos, 33 (St. Augustin, 1985). For reviews of the history of cargo cult research, see F. Steinbauer, *Melanesian Cargo Cults* (Santa Lucia, 1979); and L. Lindstrom, *Cargo Cult: Strange Stories of Desire from Melanesia and Beyond* (Honolulu, 1993).

12. Gilbert H. Herdt has been central to this discussion, both in his own works and through edited volumes. See especially, among the latter, G. Herdt, ed., *Rituals of Manhood: Male Initiation in Papua New Guinea* (Berkeley, 1982), and Herdt, ed., *Ritualized Homosexuality in Melanesia* (Berkeley, 1984), 2d ed. (Berkeley, 1991). See further, G. Herdt and J. F. P. Poole, "'Sexual Antagonism': The History of a Concept in New Guinea Anthropology," *Social Analysis* 12 (1982): 3–28. For a corrective to some of the interests reflected in these works, see Herdt, ed., *Third Sex, Third Gender: Beyond Sexual Dimorphism in Culture and History* (New York, 1994); N. C. Lutkehaus and P. B. Roscoe, *Gender Rituals: Female Initiation in Melanesia* (New York and London, 1995).

13. With respect to Papua New Guinea and Melanesia, see, among others,

the following special issues of journals: R. M. Keesing and R. Tonkinson, eds., "Reinventing Traditional Culture: The Politics of Kastom in Island Melanesia," *Mankind* 13 (1982): 297–309; M. Jolly and N. Thomas, eds., "The Politics of Tradition," *Oceania* 62, no. 4 (1992): 241–354; A. Lattas, ed., "Alienating Mirrors: Christianity, Cargo Cults and Colonialism in Melanesia," *Oceania* 63, no. 1 (1992): 11–95; R. Feinberg and L. Zimmer-Tamakoshi, eds., "The Politics of Culture in the Pacific Islands," *Ethnology* 34, no. 3 (1995): 155–244. For a useful overview of new Melanesian spiritist movements, see M. Ernst, *Winds of Change: Rapidly Growing Religious Groups in the Pacific Islands* (Suva, 1994).

I should note that despite criticisms of the term, I retain 'nativism' to indicate, largely, the creation of new traditionalisms in the context of social and cultural change. (For this reason, I would classify many so-called 'fundamentalisms' as nativistic movements). Note W. E. Arnal's creative use of the nativistic model in the concluding pages of *Jesus and the Village Scribes: Galilean Conflicts and the Setting of Q* (Minneapolis, 2001), esp. 199–203. I accept the current criticisms of the closely related term, 'revitalization movements,' as bearing a pejorative sense. While prescinding from the Weberian schema of magic/rational, R. Linton's classic article, "Nativistic Movements," *American Anthropologist* 45 (1943): 230–40 remains one of the most formally correct efforts at taxonomy in the anthropological literature. For the critique of the term, see J. Z. Smith, ed., *The HarperCollins Dictionary of Religion* (San Francisco, 1995): 763, s.v. "nativistic movements"; cf. C. Myscofski, "New Religions," ibid., pp. 771–72.

14. I rely, here, on E. Bercovitch, "The Altar of Sin: Social Multiplicity and Christian Conversion among a New Guinea People," in S. Mizruchi, ed., *Religion and Cultural Studies* (Princeton, 2001), 211–35; cf. Bercovitch, "Mortal Insights: Victim and Witch in Nalumin Imagination," in G. H. Herdt and M. Stephen, eds., *Varieties of the Religious Imagination in New Guinea* (New Brunswick, 1989), 122–59; Bercovitch, "The Agent in the Gift: Hidden Exchange in Inner New Guinea," *Cultural Anthropology* 9 (1994): 498–536. Bercovitch conducted his fieldwork during the periods August 1981–March 1982 and November 1982–December 1985. To my knowledge, the only guide to tribal groups related to or adjacent to the Atbalmin remains the physical anthropological study by K. Rieckmann et al., "Blood Groups and Hemoglobin Values in the Telefomin Area New Guinea," *Oceania* 31 (1961): 296–304. See also, T. Hays, "Mountain-Ok Bibliography," in B. Craig and D. Hyndman, eds., *Children of Afek: Tradition and Change among the Mountain-Ok of Central New Guinea*, Oceania Monographs, 40 (Sydney, 1990), 167–97. For the geography, see the excellent frontispiece map in F. Barth's classic comparative study of the region, *Cosmologies in the Making: A Generative Approach to Cultural Variation in Inner New Guinea* (Cambridge, 1987; reprint, 1993), xii. Barth's work may be used with caution as parallel comparative cultural material for the region.

15. Bercovitch, "Altar of Sin," 214–15.

16. J. Goody, Foreword, to Barth, *Cosmologies in the Making*, xi.

17. Bercovitch, "Altar of Sin," 211, 217–18 et passim.

18. Bercovitch, "Altar of Sin," 212.

19. Bercovitch, "Altar of Sin," 228.

20. Bercovitch, "Altar of Sin," 232, cf. 216.

21. Bercovitch, "Altar of Sin," 222–23. For this earlier movement, Bercovitch (232, n. 14) refers to the article by Dan Jorgensen, the dean of Telefolmin studies, "Life on the Fringe: History and Society in Telefomin," in R. Gordan, ed., *The Plight of Peripheral People in Papua New Guinea* (Cambridge, Mass., 1981), 59–79, as well as to an unpublished dissertation, R. Brumbaugh, "A Secret Cult in the West Sepik Highlands" (Ph.D. diss., State University of New York at Stonybrook, 1980), which I have not seen.

I should stress that 'Holy Spirit' is an imported term, derived from the English within Tok Pisin, the 'pidgin' lingua franca of Papua New Guinea. See D. Kulick, *Language Shift and Cultural Reproduction: Socialization, Self, and Syncretism in a Papua New Guinea Village* (Cambridge, 1992) for an important meditation on the cultural implications of the shift from indigenous languages to Tok Pisin; see also J. Verhaar, ed., *Melanesian and Tok Pisin: Proceedings of the First International Conference on Pidgins and Creoles in Melanesia* (Amsterdam, 1990) for the current state of research. (As an aside, recall the most important single study on translation in relation to conversion, V. Rafael's instant classic, *Contracting Colonialism: Translation and Christian Conversion in Tagalog Society under Early Spanish Rule* [Ithaca, 1989]).

With respect to the proximate dead and the ancestors as well as to spirit beings, 'spirit' (lowercase) may be a reasonable rough translation. Communication with the ancestors occur through both dreams and male and/or female initiations and transmit 'wisdom.' (For connotations of 'wisdom,' see, for example, F. J. P. Poole's discussion of this theme with respect to the neighboring Bimin-Kuskusmin, "Wisdom and Practice: The Mythic Making of Sacred History among the Bimin-Kuskusmin of Papua New Guinea," in F. Reynolds and D. Tracy, eds., *Discourse and Practice* [Albany, 1992], 13–50). Communication with the dead occur through spirit mediums, often in song, or, in the case of individuals, in dreams. 'Spirit possession' is not an accurate omnibus term for these diverse native indigenous religious contexts and activities—see Raymond Firth's widely cited distinctions between Melanesian "spirit possession, spirit mediumship and shamanism" in Firth, *Tikopia Ritual and Belief* (Boston, 1967): 296—it may well be à propos in some native Christian religious contexts.

22. Bercovitch, "Altar of Sin," 216.

23. Bercovitch, "Altar of Sin," 215.

24. Bercovitch, "Altar of Sin," 223–24.

25. Bercovitch, "Altar of Sin," 224.

26. Bercovitch, "Altar of Sin," 230.

27. Bercovitch, "Altar of Sin," 228.

28. Bercovitch, "Altar of Sin," 219.

29. I would give much to know if confession was also a part of indigenous Atbalmin tradition. Neither Bercovitch nor any ethnography I am familiar with for neighboring tribes notes its occurrence. It does occur elsewhere in New Guinea, for example, in the Madang District hinterlands. See the material cited below, note 41. To this brief mention must be added Kenelm Burridge's work on the Tangu of the Bogia region of the Madang District. In all of his work, especially in Burridge, *Tangu Traditions: A Study of the Way of Life, Mythology, and Developing Experience of a New Guinea People* (Oxford, 1969), he emphasizes the centrality of confession in a variety of social and religious contexts (495, s.v. 'confession'). Compare his odd generalization on traditional Melanesians who tend "to be prudish, obsessional, suspicious, and much given to wrestling with their consciences" (Burridge, *New Heaven New Earth: A Study of Millenarian Activities* [New York, 1969], 40).

30. Bercovitch, "Altar of Sin," 223.

31. The theme of the return of the ancestors bearing goods is an element in indigenous religions of the region, reconfigured in cargo cults. See the literature cited in J. Z. Smith, *Imagining Religion*, 161, n. 46.

32. See further my remarks on 'redescription' in "Dayyeinu," a "meta-reflection" to appear in the published papers of the Society of Biblical Literature Seminar on Ancient Myths and Modern Theories of Christian Origins, edited by R. Cameron and M. Miller.

33. I use the term "relative homogeneity" to reflect on the fact that among folk who live in small-scale societies with traditional kinship systems, while ethnically identical, kinship serves both to manufacture difference and to overcome that difference. I have generalized this as culture being "constituted by the double process of both making differences and relativizing those very same distinctions. One of our fundamental social projects appears to be our collective capacity to think of, and to think away, the differences we create," J. Z. Smith, *Differential Equations: On Constructing the 'Other'* (Tempe, 1992), 11, reprinted in this volume; compare the cuisine analogy in Smith, *Imagining Religion*, 39–41. In *Differential Equations*, 11–13, I explored this "fundamental social project" in terms of the Hua people who live on the slopes of Mount Michael in the Eastern Highlands province of Papua New Guinea.

34. Note that such a series of events are capable of being addressed through more dramatic mythic and ritual means. For example, see the Bimin-Kuskusmin response to first contact (Poole, "Wisdom and Practice," 29–31, 42–44 n. 8 [cited above, n. 21]); alteration of the environment, in this case, taking oil samples

(31–38); and destruction of sacra (F. J. P. Poole, "The Reason of Myth and the Rationality of History: The Logic of the Mythic in Bimin-Kuskusmin 'Modes of Thought,'" in F. Reynolds and D. Tracy, eds., *Religion and Practical Reason: New Essays in the Comparative Philosophy of Religions* [Albany, 1994], 263–326, esp. 284–306).

35. M. Sahlins, *Historical Metaphors and Mythical Realities: Structure in the Early History of the Sandwich Islands Kingdom*, Association for Social Anthropology in Oceania, Special Publications, 1 (Ann Arbor, 1981). For a later, more general statement, employing a different vocabulary, see Sahlins, "Goodbye to *Tristes Tropes*: Ethnography in the Context of Modern World History," *University of Chicago Record*, 27, no. 3 (February 4, 1993): 2–7; now reprinted, with a considerable number of revisions, in Sahlins, *Culture in Practice: Selected Essays* (New York, 2000), 471–500.

36. I presume the summary of Corinthian data in J. Murphy-O'Connor, *St. Paul's Corinth: Texts and Archaeology*, Good News Studies, 6 (Wilmington, 1983), as updated in Murphy-O'Connor, "Corinth," *Anchor Bible Dictionary* (New York, 1992), 1: 1134–39. Professor John Kloppenborg-Verbin drew my attention to the possible significance of the resettlement of Corinth at the Society of Biblical Literature's annual meeting in Nashville, 2000.

37. The translation history of the terminology is revealing. Both the Greek and the Latin shift the force of the term to the performer. The Vulgate employs the generic *magus*; the Septuagint, the rare word, *engastrimythos*, in the majority of cases. In the latter, the implication of fraud ('ventriloquist') has shifted to 'medium' as in the parallel *engastrimantis* (compare the 9th ed. of Liddell-Scott with the 1968 Supplement). I know of only one scholar, the always interesting, if often eccentric, comparative philologist, R. B. Onians, who, in an addendum, has attempted an explanation of the term as a proper translation reflecting an Israelitic and Greek conception of a spirit in the belly. See Onians, *The Origins of European Thought about the Body, the Mind, the Soul, the World, Time, and Fate* (Cambridge, 1951), 480–505, esp. 488–90, and notes. The Authorized Version translates "familiar spirit," keeping the magical/demonic sense, but shifting away from the performer. More recent scholarship has translated ʾôb more directly as 'spirit of the dead' or the 'deified spirit of the ancestors,' while rendering the associated term, yiddeʿônî, as 'all-knowing,' an "epithet of the deceased ancestors, or a designation of the dead in general." J. Tropper, "Spirit of the Dead," in K. van der Toorn, B. Becking and P. W. van der Horst, eds., *Dictionary of Deities and Demons in the Bible* (Leiden, 1995), 1524–30.

38. Tropper, "Spirit of the Dead"; cf. Tropper, "Wizard," in ibid., 1705–7.

39. See esp. J. Z. Smith, "Here, There, and Anywhere" in this volume.

40. See the important treatment of (spirits of) the dead as ʾĕlōhîm in Th. J. Lewis, *Cults of the Dead in Ancient Israel and Ugarit*, Harvard Semitic Monographs,

39 (Atlanta, 1989), 49–52, 115–17, 178–79, et passim; cf. Lewis, "The Ancestral Estate (*naḥălat ʾĕlōhîm*) in 2 Samuel 14:16," *Journal of Biblical Literature* 110 (1991): 597–612, esp. 602–3.

41. In the coastal regions of Papua New Guinea, which have a long history of being missionized by Christians, there is some focus on translating some understanding of the Christ myth into native idiom and practice. Take, for example, the Ngaing linguistic groups inhabiting the Madang region on the Rai Coast, first contacted by Europeans in 1871, missionized since at least 1885—a date that may be extended back to 1847–55. Indigenous religion focused on male ceremonies "honouring the spirits of the dead" (P. Lawrence, *Road Belong Cargo: A Study of the Cargo Movement in the Southern Madang District, New Guinea* [Melbourne, 1964], 13, 17–18, et passim). For a more complete account, see Lawrence, "The Ngaing of the Rai Coast," in P. Lawrence and M. J. Meggitt, eds., *Gods, Ghosts and Men in Melanesia* (Oxford, 1965), 198–223; reprinted in T. G. Harding and B. J. Wallace, eds., *Cultures of the Pacific* (New York, 1970, 285–315, esp. 292–96).

There was a short-lived Madang cargo movement (1956–61), led by Lagit, an indigenous, former Christian catechist from a Catholic mission, who killed a man in front of assembled villagers by slitting his throat. The incident was prearranged, we are told, as the victim went voluntarily to his death. Lagit's explanation, in the ethnographer's paraphrase, was that "it was necessary for a native to make the same sacrifice as Jesus Christ had made for the Europeans before the natives' oppressive standard of living could be improved." Lawrence, *Road Belong Cargo*, 267.

A more complicated case of translation, in both ritual and narrative idiom, ultimately involving the sequence of the synoptic Passion narrative, is from another Ngaing-speaking group "located in the hinterland of the Rai Coast" whose name has been concealed by the ethnographer, W. Kempf, in "Ritual, Power and Colonial Domination: Male Initiation among the Ngaing of Papua New Guinea," in C. Stewart and R. Shaw, eds., *Syncretism/Anti-Syncretism: The Politics of Religious Synthesis* (London and New York, 1994), 108–26.

For this group, traditional male initiation involves, above all, the display to the initiates of secret objects related to the ancestors that are usually kept hidden in water. After a last meal with his family as an uninitiated male, the novice went into seclusion for a three week period, during which he was shown the sacra and was governed by a wide-ranging set of prohibitions. He then emerged and his new status was publicly recognized.

In the early 1950s, circumcision was introduced to one village in the region as a hygenic practice by a native medical orderly. It subsequently became linked with initiation as a ritual practice, as well as with the characteristic Melanesian male rationale for penile bloodletting: removal of the dark, female blood from the bright male blood so that one's body is healthy and shining. (Kempf presumes some cultural interaction with Austronesian coastal traditions that, unlike the Ngaing peoples but like some Papua New Guinea Highland tribes, practice a variety of forms of penile bloodletting). Here, on the basis of an interchange of native traditions, a new ritual was inserted into the traditional initiatory sequence: immediately after the novice's farewell meal and before the first display of sacra. Following a public confession, usually stressing sexual misconduct, the circumcision commenced, discarding the first, dark blood, and saving the subsequent bright blood. This was bound together with a bundle of bull-roarers (one of the sacra to be displayed).

For indigenous Christians who practice these initiatory rituals, translation was required of this new ritual into their understanding of Christian idiom, informed by a sentiment widely held in cargo cults, that the European missionaries have reversed or concealed the true meaning of Scripture from the natives. To present the ethnographer's summary of this native Christian translation:

> Jesus's baptism by John the Baptist at the River Jordan has come to be associated with displaying the traditional gourd instruments. John is considered to be Jesus' classificatory mother's brother and, as such, is held to have initiated him into the domain of the secret gourd instruments which . . . are associated with water. . . . [The] men know too that Jesus was circumcised. The young men particularly interpret the crucifixion of Jesus as his ritual circumcision. The Last Supper is . . . compared with the last meal eaten by the . . . candidates the evening before their circumcision. Judas is not considered as the betrayer, but as Jesus' classificatory mother's brother. He led him before Pontius Pilate . . . [understood as] a member of an oppositional patrician [*sic*, patriclan] and thus responsible for the circumcision. Pilate is believed to have questioned Jesus thoroughly on his premarital affairs but could not establish that Jesus had sinned. This cross-examination is the equivalent of the confession conducted before circumcision. . . . Then the crucifixion took place, this being nothing but Jesus' circumcision. The three days after Jesus' death are interpreted as his three weeks of seclusion. Finally, the resurrection is identified with the public presentation of the initiates at the close of the circumcision rites. (Kempf, "Ritual, Power and Colonial Domination," 313)

Note that basic elements of the Christ myth (in its narrative form) are here refused. Congruent with my discussion above, death is not death, nor is resurrection a resurrection.

42. I have explored some of these themes elsewhere, especially in *Drudgery*

Divine: On the Comparison of Early Christianities and the Religions of Late Antiquity (Chicago, 1990), 109–14, 120–43.

43. I have been influenced here by the observations of Stan Stowers in his important unpublished contribution to the Consultation on Ancient Myths and Modern Theories of Christian Origins at the annual meeting of the Society of Biblical Literature in New Orleans, 1996, "On Construing Meals, Myths and Power in the World of Paul." I draw particular attention to three remarks with respect to the meal at Corinth. "The signals and expectations suggested by the Lord's Dinner might be read as confusing and contradictory in the context of the codes of eating in Greco-Roman culture" (Stowers: 14). "Instead of the community being constituted and tested by eating meat, it exists by eating bread that is a symbol of an absent body that points both to the significance of giving up that body and to the loyalty of the social body toward that symbol" (15). "Where is the body in the Lord's Dinner? It is present in its absence. The bread of human art is the reminder of a body that occupies no place" (17). Compare Burton Mack's remark concerning "Christ the first father of a non-ethnic genealogy," in his response to Stowers's paper at the same Consultation (5).

44. The issue of eating meat sacrificed to idols at Corinth would receive an assist from the interpretative framework Keane brings to his Sumbanese example. See above, note 3.

45. In this essay, I have not followed redescription at the level of data with an attempt at the rectification of generic scholarly categories within the study of religion, nor within the study of early Christianities. As indicated above, a prime candidate for rectification would be the broad, somewhat diffuse, category of "enthusiasm," one of a set of terms of Christian pedigree (e.g., "charismatic") that have frequently been applied to nativistic social and religious phenomena. In the history of scholarship, both in the study of religion and the study of early Christianities, 1 Corinthians has served as the canonical example for these categories.

CHAPTER SIXTEEN

A TWICE-TOLD TALE

THE HISTORY OF THE HISTORY OF
RELIGIONS' HISTORY

IN SHAKESPEARE'S curiously neglected play, *King John* (III.4, line 108), in William Broome's eighteenth-century translation of the *Odyssey* (XII.538), as well as in the title of Nathaniel Hawthorne's first published collection of short stories, the phrase, "twice-told tale," signifies tedium. By contrast, for those of us who study religion, twice-told or twice-performed is understood to be a minimal criterion for those basic building blocks of religion: myth and ritual. For us, repetition guarantees significance. Indeed, we demand more. In Jane Harrison's suggestive characterization, ritual (or myth) is "representation repeated,"[1] thus doubling the twice-told, twice-performed quality.

Harrison's formulation reminds us as well of the nature of our enterprise. As is characteristic of the human sciences in general, the little prefix *re-* is perhaps the most important signal we can deploy. It guarantees that we understand both the second-order nature of our enterprise as well as the relentlessly social character of the objects of our study. We re-present those re-peated re-presentations embedded in the cultures and cultural formations that comprise our subject matter.

I labor this point at the outset to make plain one presupposition that will guide my remarks. The history of the history of religions is not best conceived as a liberation from the hegemony of theology—our pallid version of that tattered legend of the origins of science, whether placed in fifth-century Athens or sixteenth-century Europe, that depicts science progressively unshackling itself from a once regnant religious world-view. Our variant of this twice-told tale needs to be set aside, not because such a claimed liberation has been, in so many moments of our history, an illusion, but rather because this way of retelling the tale occludes a more fundamental issue that yet divides us. In shorthand form, this is the debate between an understanding of religion based on *presence* and one based on *representation*. But, I get ahead of myself . . .

As in any historiographic enterprise, the history of the history of religions may be imagined in a variety of ways. Each is appropriate to the interests of their fashioner. While the mappings remain curiously consistent, there have been, in fact, two major opposing stratagems: the exceptionalist and the assimilationist. Each, in its own way, seeks legitimation, seeks a place for the study of religion on the map of recognized academic disciplines. The exceptionalist insists on the distinctive (or, unique) nature of the subject matter of the study of religion; the assimilationist argues for the equivalence (or, parity) of the methods of the study of religion with those of other human sciences. In either case, the mode of representation is genealogical, a narrative of founders and schools that often takes the form of an inverted tree diagram. While this mode was common in both the biological sciences and the linguistic sciences—abstaining from the debates as to which one influenced the other—it has now been subjected to strong critique in both fields in favor of a more diffuse, tangled, multicausal, and interactive representation. For example, the evolutionary biologist W. Ford Doolittle has written in an article entitled, "Uprooting the Tree of Life," that the schematization of the origins of life "look more like a forkful of spaghetti than a tree." Similarly, one might cite the strictures of Colin Renfrew and Bruce Lincoln with respect to the Indo-European tree diagram, building, in part, on Schuchardt's and Schmidt's wave theory.[2] For this reason, while in what follows I shall employ conventional periodization, I would stress that each of these has exceptionally fluid boundaries and are properly thought of as pluriform phenomena. Thus, one should, for example, talk of Renaissances, and take pain to specify which Enlightenment one is speaking of.

While this is a historiographical discussion well worth pursuing, it is also somewhat misleading. It assumes that the study of religion is best mapped by being attentive, at the outset, to the occasional instances of reflexive, metadiscourse in the field, to its defining moments, rather than the "normal science" of its quotidian praxis. If we start, so to speak, on the ground, a different constellation of characteristics emerges, which gives rise to a different sort of narrative as well as to a different sense of urgency with respect to matters of second-order discourse.

If some alien, unfamiliar with the fierce eighteenth- and nineteenth-century taxonomic controversies concerning the classification of the academic disciplines, were to observe scholars of religion in action, it would have no difficulty identifying the class to which they belong. With respect to practice, the history of religions is, by and large, a philological endeavor chiefly concerned with editing, translating and interpreting texts, the majority of which are perceived as participating in the dialectic of 'near' and 'far.' If this is the case, then our field may be redescribed as a child of the Renaissance.[3]

While there are surely precursors (the historian's always present temptation toward infinite regress), it is the various projects associated with the equally various Renaissances that set the agendum of our field. First, the sheer mastery of others' languages—a characteristic that still marks our field within the contemporary academy—whether their otherness be expressed in terms of temporal or spatial distance. Second, the etymological conviction, still regnant, that there is something of surpassing value hidden 'beneath' the words, a something that is essential, as opposed to the verbally accidental, and that may be uncovered only by decipherment; or, the comparable rhetorical conviction that values the givenness of the 'real' concealed 'behind' the words. Third, building on this etymological conviction, the tension between perceptions of unity and diversity in cultural formations was often settled by the postulation of an essential similarity in the face of accidental difference, which was to be explained by either environmental differences or the diffusing effects of historical processes. These issues became urgent because of the unanticipated increase of data for variegation, each the product of specific, European, historical causes. To list only three.

(1) The movement north and west of Greek and Hebrew manuscripts following the capture of Constantinople and the expulsion of Jews from Spain, both of these not unrelated to an expansive Islam, presented Renaissance scholars with an internal other, an ancestral past profoundly distant and different from the then European present. A past that was now only accessible through acts of imagination.

(2) The European colonial and mission adventures in the Americas as well as in Africa and Asia gave rise to a number of unanticipated consequences. The unexpected presence of the Americas shattered the classical biblical and Greco-Roman imagination of the inhabited geosphere as a tripartite world-island, thus giving rise to the first new intellectual confrontation with the problem of human and biological difference as possibly signalling otherness.[4] Were the Americas created separately? Were their inhabitants not descendants from Eden? In the case of both

the Americas and Africa, there was, as well, the production of ethno-graphic texts in which European words replaced and represented those of the native.[5] In the case of Asia, a different result was the collection and translation of significant texts in hitherto unknown languages.[6] Then too, there were, also, in Asia, contacts with kinds of Christianities, not experienced since the thirteenth century, whose difference from familiar European forms was often perceived as more problematic and therefore more threatening than native religions.

(3) This latter perception resonated with a European one in which the schismatic impulses of emergent Protestantisms raised a host of questions as to religious credibility and truth. These rival claims to authority made implausible older heresiological explanations for internal diversities.[7]

In each of these cases, languages and religions became the privileged cultural formations in which the controversies of unity and difference were framed. Indeed, as already suggested, it was most often the then reg-nant linguistic model of essence/accidence that governed these contro-versies when applied to religion. It is, therefore, here, as well, that the de-bate over what would become the question of 'religion' and 'the religions' first took on imperative force. Awareness of the plural 'religions' (both Christian and non-Christian) forced interest in the imagination of a sin-gular, generic 'religion.' As a late example, I take as emblematic of these Renaissance concerns Edward Brerewood's *Enquiries Touching the Diver-sity of Languages and Religions through the Chiefe Parts of the World* (pub-lished, posthumously, in 1614),[8] the second work, as far as I am aware, in the English language to employ the plural 'religions' in its title. There is, as well, a second sense in which Brerewood, now the individual, may be taken as emblematic. Like so many other nonclerical writers on religion prior to the mid-nineteenth century, Brerewood was an *amateur*, publish-ing not only on languages and religions, but also on antiquities (espe-cially numismatics), mathematics, and logic. One may well argue that the subsequent professionalization of religious studies, in concert with other fields undergoing professionalization, gave rise to new disciplinary horizons carrying their own methodological and theoretical interests that were, in the main, by no means peculiar to the study of religion. In particular, I think of the claimed *sui generis* nature of a field's object of re-search, a claim, in the late nineteenth and early twentieth centuries, es-pecially associated with the newly emergent social sciences.

The Renaissance pattern was modified through Enlightenment, counter-Enlightenment, and Romantic theories of language and reli-gion, which brings us to the threshold of the modern enterprise of the study of religion—although I will signal, here, only one trajectory of new elements in linguistic theory which was taken over into thinking about religion.

Enlightenment interest in language is a by-product of its preeminent concern for thought and thoughtfulness, an emphasis that must be reaffirmed by any scholar of religion, while prescinding from some of its formulations of this concern. For example, unity and uniformity were revalued as universalism; difference was stigmatized as irrational. Their sometimes vision of an abstract, universal humanity required the imagination of the possibility of an equally abstract, universal language in which all would be transparent, in which decipherment would be superfluous.[9] Language was thus conceived as a secondary tool for the expression of thought, with the development of the former the result of the progressive refinement of the latter. To quote one eighteenth-century authority, language "being entirely the invention of man, must have been exceedingly rude and imperfect at first, and must have arrived by slow degrees at greater and greater perfection, as the reasoning faculties acquired vigour and acuteness."[10] The only question was whether the perfecting of language was best achieved by controlling the denotation of signs or the regularization of grammar.

The counter-Enlightenment takes the issue of thoughtfulness in a new direction, one as yet insufficiently appropriated by scholars of religion.[11] Language, it was argued, is not a secondary naming or memorializing; it is not a translation of thought, it is not posterior to experience, rather, it is the very way in which we think and experience. The human sciences become conceptually possible largely through the acceptance of the counter-Enlightenment argument that their objects of study are holistic linguistic and language-like systems, and that, therefore, they are the study of "eminently social" human projects. This gives rise to what was already alluded to at the beginning of my presentation: an insistence that the central debates within the study of religion revolve around the relations of language and experience. Questions as to whether experience can ever be immediate or is always mediated? Whether we can experience a world independently of the conventional ways in which it is socially represented? Whether the *re-* of re-presentation remains always at the level of re-presentation? Such questions constitute the serious theoretical matters that sharply divide us in ways that cut across conventional, essentially political, divisions such as historians of religions and theologians.

For a certain sort of grand theorist in the study of religion, two aspects of Romantic theories of language proved most compelling. First, the reassertion, against the Enlightenment, of the supreme value of uniqueness, singularity, or individuality in the name of the creative, free expression of will. Second, and of greater import, the identification of poetic language, in opposition to the prosaic, as intransitive, as a nonpragmatic, autonomous totality, a thing-in-itself. In such a view, there is no gap between signifier and signified. The counter-Enlightenment's insistence on the nonsecondary character of language has now been transformed into the transparency of self-disclosure. From poetry to myth is but a small step; Schelling, most famously, made the translation:

> Each figure in mythology is to be taken for what it is, for it is precisely in this way that it will be taken for what it signifies. The signifying here is at the same time the being itself, it has passed into the object, being one with it. No sooner do we allow these beings to signify something than they are no longer anything themselves . . . Indeed, their greatest attraction lies in the fact that, whereas they only are, without any relation, absolute in themselves, they still allow signification to shine through.
>
> Mythology is not allegorical; it is tautegorical. For mythology, the gods are beings that really exist; instead of being one thing and signifying another, they signify only what they are.

Allegory, one of the prime modes of interpreting myth for more than a millennium, is here dethroned; the hermeneutics of 'speaking-otherwise' has given way to the direct apprehension of the other's speech.[12] Romanticism laid the groundwork for one of the hallmarks of influential twentieth-century theories of religion in which a still essentially philological discipline all but ignores modern linguistics and is often prepared to impeach the status of language in an effort to preserve ontology from anthropology and to maintain the privilege of unmediated, direct experience.

With this much by way of a brief background, let me turn to some implications of locating the history of religions within philology, and of resituating it within Renaissance and Romantic linguistic thought for both practice and theory.

We may recall Mircea Eliade's double critique of dominant modes of scholarship on religion, made in the course of a set of reflections on the past and future of the field. As is well known, for those outside of the history of religions, chiefly in the human sciences, his name for all that he abjured in their work was 'reductionism.' Less famously, Eliade named as his opponents within the field, the 'philologians.' I shall take up these two names from Eliade's execration text in reverse order.

From Eliade's totalizing perspective, the philologically based historians of religions persistently take parts for wholes, thereby giving priority to the local rather than to the general and typical. His fear was that the preponderance of language-based specialists within the field would result in a situation where "the History of Religions will be endlessly fragmented and the fragments reabsorbed in the different philologies."[13] To a degree, this has occurred, and has brought with it a new ethos of particularism that challenges the global ambitions that from time to time, have animated the field. But, more can be said.

There is the sheer effort involved in gaining proficiency, to the best of one's ability, in difficult languages, often first encountered in the course of graduate studies. While such language studies, taken together, constitute one of our major achievements over the past two centuries, their result has been that language instruction consumes a disproportionate amount of time in the training of the historian of religions. As certification in language ability has increasingly come to be the criterion for achieving professional status, other matters, preeminently those associated with mastering the second-order discourse of the field, get pushed to the side. Philology is the vocation; generalization and theory, the avocation. This has led to the wholesale adoption of a sort of common-sense descriptive discourse as a major rhetoric for the work of the field.

It is possible to point to a variety of practices symptomatic of this sort of discourse in which everything is treated as a self-evident instance of ostension. Texts are pointed to, paraphrased, or summarized as if their citation is, by itself, sufficient to guarantee significance. When translation is undertaken, it is without an explicit theory of translation; rather, reproduction and verbal congruence are assumed to be values in their own right. Comparisons are limited to those grounded in common genealogy or spatial contiguity.

The ostensive nature of these practices serve a protective role. In each of these, the unity, the integrity of the subject for study is preserved. Like the Mosaic altar, such practices guarantee that the scholar's work will be built of "whole stones," that the injunction, "thou shalt not lift up any iron tool upon them," (Deuteronomy 27:5–6) has been piously observed; that like the Temple of Solomon, "there was neither hammer nor axe nor any tool of iron heard in the house while it was in building" (1 Kings 6:7). By means of such practices, the handicraft of the scholar is disguised so as to give the appearance of achieving "a house not made with hands" (Acts 7:48). Such an attitude, as Bakhtin pointed out, has as one of its causes philology's focus on "dead languages, languages that were by that very fact 'unities.'"[14] But it comes as well from a deeply held ethos that Karl Mannheim characterized, in his seminal essay on the sociology of knowledge, as a "conservative" ideology, a "right wing method-ology," which tends to use "morphological categories which do not break up the concrete totality of the data of experience but seek rather to pre-serve it in all of its uniqueness." Opposed to this, Mannheim wrote, is "the analytical approach characteristic of parties of the left [which] broke down every concrete totality in order to arrive at smaller, more gen-eral units which may then be recombined."[15] Here, the scholar's "tools" have indeed been busy with the altar. The result can no longer be thought of as 'natural' but rather stands forth, marked as a construction. Whether this fabrication be judged as informative or as a lie depends not on pre-sumptions of congruence but on the exercise of a critical intelligence that assesses the cognitive gain or loss made possible by the constructive difference and distance from what Mannheim termed "the concrete to-tality." The fabrication is, necessarily, a representation rather than a claimed presence.

I would note as well Mannheim's description of the analytical approach as seeking "smaller, more general units." Scholars of religion have made insufficient use of the notion of 'generalization,' a neo-Latin coinage, growing out of the Aristotelian taxonomic distinction between genus and species, the latter giving rise to 'specialization' as the proper antonym to 'generalization.' In handbooks of logic, the 'general' is placed in opposition to the 'universal' by its admission to significant exceptions. Generalization is understood to be a mental, comparative, taxonomic ac-tivity that directs attention to cooccurrences of selected stipulated char-acteristics while ignoring others. Both of these qualifications, not uni-versal and highly selective, are central to generalization. Indeed, they are frequently exaggerated, leading to the pejorative sense of 'generality' as exhibiting vagueness or indeterminacy. Employed correctly, these same characteristics insure that generalities are always corrigible.[16] By this un-derstanding, our object of interest would then be 'religion' as the general name of a generic anthropological category, a nominal, intellectual con-struction, surely not to be taken as a 'reality.' After all, there are no exis-tent genera.

It is here that we begin to get an assist from modern linguistic theo-ries. The scholarly imagination of 'religion' as an intellectual category es-tablishes a disciplinary horizon that should play the same sort of role as 'language' in linguistics or 'culture' in anthropology. In each case, the generic category supplies the field with a theoretical object of study, different from, but complimentary to, their particular subject matters. Taking up only the analogy to language, Hans Penner has persistently reminded us of the relevance of the Saussurean project,[17] which was

369

undertaken to "show the linguist what he is doing," in conscious opposition to what Saussure termed the "philologies" and languages' "ethnographic aspect[s]."[18] As described by one scholar of language:

> Saussure was doubtless one of the first to render explicit, for linguistics, the necessity of accomplishing what Kant terms the Copernican revolution. [Saussure] distinguished the *subject matter* of linguistics, the linguist's field of investigation—which includes the whole set of phenomena closely or distantly related to language use—from its *object* . . . The role of general linguistics . . . is to define certain concepts that allow us to discern in the particular investigation of any particular language, the object within the subject matter.[19]

It is important to recall that Saussure's distinction between 'language' and 'speech' is maintained, methodologically, by most forms of contemporary linguistics, although there is sharp disagreement as to their definitions as well as over the appropriate criteria for distinguishing the empirical subject matter from the theoretical object of research. That is to say, the formulation is both arguable and corrigible. It is this very process of argumentation concerning this object that has resulted in some of the most significant theoretical advances in linguistics.

To come at the same point from a different angle. The field of religious studies has been more persistent than many of its academic neighbors in continuing to maintain one strand of nineteenth-century neo-Kantian thought, which argued that the distinction between the natural sciences and the human sciences was a matter of explanation as opposed to interpretation. The former, in one of its earlier formulations, being understood as privileging the general (through subsumption to law-like statements); the latter, as privileging the individual, or more strongly, the unique. Each was thought to have its own sort of data, its own appropriate subject matter. Far more fruitful is the alternative proposal, from another strand of contemporaneous neo-Kantian thought, that holds these two approaches to be alternative ways of construing the same datum, the same subject matter.[20] In either proposal, the term 'reduction' has come to stand, nowhere more so than in the study of religion, as the ambivalent cipher for this difference, perceived as being highly valued by the natural sciences and abjured by the majority of the human sciences. Such a view—at times raised to the level of an ethical proscription—is, and has been for some time, utterly inadequate.

Both explanations and interpretations are occasioned by surprise. It is the particular subject matter that provides the scholar with an occasion for surprise. Surprise, whether in the natural or the human sciences, is always reduced by bringing the unknown into relations to the known. The process by which this is accomplished, in both the natural and the human sciences, is translation: the proposal that the second-order conceptual language appropriate to one domain (the known/the familiar) may translate the second-order conceptual language appropriate to another domain (the unknown/the unfamiliar). Perhaps the strongest example of this procedure in the study of religion is Durkheim's translation of the language appropriate to religion (for him, the unknown) into the language appropriate for society (the known). The point at which one may differ from Durkheim's project is with respect to his acceptance of the goal of explanatory simplicity. Better, here, is Lévi-Strauss's formulation: "scientific explanation consists not in a movement from the complex to the simple but in the substitution of a more intelligible complexity for another which is less."[21]

While the adequacy of any translation proposal may be debated, an argument made more difficult by the lack of elaborated theories of translation by scholars of religion, the only grounds for rejecting such a procedure is to attack the possibility of translation itself, most often attempted through appeals to incommensurability. Such appeals, if accepted, must entail the conclusion that the enterprise of the human sciences is, strictly speaking, impossible.[22]

I would note only two implications of translation. First, translation, as an affair of language, is a relentlessly social activity, a matter of public meaning rather than of individual significance. Here, for the study of religion, the public is, first of all, the academic community, and therefore, a central issue becomes one of specifying the relations between the study of 'religion' and other disciplinary endeavors, a matter of locating oneself with respect to one's conversation partners, those with whom one will work out appropriate translation languages. Second, whether of a conceptual or natural language, whether intercultural or intracultural, translation is never fully adequate. To pick up again Schelling's term (borrowed from Coleridge), translation can never be "tautegorical." There is always discrepancy. (To repeat the old tag: "To translate is to traduce.") Central to any proposal of translation are questions as to appropriateness and 'fit,' questions that must be addressed through the double methodological requirement of comparison and criticism.

Indeed, the cognitive power of any translation, model, map, generalization or redescription—as, for example, in the imagination of 'religion'—is, by this understanding, a result of its *difference* from the subject matter in question and not its congruence. This conclusion has, by and large, been resisted throughout the history of the history of religions. But this resistence has carried a price. Too much work by scholars of religion takes the form of a paraphrase, our style of ritual repetition, which is a particularly weak mode of translation, insufficiently different from its subject matter for purposes of thought. To summarize: a theory, a model, a conceptual category, a generalization cannot be simply the data writ large.

The alternative would be to persist in a view that would make our "twice-told tale" truly tedious, to persist in denying that a science depends on the construction of its theoretical object of study, insisting rather that it is founded on the discovery of a unique reality that eludes any translation other than paraphrase. It is to accede to the odd sort of "tautegorical" claim that last appeared in the 1960–61 description of the History of Religions field at the University of Chicago: "It is the contention of the discipline of History of Religions that a valid case can be made for the interpretation of transcendence as transcendence."[23] This expression, with its implied acceptance of incommensurability, denies the legitimacy of translation, and the cognitive value of difference. It condemns the field to live in the world of Borges's Pierre Menard, in which a tale must always be identically "twice-told," where a word can only be translated by itself.[24]

Notes

1. J. Harrison, *Ancient Art and Ritual,* 2d ed. (Oxford, 1918), 42.

2. The tree or inverted tree diagram has had a long history in biological and linguistic representations. For an important collective volume on the image with rich bibliographies, see, H. M. Hoenigswald and L. F. Wiener, eds., *Biological Metaphor and Cladistic Classification: An Interdisciplinary Perspective* (Philadelphia, 1987). I have taken the quotation by W. Ford Doolittle, "Uprooting the Tree of Life," *Scientific American* (February, 2000) from *The New York Times,* June 13, 2000, D2. For the strictures on the tree diagram in Indo-European linguistics, see C. Renfrew, *Archaeology and Language: The Puzzle of Indo-European Origins* (Cambridge, 1987); and B. Lincoln, *Theorizing Myth: Narrative, Ideology and Scholarship* (Chicago, 1999), esp. 211–16. The theoretical basis of the rival "wave theory" was revisited in E. Pulgram's classic article, "Family Tree, Wave Theory, and Dialectology," *Orbis* 2 (1953): 67–72. The theory ultimately depends on the works of H. Schuchardt, *Der Vokalismus des Vulgärlateins* (Leipzig, 1868), vol. 3; and J. Schmidt, *Die Verwandtschaftsverhältnisse der indogermanischen Sprachen* (Weimar, 1872).

3. In this brief sketch of Renaissance linguistics, I have relied, above all, on

M.-L. Demonet, *Les voix du signe: Nature du langage à la Renaissance, 1480–1580* (Paris and Geneva, 1992).

4. On the issues engendered by the novelty of the Americas, see J. Z. Smith, "What a Difference a Difference Makes," in J. Neusner and E. S. Frerichs, eds., *"To See Ourselves As Others See Us": Christians, Jews. "Others" in Late Antiquity* (Chico, 1985), 3–48; and Smith, "Close Encounters of Diverse Kinds," in S. Mizruchi, ed., *Religion and Cultural Studies* (Princeton, 2001), both reprinted in this volume.

5. On the production of ethnographic texts focusing on indigenous American and African religions, Ramón Pané, *Relación acera de las antigüedades de los indios* (ca. 1495) seems to be the earliest for the American. See, among others, E. G. Bourne, "Columbus, Ramon Pane and the Beginnings of American Anthropology" (Worcester, Mass., 1906: offprint, *Proceedings of the American Antiquarian Society*); *Fray Ramón Pané; Relación . . .* , ed. J. J. Arrom (Mexico City, 1988). H. Louis Gates has given an oral report of the Mellon-Harvard-Timbucto project which recovered a 1453 Arabic manuscript produced at the University of Timbucto on African indigenous religions which would represent an early example from a different expansionist movement.

6. While scattered throughout the work, the most convenient guide to Asian language materials and translations in Europe remains D. Lach's multivolume study, *Asia in the Making of Europe* (Chicago, 1965–93).

7. On the issue of external and internal diversities, see J. Z. Smith. "Religion, Religions, Religious," in M. C. Taylor, ed., *Critical Terms for Religious Studies* (Chicago, 1998), esp. pp. 270–76, reprinted in this volume.

8. E. Brerewood, *Enquiries Touching the Diversity of Languages and Religions through the Chiefe Parts of the World* (London, 1614). Samuel Purchas, *His Pilgrimage, or, Relations of the World and the Religions observed in all Ages and all Places discovered* (London, 1613) appears to be the earliest English work to employ the plural, 'religions,' in its title.

9. While a number of complex linguistic issues recur in Enlightenment thought—compare, for example, H. Aarsleff, *From Locke to Saussure: Essays on the Study of Language and Intellectual History* (Minneapolis, 1982) and Aarsleff, *The Study of Language in England, 1780–1860* (Minneapolis, 1983) with L. Formigari, *L'esperienza e il segno: La filosofia del linguaggio tra Illuminismo e Restaurazione* (Rome, 1990)—I focus, here, on the issue of universality, on which see U. Eco, *The Search for the Perfect Language* (Oxford, 1997).

10. "Language," *Encyclopaedia Britannica*, 1st ed. (Edinburgh, 1771), 3: 863.

11. I have taken the term 'counter-Enlightenment' from I. Berlin. For the linguistic theories here summarized, see esp. Berlin, *The Magus of the North: J. G. Hamann and the Origins of Modern Irrationalism* (New York, 1994).

12. For Romantic language theories, I have relied primarily on T. Todorov,

Theories of the Symbol (Ithaca, 1982), esp. 147–221. The two passages from Schelling are translated in Todorov, 210 and 163–64. Note that the indebtedness of Schelling to Coleridge's use of the term "tautegorical" (S. T. Coleridge, *Aids to Reflection* [reprint, London, 1913], 136) is acknowledged in a footnote to the latter passage (Schelling, *Introduction à la Philosophie de la mythologie*, trans. V. Jankélevitch [Paris, 1946], 1: 238, n 1).

13. M. Eliade, "Crisis and Renewal in History of Religions," *History of Religions* 5 (1965): 17.

14. M. Bakhtin, "Discourse in the Novel," in *The Dialogic Imagination: Four Essays by M. M. Bakhtin*, ed. M. Holquist (Austin, 1981), 271.

15. K. Mannheim, *Ideology and Utopia* (New York, 1936), 274.

16. See, for example, J. S. Mill, *A System of Logic*, 10th ed. (London, 1879), 2: 127–41, 360–80. A good sense of the semantic range of the term can be gained from the *Oxford English Dictionary*, s.v. "general," "generality," "generalization," "generalize."

17. H. H. Penner, *Impasse and Resolution: A Critique of the Study of Religion* (New York, 1989), esp. pp. 130–34.

18. F. de Saussure, letter to A. Meillet, dated January 4, 1894, as quoted in E. Benveniste, *Problems in General Linguistics* (Coral Gables, 1971), 33–34.

19. O. Ducrot and T. Todorov, *Encyclopedic Dictionary of the Sciences of Language* (Baltimore, 1979), 118.

20. On this issue, see the references in J. Z. Smith, *To Take Place: Toward Theory in Ritual* (Chicago, 1987), 33–34 and 138–39, notes 48–51.

21. C. Lévi-Strauss, *La Pensée sauvage* (Paris, 1962), 328. Compare the different translation of this sentence in Lévi-Strauss, *The Savage Mind* (Chicago, 1966), 248.

22. For a preliminary account, see R. Feleppa, *Convention, Translation and Understanding: Philosophical Problems in the Comparative Study of Culture* (Albany, 1988). Once again, Hans Penner, reflecting the work of Donald Davidson, persistently urges confidence in the possibility of translation. "To interpret means to translate. The notion then that someone speaks an uninterpretable language is incomprehensible—language *entails* translatability." H. H. Penner, "Interpretation," in W. Braun and R. T. McCutcheon, eds., *Guide to the Study of Religion* (London and New York), 69. See further, Penner, "Holistic Analysis: Conjectures and Refutations," *Journal of the American Academy of Religion* 62 (1994): 977–96 and Penner, "Why Does Semantics Matter to the Study of Religion?" *Method & Theory in the Study of Religion* 7 (1995): 221–49.

23. University of Chicago, the Divinity School, *Announcements for Sessions of 1960–1961* (Chicago, 1960), 3.

24. J. L. Borges, "Pierre Menard, Author of the *Quixote*," in Borges, *Collected Fictions* (New York, 1998), 88–95.

CHAPTER SEVENTEEN

GOD SAVE THIS
HONOURABLE COURT

RELIGION AND CIVIC DISCOURSE

MY FRIEND AND sometimes colleague, Professor William Scott Green, at the University of Rochester, has established, with epigrammatic precision the contours of this essay when he observed that the study of religion is the only humanistic field in the American academy whose subject matter is explicitly governed by the United States Constitution. On another occasion, articulating one aspect of the common-sense sort of distinction between religion and the study of religion, Green noted, with no small bitterness, that in preparation for Easter news reporters always contact the local bishop to inquire about the significance of the holiday, while they call the local college's department of religion to find out why there are Easter bunnies and Easter eggs. The first observation suggests the gravity of the enterprise; the second, its simultaneous marginalization. What ever religion 'is,' its definition seems to be thought to lie with others—with courts and practitioners—and not with the academic field charged with its study. This odd displacement is only encouraged when scholars of religion at times assume the stance that their subject matter is by nature undefinable. But this latter is not the issue of this essay.[1] Rather, I wish to look at the consequences of some legal understandings of religion from the point of view of a student of religion.

Let me begin with some items many of us will have encountered on the instructions for filing Internal Revenue Service schedule SE, the form you use to figure your Social Security tax if you are self-employed. Nearly three-quarters of the instruction page is taken up with matters organized under headings such as "Employees of Churches and Church Organizations," "Ministers and Members of Religious Orders," and "Members of Certain Religious Sects." The second of these topics contains a new provision from the 2000 tax law. "If you are a minister, a member of a religious order not under a vow of poverty, or a Christian Science practitioner who previously elected exemption from social security coverage and self-employment tax, you can now revoke that exemption." The section entitled "Members of Certain Religious Sects" begins:

> If you have conscientious objections to social security insurance because of your membership in and belief in the teachings of a religious sect recognized as being in existence at all times since December 31, 1950, and which has provided a reasonable level of living for its dependent members, you are exempt from SE [self-employment] tax if you received IRS approval by filing **Form 4029** . . . See Pub[lication] 517 [i.e., "Social Security and Other Information for Members of the Clergy and Religious Orders]."

The Internal Revenue Service is, both de facto and de jure, America's primary definer and classifier of religion. It reproduces the imperial Roman government's efforts at distinguishing licit and illicit religions as subtypes of a wider legal concern for distinctions between licit and illicit associations.

How does the Internal Revenue Service fulfill these defining and classifying functions? We see this most clearly in the regulations governing the tax-exempt status of religious organizations in section 501(c)(3) of the Internal Revenue Code, a subset of provisions for the larger tax-exempt category of "nonprofit" organizations. (The same criteria likewise govern the tax-deductible status of contributions to such organizations [section 170]). The main criterion is that a religious organization "must be organized and operated exclusively for religious purposes," with exclusivity and purpose specified in the same general terms that apply to all tax-exempt organizations: no individual financial benefit and no substantial political lobbying or participation in political campaigns. However, there is one important difference. All other sorts of tax-exempt groups file annually both a statement of activities and an informational tax return; however, "churches, their integrated activities, and conventions or associations of churches, and organizations claiming to be churches" do not have to submit these documents. In Department of the Treasury Regulation 1.511–2(a)(3)(ii), 'church' for the purpose of this rule, is defined as the following: "The term 'church' includes a religious order or a religious organization if such order or organization is (a) an internal part of a church, and (b) is engaged in carrying out the functions of a church." The Regulation continues but scarcely clarifies: "A religious order or organization shall be considered to be engaged in carrying out the functions of a church if its duties include the ministration of sacerdotal functions and the conduct of religious worship. What constitutes the conduct of religious worship or the ministration of sacerdotal functions depends on the tenets and practices of a particular religious body constituting a church."[2]

In this passage, as elsewhere in government documents, legal discourse appears to stammer in a setting that, at least putatively, recognizes religious pluralism and remains antiestablishmentarian. At first glance, what we read appears to be a set of tautologies masked as definitions in violation of the first rule of lexicography, "a word may not be defined in terms of itself." Surely, it is singularly uninformative to assert with the Internal Revenue Service that a religious organization must be organized for religious purposes or that a church must be a part of a church or engaged in carrying out the functions of a church! The circularity of these definitions suggests, at the practical level, that the Internal Revenue Service is reluctant, in most cases, to adjudicate the claims of religious organizations, except those it judges to be extraordinarily or patently fraudulent (for example, mail order ministries such as the Universal Life Church, founded in 1962).

For the student of religion, something more fundamental is at work: a notion of self-evidence derived from using lay understandings of varied forms of Christianities to serve as what cognitive scientists term a "prototype." A prototype functions in classification by providing an image of a commonplace example that then serves as an ideal or typical exemplar of a category with decisions as to whether another object is a member of the same category being based on matching it against features of the prototype (for example, employing a robin as the prototype for "bird"). While matters are no longer quite so blunt as stated by Justice Gilbert, writing for the Georgia Supreme Court in 1922 in *Wilkerson v Rome*, "Christianity is the only religion known to American law," or Thomas MacIntyre Cooley's observation in his influential handbook on constitutional law (4th ed., 1938), "The Christian religion is, of course, recognized by the government," the unproblematized use in tax law of terms such as "church," "sect," "religious organization," "religious orders," "ministers," "sacerdotal," and so forth suggests that the features of other religions are routinely being matched against some Christian prototype.

Matters are more complex at the level of the United States Supreme Court, which will be my focus for the remainder of this essay—not on the Court as the ultimate authority on the United States Constitution, most especially the First Amendment's negative guarantee with respect to religion and Article VI's prohibition of religious tests as a qualification for Federal office (initially designed to protect Christians from Christians), but rather on the Court as the legally authorized interpreter of religion. For this reason I shall draw, in what follows, on the opening narrative statements as to the facts of the case in the majority's decision, rather than on the legal reasonings of the decision itself.

For the Supreme Court, classification by prototype continues to be common. Let me give as an example the 1993 case of *The Church of Lukumi Babalu Aye, Inc., and Ernesto Pichado v City of Hialeah* (508 US 520). This is a case that should never have come before the Court, but rather should have been settled in the lower courts in the petitioner's favor. The issue was one of "free exercise," a matter less frequently litigated than "establishment" cases before the Court. A Cuban American Santeria church leased property and planned to construct a religious complex in which, among other things, animal sacrifice would be performed. The Hialeah City Council subsequently issued a set of resolutions prohibiting animal sacrifice and the possession of animals intended for ritual killing. The Supreme Court unanimously declared these resolutions to be in violation of the Constitution's free exercise clause.

There are many interesting features specific to this decision that would well repay discussion, including the multiple concurrent opinions and the Court's clear consciousness of the contemporary 1993 Congressional debates concerning the Religious Freedom Restoration Act, which sought to set aside the implications of an earlier, 1990, free exercise decision (*Employment Division, Department of Human Resources of Oregon v Smith* [494 US 872]). The Court subsequently invalidated the act in a 1997 decision (*City of Boerne v Flores* [521 US 519]).

From a different perspective, the student of religion might note, as the Court need not, that the Court's deliberative processes evidence little interest in the divisive sociopolitical environment that resulted in the City Council's actions, in particular, the racial and economic class distinctions between the two Cuban immigrant groups, the upper- and middle-class Hispanic Catholic opponents and the working-class, black Santerians. This division made all the more remarkable the opponents' odd argument that Santeria ought to be dismissed as a religion because it was illegal in Castro's Cuba—perhaps the only occasion at which this group of Cuban Americans have cited Castro's perspicacity in religious questions! Indeed, there is no sign of the Justices' awareness of the massive influence of Santeria in Cuba (one of the reasons, after all, for the papal visit, in the late 90s, to the island), nor of its historical and structural relations to other Afro-Caribbean religions. However, for the purposes of this essay, I want to focus only on the Court's familiarizing attempts to "place" Santeria in relation to the Christian prototype and to "place" animal sacrifice with respect to that prototype of religion on the basis of information the Court cites from both the Florida District Court records of the case (723 F. Supp [SD Fla. 1989]) and standard reference works, including, most prominently, the *Encyclopedia of Religion* (1987), edited by Mircea Eliade.

Let me quote, with only occasional abridgement, the first three framing paragraphs of Justice Kennedy's majority opinion, commenting on each in turn. The decision begins:

> This case involves practices of the Santeria religion, which originated in the 19th century. When hundreds of thousands of members of the Yoruba people were brought as slaves from western Africa to Cuba, their traditional African religion absorbed significant elements of Roman Catholicism. The resulting syncretism, or fusion, is Santeria, 'the way of the saints.' The Cuban Yoruba express their devotion to spirits, called *orishas*, through the iconography of Catholic saints, Catholic symbols are often present at Santeria rites, and Santeria devotees attend the Catholic sacraments. 723 FSupp. 1467, 1469–1470 (SD Fla. 1989); 13 Encyclopedia of Religion, 66 (M. Eliade ed. 1987); 1 Encyclopedia of the American Religious Experience 183 (C. Lippy & P. Williams eds. 1988).

Kennedy's first domesticating paragraph is preeminently genealogical. While measured on the time scale of familiar western religions, Santeria is relatively new; Justice Kennedy portrays it as being a combination of two more archaic elements, "traditional African religion" and "Roman Catholicism." While its devotion to "spirits," *orishas* in Yoruba, clearly mark it as "African" (indeed, Justice Kennedy employs the curious locution, "the Cuban Yoruba" as if the tribal identification remained intact), Catholic elements, in Justice Kennedy's domesticating representation, clearly prevail. As this paragraph is largely composed of paraphrase and unmarked direct quotation from Joseph M. Murphy's article on Santeria in the Eliade *Encyclopedia*, it is significant that the last sentence by Kennedy, "Catholic symbols are often present at Santeria rites, and Santeria devotees attend Catholic sacraments" carries the reverse implication in Murphy. "Despite the frequent presence of Catholic symbols in Santeria rites and the attendance of santeros at Catholic sacraments, Santeria is essentially an African way of worship drawn into a symbiotic relationship with Catholicism."

The second paragraph faces up to the difficulty caused by Kennedy's familiarizing interpretation. If Santeria is but an ethnically colored Catholicism, in principle no different than Justice Kennedy's Irish Catholicism, what about animal sacrifice?

> The Santeria faith teaches that every individual has a destiny from God, a destiny fulfilled with the aid and energy of the *orishas*. The basis of the Santeria religion is the nurture of a personal relation with the *orishas*, and one of the principal forms of devotion is an animal sacrifice. 13 Encyclopedia of Religion, *supra*, at 66.

Let me interrupt Kennedy at this point to note further elements of domestication. He now uses Protestant nomenclature, thoroughly assimilated in American discourse, of "the Santeria faith" along with "the Santerian religion," and emphasizes that the presupposition of this faith is "that every individual has a destiny from God." Again reverting to American Protestant language, Kennedy asserts that the "basis of the Santerian religion is the nurture of a personal relation with the *orishas*," without a hint that this evangelical-sounding "personal relation" is one of spirit-possession. Kennedy's sources, strategically not quoted at this point in his decision, state that this relation culminates in a lengthy initiation in which the "*orisha* is 'enthroned' in the head of the devotee and is 'sealed' as a permanent part of the devotee's personality." Furthermore, again unnoted by Kennedy, this "personal relation with the *orishas*" is regularly effected, in Santeria, through divinatory procedures, spirit mediumship, and spirit possession as well as by sacrifice, understood, in native practice, as an intimate, divine/human sharing of food. Kennedy prefers a blander understanding of the latter, interpreting sacrifice as a mode of worship, a form of personal "devotion." Despite this attempt at familiarization, animal sacrifice remains stubbornly alien, and thus requires further efforts at placement.

> The sacrifice of animals as part of religious rituals has ancient roots. See generally 12 *id.*, at 554–556. Animal sacrifices are mentioned throughout the Old Testament, see 14 Encyclopaedia

Judaica 600, 600–606 (1971), and it played an important role in the practice of Judaism before the destruction of the second Temple in Jerusalem, see *id.*, at 605–612. In modern Islam, there is an annual sacrifice commemorating Abraham's sacrifice of a ram in the stead of his son. See C. Glassé, Concise Encyclopedia of Islam 178 (1989); 7 Encyclopedia of Religion, *supra*, at 456.

Note that, despite Justice Kennedy's citation here of the article on sacrifice by Joseph Henninger in the Eliade *Encyclopedia,* the justice's illustrations of sacrifice contain no allusion to its role in traditional religions, including those of Africa. "Ancient roots," antiquity, is normatively represented, in his account, by the religion of Israel as described in the "Old Testament." As Kennedy continues his history, he clearly has in mind some version of the triple formulation of the "Abrahamic tradition," encapsulated in President Bush's reiterated phrase, "churches, synagogues or mosques" (the order is not without significance), a formation as problematic as its predecessor, "the Judeo-Christian tradition," which first came to prominence at the 1939–40 New York World's Fair in Flushing, New York. The "Abrahamic tradition" maps Christianity as the center, Judaism the near neighbor, and Islam the far. In Kennedy's account, animal sacrifice is on the map of recognizable religious practice because Jews once practiced it, and Muslims still do, but only once a year. These two traditions are linked as the Islamic practice is held to commemorate an event in biblical tradition, although Kennedy does not note that Abraham's son who was spared by the substitution of a ram is frequently held to be Ishmael and not Isaac. Kennedy need not speak the obvious exception: Christianity, as he thinks of it, did not and does not perform animal sacrifice. (Parenthetically, Kennedy does not record the ambivalence in Islam to sacrifice. For the student of religion, it is notable that metaphorical sacrificial language dominates most Christianities, which lack rituals of sacrifice, while it is distinctly muted in both Judaism and Islam, which have real histories of animal sacrifice).

Almost in passing, Kennedy announces in the first sentence of his third framing paragraph the logic of Santerian sacrifice: "The *orishas* are powerful but not immortal. They depend for survival on the sacrifice." That is to say, as in Numbers 28, sacrifice provides superhuman beings with their necessary food. But this rationale—apparently as estranging to Kennedy as it is correct—is quickly overcome by a flood of (largely irrelevant) information in the rest of the paragraph, which enumerates, in considerable detail, the occasions for sacrifice, the sorts of animals commonly sacrificed, and the procedures for killing, cooking, and eating the animal.

> According to Santeria teaching, the *orishas* are powerful but not immortal. They depend for survival on the sacrifice. Sacrifices are performed at birth, marriage, and death rites, for the cure of the sick, for the initiation of new members and priests, and during an annual celebration. Animals sacrificed in Santeria rituals include chickens, pigeons, doves, ducks, guinea pigs, goats, sheep, and turtles. The animals are killed by the cutting of the carotid arteries in the neck. The sacrificed animal is cooked and eaten, except after healing and death rituals. See 723 F. Supp., at 1471–1472; 13 Encyclopedia of Religion, *supra*, at 66; M. González-Wippler, The Santeria Experience 105 (1982).

What Justice Kennedy has undertaken in this initial statement of fact, or more properly, of data, that is to say, facts accepted for purposes of the argument, is an essay in familiarization, largely enabled by the deployment of a Christian prototype. That which initially appeared strange— Santerian animal sacrifice—has been reduced to an instance of the known. In favor of Kennedy's procedure, the heavy social and political cost of leaving the practice in the realm of the exotic is indicated by the comments of Hialeah officials cited in the body of the Court's opinion.

> Councilman Mejides indicated that he was "totally against the sacrificing of animals" and distinguished [the Jewish practice of] kosher slaughter because it had a "real purpose." The "Bible says we are allowed to sacrifice an animal for consumption," he continued, "but for any other purpose, I don't believe that the Bible allows that.". . . The chaplain of the Hialeah Police Department told the city council that Santeria was a sin, "foolishness," and the worship of "demons." He advised the city council: "We need to be helping people and sharing with them the truth that is found in Jesus Christ"; He concluded: "I would exhort you . . . not to permit this Church to exist."

Kennedy's redescription of Santeria is an effort, at one and the same time, both similar and different to that familiarizing project undertaken by the study of religion as it works through the necessary tension between the near and the far.

The relations between the near and the far, the familiar and the exotic, have been a preoccupation of western students of religion ever since the Ionian ethnographers. Although the presuppositions and techniques have altered over time, the fundamental devices have remained the same: comparison, translation, and redescription. These projects work with difference, relaxing it, but never overcoming it. Because nothing is ever quite the same as another, these efforts require judgment and criticism.

Translation and difference and criticism challenge, each in their own way, the confidence attendant on the deployment of some form of Christianity as a prototype, whether practiced by the Internal Revenue Service, the United States Supreme Court, a scholar of religion, the daily press, or ourselves as citizens.

What is more, in the three paragraphs cited from Justice Kennedy, terms such as 'religion,' 'syncretism,' and 'sacrifice' are employed as if they were self-evident. In his decision, they are innocent of either controversy or entailments; they have no history. There is no hint of the problematics of redescription, of translation, here, at the level of a second-order theoretical language.

I contrast this to the strongest example of these processes in the study of religion that I know: Durkheim's translation in *Elementary Forms of Religious Life* (1912) of the language appropriate to religion (for him, in this work, functioning as the unknown) into the language appropriate to society (for him, the known). From the precising definitions on the very first page to the redescription of aboriginal rituals in the final part, Durkheim has taken care.

For the purposes of this essay, this is not the aspect of Durkheim I need to stress.[3] Rather, I want to use his work to illustrate the contrary impulse to familiarization, one that is equally imperative in the human sciences in general, and the study of religion in particular, namely, defamiliarization. This is a process of making the familiar seem strange in order to enhance our perception of the familiar—equally a matter of redescription. For it is the aforementioned requirements of difference and criticism, as well as the process of defamiliarization, that prevent the study of religion from being an exercise in the transmission of a religious tradition.

To illustrate defamiliarization, allow me to introduce a second Supreme Court case, *Lynch v Donnelly* (465 US 668), decided in 1984.[4] The case concerns a Christmas nativity display (a crèche) erected by the City of Pawtucket, Rhode Island, at their downtown shopping center. By a narrow margin, 5–4, the Court ruled in favor of the City that the exhibit was not primarily religious in that (1) it contained secular as well as religious symbols, for example, the infant Jesus along with a talking wishing well, and (2) that it was erected for a secular, commercial purpose.

The first criterion was thought crucial, inasmuch as five years later, in 1989, in *Allegheny County v ACLU* (492 US 573), the Court found the erection of a crèche in the county's courthouse square, accompanied by a banner proclaiming "Gloria in excelsis Deo," to be an illicit entanglement of religion and state; but found permissible a second civic display, one block away, likewise on government property, containing a Christmas tree, a menorah, and a banner reading "During this holiday season the city . . . salutes liberty. Let these festive lights remind us that we are keepers of the flame of liberty and our legacy of freedom." This second display was judged proper in that, unlike the first, it contained a mixture of sacred and secular objects (the Christmas tree and the menorah on the one hand, the banner on the other), and was erected, at least in part, for the secular purpose of fostering patriotism. (I leave aside the additional issue of the possible ameliorating effects of displaying, together, symbols from two religions).

I quote, without intervening comment, two extracts from the majority opinion in *Lynch v Donnelly*, written by Chief Justice Burger. The first may be taken as an ethnographic description, the second as a statement by native informants.

The first, descriptive statement is based on a summary by Judge Pettine when the case was decided, previously, by the U.S. District Court of Rhode Island.

> Each year, in cooperation with the downtown retail merchants association, the city of Pawtucket, R.I. . . . erects a Christmas display as part of its observance of the Christmas holiday season. The display is situated in a park owned by a non-profit organization and located in the heart of the shopping district. The display comprises many figures and decorations traditionally associated with Christmas, including, among other things, a Santa Claus house, reindeer pulling Santa's sleigh, candy striped poles, a Christmas tree, carolers, cut out figures representing such characters as a clown, an elephant, a teddy bear, a talking wishing well, hundreds of colored lights, a large banner that reads "Seasons Greetings," and a creche. The creche has been on display for forty or more years. It consists of the traditional figures including the Infant Jesus, Mary and Joseph, angels, shepherds, kings and animals, all ranging in height from five inches to five feet. The creche is positioned in a central and highly visible location, an almost life sized tableau marked off by a white picket fence.

As part of the argument for the propriety of the exhibit, that it was not an unconstitutional mingling of state and church, the City had argued that it was not erected for religious purposes. As I have indicated, the second statement may be taken as if it were one by native informants. It was offered by David Freeman, professor of philosophy at the University of Rhode Island, who had appeared as an expert witness for the City in the U.S. district court hearing of the case.

> The display engenders a friendly community spirit of goodwill in keeping with the season. The display brings into the central city shoppers and serves commercial interests and benefits merchants and their employees. It promotes pre-Christmas retail sales and helps engender goodwill and neighborliness commonly associated with the Christmas season. It invites people to participate in the Christmas spirit, brotherhood, peace, and to let loose with their money.

I propose we undertake a thought experiment in the service of defamiliarization in which we replace one of the members of the Supreme Court with Émile Durkheim. We will instruct him to ignore the constitutional question of government and religion (inasmuch as Durkheim's translation language of 'church' and 'society' is not equivalent to the American vocabulary of 'church and state'), asking him only to argue the question whether, from the point of view of his redescriptive theory and solely on the basis of the two extracts I have quoted, the *totality* of the Pawtucket display constitutes a religion. A number of Durkheimian interpretative possibilities present themselves—I shall offer ten—no one of which is necessarily correct. Interpretation, whether in the human sciences or in a court of law, is a matter of persuasion not of truth. Persuasion depends on the power of the relations argued between the stipulated data (in this instance, the two reports) and the rhetorical-interpretative frame placed upon them (in the present experiment, that of Durkheim).

Let us begin by granting for purposes of argument the finding of fact by the Court: that the display consists of the copresence of sacred and secular items. In the Court's reasoning, religion would be present only if the exhibit consisted entirely of sacred symbols; that is to say, for the Court, following some generalized Christian prototype, religion is the sacred. Durkheim might reject both the Court's premise and its conclusion, while accepting its finding of fact. For Durkheim, religion is the oppositional relationship of sacred to profane. The presence of both are required for there to be religion. I assume, in arguing this understanding, that he might accept the Court's categorization the nativity scene as sacred, what the Court termed "the traditional figures," and note their separation from the other items in the display by the "picket fence" as guarding it against profanation. But I doubt Durkheim would remain content with this initial move.

Durkheim would surely go on to argue that, conceptually, one must start an interpretation of any group's religion with their beliefs rather than with their rites or symbols. Here, as Durkheim does persistently with respect to Australian data, the scholar must reject the native's claimed pragmatic results in favor of a social scientific interpretation; an interpretation from the outside, dependent on the scientist's theories and comparative knowledge. That is to say, translation is required.

In the case at hand, the native informant predictably stressed the economic and pragmatic consequences of the display. This understanding was, from Durkheim's view, erroneously accepted as true by the Court. The informant claimed that the exhibit "benefits merchants and their employees," it "serves commercial interests," it "promotes retail sales," it causes folk to "let loose with their money." Durkheim might remark that embedded in this economic discourse is a second language of sociality, specifically tied to a particular season. Rather than holding this to be a secondary effect of the economic initiatives, he would hold it to be the primary cause for the display. The scene "engenders a friendly community spirit of goodwill in keeping with the season," it brings members of the society "into the central city," it "helps engender goodwill and neighborliness commonly associated with the Christmas season," "it invites people to participate in the Christmas spirit, brotherhood [and] peace." As translated by Durkheim, members of the Pawtucket society usually live dispersed in their separate homes, following individual biological and economic pursuits. For Durkheim, this is the fundamental, social translation of the profane. By contrast, in the shopping center, these same folk come together to "participate" in what Durkheim would define as a "moral community," his translation of the sacred. For Durkheim, the alternation between these two types of time, one individual, the other collective, is in fact the social origin of the distinction between the profane and the sacred. It is this temporal opposition that marks the two qualities; it is never an inherent distinction between objects. This collectivity needs to be periodically refreshed and renewed. (Durkheim may be credited with introducing the potent prefix, *re-*, as a centrally important element in the understanding of religion). The coming together "into the central city" is a ritual that resignifies the sacred. In Durkheim's sense of the term, this coming together in the shopping center constitutes Pawtucket's 'church.'

From this perspective, Durkheim might go on to argue two reinterpretations of the native informants' account. Both would reject the Court's understanding that Pawtucket's beliefs are secular. On the one hand, Durkheim might argue that, in religion, the experience of the collectivity is objectified, often as an impersonal force, sometimes as a supernatural being. In the native's erroneous understanding, it is this force (or being) rather than the coming together that is thought to "engender" the powerfully experienced sentiments of collective life. In Pawtucket, this objectification is variously named the "Season," the "Christmas Season," or the "Christmas Spirit." This is a sacred power in that it can be profaned. Think of the canonical example of Scrooge.

Alternatively, Durkheim might argue that as these sentiments are "engendered" by this periodic coming together, seasonal shopping in Pawtucket constitutes that society's religious ritual.

Taking a different tack, Durkheim might question the Court's literal acceptance of the native informant's claim of commercial motivation. He might note that, unlike what occurs in profane time, where money is spent shopping largely to meet the needs of sustinence, whether individual or those of a biological family, here, in this season, money is being spent on gifts for family, for a socially constructed extended family, and for others. This recognition of nonutilitarian mutual obligations between social actors who are not biologically related marks for Durkheim a moral community, which, when named in religious idiom, is what he calls a 'Church.' (Note that the French, *l'Église* from the Greek *ekklesia* carries a social, associative sense not found in the English 'church,' which refers to divine ownership of a building.)[5]

Given this translated understanding of Pawtucket's religious beliefs, Durkheim might next turn his attention to a revaluation of the description of the display, bearing in mind, again, his injunction that the scientist must know how to "get beneath" the symbols to the social realities they represent, while rejecting the interpretations offered by their believers, which are "almost always false."

The ritual nature of the entire display is signalled by the notice that the display is erected "each year," some items for "forty years." It is repetitive and periodic. This said, Durkheim might remind the Court that such objects are best understood as collective representations; that, if religious, they will exhibit an opposition between sacred and profane; and that, rather than being inherent in the object, sacrality is arbitrarily "superadded" by society. Durkheim might recognize, as did the Court, an apparent distinction between two groups of representations: the nativity scene and everything else. But as a first move he might reverse the Court's evaluation of the nativity scene as self-evidently sacred.

Within the group of 'everything else,' classified as secular by the Court, Durkheim might note three central objects: the banner "Seasons Greetings," the Christmas tree, and the figure of Santa Claus. For Durkheim, as already suggested, the banner marks both sacred time (i.e., collective time) and the objectification, as the "Season," of the power of socially renewed collectivity. Both the Christmas tree and Santa Claus are collective representations of gift-giving, that mutual, moral obligation within the framework of a socially constructed community which marks, for Durkheim, a 'Church.' The other representations are all associated with these three.

Each of these three primary representations can be profaned, a sign of their sacrality. For a familiar example, in the case of Santa Claus, despite his present iconic origins in a Coca-Cola ad campaign, think of the drunk Santa Claus in the opening scene of *Miracle on 34th Street*. For a more complex example, one of deliberate profanation, I refer to the French incident on Christmas Eve, 1951, when a figure of Santa Claus was hung by the neck from the railing of the Dijon Cathedral, followed by the burning of the effigy in the cathedral square. These acts were undertaken with the prior agreement of the clergy in front of several hundred sunday school children as a protest against the "Americanization" of Christmas.[6]

With these various "other" objects established as the collective representations of the Church of Pawtucket, Durkheim can turn to the nativity scene. Anticipating a possible objection—the "white picket fence"—Durkheim might here argue that the Christian scene is profane relative to the collective representations of the Church of Pawtucket and is therefore being separated from them. After all, divisiveness, as opposed to collectivity, is, for Durkheim, the hallmark of the profane. The very fact that there is a lawsuit concerning the nativity scene is, in itself, sufficient demonstration of its profanity. Besides, remember the alternation of times. From the coming together at the shopping center, the members of the Church of Pawtucket disperse to their individual homes and denominational houses of worship, a dispersal that likewise marks the profane.

Alternatively, Durkheim might again invoke the requirement to "get beneath" the symbols while rejecting the interpretations of believers. If so, the nativity scene might be reinterpreted as a collective representation of Pawtucket's religion as understood by Durkheim. In Joseph, Mary, and Jesus we are presented with an ideal extended family, one surely not bound together by blood. Jesus and the kings are presented as an ideal of mutual gift-giving, and so on.

This sort of interpretation might lead Durkheim to suggest, consistent with his understanding of Australian aboriginal organizations, that there are, in fact, two religions in Pawtucket. The first, which is a relatively more inclusive 'tribal' or 'pantribal' one, is that objectified as the Season. The second, that of a relatively more limited "clan," is represented by the Christian figures as Durkheim might redescribe them. Both, properly translated and explained, compliment each other. Both are representations of the Church of Pawtucket.

I have undertaken this exercise in Durkheimian translation in order to make a simple point. The disciplined study of any subject is, among other things, an assault on self-evidence, on matters taken for granted, nowhere more so than in the study of religion. The future of our increasingly diverse societies will call on all our skills at critical translation; all our abilities to occupy the contested space between the near and the far; all our capacities for the dual project of making familiar what, at first encounter, seems strange, and making strange what we have come to think of as all-too-familiar. Each of these endeavors needs to be practiced and refined in the service of an urgent civic and academic agendum: that difference be negotiated but never overcome.

Notes

1. See, especially, Smith, "Religion, Religions, Religious," reprinted in this volume.

2. I am indebted to the discussion of the Internal Revenue Code in B. N. Evans, *Interpreting the Free Exercise of Religion: The Constitution and American Pluralism* (Chapel Hill, 1997), esp. 139–43.

3. See, especially, Smith, "Topography of the Sacred," and "Manna, Mana Everywhere and /-/-/," reprinted in this volume. All Durkheim quotations and references, below, are from the K. Fields translation of E. Durkheim, *The Elementary Forms of Religious Life* (New York, 1995).

4. While I have a different set of interests, see the important monograph on *Lynch v Donnelly* by W. F. Sullivan, *Paying the Words Extra: Religious Discourse in the Supreme Court of the United States*, Harvard University, Center for the Study of World Religions, Religions of the World (Cambridge, Mass., 1994). Professor Sullivan has a law degree as well as a Ph.D. in the History of Religions.

5. Compare this understanding with several recent (critical) studies of Christmas and consumerism, including L. E. Schmidt, *Consumer Rites: The Buy-*

ing and Selling of American Holidays (Princeton, 1995); S. Nissenbaum, *The Battle for Christmas* (New York, 1996); and the collection coedited by R. Horsley and J. Tracy, *Christmas Unwrapped: Consumerism, Christ, and Culture* (Harrisburg, 2001). From a quite different perspective, I much appreciate the analyses and comparisons of Christmas and Easter in T. Caplow, H. M. Bahr, and B. A. Chadwick, *All Faithful People: Change and Continuity in Middletown's Religion*, Middletown III Project (Minneapolis, 1983), 182–98; cf. T. Caplow and M. H. Williamson, "Decoding Middletown's Easter Bunny: A Study in American Iconography," *Semiotica* 32 (1980): 221–32.

6. C. Lévi-Strauss, "Le Père Noël supplicié," *Les Temps modernes* 77 (1952): 1572–90.

APPENDIX

JONATHAN Z. SMITH: PUBLICATIONS, 1966–2003

THIS LISTING includes all publications on the study of religion and on education. It does not include book reviews; articles, reports, and speeches in school, college, and university publications; or juvenilia.

1966

"The Garments of Shame." *History of Religions* 5 (1966): 217–38. Reprinted in Smith, *Map Is Not Territory* (1978), 1–23.

1968

"The Prayer of Joseph." In *Religions in Antiquity: Essays in Honor of E. R. Goodenough*, ed. J. Neusner, 253–94. Studies in the History of Religion, 15. Leiden: E. J. Brill, 1968. Reprinted in Smith, *Map Is Not Territory* (1978), 24–66.

1969

"The Glory, Jest and Riddle: James George Frazer and The Golden Bough." Ph.D. diss., Yale University.

"Earth and Gods." *Journal of Religion* 49 (1969): 103–27. Reprinted in Smith, *Map Is Not Territory* (1978), 104–28.

"Coup d'essai." *Criterion* 9 (1969): 19–20.

1970

"Archaeology and Babylonian Jewry." Jacob Neusner and J. Z. Smith, in J. A. Sanders, ed., *Near Eastern Archaeology in the Twentieth Century: Essays in Honor of Nelson Glueck* (Garden City: Doubleday, 1970), 331–47. (My contribution consists of an addendum [344–47] on Aramaic magical bowls with the divorce of demons motif.)

"Birth Upside Down or Rightside Up?" *History of Religions* 9 (1970): 281–303. Reprinted in Smith, *Map Is Not Territory* (1978), 147–71. German translation, in W. Meeks, ed., *Zur Soziologie des Urchristentums*, Theologische Bücherei, Historische Theologie, 62 (Munich: Kaiser Verlag, 1978), 284–309.

"The Influence of Symbols upon Social Change: A Place on Which to Stand." *Worship* 44 (1970): 457–74. Reprinted in Smith, *Map Is Not Territory* (1978), 129–46; and, J. D. Shaughnessy, ed., *The Roots of Ritual* (Grand Rapids: W. B. Eerdmans, 1973), 121–43.

1971

"Adde Parvum Parvo Magnus Acervus Erit." *History of Religions* 11 (1971): 67–90. Reprinted in Smith, *Map Is Not Territory* (1978), 240–64.

"Native Cults in the Hellenistic Period." *History of Religions* 11 (1971): 236–49.

"The Wobbling Pivot." *Journal of Religion* 52 (1972): 134–49. Reprinted in Smith, *Map Is Not Territory* (1978), 88–103.

"I Am a Parrot (Red)." *History of Religions* 11 (1972): 391–413. Reprinted in Smith, *Map Is Not Territory* (1978), 265–88.

1973

"When the Bough Breaks." *History of Religions* 12 (1973): 342–71. Reprinted in Smith, *Map Is Not Territory* (1978), 208–39.

"Basic Problems in the Study of Religion." In L. T. Johnson, ed., *Teaching Religion to Undergraduates* (New Haven: Society for Religion in Higher Education, 1973), 47–53.

1974

"Animals and Plants in Myth and Legend." *Encyclopaedia Britannica*, 15th ed. (1974 printing), *Macropaedia*, 1: 911–18; "Healing Cults," 8: 685–87; "Hellenistic Religions," 8: 749–51 (rev. ed., 1990).

"Agriculturalists and Pastoralists, Religion of." *Encyclopaedia Britannica*, 15th ed. (1974 printing), *Micropaedia*, I: 145; "Animal Worship," I: 386; "Blessingway Rites," II: 81; "Cannibalism," II: 511–12; "Churinga," II: 927; "Corn Mother," III: 158; "Dema Deities," III: 454; "Dreaming, The," III: 660; "Earth Mother," III: 752; "Guardian Spirits," IV: 772; "Headhunting," IV: 971; "Hieros Gamos," V: 33; "High God," V: 35–36; "Hunters and Gatherers, Religion of," V: 216–17; "Kachina doll," V: 653; "Lunar Deities," VI: 388; "Mana," VI: 549; "Master of the Animals," VI: 679; "Maui, or Maui-tiki-tiki," VI: 702; "Medicine Society," VI: 748; "Mother Goddess," VII: 53; "Multiple Souls," VII: 96; "Nagual," VII: 165; "Nagualism," VII: 165; "New Year Festivals, primitive," VII: 308; "Phallic Cults," VII: 925; "Rice Mother," VIII: 565; "Sacred Clown," VIII: 754–55; "Sand Painting," VIII: 851; "Sky God," IX: 263; "Solar Deities," IX: 330; "Soul" (revision of existing entry),

IX: 363–64; "Soul Loss," IX: 364; "Taboo," IX: 756; "Trickster," X: 119; "Vegetation Deities," X: 378; "Vision Quest," X: 461; "World Tree," X: 752.

1975

"Good News Is No News: Aretalogy and Gospel." In J. Neusner, ed., *Christianity, Judaism, and Other Greco-Roman Cults: Studies for Morton Smith at Sixty,* Studies in Judaism in Late Antiquity, 12 (Leiden: E. J. Brill, 1975), 1: 21–39. Reprinted in Smith, *Map Is Not Territory* (1978), 190–207. An earlier version was published later: "No News Is Good News: The Gospel as Enigma." In K. Bolle, ed., *Secrecy in Religions,* Studies in the History of Religions, 49 (Leiden: E. J. Brill, 1989), 66–80.

"The Social Description of Early Christianity." *Religious Studies Review* 1 (1975): 19–25.

"Wisdom and Apocalyptic." In B. Pearson, ed., *Religious Syncretism: Essays in Conversation with Geo Widengren,* Series on Formative Contemporary Figures, 1 (Missoula: Scholars Press, 1975), 131–56. Reprinted in Smith, *Map Is Not Territory* (1978), 67–87; and in P. D. Hanson, ed., *Visionaries and Their Apocalypses,* Issues in Religion and Theology, 2 (Philadelphia: Fortress Press, 1983): 101–20.

1976

"A Pearl of Great Price and a Cargo of Yams." *History of Religions* 16 (1976): 1–19. Reprinted in Smith, *Imagining Religion* (1982), 90–101, 156–62.

"The Temple and the Magician." In J. Jervell and W. Meeks, eds., *God's Christ and His People: Essays Honoring Nils A. Dahl* (Oslo: Oslo Universitetsforlaget, 1976), 233–47. Reprinted in Smith, *Map Is Not Territory* (1978), 172–89.

1978

Map Is Not Territory: Studies in the History of Religions. Studies in Judaism in Late Antiquity, 23 (Leiden: E. J. Brill, 1978). (A collection of previously published essays and one new essay.)

"Map Is Not Territory." In Smith, *Map Is Not Territory* (1978), 289–309.

"Too Much Kingdom/Too Little Community." *Zygon* 13 (1978): 123–30.

"Towards Interpreting Demonic Powers in Hellenistic and Roman Antiquity." *Aufstieg und Niedergang der römischen Welt* (Berlin: W. de Gruyter, 1978), II. 16.1: 425–39.

1979

"Sacred Persistence: Towards a Redescription of Canon." In W. S. Green, ed., *Approaches to Ancient Judaism,* Brown Judaic Studies, 1 (Missoula: Scholars Press, 1979), 1: 11–28. Reprinted in Smith, *Imagining Religion* (1982), 36–52, 141–43.

1980

"The Bare Facts of Ritual." *History of Religions* 20 (1980): 112–37. Reprinted in Smith, *Imagining Religion* (1982), 53–65, 143–45; and in R. L. Grimes, ed.,

Readings in Ritual Studies (Upper Saddle River: Prentice Hall, 1996), 473–83. German translation in A. Belliger and D. J. Krieger, eds., *Ritualtheorien: Ein einführendes Handbuch* (Opladen-Wiesbaden: Westdeutscher Verlag, 1998), 213–26.

"Fences and Neighbors: Some Contours of Early Judaism." In W. S. Green, ed., *Approaches to Early Judaism*, Brown Judaic Studies, 9 (Missoula: Scholars Press, 1980), 2: 1–25. Reprinted in Smith, *Imagining Religion* (1982), 1–18, 135–39.

"Samuel Sandmel: A Man of Largess." *Criterion* 19 (1980), 28–29. Reprinted in F. E. Greenspahn, E. Hilgert, B. L. Mack, eds., *Nourished with Peace: Studies in Hellenistic Judaism in Memory of Samuel Sandmel*. Scholar's Press Homage Series, 9 (Chico: Scholars Press, 1980), 9–12.

"What Is a Classic?" With a response by G. Anastapolo. Chicago: Chicago Program in Continuing Education, 1980.

1981

"St. Peter." *World Book* (1981 edition).

1982

Imagining Religion: From Babylon to Jonestown. Chicago Studies in the History of Judaism (Chicago: University of Chicago Press, 1982). Korean translation in preparation. (A collection of previously published essays and three new essays.)

"In Comparison a Magic Dwells." In Smith, *Imagining Religion* (1982), 19–35. Reprinted in K. C. Patton and B. C. Ray, eds., *A Magic Still Dwells: Comparative Religion in the Postmodern Age* (Berkeley: University of California Press, 2000), 23–44.

"The Unknown God: Myth in History." In Smith, *Imagining Religion* (1982), 66–89, 145–56.

"The Devil in Mr. Jones." In Smith, *Imagining Religion* (1982), 102–20. Reprinted in R. T. McCutcheon, ed., *The Insider/Outsider Problem in the Study of Religion: A Reader*, Controversies in the Study of Religion (London: Cassell, 1999), 370–89.

1983

"Mythos und Geschichte." In H.-P. Duerr, ed., *Alcheringa, oder beginnende Zeit: Mircea Eliade zum 75. Gerburtstag* (Frankfurt am Main: Qumran Verlag, 1983), 27–48.

"No Need to Travel to the Indies: Judaism and the Study of Religion." In J. Neusner, ed., *Take Judaism, for Example: Studies towards the Comparison of Religions*, Chicago Studies in the History of Judaism (Chicago: University of Chicago Press, 1983), 215–26; reprinted (Atlanta, 1992) in the series South Florida Studies in the History of Judaism, 51.

"Why the College Major? Questioning the Great Unexplained Aspect of Undergraduate Education." *Change*, 15, no. 5 (1983): 12–15. Excerpt reprinted in "The Best of Change: 25th Anniversary Issue." *Change* 26 (1994).

1984

"Here and Now: Prospects for Graduate Education." In J. Neusner, ed., *New Humanities and Academic Disciplines: The Case of Jewish Studies* (Madison: University of Wisconsin Press, 1984), 33–45.

1985

"What a Difference a Difference Makes." In J. Neusner and E. Frerichs, eds., *"To See Ourselves As Others See Us": Christians, Jews, 'Others' in Late Antiquity*, Scholars Press Studies in the Humanities, 8 (Chico: Scholars Press, 1985), 3–48.

"The Prayer of Joseph." In J. H. Charlesworth, ed., *The Old Testament Pseudepigrapha* (Garden City: Doubleday, 1985), 2: 699–714.

Commission on the Baccalaureate Degree, *Integrity and the College Curriculum: A Report to the Academic Community* (Washington, DC: Association of American Colleges, 1985). (Responsible for drafting chapters 4, "Study in Depth," and 6, "Profession of College Teaching.")

"Commentary on William J. Bennett's *To Reclaim a Legacy*." *American Journal of Education* 93 (1985): 541–46.

"Symposium on the Academic Vocation." *Cresset* 48 (1985): 8–10.

1986

"Jerusalem: The City as Place." In P. Hawkins, ed., *Civitas: Religious Interpretations of the City*, Scholars Press Studies in the Humanities, 10 (Baltimore: Scholars Press, 1986), 25–38.

"The Domestication of Sacrifice." In R. G. Hamerton-Kelly, ed., *Violent Origins: Ritual Killing and Cultural Formation. Conversations between W. Burkert, R. Girard and J. Z. Smith* (Stanford: Stanford University Press, 1986), 278–304.

"Towards Imagining New Frontiers." *Forum for Honors* 16 (1986): 3–7.

"Reforming Undergraduate Education: A Retrospective." In J. W. Reed, ed., *Reforming the Undergraduate Curriculum* (Rutgers: Rutgers University Press, 1986), 1–21.

"The New Liberal Arts." *International Journal of Social Education* 1 (1986–87): 7–17.

1987

To Take Place: Toward Theory in Ritual. Chicago Studies in the History of Judaism. (Chicago: University of Chicago Press, 1987). Norwegian translation, *Å finne sted: Rommets dimensjon i religiøse ritualer.* Pax Labyrint. Oslo: Pax Forlag, 1998.

"Ages of the World." In M. Eliade, ed., *The Encyclopedia of Religion* (New York: Macmillan, 1987), 1: 128–33; "Dying and Rising Gods," 4: 521–27; "Golden Age," 6: 69–73; "Sleep," 13: 361–65.

"atonement," "fast," "foreordination," "martyr," "sacrifice," "tithe," revisions of existing entries in *World Book* (1987 edition).

"Puzzlement." In T. March, ed., *Interpreting the Humanities*, 1986 (Princeton:

Woodrow Wilson Foundation, 1987), 53–68. Reprinted in *Liberal Education* 73 (1987): 14–20; *Maine Scholar* 1 (1988): 3–16; *Kettering Review* (Dec. 1990): 6–12.

1988

"'Religion' and 'Religious Studies': No Difference at All." *Soundings* 71 (1988): 231–44.

"Narrative into Problems: The College Introductory Course and the Study of Religion." *Journal of the American Academy of Religion* 56 (1988): 727–39.

1989

"No News Is Good News: The Gospel as Enigma." See "Good News Is No News: Aretalogy and Gospel" (1975).

"cult," "Golden Rule," "hermit," "Lord's Prayer," "saint," revisions of existing entries in *World Book* (1989 edition).

1990

Drudgery Divine: On the Comparison of Early Christianities and the Religions of Late Antiquity (London: School of Oriental and African Studies, 1990); Jordan Lectures in Comparative Religion, 14; and (Chicago: University of Chicago Press, 1990), Chicago Studies in the History of Judaism. Chapter 2, "On Comparison," has been reprinted in C. Ando, ed., *Roman Religion*, Edinburgh Readings on the Ancient World, 3 (Edinburgh: Edinburgh University Press, 2003), 23–38.

"Connections." *Journal of the American Academy of Religion* 58 (1990): 1–15.

Association of American Colleges. *The Challenge of Connecting Learning: Project on Liberal Learning, Study-in-Depth, and the Arts and Sciences Major.* Liberal Learning and the Arts and Sciences Major, vol. 1 (Washington, D.C.: Association of American Colleges and Universities, 1990). (Principal author.)

1991

"A Slip in Time Saves Nine: Prestigious Origins Again." In J. Bender and D. E. Welby, eds., *Chronotypes: The Construction of Time* (Stanford: Stanford University Press, 1991), 67–76.

"The Introductory Course: Less Is Better." In M. Jurgensmeyer, ed., *Teaching the Introductory Course in Religious Studies: A Sourcebook*, 185–92. Atlanta: Scholars Press, 1991.

1992

"Scriptures and Histories (An Essay in Honor of Wilfred Cantwell Smith)." *Method & Theory in the Study of Religion* 4 (1992): 97–105.

Differential Equations: On Constructing the "Other." University Lecture in Religion, 13 (Tempe: Arizona State University, 1992).

1993

"To Double Business Bound." In C. G. Schneider and W. S. Green, eds., *Strength-*

ening the College Major, New Directions for Higher Education, 84 (San Francisco:Jossey-Bass, 1993), 13–23.

1995

General editor, *The HarperCollins Dictionary of Religion* (San Francisco: HarperSanFrancisco, 1995). Prepared under the sponsorship of the American Academy of Religion. [Also available in electronic form, beliefnet.com].

introduction, pronunciation guide, all charts, maps, figures and captions as well as most cross-references and blind entries.

Entries: Aaron; Abelard; ablution; abortion; abstinence; Abrahamic religions; accretions; acculturation; Adam and Eve; Adonai; adoptionism; adultery; aeon; affliction; African traditional religions; ages of the world; agriculture, religious aspects of; Agrippa of Nettesheim; A.H.; akedah; Albertus Magnus; Alcoholics Anonymous; Alcuin; allegory; almsgiving; alphabet mysticism; altered states of consciousness; Amana Society; Ambrose; A.M.; American Indian; amulet or talisman; Anabaptists; ancestor rites; ancestor worship; androgyny; angels; aniconic; ankh; anointing; Anselm; antediluvian/postdiluvian; anthropogony; antinomianism; Aphrahat; Apollonius of Tyana; apostasy; apotheosis; apotropaic ritual; Aquinas; archaic; Arius; Apocrypha; apple; archangels; Ark; Arminius; ascension; ascension rituals; atonement; augurs; Augustine of Canterbury; Ave Maria; Babel, Tower of; Babism; Babylon, Whore of; Babylonian Captivity; Baha'i; Barclay, Robert; Barth, Karl; Basil of Caesarea; B.C./A.D.; B.C.E./C.E.; Becket, Thomas; Bede; Beelzebub; Behemoth; Bellarmine; Benedict of Nursia; Bernadette of Lourdes; Bernard of Clairvaux; Bethel; Beza; bilocation; birth control; blasphemy; blessing; blood; bodily secretions; Boehme; Bogomils; Bonaventura; Bonhoeffer; Boniface; Book of Common Prayer; born again; Branch Davidians; breath; Bridget of Sweden; British Israelites; brotherhood; Browne, Robert; Bruno; Bucer; Buchman; Bultmann; burial; Cain, mark of; Calvary, Mount; Calvin; Campbell; Canisius; cantor; cannibalism; canon; Cassian; casuistry; Catherine of Siena; celibacy; Channing; chant; chaos; chaos, return to; charismatic leadership; charm; chastity; cherub; chiliasm; Chrysostom; chthonic; church/sect; Church of God in Christ; Church of Scientology; circumambulation; circumcision; civic cults; Clare of Assisi; Clement of Alexandria; cliterodechtomy; clowns; Colette of Corbie; commandments; Cone, James H.; consecration; contagion; contagious magic; conversion; cosmogony; cosmology; covenant; creation out of nothing; creed; cremation; criticism, higher; criticism, lower; crucifix; crucifixion; curse; cyclical time; Cyril of Alexandria; Cyril of Jerusalem; damnation; dance; Darby; David; dead, rituals with respect to; death; deification; descent to Hades; descent to the underworld; devil worshippers; devotion; dialogue; diaspora;

diffusion; Dionysius the Areopagite; divination; divine combat; divine man; divine right; divinity; divorce; domestic ritual; Dominic of Osna; do ut des; doxology; drum; Duns Scotus; dynastic leadership; Earthmother; eating together; Ecce homo; ecstasy; Eckhart; Eddy; Eden; edict of Milan; Edwards; egg, cosmic; Elijah; Elohim; emanation; emergence; emic/etic; Enoch; Ephraem Syrus; epic; epiphany; epiphenomenon; Erasmus; eschatology; Essenes; eternal; eternity; Ethical Culture; etiology; eunuch; Eusebius; Evagrius Ponticus; Eve; evil; excommunication; exegesis; Exodus; exorcism; expiation; Ezra; faith; Fall; faith healing; fallen angels; familiar; fanatic; fasting; fatalism; fate; fear; feet washing; fertility rites; festal cycle; Feuerbach; Ficino; fideism; fire; fire ritual (Japan); firewalking; firewalking (Japan); firmament; flagellation; flood stories; food; fortunate fall; foundation rites; foundation sacrifice; founded religions; Fox; Francis de Sales; Francis of Assisi; Freemasonry; free will; fundamentalism; Gabriel; Galilee; gender roles; gentile; geomancy; ghost; glory; god; God; G-d; goddess; Goddess; godhead; Gog and Magog; golden age; golden calf; golden rule; golem; Good Samaritan; Good Shepherd; gospel; grace; Graham, William (Billy); Grail, Holy; grave, graveyard; Great White Brotherhood; Gregory I; Gregory Palamas; ground of (all) being; guardian angel; guardian spirit; Gurney; hagiography; hallucinogens; halo; happy hunting ground; harrowing of Hell; harvest rituals; healing; heathen; heaven and hell; Helwys; hermit; heterodoxy; hexagram; Hicks; hierophany; high god; Hildegard of Bingen; history of religion(s); hocus-pocus; holocaust; holy books; Holy Ghost; holy of holies; holy persons; Holy Rollers; Holy Spirit; homiletics; homosexuality; Hooker; horoscope; hunting, religious aspects of; Hus(s); Hut(t)er; hymn; hypostasis; iconoclasm; idolatry; Ignatius of Loyola; IHC: images; imago Dei; immanence; immortality; incantation; incense; ineffable; inerrancy; infallibility; infanticide; infibulation; infinite; initiation rituals; inquisition; Inquisition, Spanish; inspiration; intention; intercession; intensification rites; invisibility; invulnerability; Iranian religion; Irenaeus; Ishmael; islands of the blessed; Israelite religion; Jacob-Israel; Jacob's Ladder; Jainism; James; Jansen; Jehovah; Jerome; Jew; Joachim of Fiore; Job; John; John Canoe; John of the Cross; John the Divine; Jordan, river; journey to the otherworld; Judas Iscariot; Judea; Judeo-Christian tradition; Judgement Day; Julian "the Apostate"; Julian of Norwich; justification by faith alone; Justin Martyr; Kierkegaard; kingdom of God; kingship, sacred; kneeling; Knox; kratophany; Kwanzaa; language, sacred; Last Supper; lectionary; Lee, Ann; legend; libation; life crisis rituals; life cycle rituals; light/darkness; lights; Lilith; limbo; Lord's Day; Lost Tribes; Lucifer; Luke; Lull; Maccabees; macrocosm; Madonna; Magnificat; mana; -mancy; manifest/latent; manna; maranatha; Mark; marriage; marriage, sacred; martial arts; Mary, pilgrimage sites; masks;

master/mistress of the animals; Matthew; meditation; Menno Simons; menstrual blood; Merton; Messiah; messianic; Methodism; Miller, William; Minoan religion; miracle; miracle plays; mission, missionary movements; mock king; Mohammedan; Mohammedanism; Molinos; monasticism; monk; monsters; Montanus; Moody; Moroni; Moses; motif; mountains, sacred; mourning; mutilation; Mycenaean religion; mystery play; naming rituals; Nazareth; necromancy; neophyte; Nestorius; New Covenant; New Jerusalem; Newman; new year festivals; Niebuhr, Reinhold; nimbus; Noah; Non-Conformist; non-periodic rites; nudity; number symbolism; numinous; nun; nymph; oceanic feeling; occultation; Old Catholic churches; omen; omnipotence; omnipresence; omniscience; Opus Dei; oracle; orant; ordeal; ordination; orgy; orientation; Origen; Otto; Pachomius; pagan; Pan-Babylonian; paradise; Parham; Parsi; Passion; path; path of (ritual) action; patriarchal; patriarchs; Pelagius; penance; penile bloodletting; Pentateuch; perfectionism; periodic rites; phallic worship; Photius; Pinkster festival; plausibility structure; pluralism, religious; Plymouth Brethren; pneuma; Porphyry; possession; power; praxis; prayer; preacher; preaching; preexistence; priesthood; profanation; profane; promised land; prophet; Prophet, The; Prophets; prostration; Protestantism; providence; pseudepigrapha; psyche; psychedelic substances; psychoactive plants; purification; Queen of Heaven; Qumran; Rahner; Rauschenbusch; rebellion, rituals of; rebirth; Red Sea; Reform Judaism; reincarnation; relics; remnant; repentance; resurrection; revelation; Revelation, Book of; revenant; reversal; rites de passage; Russel, Charles; Ruusbruec; Sabbath; sacrifice; sage; saint; salvation; Salvation Army; salvation, religions of; sanctification; sanctification, religions of; Sanskrit; Saturnalia; savior; scapegoat; Schleiermacher; Schweitzer; Scofield; secret societies; Sect Shinto; semiotics; Semites; Separatist; Sermon on the Mount; Servetus; sexuality and religion; shamanism; shapeshifting; Shriners; Shrine Shinto; Simon, Richard; sin; Sinai; sisterhood; 613 commandments; 666; Skinwalker; sky; Smith, Joseph; smoke; Smyth; Socinus; Solomon; soma; soteriology; soul; soul-loss; Spener; spirits; state religion; subincision; suffering; Suffering Servant; sui generis; supernatural beings; Suso; Swedenborg; Symeon; tabernacle; tale type; talisman; tasks, heroic; Tatian; Tauler; Teihard de Chardin; Templars; temple; ten commandments; Tertullian; Teresa of Avila; tests, heroic; tetragrammaton; theocracy; theodicy; theophany; Thérèse of Lisieux; theriomorphic; Thomas à Kempis; Thomism; Tillich; tradition; trance; transcendence; transfiguration; translation; transvestism; tremendum; trickster; Tyndale; typology; unleavened bread; usury; veil; vernacular; Via Dolorosa; vision; voluntary association; Votan; votive offering; vow; Wandering Jew; Watts; Wesley, Charles; Wesley, John; White, Helen G.; Wholly Other; wilderness wandering; Williams; Woden; world religions;

World's Parliament of Religions; worldview; Worldwide Church of God; Wyclif; yeshiva; Yezidis; YHWH; Zen; Zion; Zwingli.

"Wisdom's Place." In J. J. Collins and M. Fishbane, eds., *Death, Ecstasy and Other Worldly Journeys* (Albany: State University of New York Press, 1995), 3–13.

"Trading Places." In M. Meyer and P. Mirecki, eds., *Ancient Magic and Ritual Power*, Religion in the Graeco-Roman World, 129 (Leiden: E. J. Brill, 1995): 13–27.

"Afterword: Religious Studies, Whither (Wither) and Why?" *Method & Theory in the Study of Religion* 7 (1995): 404–14.

"Double Play: Socrate's Apology and the Study of the Humanities." In Ph. Desan, ed., *Engaging the Humanities* (Chicago: University of Chicago College, 1995; 2d ed., 1997), 57–60.

1996

"Social Formations of Early Christianities: A Response to Ron Cameron and Burton Mack." *Method & Theory in the Study of Religion* 8 (1996): 271–78.

"A Matter of Class: Taxonomies of Religion." *Harvard Theological Review* 89 (1996): 387–403.

"Nothing Human Is Alien to Me." *Religion* 26 (1996): 297–309.

1997

"Review Essay: The Rise of Christianity." *American Journal of Sociology* 102 (1997): 1663–65.

"Are Theological and Religious Studies Compatible?" *Bulletin of the Council of Societies for the Study of Religion* 26 (1997): 60–61.

"The Aims of Education." In J. Boyer, ed., *The Aims of Education* (Chicago: University of Chicago College, 1997), 215–31.

1998

"Constructing a Small Place." In B. Z. Kedar and R. J. Zwi Werblowsky, eds., *Sacred Space: Shrine, City, Land* (New York: Academic Press and Jerusalem: Israel Academy of Arts and Sciences, 1998), 18–31.

"Canons, Catalogues and Classics." In A. van der Kooij and K. van der Toorn, eds., *Canonization and Decanonization*, Studies in the History of Religions, 82 (Leiden: E. J. Brill, 1998), 295–311.

"Religion, Religions, Religious." In M. Taylor, ed., *Critical Terms for Religious Studies* (Chicago: University of Chicago Press, 1998), 269–84.

"Cross-cultural Reflections on Apocalyptism." In A. Y. Collins, ed., *Ancient and Modern Perspectives on the Bible and Culture: Essays in Honor of H. D. Betz* (Atlanta: Scholars Press, 1998), 281–85.

"Teaching the Bible in the Context of General Education." *Teaching Theology & Religion* 1 (1998): 73–78.

2000

"Classification." In W. Braun and R. T. McCutcheon, eds., *Guide to the Study of Religion* (London and New York: Cassell, 2000), 35–45.

"Epilogue: The 'End' of Comparison: Rectification and Redescription." In K. C. Patton and B. C. Ray, eds., *A Magic Still Dwells: Comparative Religion in the Postmodern Age* (Berkeley: University of California Press, 2000), 237–41.

"Acknowledgments: Morphology and History in Mircea Eliade's *Patterns in Comparative Religion* (1949–1999). Part 1, The Work and Its Contexts." *History of Religions* 39 (2000): 315–31.

"Acknowledgments: Morphology and History in Mircea Eliade's *Patterns in Comparative Religion* (1949–1999). Part 2, The Texture of the Work." *History of Religions* 39 (2000): 332–51.

"Bible and Religion." *Bulletin of the Council of Societies for the Study of Religion* 29 (2000): 87–93.

"Alternative Visions of General Education." Transcript of paper presented at AACU's Network for Academic Renewal Spring 2000 Conference, General Education in the New Millennium: Opportunities, Principles, Politics. http://www.aacu-edu.org/ (paper no longer posted).

2001

"Close Encounters of Diverse Kinds." In S. L. Mizruchi, ed., *Religion and Cultural Studies* (Princeton: Princeton University Press, 2001), 3–21.

"A Twice-told Tale: The History of the History of Religions' History." *Numen* 48 (2001): 131–46.

"Foreword." In R. C. Neville, ed., *Religious Truth* (Albany: State University of New York Press, 2001), xi–xii.

"On the Occasion of Frank Reynolds' Retirement." *Criterion* 40 (2001): 9–12.

2002

"Religion Up and Down, Out and In: The Relation of Text to Artifact." In B. M. Gitlin, ed., *Sacred Time, Sacred Place: Archaeology and the Religion of Israel* (Winona Lake, Wisc.: Eisenbrauns, 2002), 3–10.

"Manna, Mana Everywhere and /-/-/." In N. K. Frankenberry, ed., *Radical Interpretation in Religion* (Cambridge: Cambridge University Press, 2002), 188–212.

"Great Scott! Thought and Action One More Time." In P. Mirecki and M. Meyer, eds., *Magic and Ritual in the Ancient World*, Religions in the Graeco-Roman World, 141 (Leiden: E. J. Brill, 2002), 73–91.

"A Private Sector Perspective on the American Academy of Religion Census of Religion and Theology Programs." *Religious Studies News* 17, no. 2 (2002): 7, 23.

2003

"Here, There, and Anywhere." In S. Noegel, J. Wallker, and B. Wheeler, eds., *Prayer, Magic, and the Stars in the Ancient and Late Antique World*, Magic in History, 8 (University Park: Pennsylvania State University Press, 2003), 21–36.

NAME INDEX

Acosta, Joseph de, 180–81, 272, 273–74, 310

Adams, Charles J., 175

Adler, Max, 3

Agamben, Giorgio, 107

Amrine, Frederick, 65

Annius of Viterbo, 309

Arber, Agnes, 65

Aristotle, 6, 117

Asclepiades of Myrlea, 63

Athenaeus, 257

Augustine, 264, 272

Bakhtin, Mikhail M., 368

Barth, Frederick, 343

Baxter, Richard, 182–83

Baetke, Walter, 103

Benveniste, Émile, 110

Bercovitch, Eytan, 342–46

Berlin, Isaiah, 316

Bernier, François, 314

Black, Max, 29

Bodenheimer, Frederick S., 119

Bodin, Jean, 309

Boemus, Joannes, 181

Borges, Jorge L., 209, 372

Bourgeaud, Philippe, 109

Boyer, Pascal, 127

Brerewood, Edward, 182, 186, 192, 310, 363

Brother Julian of Hungary, 309

Bullard, Thomas E., 304–6

Burger, Chief Justice Warren, 384–85

Burns, Robert, 252–53

Caillois, Roger, 83–84, 103

Capps, Walter, 9, 185–86

Case, Shirley J., 205

Cassirer, Ernst, 4–5, 65

Chance, David, 305

Chase, Agnes, 102

Childs, Brevard S., 7

Chomsky, Noam, 65

Christian, William A., 193

SUBJECT INDEX

Subject Index